# A-Z GLASGOW  Deluxe

CW00350085

## CONTENTS

## REFERENCE

| | | | | |
|---|---|---|---|---|
| Motorway | **M8** | Map Continuation **86** | Large Scale City Centre **4** | |
| A Road | **A77** | Car Park  Selected | P | |
|   Under Construction | | Church or Chapel | † | |
|   Proposed | | Cycle Route | 🚲 | |
| | | Fire Station | ■ | |
| B Road | **B812** | Hospital | Ⓗ | |
| Dual Carriageway | | House Numbers (A and B Roads only) | 13 8 | |
| One Way Street | → | Information Centre | 🅸 | |
| Traffic flow on A Roads is also indicated by a heavy line on the driver's left. | → | National Grid Reference | ⁶60 | |
| Junction Name | TOWNHEAD INTERCHANGE | Police Station (Open 24 Hours) | ▲ | |
| Restricted Access | | Post Office | ★ | |
| Pedestrianized Road | | Toilet | ▽ | |
| Track/Footpath | |   with facilities for the Disabled | ♿ | |
| Residential Walkway | | Viewpoint | ✳ ✸ | |
| Railway | Level Crossing / Station / Tunnel | Educational Establishment | ◩ | |
| | | Hospital or Hospice | ◩ | |
| Underground Station | Ⓤ | Industrial Building | ◩ | |
| Local Authority Boundary | | Leisure or Recreational Facility | ◩ | |
| Posttown Boundary | | Place of Interest | ◩ | |
| Postcode Boundary within Posttowns | | Public Building | ◩ | |
| Built-up Area | MILL ST. | Shopping Centre or Market | ◩ | |
| | | Other Selected Buildings | ◩ | |

## SCALE

| Map Pages 6-165  1:13,368 | Map Pages 4-5  1:6,684 |
|---|---|
| 0         ¼         ½ Mile | 0        ⅛        ¼ Mile |
| 0  250  500  750 Metres | 0  100  200  300  400 Metres |
| 4¾ inches (12.06 cm) to 1 mile   7.49 cm to 1 km | 9½ inches (24.11 cm) to 1 mile   14.98 cm to 1 km |

## Copyright of Geographers' A-Z Map Company Limited

Head Office:
Fairfield Road, Borough Green, Sevenoaks, Kent TN15 8PP
Telephone 01732 781000 (Enquiries & Trade Sales)
         01732 783422 (Retail Sales)
www.a-zmaps.co.uk

Copyright © Geographers' A-Z Map Co. Ltd.

Ordnance Survey® This product includes mapping data licensed from Ordnance Survey® with the permission of the Controller of Her Majesty's Stationery Office.
© Crown Copyright 2002. All rights reserved.
  Licence number 100017302

Edition 2  2002  Edition 2a 2005 (Part Revision)

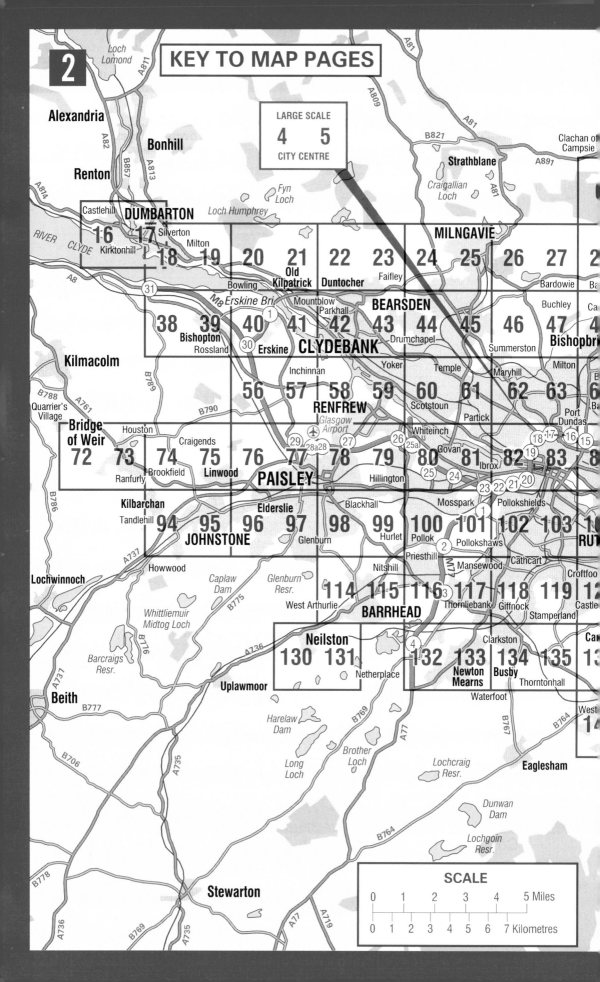

**2**

# KEY TO MAP PAGES

LARGE SCALE
**4    5**
CITY CENTRE

Loch Lomond

Alexandria

Bonhill

Renton

Castlehill

**DUMBARTON**  **16**  **17** Silverton

Kirktonhill

Milton

Strathblane

Craigallian Loch

Clachan of Campsie

RIVER CLYDE

**18**  **19**  **20**  **21** Old Kilpatrick  **22**  **23** Faifley  **24**  **25**  **26**  **27**

Bowling

Erskine Bri.

Mountblow

Parkhall

**BEARSDEN**

Bardowie

Buchley

Ca.

MILNGAVIE

**38**  **39** Bishopton  **40**  **41**  **42**  **43**  **44**  **45**  **46**  **47**  **Bishopbr**

Rossland

Erskine

**CLYDEBANK**

Drumchapel

Summerston

Kilmacolm

Inchinnan

Yoker

Temple

Maryhill

Milton

**56**  **57**  **58**  **59**  **60**  **61**  **62**  **63**

Quarrier's Village

**RENFREW**

Glasgow Airport

Scotstoun

Partick

Port Dundas

Bridge of Weir

Houston

Craigends

Whiteinch

**72**  **73**  **74**  **75**  **76**  **77**  **78**  **79**  **80**  **81**  **82**  **83**

Brookfield

Linwood

**PAISLEY**

Hillington

Govan

Ibrox

Ranfurly

Blackhall

Mosspark

Pollokshields

Kilbarchan

Elderslie

Hurlet

Pollok

**94**  **95**  **96**  **97**  **98**  **99**  **100**  **101**  **102**  **103**

Tandlehill

**JOHNSTONE**

Glenburn

Pollokshaws

Cathcart

**RUT**

Lochwinnoch

Howwood

Caplaw Dam

Glenburn Resr.

Nitshill

Priesthill

Mansewood

Croftfoot

**114**  **115**  **116**  **117**  **118**  **119**  **12**

West Arthurlie

**BARRHEAD**

Thornliebank

Giffnock

Stamperland

Castle

Whittliemuir Midtog Loch

Clarkston

Ca.

Beith

Barcraigs Resr.

Neilston

**130**  **131**  **132**  **133**  **134**  **135**  **13**

Netherplace

Newton Mearns

Busby

Thorntonhall

Uplawmoor

Waterfoot

West

**14**

Harelaw Dam

Brother Loch

Lochcraig Resr.

Eaglesham

Long Loch

Dunwan Dam

Stewarton

Lochgoin Resr.

## SCALE

0    1    2    3    4    5 Miles

0  1  2  3  4  5  6  7 Kilometres

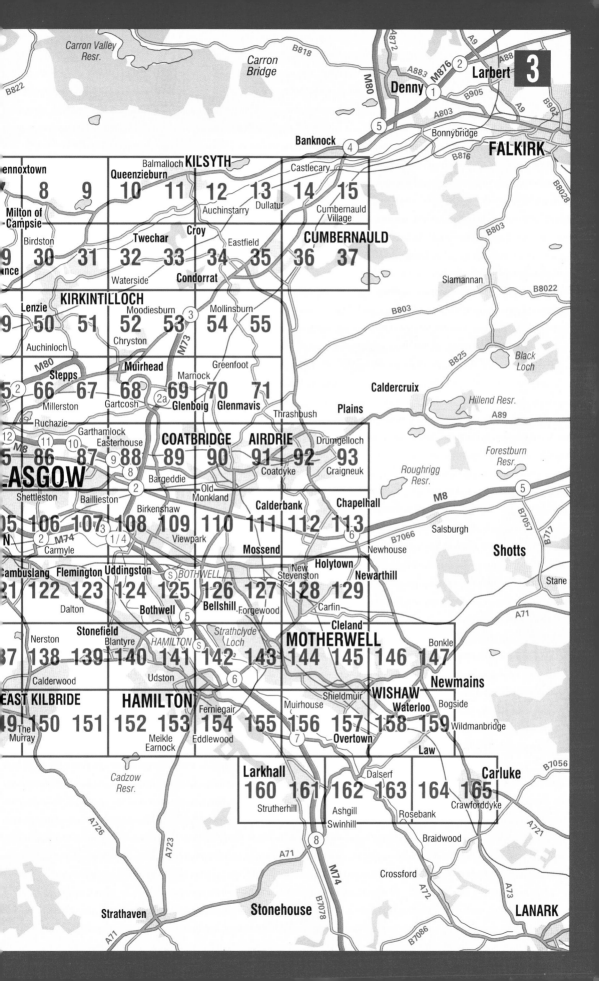

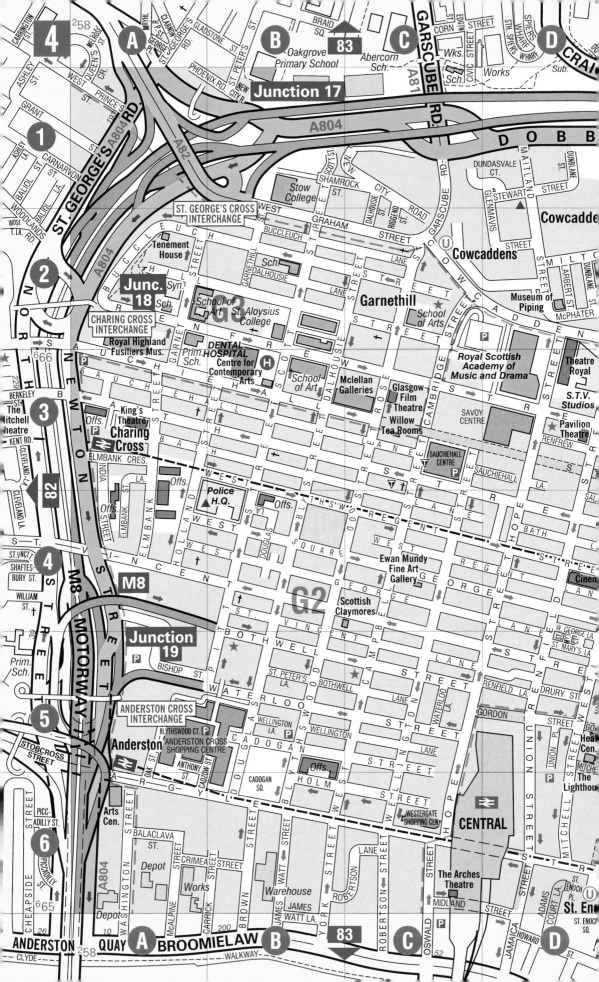

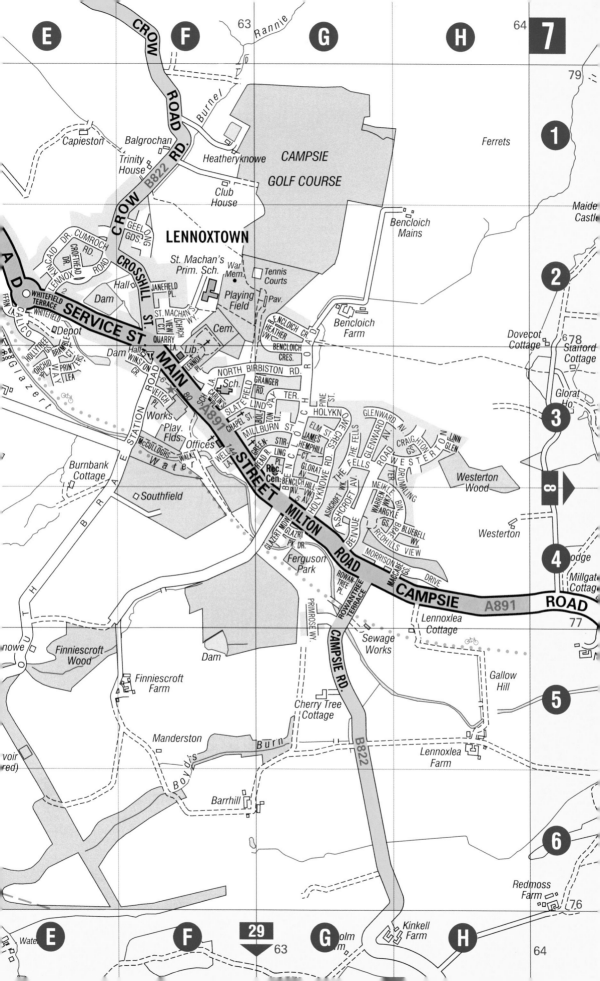

63 Rannie 64 79

1

CROW ROAD

Burnel

Capieston

Balgrochan

Trinity House

Heatheryknowe

CAMPSIE GOLF COURSE

Ferrets

Maide Castle

B822 CROW RD.

Club House

Bencloich Mains

2

CROSSHILL ST.

LENNOXTOWN

GEELONG GDS.

CUMROCH RD.

CAID DR.

CROFTHEAD DR.

KINCAID DR.

LENNOX ROAD

St. Machan's Prim. Sch.

War Mem.

Tennis Courts

Dovecot Cottage

678

Stanford Cottage

WHITEFIELD TERRACE

SERVICE ST.

Dam

Hall

JANEFIELD PL.

CHURCH VIEW

ST. MACHAN'S

Playing Field

Pav.

BENCLOICH CR.

HEATHER VW.

Bencloich Farm

ROAD

Glorat Ho.

3

FIRN CALICO

WHITEFIELD

Depot

QUARRY

Cem.

Lib.

LENNOX

NORTH BIRBISTON RD.

Sch.

GRANGER RD.

TER.

PINE ST.

HOLYKNO

Glenward Av.

GLENWARD

CRAIGHTON GS.

WESTERTON

LINN GLEN

Westerton Wood

HOLLYTREE

BRAMBLE CT.

ORCHARD WAY

PRINTERS LEA

WINSTON CR.

Dam

Hall

VEITCH PL.

Works

STATION ROAD

B82

A891

SLATE FIELD

CHAPEL ST.

LIND DR.

MULBURN ST.

COLT TER.

GREEN R.

STIR.

HEAD R.

LING PL.

ELM ST.

JAMES ST.

HEMPHILL CT.

GLORAT AV.

THE FELLS

GLENWARD

ROWANTER.

DRUMLING

8

Glazert

McCULLOCHS

Play. Flds

Offices

144

WELLS LA.

REC. CEN.

BENCLOICH HILL AV.

HOLYKNOWE RD.

THE FELLS

ASHCROFT AV.

ASHCROFT WK.

MEIKLE BIN TER.

WARREN WK.

ARGYLE GS.

BLUEBELL WY.

REDHILLS VIEW

Westerton

4

Burnbank Cottage

BRAE

Water

WALK

MILTON ROAD

STREET

Southfield

GLAZERT MOTOR PK. DR.

Ferguson Park

PRIMROSE WY.

ROWANTREE PL.

ROWANTREE TERRACE

BENNUE

MORRISON GS.

MACCABE GS.

DRIVE

CAMPSIE A891 ROAD

Lodge

Millgate Cottage

77

Lennoxlea Cottage

5

knowe

Finniescroft Wood

Finniescroft Farm

Dam

CAMPSIE RD.

Cherry Tree Cottage

Sewage Works

Gallow Hill

Lennoxlea Farm

voir red)

Manderston

Burn

B822

Boyd's

Barrhill

6

Redmoss Farm

76

Water

Holm

Kinkell Farm

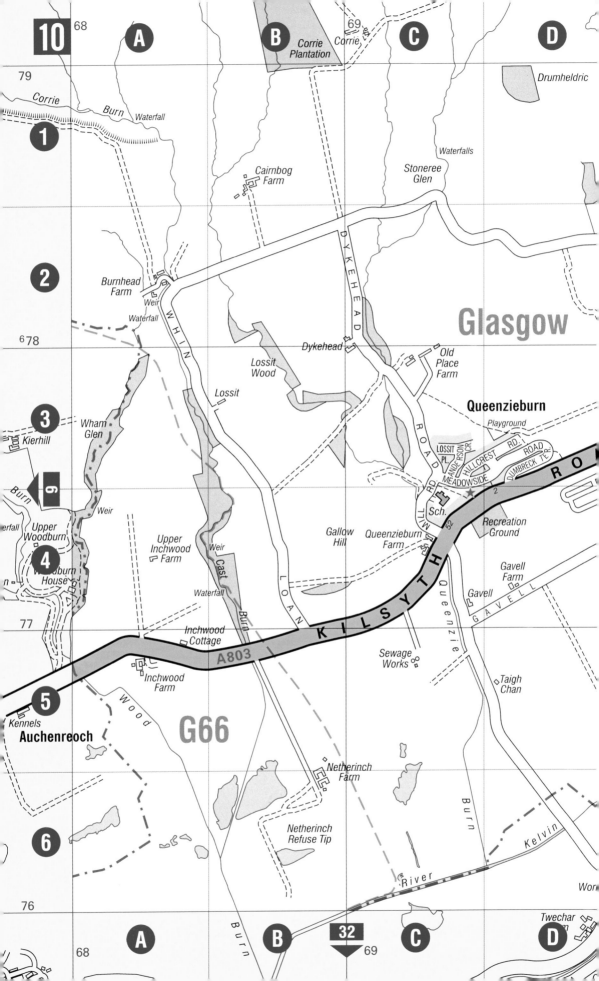

Prim. Sch.
BOG RD.
LABURNUM
MAPLE
LAUREL SQ.
ROAD
CEDAR RD.
LARCH DR.
ALMOND DR.
CHERRY

BALLINKIER
HILLHEAD AV.
HOLLAND AV.
BUSH
AUCHINCLOCH DR.
KELVINVIEW AV.
ENVIEW
HILLHEAD
LINDEN DR.
HOLLY RD.
ASH PL.
WILLOW DR.
HAZEL
CASTLEHILL CR.
HAWTHORN DR.
ROAD

Football Grd.
Castlecary Bridge
AVENUE
CUMBERNAULD
CASTLEVIEW ST.
MARGARET AV.
GARNGREW RD.
79
Longcroft Holdings

**BANKNOCK**

Sub.

Woodneuk

Works

**Haggs**

Castlecary Mill Farm

**Longcroft**

Bonny Water

Forth and Clyde Canal

Bowling Green Pav.
Rec. Grd.
THORNDALE GDNS.
ALLANDALE COTTS.
★
**1**

B816

DUNDAS COTTS.

**Allandale**

Woodend

**2**

Thorn

678

**Castlecary**

CASTLEVIEW

CASTLE COURT

GARNHALL FARM RD.

A80

ROAD

BRIDGEND CT.

CASTLECARY LOW WOOD

**3**

Dunns Wood

Castle Glen

Waterfalls

Castle Cary

Waterfall

Upper Glen Plantation

Purification Works

Waterfall

West Craig

**4**

Bandominie Strip

77

Bandominie

Walton Burn

Red Burn

WEST

WHITELEES RD.
CASTBURN RD.
BRAES BURN
BRAESBURN RD.
BURN PL.
BURN CT.
RED BURN CT.
ROSEBURN CT.
REDBURN PL.
BIRKENBURN
WHITELEES ROAD

Off. Sub.

Waterfall

Bandominie South Wood

**5**

**G67**

Whitelees Prim. Sch.

LILAC HILL
LILAC CT.
LILAC AV.
LILAC PL.
CHESTNUT CT.
CHESTNUT CT.
HORNBEAM RD.
Sub.

ROAD

WHITELEES ROUNDABOUT

MAPLE RD.
MAPLE CT.
FOREST ROAD
MOSS RD.

Sub.

Kilt Farm

Kilt Bridge

Walton Burn

**6**

76

THORN ROAD
PINE RD.
PINE GRO.
PINE CR.
Prim. Sch.
ALMOND RD.
ALMOND DR.
ELM DR.
OAK
Bowling Greens
Sub.

St. Lucy's Prim. Sch.

Comm.

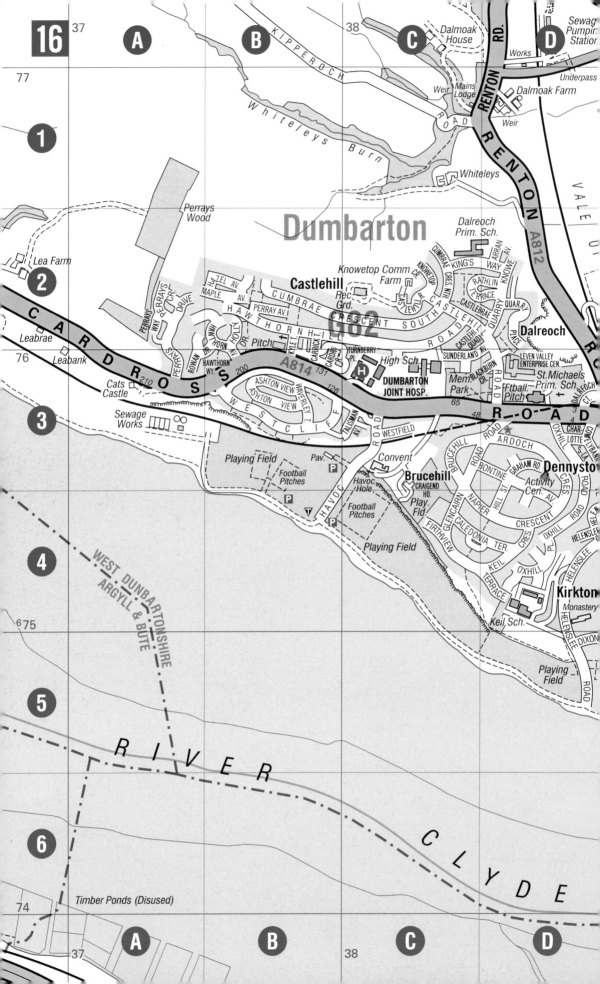

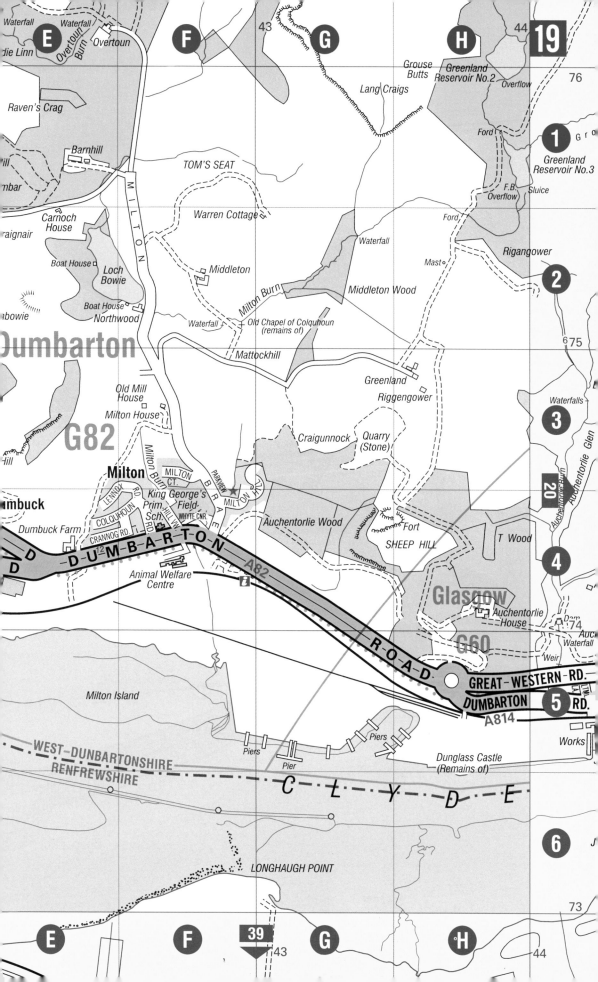

Waterfall    Waterfall
die Linn    Overtoun Burn
Overtoun

Grouse
Butts    Greenland
Reservoir No.2
Overflow

Lang Craigs

Raven's Crag

**1**

Greenland
Reservoir No.3

Ford

Barnhill    TOM'S SEAT    Rigangower

mbar

Warren Cottage    Mast    F.B.
Overflow    Sluice

Ford

Carnoch
House

Craignair

**2**

Waterfall

Boat House    Loch
Bowie    Middleton    Middleton Wood

675

bowie    Boat House
Northwood    Milton Burn    Old Chapel of Colquhoun
(remains of)    Greenland
Riggengower

**Dumbarton**    Waterfall

Mattockhill    Waterfalls

Old Mill
House    Greenland
Riggengower    **3**

**G82**    Milton House    Craigunnock    Quarry
(Stone)    Auchentorlie Glen

Hill    Milton    KING GEORGE'S FIELD    **20**    Auchentorlie Burn

mbuck    LENNOX RD.    COLQUHOUN RD.    MILTON CT.    Auchentorlie Wood    Fort    T Wood

Dumbuck Farm    CRANNOG RD.    WHYTE CNR.    SHEEP HILL    **4**

**D D**    **DUMBARTON**    A82    **Glasgow**
Animal Welfare
Centre    **ROAD**    Auchentorlie
House    **G60**

Milton Island    Auc
Waterfall
Weir

**GREAT WESTERN RD.**
**DUMBARTON**    **5** **RD.**
A814    Works

**WEST DUNBARTONSHIRE**
**RENFREWSHIRE**    Piers    Piers
Pier    Pier    Dunglass Castle
(Remains of)

**C L Y D E**

**6**

LONGHAUGH POINT    73

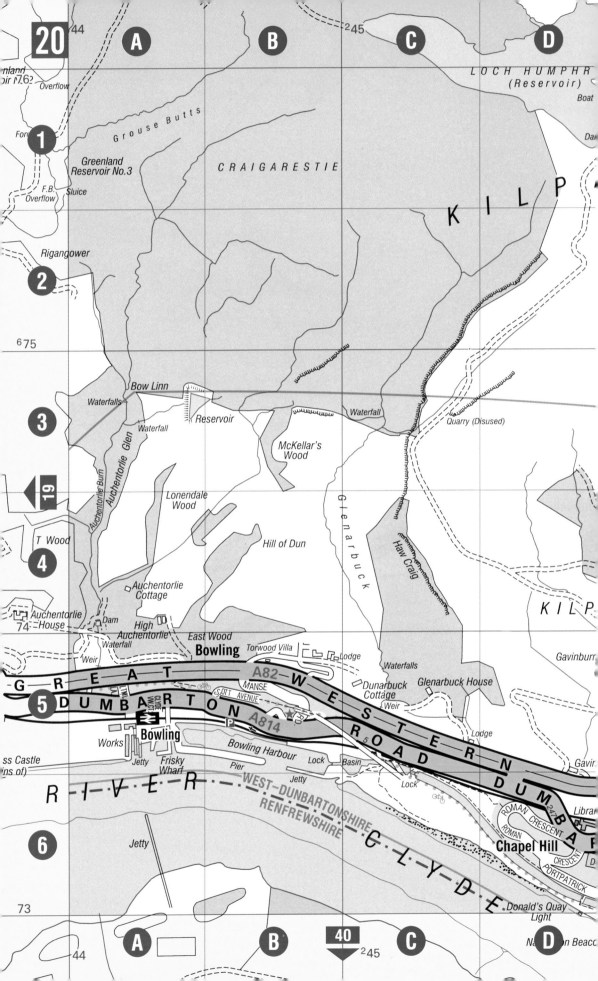

44
A
B
245
C
D

LOCH HUMPHR
(Reservoir)
Boat

nland
oir N 762
Overflow

Grouse Butts

Fo
1

F.B.
Overflow
Sluice

Greenland
Reservoir No.3

CRAIGARESTIE

KILP

Da

Rigangower
2

675

Bow Linn

Waterfalls

Waterfall

Reservoir

Waterfall

Waterfall

Quarry (Disused)

3

McKellar's
Wood

Auchentorlie Glen

Auchentorlie Burn

19

Lonendale
Wood

Glenarbuck

Haw Craig

T Wood
4

Hill of Dun

KILP

Auchentorlie
Cottage

Auchentorlie
House
74

Dam

High
Auchentorlie

East Wood

Waterfall

Weir

Bowling

Torwood Villa

Lodge

Waterfalls

Dunarbuck
Cottage

Glenarbuck House

Gavinburr

G R E A T        W E S T E R N        R O A D
A82
MANSE
SCOTT    AVENUE
CLYDE WAY

Lodge

5
D U M B A R T O N
A814
P

Weir

Lodge

DUM

Works

Bowling

Frisky
Wharf

Bowling Harbour

Pier

Lock

Basin

Lock

Gavir.

ss Castle
ns of)

Jetty

Jetty

R    I    V    E    R
WEST-DUNBARTONSHIRE
RENFREWSHIRE
C L Y D E

Lock

Library

ROMAN CRESCENT
ROMAN

6

Jetty

Chapel Hill

CRESCENT
PORTPATRICK

73

Donald's Quay
Light

44
A
B
40
245
C
D

Na    n Beac

76

**E R I C K   H I L L S**

**1**

Loch Humphrey Burn

GREENSIDE RESERVOIR

**Dumbarton**

IROCH

**G82**

**2**

THE SLACKS

6 75

Loch Humphrey

**3**

22

Burn

**4**

Ford
Waterfall

**R I C K   B R A E S**

e Grid

74

Craigleith

**Glasgow**

Blackmailing

Blackmailing
Reservoir
(Covered)

**5**

**G60**

Filter
Beds

Waterfall

Drums

Lodge

Hole
Cottage

Mount
Pleasant

**6**

Netherclose

Carleith

CRESCENT

Cemy.

A82   R O A D

A814

Carleith

FM 73

RUSSE

PL

GAVINBURN PL
GAVINBURN PL

ROAD

Halls

CHURCH
MANSFIELD KIRKTON

THISTLENEUK

MOUNT

PEACOCK PL

PLEASANT   RD.

North
Dalnottar
Cemetery

Clydebank
Crematorium

Old
atrick

KILPATRICK CT.
CHERRYSIDE CT.

HILLER

STA.

RD.

41

Carleith
Prim. Se

MT. PLEASANT
HO. ASHTREE
CT.

LISSET

Kilpatrick

47

48

M 0

Dal

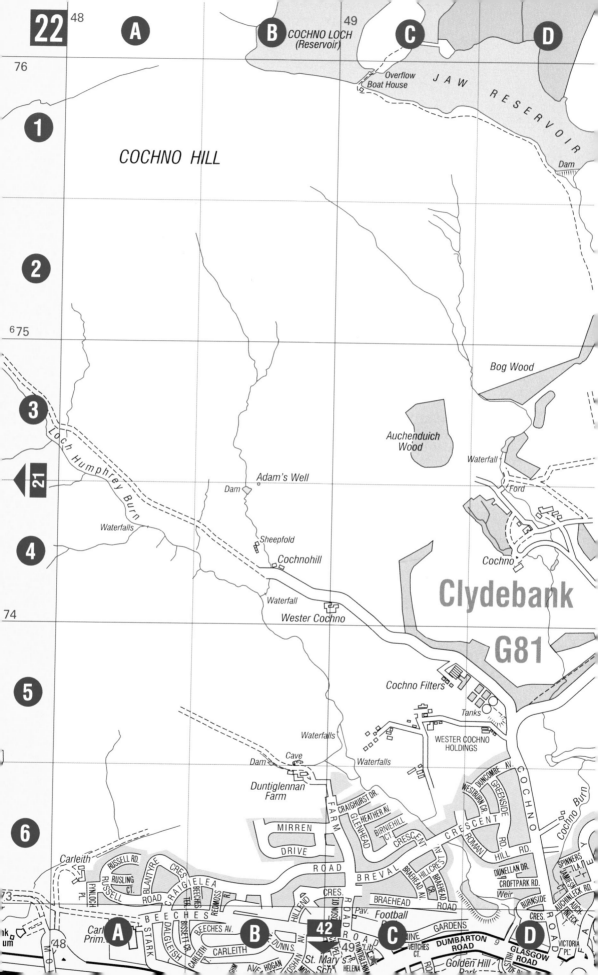

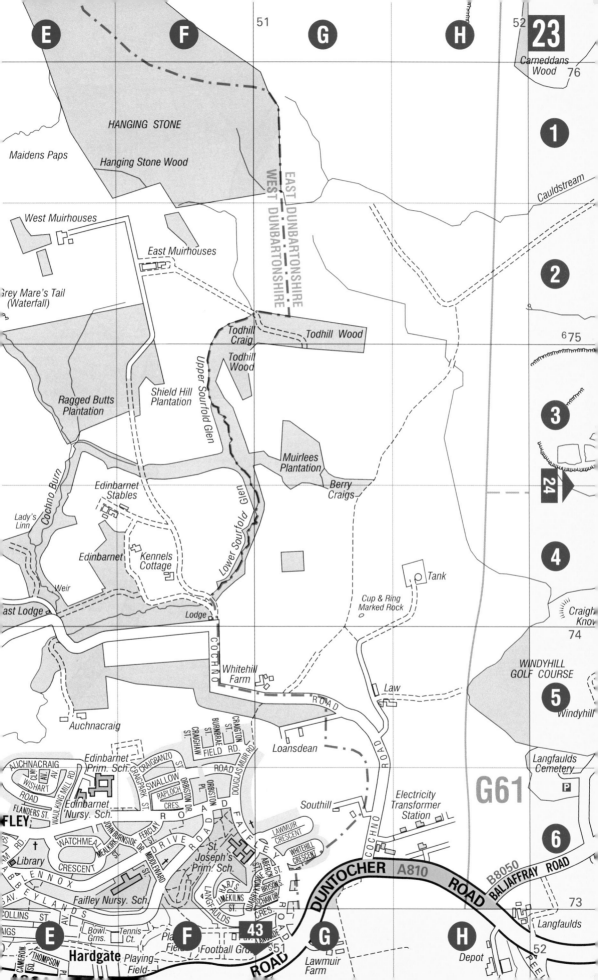

Carneddans
Wood 76

**1**

HANGING STONE

Maidens Paps

Hanging Stone Wood

Cauldstream

West Muirhouses

**2**

East Muirhouses

EAST DUNBARTONSHIRE
WEST DUNBARTONSHIRE

Grey Mare's Tail
(Waterfall)

Todhill
Craig

Todhill Wood

6 75

Todhill
Wood

Upper Sourfold Glen

**3**

Ragged Butts
Plantation

Shield Hill
Plantation

Muirlees
Plantation

Cochno Burn

Edinbarnet
Stables

Berry
Craigs

**24**

Lady's
Linn

Edinbarnet

Kennels
Cottage

Lower Sourfold Glen

**4**

Weir

Tank

Craigh
Know

East Lodge

Lodge

Cup & Ring
Marked Rock

74

Whitehill
Farm

Law

WINDYHILL
GOLF COURSE

**5**

Windyhill

Auchnacraig

COCHNO

ROAD

Loansdean

Langfaulds
Cemetery

P

Craigton
St.

Burnbrae
St.

Craighaw
St.

FIELD
RD.

DOUGLASMUIR RD.

ROAD

COCHNO

Electricity
Transformer
Station

**G61**

**6**

Auchnacraig
CLN AV
WISHART
ROAD

Edinbarnet
Prim. Sch.

Walking Mill Rd.

Craiganzo
St.

Craigpark St.

Swallow

Raploch
Cres.

Orbiston
Pl.

Orbiston Dr.

Southill

Edinbarnet
Nursy. Sch.

Flanders St.

John Burnside

Ferglay St.

Mealkirk St.

Drive

Fairley
Road

St.
Joseph's
Prim. Sch.

Lawmuir
Crescent

Whitehill
Crescent

B8050

BALJAFFRAY ROAD

73

**FLEY**

Watchmea
Crescent

Middleyard St.

Aberch St.

**DUNTOCHER** A810 **ROAD**

Library

LENNOX

BAYLANDS

Faifley Nursy. Sch.

Harts
Langfaulds
Limekilns
St.

Quarry Knowe St.
Bryson's
St.
Schaw Dr.
Cres.

Langfaulds

Cameron
Sq.
Thompson St.

Collins
St.

Bowl.
Grns.

Tennis
Ct.

Pla

Football Gro

351

**Hardgate**

Playing
Field

ROAD

Lawmuir
Farm

Depot

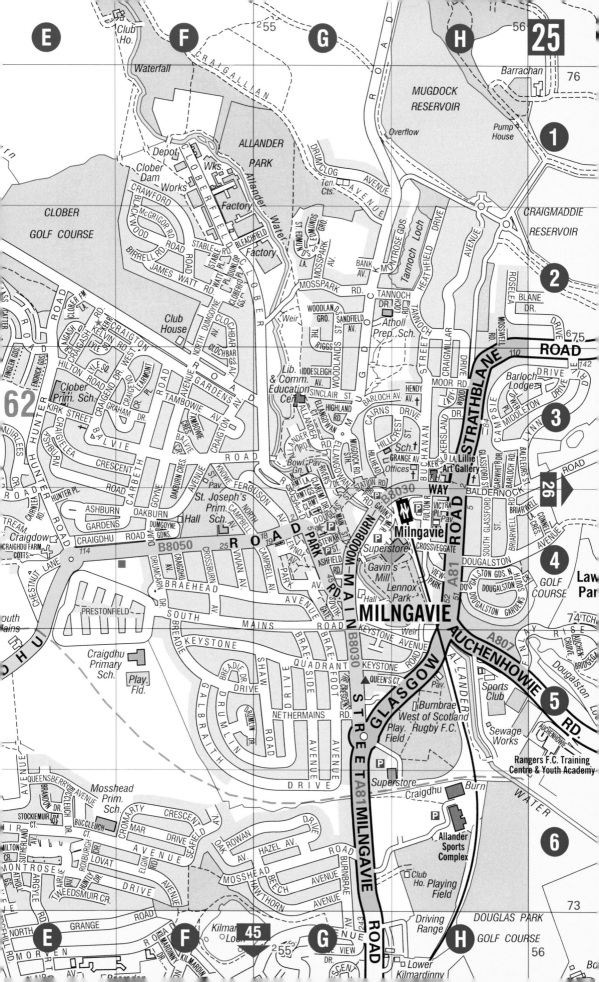

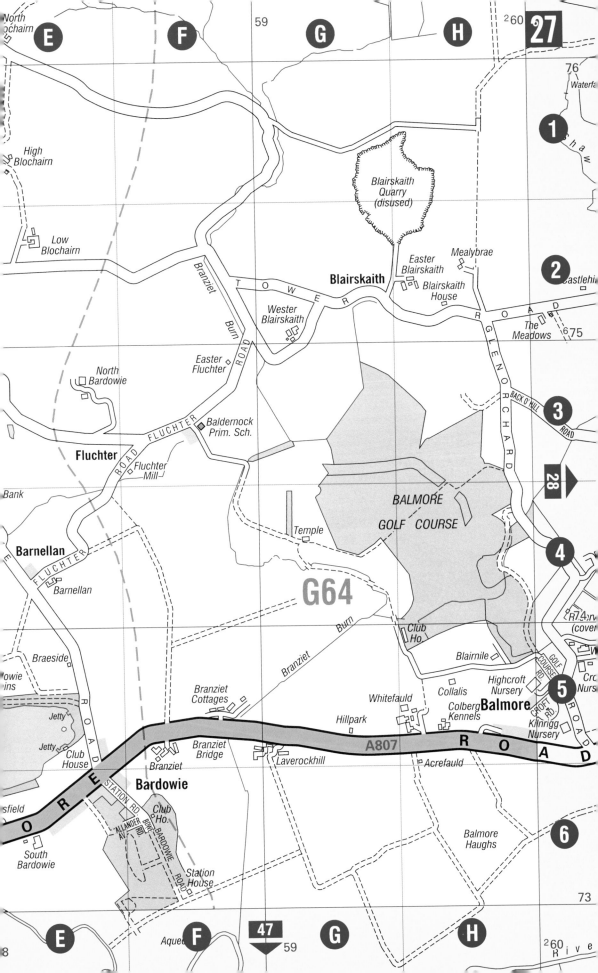

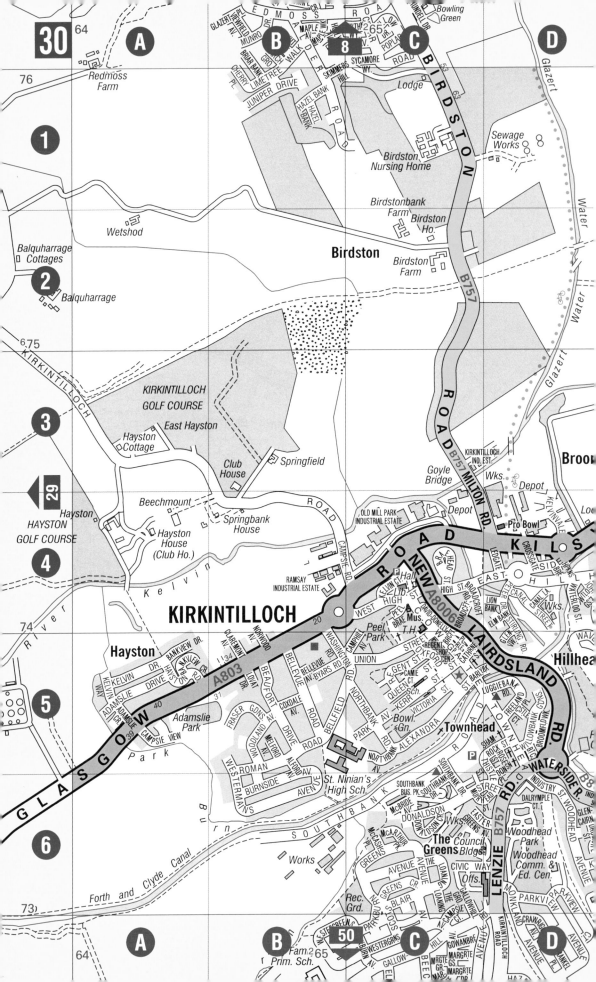

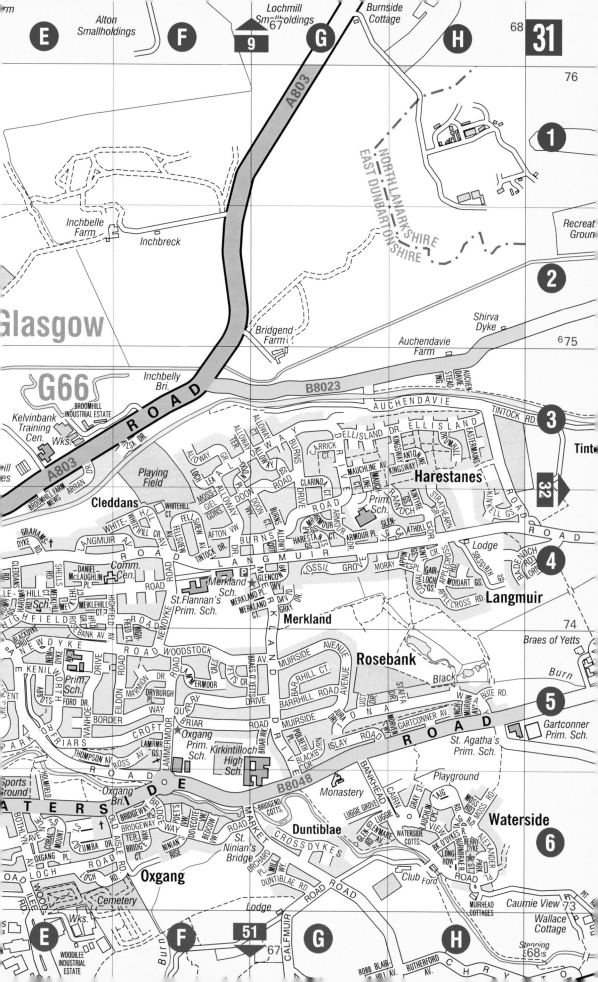

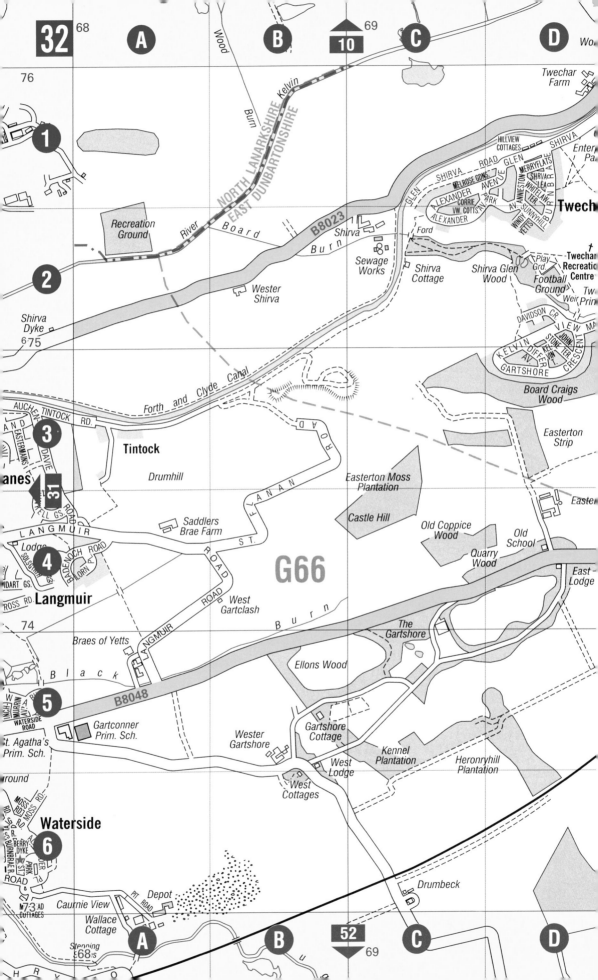

A    B    **10**    C    D

76

1

Wood

Kelvin

Burn

NORTH LANARKSHIRE
EAST DUNBARTONSHIRE

River    Board    B8023    Shirva

2    Recreation
Ground

Wester
Shirva

Sewage
Works

Shirva
Cottage

Ford

Shirva Glen
Wood

HILLVIEW
COTTAGES

SHIRVA    GLEN

SHIRVA
ROAD

MELROSE GDNS.    MERRYFLATS

ALEXANDER    AVENUE    PARK    SHAVAR
CORRIE    WHITELAW
ALEXANDER    VW. COTTS.    SUNNYHILL
ALEXANDER    WINDY    YETTS

Enter
Pa.

Twechar
Farm

Twech

Play
Grd.

Twechar
Recreation
Centre

Football
Ground

Tw.
Prin

Weir

Shirva
Dyke
6    75

DAVIDSON CR.    VIEW

KELVIN    STONE    JOHN    CRESCENT
DIFFER    AV.    TER    TER
GARTSHORE

Board Craigs
Wood

Easterton
Strip

AUCHE    TINTOCK    RD.
AND
EASTERMAINS    DAVIE

3    Tintock

Drumhill

Forth    and    Clyde    Canal

ROAD

Easterton Moss
Plantation

Castle Hill

Old Coppice
Wood

Old
School

Easter

31     anes

LANGMUIR

Lodge

4    Langmuir

ROSS    RD.

Saddlers
Brae Farm

ST.    TANAN

LANGMUIR    ROAD

ROAD

West
Gartclash

G66

Quarry
Wood

East
Lodge

74

Braes of Yetts

B8048

Gartconner
Prim. Sch.

Black

Burn

The
Gartshore

Ellons Wood

Gartshore
Cottage

Kennel
Plantation

Heronryhill
Plantation

St. Agatha's
Prim. Sch.

Wester
Gartshore

West
Lodge

5

6    Waterside

BERRY
DYKE

Depot
PIT
ROAD

West
Cottages

Caurnie View

Wallace
Cottage

N    73
COTTAGES

Stepping
S. 68

Drumbeck

Hope Park
Quarry
(dis.)

76

❶

Drumglass
Cottages

Sew
Wor

G65

Bar Hill

Creecyhill
Wood

Cailhead
Plantation

E y r e l a n   G l e n

ar
em.

Bar Hill

Barhill
Wood

B u r n

❷

anse
Pavs
Bowl
Gn.

B o a r d

Westerboard
Cottages

Woodside
Cottages

Works

Easter Board

Depot

675

West Board
Farm

Works

Glasgow

Boardloch
Wood

Drumgrew
Plantation

EAST DUNBARTONSHIRE
NORTH LANARKSHIRE

B u r n

❸

[34] ▶

BLACKWOOD WEST
ROUNDABOUT

KINGSH
LITTLEMILL
RAITH
BARONY PL.
SEAFIE
CRES

B o a r d

B8048

HUNT HILL
ROUNDABOUT

Drumgrew

Blackwood

CARDOWAN DRIVE
BLACKWOOD ROAD

❹

74

B8048

DRUMGREW
ROUNDABOUT

HUNT HILL

WELLESLEY PL.
WELLESLEY DR.
ARTEN WH
DEVON

Works

Black
Wood

❺

Little Drum
Plantation

LITTLE DRUM ROAD

ORCHARDTON WOODS
INDUSTRIAL PARK

P A R K

G68

G a r t s h o r e   M o s s

D R U M

M A I N S

Orchardton
Plantation

❻

ROAD

Grayshill
Wood

Abattoir

Newla
Far

GRAYSHILL ROAD
GRAYSHILL RD.
GRAYSHILL ROAD

73

ORCHARDTON

TFIELD
STRIAL
AREA

72

GRAYSHI

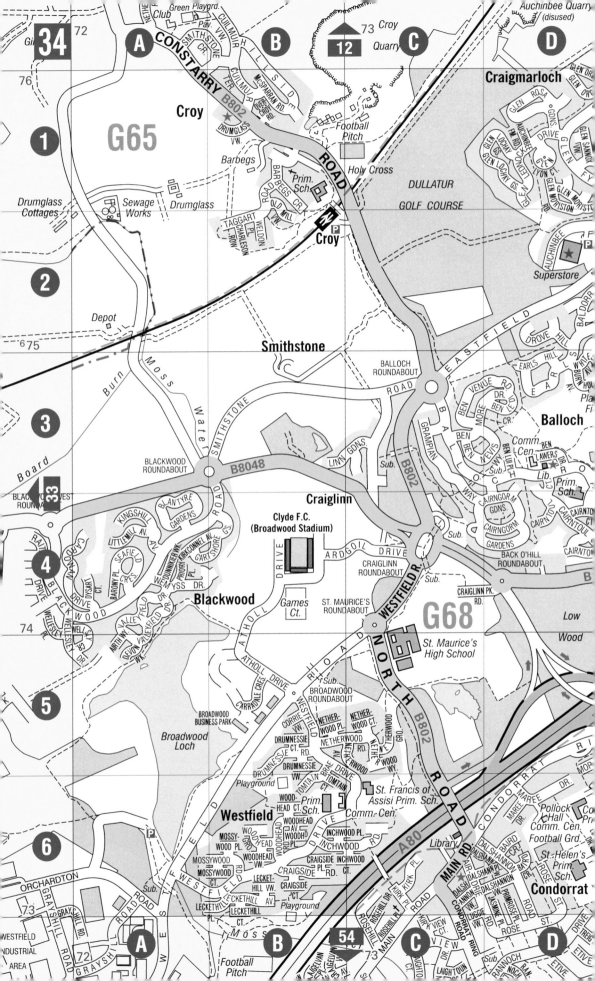

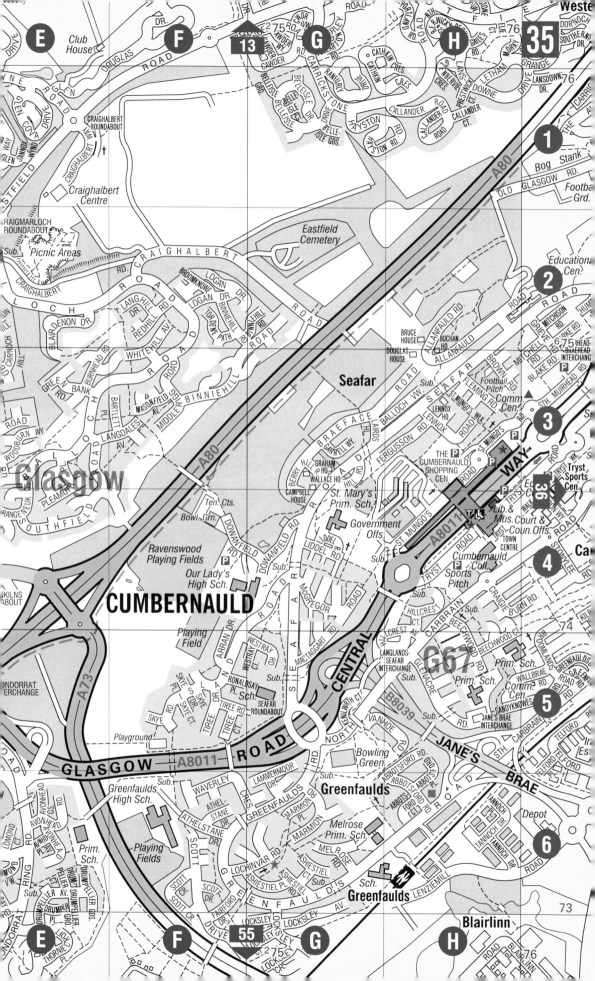

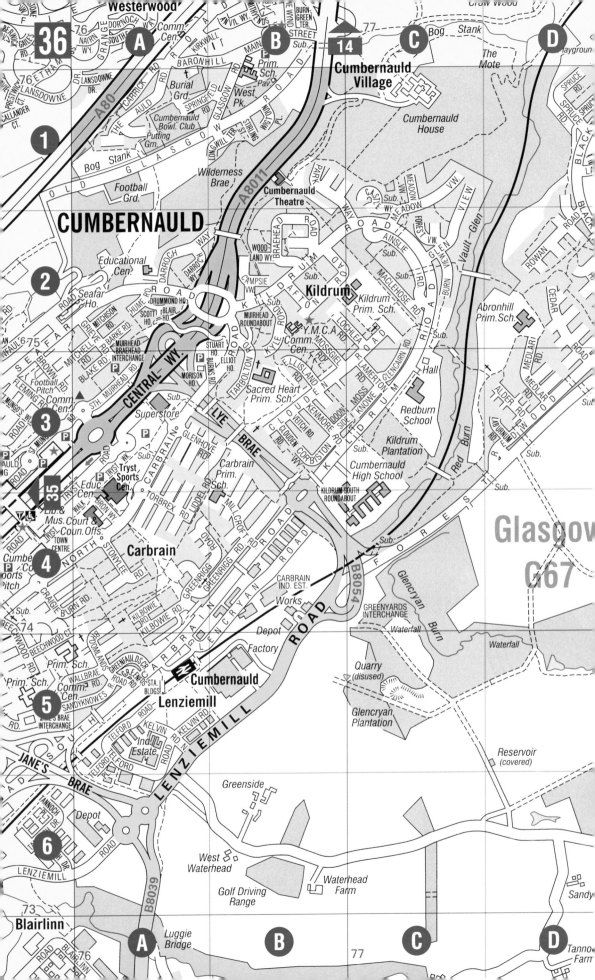

E  Prim. Sch.  F  G  H  ²80  37

Walton

Kilt
Bridge

79

15

76

ROAD

HORNBEAM RD.
ALMOND
MAPLE
MAPLE CT.
Sub.
Sub.

AV'
ROAD
Sub.
Sub.

PINE GRO.
PINE RD.
PINE CR.
PINE PL.
PINE
ELM DR.
HAWTHORN RD.
OAK RD.
GEAN CT.
ALMOND RD.
ALMOND RD.

Bowling
Greens

Sub.

St. Lucy's
Prim. Sch.

Lib.

Comm.
Cen.

Glenhead
Wood

Abronhill
High Sch.

OAK ROAD

BIRCH ROAD
BIRCH RD.
Comm.
Cen.
Glenhead
Wood

Glenhead

1

Crowbank

MOSS ROAD
LIME CRESCENT
LIME CRES.
OIL
onhill
otball
Grd.
s.
ROAD
Sub.
Subs.
DI
Sub.
Sub.
BLACKTHORN
ROUNDABOUT

2

675

Mid
orest

Forest
Plantation

3

FANNYSIDE

MUIR

Forest
Plantation

Forest
Plantation

4

74

Glencryan  Burn

5

PALACERIGG
GOLF COURSE

PALACERIGG
COUNTRY PARK

FANNYSIDE

LOCHS

Palacerigg
Cottage

Visitor
Cen.

Picnic
Area

6

Cattle
Grid

Palacerigg
House

Club
House

P

PALACERIGG
(CUMBERNAULD)
GOLF COURSE

73

E  F  G  H  Herd's  ²80
Hill

Cherrybank
Nurseries

Picnic Area

Picnic
Area

79

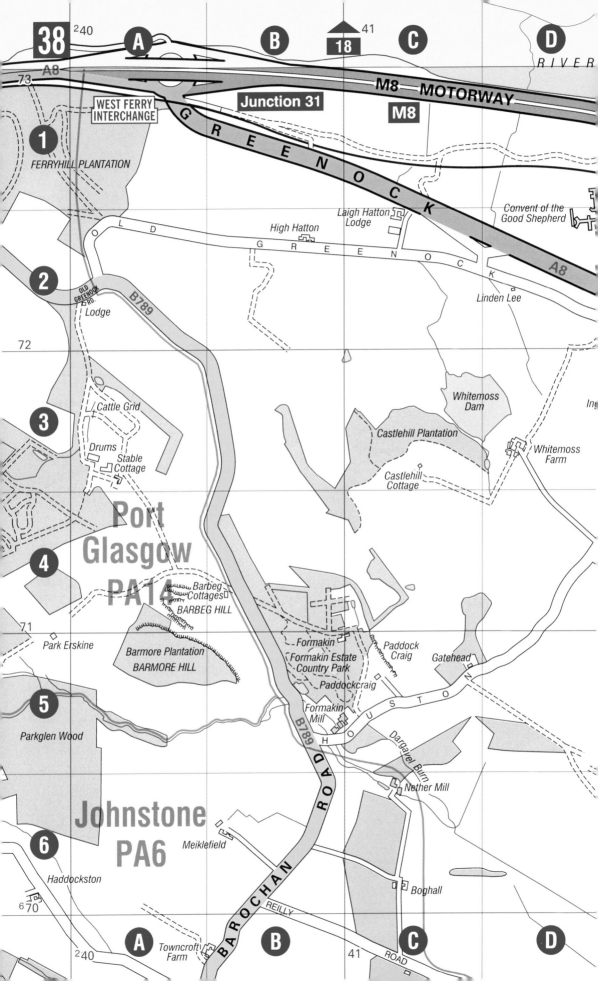

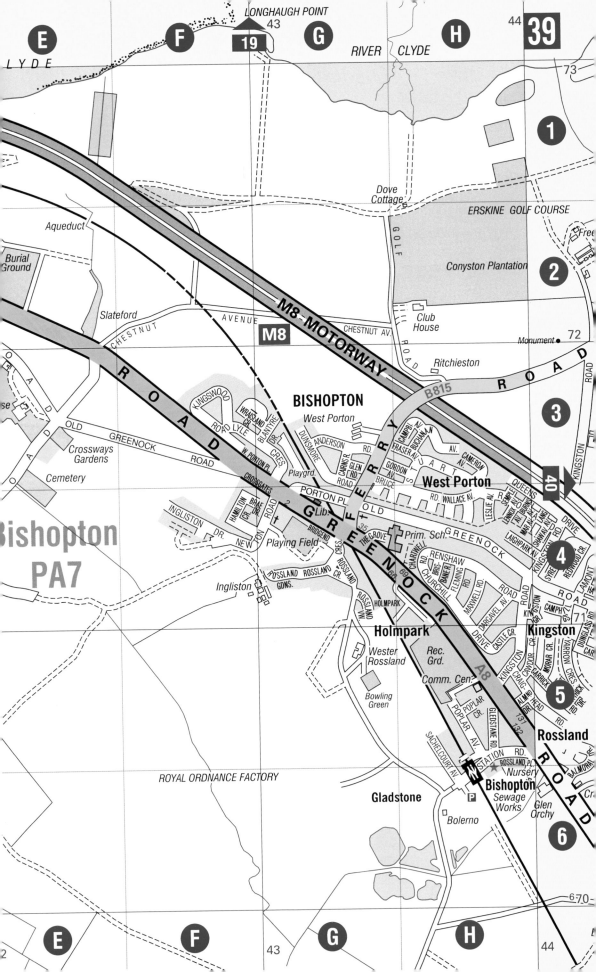

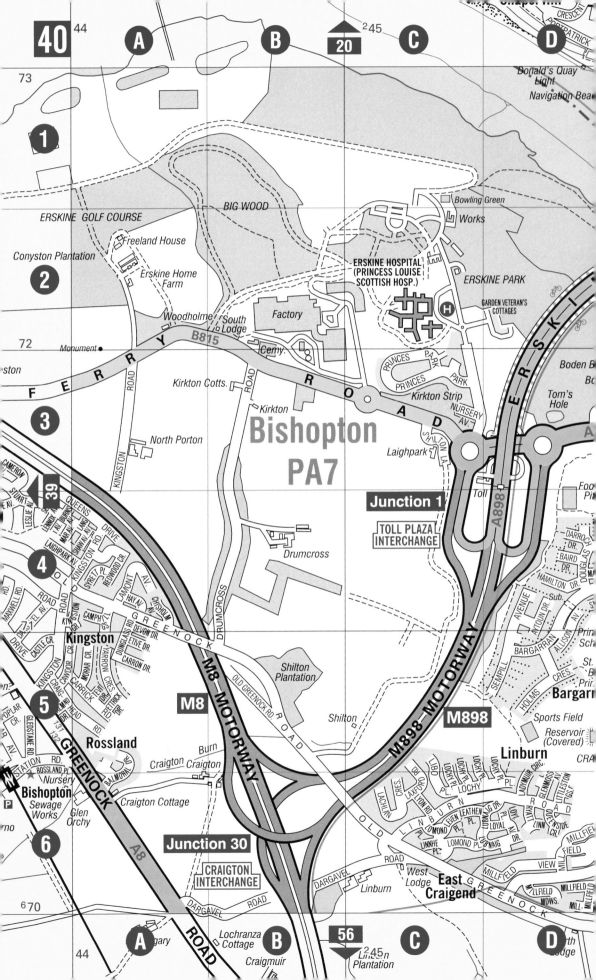

**A**     **B**     **C**     **D**

245
20

**1**

73

Donald's Quay
Light
Navigation Bea

*BIG WOOD*

Bowling Green
Works

*ERSKINE GOLF COURSE*

Freeland House

**2** *Conyston Plantation*

Erskine Home
Farm

ERSKINE HOSPITAL
(PRINCESS LOUISE
SCOTTISH HOSP.)

*ERSKINE PARK*

GARDEN VETERAN'S
COTTAGES

Woodholme South
Lodge

Factory

72 Monument ●

*Cemy.*

ston

B815

**H**

PRINCES
PARK

PRINCES PARK

Boden B
Bo

FERRY ROAD

Kirkton Cotts.

Kirkton

Kirkton Strip

Tom's
Hole

North Porton

**3**

**Bishopton
PA7**

Laighpark

NURSERY
AV.

SHILTON LA.

ERSKI

CAMERON

39

QUEENS

Drumcross

**Junction 1**

Toll

A898

**TOLL PLAZA
INTERCHANGE**

Foo
Pi

DARRO
DR.

BAIRD
DR.

**4**

LAIGHPARK AV.

KINGSTON

CHISHOLM

GREENOCK

DRUMCROSS

HAMILTON DR.
Sub.

DOUGLAS DR.

Pri
Sch

**Kingston**

DEVON DR.

ETIVE DR.
YARROW CRES.
CARRON DR.

*Shilton
Plantation*

AVENUE

AYTOUN DR.

ALLISON AV.

Prin
Pri

BARGARRAN CRES.

St.

**Bargarr**

OLD GREENOCK ROAD

**M8**

**M898**

Sports Field

**5**

GREENOCK

GLEDSTANE RD.

*Shilton*

Reservoir
(Covered)

**Linburn**

CRA

**Rossland**

Burn

Craigton Craigton

LACHLAN CRES.

LIBO PL.

LAXFORD PL.

LOCHY PL.

LOCHY PL.

LOCHY
PL.

LADYMUIR CIRC.

GLENMOSS AV.

LITTLESTON

ROAD

**Bishopton**

N

ROSSLAND PL.

Nursery

BALMORAL

*Craigton Cottage*

A8

OLD LINBURN

LINNHE PL.

LEVEN
PL.

LEATHEN
PL.

LUBNAIG DR.

LOMOND

ROAD

LOYAL
PL.

RYAT
PL.

QUEENSIDE
CR.

LINN
DR.

MILLFIELD

MILLFIELD

P Sewage
Works

Glen
Orchy

LOMOND

LINNHE PL.

LOMOND PL.

LUBNAIG DR.

ROAD

VIEW

MILL
FIELD

MILLFIELD

rno

**6**

**Junction 30**

West
Lodge

**East
Craigend**

ILLFIELD

MILLFIELD
MDWS.

MILL

670

**CRAIGTON
INTERCHANGE**

DARGAVEL

ROAD

*Linburn*

GREENOCK

6 70

**A**     **B**     **C**     **D**

*Lochranza
Cottage*

56

245

ROAD

*Craigmuir*

Lin
Plantation

44

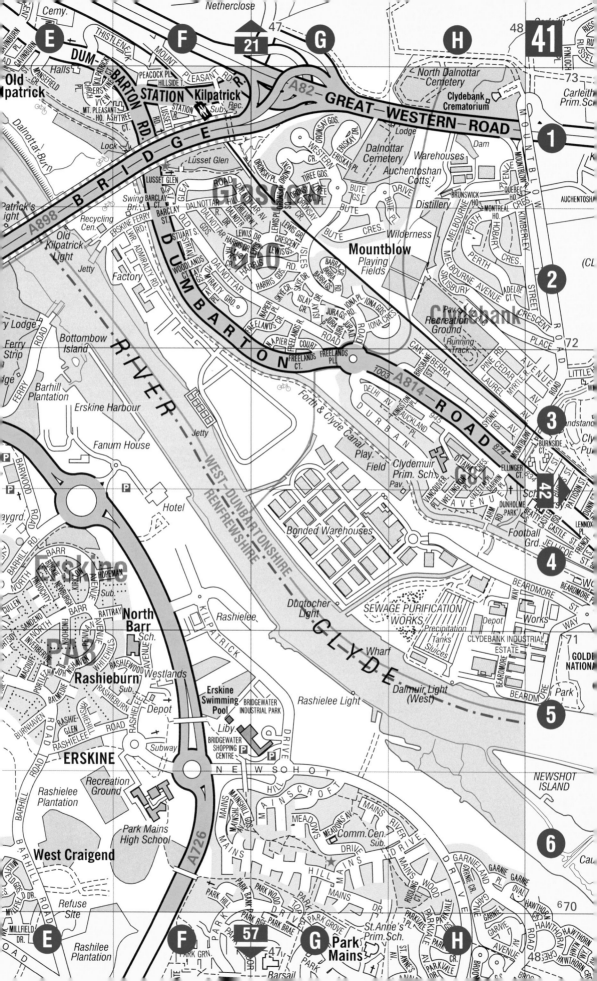

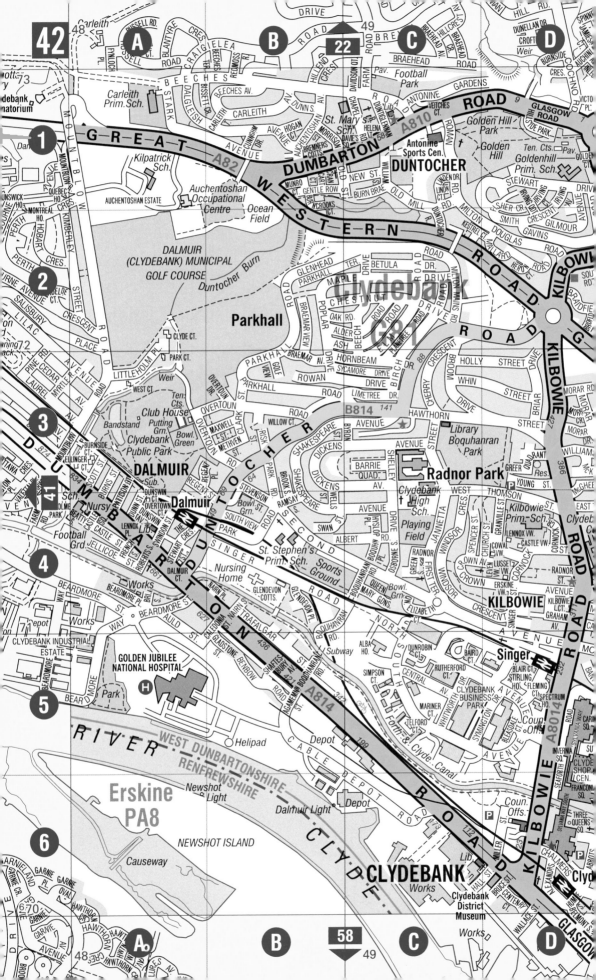

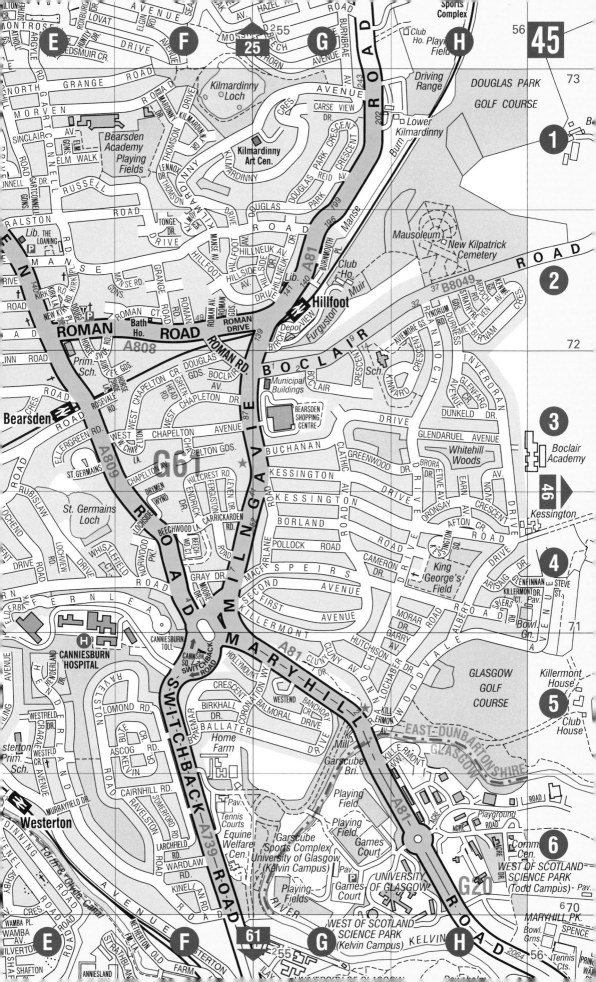

A    B    26    C    D

57

73
DOUGLAS PARK
GOLF COURSE

**1**

Boclair

G62

WATER

AUCHENHOWIE ROAD

BALMORE

A807

BALMORE RD.

B8049

Crow Hill   Hillside   Temple of Boclair

BOCLAIR

ROAD

w Kilpatrick
Cemetery

**2**

ARDOCH RD.   STRATHYRE   ANETH   BONAM   CRES.

GLENFARG CT.

72

West Millichen

East Millichen Cotts.

ROAD   A879

Sur

INVERORA

G61

Kelvin View
Rosehill

Birkwood

MILLICHEN

East Millichen

KELVIN

**3**

AVENUE

itehill
oods

Boclair
Academy

EAST DUNBARTONSHIRE   GLASGOW

Shielburn

RIVER

Glasgow

FARN   AV N CR   ROAD

**45**

CRESCENT

RIVER

Kessington

TEMPLEHILL
WOOD

**4**

ARISAIG DR.   GLENFINNAN   STEVE ST.
KILLERMONT CT.   Pav.

RIVER

SPIERS RD.   Bowl. Gn.

AVENUE

71

WOODVALE

GLASGOW
GOLF
COURSE

G23

G20

**5**

Killermont
House
Club House

Blackhill
Farm

Cawder
Cuilt

Summerston

BLACKHILL

Sandyflat
Riding Sch.

Playing
Field
John Paul
Academy

WEST OF SCOTLAND
SCIENCE PARK
(Todd Campus)

**6**

ACRE   ROAD

Playground
ROAD

Comm.
Cen.   Caldercuilt
Play. Field

DRIVE

Pav.

CALDERCUILT ROAD

ARROCHAR   ST.

CARNOCH S.
ARDESSIE S.
GEARY
DRKN CT.
CHATTON S.
CRAIGBO ST.
ROTHES
LITTLETON S.
FERNDALE GS.
FERNDALE DR.

MILOVAIG

CABRE'S   ZE ST.
ELPHIN
LEWISTON RD.

STAFIN DR.   BALMARTIN   HARRIS RD.

CONSER S.   STAFIN RD.

INVERSHIEL RD.

St. Blane's
Prim. Sch.
Football
Grd

SHIEL   BRIDGE GS.   HARBURN
LETTERFEARN DR.   NEWTON
Games
Ct.   Sch
ABERCORN
FOXHILLS PL.
HOY-
LAKE PL.   PIDUNSYRE PL.

HAWTHORNDEN
HOPETOUN PL.   WESTERKIRK DR.
BROUGHTON GDS.
PENCAITLND.
NEWSTEAD
GDS.

CROSS-POINT DR.
LYNNE DR.
LYTHAM DR.
MUIR-
FIELD CR.

INVER   GLEN
BERVIE RD.

TULSTA RD.
WENTWN   DR.

CROSSFD.

BROUGHTON ROAD

LAMBHILL
CEMETERY

MARYHILL PARK

Bowl.
Grns.   SPENC.
WHITTON
ST.   PRINCE OF
WALES   ST.
Tennis
Cts.   BARRA
ROSE-DALE

FERNDALE GS.

GU
GORSTAN
PTH.
Shopping

Comm.
Cen.

**62**

BROUGHTON

WESTERN
NECROPOLIS

ST. KENT
CEME

MARYHILL RD.   56

A    B    57    C    D

670

South Bardowie

E

F

59

27

G

H

260

73

1

Aqueduct

River Kelvin

Sand Pit

Buchley Cottages

2

Buchley Cottages

Bonded Warehouses

Buchley Lodge

ROAD

72

Buchley Farm

Pumping Station

ROAD

ROAD

BALMUILDY

WILDERNESS PLANTATION

3

...uildy ...ge

Easter Balmuildy

Brick Factory

BALMUILDY

Balmuildy Cottages

Avalon Kennels

G64

MAVIS

48

WE...

Refuse Disposal Plant

4

BISHOPBRIGGS

Bishopbriggs

71

Works

ROAD

GOLF COURSE

Turnbull High Sch.

5

ST. MARY'S

ROAD

A879

1283

Parkholm Farm

LOCHFAULD

Lochfauld

Forth & Clyde Canal

ROAD

Football Pitch

Playing Field

BALMORE

ROAD

G22

St. Mary's Kenmure

Kenmure Farm

6

POSSIL LOCH (Bird Sanctuary)

CASTLEBAY DR.

670

E

F

SHELDAIG

63

CASTLEBAY

G

CATHAY

CASTLE...

STREET

H

SCARAWAY DR.

260

HILLSWICK

ST.

59

SKERRAY

STREET

RAASAY

CATHAY

STREET

SCARAWAY

ST.

SCARAWAY

58

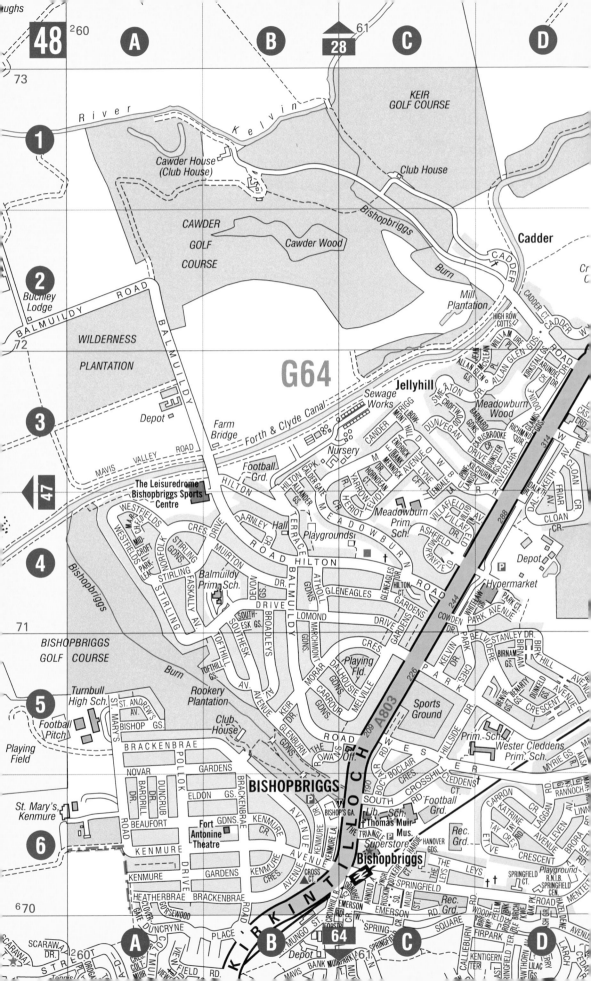

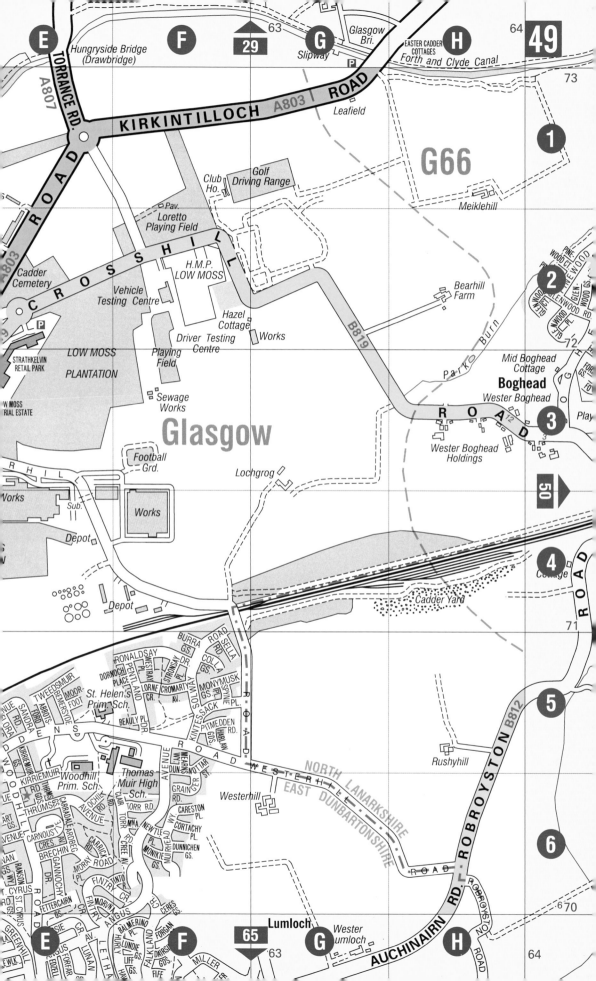

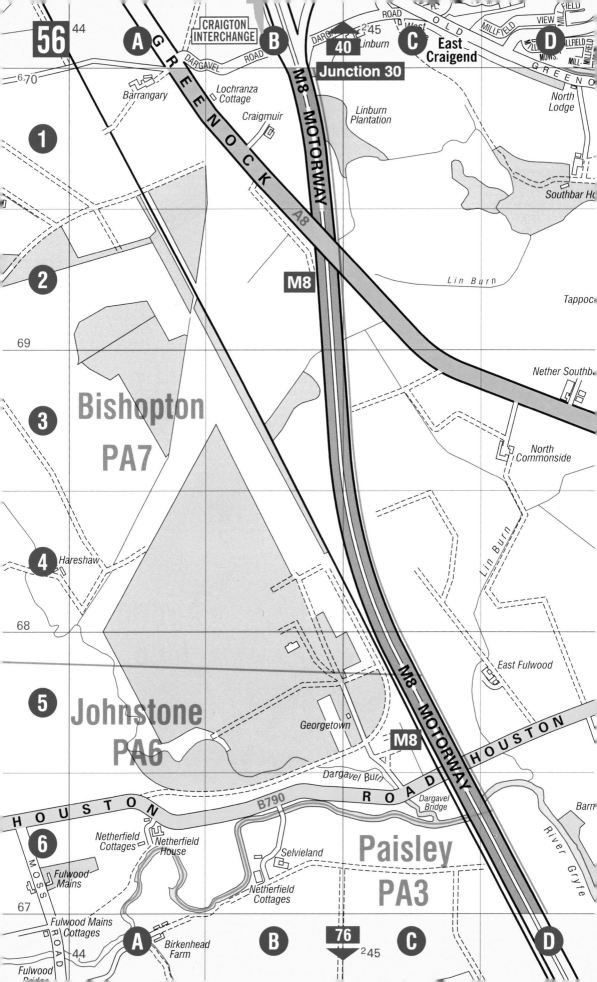

**56** 44

A **GREENOCK** B **M8 MOTORWAY** C **D**

CRAIGTON INTERCHANGE

DARGAVEL ROAD

40 — Linburn
**Junction 30**

West

OLD

ROAD

MILLFIELD

VIEW

MILLFIELD

MOWS.

GREENO

East Craigend

6·70

Barrangary

Lochranza Cottage

Craigmuir

Linburn Plantation

North Lodge

**1**

Southbar Ho

**2**

A8

M8

*Lin Burn*

Tappoc

69

Nether Southb

**Bishopton PA7**

**3**

North Commonside

*Lin Burn*

**4** Hareshaw

68

East Fulwood

M8 — MOTORWAY

**Johnstone PA6**

**5**

Georgetown

M8

HOUSTON

HOUSTON

ROAD

Dargavel Burn

Dargavel Bridge

**Paisley PA3**

River Gryfe

Barn

67

HOUSTON

B790

Netherfield Cottages

Netherfield House

Selvieland

Netherfield Cottages

**6**

MOSS

Fulwood Mains

Fulwood Mains Cottages

ROAD

44

Fulwood Bridge

A Birkenhead Farm

B

76
245

C

D

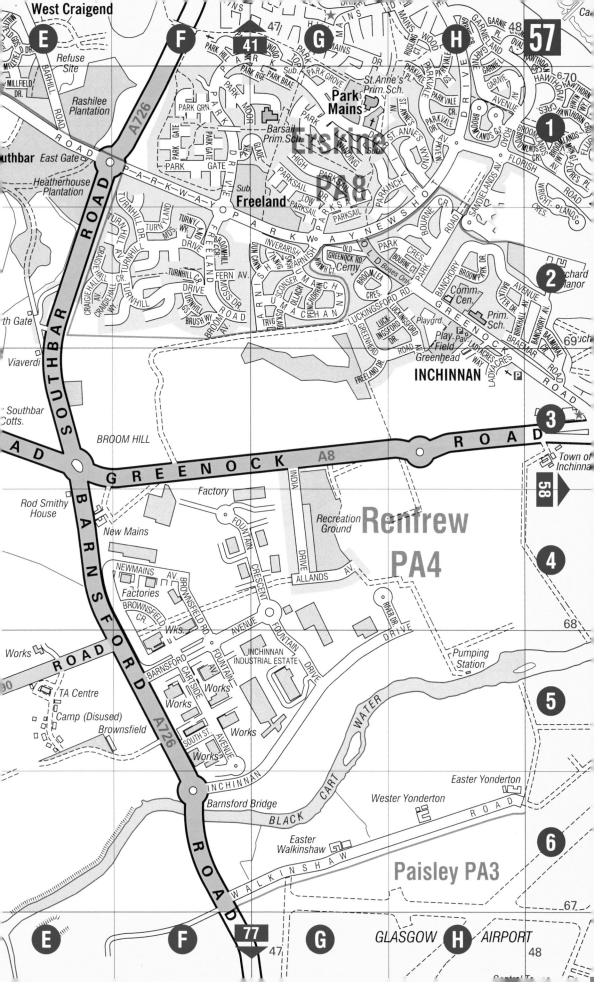

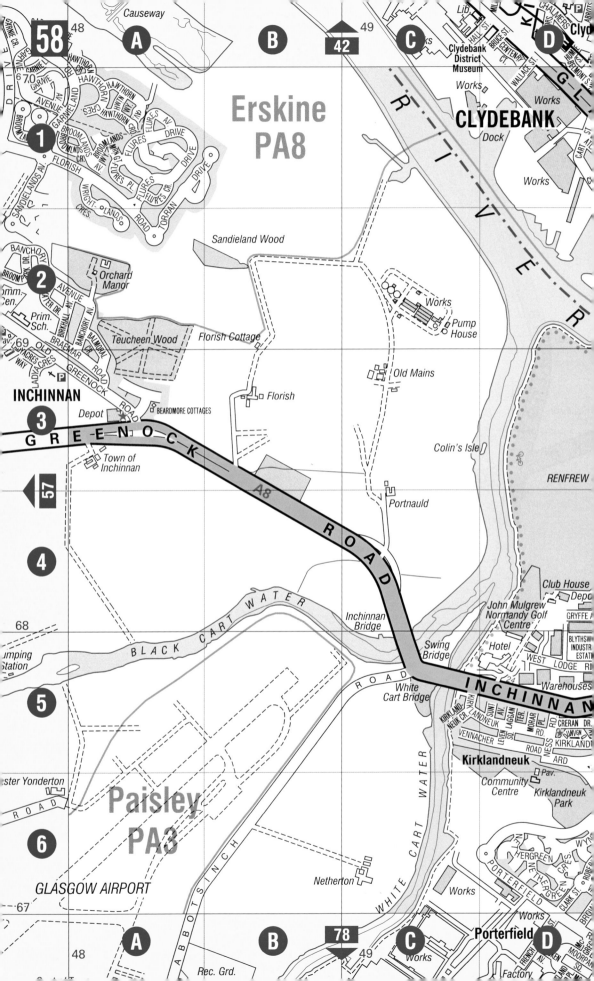

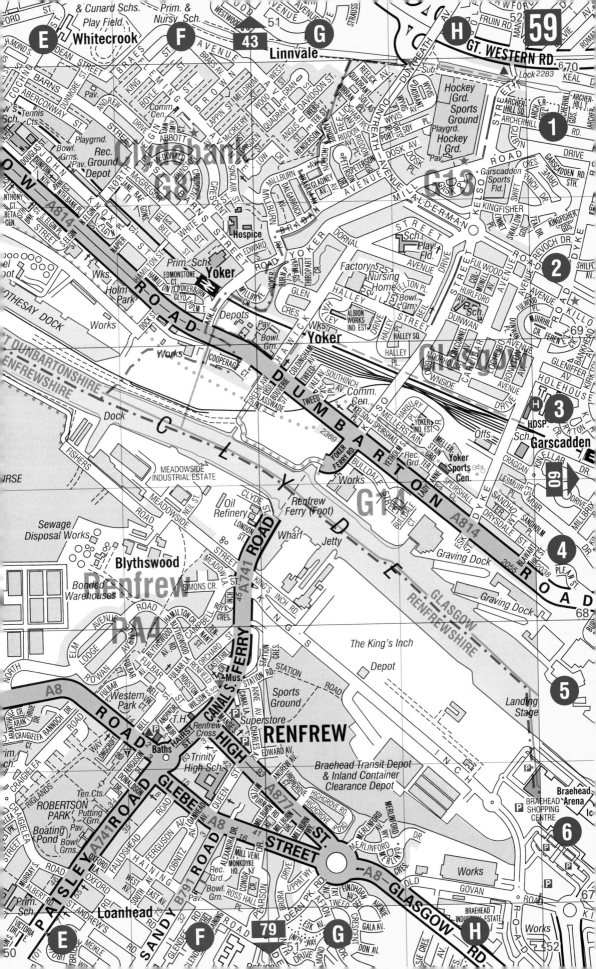

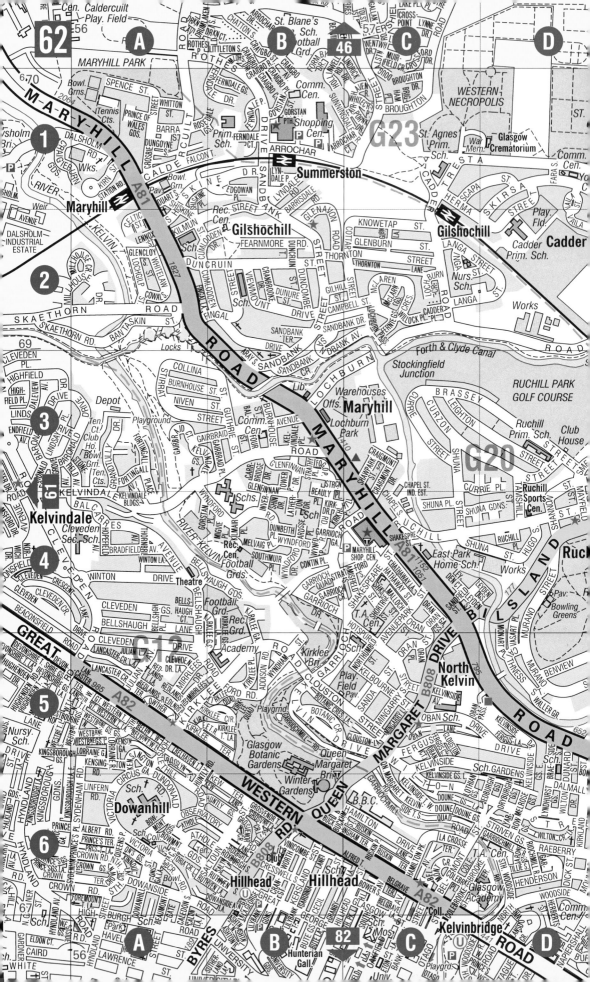

E  F  ▲ 47  59  G  H  260  **63**

670

POSSIL LOCH
(Bird Sanctuary)

Forth & Clyde Canal

SHELDAIG
AULTBEA
HILLSWICK
ROAD

CATHAY
CASTLE
STREET
SCARAWAY
CATHAY
SCARAWA
DR.

❶

**1**

SKERRAY
RAASAY
LONGAY
STORNOWAY
SHAPINSAY S.
SHAPINSAY'S.
VALLAY S.
MINGULAY
CRES.
TOROGAY
SHILL

BALMORE
INDUSTRIAL
ESTATE

GLENTANAR

DRYNOCH PL.
Sch.

EGILSAY
LONGAY
CR.
EGILSA ST.
EGILSAY
CR.
TOROGAY
TER.
ROGAY

**Milton**

RONAY
ENSAY ST.
MINGULAY
STREET
Tennis
Pav.  Cts.
Milton Park
Bowl.-Grns.

Prim.
Sch.

**❷**

LIDDESDALE
BIRSAY
LOSKIN
DR.
*St. Augustine's
Prim. & Sec. Schs.*

SCALPAY
SCALPAY PL.
SCALPAY
PASS.
RONALDSAY PASS.
SCALPAY PASS.

Comm.
Cen.
Library

LIDDESDALE TER.
Milton
Sch.
Milton
SQ.

**Colston**

ROAD

STREET

**Lambhill**
Lambhill
Bridge
STRACHUR
ST.
KYADALE
A879
KILFINAN ST
RoAD
ASHDENE

ERIBOLL
GREEN-MOUNT
ERIBOLL
ST.
ROAD
ASHGILL

KING'S
PL.
CLADDENS
BRACKEN ST.
HODGE CT.
LAMB
BROADHOLM

EGILSAY
ROAD
BERNERAY
Hockey
Playing
Fields

RONALDSAY
STREET
WESTRAY
WESTRAY
(SQ.)

CROWHILL
GLENHEAD

ASHGILL
PL.
HARMETRAY ST.
EDAY ST.
STREET

WESTRY
ST.

Chirnsyde
Sports Cen.
Playing
Field
Chirnsyde
Prim.
Sch.

EVERARD
CT.
EVERARD
QUA
69
EVERARD

**❸**

**Glasgow**

HAYWOOD
STREET
CHAPELTON
COLTMUIR
GADLOCH
CLADDENS QUAD.

**G22**

STREET
GLEN
EED
CR.
BUCKLEY ST.
KIPPEN
Sch.
STREET

Wo

Depot
PARKBRAE
PARKBRAE
PARKBRAE
DR.
PARKBRAE
PL.
Prim.
Sch.
Comm.
Cen.

BILSLAN'S
CT.
HAYSTON
CRES.
REDMOSS
ST.

BALMORE
PL.
**Possilpark &
Parkhouse**

LOMOND ST.  DENMARK

DENMARK
STREET
INDUS.
CENTRE

ASHFIELD
WAL  PA
WALNUT CR.
NUT PL.
WALNUT
HAWTHORN
QUAD.
CYPRESS ST.
SPRUCE ST.

**Ashfield**
Cowlairs
Nth. Junc.

CARRON
CR.
Sch.
CAR
CARRON PL.

64 ▶

**❹**

B808

**DRIVE**
**ROAD**

**HAWTHORN**
B808

STREET

Possil Park
Trading Cen.

73

MANSION
STREET
Sch.
Comm.
Cen.
Football
Grd.
20
Ind.
Est.

Depot
Keppoch
L Park
Hawthorn
Prim.
Sch.
Depot
**STREET**
**Possil
Park**
Saracen
Park

CHESTNUT ST.
CHRIS PL.
ROAD
NLVS PL.
BLACKTHORN
MEMEL
Comm.
Cen.
ELMVA
68
Cowlairs
West
Junc.

**❺**

Football
Ground
P

STRONEND
ST.
BALGAIR
PANMURE PL.
WESTER
COMMON DR.
BALGLASS
BARDOWIE
BARGAIR
ST.
BURMOLA
ST.
SUNNYLAW
CLOSEBURN

STREET
CARBETH
STREET
HOBART
STREET
BARDOWIE
ST.
DENMARK

ASHFIELD
ST.
FRUIN
FRUIN ST.
GLEN
GLENDVL
COULIN
GS.
TROOL
GS.
GS.
KIN.
BISHOT PH.

TORR ST.
LOCHSLOY CT.
SLOY
PL.
BRAEMORE GS.
FINLAS
STREET

COWLAIRS
INDUSTRIAL
ESTATE

CRICHTON
CRICHTON
PL.
Depo
Cowlairs

WESTER
COMMON
RD.
Schs.

Millennium
Cen.
Lib.

ALLANDER
STONYHURST
BAR-LOCH
REDNOCK

KIN.
BUCK
PASS.
BUCK
PL.

MORRIN
MORRIN PATH

**Cowlairs**

ck Thistle F.C.
(Firhill Park)

Wester
Common
Prim. Sch.

PANMURE
STONYHURST
DERWENT
ST.
SALMONA
ST.
HAMILTONH.
CRE.
HAMILTONH.
CR.

DARVAN
AUCKLAND
DARTFORD
DENHAM ST.
BONHILL

STREET
KILLEARN
STREET

STREET
KESSOCK
PL.
MONAR PL.
KESSOCK
DR.

KIN.
KIN.
ST.
ST.
KILLEARN ST.
CARLISLE
Depot
INVERURIE
ST.
GOURLAY
GOURLAY ST.
ST.
KEPPOCH
ROAD
Sch.
Prim.
Sch.

**Firhill**

ELLESMERE
ROAD
ELLESMERE
CALLANDER
ST.

CLEGHORN
ST.
ELTHAM ST.
APPLEBY
ST.

**Hamiltonhill**
Works

St. Teresa's
Prim. Sch.

Keppoch
Prim.
Sch.

**COWLAIRS PARK**
**(Rec. Grd.)**

**G21**

P

❻

**6**

Works

NAL
GEN
ANCROFT ST.
HOPEHILL
GS.
A81

**CARSCUBE**

OAKBANK
INDUS. EST.
DAWSON PL.
BAIRD BRAE

APPLECROSS
WSON
RD.
CRAIGHALL
RD.
A879

Warehouse

KEPPOCHHILL
COLD
STREAM
MASTERTON ST.

SCONE
ST.
PEATHILL
ST.
PINKSTON
COXHILL ST.
KEPPOCHHILL

FOUNTAINWELL PL.
ROY
DRIVE
FOUNTAINWELL PL.
KEYHILL
Sighthill
Prim.
Sch.
KEPHILL
Play
Fld.
EAGLE
HEIGHTS

**SIGHTH**
**CEMETE**
67
Monu
260

HILL
GROVEPARK
GS.
GROVEPARK
ST.
WOODSIDE TER.
WINDSOR TER.
Sch.
Depo

CEDAR
PK. GS.
CAITHNESS
FARM
BURNS
SAWMILLFIELD
ST.

ROAD
POSSIL
CALLANDER
BARR ST.
RODNEY
CRAIGHALL
124
BORRON
G4

VINTNER
HARVEY
Distillery
PORT DUNDAS
INDUS. EST.

FOUNTAINWELL
Sub.
Sch.
ARY
HUNTINGDON
FOUNTAINWELL
RD.
TINGDON
SQUARE
RD.
Youth
Si

E  F  ▲ 83  59  G  H
**ROAD**  **CRAIGHALL**  **ROAD**

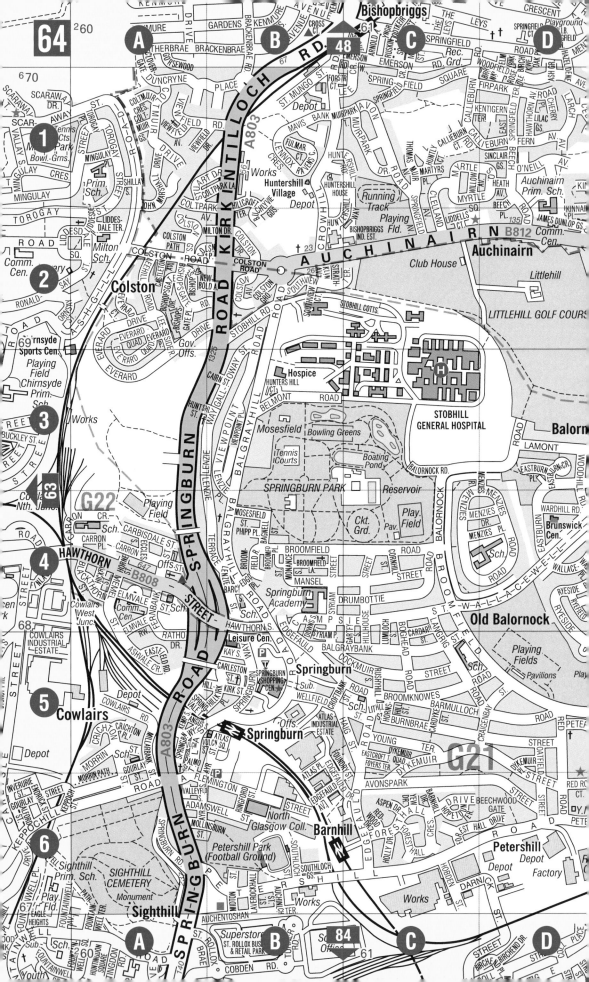

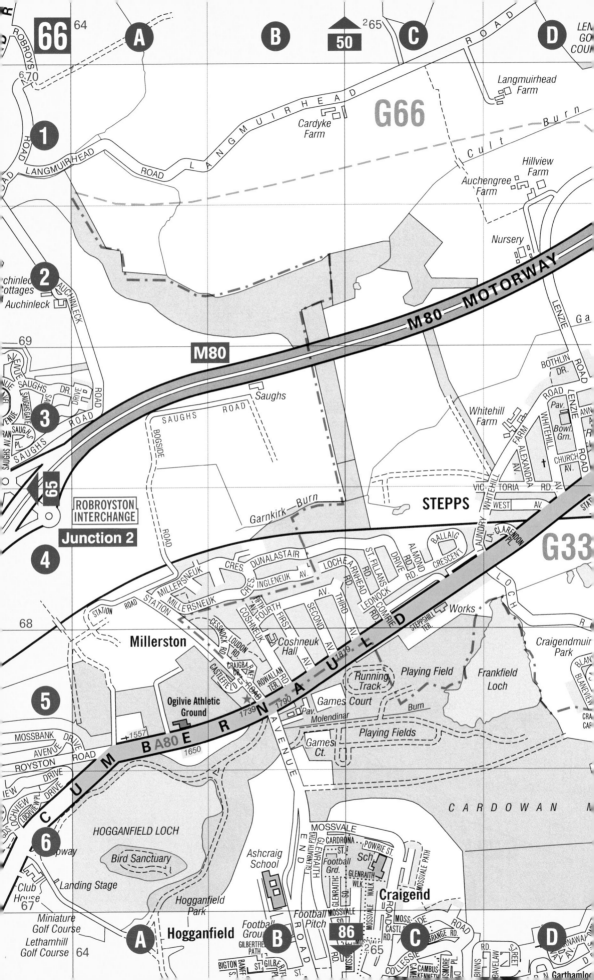

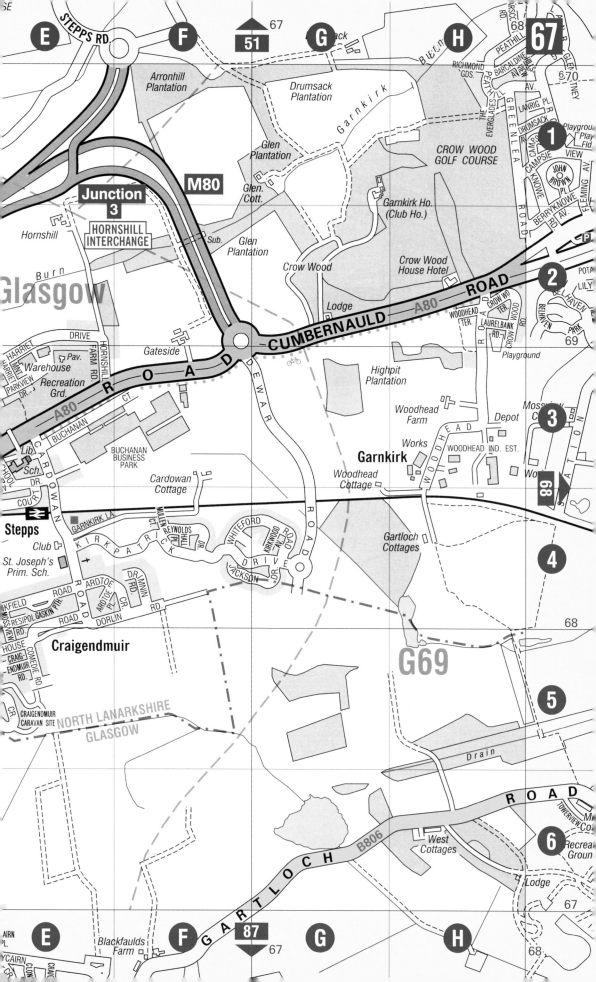

Arronhill
Plantation

Drumsack
Plantation

Garnkirk

Glen
Plantation

CROW WOOD
GOLF COURSE

Glen.
Cott.

Glen Plantation

Sub.

M80

Junction
3
HORNSHILL
INTERCHANGE

Hornshill

Burn

Garnkirk Ho.
(Club Ho.)

**1**

Crow Wood

Crow Wood
House Hotel

**Glasgow**

Lodge

Woodhead
TER.

CUMBERNAULD   ROAD

A80

**2**

Laurelbank
RD.

Playground

69

DRIVE

Gateside

Highpit
Plantation

HARRIET

Pav.

Warehouse

Recreation
Grd.

A80   ROAD

Woodhead
Farm

Depot

Mossview
C

**3**

PARKVIEW
DR.

BUCHANAN

Works

Woodhead

WOODHEAD IND. EST.

68

BUCHANAN
BUSINESS
PARK

Cardowan
Cottage

**Garnkirk**

Woodhead
Cottage

Lib.
Sch.
COURT

Wo

CARDOWAN
DR.
GARNKIRK LA.

KIRKPATRICK

NILLEN
CT.

REYNOLDS
PL.
HILL
DR.

WHITEFORD

KIRKWOOD
ROAD

ROAD

Gartloch
Cottages

**4**

**Stepps**

Club

St. Joseph's
Prim. Sch.

JACKSON
DRIVE
DR.

ARDTOE
PL.
DRUMIN
RD.

KFIELD
ROAD
RESIPOL
RD.

**Craigendmuir**

ARDTOE
CR.
DORLIN
RD.

GASKIN PTH.

MOSS
VIEW RD.
HOUSE

68

**G69**

CRAIG-
ENDMUIR
RD.

COMEDIE RD.

CR.

CRAIGENDMUIR
CARAVAN SITE

NORTH LANARKSHIRE
GLASGOW

**5**

Drain

ROAD

TOWERVIEW Co.

**6**

B806

GARTLOCH

West
Cottages

Recrea
Groun

Lodge

67

Blackfaulds
Farm

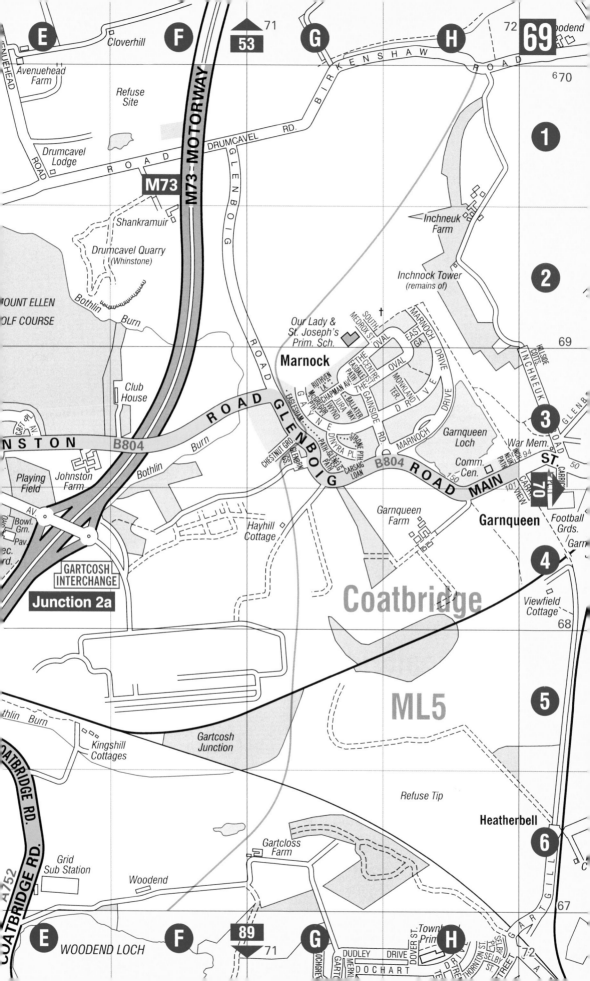

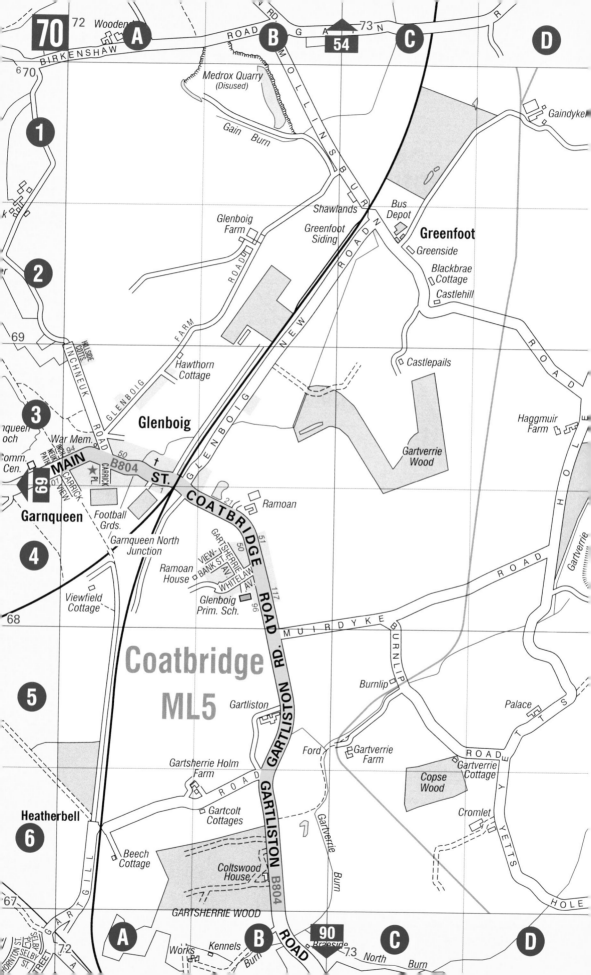

Black Craig

Cleddans
East Lodge
West Lodge
Hairstanes Cottage

Plantation

Douglas Plantation

76

House

670

Cullochrig

**1**

Brackenhirst Plantation

East Lodge Wood

East Gartmillan

Glenmill

Shank Burn

Foot o' Loan Wood

West Gartmillan

Arderyth

Glenmill Wood

Drumbowie Farm

**2**

69

Greenfield

Firknowe

ROAD

BRACKENHIRST

Reservoir (covered)

**3**

Brackenhirst GDNS.

Ryding

B802

Gas Storage Depot

Brackenhirst Farm

**Airdrie ML6**

Laverock Knowe

**4**

Ryden Mains

Cemetery

**New Monkland**

Norwood

Rochsoles

Crowhill Plantation

68

Cemetery

New Monkland Prim. Sch.

CRATHIE

B803

MORAL TREE
BANCHORY
STRYRE GDS.
GRANT GS.
DUNNET
NIGG
AV.

CULZEAN
DRIVE
WINDSOR
IRVINE ST.
APRIN WY.
HAWKWD.
MAINS
MAINS
MELDRUM

**5**

Comm. Cen.
CLEDDANS VW.
173

QUARRYSIDE ST.

LOCHBUIE LA.

MELDRUM

190

LOCHDON

GLENVIEW ST.

AIRDRIE GOLF COURSE

KIRKSTYLE PL.

MACARTHUR

WADDELL AV.
AV.

Playground

Football Ground

Bowl. Grn.

91

92  227

**GLENMAVIS**

GLENWELL ST.

Blackwalk Plantation

Roughcraig Glen

CRES.

**6**

Braidenhill Farm

Dryflat

B803

**COATBRIDGE**

ROAD

**GLENMAVIS**

B802

South Lodge

STRATHSPEY CR.
STRATHBLANE CR.
STRTHMORE CR.
STRTHON.
STRATHCON
CR.

PARK

DRIVE

STRTHAVEN CR.
STRTHMORE CR.
STRATHPEFFER

67

BRAES

STAINEY
PL. 76

Cemy.

ROAD

Club Ho.

**Golfhill**

LOCHEARN CR.
LOCHGOILE
BLUEBELL
WAY

TIMMEL
CR.

103

RINGHORN

Virtuewell Glen

Golfhill Prim. Sch.

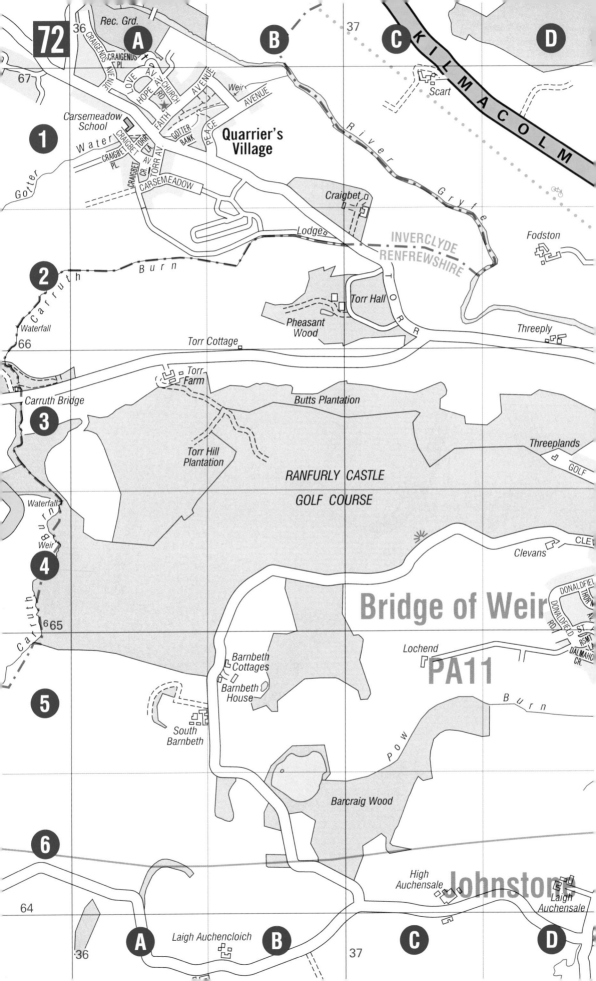

36  A  B  37  C  KILMACOLM  D

67

Rec. Grd.

CRAIGENDS PL
CRAIGENDS

AVENUE

Scart

Weir

AVENUE

1

Carsemeadow School

Water

LOVE AV.
HOPE AV.
CHURCH RD.
FAITH

GOTTER BANK

AVENUE

PEACE

Quarrier's Village

Craigbet

River
Gryfe

Fodston

CRAIGBET
TORR AV.
CRAIGBET PL
CRAIGBET CR.
TORR AV.

CARSEMEADOW

Lodge

INVERCLYDE
RENFREWSHIRE

Gotter

Burn

2

Carruth

TORR

Torr Hall

66

Waterfall

Torr Cottage

Pheasant Wood

Threeply

Carruth Bridge

Torr Farm

Butts Plantation

3

Torr Hill Plantation

Threeplands

GOLF

RANFURLY CASTLE

GOLF COURSE

Waterfall

Burn

Clevans

CLE

4

Weir

Bridge of Weir

DONALDFIEL
THORN
DONALDFIELD RD.
ST.
BSMT
DALMAHO
CR.

Carruth

65

Lochend

PA11

5

Barnbeth Cottages

Barnbeth House

Burn

South Barnbeth

POW

Barcraig Wood

6

High Auchensale

Johnstone

64

Laigh Auchensale

36  A  Laigh Auchencloich  B  37  C  D

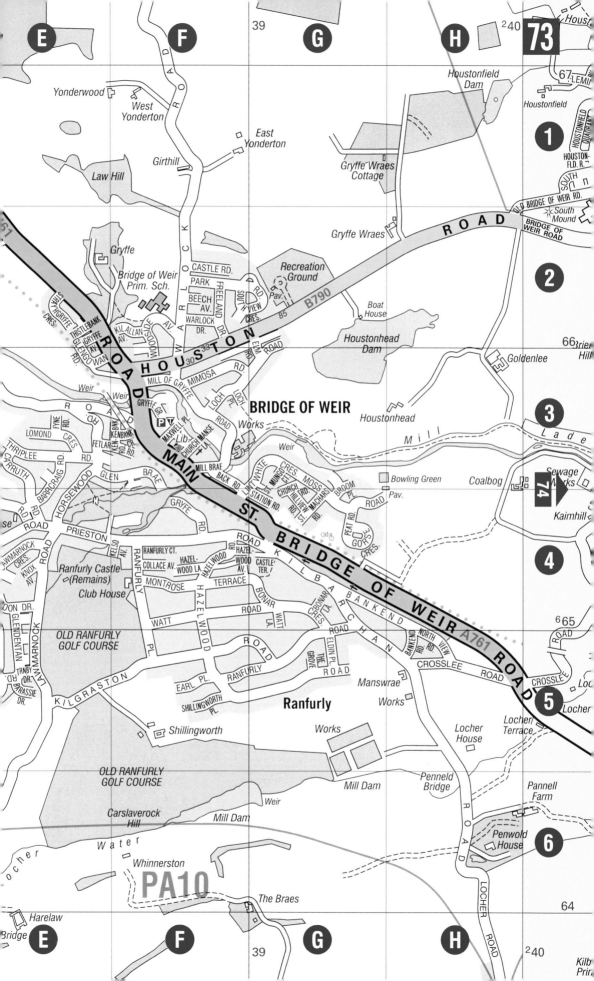

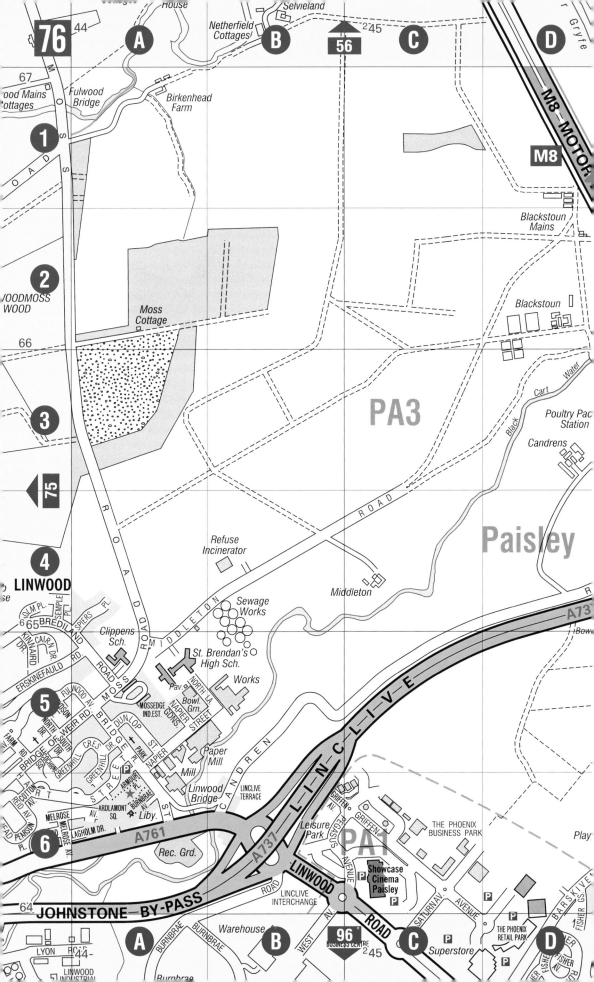

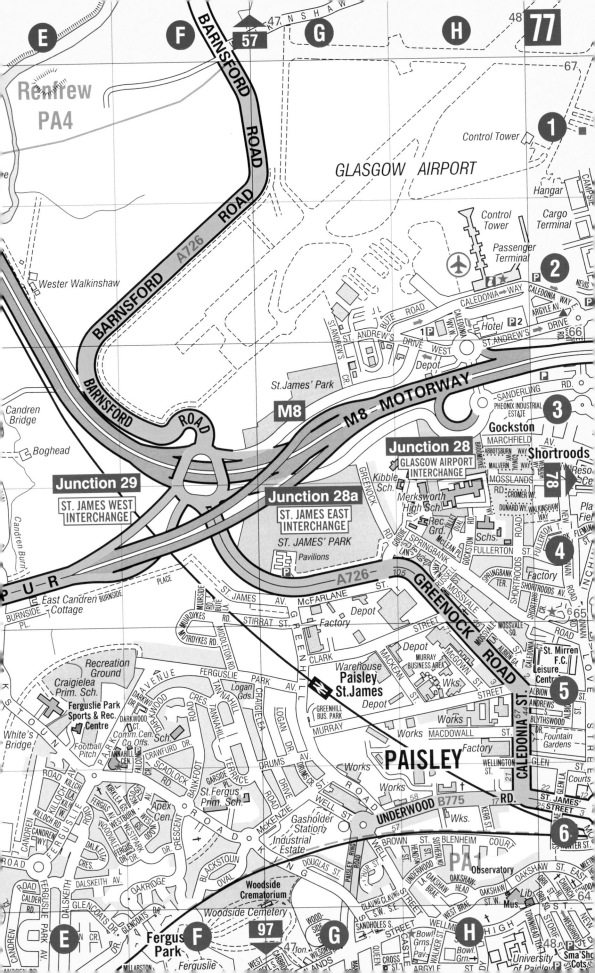

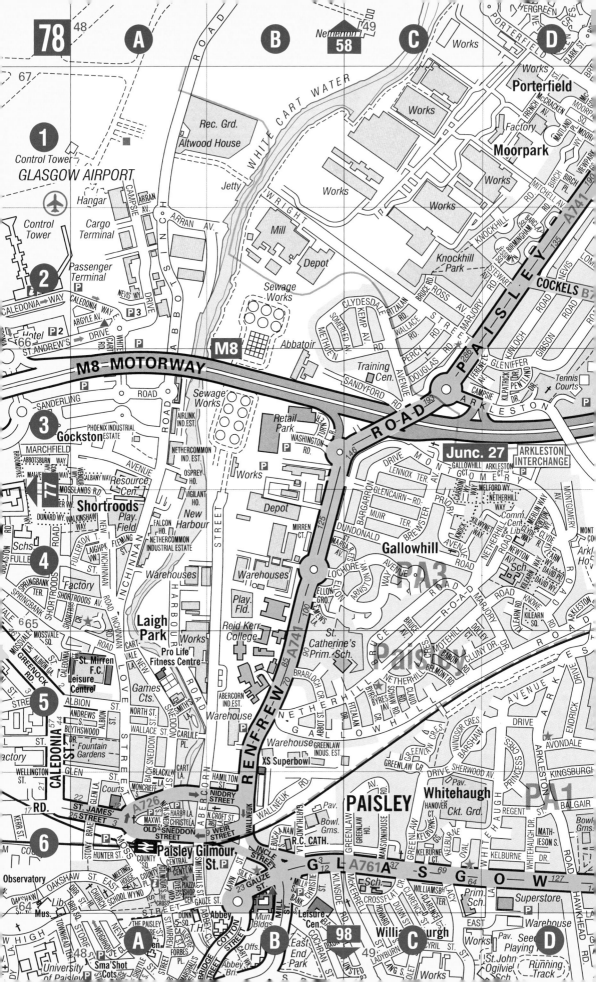

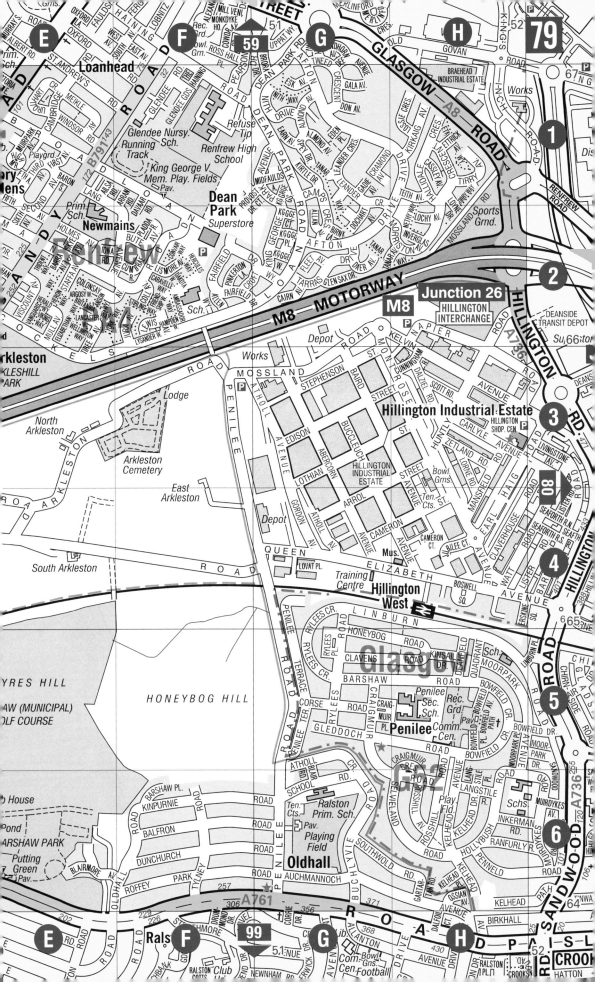

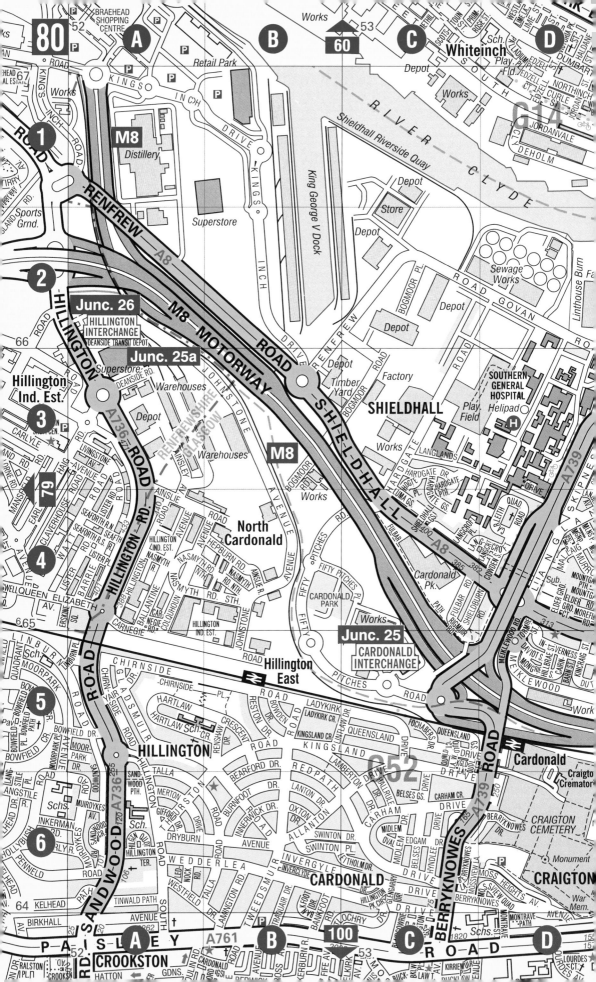

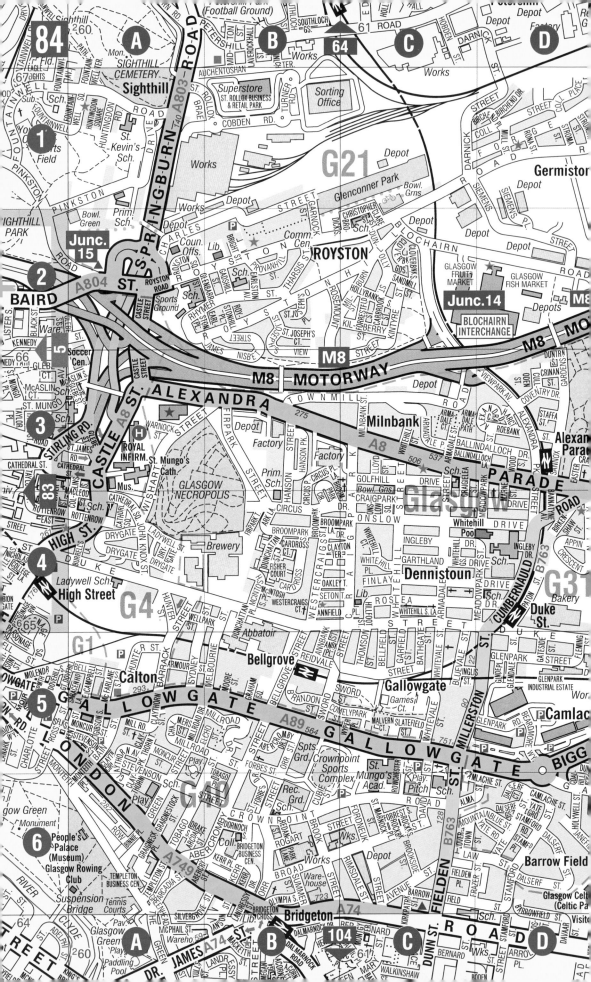

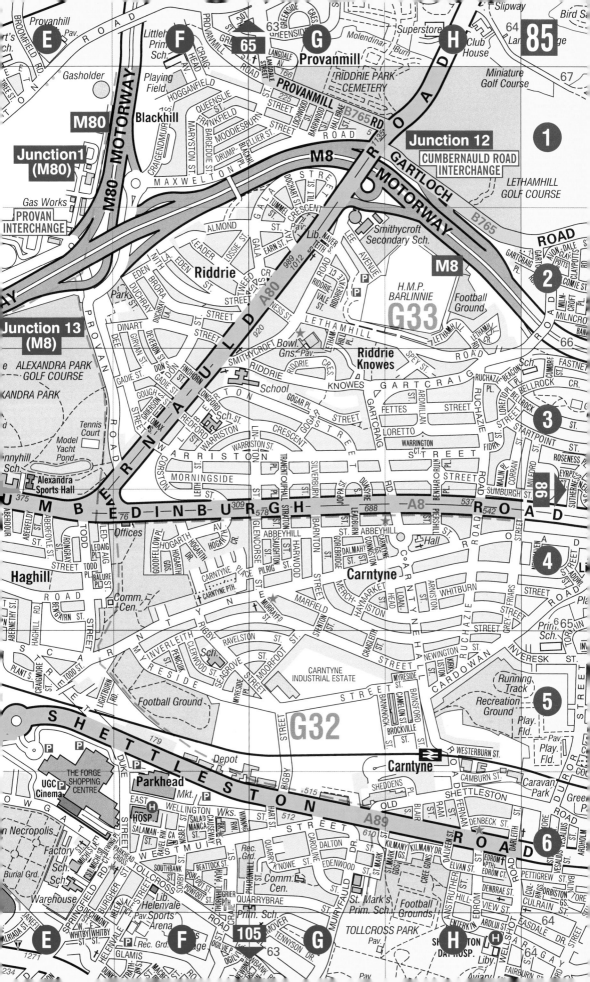

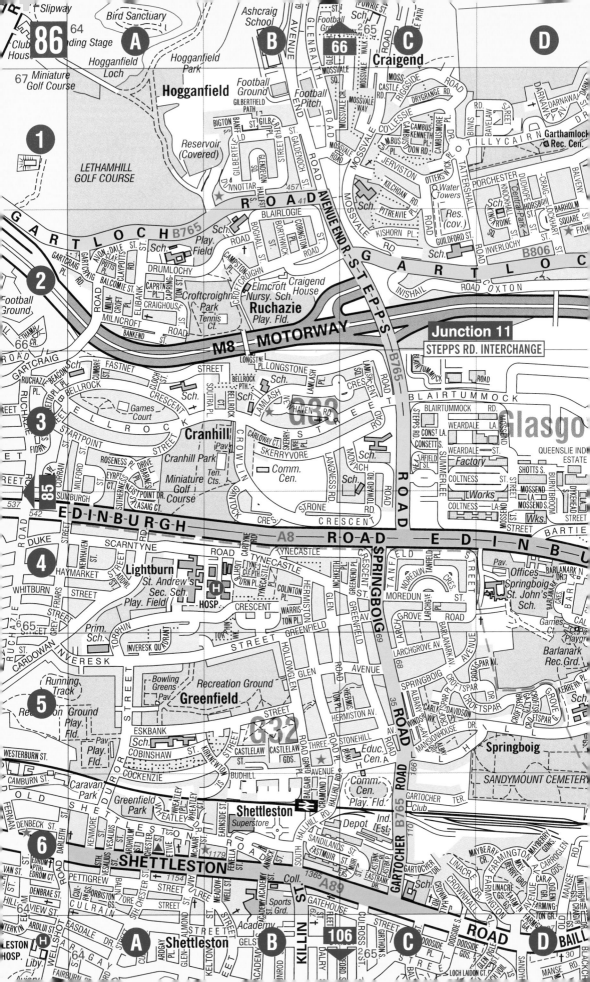

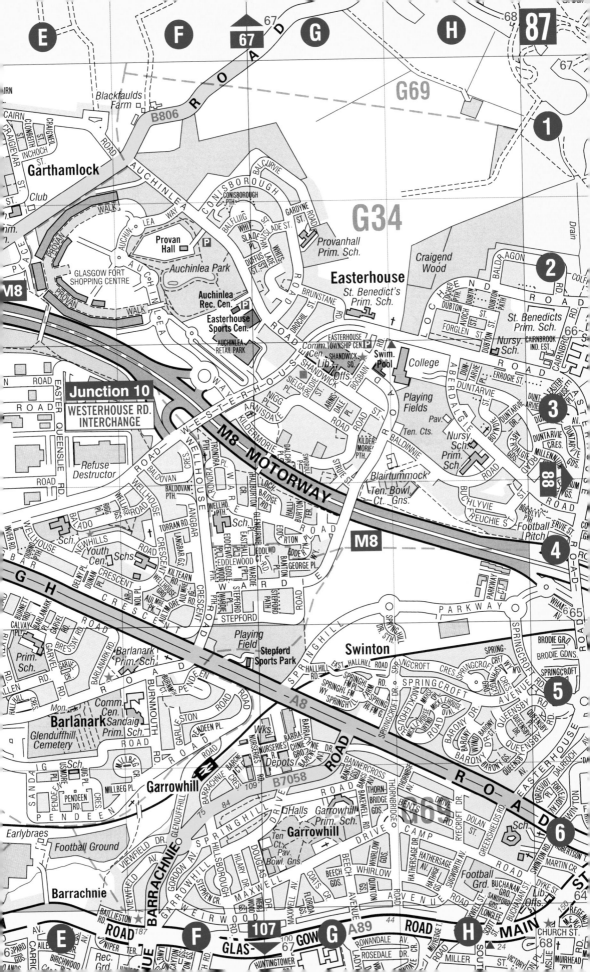

**88**

A  B  C  D

1  2  3  4  5  6

**BISHOP LOCH**

Glasgow

M73

Lochwood Farm
Lochwood Cottages
Baillie Moss Wood

ROAD

Drain

68 Lodge
67

Recreation Ground

68

Burn

Lochwood Plantation
AUCHINGILL ROAD
Sch.
MYROCH ROAD
DINDUFF ST.
STOBO ST.
SKELBO PATH
AUCHINGILL
COLFIN ST.
CALCOTS PL.
CALCOTS PL.
LIFT PTH.
LOCH-FRED
DRUMLANRIG
DALLEA
DALLEA PL.
GLASSEL RD.
OAKWOOD CR.
OAKWOOD
TWIN-LAW
CANOMBIE ST.
CORPACH PL.
ABBEYCRAG
GLENFELG QUADRANT
ABBEYGREEN ST.
ABBEYCRAG RD.
DUNPHAIL DR.
DUNPHAIL
ALLWCH PL.
LAIRIG
DUNPHAN
Drain

BALDRAGON
DUBTON ST.
DUBTON ST.
WESTERHOUSE RD.
ERROGIE ST.
St. Benedicts Prim. Sch.
Nursy. Sch.
CAIRNBROOK IND. EST.
CAIRNBROOK RD.
Lochend Secondary Sch.
GLENGYRE ST.
GLASSEL RD.
AVENUE
St. Clare's Prim. Sch.
AUCHENCROW ST.
BRUCEFIELD PL.
COMMONHEAD
NETHERHOUSE RD.
NETHERHOUSE
Heatheryknowe
HEATHERYKNOWE ROAD

**G34**
Playing Field

66
CHERUSTARVIE
DUNTARVIE AV.
DUNTARVIE CRES.
DUNTARVIE GDNS.
CORSE-HILL PL.
CORSEHILL ST.
CORSE-HILL PATH
Rogerfield Prim. Sch.
DALSWINTON ST.
DALSWINTON
TORDUN PTH.
DUNSKAITH ST.
DUNSKAITH
Schs.
Commonhead

**87**
ABERDALGIE ROAD
BOYND
RICHLYVIE
FREUCHIE ST.
Football Pitch
BUCHLYVIE PTH.
TERVIE PL.
MILLENNIUM CT.
MILLENNIUM GS.
MILLENNIUM ROAD
DENMILNE ST.
DENMILNE ST.
FINLARIG ST.
LENTRAN ST.
DENMILNE PATH
COLLREE GDNS.

4
PARKWAY CT.
KWAY 65
WHAMFLET AV.
ROGERFIELD ROAD
EASTERHOUSE ROAD
**Junction 9**
**EASTERHOUSE RD. INTERCHANGE**
Whitehall
Rogerfield Farm
ROAD
**West Maryston**
DENMILNE RD.
Netherhouse

**G69**
Greenwells

Swinton
SPRING-CROFT
SPRINGCROFT GS.
BRODIE GRO.
BRODIE GDNS.
SPRINGCROFT ROAD
**Easterhouse**
RHINDMUIR CT.
RHINDMUIR
LONG ROW
RHINDMUIR DRIVE
RHINDMUIR AV.
RHINDMUIR
Sch.
RHINDMUIR WYND
RHINDMUIR GRO.
RHINDMUIR RD.
RHINDMUIR VW.
**M8**
M73

5
QUEENSBY DR.
QUEENSBY PL.
QUEENSBY RD.
QUEENSBY AV.
BARONY GDNS.
Football Grd.
DALREOCH PATH
FAULDSPARK CR.
MAINHILL PL.
MAINHILL AV.
MAINHILL ROAD
CRESCENT
MANSE ROAD
Hall
**Junction 8 (M8)**
ROA
Depot
A89 501
**COATBRIDG**
ROSLYN DR.
MELROSE
CAMPSIE CR.
LORD WY.
BRAESIDE
Pav. AV.
Recreation Ground
Playgd.
**BARGEDDIE**
MAINHILL
QUEENS
ABERCROMBIE

6
**EDINBURGH RD.**
GREENSHEILDS RD.
ROBERTSON T.
MARTIN CR.
SWINTON
FORTEVIOT
FORFAR AV.
FAULDS GS.
GLENBURN
GLENBURN CR.
GLEN-BURN WK.
FAULDS AV.
RHINDSDALE CR.
SWINTON AV.
MAINHILL
RHDHO.
CROSSVIEW AV.
CROSSVIEW
**COATBRIDGE RD.**
**GLASGOW & EDINBURGH RD.**
**BAILLIESTON INTERCHANGE**
A8
**Junc. 2 (M73)**
MAINHILL
BREDISHOLM ROAD
ABERCROMBIE ROAD
Memor. Hall

24
68
VICTORY ST.
MAIN STREET
A89
CHURCH ST.
MUIRHEAD
P Superstore
Memorial Park
**Crosshill**
BREDISHOLM ROAD
**BAILLIESTON**
REGENTS
BREDISHOLM
DYKE ST.
ELLISMUIR PL.
ELLISMUIR TER.
THORNYBURN DR.
RAVENSWOOD RD.
64
LONGLEE
BUCHANAN GRO.
BUCHANAN ST.
Lib. Offs.

108

69

A  B  C  D

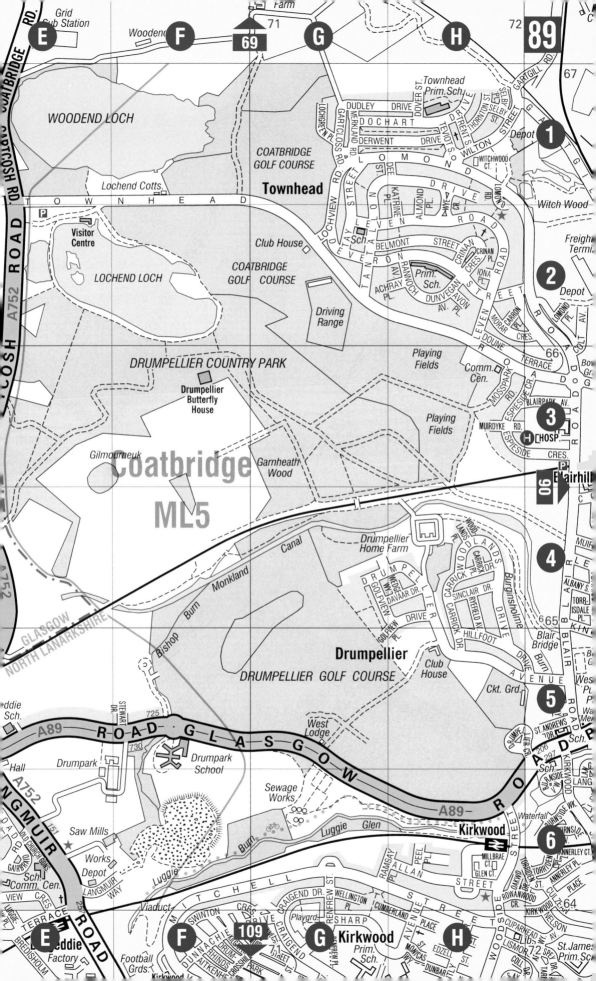

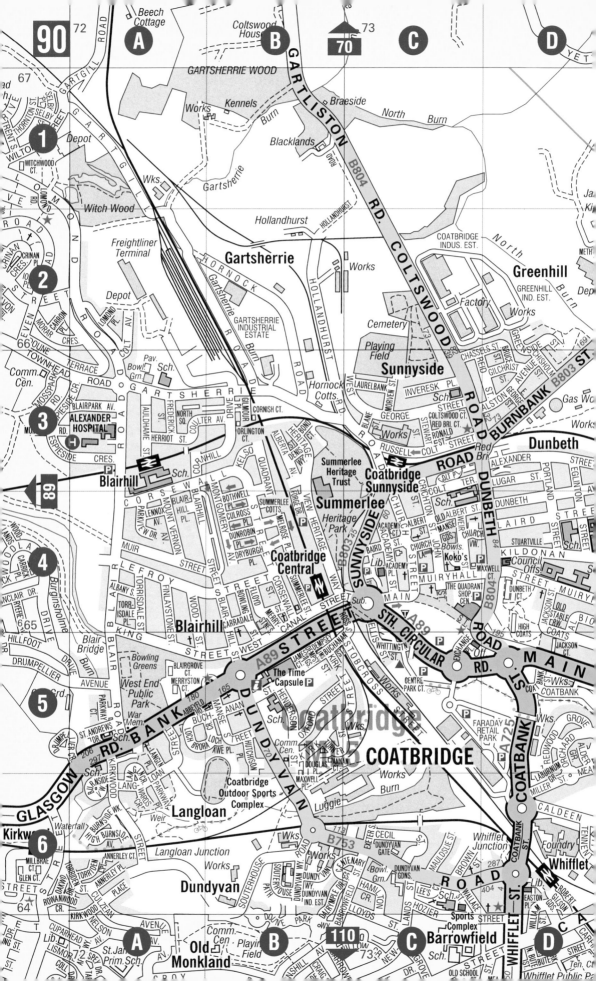

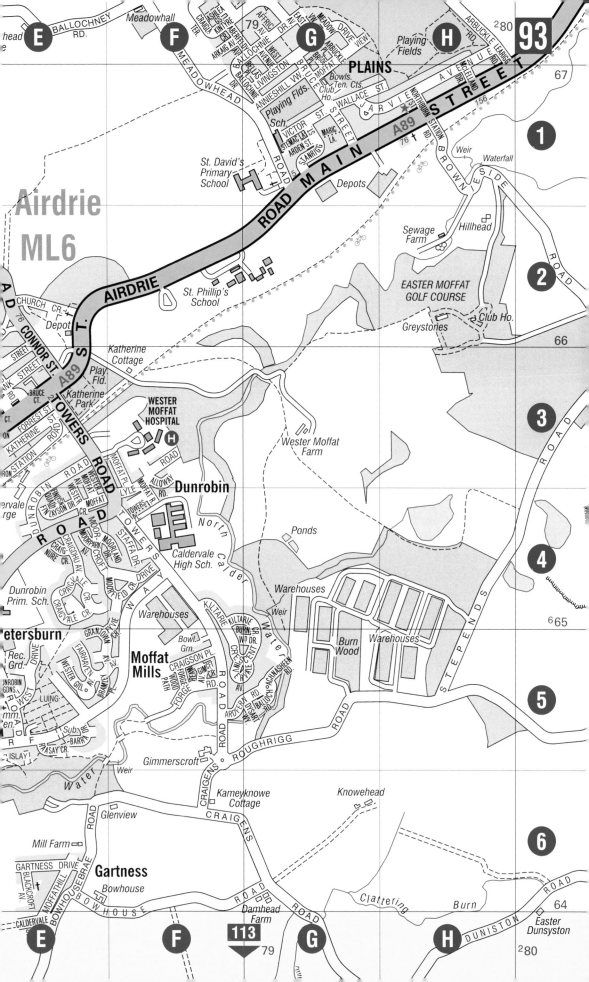

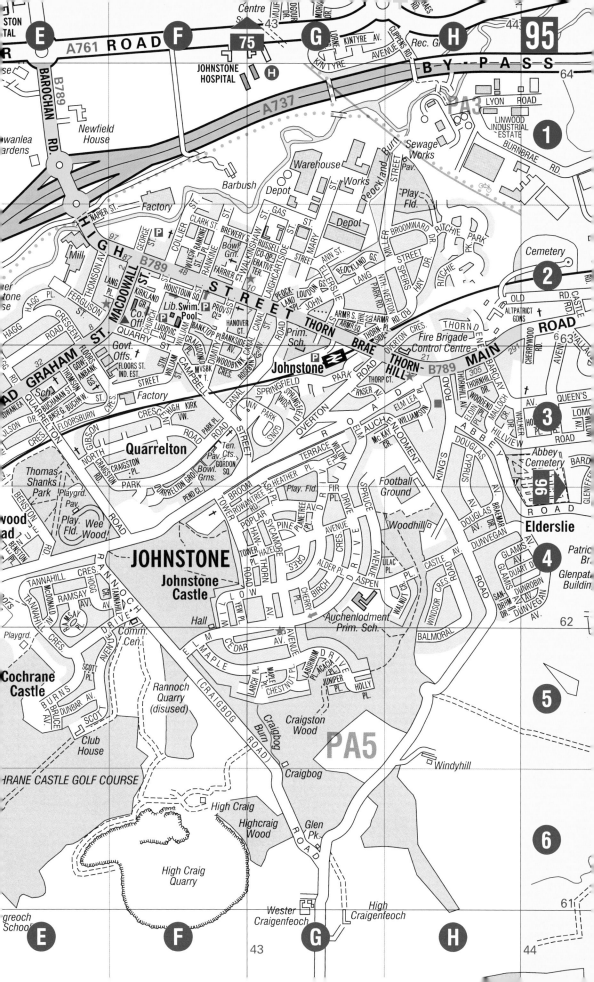

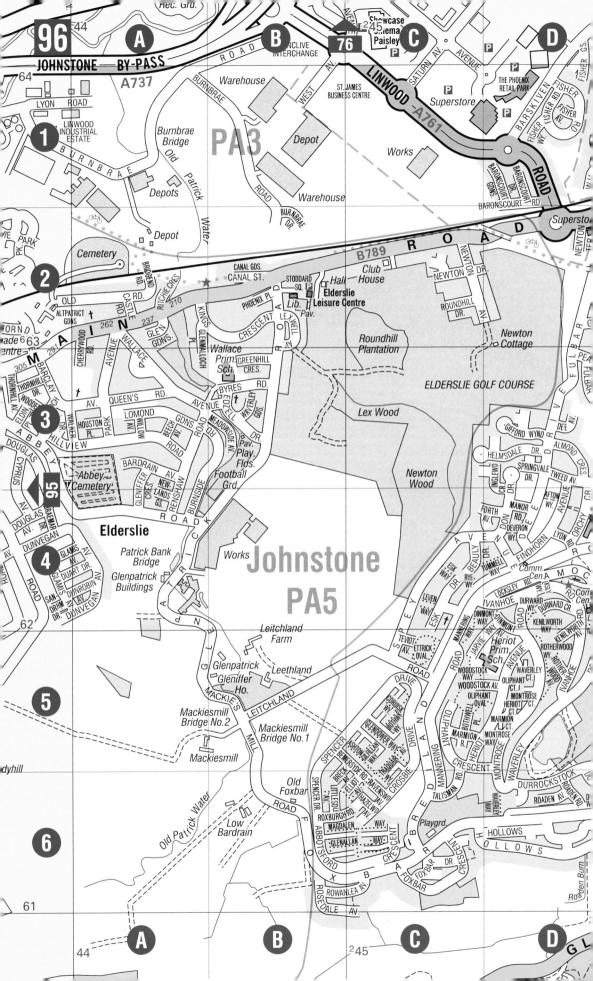

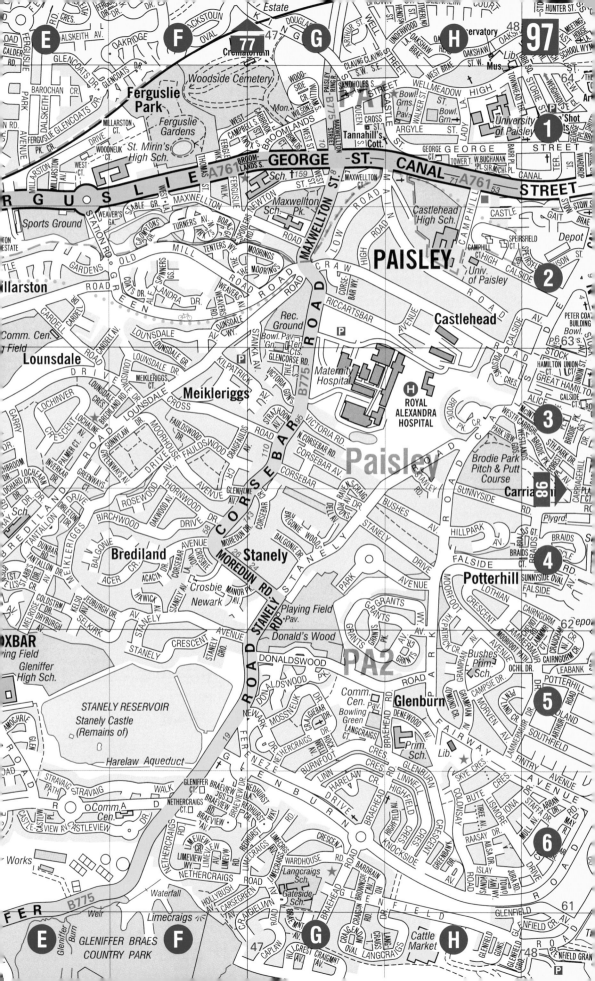

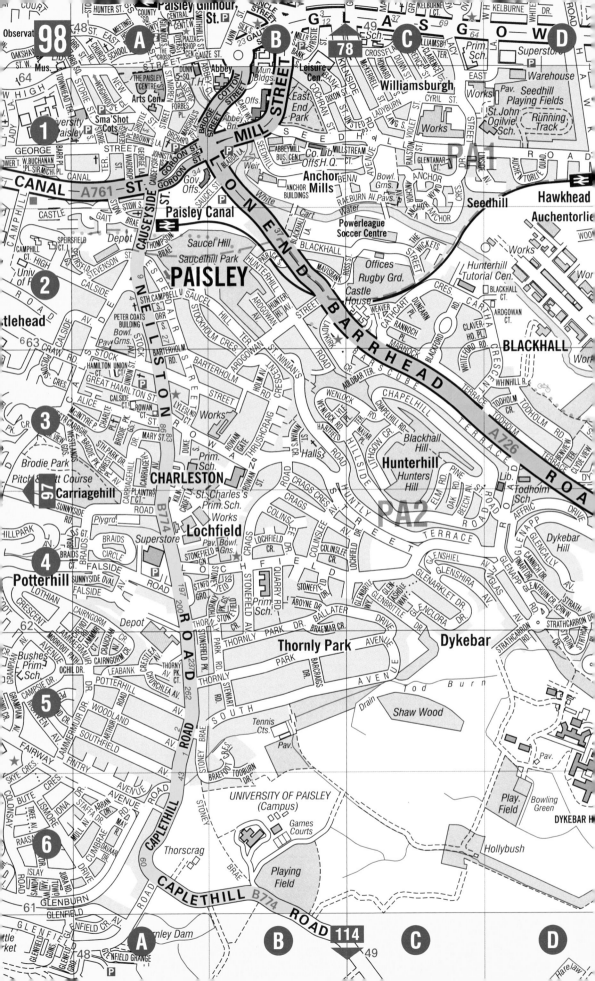

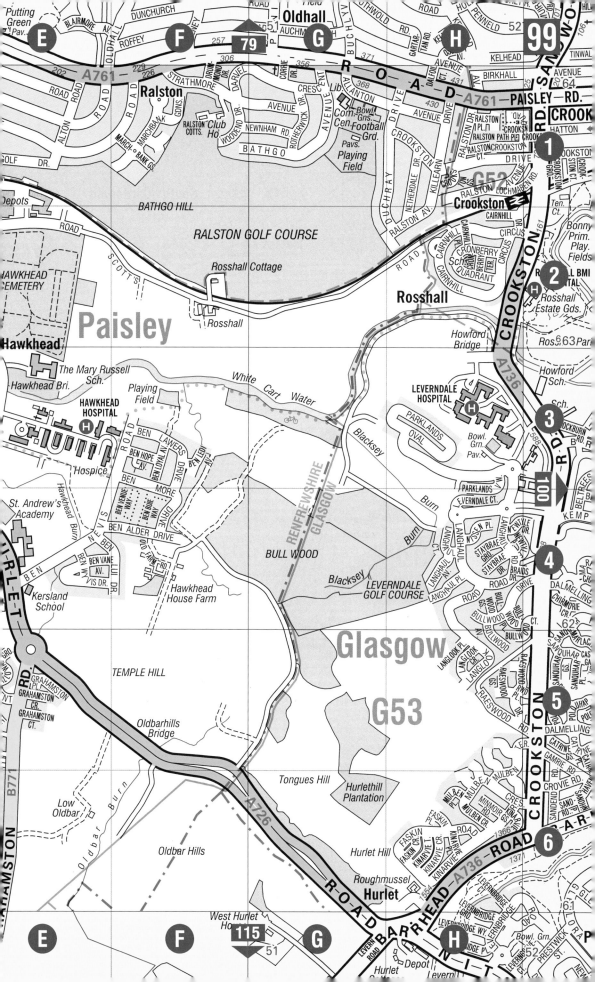

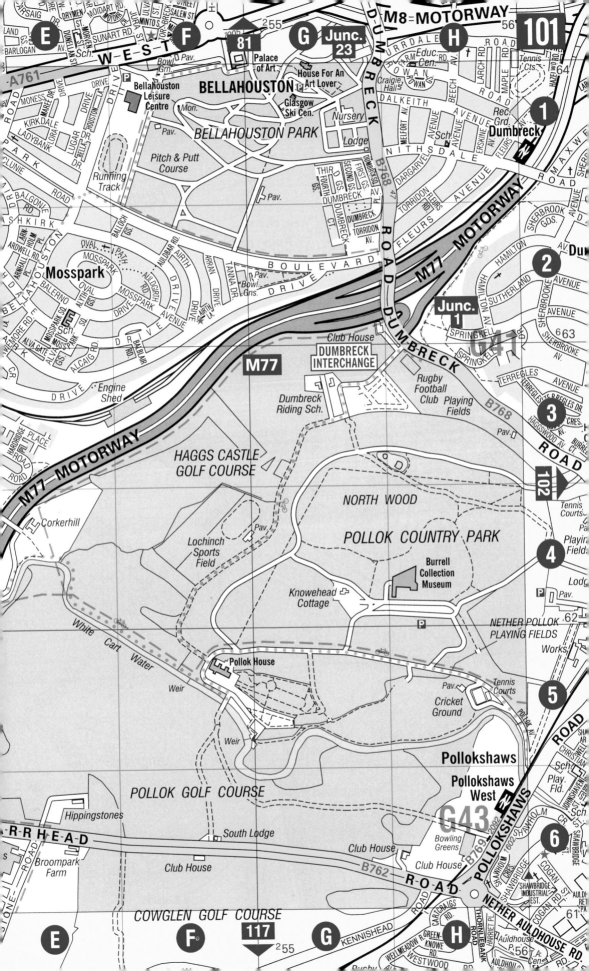

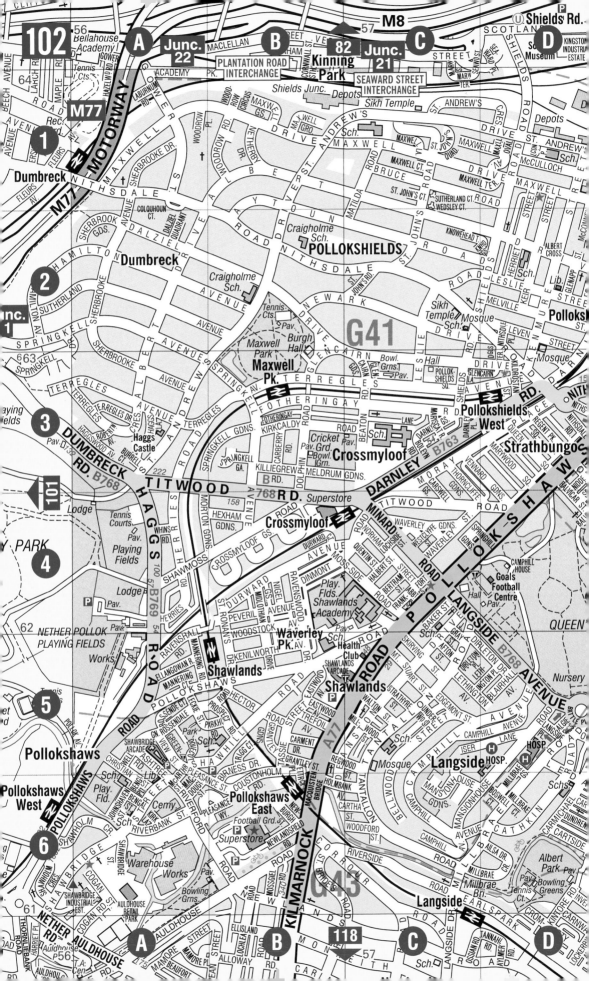

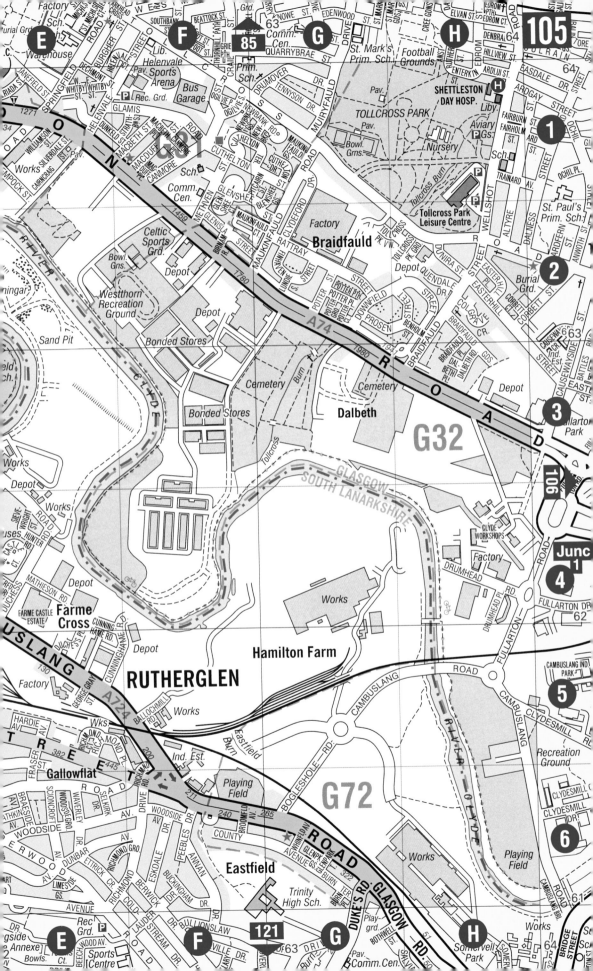

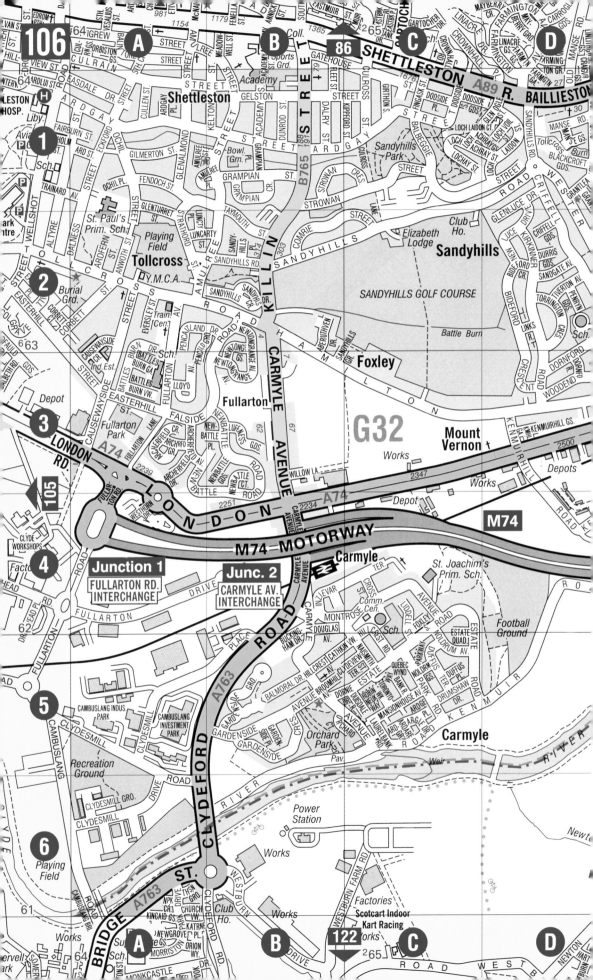

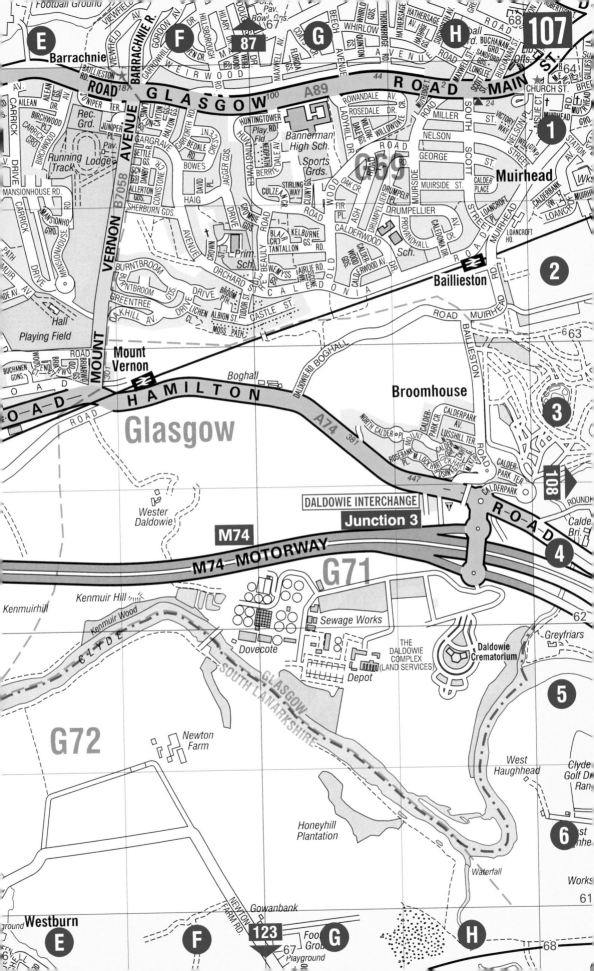

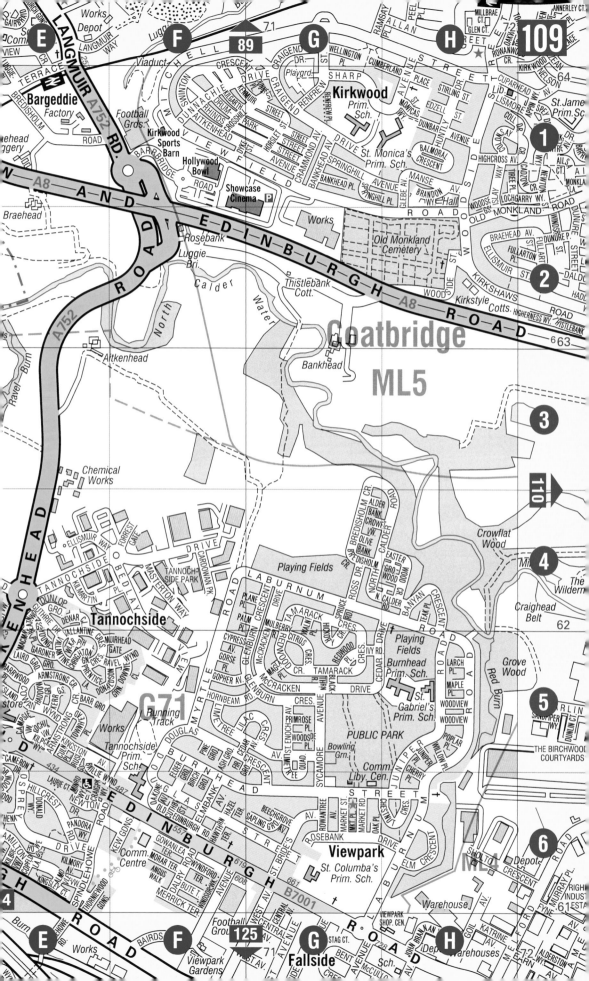

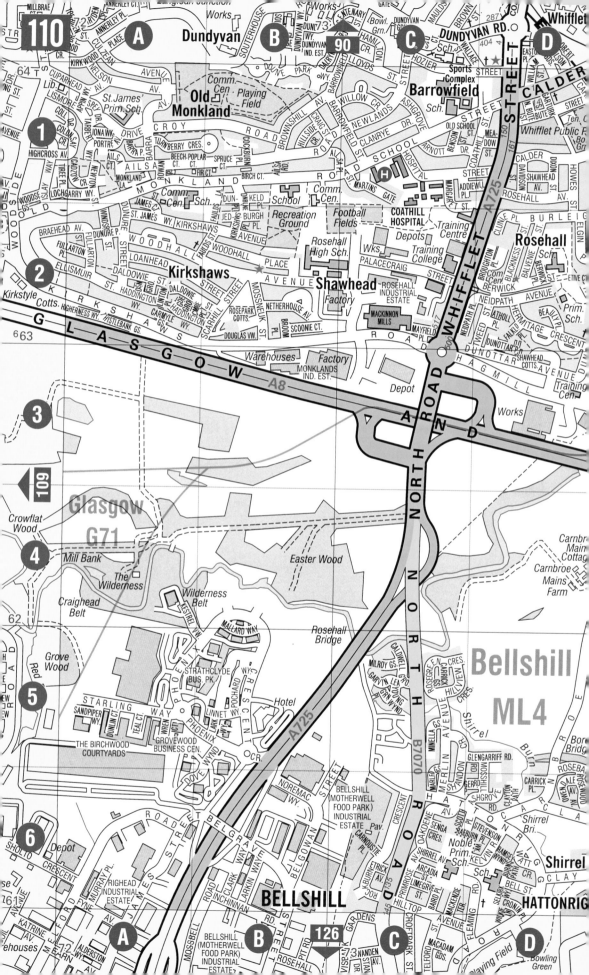

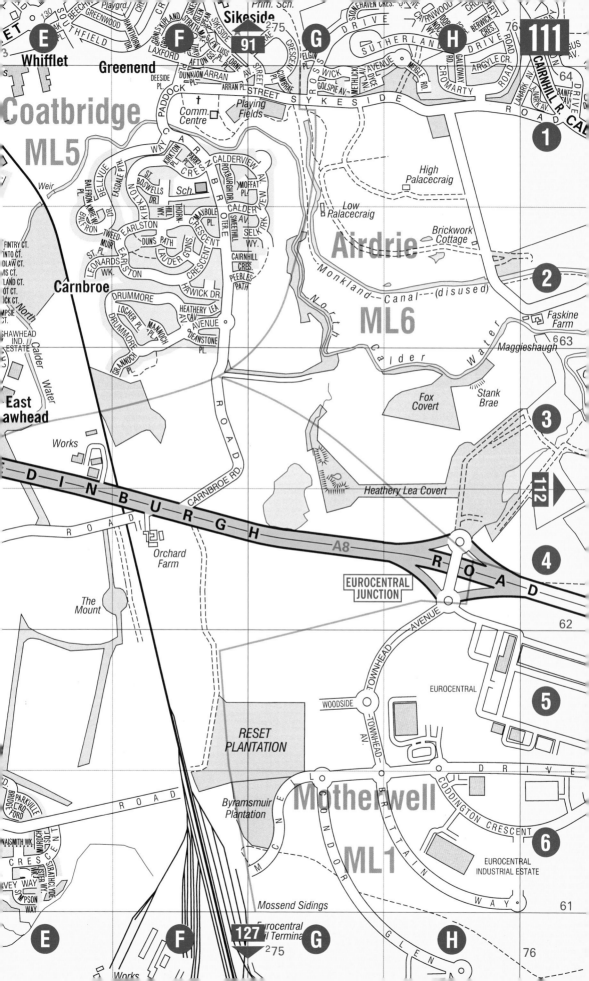

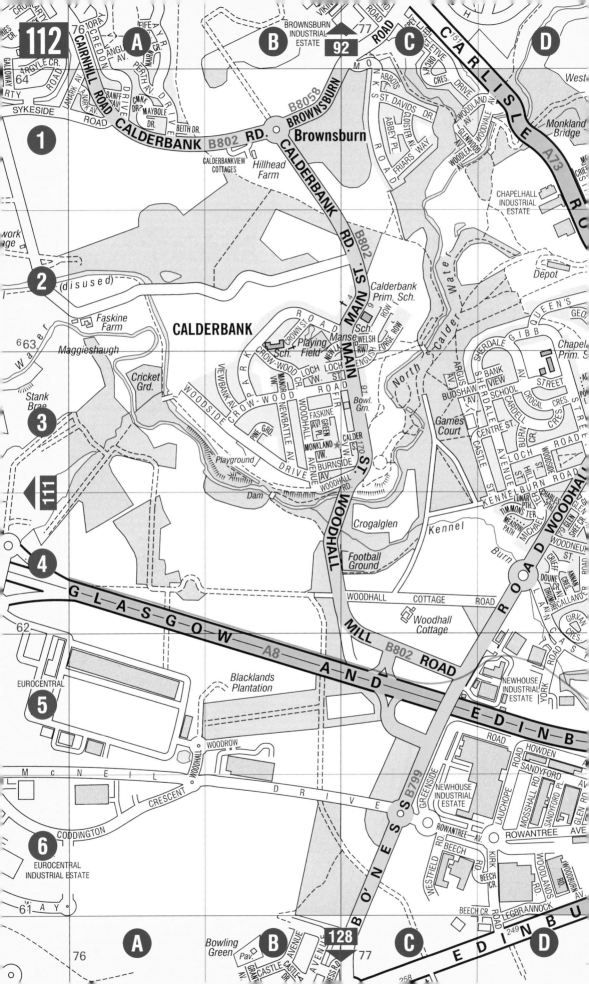

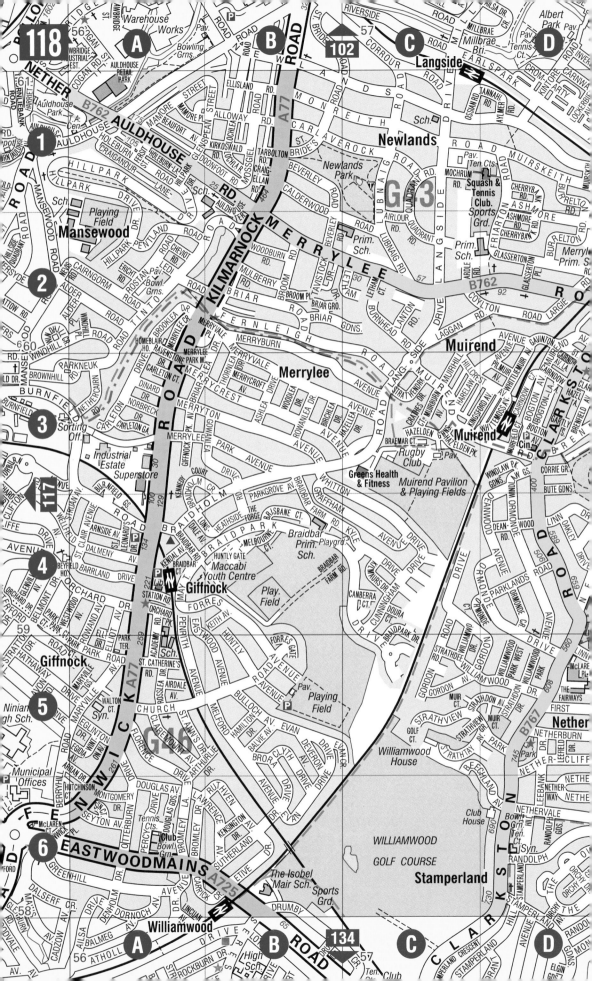

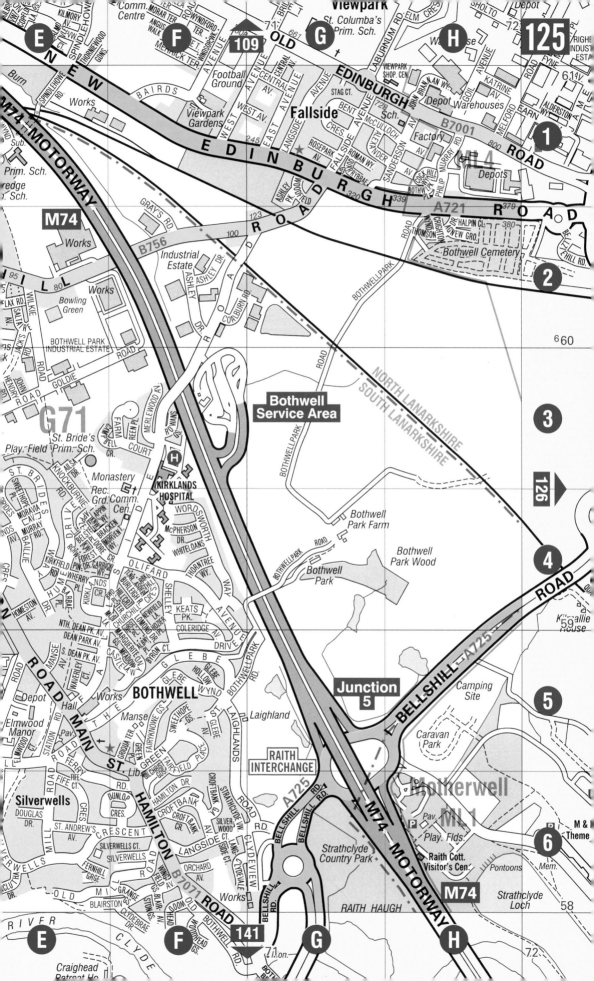

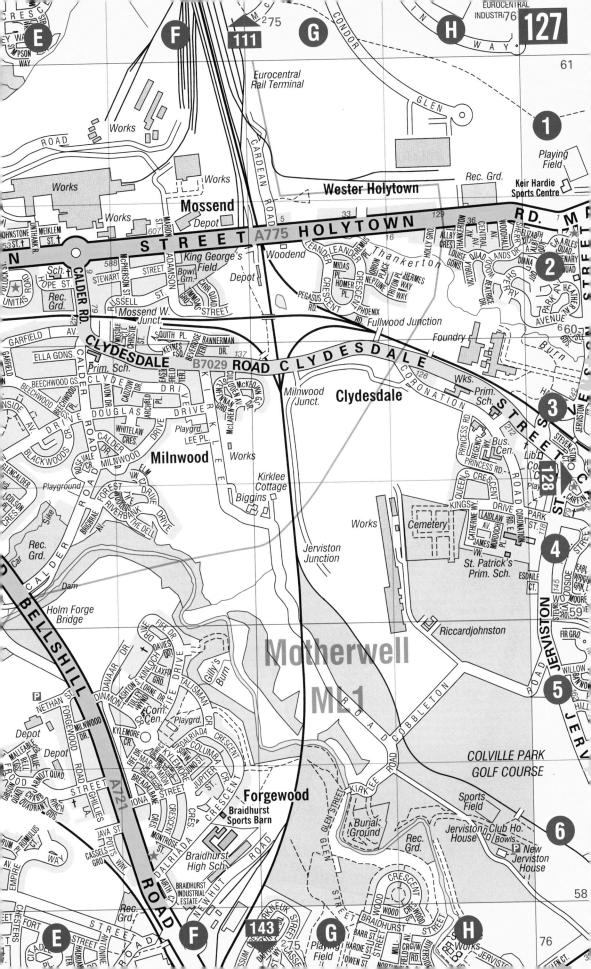

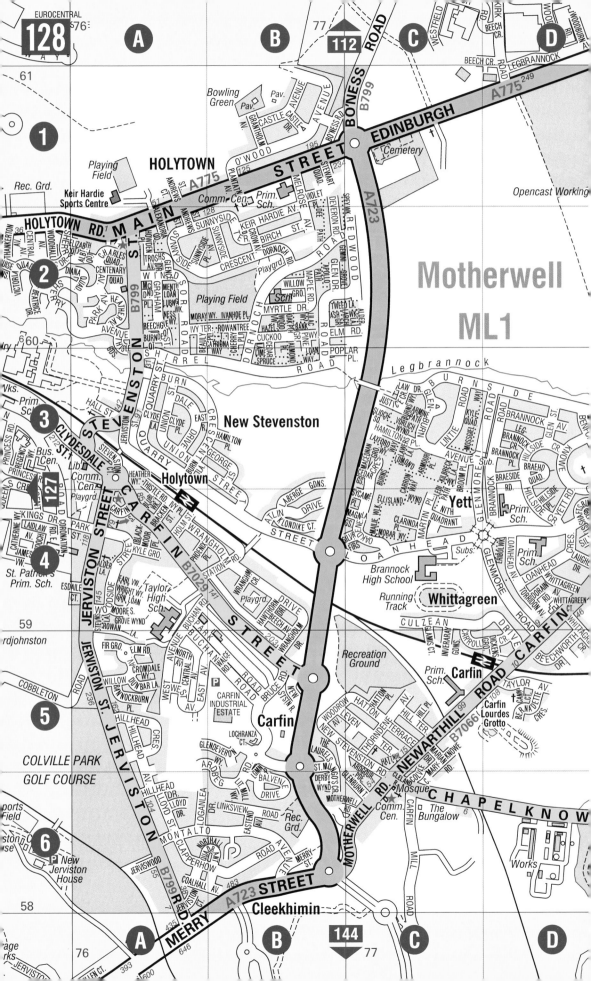

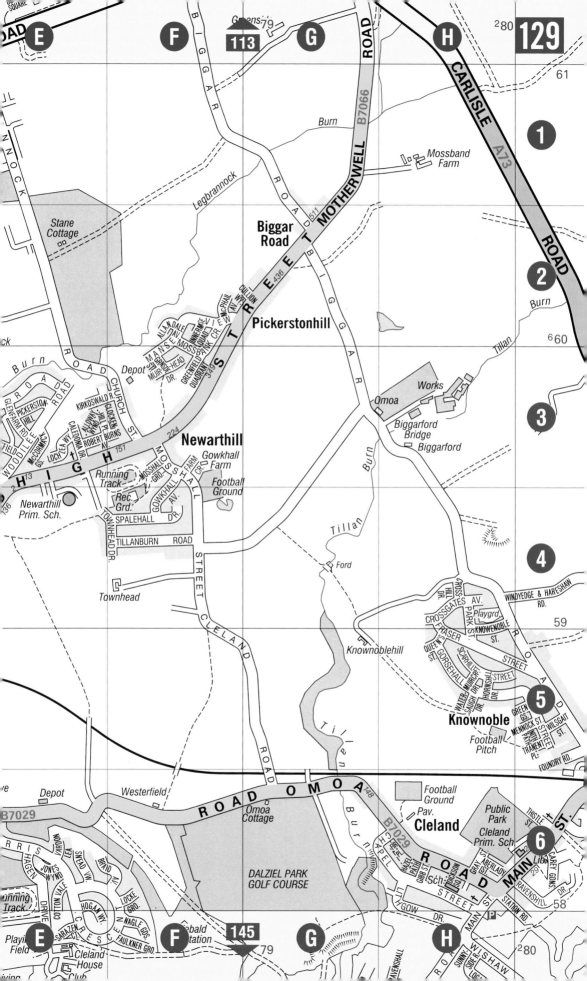

**1**

CARLISLE ROAD A73

MOTHERWELL ROAD B7066

Burn

Mossband Farm

**2**

Burn

Biggar Road

511

Legbrannock

Stane Cottage

Pickerstonhill

Tillan

660

**3**

MACPHAIL AV.
CULLION WAY
INNERMUIR CR.
ALLAN DALE
DAV.
MOSSBANK
SEMPLE VIEW
GROVE
MUIRS-HEAD
DR.
GREENFIELD
QUADRANT
349

Depot

BIGGAR ROAD

436

Works

Omoa

Biggarford Bridge
Biggarford

ROAD
Burn
GLENFARM RD.
PICKERSTON HILL
WOODILEE
McCORMACK
LOCH LEA
GS.
KIRKOSWALD R.
CLOCKEN
CALEDONIA DR.
HILL PL.
ALLOWAY
RD.
ROBERT BURNS AV.
CHURCH ST.
151

224

**Newarthill**

HIGH
73
136

Running Track

Rec. Grd.

Newarthill Prim. Sch.

MOSSHALL GRO.
GOWKHALL
FARM CR.
MOSSHALL
GOWKHALL AV.
SPALEHALL DR.
TOWNHEAD DR.

Gowkhall Farm

Football Ground

Tillan

**3**

STREET

Burn

Ford

**4**

TILLANBURN ROAD

Townhead

STREET

CLELAND

Knownoblehill

Tillan

CROSS HILL DR.
CROSSGATES
PARK ST.
Playgrd.
FRASER ST.
KNOWNOBLE ST.
QUEEN'S
GORSEHALL
SCARHILL
WATERLOO
MURCROFT
SLOUGH DR.
HORNSHILL DR.
STREET
59

ROAD

**4**

**5**

**Knownoble**

Football Pitch

GREEN ST.
MENNOCK ST.
TRANENT PL.
WILSGAIT ST.
STREET
FOUNDRY RD.

**5**

ROAD

Depot

Westerfield

ROAD   OMOA

748

Omoa Cottage

Burn

B7029

Football Ground

Pav.

Public Park

**Cleland**

Cleland Prim. Sch.

THISTLE ST.
MAIN ST.

**6**

B7029

ROAD

CHAPEL

HAZEL PATH
COBB ST.
DICKSON ST.
ABERLADY ST.
GRAY ST.
Sch.
LITTLEGOW DR.

MAIN STREET

SUNNYSIDE
Lib.
CAREY GDNS.
RAVENSHILL DR.
STATION RD.
58

ROAD

**E**
Playing Field
Cleland House Club

DRIVE
RUNNING Track
MORRIS HAGEN
JONES WYND
NORTON LEA
SNEAD VW.
BRAID AV.
LOCKE GRO.
NAGLE GDS.
COTTON VALE
SARAZEN CT.
HOGAN WY.
CRES.
FAULKNER GRO.

**F** Archibald Station

**G**

**H**

145
79

DALZIEL PARK GOLF COURSE

WISHAW
280
RAVENSHALL

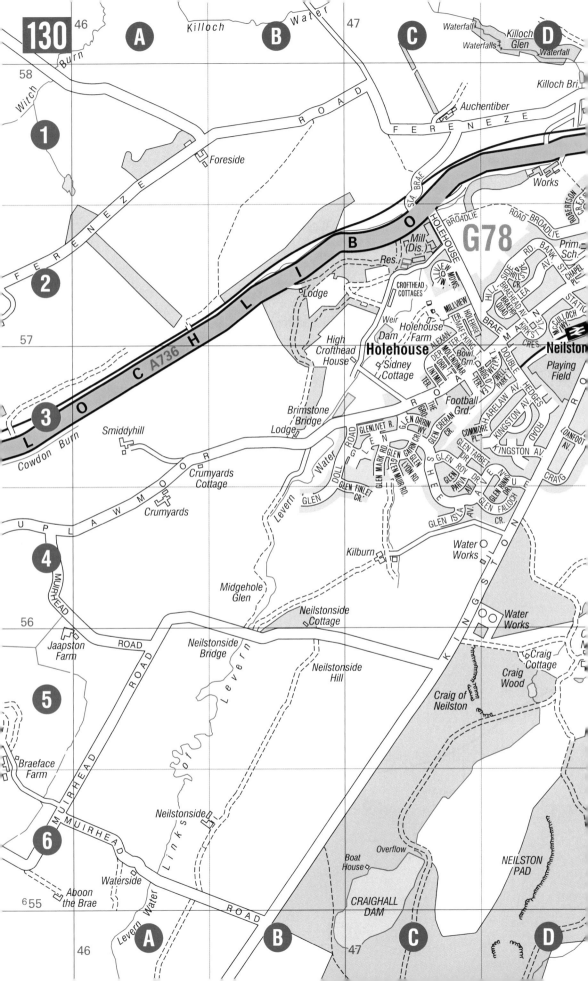

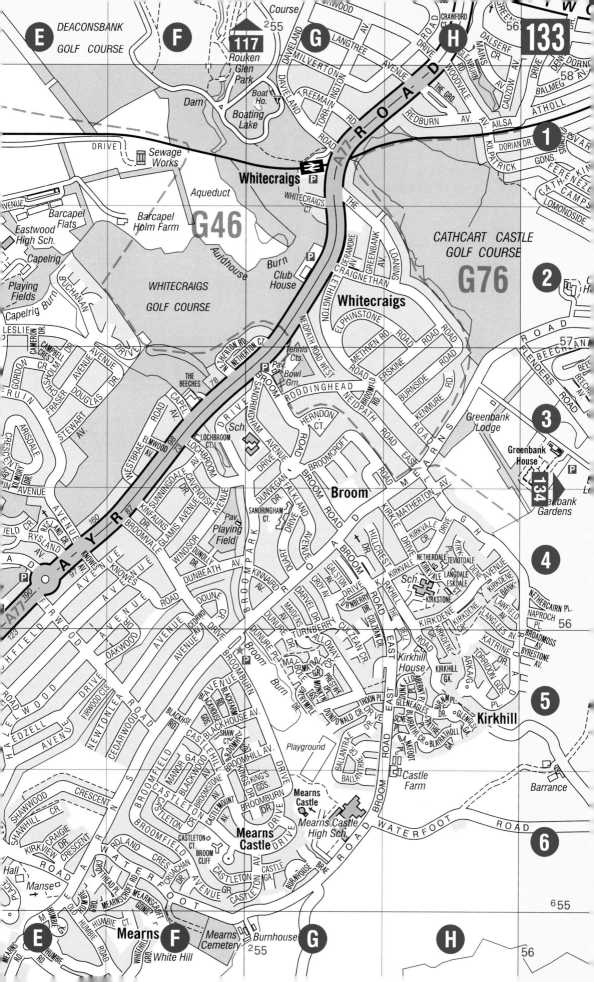

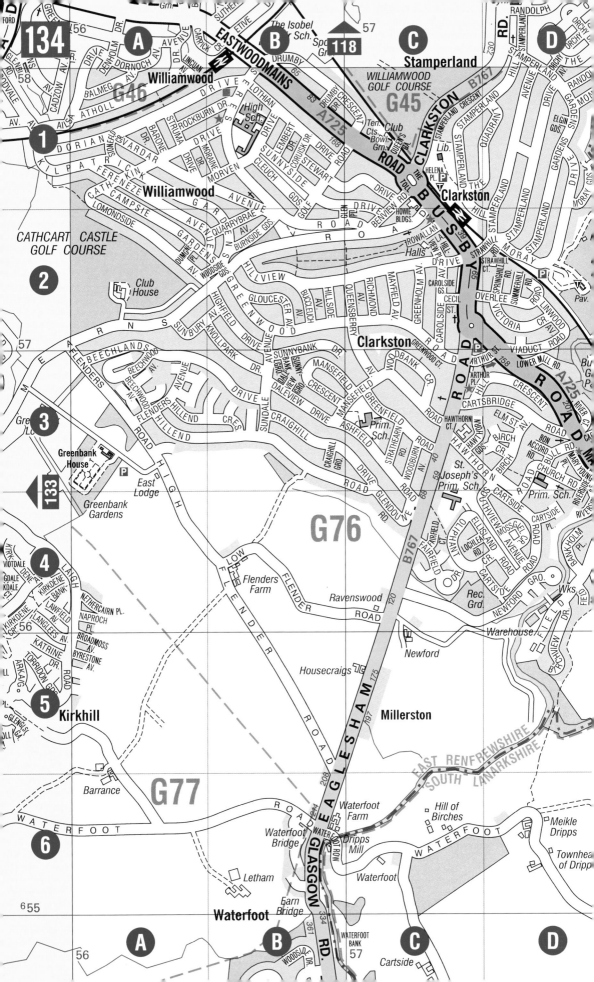

A   B   C   D

61
120

CATHKIN BRAES
GOLF COURSE

58

G45

Curling
Pond

1

GALLOWHILL
THE
WILLOWS
FAIR OAKS HIGH
BEECHES
GREEN
SIDE

CATHKIN

ROAD

B759

Muir
Farm

BUSBY R.
KIRK
MANSE
SYCMWE
GLEBE
AV.
CRAIGHILL PARK
CRAGWELL PARK
WATERSIDE

CARMUNNOCK

GLASGOW
SOUTH LANARKSHIRE

37

2

Prim.
Sch.

WATT
GDNS.

KITTOCHSIDE

ROAD

57

WATERSIDE

Parklea

Bellcraig

Highflat
Farm

3

ROAD

135

KITTOCHSIDE

Braefoot

Rockcrest

G76

ROAD

4

Waters

Waterbank

Stepends
Bridge

56

Philipshill Sewage
Works

Wester
Kittochside

Kittochside

ROAD

Kittochside
Farm

CAIRNMUI

Eastend

CARMUNNOCK

Dykehead
Farm

KITTOCHSIDE
RD.

Kittochside

Cemetery

Mill
Cottage

Museum of
Scottish
Country Life

GLEN RD

McCALLUM

AVENUE

5

Philipshill

STEWARTFIELD

GLEN

ROAD

MACIVOR

MACDONALD

McKAY PL.

McCALLUM

MACKENZIE
GDNS.

MAC-NEILL DR.

MACNEILL GS.

CRESCENT

Super-
Co

EAST
KILBRIDE

A725

ROAD

Kingsknowe

CASTERFIELD RD.

PHILIPSHILL

PHILIPSHILL
GATE

Hotel

Government
Offices

Rough
Hill

Castle Hill

Castleglen

CASTLEGLEN
PARK

CASTLEHILL

DAVIE'S

MIN-
STERS

ACRE

Kittoch   Water

GLEN   ROAD

HAWBANK

RENNIE
PL.

WATT

JAMES

PLACE

6

ehead
out

gpark

55

GLASGOW SOUTHERN ORBITAL

BARBANA

A726

ROAD

REDWOOD

Ind. Est.

PEEL PARK
(IND. EST.)

REDWOOD
CRESCENT

Q-U-E-E-N-S-W-A-Y

A726

GLENBURN WY.

GLENBURN

GLENBURN
WY.

WESTGARTH
PLACE

SPRINGBURN PL.

DIXON
PLACE

ROAD

College
Milton

ARROTSH

ROAD

We
Ma

Industrial   Estate

148

61 MILTON

E-A-S-T

A   B   C   D

6   55
260

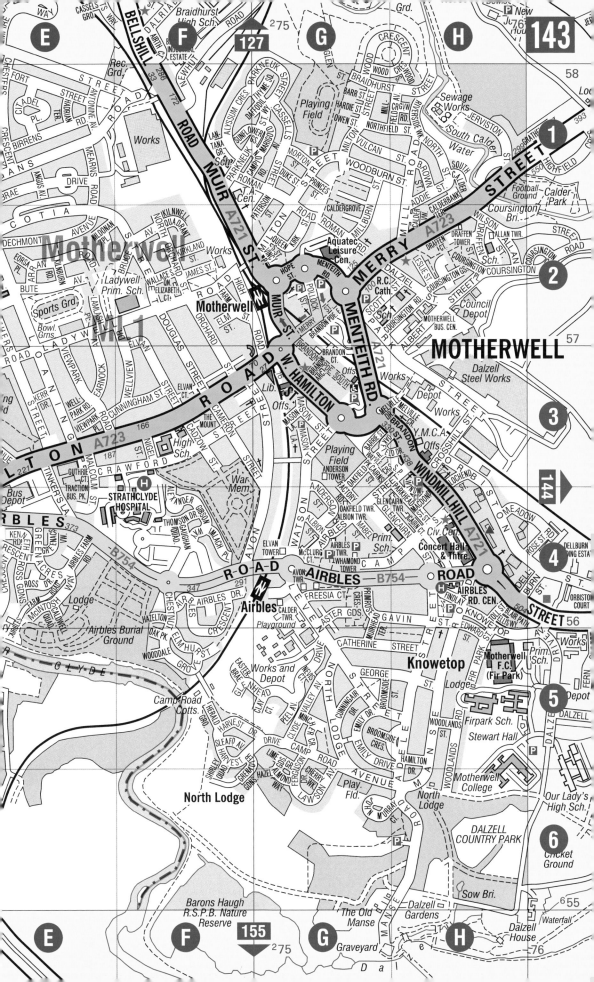

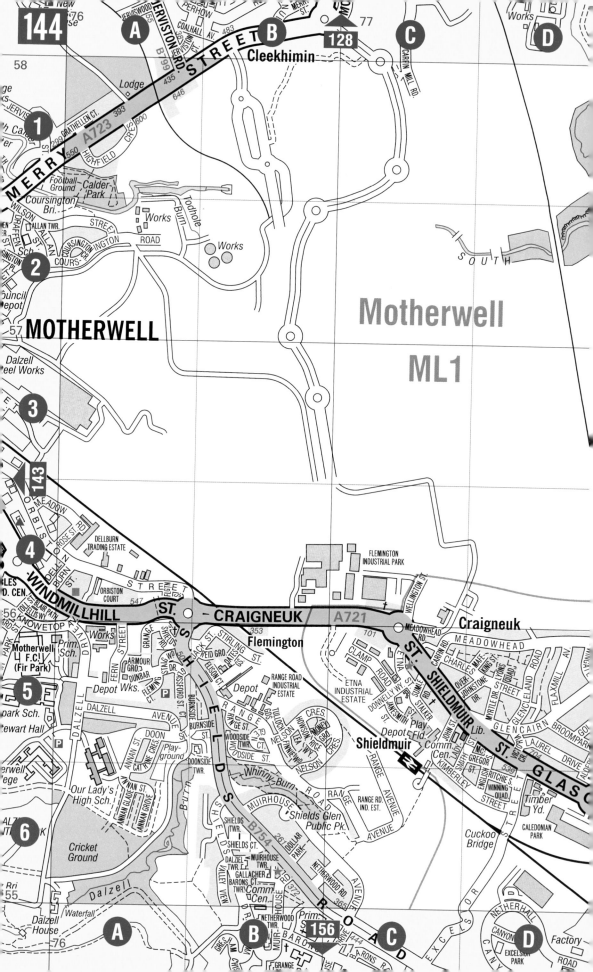

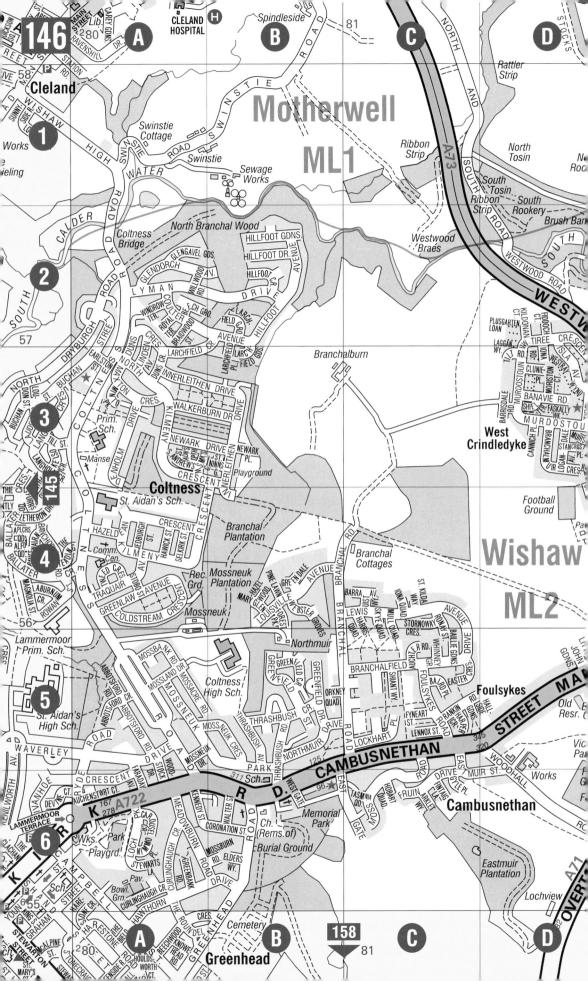

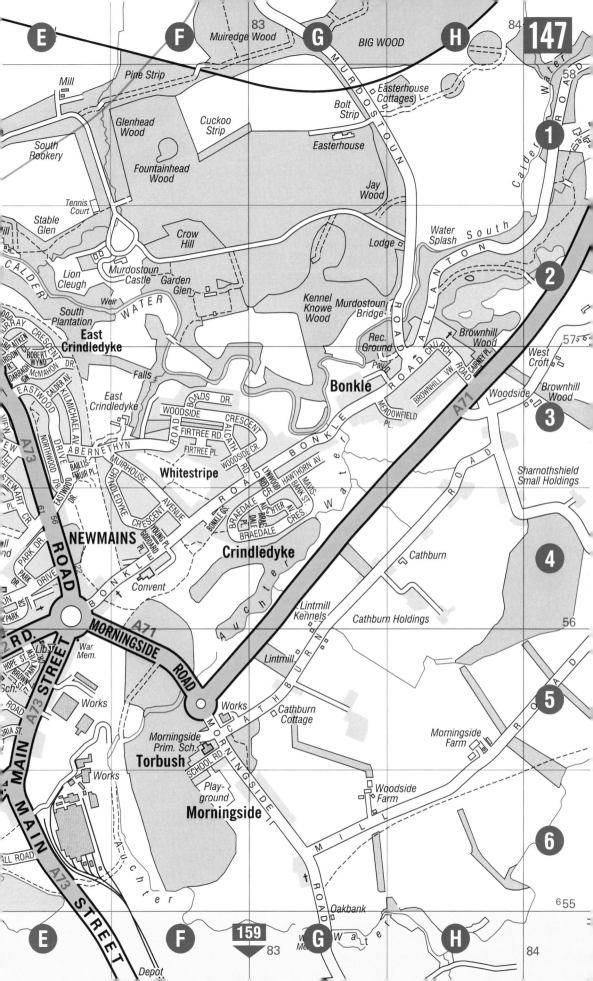

E F 83 Muiredge Wood G BIG WOOD H 84 58

1

MURDOSTOUN ROAD

Mill
Pine Strip
South Rookery
Glenhead Wood
Cuckoo Strip
Fountainhead Wood

Easterhouse Cottages
Bolt Strip
Easterhouse

Jay Wood

Calder Water

Tennis Court
Stable Glen
Crow Hill
Lodge
Water Splash
South

2

CALDER
Lion Cleugh
Murdostoun Castle
Garden Glen
Weir
WATER
South Plantation

East Crindledyke

Kennel Knowe Wood
Murdostoun Bridge
Rec. Ground
Pav

ALLANTON ROAD
CHURCH ROAD
Brownhill Wood
CAIRNEY PL.
West Croft
57

Falls
East Crindledyke

MURRAY CRESCENT
AITKEN
HARRISON CT.
ROBERT WYND
DARRAGH GN.
McMAHON
EASTWOOD
CALDER AV.
KILMICHAEL AV.
ABERNETHYN
MUIRHOUSE
MUIR PL.
BAILLIE

Whitestripe

WOODSIDE ROAD
BONDS DR.
CRESCENT
ALCATH
FIRTREE RD.
FIRTREE PL.
WOODSIDE CR.

Bonkle
MEADOWFIELD PL.
BROWNHILL VW.

Woodside
Brownhill Wood
3

NORTHWOOD DRIVE
EASTWOOD DR.
CRINDLEDYKE CRESCENT
AVENUE
YOUNG PL.
GODDARD
BONKLE CS.
BRAEDALE PL.
BRAEDALE
LYNWOOD RD.
MAVIS CR.
HAWTHORN AV.
BANK ST.
BACHTER AV.
BRAE
DALE CRES.

BONKLE ROAD

A73

A73 ROAD
STEWART CR.
PL.
PARK DR.
PARK DR.
DRIVE

NEWMAINS
Convent
Crindledyke

Auchter Water

A71

Sharnothshield Small Holdings

Cathburn
4
56

CATHBURN

Lintmill Kennels
Cathburn Holdings
Lintmill

MORNINGSIDE ROAD
War Mem.
HOPE ST.
MARY ST.
BROWNLIE
Sch.
Works

Works
Cathburn Cottage

Morningside Farm
5

MAIN STREET
A73
ROAD
VICTORIA ST.

Works
Morningside Prim. Sch.

Torbush
SCHOOL RD.
MORNINGSIDE ROAD
Woodside Farm

ROAD

Play-ground
Morningside

MILL ROAD

6

Auchter

Oakbank

W Water

655

Depot

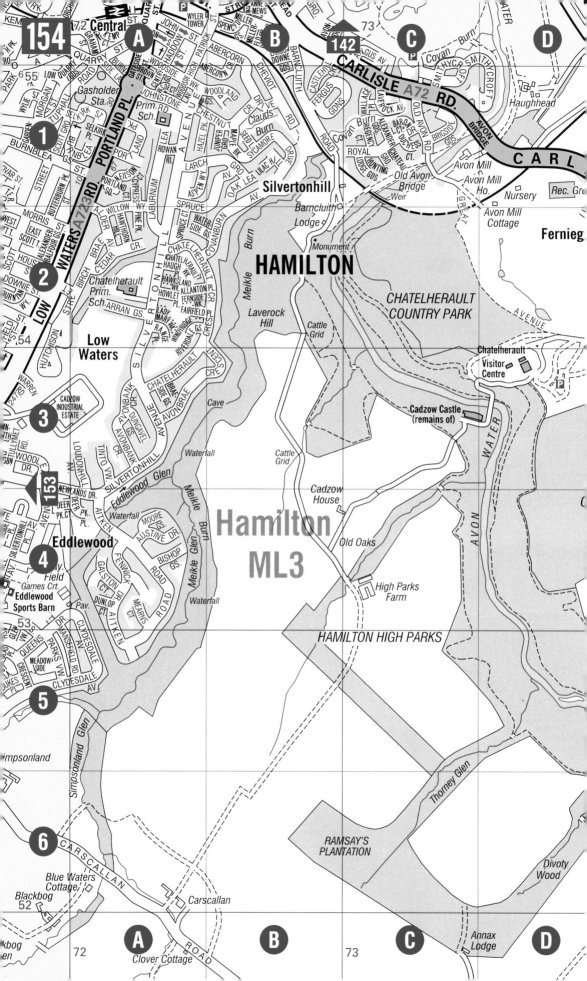

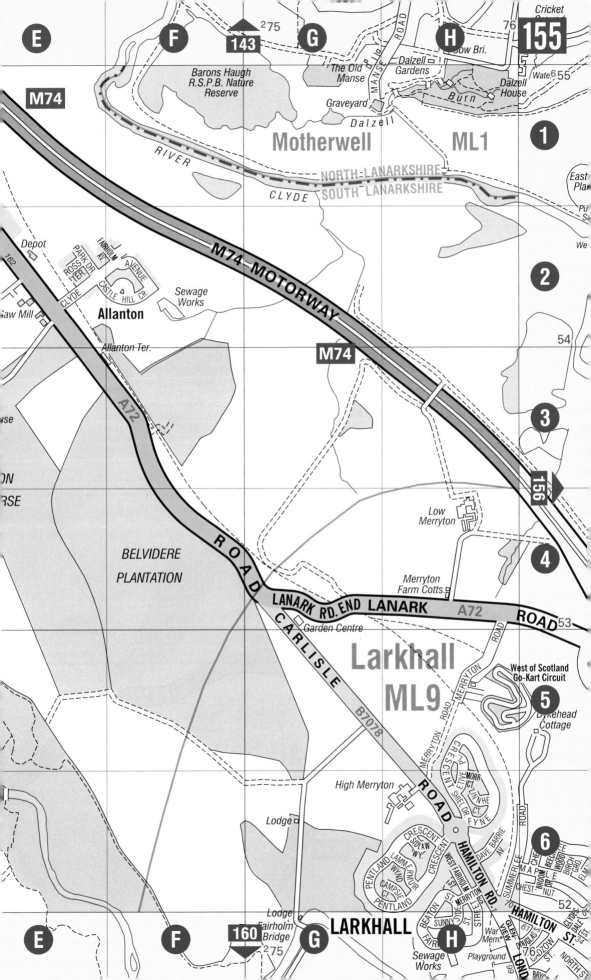

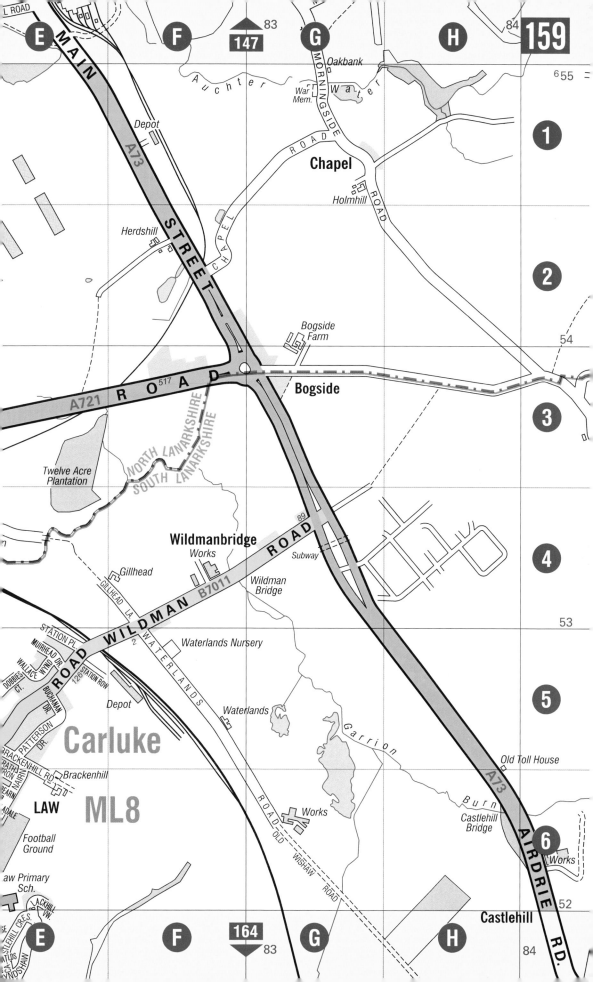

6 55

1

Oakbank

War Mem.

Chapel

Holmhill

Depot

A73

Herdshill

2

Bogside Farm

Bogside

517

A721 ROAD

3

54

North Lanarkshire

South Lanarkshire

Twelve Acre Plantation

89

Wildmanbridge

Works

Gillhead

Subway

Wildman Bridge

B7011

4

GILLHEAD LA.

WILDMAN  ROAD

Waterlands Nursery

53

STATION PL.

2

WATERLANDS

MUIRHEAD DR.

WALLACE WYND

126 STATION ROW

Depot

DOBBIES CT.

BUCHANAN DR.

Waterlands

Carluke

PATTERSON DR.

5

Garrion

BRACKENHILL RD.

Brackenhill

STRATH...

NAIRN

...EARN

LAW  ML8

Old Toll House

A73

...DALE

Football Ground

OLD  WISHAW  ROAD

ROAD

Works

Castlehill Bridge

Burn

6

...aw Primary Sch.

...ACKHILL CRES.

BLACKHILL VW.

Works

AIRDRIE RD.

52

Castlehill

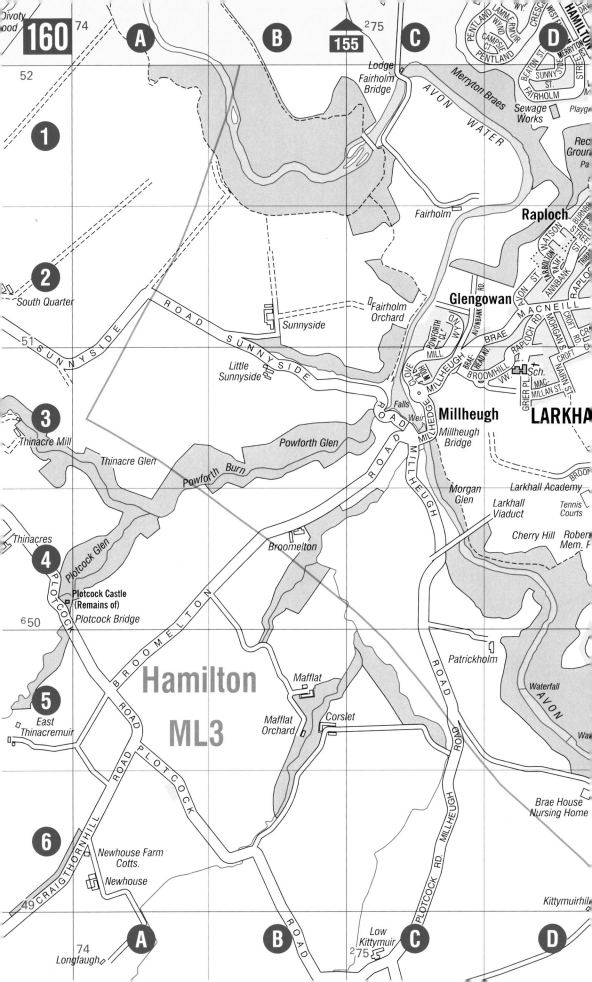

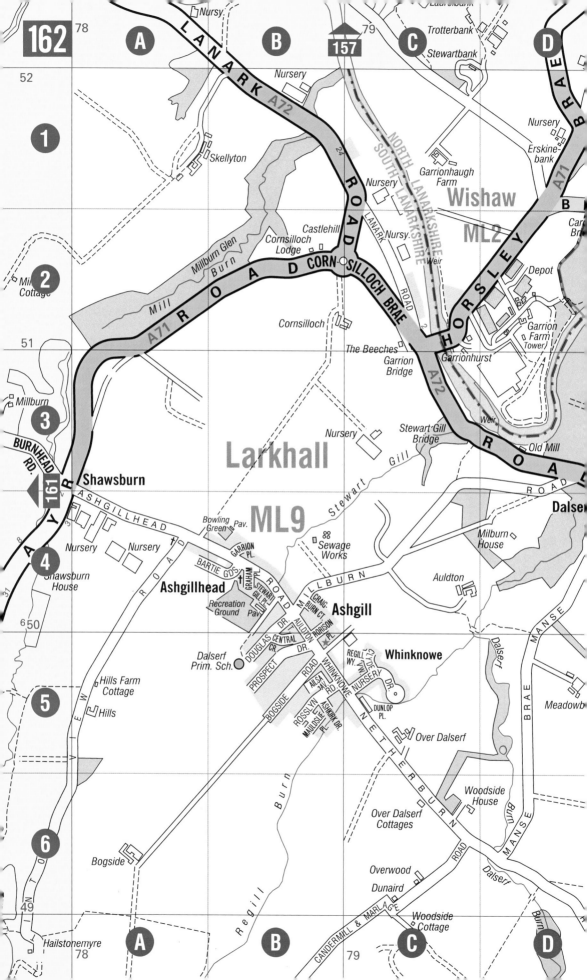

E · F · G · H

**158**

**81**
Shawgill

BIRKS ROAD

ROAD

101
100

82

Birks

Anstruther CT · Anstruther · CARMICHAEL · Michael JW
Braefoot · Michael ST
WESTEND CT
BRAEFOOT CR · BRAEFOOT
BIRKS CT
SWAN WY
MURRAY RD
KINGSHAW WY
SHAWGILL CT · SWAN WY
52 S
MANSE CT
STILEHILL LA
WATLDS
STILEHILL VIEW
SMITHS WY
HILL VW

**1**

STRAVENHOUSE ROAD

ROAD

Comm. Cen.
**Law of Mauldslie**

La

Jollyfield

B7011

MAULDSLIE

N L E E

West Brownlee

Brownlee House

Binniesbrig

BIRKS ROAD

Stravenhouse Farm

QUARRY RD

ROAD

**2**

51

Bowmanhirst
Castlehill
Nursery

Gill

**Carluke**

**ML8**

Mauldslie Mains

QUARRY

**3**

Mauldslie Cottage
**164**

RIVER

CLYDE

Rams

Dalserf House

Mauldslie Stables

Works

Mauldslie Bridge

Mauldslie House

East Lodge

Nursery

ROAD

**4**

JOCK'S GILL WOOD

6 50

Mauldslie View
Nursery

L A N A R K

Gill

Hotel
Nurseries

Haugh Hill

Jock's Burn

Gillbank

**5**

A72

**Rosebank**

Annsfield

Nursery

Nursery

Milton-Lockhart Farm

**6**

Dalpatrick

Nursery

RIVER

CLYDE

Sandilandgate

49

Hazelwood Cottage

ROAD

Overton Wood

Carcain Gill

**81**

Milton Lockhart Bri.

Waterfall

Townhead

82

**E** · **F** · **G** · **H**

80

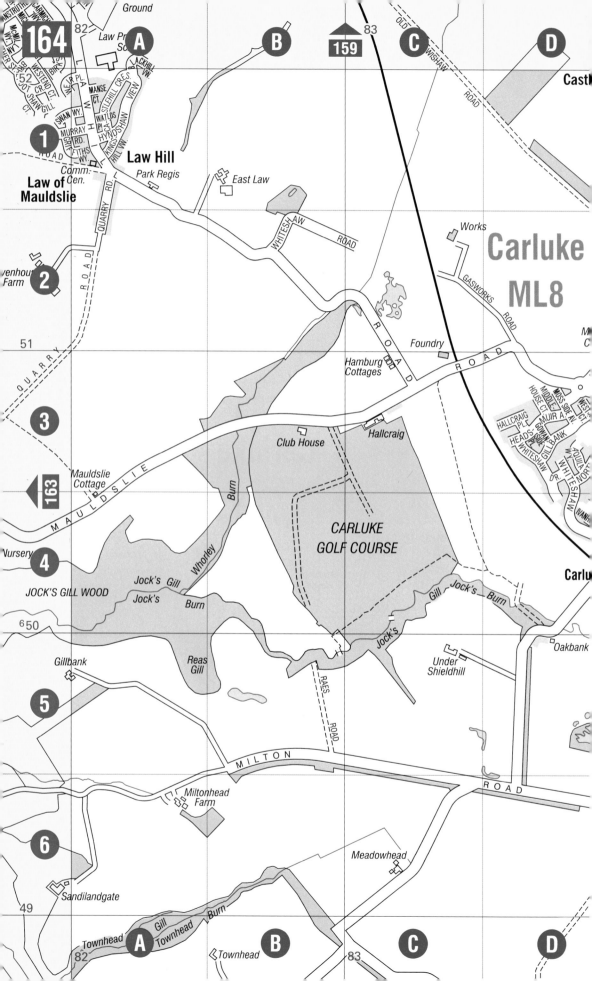

**164** 82

Law Hill

Law of Mauldslie

Park Regis

East Law

WHITESHAW ROAD

Carluke ML8

Works

Comm. Cen.

QUARRY ROAD

51

QUARRY

ROAD

159

OLD WISHAW ROAD

Cast

GASWORKS ROAD

Foundry

Hamburg Cottages

HALLCRAIG PL

HEADS SIDE
WHITESHAM

MIDDLE HOUSE CT
MUIR AV
GOWAN
GILLBANK

MOSS SIDE AV
WEST CT

AQUILA NORTH WY
WHITESHAW DR
NANTH

163

Mauldslie Cottage

MAULDSLIE

Club House

Hallcraig

CARLUKE GOLF COURSE

Carlu

Nursery

JOCK'S GILL WOOD

Jock's Gill

Whorley

Burn

Jock's

Jock's Gill Burn

Jock's Burn

Under Shieldhill

Oakbank

6 50

Gillbank

Reas Gill

RAES ROAD

MILTON

ROAD

Miltonhead Farm

Meadowhead

49

Sandilandgate

Townhead Gill

Townhead

Townhead Burn

82

83

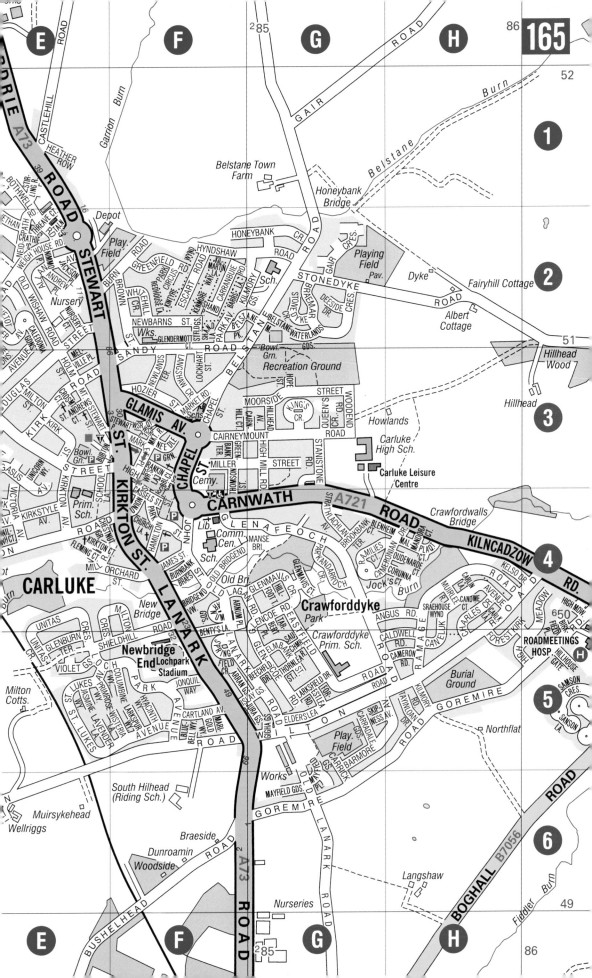

# INDEX

Including Streets, Places & Areas, Industrial Estates, Selected Flats & Walkways,
Junction Names, Stations and Selected Places of Interest.

## HOW TO USE THIS INDEX

1. Each street name is followed by its Postal District and then by its Locality abbreviation(s) and then by its map reference; e.g. **Abbeycraig Rd.** G34: Glas . . . .2B **88** is in the Glasgow 34 Postal District and the Glasgow Locality and is to be found in square 2B on page **88**. The page number is shown in bold type.

2. A strict alphabetical order is followed in which Av., Rd., St., etc. (though abbreviated) are read in full and as part of the street name; e.g. **Adams Pl.** appears after **Adamson St.** but before **Adamswell St.**

3. Streets and a selection of flats and walkways too small to be shown on the maps, appear in the index with the thoroughfare to which it is connected shown in brackets; e.g. **Abbey Wlk.** G69: Barg . . . .6D **88** (off Abercrombie Cres.)

4. Addresses that are in more than one part are referred to as not continuous.

5. Places and areas are shown in the index in BLUE TYPE and the map reference is to the actual map square in which the town centre or area is located and not to the place name shown on the map; e.g. **AIRDRIE** . . . .3H **91**

6. An example of a selected place of interest is Auchinvole Castle . . . .5G **11**

7. Junction names are shown in the index in CAPITAL LETTERS; e.g. **ANDERSTON CROSS INTERCHANGE** . . . .5A **4**

8. An example of a station is Airbles Station (Rail) . . . .4G **143**. Included are Rail (**Rail**) and Underground (**Und.**) Stations.

9. Map references shown in brackets; e.g. **Adams Ct. La.** G1: Glas . . . .5F **83** (6D **4**) refer to entries that also appear on the large scale pages **4** & **5**.

## GENERAL ABBREVIATIONS

| | | | |
|---|---|---|---|
| **Arc.** : Arcade | **Ct.** : Court | **Junc.** : Junction | **Rdbt.** : Roundabout |
| **Av.** : Avenue | **Cres.** : Crescent | **La.** : Lane | **Shop.** : Shopping |
| **Bk.** : Back | **Cft.** : Croft | **Lit.** : Little | **Sth.** : South |
| **Blvd.** : Boulevard | **Dpt.** : Depot | **Lwr.** : Lower | **Sq.** : Square |
| **Bri.** : Bridge | **Dr.** : Drive | **Mans.** : Mansions | **Sta.** : Station |
| **Bldg.** : Building | **E.** : East | **Mkt.** : Market | **St.** : Street |
| **Bldgs.** : Buildings | **Ent.** : Enterprise | **Mdw.** : Meadow | **Ter.** : Terrace |
| **Bus.** : Business | **Est.** : Estate | **Mdws.** : Meadows | **Twr.** : Tower |
| **Cvn.** : Caravan | **Fld.** : Field | **M.** : Mews | **Trad.** : Trading |
| **Cen.** : Centre | **Gdn.** : Garden | **Mt.** : Mount | **Up.** : Upper |
| **Chu.** : Church | **Gdns.** : Gardens | **Mus.** : Museum | **Va.** : Vale |
| **Circ.** : Circle | **Ga.** : Gate | **Nth.** : North | **Vw.** : View |
| **Cir.** : Circus | **Gt.** : Great | **Pde.** : Parade | **Vs.** : Villas |
| **Cl.** : Close | **Grn.** : Green | **Pk.** : Park | **Vis.** : Visitors |
| **Coll.** : College | **Gro.** : Grove | **Pas.** : Passage | **Wlk.** : Walk |
| **Comn.** : Common | **Hgts.** : Heights | **Pl.** : Place | **W.** : West |
| **Cnr.** : Corner | **Ho.** : House | **Quad.** : Quadrant | **Yd.** : Yard |
| **Cott.** : Cottage | **Ind.** : Industrial | **Ri.** : Rise | |
| **Cotts.** : Cottages | **Intl.** : International | **Rd.** : Road | |

## LOCALITY ABBREVIATIONS

| | | | |
|---|---|---|---|
| Air : **Airdrie** | Carm : **Carmyle** | Hag : **Haggs** | N'hill : **Newarthill** |
| Alla : **Allandale** | C'cry : **Castlecary** | Ham : **Hamilton** | N'hse : **Newhouse** |
| Anna : **Annathill** | Chap : **Chapelhall** | Hard : **Hardgate** | Newm : **Newmains** |
| Ashg : **Ashgill** | Chry : **Chryston** | Hill : **Hillington Ind. Est.** | New S : **New Stevenston** |
| Auch : **Auchinloch** | Clar : **Clarkston** | Holy : **Holytown** | Newt : **Newton** |
| Bail : **Baillieston** | Cle : **Cleland** | Hous : **Houston** | Newt M : **Newton Mearns** |
| Balder : **Baldernock** | Clyd : **Clydebank** | How : **Howwood** | Old K : **Old Kilpatrick** |
| Balm : **Balmore** | Coat : **Coatbridge** | Inch : **Inchinnan** | Over : **Overtown** |
| Bank : **Banknock** | Crsfd : **Crossford** | John : **Johnstone** | Pais : **Paisley** |
| Bant : **Banton** | C'lee : **Crosslee** | Kilb : **Kilbarchan** | Plain : **Plains** |
| Bard : **Bardowie** | Croy : **Croy** | Kils : **Kilsyth** | Q'riers : **Quarriers Village** |
| Barg : **Bargeddie** | Cumb : **Cumbernauld** | Kirk : **Kirkintilloch** | Quar : **Quarter** |
| Barr : **Barrhead** | Dals : **Dalserf** | Lang : **Langbank** | Queen : **Queenzieburn** |
| Bear : **Bearsden** | Denn : **Dennyloanhead** | Lark : **Larkhall** | Renf : **Renfrew** |
| Bell : **Bellshill** | Dull : **Dullatur** | Law : **Law** | Rent : **Renton** |
| Birk : **Birkenshaw** | Dumb : **Dumbarton** | Len : **Lennoxtown** | Rigg : **Riggend** |
| B'rig : **Bishopbriggs** | Dun : **Duntocher** | Lenz : **Lenzie** | Roger : **Rogerton** |
| B'ton : **Bishopton** | E Kil : **East Kilbride** | Lin : **Linwood** | Rose : **Rosebank** |
| Blan : **Blantyre** | Eld : **Elderslie** | Loch : **Lochwinnoch** | Ruth : **Rutherglen** |
| B'bri : **Bonnybridge** | Ersk : **Erskine** | Longc : **Longcroft** | Shaw : **Shawsburn** |
| Both : **Bothwell** | Faif : **Faifley** | Mille : **Millerston** | Step : **Stepps** |
| Bowl : **Bowling** | Fern : **Ferniegair** | Miln : **Milngavie** | Tann : **Tannochside** |
| Bri W : **Bridge of Weir** | Flem : **Flemington** | Milt : **Milton** | T'bnk : **Thornliebank** |
| Brkfld : **Brookfield** | G'csh : **Gartcosh** | Milt C : **Milton of Campsie** | T'hall : **Thorntonhall** |
| Busby : **Busby** | Gart : **Gartness** | Mollin : **Mollinsburn** | Torr : **Torrance** |
| C'bnk : **Calderbank** | Giff : **Giffnock** | Mood : **Moodiesburn** | Twe : **Twechar** |
| Camb : **Cambuslang** | Glas : **Glasgow** | Moss : **Mossend** | Udd : **Uddingston** |
| Cam G : **Campsie Glen** | Glas A : **Glasgow Airport** | Moth : **Motherwell** | View : **Viewpark** |
| Card : **Cardross** | Glass : **Glassford** | Muirh : **Muirhead** | Water : **Waterfoot** |
| Carf : **Carfin** | Glenb : **Glenboig** | Neil : **Neilston** | Wis : **Wishaw** |
| Carl : **Carluke** | Glenm : **Glenmavis** | Ners : **Nerston** | |
| Crmck : **Carmunnock** | Grng : **Greengairs** | Neth : **Netherlee** | |

---

## A

| | | |
|---|---|---|
| **Abbey Cl.** PA1: Pais . . . . . . . . . .1A **98** | **Abbeylands Rd.** G81: Faif . . . . . . .6E **23** | **Abbotsford Av.** G73: Ruth . . . . . . .6D **104** |
| **Abbeycraig Rd.** G34: Glas . . . . . .2B **88** | **Abbeymill Bus. Cen.** | ML3: Ham . . . . . . . . . . . . . . .3F **141** |
| **Abbeydale Way** G73: Ruth . . . . . .4E **121** | PA1: Pais . . . . . . . . . . . . . . .1B **98** | ML9: Lark . . . . . . . . . . . . . . .4E **161** |
| **Abbey Dr.** G14: Glas . . . . . . . . . .5E **61** | **Abbey Pl.** ML6: Air . . . . . . . . . . .1C **112** | **Abbotsford Brae** G74: E Kil . . . . .6G **137** |
| **Abbeyfield Ho.** G46: Giff . . . . . . .4H **117** | **Abbey Rd.** PA5: Eld . . . . . . . . . . .3H **95** | **Abbotsford Ct.** G67: Cumb . . . . . . .6H **35** |
| ML5: Coat . . . . . . . . . . . . . . .5A **90** | **Abbey Wlk.** G69: Barg . . . . . . . . .6D **88** | **Abbotsford Cres.** |
| **Abbeygreen St.** G34: Glas . . . . . .2C **88** | (off Abercrombie Cres.) | ML2: Wis . . . . . . . . . . . . . . .5A **146** |
| **Abbeyhill St.** G32: Glas . . . . . . . .4G **85** | ML9: Lark . . . . . . . . . . . . . . .1F **161** | ML3: Ham . . . . . . . . . . . . . . .3F **141** |
| | (off Duncan Graham St.) | PA2: Pais . . . . . . . . . . . . . . .6B **96** |
| | **Abbotsburn Way** PA3: Pais . . . . . . .3H **77** | **Abbotsford Dr.** G66: Kirk . . . . . . . .5E **31** |
| | **Abbotsford** G64: B'rig . . . . . . . . . .5E **49** | **Abbotsford La.** ML4: Bell . . . . . . .1B **126** |

| | |
|---|---|
| **Abbotsford Pl.** G5: Glas . . . . . . . . .1F **103** |
| (not continuous) |
| G67: Cumb . . . . . . . . . . . . . . .6H **35** |
| ML1: Holy . . . . . . . . . . . . . . .2A **128** |
| (off Ivy Ter.) |
| **Abbotsford Rd.** G61: Bear . . . . . . . .1C **44** |
| G67: Cumb . . . . . . . . . . . . . . .6H **35** |
| G81: Clyd . . . . . . . . . . . . . . .6D **42** |
| ML2: Wis . . . . . . . . . . . . . . .5A **146** |
| ML3: Ham . . . . . . . . . . . . . . .3E **141** |
| ML6: Chap . . . . . . . . . . . . . . .4E **113** |

Abbotshall Av.—Allerdyce Ct.

bbotshall Av. G15: Glas 4G 43
bbotsinch Rd. PA4: Renf 6A 58
bbotsinch Rd. PA3: Glas A 2A 78
bbots Ter. ML6: Air 1C 112
bbot St. G41: Glas 4C 102
PA3: Pais 5B 78
bbott Cres. G81: Clyd 1F 59
BC Cinema 3D 118
berconway St. G81: Clyd 1E 59
bercorn Av. G52: Hill 3G 79
bercorn Cres. ML3: Ham 1B 154
bercorn Dr. ML3: Ham 6B 142
bercorn Ind. Est. PA3: Pais 5B 78
bercorn Pl. G23: Glas 6C 46
bercorn Rd. G77: Newt M 3C 132
bercorn St. G81: Faif 6G 23
PA3: Pais 6A 78
bercrombie Cres. G69: Barg 6D 88
bercrombie Dr. G61: Bear 5B 24
bercrombie Ho. G75: E Kil 2A 148
bercrombie Pl. G65: Kils 2F 11
bercromby Cres. G74: E Kil 6B 138
bercromby Dr. G40: Glas 5B 84
bercromby Pl. G74: E Kil 6B 138
bercromby St. G40: Glas 6A 84
(not continuous)
berdalgie Path G34: Glas 3H 87
(off Aberdalgie Rd.)
berdalgie Rd. G34: Glas 3H 87
berdeen Rd. ML6: Chap 1D 112
berdour St. G31: Glas 4E 85
berfeldy Av. ML6: Plain 1F 93
berfeldy St. G31: Glas 4E 85
berfoyle St. G31: Glas 4E 85
berlady Rd. G51: Glas 4E 81
berlady St. ML1: Cle 6H 129
bernethy Dr. PA3: Lin 6G 75
bernethyn Rd. ML2: Newm 3E 147
bernethy Pk. G74: E Kil 1F 149
bernethy Pl. G77: Newt M 5H 133
bernethy St. G31: Glas 5E 85
beruthven Dr. G32: Glas 2B 106
biegail Pl. G72: Blan 6B 124
boukir St. G51: Glas 3E 81
boyne Dr. PA2: Pais 4B 98
boyne St. G51: Glas 5F 81
BRONHILL 1E 37
cacia Dr. G78: Barr 2C 114
PA2: Pais 4F 97
cacia Pl. PA5: John 5G 95
cacia Way G72: Flem 2E 123
cademy Ct. ML5: Coat 4C 90
cademy Pk. G51: Glas 1A 102
ML6: Air 4A 92
cademy Pl. ML5: Coat 4C 90
cademy Rd. G46: Giff 5A 118
cademy St. G32: Glas 1B 106
ML5: Coat 4C 90
ML6: Air 4A 92
ML9: Lark 2E 161
cademy Ter. ML4: Bell 2D 126
cer Cres. PA2: Pais 4E 97
cer Gro. ML6: Chap 2E 113
chamore Cres. G15: Glas 3G 43
chamore Dr. G15: Glas 3G 43
chamore Gdns. G15: Glas 3G 43
chamore Rd. G15: Glas 3G 43
chnasheen Rd. ML6: Air 5G 93
chray Dr. PA2: Pais 4E 97
chray Pl. G62: Miln 2D 24
ML5: Coat 2H 89
chray Rd. G67: Cumb 6D 34
corn Ct. G40: Glas 1B 104
corn St. G40: Glas 1B 104
credyke Cres. G21: Glas 2E 65
credyke Pl. G21: Glas 3E 65
credyke Rd. G21: Glas 2D 64
G73: Ruth 5B 104
cre Rd. G20: Glas 6H 45
cres, The ML9: Lark 3F 161
cre Valley Rd. G64: Torr 3D 28
dam Av. ML6: Air 4B 92
dams Ct. La. G1: Glas 5F 83 (6D 4)
damslie Cres. G66: Kirk 5A 30
damslie Dr. G66: Kirk 5A 30
damson St. ML4: Moss 2F 127
dams Pl. G65: Kils 3H 11
damswell St. G21: Glas 6A 64
damswell Ter. G69: Mood 5E 53
ddie St. ML1: Moth 1H 143
ddiewell Pl. ML5: Coat 1C 110
ddiewell St. G32: Glas 4A 86
ddison Gro. G46: T'bnk 3F 117
ddison Pl. G46: T'bnk 3F 117
ddison Rd. G12: Glas 5B 62
G46: T'bnk 3E 117
delaide Ct. G81: Clyd 2H 41
delaide Rd. G75: E Kil 4D 148
dele St. ML1: Moth 5H 143
delphi Cen. G5: Glas 6H 83
Adelphi St. G5: Glas 6H 83
(Commercial Rd., not continuous)
G5: Glas 6G 83
(Gorbals St.)
Admiral St. G41: Glas 6C 82
Admiralty Gdns. G60: Old K 2F 41
Admiralty Gro. G60: Old K 2F 41
Admiralty Pl. G60: Old K 2F 41
Advance Pl. *PA11: Bri W 3F 73*
*(off Main St.)*
Advie Pl. G42: Glas 5F 103
Affric Av. ML6: Plain 1G 93
Affric Dr. PA2: Pais 4D 98
Afton Cres. G61: Bear 4H 45
Afton Dr. PA4: Renf 6G 59
Afton Gdns. G72: Blan 3H 139
ML5: Coat 6F 91
Afton Rd. G67: Cumb 2B 36
Afton St. G41: Glas 5C 102
ML9: Lark 3G 161
Afton Vw. G66: Kirk 4F 31
Afton Way PA2: Pais 4D 96
Agamemnon St. G81: Clyd 5B 42
Agate Ter. *ML4: Bell 3C 126*
*(off Diamond St.)*
Agnew Av. ML5: Coat 4E 91
Agnew Gro. ML4: Bell 2H 125
Agnew La. G42: Glas 4E 103
Aigas Cotts. *G13: Glas 4F 61*
*(off Fern La.)*
Aikenhead Rd. G42: Glas 2F 103
G44: Glas 1G 119
Aikman Pl. G74: E Kil 5B 138
Aikman Rd. ML1: Moth 4D 142
Ailart Loan *ML2: Newm 3D 146*
*(off Tiree Cres.)*
Ailean Dr. G32: Glas 1E 107
Ailean Gdns. G32: Glas 1E 107
Aillort Pl. G74: E Kil 6G 137
Ailort Av. G44: Glas 2E 119
Ailsa Av. ML1: Moth 2D 142
ML9: Ashg 5B 162
Ailsa Ct. ML3: Ham 2B 152
ML5: Coat 1A 110
Ailsa Cres. ML1: Moth 2D 142
Ailsa Dr. G42: Glas 6D 102
G46: Giff 1H 133
G66: Kirk 3F 31
G71: Both 3E 125
G73: Ruth 2B 120
G81: Hard 1E 43
PA2: Pais 6H 97
Ailsa Pl. ML5: Coat 1B 110
Ailsa Rd. G64: B'rig 5D 48
ML5: Coat 1A 110
PA4: Renf 1E 79
Ailsa Twr. G72: Camb 4G 121
Ainslie Av. G52: Hill 3A 80
Ainslie Rd. G52: Hill 4A 80
(not continuous)
G67: Cumb 2C 36
Airbles Cres. ML1: Moth 4F 143
Airbles Dr. ML1: Moth 4F 143
Airbles Farm Rd.
ML1: Moth 5E 143
Airbles Rd. ML1: Moth 4E 143
Airbles Station (Rail) 4G 143
Airbles St. ML1: Moth 4G 143
Airbles Twr. ML1: Moth 4G 143
Airdale Av. G46: Giff 5A 118
AIRDRIE 3H 91
Airdriehill Rd. ML6: Air 1C 92
Airdriehill St. ML6: Air 1C 92
Airdrie Leisure Cen. 2C 92
Airdrie Rd. G65: Kils 2H 11
G67: Cumb 1D 54
(Condorrat Ring Rd.)
G67: Cumb 6C 34
(Main Rd.)
G67: Mollin 3H 53
ML6: Air, Plain 2F 93
ML8: Carl 6H 159
Airdrie Station (Rail) 4A 92
Airdrie United F.C. 5C 92
Aird's La. *G1: Glas 5G 83*
*(off Bridgegate)*
Airgold Dr. G15: Glas 3H 43
Airgold Pl. G15: Glas 3H 43
Airlie Av. G61: Bear 6E 25
Airlie Dr. ML4: Bell 1C 126
Airlie Gdns. G73: Ruth 3F 121
Airlie La. G12: Glas 6H 61
Airlie Rd. G69: Bail 2G 107
Airlie St. G12: Glas 6G 61
Airlink Ind. Est.
PA3: Glas A 3A 78
Airlour Rd. G43: Glas 2C 118
Airth Ct. ML1: Moth 6F 127
Airth Dr. G52: Glas 2F 101
Airth La. G52: Glas 2F 101
Airth Pl. *G52: Glas 2F 101*
*(off Airth La.)*
Airthrey Av. G14: Glas 6E 61
Airthrey La. *G14: Glas 5E 61*
*(off Airthrey Av.)*
Airth Way G68: Cumb 5A 34
Aitchison Ct. ML6: Air 3H 91
Aitchison St. ML6: Air 4G 91
Aitkenbar Circ. G82: Dumb 2H 17
Aitkenbar Dr. G82: Dumb 1H 17
Aitken Cl. ML2: Newm 2E 147
Aitkenhead Av. ML5: Coat 1F 109
Aitkenhead Rd.
G69: Barg, Tann 5E 109
G71: Barg, Tann 5E 109
ML6: Chap 3D 112
Aitken Rd. ML3: Ham 4A 154
Aitken St. G31: Glas 4D 84
ML6: Air 2A 92
Alasdair Ct. G78: Barr 5E 115
Alba Gdns. ML8: Carl 2E 165
Alba Ho. G81: Clyd 5C 42
Albans Cres. ML1: Moth 1D 142
Albany G74: E Kil 5C 138
Albany Av. G32: Glas 5C 86
Albany Cotts. *G13: Glas 4F 61*
*(off Fern La.)*
Albany Dr. G73: Ruth 1D 120
Albany Pl. G71: Both 5F 125
Albany Quad. G32: Glas 5C 86
Albany Rd. ML3: Ham 4G 153
Albany St. G40: Glas 1C 104
ML5: Coat 4A 90
Albany Ter. G72: Camb 4G 121
Albany Way PA3: Pais 3A 78
Albany Wynd *ML9: Lark 1F 161*
*(off Duncan Graham St.)*
Alba Way ML3: Ham 5G 153
*ML9: Lark 4G 161*
*(off Keir Hardie Rd.)*
Alberta Av. G75: E Kil 3D 148
ML5: Coat 3B 90
Alberta Cres. G75: E Kil 3E 149
Alberta Pk. G75: E Kil 3F 149
Alberta Pl. G75: E Kil 3F 149
Albert Av. G42: Glas 4D 102
Albert Bri. G5: Glas 6G 83
Albert Cres. ML6: Air 4B 92
Albert Cross G41: Glas 2D 102
Albert Dr. G41: Glas 3A 102
G61: Bear 4H 45
G73: Ruth 2D 120
ML9: Lark 3F 161
Albert Pl. ML6: Air 3B 92
Albert Quad. ML1: Holy 2A 128
Albert Rd. G12: Glas 6H 61
G42: Glas 4E 103
G66: Lenz 4C 50
G81: Clyd 4B 42
PA4: Renf 6E 59
PA5: Brkfld 6C 74
Albert St. ML1: Moth 2H 143
ML3: Ham 3F 141
ML5: Coat 4C 90
(not continuous)
Albert Ter. ML3: Ham 3E 141
Albion Ct. *ML5: Coat 5E 91*
*(off Clifton Pl.)*
Albion Ga. G1: Glas 4H 83 (6G 5)
PA3: Pais 5H 77
Albion Rovers F.C. 5E 91
Albion St. G1: Glas 5H 83 (6G 5)
G69: Bail 2F 107
ML1: Moth 4G 143
ML5: Coat 4D 90
PA3: Pais 5A 78
Albion Twr. ML1: Moth 4G 143
Albion Way G75: E Kil 6H 149
Albion Works Ind. Est.
G13: Glas 2G 59
Alcaig Rd. G52: Glas 3E 101
Alcath Rd. ML2: Newm 3F 147
Alclutha Av. G82: Dumb 4H 17
Alder Av. G66: Lenz 2B 50
ML3: Ham 2A 154
Alder Bank G71: View 4G 109
Alder Ct. G75: E Kil 6E 149
G78: Barr 6E 115
Alder Cres. G75: E Kil 6E 149
Alder Ga. G72: Flem 2E 123
Alder Gro. ML5: Coat 5D 90
Alder La. ML1: Holy 2C 128
ML1: New S 4A 128
Alderman Pl. G13: Glas 3C 60
Alderman Rd. G13: Glas 2H 59
Alder Pl. G43: Glas 2A 118
G75: E Kil 6E 149
PA5: John 4G 95
Alder Rd. G43: Glas 2H 117
G66: Milt C 6B 8
Alder Rd. G67: Cumb 3D 36
G81: Clyd 2B 42
G82: Dumb 3E 17
Alderside Gdns. G71: Udd 6C 108
Alderside Pl. G71: Both 4F 125
Alderstocks G75: E Kil 6G 149
Alderston Pl. ML4: Bell 3A 126
Alderston Way ML4: Bell 1A 126
Aldersyde Av. ML2: Wis 5D 144
Aldersyde Pl. G72: Blan 6A 124
Alexander Av. G65: Twe 2C 32
G71: View 1G 125
Alexander Balfour Gdns.
ML3: Ham 2H 153
Alexander Cres. G5: Glas 1G 103
Alexander Gdns. ML3: Ham 1C 154
Alexander Gibson Way
ML1: Moth 4F 143
Alexander Pl. G66: Kirk 6H 31
Alexander St. G81: Clyd 6D 42
G82: Dumb 3G 17
ML2: Wis 6F 145
ML5: Coat 3D 90
ML6: Air 4G 91
Alexander Ter. G78: Neil 3C 130
Alexandra Av. G33: Step 3D 66
G66: Lenz 3C 50
Alexandra Ct. G31: Glas 3D 84
Alexandra Dr. PA2: Pais 2F 97
PA4: Renf 6F 59
Alexandra Gdns. G66: Lenz 3C 50
Alexandra Pde. G31: Glas 3A 84
Alexandra Parade Station (Rail)
3D 84
Alexandra Pk. G66: Lenz 3C 50
Alexandra Pk. St. G31: Glas 3D 84
Alexandra Rd. G66: Lenz 3C 50
Alexandra Sports Hall 3E 85
Alexandra St. G66: Kirk 5C 30
Alford Av. G66: Kirk 5B 30
Alford Pl. PA3: Lin 5E 75
Alford Quad. ML2: Wis 4H 145
Alford St. G21: Glas 6H 63
Alfred La. *G12: Glas 6C 62*
*(off Cecil St.)*
Alfred Ter. G12: Glas 6C 62
Algie St. G41: Glas 5D 102
Algoma Pl. G75: E Kil 3D 148
Alice Av. ML4: Bell 3C 126
Alice St. PA2: Pais 3A 98
Aline Ct. G78: Barr 3D 114
Alison Lea G74: E Kil 6B 138
Allan Av. ML8: Carl 2E 165
PA4: Renf 2G 79
Allan Ct. G75: E Kil 4A 148
Allan Cres. G82: Dumb 1H 17
ALLANDALE 1H 15
Allandale Av. ML1: N'hill 2F 129
Allandale Cotts. FK4: Alla 1H 15
Allandale Path *G72: Blan 2B 140*
*(off Winton Cres.)*
Allander Av. G62: Bard 6F 27
Allander Dr. G64: Torr 5C 28
Allander Gdns. G64: B'rig 3B 48
Allander Ho. *G67: Cumb 4H 35*
*(in Cumbernauld Shop. Cen.)*
Allander Rd. G62: Miln 3G 25
Allander Sports Complex 6H 25
Allander St. G22: Glas 5G 63
Allander Wlk. *G67: Cumb 4H 35*
*(in Cumbernauld Shop. Cen.)*
Allands Av. PA4: Inch 4G 57
Allanfauld Rd. G65: Kils 1H 11
G67: Cumb 3H 35
Allan Glen Gdns. G64: B'rig 3C 48
Allan Pl. G40: Glas 3D 104
G75: E Kil 4A 148
G82: Dumb 3G 17
Allanshaw Gdns. ML3: Ham 6F 141
Allanshaw Gro. ML3: Ham 1F 153
Allanshaw Ind. Est.
ML3: Ham 6G 141
Allanshaw St. ML3: Ham 6G 141
Allan St. G40: Glas 3D 104
ML1: Moth 2H 143
ML5: Coat 6H 89
ALLANTON 2E 155
Allanton Av. PA1: Pais 1G 99
Allanton Dr. G52: Glas 6B 80
Allanton Gro. ML2: Wis 4H 145
Allanton Lea ML3: Ham 3G 153
Allanton Pl. ML3: Ham 2A 154
Allanton Rd. ML2: Newm 2H 147
Allanton Ter. ML3: Fern 3F 155
Allan Twr. ML1: Moth 2H 143
Allbany Cres. ML1: Holy 2H 127
Allendale G74: E Kil 6E 137
Allender Rd. G61: Bear 4D 44
Allen Way PA4: Renf 2F 79
Allerdyce Ct. G15: Glas 6G 43

Allerdyce Dr.—Arklet Rd.


Allerdyce Dr. G15: Glas 6H 43
Allerdyce Pl. G15: Glas 6H 43
Allerdyce Rd. G15: Glas 6G 43
Allershaw Pl. ML2: Wis 3F 157
Allershaw Rd. ML2: Wis 3F 157
Allershaw Twr. ML2: Wis 3F 157
Allerton Gdns. G69: Bail 1F 107
Alleysbank Rd. G73: Ruth 4D 104
Allison Av. PA8: Ersk 5D 40
Allison Dr. G72: Camb 1A 122
Allison Pl. G42: Glas 3E 103
G69: G'csh 5C 68
G77: Newt M 5C 132
Allison St. G42: Glas 3E 103
Allnach Pl. G34: Glas 3C 88
Alloway Av. PA2: Pais 5D 98
Alloway Ct. G66: Kirk 3G 31
Alloway Cres. G73: Ruth 2B 120
PA2: Pais 5D 98
Alloway Dr. G66: Kirk 3F 31
G73: Ruth 2B 120
G77: Newt M 5G 133
G81: Clyd 4E 43
PA2: Pais 5D 98
Alloway Gdns. G66: Kirk 3G 31
ML3: Ham 2B 152
Alloway Gro. G66: Kirk 3F 31
PA2: Pais 5E 99
Alloway Quad. G66: Kirk 4G 31
Alloway Rd. G43: Glas 1B 118
G74: E Kil 5D 138
ML6: Air 3F 93
Alloway St. ML9: Lark 3G 161
Alloway Ter. G66: Kirk 3F 31
Alloway Wynd ML1: N'hill 3E 129
Almada Gro. ML3: Ham 5H 141
Almada La. ML3: Ham 5H 141
Almada St. ML3: Ham 5G 141
Alma St. G40: Glas 6C 84
Almond Av. PA4: Renf 1G 79
Almond Bank G61: Bear 5C 44
Almond Cres. PA2: Pais 3D 96
Almond Dr. FK4: Bank 1E 15
G66: Lenz 2B 50
G74: E Kil 2B 150
PA7: B'ton 5H 39
Almond Pl. ML1: Holy 3B 128
ML5: Coat 2H 89
Almond Rd. G33: Step 4C 66
G61: Bear 5D 44
G67: Cumb 6F 15
Almond St. G33: Glas 2F 85
Almond Va. G71: Tann 6E 109
Almond Vw. G15: Glas 5B 44
Almond Way ML1: Moth 6G 143
Alness Cres. G52: Glas 2E 101
Alness St. ML3: Ham 2H 153
Alness Ter. ML3: Ham 1H 153
Alpine Gro. G71: Tann 6D 108
Alsatian Av. G81: Clyd 5F 43
Alsh Ter. ML3: Ham 2E 153
Alston Av. ML5: Coat 3D 90
Alston Gdns. G61: Bear 5B 24
Altnacreag Gdns. G69: Mood 4E 53
Alton Ct. *G66: Kirk* *5E 31*
*(off Highfield Rd.)*
Alton Rd. PA1: Pais 1E 99
Altpatrict Gdns. PA5: Eld 2H 95
Altyre St. G32: Glas 2H 105
Alva Gdns. G52: Glas 3E 101
G61: Bear 6D 24
Alva Ga. G52: Glas 2E 101
Alva Pl. G66: Lenz 3E 51
Alwyn Av. PA6: C'lee 3D 74
Alwyn Ct. G74: E Kil 6G 137
Alyssum Cres. ML1: Moth 1F 143
Alyth Cres. G76: Clar 1E 135
Alyth Gdns. G52: Glas 2E 101
G76: Clar 1E 135
Ambassador Way PA4: Renf 2F 79
Amber Ter. ML4: Bell 3C 126
Ambleside G75: E Kil 5B 148
Ambleside Ri. ML3: Ham 6G 153
Ambrose Ct. *ML3: Ham* *5F 141*
*(off Burnbank Rd.)*
Amethyst Av. ML4: Bell 3C 126
AMF Bowling 4D 82
Amisfield St. G20: Glas 4C 62
Amochrie Dr. PA2: Pais 5E 97
Amochrie Glen PA2: Pais 5E 97
Amochrie Rd. PA2: Pais 4D 96
Amochrie Way *PA2: Pais* *4D 96*
*(off Amochrie Rd.)*
Amulree Pl. G32: Glas 1A 106
Amulree St. G32: Glas 2A 106
Ancaster Dr. G13: Glas 3F 61
Ancaster La. G13: Glas 3F 61
Anchor Av. PA1: Pais 1C 98
Anchor Bldgs. PA1: Pais 1B 98
Anchor Cres. PA1: Pais 2C 98
Anchor Dr. PA1: Pais 1C 98
Anchor La. G2: Glas 4G 83 (5E 5)
ANCHOR MILLS 1C 98
Anchor Wynd PA1: Pais 2C 98
Ancroft St. G20: Glas 6E 63
Andersen Ct. G75: E Kil 5G 149
Anderside G75: E Kil 6G 149
Anderson Av. G65: Kils 2F 11
Anderson Ct. G77: Newt M 5C 132
ML4: Bell 2D 126
Anderson Cres. G65: Queen 3C 10
Anderson Dr. G77: Newt M 5C 132
PA4: Renf 5F 59
Anderson Gdns. G72: Blan 6C 124
Anderson La. ML6: Air 3A 92
Anderson Rd. PA7: B'ton 3G 39
Anderson St. G11: Glas 1H 81
ML1: Moth 4G 143
ML3: Ham 4D 140
ML6: Air 3A 92
Anderson Twr. ML1: Moth 3G 143
ANDERSTON 4D 82
ANDERSTON CROSS INTERCHANGE 5A 4
Anderston Cross Shop. Cen.
G2: Glas 4E 83 (5A 4)
Anderston Quay
G3: Glas 5D 82 (6A 4)
Anderston Station (Rail) 4E 83 (5A 4)
Andrew Av. G66: Lenz 4D 50
PA4: Renf 6G 59
Andrew Dr. G81: Clyd 1E 59
Andrew Pl. ML8: Carl 2E 165
Andrew Sillars Av. G72: Camb 2B 122
Andrews St. PA3: Pais 5A 78
Andrew St. G74: E Kil 2H 149
Anford Pl. G72: Blan 2C 140
Angela Way G71: Udd 1D 124
Angle Ga. G14: Glas 5D 60
Angus Av. G52: Glas 2C 100
G64: B'rig 1E 65
G74: E Kil 1B 150
ML1: Moth 1E 143
ML3: Ham 6C 142
ML6: Air 6A 92
Angus Gdns. G71: Tann 5D 108
Angus Oval G52: Glas 1B 100
Angus Pl. G52: Glas 1B 100
G74: E Kil 1B 150
Angus Rd. ML8: Carl 4G 165
Angus St. G21: Glas 5A 64
G81: Clyd 1G 59
Angus Wlk. G71: View 6F 109
Anish Pl. G15: Glas 3G 43
Annan Av. G75: E Kil 4A 148
Annan Ct. ML5: Coat 5B 90
Annan Cres. ML6: Chap 4D 112
Annandale St. G42: Glas 2F 103
Annan Dr. G61: Bear 4C 44
G73: Ruth 6F 105
Annan Glade ML1: Moth 6A 144
Annan Gro. ML1: Moth 6A 144
Annan Ho. *G67: Cumb* *4H 35*
*(in Cumbernauld Shop. Cen.)*
Annan Pl. PA5: John 5C 94
Annan St. G42: Glas 5E 103
ML1: Moth 6A 144
Annan Way *G67: Cumb* *4H 35*
*(in Cumbernauld Shop. Cen.)*
ANNATHILL 5B 54
Annathill Gdns. ML5: Anna 5B 54
Annbank St. G31: Glas 5B 84
ML9: Lark 2D 160
Ann Ct. ML3: Ham 4E 141
Anne Av. PA4: Renf 5F 59
Anne Cres. G66: Lenz 4D 50
Annerley Ct. ML5: Coat 6A 90
Annerley Pl. ML5: Coat 6A 90
Anne's M. ML3: Ham 6B 142
Annette St. G42: Glas 3E 103
Annfield Gdns. G72: Blan 6A 124
Annfield Pl. G31: Glas 4B 84
Annick Dr. G61: Bear 4C 44
Annick St. G32: Glas 6B 86
G72: Camb 2D 122
Anniesdale Av. G33: Step 3D 66
Annieshill Vw. ML6: Plain 1G 93
ANNIESLAND 3F 61
Anniesland Cres. G14: Glas 4A 60
Anniesland Ind. Est. G13: Glas 1E 61
Anniesland Rd. G13: Glas 3C 60
G14: Glas 4A 60
Anniesland Station (Rail) 3F 61
Annieston G65: Twe 1D 32
Anniversary Av. G75: E Kil 4E 149
Annsfield Rd. ML3: Ham 4G 153
Ann St. ML3: Ham 4E 141
PA5: John 2G 95
Ansdell Av. G72: Blan 2A 140
Anson St. G40: Glas 1B 104
Anson Way PA4: Renf 2E 79
Anstruther Ct. ML8: Law 6D 158
Anstruther St. G32: Glas 6H 85
ML8: Law 6D 158
Antermony Rd. G66: Milt C 5C 8
Anthony Ct. G81: Clyd 1E 59
Anthony St. G2: Glas 4E 83 (5A 4)
Antigua Way G75: E Kil 2C 148
Anton Cres. G65: Kils 3A 12
Antonine G66: Kirk 3H 31
Antonine Av. ML1: Moth 1E 143
Antonine Gdns. G81: Dun 1C 42
Antonine Rd. G61: Bear 1B 44
G68: Dull 5E 13
Antonine Sports Cen. 1C 42
Antrim La. ML9: Lark 1F 161
Anwoth St. G32: Glas 2A 106
Apartments, The *G46: Giff* *6H 117*
*(off Milverton Rd.)*
Apollo Path ML1: Holy 2B 128
Appin Ct. G66: Kirk 4H 31
Appin Cres. G31: Glas 4D 84
Appin Rd. G31: Glas 4D 84
Appin Ter. G73: Ruth 3F 121
ML3: Ham 5C 140
Appin Way G71: Both 4E 125
ML5: Coat 1A 110
ML6: Glenm 5H 71
Appleby Cl. G75: E Kil 5B 148
Appleby St. G22: Glas 6F 63
Applecross Gdns. G69: Mood 4D 52
Applecross Quad. ML2: Wis 4H 145
Applecross Rd. G66: Kirk 4H 31
Applecross St. G4: Glas 6F 63
Appledore Cres. G71: Both 4E 125
Appleyard Ct. ML4: Bell 4B 126
Apsley La. G11: Glas 1G 81
Apsley St. G11: Glas 1G 81
Aqua Av. ML3: Ham 1C 152
Aqua Ct. ML3: Ham 1C 152
Aquatec Leisure Cen. 2G 143
Aquila Way ML8: Carl 3D 164
Araburn Dr. G75: E Kil 6G 149
Aranthrue Cres. PA4: Renf 5E 59
Aranthrue Dr. PA4: Renf 5E 59
Aray St. G20: Glas 3B 62
Arbroath Av. G52: Glas 1B 100
Arbroath Gro. ML3: Ham 1F 153
Arbuckle Pl. ML6: Plain 1G 93
Arbuckle Rd. ML6: Plain 1H 93
Arcadia St. G40: Glas 6A 84
ML4: Bell 6C 110
Arcan Cres. G15: Glas 5B 44
Archerfield Av. G32: Glas 3A 106
Archerfield Cres. G32: Glas 3A 106
Archerfield Dr. G32: Glas 3A 106
Archerfield Gro. G32: Glas 3A 106
Archerhill Av. G13: Glas 1A 60
Archerhill Cotts. G13: Glas 1A 60
Archerhill Cres. G13: Glas 1B 60
Archerhill Gdns. G13: Glas 1A 60
Archerhill Rd. G13: Glas 1H 59
Archerhill Sq. G13: Glas 1H 59
Archerhill Ter. G13: Glas 1A 60
(not continuous)
Arches Theatre 4F 83 (6C 4)
Archibald Ter. G66: Milt C 5B 8
Archiebald Pl. ML4: Bell 3F 127
Arch Way G65: Kils 2H 11
Ardargie Dr. G32: Carm 5C 106
Ardargie Gro. G32: Carm 5C 106
Ardargie Pl. G32: Carm 5C 106
Ardbeg Av. G64: B'rig 6E 49
G73: Ruth 4G 121
Ardbeg Rd. ML1: Carf 5B 128
Ardbeg St. G42: Glas 3E 103
Ardconnel St. G46: T'bnk 3F 117
ARDEN 3D 116
Arden Av. G46: T'bnk 5E 117
Ardenclutha Av. ML3: Ham 5F 141
Arden Ct. ML3: Ham 2H 153
*ML6: Air* *3F 91*
*(off Monkscourt Av.)*
Ardencraig Dr. G45: Glas 5B 120
Ardencraig Gdns. G45: Glas 5C 120
Ardencraig Pl. G45: Glas 4A 120
Ardencraig Quad. G45: Glas 5B 120
Ardencraig Rd. G45: Glas 6G 119
Ardencraig St. G45: Glas 4C 120
Ardencraig Ter. G45: Glas 5B 120
Ardencraig Workspace
G45: Glas 5C 120
Arden Dr. G46: Giff 5H 117
Arden Gro. G65: Kils 1G 11
Ardenlea G71: Tann 6D 108
Ardenlea St. G40: Glas 2D 104
Arden Pl. G46: T'bnk 5E 117
Arden Rd. ML3: Ham 1G 153
Arden St. ML6: Plain 1G 93
Arden Ter. ML3: Ham 1G 153
Ardery St. G11: Glas 1G 8
Ardessie St. G23: Glas 6B 4
Ardfern Rd. ML6: Air 5F 9
Ardfern St. G32: Glas 2A 10
Ardgay Pl. G32: Glas 1A 10
Ardgay St. G32: Glas 1A 10
Ardgay Way G73: Ruth 4D 12
Ardgoil Dr. G68: Cumb 4B 3
Ardgour Ct. G72: Blan 3D 14
Ardgour Dr. PA3: Lin 6G 7
Ardgour Pde. ML1: Carf 6C 12
Ardgowan Av. PA2: Pais 2B 9
Ardgowan Ct. PA2: Pais 2D 9
Ardgowan Dr. G71: Tann 6D 10
Ardgowan St. PA2: Pais 3B 9
Ardgowan Ter. La. *G3: Glas* *2B 8*
*(off Radnor St*
Ardgryfe Cres. PA6: Hous 1D 7
Ardholm St. G32: Glas 6A 8
Ardhu Pl. G15: Glas 3A 4
Ardlamont Sq. PA3: Lin 6A 7
Ard La. *ML2: Newm* *3D 14*
*(off Clunie Pl*
Ardlaw St. G51: Glas 5F 8
Ardle Rd. G43: Glas 2C 11
Ard Loan *ML1: Holy* *2A 12*
*(off Howden P*
Ardlui Gdns. G62: Miln 2D 2
Ardlui St. G32: Glas 1H 10
Ardmaleish Cres. G45: Glas 5A 12
Ardmaleish Dr. G45: Glas 5H 11
Ardmaleish Rd. G45: Glas 5H 11
Ardmay Cres. G44: Glas 6G 10
Ardmillan St. G33: Glas 3H 8
Ardmory Av. G42: Glas 6H 10
Ardmory La. G42: Glas 6A 10
Ardmory Pl. G42: Glas 6A 10
Ardnahoe Av. G42: Glas 5H 10
Ardnahoe Pl. G42: Glas 5H 10
Ardneil Rd. G51: Glas 5F 8
Ardnish St. G51: Glas 4E 8
Ardoch Cres. G82: Dumb 3D 1
Ardoch Gdns. G72: Camb 1H 12
Ardoch Gro. G72: Camb 1H 12
Ardoch Path *ML2: Newm* *3D 14*
*(off Tiree Cres*
Ardochrig G75: E Kil 6H 14
Ardoch Rd. G61: Bear 2H 4
Ardoch St. G22: Glas 5F 6
Ardoch Way G69: Mood 5D 5
Ardo Gdns. G51: Glas 6G 8
Ardressie Pl. G20: Glas 4B 6
Ard Rd. PA4: Renf 5D 5
Ardshiel Rd. G51: Glas 4E 8
Ardsloy La. G14: Glas 5A 6
Ardsloy Pl. G14: Glas 5A 6
Ard St. G32: Glas 1A 10
Ardtoe Cres. G33: Step 4E 6
Ardtoe Pl. G33: Step 4E 6
Arduthie Rd. G51: Glas 4E 8
Ardwell Rd. G52: Glas 2E 10
Argosy Way PA4: Renf 2E 7
Argus Av. ML6: Chap 3C 11
Argyle Av. PA3: Glas A 2A 7
Argyle Cres. ML3: Ham 6D 14
ML6: Air 1H 11
Argyle Dr. ML3: Ham 5E 14
Argyle Gdns. G66: Len 4G
Argyle Rd. G61: Bear 6E 2
Argyle St. G1: Glas 4G 83 (6E 5
G2: Glas 4E 83 (6A 4
G3: Glas 2B 8
PA1: Pais 1H 9
Argyle Street Station (Rail)
5G 83 (6E 5
Argyll Arc. G1: Glas 4G 83 (6D 4
Argyll Av. G82: Dumb 1C 1
PA4: Renf 5D 5
Argyll Gdns. ML9: Lark 2F 16
Argyll Pl. G65: Kils 3A 1
G74: E Kil 6C 13
G82: Dumb 1C 1
ML4: Bell 5B 12
Argyll Rd. G81: Clyd 1D 5
Arisaig Dr. G52: Glas 2D 10
G61: Bear 4H 4
Arisaig Pl. G52: Glas 2E 10
Arisdale Cres. G77: Newt M 3E 13
Arkaig Av. ML6: Plain 1F 9
Arkaig Pl. G77: Newt M 5H 13
Arkaig St. ML2: Wis 2H 15
Ark La. G31: Glas 4B 8
ARKLESTON 3E 7
Arkleston Ct. PA3: Pais 3D 7
Arkleston Cres. PA3: Pais 4D 7
ARKLESTON INTERCHANGE 3C 7
Arkleston Rd. PA1: Pais 5D 7
PA4: Renf 3C 7
Arkle Ter. G72: Camb 4G 12
Arklet Rd. G51: Glas 5E 8

Arklet Way—Avonside Gro.


klet Way ML2: Wis 6C 146
kwrights Way PA1: Pais 2F 97
lington Baths Club 1D 82
lington Pl. *G3: Glas 2D 82*
*(off Arlington St.)*
lington St. G3: Glas 2D 82
nadale Ct. G31: Glas 3C 84
nadale Path G31: Glas 3C 84
nadale Pl. G31: Glas 3C 84
nadale St. G31: Glas 4C 84
mine Path ML1: N'hill 3C 128
mour Av. ML6: Air 4G 91
nour Ct. G66: Kirk 4G 31
G72: Blan 3H 139
mour Dr. G66: Kirk 4G 31
mour Gdns. G66: Kirk 4G 31
mour Gro. ML1: Moth 5A 144
mour Pl. G66: Kirk 4G 31
ML1: N'hill 3C 128
PA3: Lin 6A 76
PA5: John 2G 95
mour Sq. PA5: John 2G 95
mour St. G4: Glas 5A 84
PA5: John 2G 95
mstrong Cres. G71: Tann 5E 109
mstrong Gro. G75: E Kil 4F 149
nbrae Rd. G65: Kils 2F 11
ngask Rd. G51: Glas 4E 81
nhall Pl. G52: Glas 2E 101
nhem St. G72: Camb 2D 122
nholm Pl. G52: Glas 2E 101
nisdale Pl. G34: Glas 3G 87
nisdale Rd. G34: Glas 3G 87
nisdale Way G73: Ruth 3D 120
nish PA8: Ersk 2G 57
niston St. G32: Glas 4H 85
niston Way PA3: Pais 4C 78
nold Av. G64: B'rig 6C 48
nol Pl. G33: Glas 4F 87
nott Dr. ML5: Coat 1C 110
nott Quad. ML1: Moth 6E 127
nott Way G72: Camb 1A 122
nprior Cres. G45: Glas 4H 119
nprior Gdns. G69: Mood 5D 52
nprior Quad. G45: Glas 3H 119
nprior Rd. G45: Glas 3H 119
nprior St. G45: Glas 3H 119
nside Av. G46: Giff 4A 118
num Gdns. ML8: Carl 4F 165
num Pl. ML8: Carl 4F 165
nwood Dr. G12: Glas 4G 61
on Ter. G72: Camb 4H 121
os Dr. G52: Glas 2D 100
os La. G52: Glas 3D 100
an G74: E Kil 2C 150
an Av. G82: Dumb 2D 16
ML5: Coat 1F 111
PA3: Glas A 1A 78
(not continuous)
an Dr. G46: Giff 5A 118
G52: Glas 2F 101
G66: Kirk 3E 31
G67: Cumb 5F 35
ML6: Air 2H 91
ML6: Glenm 4H 71
PA2: Pais 6A 98
PA5: John 4D 94
an Gdns. ML3: Ham 2A 154
ML8: Carl 5F 165
an La. G69: Mood 5E 53
an Path *ML9: Lark 4G 161*
*(off Stuart Dr.)*
an Pl. G81: Clyd 5E 43
ML5: Coat 1F 111
PA3: Lin 5G 75
an Rd. ML1: Moth 2E 143
PA4: Renf 1F 79
an Twr. G72: Camb 4G 121
an Vw. G65: Kils 3H 11
anview St. ML6: Chap 4E 113
an Way G71: Both 5D 124
G73: Ruth 2B 120
ochar Ct. G23: Glas 1B 62
ochar Dr. G23: Glas 6B 46
ochar Path *G23: Glas 6B 46*
*(off Arrochar Rd.)*
ochar St. G23: Glas 6B 46
ol Pl. G40: Glas 1D 104
ol St. G52: Hill 4G 79
(not continuous)
otshole Ct. G74: E Kil 6D 136
otshole Rd. G74: E Kil 1D 148
owsmith Av. G13: Glas 1D 60
hur Av. G78: Barr 6D 114
ML6: Air 5H 91
THURLIE 6D 114
hurlie Av. G78: Barr 5E 115
hurlie Dr. G46: Giff 5A 118
G77: Newt M 6D 132
hurlie Gdns. G78: Barr 5E 115
Arthurlie St. G51: Glas 4F 81
G78: Barr 5E 115
Arthur Pl. G76: Busby 3C 134
Arthur Rd. PA2: Pais 5A 98
Arthur St. G3: Glas 2B 82
G76: Busby 3C 134
ML3: Ham 4H 141
PA1: Pais 6G 77
Arundel Dr. G42: Glas 6E 103
G64: B'rig 3D 48
Ascaig Cres. G52: Glas 3E 101
Ascog Rd. G61: Bear 5F 45
Ascog St. G42: Glas 3E 103
Ascot Av. G12: Glas 3F 61
Ascot Ct. G12: Glas 3G 61
Ash Av. G75: E Kil 5E 149
Ashbank Cres. ML6: Chap 2E 113
Ashburn Gdns. G62: Miln 4E 25
Ashburn Loan ML9: Lark 1F 161
Ashburn Rd. G62: Miln 3E 25
Ashburton La. *G12: Glas 3H 61*
*(off Ashburton Rd.)*
Ashburton Pk. G75: E Kil 4C 148
Ashburton Rd. G12: Glas 3H 61
Ashbury Ct. *PA3: Lin 6H 75*
*(off Melrose Av.)*
Ashby Cres. G13: Glas 6E 45
Ash Ct. G75: E Kil 5E 149
Ashcroft G74: E Kil 4D 138
Ashcroft Av. G66: Len 4G 7
Ashcroft Dr. G44: Glas 1A 120
Ashcroft Wlk. G66: Len 4G 7
Ashdale Dr. G52: Glas 2E 101
Ashdene St. G22: Glas 2F 63
Asher Rd. ML6: Chap 3E 113
Ashfield G64: B'rig 4C 48
Ashfield Rd. G62: Miln 4G 25
G76: Clar 3C 134
ML8: Law 5D 158
Ashfield Station (Rail) 4G 63
Ashfield St. G22: Glas 5G 63
(not continuous)
ASHGILL 4B 162
ASHGILLHEAD 4A 162
Ashgillhead Rd. ML9: Shaw 4A 162
Ashgill Pl. G22: Glas 3G 63
Ashgill Rd. G22: Glas 2F 63
Ash Gro. G64: B'rig 1D 64
G66: Lenz 2B 50
Ashgrove G69: Mood 6D 52
Ash Gro. G71: View 5F 109
Ashgrove ML5: Coat 1C 110
ML6: Air 4D 92
Ash Gro. ML8: Law 5D 158
Ashgrove Rd. ML4: Bell 6D 110
Ashgrove St. G40: Glas 3C 104
Ashiestiel Ct. G67: Cumb 6G 35
Ashiestiel Pl. G67: Cumb 6G 35
Ashiestiel Rd. G67: Cumb 6G 35
Ashkirk Dr. G52: Glas 2E 101
ML9: Ashg 5B 162
Ashland Av. ML3: Ham 5H 153
Ashlea Dr. G46: Giff 3B 118
Ashlea Gdns. ML6: Plain 1F 93
Ashley Dr. G71: Both 2F 125
Ashley La. G3: Glas 1A 4
Ashley Pk. G71: View 1G 125
Ashley Pl. G72: Blan 1A 140
Ashley St. G3: Glas 2D 82 (1A 4)
Ashmore Rd. G43: Glas 2D 118
G44: Glas 2D 118
Ash Pl. FK4: Bank 1E 15
G75: E Kil 5E 149
PA5: John 4G 95
Ash Rd. G67: Cumb 6D 14
(not continuous)
G69: Bail 2G 107
G81: Clyd 2B 42
G82: Dumb 3F 17
Ashton Gdns. G69: G'csh 3E 69
Ashton Grn. G74: E Kil 1G 149
Ashton La. G12: Glas 6B 62
(not continuous)
Ashton La. Nth. G12: Glas 1B 82
Ashton Rd. G12: Glas 1B 82
G73: Ruth 4C 104
Ashton St. ML1: Moth 5F 127
Ashton Vw. G82: Dumb 3B 16
Ashton Way PA2: Pais 5C 96
Ashtree Ct. G60: Old K 1F 41
Ashtree Gro. G77: Newt M 6C 132
Ashtree Pk. ML2: Wis 6E 145
Ashtree Rd. G43: Glas 5A 102
Ashvale Cres. G21: Glas 5A 64
Ash Wlk. G73: Ruth 4E 121
ML1: Holy 2B 128
Ashwood ML2: Wis 2E 157
Ashworth Ter. ML3: Ham 5E 141
Ash Wynd G72: Flem 3E 123
Aspen Dr. G21: Glas 6C 64
Aspen Pl. G72: Flem 2E 123
PA5: John 4G 95
Aspen Way ML3: Ham 1A 154
Asquith Pl. ML4: Bell 2F 127
Aster Dr. G45: Glas 4C 120
Aster Gdns. G53: Glas 4C 116
ML1: Moth 4G 143
Athelstane Dr. G67: Cumb 6F 35
Athelstane Rd. G13: Glas 2C 60
Athena Way G71: Tann 6E 109
Athole Gdns. G12: Glas 6A 62
Athole La. G12: Glas 6A 62
Atholl Av. G52: Hill 3G 79
(not continuous)
G64: Torr 4D 28
Atholl Ct. G66: Kirk 4H 31
G72: Blan 3D 140
Atholl Cres. PA1: Pais 5G 79
Atholl Dr. G46: Giff 1A 134
G68: Cumb 5B 34
Atholl Gdns. G46: Glas 5F 117
G61: Bear 6E 25
G64: B'rig 4B 48
G73: Ruth 3G 121
Atholl La. G69: Mood 5E 53
Atholl Pl. G46: Glas 4F 117
ML5: Coat 2D 110
PA3: Lin 5G 75
Atholl St. ML3: Ham 3F 141
Atholl Ter. *G46: Glas 5F 117*
*(off Woodlands Pk.)*
G71: Tann 4D 108
Atlas Ind. Est. G21: Glas 5B 64
Atlas Pl. G21: Glas 5B 64
Atlas Rd. G21: Glas 5A 64
Atlas Sq. G21: Glas 5B 64
Atlas St. G81: Clyd 1D 58
Atlin Dr. ML1: New S 4B 128
Attercliffe Av. ML2: Wis 1C 156
Attlee Av. G81: Clyd 6F 43
Attlee Pl. *G81: Clyd 6F 43*
*(off Attlee Av.)*
Attow Rd. G43: Glas 2H 117
Auburn Dr. G78: Barr 6F 115
Auchans Rd. PA6: Hous 3F 75
AUCHENBACK 6F 115
Auchenbothie Cres. G33: Glas 3G 65
Auchenbothie Pl. G33: Glas 4F 65
Auchencrow St. G34: Glas 3B 88
Auchencruive G62: Miln 5A 26
Auchendavie Rd. G66: Kirk 3H 31
Auchendavie Steading
G66: Kirk 3H 31
Auchengeich Rd. G69: Mood 3B 52
Auchengilloch G75: E Kil 6G 149
Auchengleich Gdns.
G69: Mood 5D 52
Auchenglen Dr. G69: Mood 5D 52
Auchengreoch Av. PA5: John 5D 94
Auchengreoch Rd. PA5: John 5D 94
Auchenhowie G62: Miln 5A 26
Auchenhowie Rd.
G62: Bard, Miln 5H 25
Auchenkilns Rd. G67: Cumb 1F 55
Auchenkilns Rdbt. G68: Cumb 4E 35
Auchenlodment Rd. PA5: John 3G 95
AUCHENREOCH 5H 9
Auchenreoch Av. G82: Dumb 1H 17
Auchenstewart Ct. ML2: Wis 6A 146
AUCHENTIBBER 6F 139
Auchentibber Rd. G72: Blan 6F 139
AUCHENTORLIE 2D 98
Auchentorlie Quad. PA1: Pais 1D 98
Auchentorlie St. G11: Glas 1F 81
Auchentoshan Av. G81: Dun 1B 42
Auchentoshan Est. G81: Clyd 1A 42
Auchentoshan Ter. G21: Glas 1B 84
AUCHINAIRN 1D 64
Auchinairn Gdns. G64: B'rig 1F 65
Auchinairn Rd. G64: B'rig 1F 65
Auchinbee Farm Rd.
G68: Cumb 1D 34
Auchinbee Way G68: Cumb 2D 34
Auchincampbell Rd.
ML3: Ham 6H 141
Auchincloch Dr. FK4: Bank 1F 15
Auchineden Ct. G61: Bear 6C 24
Auchingill Path *G34: Glas 2B 88*
*(off Auchingill Pl.)*
Auchingill Pl. G34: Glas 2B 88
Auchingill Rd. G34: Glas 2A 88
(not continuous)
Auchingramont Ct. ML3: Ham 6H 141
Auchingramont Rd. ML3: Ham 5H 141
Auchinlea Retail Pk. G34: Glas 3F 87
Auchinlea Rd. G34: Glas 1F 87
Auchinlea Way G34: Glas 2F 87
Auchinleck Av. G33: Glas 3G 65
Auchinleck Cres. G33: Glas 3G 65
Auchinleck Dr. G33: Glas 3G 65
Auchinleck Gdns. G33: Glas 3G 65
Auchinleck Rd. G33: Glas 2H 65
G81: Hard 6D 22
Auchinleck Ter. G81: Hard 6D 22
AUCHINLOCH
Banknock 1C 14
Lenzie 5D 50
Auchinloch Rd. G66: Lenz 3D 50
Auchinloch St. G21: Glas 6B 64
AUCHINRAITH 3C 140
Auchinraith Av. ML3: Ham 3F 141
Auchinraith Rd. G72: Blan 3B 140
Auchinraith Ter. G72: Blan 3C 140
(not continuous)
AUCHINSTARRY 5A 12
Auchintibber Ct. G72: Blan 4C 140
Auchinvole Castle 5G 11
Auchinvole Cres. G65: Kils 3F 11
Auchmannoch Av. PA1: Pais 6G 79
Auchnacraig Rd.
G81: Faif, Hard 5E 23
Auchter Av. ML2: Newm 4G 147
Auchter Rd. ML2: Wis 5C 146
Auckland Pk. G75: E Kil 3C 148
Auckland Pl. G81: Clyd 3H 41
Auckland St. G22: Glas 6F 63
Auldbar Rd. G52: Glas 2F 101
Auldbar Ter. PA2: Pais 3C 98
Auldburn Pl. G43: Glas 1H 117
Auldburn Rd. G43: Glas 1H 117
Auldearn Rd. G21: Glas 2E 65
Auldgirth Rd. G52: Glas 2F 101
Auldhame St. ML5: Coat 3A 90
Auldhouse Av. G43: Glas 1H 117
Auldhouse Ct. G43: Glas 1H 117
Auldhouse Gdns. G43: Glas 1H 117
Auldhouse Retail Pk.
G43: Glas 6A 102
Auldhouse Rd. G43: Glas 1H 117
G75: E Kil 6F 149
Auldhouse Ter. G43: Glas 1B 118
Auld Kirk Mus. 4C 30
Auld Kirk Rd. G72: Camb 4C 122
Auldkirk, The G76: Busby 4E 135
Auldmurroch Dr. G62: Miln 3D 24
Auld Rd., The G67: Cumb 1A 36
Auld's Brae ML6: Air 3A 92
Auld St. G81: Clyd 4A 42
Auldton Ter. ML9: Ashg 4B 162
Aultbea St. G22: Glas 1F 63
Aultmore Gdns. G33: Glas 4F 87
Aultmore Pk. G33: Glas 4F 87
Aultmore Rd. G33: Glas 4F 87
Aursbridge Cres. G78: Barr 5F 115
Aursbridge Dr. G78: Barr 5F 115
Aurs Cres. G78: Barr 5F 115
Aurs Dr. G78: Barr 6F 115
Aurs Glen G78: Barr 6E 115
Aurs Pl. G78: Barr 5G 115
Aurs Rd. G78: Barr 4F 115
Austen La. G13: Glas 4E 61
Austen Rd. G13: Glas 4E 61
Austine Dr. ML3: Ham 4A 154
Avenel Rd. G13: Glas 6E 45
Avenue End Rd. G33: Glas 5B 66
Avenuehead Rd. G69: Mood 6D 52
Avenuepark St. G20: Glas 5C 62
Avenue St. G40: Glas 6C 84
G73: Ruth 4D 104
Avenue, The (Shop. Cen.)
G77: Newt M 5D 132
Aviemore Gdns. G61: Bear 2H 45
Aviemore Rd. G52: Glas 3E 101
Avoch St. G34: Glas 2H 87
Avon Av. G61: Bear 4H 45
ML8: Carl 3E 165
Avonbank Cres. ML3: Ham 3A 154
Avonbank Rd. G73: Ruth 6B 104
ML9: Lark 2C 160
Avonbrae Cres. ML3: Ham 3A 154
Avon Bri. ML3: Ham 1C 154
Avonbridge Dr. ML3: Ham 6B 142
Avondale Av. G74: E Kil 2H 149
Avondale Dr. PA1: Pais 5D 78
Avondale Pl. G74: E Kil 3A 150
Avondale St. G33: Glas 2A 86
Avon Dr. ML4: Bell 3E 127
PA3: Lin 5H 75
Avonhead G75: E Kil 6G 149
Avonhead Av. G67: Cumb 6E 35
Avonhead Gdns. G67: Cumb 6E 35
Avonhead Pl. G67: Cumb 6E 35
Avonhead Rd. G67: Cumb 6E 35
Avon Ho. ML3: Ham 4A 142
Avon Pl. ML5: Coat 2H 89
ML9: Lark 6F 161
Avon Rd. G46: Giff 5H 117
G64: B'rig 1C 64
ML9: Lark 5E 161
Avonside Gro. ML3: Ham 6B 142

# Avonspark St.—Barnes St.



**Avonspark St.** G21: Glas 6C **64**
**Avon St.** ML1: Moth 4F **143**
ML3: Ham 6A **142**
ML9: Lark 2D **160**
**Avon Twr.** ML1: Moth 4G **143**
**Avon Wlk.** *G67: Cumb 3H 35*
*(in Cumbernauld Shop. Cen.)*
**Avon Wynd** ML2: Newm 3D **146**
**Aylmer Rd.** G43: Glas 1D **118**
**Ayr Dr.** ML6: Air 6A **92**
**Ayr Rd.** G46: Giff 2G **133**
G77: Newt M 6A **132**
ML9: Lark, Shaw 6H **161**
**Ayr St.** G21: Glas 5B **64**
**Ayton Pk. Nth.** G74: E Kil 6B **138**
**Ayton Pk. Sth.** G74: E Kil 6B **138**
**Aytoun Dr.** PA8: Ersk 4D **40**
**Aytoun Rd.** G41: Glas 1B **102**
**Azalea Gdns.** G72: Flem 2E **123**

## B

**Babylon Av.** ML4: Bell 4C **126**
**Babylon Dr.** ML4: Bell 4C **126**
**Babylon Pl.** ML4: Bell 5C **126**
**Babylon Rd.** ML4: Bell 4C **126**
**Backbrae St.** G65: Kils 3H **11**
(not continuous)
**Back Causeway** G31: Glas 6F **85**
**Backmuir Cres.** ML3: Ham 3F **141**
**Backmuir Pl.** ML3: Ham 3F **141**
**Backmuir Rd.** G15: Glas 3B **44**
ML3: Ham 3F **141**
**Bk. o'Barns** ML3: Ham 5A **142**
**Bk. o'Dykes Rd.** G66: Kirk 6H **31**
**Back o' Hill** PA6: C'lee 2B **74**
**Back o' Hill Rd.**
G64: Balm, Torr 3H **27**
**BACK O'HILL RDBT.** **4D 34**
**Back Row** ML3: Ham 5A **142**
**Bk. Sneddon St.** PA3: Pais 6A **78**
**Badenheath Pl.** G68: Cumb 2H **53**
**Badenheath Ter.** G67: Mollin 3H **53**
**Badenoch Rd.** G66: Kirk 4H **31**
**Bagnell St.** G21: Glas 4B **64**
**Bahamas Way** G75: E Kil 2C **148**
**Bailie Dr.** G61: Bear 6D **24**
**Bailie Fyfeway** ML2: Over 4H **157**
**Baillie Dr.** G71: Both 4E **125**
G74: E Kil 5B **138**
**Baillie Gdns.** ML2: Wis 5C **146**
**Baillie Pl.** G74: E Kil 5C **138**
**Baillies La.** ML6: Air 4A **92**
**Bailliesmuir Pl.** ML2: Newm 3E **147**
**BAILLIESTON** **6A 88**
**Baillieston Rd.** G32: Glas 1D **106**
G71: Udd 2H **107**
**Baillieston Station (Rail)** **2H 107**
**Baillie Wynd** G71: Tann 5E **109**
**Bainsford St.** G32: Glas 5H **85**
**Bain St.** G40: Glas 5A **84**
**Baird Av.** G52: Hill 3G **79**
ML6: Air 1B **92**
ML9: Lark 5F **161**
**Baird Brae** G4: Glas 6F **63**
**Baird Ct.** G81: Clyd 5C **42**
**Baird Cres.** G67: Cumb 6D **34**
(not continuous)
**Baird Dr.** G61: Bear 2D **44**
PA8: Ersk 4D **40**
**Baird Hill** G75: E Kil 3F **149**
**Baird Pl.** ML2: Wis 5C **146**
ML4: Bell 6C **110**
**Bairds Av.** G71: View 1F **125**
**Bairds Cres.** ML3: Ham 6G **141**
**Bairdsland Vw.** ML4: Bell 2D **126**
**Baird St.** G4: Glas 2H **83** (2G **5**)
ML5: Coat 4C **90**
**Baker St.** G41: Glas 4C **102**
**Bakewell Rd.** G69: Bail 6G **87**
**Balaclava St.** G3: Glas 4E **83** (6A **4**)
**Balado Rd.** G33: Glas 4E **87**
**Balbeggie St.** G32: Glas 1C **106**
**Balbeg St.** G51: Glas 5E **81**
**Balblair Rd.** G52: Glas 3F **101**
**Balcarres Av.** G12: Glas 4A **62**
**Balcary Pl.** ML6: Chap 4E **113**
**Balcastle Gdns.** G65: Kils 1F **11**
**Balcastle Rd.** G65: Kils 2E **11**
**Balcomie St.** G33: Glas 2A **86**
**Balcomie Ter.** ML3: Ham 3F **153**
**Balcurvie Rd.** G34: Glas 1G **87**
**BALDERNOCK** **3D 26**
**Baldernock Rd.**
G62: Balder, Miln 4H **25**
**Baldinnie Rd.** G34: Glas 3H **87**
**Baldoran Dr.** G66: Milt C 5B **8**
**Baldorran Cres.** G68: Cumb 2D **34**
**Baldovan Cres.** G33: Glas 3F **87**
**Baldovan Path** G33: Glas 4F **87**
**Baldovie Rd.** G52: Glas 1C **100**
**Baldragon Rd.** G34: Glas 2H **87**
**Baldric Rd.** G13: Glas 3C **60**
**Baldwin Av.** G13: Glas 2D **60**
**Balerno Dr.** G52: Glas 2E **101**
**Balfleurs St.** G62: Miln 3H **25**
**Balfluig St.** G34: Glas 2F **87**
**Balfour St.** G20: Glas 3B **62**
**Balfour Ter.** G75: E Kil 4H **149**
**Balfour Wynd** ML9: Lark 4F **161**
**Balfron Cres.** ML3: Ham 6D **140**
**Balfron Dr.** ML5: Coat 2E **111**
**Balfron Rd.** G51: Glas 4E **81**
PA1: Pais 6F **79**
**Balgair Dr.** PA1: Pais 6D **78**
**Balgair Pl.** G22: Glas 5F **63**
**Balgair St.** G22: Glas 4F **63**
**Balgair Ter.** G32: Glas 6B **86**
**Balglass Gdns.** G22: Glas 5F **63**
**Balglass St.** G22: Glas 5F **63**
**Balgonie Av.** PA2: Pais 4E **97**
**Balgonie Dr.** PA2: Pais 4G **97**
**Balgonie Rd.** G52: Glas 1E **101**
**Balgonie Woods** PA2: Pais 4G **97**
**Balgownie Cres.** G46: T'bnk 5G **117**
**Balgraybank St.** G21: Glas 5B **64**
**Balgray Cres.** G78: Barr 5F **115**
**Balgrayhill Rd.** G21: B'rig, Glas 3B **64**
**Balgray Rd.** G77: Newt M 4A **132**
**Balintore St.** G32: Glas 6A **86**
**Baliol La.** G3: Glas 2A **4**
**Baliol St.** G3: Glas 2D **82** (1A **4**)
**Baljaffray Rd.** G61: Bear 6H **23**
**Baljaffray Shop. Cen.**
G61: Bear 5C **24**
**Ballagan Pl.** G62: Miln 3D **24**
**Ballaig Av.** G61: Bear 2D **44**
**Ballaig Cres.** G33: Step 4C **66**
**Ballantay Quad.** G45: Glas 4C **120**
**Ballantay Rd.** G45: Glas 4C **120**
**Ballantay Ter.** G45: Glas 4C **120**
**Ballantine Av.** G52: Hill 4A **80**
**Ballantrae** G74: E Kil 1F **149**
**Ballantrae Cres.** G77: Newt M 6G **133**
**Ballantrae Dr.** G77: Newt M 5G **133**
**Ballantrae Rd.** G72: Blan 4C **140**
**Ballantrae Wynd** *ML1: Holy 2A 128*
*(off Beauly Pl.)*
**Ballater Cres.** ML2: Wis 4H **145**
**Ballater Dr.** G61: Bear 5F **45**
PA2: Pais 4B **98**
PA4: Inch 2H **57**
**Ballater Pl.** G5: Glas 1H **103**
**Ballater St.** G5: Glas 6G **83**
**Ballater Way** ML5: Glenb 3G **69**
**Ballayne Dr.** G69: Mood 4E **53**
**Ballerup Ter.** G75: E Kil 5G **149**
**BALLIESTON** **1A 108**
**Ballindalloch Dr.** G31: Glas 3C **84**
**Ballindalloch La.** G31: Glas 3C **84**
**Ballinkier Av.** FK4: Bank 1E **15**
**BALLOCH** **3D 34**
**Balloch Gdns.** G52: Glas 2F **101**
**Ballochmill Rd.** G73: Ruth 5F **105**
**Ballochmyle** G74: E Kil 5D **138**
**Ballochmyle Cres.** G53: Glas 5A **100**
**Ballochmyle Dr.** G53: Glas 5A **100**
**Ballochmyle Gdns.** G53: Glas 5A **100**
**Ballochmyle Pl.** G53: Glas 5A **100**
**Ballochney La.** ML6: Air 1G **91**
**Ballochney Rd.** ML6: Air 1E **93**
**Ballochney St.** ML6: Air 1G **91**
**Ballochnie Dr.** ML6: Plain 1F **93**
**Balloch Rd.** G68: Cumb 3C **34**
ML6: Air 5G **93**
**BALLOCH RDBT.** **3C 34**
**Balloch Vw.** G67: Cumb 3H **35**
**Ballogie Rd.** G44: Glas 6F **103**
**BALMALLOCH** **2G 11**
**Balmalloch Rd.** G65: Kils 2F **11**
**Balmartin Rd.** G23: Glas 6B **46**
**Balmedie** PA8: Ersk 5E **41**
**Balmeg Av.** G46: Giff 1A **134**
**Balmerino Pl.** G64: B'rig 1F **65**
**Balmoral Av.** ML6: Glenm 4H **71**
**Balmoral Cres.** ML5: Coat 1H **109**
PA4: Inch 2A **58**
**Balmoral Dr.** G32: Carm 5B **106**
G61: Bear 5G **45**
G72: Camb 2G **121**
PA7: B'ton 6A **40**
**Balmoral Gdns.** G71: Tann 4D **108**
G72: Blan 5A **124**
**Balmoral Path** *ML9: Lark 3G 161*
*(off Alloway St.)*
**Balmoral Pl.** G74: E Kil 2E **149**
**Balmoral Rd.** PA5: Eld 5H **95**
**Balmoral St.** G14: Glas 6B **60**
**BALMORE** **5A 28**
**Balmore Dr.** ML3: Ham 3E **153**
**Balmore Ind. Est.** G22: Glas 1F **63**
**Balmore Pl.** G22: Glas 3F **63**
**Balmore Rd.** G23: Glas 1D **46**
G62: Balm, Bard 6D **26**
G64: Balm, Torr 5H **27**
**Balmore Sq.** G22: Glas 4F **63**
**Balmuildy Rd.** G23: Glas 3E **47**
G64: B'rig 3G **47**
**BALORNOCK** **3D 64**
**Balornock Rd.** G21: Glas 4C **64**
**Balruddery Pl.** G64: B'rig 1F **65**
**Balshagray Av.** G11: Glas 6F **61**
**Balshagray Cres.** G14: Glas 1E **81**
**Balshagray Dr.** G11: Glas 6F **61**
**Balshagray La.** G11: Glas 1F **81**
**Balshagray Pl.** G11: Glas 6F **61**
**Baltic Ct.** G40: Glas 2C **104**
**Baltic La.** G40: Glas 2C **104**
**Baltic Pl.** G40: Glas 1C **104**
**Baltic St.** G40: Glas 1C **104**
(not continuous)
**Balure Pl.** G31: Glas 4E **85**
**Balvaird Cres.** G73: Ruth 6C **104**
**Balvaird Dr.** G73: Ruth 6C **104**
**Balvenie Dr.** ML1: Carf 6B **128**
**Balvenie St.** ML5: Coat 2D **110**
**Balveny St.** G33: Glas 1D **86**
**Balvicar Dr.** G42: Glas 4D **102**
**Balvicar St.** G42: Glas 3D **102**
**Balvie Av.** G15: Glas 6A **44**
G46: Giff 5B **118**
**Balvie Cres.** G62: Miln 3F **25**
**Balvie Rd.** G62: Miln 3E **25**
**Banavie La.** G11: Glas 6G **61**
**Banavie Rd.** G11: Glas 6G **61**
ML2: Newm 3D **146**
**Banchory Av.** G43: Glas 2H **117**
ML6: Glenm 4H **71**
PA4: Inch 2H **57**
**Banchory Cres.** G61: Bear 5G **45**
**Banchory Rd.** ML2: Wis 4H **145**
**Baneberry Path** G74: E Kil 5F **137**
**Banff Av.** ML6: Air 1A **112**
**Banff Pl.** G75: E Kil 3E **149**
**Banff Quad.** ML2: Wis 4H **145**
**Banff St.** G33: Glas 1B **86**
**Bangorshill St.** G46: T'bnk 3F **117**
**Bank Av.** G62: Miln 2G **25**
**Bankbrae Av.** G53: Glas 1A **116**
**Bankend** PA11: Bri W 4G **73**
**Bankend Rd.** G82: Dumb 3F **17**
PA11: Bri W 5H **73**
**Bankend St.** G33: Glas 2A **86**
**Bankfield Dr.** ML3: Ham 4H **153**
**Bankfoot Dr.** G52: Glas 6B **80**
**Bankfoot Pl.** G77: Newt M 5H **133**
**Bankfoot Rd.** G52: Glas 1B **100**
PA3: Pais 6F **77**
**Bankglen Rd.** G15: Glas 3B **44**
**Bankhall St.** G42: Glas 3F **103**
**BANKHEAD** **1B 120**
**Bankhead Av.** G13: Glas 3A **60**
ML4: Bell 4D **126**
ML5: Coat 1G **109**
ML6: Air 4D **92**
**Bankhead Dr.** G73: Ruth 6C **104**
**Bankhead Pl.** ML5: Coat 1G **109**
ML6: Air 4D **92**
**Bankhead Rd.** G66: Kirk 6G **31**
G73: Ruth 1B **120**
G76: Crmck 2H **135**
**Bankholm Pl.** G76: Busby 4D **134**
**Bankier Rd.** FK4: Bank 1E **15**
**Bank La.** PA1: Pais 6B **78**
**BANKNOCK** **1E 15**
**Banknock St.** G32: Glas 5G **85**
**Bank Pk.** G75: E Kil 3F **149**
**Bank Rd.** G32: Carm 5C **106**
**Bankside Av.** PA5: John 2F **95**
**Banks Rd.** G66: Kirk 4D **30**
**Bank St.** G12: Glas 1C **82**
G72: Camb 1A **122**
G78: Barr 5E **115**
G78: Neil 2D **130**
ML5: Coat 5A **90**
ML6: Air 3A **92**
PA1: Pais 1B **98**
(not continuous)
**Banktop Pl.** PA5: John 2F **95**
**Bank Vw.** ML6: Chap 3D **112**
**Bankview Cres.** G66: Kirk 5A **30**
**Bankview Dr.** G66: Kirk 5A **30**
**Bank Way** *ML9: Lark 1F 161*
*(off Carrick Pl.)*
**Bannatyne Av.** G31: Glas 4D **84**
**Bannercross Av.** G69: Bail 6G **87**
**Bannercross Dr.** G69: Bail 5G **87**
**Bannercross Gdns.** G69: Bail 6G **87**
**Banner Dr.** G13: Glas 6C **44**
**Bannerman Dr.** ML4: Bell 2F
**Bannerman Pl.** G81: Clyd 5D
**Banner Rd.** G13: Glas 6C
**Bannockburn Dr.** ML9: Lark 4G
**Bannockburn Pl.** ML1: New S 5A
**Bantaskin St.** G20: Glas 2A
**BANTON** 1G
**Banton Pl.** G33: Glas 4G
**Banton Rd.** G65: Kils 2E
**Banyan Cres.** G71: View 4H
**Barassie** G74: E Kil 6F
**Barassie Ct.** G71: Both 5D
**Barassie Cres.** G68: Cumb 5H
**Barassie Dr.** PA11: Bri W 5E
**Baraston Rd.** G64: Torr 2B
**Barbados Grn.** G75: E Kil 2C
**Barbana Rd.** G74: E Kil 1A
**Barbegs Cres.** G65: Croy 1B
**Barberry Av.** G53: Glas 5B
**Barberry Gdns.** G53: Glas 5B
**Barberry Pl.** G53: Glas 5C
**Barbeth Gdns.** G67: Cumb 1D
**Barbeth Pl.** G67: Cumb 1C
**Barbeth Rd.** G67: Cumb 1C
**Barbeth Way** G67: Cumb 1C
**Barbrae Pl.** G71: Both 4E
**Barbreck Rd.** G41: Glas 3D
**Barcaldine Av.** G69: Chry 1H
**Barcapel Av.** G77: Newt M 2E
**Barchan's Rd.** PA10: Kilb 3B
**Barclay Av.** PA5: Eld 3H
**Barclay Ct.** G60: Old K 1F
**Barclay Rd.** ML1: Moth 3D
**Barclay Sq.** PA4: Renf 2D
**Barclay St.** G21: Glas 4B
G60: Old K 2F
**Barcloy Pl.** ML6: Chap 4E
**Barcraigs Dr.** PA2: Pais 5B
**Bard Av.** G13: Glas 1B
**BARDOWIE** 6F
**Bardowie Ind. Est.** *G22: Glas 5G*
*(off Bardowie*
**Bardowie Rd.** G62: Bard 6F
**Bardowie St.** G22: Glas 5F
(not continuo
**Bardrain Av.** PA5: Eld 3A
**Bardrain Rd.** PA2: Pais 6G
**Bardrill Dr.** G64: B'rig 6A
**Bardykes Rd.** G72: Blan 1H
**Barefield St.** ML9: Lark 1E
**Barfillan Dr.** G52: Glas 6E
**Bargany Rd.** G53: Glas 4A
**Bargaran Rd.** G53: Glas 2B
**BARGARRAN** 5D
**Bargarran Rd.** PA8: Ersk 5D
**Bargarran Sq.** PA8: Ersk 4D
**Bargarron Dr.** PA3: Pais 4C
**BARGEDDIE** 6D
**Bargeddie Station (Rail)** 1E
**Bargeddie St.** G33: Glas 1F
**Barhill Cotts.** *G65: Twe 1D*
*(off Main*
**Barhill La.** G65: Twe 1D
**Bar Hill Pl.** G65: Kils 3F
**Barhill Ter.** G65: Twe 1E
**Barholm Sq.** G33: Glas 1D
**Barke Rd.** G67: Cumb 2A
**Barkly Ter.** G75: E Kil 3E
**BARLANARK** 5E
**Barlanark Av.** G32: Glas 4C
**Barlanark Cres.** G33: Glas 4D
**Barlanark Dr.** G33: Glas 4D
**Barlanark Pl.** G32: Glas 5C
G33: Glas 4E
**Barlanark Rd.** G33: Glas 4D
**Barlandfauld St.** G65: Kils 3A
**Barleybank** G66: Kirk 5C
**Barlia Dr.** G45: Glas 4A
**Barlia Gdns.** G45: Glas 4A
**Barlia Gro.** G45: Glas 4A
**Barlia Sports Complex** 4A
**Barlia St.** G45: Glas 4A
**Barlia Ter.** G45: Glas 4A
**Barloan Cres.** G82: Dumb 2G
**Barloan Pl.** G82: Dumb 2G
**Barloch Av.** G62: Miln 3G
**Barloch Rd.** G62: Miln 3H
**Barloch St.** G22: Glas 5G
**Barlogan Av.** G52: Glas 6E
**Barlogan Quad.** G52: Glas 6E
**Barmore Av.** ML8: Carl 5G
**BARMULLOCH** 5E
**Barmulloch Rd.** G21: Glas 5C
**Barnard Gdns.** G64: B'rig 3C
**Barnbeth Rd.** G53: Glas 3B
**Barncluith Ct.** ML3: Ham 6B
**Barncluith Rd.** ML3: Ham 6B
**BARNELLAN** 4E
**Barnes Pl.** G33: Glas 3A
**Barnes St.** G78: Barr 5D

Beltane St.—Blaven Ct.


Beltane St. G3: Glas . . . . . . . . . . . .3D 82
ML2: Wis . . . . . . . . . . . . . . . .1G 157
Beltrees Av. G53: Glas . . . . . . . . .4A 100
Beltrees Cres. G53: Glas . . . . . . .4A 100
Beltrees Rd. G53: Glas . . . . . . . . .4A 100
Belvidere Cres. G64: B'rig . . . . . . .5D 48
ML4: Bell . . . . . . . . . . . . . . . .3D 126
Belvidere Rd. ML4: Bell . . . . . . . .3C 126
Belvoir Pl. G72: Blan . . . . . . . . . .1B 140
Bemersyde G64: B'rig . . . . . . . . . . .5E 49
Bemersyde Av. G43: Glas . . . . . . .2H 117
Bemersyde Pl. ML9: Lark . . . . . . .4E 161
Bemersyde Rd. PA2: Pais . . . . . . . .5B 96
Ben Aigan Pl. G53: Glas . . . . . . . .3C 116
Ben Alder Dr. PA2: Pais . . . . . . . . .4F 99
Benalder St. G11: Glas . . . . . . . . . .2A 82
Benarty Gdns. G64: B'rig . . . . . . . .5D 48
Benbecula G74: E Kil . . . . . . . . . .2C 150
Benbow Rd. G81: Clyd . . . . . . . . . .5B 42
Ben Buie Way PA2: Pais . . . . . . . . .4F 99
Bencloich Av. G66: Len . . . . . . . . . .3G 7
Bencloich Cres. G66: Len . . . . . . . . .2G 7
Bencloich Rd. G66: Len . . . . . . . . . .3G 7
Bencroft Dr. G44: Glas . . . . . . . . .2A 120
Ben Donich Pl. G53: Glas . . . . . . .3D 116
Ben Edra Pl. G53: Glas . . . . . . . .3D 116
Benford Av. ML1: N'hill . . . . . . . .3D 128
Benford Knowe ML1: N'hill . . . . . .3E 129
Bengairn St. G31: Glas . . . . . . . . . .4E 85
Bengal Pl. G43: Glas . . . . . . . . . .6A 102
Bengal St. G43: Glas . . . . . . . . . .6A 102
Ben Garrisdale Pl. G53: Glas . . . .3D 116
Ben Glas Pl. G53: Glas . . . . . . . .3D 116
Benhar Pl. G33: Glas . . . . . . . . . . .4H 85
Benholm St. G32: Glas . . . . . . . . .2H 105
Ben Hope Av. PA2: Pais . . . . . . . . .3F 99
Ben Laga Pl. G53: Glas . . . . . . . .3D 116
Ben Lawers Dr. G68: Cumb . . . . . .3D 34
PA2: Pais . . . . . . . . . . . . . . . . .3F 99
Ben Ledi Av. PA2: Pais . . . . . . . . . .3F 99
Ben Ledi Cres. G68: Cumb . . . . . . .3D 34
Ben Loyal Av. PA2: Pais . . . . . . . . .3F 99
Ben Lui Dr. PA2: Pais . . . . . . . . . . .4E 99
Ben Lui Pl. G53: Glas . . . . . . . . . .3D 116
G68: Cumb . . . . . . . . . . . . . . . .3D 34
Ben Macdui Gdns.
G53: Glas . . . . . . . . . . . . . . . .3D 116
Ben More Dr. G68: Cumb . . . . . . . .3C 34
PA2: Pais . . . . . . . . . . . . . . . . .3F 99
Benmore Twr. G72: Camb . . . . . .4G 121
Bennan Sq. G42: Glas . . . . . . . . .3G 103
Benn Av. PA1: Pais . . . . . . . . . . . .1B 98
Ben Nevis Rd. PA2: Pais . . . . . . . .4E 99
Ben Nevis Way G68: Cumb . . . . . . .3C 34
Benny Lynch Ct. G5: Glas . . . . . . .6G 83
Benson St. ML5: Coat . . . . . . . . . .1C 110
Benston Pl. PA5: John . . . . . . . . . .4E 95
Benston Rd. PA5: John . . . . . . . . . .4E 95
Bent Cres. G71: View . . . . . . . . .1G 125
Bentfoot Rd. ML2: Over . . . . . . . .5A 158
Benthall St. G5: Glas . . . . . . . . . .1H 103
Bentinck St. G3: Glas . . . . . . . . . . .2C 82
Bent Rd. ML3: Ham . . . . . . . . . . .1G 153
ML6: Chap . . . . . . . . . . . . . . . .2D 112
Bents Rd. G69: Bail . . . . . . . . . . . .6H 87
Benty's La. ML8: Carl . . . . . . . . . .5F 165
Ben Uird Pl. G53: Glas . . . . . . . .3D 116
Ben Vane Av. PA2: Pais . . . . . . . . .4E 99
Ben Venue Rd. G68: Cumb . . . . . . .3C 34
Ben Venue Way PA2: Pais . . . . . . . .4F 99
Benvie Gdns. G64: B'rig . . . . . . . . .5D 48
Benview Rd. G76: Clar . . . . . . . . .2C 134
Benview St. G20: Glas . . . . . . . . . .5D 62
Benview Ter. PA2: Pais . . . . . . . . . .3D 98
Ben Vorlich Dr. G53: Glas . . . . . .2D 116
Ben Vorlich Pl. G53: Glas . . . . . .3D 116
Benvue Rd. G66: Len . . . . . . . . . . . .4G 7
Ben Wyvis Dr. PA2: Pais . . . . . . . . .4E 99
Berelands Cres. G73: Ruth . . . . . .6A 104
Berelands Pl. G73: Ruth . . . . . . . .6A 104
Berenice Pl. G82: Dumb . . . . . . . . .3C 18
Beresford Av. G14: Glas . . . . . . . . .5E 61
Berkeley St. G3: Glas . . . . .3C 82 (3A 4)
Berkley Dr. G72: Blan . . . . . . . . .6A 124
Berkley Ter. La. *G3: Glas . . . . . . . .3D 82*
*(off Granville St.)*
Berl Av. PA6: C'lee . . . . . . . . . . . .3C 74
Bernadette Cres. ML1: Carf . . . . .5D 128
Bernadette St. ML1: N'hill . . . . . .4D 128
Bernard Path *G40: Glas . . . . . . . .1C 104*
*(off Bernard Ter.)*
Bernard St. G40: Glas . . . . . . . . . .1C 104
Bernard Ter. G40: Glas . . . . . . . . .1C 104
Berneray St. G22: Glas . . . . . . . . . .2G 63
Bernisdale Dr. G15: Clyd . . . . . . . .4F 43
Bernisdale Gdns. G15: Clyd . . . . . .4F 43
Bernisdale Pl. G15: Clyd . . . . . . . .4F 43
Berridale Av. G44: Glas . . . . . . . .2E 119
Berriedale G75: E Kil . . . . . . . . . .3A 148
Berriedale Av. G69: Bail . . . . . . . .1G 107
Berriedale Quad. ML2: Wis . . . . .4H 145
Berryburn Rd. G21: Glas . . . . . . . . .5E 65
Berry Dyke G66: Kirk . . . . . . . . . . .6H 31
Berryhill Dr. G46: Giff . . . . . . . . . .5H 117
Berryhill Rd. G46: Giff . . . . . . . . .6H 117
Berry Hill Rd. G67: Cumb . . . . . . . .3G 35
Berryknowe *G66: Kirk . . . . . . . . . . .6H 31*
*(off Bk. o'Dykes Rd.)*
Berryknowe Av. G69: Chry . . . . . . .2A 68
Berryknowes Av. G52: Glas . . . . . .6C 80
Berryknowes Dr. G52: Glas . . . . . .6D 80
Berryknowes La. G52: Glas . . . . . .6C 80
Berryknowes Rd. G52: Glas . . . . .1C 100
Bertram St. G41: Glas . . . . . . . . .4C 102
ML3: Ham . . . . . . . . . . . . . . . .3E 141
ML9: Lark . . . . . . . . . . . . . . . .4G 161
Bervie St. G51: Glas . . . . . . . . . . . .5F 81
Berwick Cres. ML6: Air . . . . . . . . . .6H 91
PA3: Lin . . . . . . . . . . . . . . . . . .4F 75
Berwick Dr. G52: Glas . . . . . . . . .1B 100
G73: Ruth . . . . . . . . . . . . . . . .6F 105
Berwick Pl. G74: E Kil . . . . . . . . .6C 138
ML5: Coat . . . . . . . . . . . . . . . .2D 110
Berwick St. ML3: Ham . . . . . . . . .4F 141
ML5: Coat . . . . . . . . . . . . . . . .2D 110
Bessemer Dr. G75: E Kil . . . . . . . .6A 150
Beta Cen. G81: Clyd . . . . . . . . . . . .2E 59
Betula Dr. G81: Clyd . . . . . . . . . . . .2C 42
Bevan Gro. PA5: John . . . . . . . . . . .3E 95
Beveridge Ter. ML4: Bell . . . . . . . .3F 127
Beverley Rd. G43: Glas . . . . . . . .1B 118
Bevin Av. G81: Clyd . . . . . . . . . . . .6F 43
Bideford Cres. G32: Glas . . . . . . .2D 106
Bield, The ML2: Wis . . . . . . . . . . .1A 158
BIGGAR ROAD . . . . . . . . . . . . . .2G 129
Biggar Rd. ML1: N'hse . . . . . . . . .5F 113
ML6: Chap . . . . . . . . . . . . . . . .4E 113
Biggar St. G31: Glas . . . . . . . . . . . .5D 84
Bigton St. G33: Glas . . . . . . . . . . . .1B 86
Billings Rd. ML1: Moth . . . . . . . .4D 142
Bilsland Ct. G20: Glas . . . . . . . . . . .4F 63
Bilsland Dr. G20: Glas . . . . . . . . . .4D 62
Binend Rd. G53: Glas . . . . . . . . . .5C 100
Binniehill Rd. G68: Cumb . . . . . . . .2F 35
Binnie Pl. G40: Glas . . . . . . . . . . . .6A 84
Binns Rd. G33: Glas . . . . . . . . . . . .1C 86
Birch Av. G76: Busby . . . . . . . . . .3D 134
Birch Brae ML3: Ham . . . . . . . . . .2A 154
Birch Ct. ML5: Coat . . . . . . . . . . .1B 110
Birch Cres. G76: Busby . . . . . . . .3D 134
PA5: John . . . . . . . . . . . . . . . . .4G 95
Birch Dr. G66: Lenz . . . . . . . . . . . .2D 50
G72: Camb . . . . . . . . . . . . . . . .1C 122
Birchend Dr. G21: Glas . . . . . . . . . .1D 84
Birchend Pl. G21: Glas . . . . . . . . . .1D 84
Birchfield Dr. G14: Glas . . . . . . . . .5B 60
Birchfield Rd. ML3: Ham . . . . . . . .6F 141
Birch Gro. G71: View . . . . . . . . . .6F 109
ML9: Lark . . . . . . . . . . . . . . . .6A 156
Birchgrove PA6: Hous . . . . . . . . . .2D 74
Birch Knowe G64: B'rig . . . . . . . . .1D 64
Birchlea Dr. G46: Giff . . . . . . . . .3B 118
Birchmount Ct. ML6: Air . . . . . . . . .3D 92
Birch Pl. G72: Blan . . . . . . . . . . . .1B 140
G72: Flem . . . . . . . . . . . . . . . .3F 123
PA4: Renf . . . . . . . . . . . . . . . . .1D 78
Birch Quad. ML6: Air . . . . . . . . . . .4D 92
Birch Rd. G67: Cumb . . . . . . . . . . .2E 37
G81: Clyd . . . . . . . . . . . . . . . . .3C 42
G82: Dumb . . . . . . . . . . . . . . . .3F 17
Birch St. G5: Glas . . . . . . . . . . . .2H 103
ML1: Holy . . . . . . . . . . . . . . . .2B 128
Birch Vw. G61: Bear . . . . . . . . . . .2G 45
Birchview Dr. G76: Busby . . . . . . .5D 134
Birch Way PA4: Renf . . . . . . . . . . .1D 78
Birchwood Av. G32: Glas . . . . . . .1E 107
Birchwood Courtyards, The
ML4: Bell . . . . . . . . . . . . . . . .5A 110
Birchwood Dr. PA2: Pais . . . . . . . . .4E 97
Birchwood Pl. G32: Glas . . . . . . . .1E 107
Birdsfield Ct. ML3: Ham . . . . . . . .3D 140
Birdsfield Dr. G72: Blan . . . . . . . .3B 140
Birdsfield St. ML3: Ham . . . . . . . .3D 140
BIRDSTON . . . . . . . . . . . . . . . . . .2C 30
Birdstone Rd. G66: Kirk . . . . . . . . .3C 30
Birdston Rd. G21: Glas . . . . . . . . . .3E 65
G66: Milt C . . . . . . . . . . . . . . . . .5C 8
Birgidale Rd. G45: Glas . . . . . . . .5H 119
Birgidale Ter. G45: Glas . . . . . . . .5H 119
Birkdale G74: E Kil . . . . . . . . . . .6E 137
Birkdale Ct. G71: Both . . . . . . . .5D 124
Birkdale Cres. G68: Cumb . . . . . . .5H 13
Birkdale Wood G68: Cumb . . . . . . .5A 14
Birkenburn Rd. G67: Cumb . . . . . . .5F 15
Birken Rd. G66: Lenz . . . . . . . . . . .3E 51
BIRKENSHAW
Glasgow . . . . . . . . . . . . . . .5D 108
Larkhall . . . . . . . . . . . . . . . . .6F 161
Birkenshaw Ind. Est.
G71: Tann . . . . . . . . . . . . . . . .4C 108
Birkenshaw Rd. G69: G'csh . . . . . .1G 69
ML5: Glenb . . . . . . . . . . . . . . .6A 54
Birkenshaw Sports Hall . . . . . . .4D 108
Birkenshaw St. G31: Glas . . . . . . . .4D 84
Birkenshaw Way *PA3: Pais . . . . . . .3A 78*
*(off Mossland Rd.)*
Birkfield Pl. ML8: Carl . . . . . . . . .4H 165
Birkhall Av. G52: Glas . . . . . . . . . .1H 99
PA4: Inch . . . . . . . . . . . . . . . . .2H 57
Birkhall Dr. G61: Bear . . . . . . . . . .5F 45
Birkhill Av. G64: B'rig . . . . . . . . . .5D 48
Birkhill Gdns. G64: B'rig . . . . . . . .5D 48
Birkhill Rd. ML3: Ham . . . . . . . . .4H 153
Birkmyre Rd. G51: Glas . . . . . . . . . .5F 81
Birks Ct. ML8: Law . . . . . . . . . . .1H 163
Birkshaw Brae ML2: Wis . . . . . . .3G 157
Birkshaw Pl. ML2: Wis . . . . . . . . .3G 157
Birkshaw Twr. ML2: Wis . . . . . . . .3F 157
Birks Rd. ML8: Carl . . . . . . . . . . .1G 163
ML9: Lark . . . . . . . . . . . . . . . .6F 161
Birkwood St. G40: Glas . . . . . . . .3D 104
Birmingham Rd. PA4: Renf . . . . . . .2D 78
Birnam Av. G64: B'rig . . . . . . . . . .5D 48
Birnam Cres. G61: Bear . . . . . . . . .2H 45
Birnam Pl. G77: Newt M . . . . . . .5H 133
ML3: Ham . . . . . . . . . . . . . . . .6C 140
Birnam Rd. G32: Glas . . . . . . . . . .2F 105
Birness Dr. G43: Glas . . . . . . . . .5B 102
Birnie Ct. G21: Glas . . . . . . . . . . . .5E 65
BIRNIEHILL . . . . . . . . . . . . . . .3H 149
Birniehill Ct. G81: Hard . . . . . . . . .6C 22
BIRNIEHILL RDBT. . . . . . . . . . .3A 150
Birnie Rd. G21: Glas . . . . . . . . . . . .5E 65
Birnock Av. PA4: Renf . . . . . . . . . .2G 79
Birrell Rd. G62: Miln . . . . . . . . . . .2F 25
Birrens Rd. ML1: Moth . . . . . . . .1E 143
Birsay Rd. G22: Glas . . . . . . . . . . .2F 63
BISHOPBRIGGS . . . . . . . . . . . . . . .6C 48
Bishopbriggs Ind. Est.
G64: B'rig . . . . . . . . . . . . . . . . .2C 64
Bishopbriggs Station (Rail) . . . . .6C 48
Bishopdale G74: E Kil . . . . . . . . .6E 137
Bishop Gdns. G64: B'rig . . . . . . . . .5A 48
ML3: Ham . . . . . . . . . . . . . . . .4A 154
Bishopmill Pl. G21: Glas . . . . . . . .5E 65
Bishopmill Rd. G21: Glas . . . . . . . .4E 65
Bishop's Ga. G64: B'rig . . . . . . . . .6B 48
G74: T'hall . . . . . . . . . . . . . . .6G 135
(not continuous)
Bishopsgate Dr. G21: Glas . . . . . . .2A 64
Bishopsgate Gdns. G21: Glas . . . . .2A 64
Bishopsgate Pl. G21: Glas . . . . . . .2A 64
Bishopsgate Rd. G21: Glas . . . . . . .2A 64
Bishops Pk. G74: T'hall . . . . . . . .6F 135
Bishop St. G2: Glas . . . . . . .4E 83 (5A 4)
BISHOPTON . . . . . . . . . . . . . . . . .4G 39
Bishopton Station (Rail) . . . . . . . .6H 39
Bisset Ct. *PA5: John . . . . . . . . . . .4E 95*
*(off Tannahill Cres.)*
Bissett Cres. G81: Dun . . . . . . . . . .1A 42
Blackadder Pl. G75: E Kil . . . . . . .4A 148
Blackbog Rd. ML6: Rigg . . . . . . . . .5G 55
Blackbraes Rd. G74: E Kil . . . . . .5B 138
Blackbull Cl. ML8: Carl . . . . . . . . .3F 165
Blackburn Cres. G66: Kirk . . . . . . .5G 31
G82: Dumb . . . . . . . . . . . . . . . .3D 16
Blackburn Sq. G78: Barr . . . . . . . .6F 115
Blackburn St. G51: Glas . . . . . . . . .5B 82
Blackbyres Ct. G78: Barr . . . . . . . .3F 115
Blackbyres Rd. G78: Barr . . . . . . .1E 115
Blackcraig Av. G15: Glas . . . . . . . .4A 44
Blackcroft Av. ML6: Gart . . . . . . . . .6E 93
Blackcroft Gdns. G32: Glas . . . . .1D 106
Blackcroft Rd. G32: Glas . . . . . . .1D 106
Blackdyke Rd. G66: Kirk . . . . . . . . .5E 31
Blackfarm Rd. G77: Newt M . . . . .5F 133
Blackfaulds Rd. G73: Ruth . . . . . .5A 104
Blackford Rd. PA2: Pais . . . . . . . . .3C 98
Blackfriars St. G1: Glas . . . .4H 83 (6G 5)
BLACKHALL . . . . . . . . . . . . . . . . .2C 98
Blackhall Ct. PA2: Pais . . . . . . . . .2D 98
Blackhall La. PA1: Pais . . . . . . . . .2B 98
Blackhall St. PA1: Pais . . . . . . . . .2B 98
BLACKHILL . . . . . . . . . . . . . . . . . .1F 85
Blackhill Pl. G33: Glas . . . . . . . . . .1F 85
Blackhill Rd. G23: Glas . . . . . . . . .5B 46
Blackhill Vw. ML8: Law . . . . . . . .6E 159
Blackhouse Av. G77: Newt M . . . .5F 133
Blackhouse Gdns.
G77: Newt M . . . . . . . . . . . . .5F 133
Blackhouse Rd. G77: Newt M . . . .5F 133
Blackie St. G3: Glas . . . . . . . . . . . .2B 82
Blacklands Pl. G66: Lenz . . . . . . . .3E 51
Blacklands Rd. G74: E Kil . . . . . . .2F 149
Blacklaw Dr. G74: E Kil . . . . . . . .2B 150
Blacklaw La. PA3: Pais . . . . . . . . . .6A 78
Blackmoor Pl. ML1: New S . . . . . .4A 128
Blackmoss Dr. ML4: Bell . . . . . . .3B 126
Blackness St. ML5: Coat . . . . . . .2D 110
Blackstone Av. G53: Glas . . . . . . .5C 100
Blackstone Cres. G53: Glas . . . . .4C 1
Blackstoun Av. PA3: Lin . . . . . . . . .5H
Blackstoun Oval PA3: Pais . . . . . . .6F
Blackstoun Rd. PA3: Pais . . . . . . . .3E
Black St. G4: Glas . . . . . . . .2H 83 (2H
ML6: Air . . . . . . . . . . . . . . . . . .2B
Blackswell La. ML3: Ham . . . . . . . .6B 1
Blackthorn Av. G66: Lenz . . . . . . . .2A
Blackthorn Gro. G66: Lenz . . . . . . .2B
Blackthorn Rd. G67: Cumb . . . . . . .1D
G71: View . . . . . . . . . . . . . . . . .5G 1
BLACKTHORN RDBT. . . . . . . . . . . .2E
Blackthorn St. G22: Glas . . . . . . . .4A
BLACKWOOD . . . . . . . . . . . . . . . .4A
Blackwood G75: E Kil . . . . . . . . . . .6F 1
Blackwood Av. G77: Newt M . . . . .6F 1
PA3: Lin . . . . . . . . . . . . . . . . . .6G
Blackwood Gdns. ML1: Moth . . . . .6E 1
Blackwood Rd. G62: Miln . . . . . . . .1F
G68: Cumb . . . . . . . . . . . . . . . . .4H
BLACKWOOD RDBT. . . . . . . . . . . .3A
Blackwoods Cres. G69: Mood . . . .5D
ML4: Bell . . . . . . . . . . . . . . . . .3E 1
Blackwood St. G13: Glas . . . . . . . .2E
G78: Barr . . . . . . . . . . . . . . . . .5D 1
Blackwood Ter. PA5: John . . . . . . .5D
BLACKWOOD W. RDBT. . . . . . . . . .4H
Bladda La. PA1: Pais . . . . . . . . . . .1B
Blades Ct. G69: G'csh . . . . . . . . . .3E
Bladnoch Dr. G15: Glas . . . . . . . . .5C
Blaeloch Av. G45: Glas . . . . . . . . .6G 1
Blaeloch Dr. G45: Glas . . . . . . . . .6F 1
Blaeloch Ter. G45: Glas . . . . . . . . .6F 1
Blaeshill Rd. G75: E Kil . . . . . . . .3A 1
Blairardie Dr. G13: Glas . . . . . . . . .6B
G15: Glas . . . . . . . . . . . . . . . . .6B
Blairathol Av. G11: Glas . . . . . . . . .6G
Blairathol Gdns. G11: Glas . . . . . . .6G
Blairatholl Cres. G77: Newt M . . .5H 1
Blair Atholl Dr. ML9: Lark . . . . . .4G 1
Blairatholl Ga. G77: Newt M . . . .5H 1
Blairbeth Dr. G44: Glas . . . . . . . . .6F 1
Blairbeth Pl. *G73: Ruth . . . . . . . .2D 1*
*(off Blairbeth R*
Blairbeth Rd. G73: Ruth . . . . . . . .2C 1
Blairbeth Ter. G73: Ruth . . . . . . . .2E 1
Blair Ct. G81: Clyd . . . . . . . . . . . .5D
Blair Cres. G69: Bail . . . . . . . . . . .2G 1
Blairdardie Rd. G15: Glas . . . . . . .6B
Blairdenan Av. G69: Mood . . . . . . .4E
Blairdenon Dr. G68: Cumb . . . . . . .2E
Blair Dr. G66: Milt C . . . . . . . . . . . .6
Blair Gdns. G64: Torr . . . . . . . . . .4D
G77: Newt M . . . . . . . . . . . . . . .4B 1
Blairgowrie Rd. G52: Glas . . . . . . .1C 1
Blairgrove Ct. ML5: Coat . . . . . . . .5A
Blairhall Av. G41: Glas . . . . . . . . .5D 1
BLAIRHILL . . . . . . . . . . . . . . . . . .4B
Blairhill Av. G66: Kirk . . . . . . . . . .1G
Blairhill Pl. ML5: Coat . . . . . . . . . .4A
Blairhill Station (Rail) . . . . . . . . . .3A
Blairhill St. ML5: Coat . . . . . . . . . .4A
Blairholm Dr. ML4: Bell . . . . . . . .4D 1
Blair Ho. G67: Cumb . . . . . . . . . . .2A
BLAIRLINN . . . . . . . . . . . . . . . . . .1H
Blairlinn Ind. Est. G67: Cumb . . . .1H
Blairlinn Rd. G67: Cumb . . . . . . . .1H
Blairlogie St. G33: Glas . . . . . . . . .2B
Blairmore Av. PA1: Pais . . . . . . . . .6E
Blairpark Av. ML5: Coat . . . . . . . .3A
Blair Path ML1: Moth . . . . . . . . . .4H 1
Blair Rd. ML5: Coat . . . . . . . . . . .4A
PA1: Pais . . . . . . . . . . . . . . . . . .6G
BLAIRSKAITH . . . . . . . . . . . . . . . .2H
Blairston Av. G71: Both . . . . . . . .6E 1
Blairston Gdns. G71: Both . . . . . .6F 1
Blair St. G32: Glas . . . . . . . . . . . .6H
Blairtum Dr. G73: Ruth . . . . . . . . .2D 1
Blairtummock Rd. G33: Glas . . . . .3C
(not continuo
Blake Rd. G67: Cumb . . . . . . . . . . .3A
Blane Dr. G62: Miln . . . . . . . . . . . .2H
Blanefield Gdns. G13: Glas . . . . . . .1F
Blane St. ML5: Coat . . . . . . . . . . .3C
Blaneview G33: Step . . . . . . . . . . .5D
BLANTYRE . . . . . . . . . . . . . . . . .3A 1
Blantyre Ct. PA8: Ersk . . . . . . . . . .4E
Blantyre Cres. G81: Dun . . . . . . . .6A
Blantyre Dr. PA7: B'ton . . . . . . . . .3G
Blantyre Farm Rd. G71: Udd . . . .2A 1
G72: Blan . . . . . . . . . . . . . . . . .6A 1
BLANTYREFERME . . . . . . . . . . . .1B 1
Blantyre Gdns. G68: Cumb . . . . . .4A
Blantyre Ind. Est. G72: Blan . . . . .4C 1
Blantyre Mill Rd. G71: Both . . . . .5D 1
Blantyre Rd. G71: Both . . . . . . . . .5E 1
Blantyre Sports Cen. . . . . . . . . . .1C 1
Blantyre Station (Rail) . . . . . . . . .1C 1
Blantyre St. G3: Glas . . . . . . . . . .2B
Blaven Ct. G69: Bail . . . . . . . . . . .1A 1

Blawart Hill St.—Brenfield Rd.


awart Hill St. G14: Glas 4H 59
eachfield G62: Miln 2F 25
easdale Ct. G81: Clyd 5D 42
enheim Av. G33: Step 3D 66
G75: E Kil 4E 149
enheim Ct. G33: Step 3D 66
G65: Kils 2H 11
ML8: Carl 4G 165
PA1: Pais 6H 77
.OCHAIRN INTERCHANGE 3C 84
ochairn Rd. G21: Glas 2C 84
uebell Gdns. G45: Glas 5C 120
ML1: Moth 5E 127
uebell Wlk. ML1: New S 4A 128
uebell Way G66: Len 4H 7
ML6: Air 1H 91
ML8: Carl 5F 165
ueknowes Rd. ML8: Law 6D 158
(not continuous)
uevale St. G31: Glas 5C 84
yth Pl. G33: Glas 5D 86
yth Rd. G33: Glas 5E 87
.YTHSWOOD 4F 59
ythswood Av. PA4: Renf 5F 59
ythswood Ct. G2: Glas 4E 83 (5A 4)
ythswood Dr. PA3: Pais 5H 77
ythswood Ind. Est. PA4: Renf 5D 58
ythswood Rd. PA4: Renf 5F 59
ythswood Sq. G2: Glas 3E 83 (4B 4)
ythswood St. G2: Glas 4E 83 (6B 4)
oardwalk, The G75: E Kil 4A 150
obbins Ga. PA1: Pais 2F 97
oclair Av. G61: Bear 3F 45
oclair Cres. G61: Bear 3G 45
G64: B'rig 5C 48
oclair Rd. G61: Bear 3G 45
G62: Miln 1B 46
G64: B'rig 6C 48
oclair St. G13: Glas 1E 61
odden Sq. ML1: N'hse 6E 113
oden Ind. Est. G40: Glas 1D 104
oden Quad. ML1: Moth 5D 126
oden St. G40: Glas 1C 104
odmin Gdns. G69: Mood 4D 52
ogany Ter. G45: Glas 5A 120
ogbain Rd. G34: Glas 3G 87
oggknowe G71: Tann 5B 108
oghall Rd. G71: Udd 3G 107
ML8: Carl 6H 165
oghall St. G33: Glas 2B 86
OGHEAD 3H 49
oghead Av. G82: Dumb 3H 17
oghead Rd. G21: Glas 4C 64
G66: Lenz 3A 50
G82: Dumb 3G 17
ogleshole Rd. G72: Camb 6G 105
ogmoor Pl. G51: Glas 2C 80
ogmoor Rd. G51: Glas 3B 80
og Rd. FK4: Bank 1E 15
OGSIDE 3G 159
ogside Rd. G33: Mille 3A 66
G65: Kils 4H 11
ML9: Ashg 5B 162
ogside St. G40: Glas 1D 104
ogstonhill Rd. PA6: Hous 1B 74
ogs Vw. ML4: Bell 4B 126
ogton Av. G44: Glas 3D 118
ogton Av. La. G44: Glas 3D 118
oleyn Rd. G41: Glas 3C 102
olingbroke G74: E Kil 5C 138
olivar Ter. G42: Glas 5G 103
olton Dr. G42: Glas 5F 103
olton Ter. G66: Len 3G 7
on Accord Rd. G76: Busby 3D 134
on Accord Sq. G81: Clyd 1D 58
onar Cres. PA11: Bri W 4G 73
onar La. PA11: Bri W 4G 73
onawe St. G20: Glas 5D 62
onds Dr. ML2: Newm 3F 147
o'ness Rd. ML1: Holy 1C 128
oness St. G40: Glas 1D 104
onhill Rd. G82: Dumb 3G 17
onhill St. G22: Glas 6F 63
ONKLE 3G 147
onkle Gdns. ML2: Newm 4F 147
onkle Rd. ML2: Newm 4F 147
onnar St. G40: Glas 2C 104
onnaughton Rd. G61: Bear 1B 44
onnyholm Av. G53: Glas 2A 100
onnyrigg Dr. G43: Glas 2G 117
onnyton La. ML3: Ham 4F 153
ontine Av. G82: Dumb 3D 16
onyton Av. G13: Glas 3H 59
oon Dr. G15: Glas 5B 44
oquhanran Pl. G81: Clyd 4C 42
oquhanran Rd. G81: Clyd 5B 42
(not continuous)
orden La. G13: Glas 4E 61
orden Rd. G13: Glas 4E 61
order Way G66: Kirk 5E 31
Boreland Dr. G13: Glas 2A 60
ML3: Ham 1C 152
Boreland Pl. G13: Glas 3B 60
Bore Rd. ML6: Air 2B 92
Borgie Cres. G72: Camb 2A 122
Borland Dr. ML9: Lark 5F 161
Borland Rd. G61: Bear 4G 45
Borron St. G4: Glas 6G 63
Borrowdale G75: E Kil 6B 148
Borthwick Dr. G75: E Kil 4A 148
Borthwick St. G33: Glas 2B 86
Bosfield Cnr. G74: E Kil 6H 137
Bosfield Pl. G74: E Kil 6H 137
Bosfield Rd. G74: E Kil 6G 137
Boswell Ct. G42: Glas 6D 102
Boswell Dr. G72: Blan 2B 140
Boswell Pk. G74: E Kil 5C 138
Boswell Sq. G52: Hill 4H 79
Bosworth Rd. G74: E Kil 5B 138
Botanic Cres. G20: Glas 5B 62
Botanic Cres. La. G20: Glas 5B 62
Bothlin Dr. G33: Step 3D 66
Bothlyn Av. G66: Kirk 6E 31
Bothlyn Cres. G69: G'csh 2D 68
Bothlyn Rd. G69: Chry 1B 68
BOTHWELL 5E 125
Bothwell Bri. G71: Both 1G 141
Bothwell Castle 4B 124
Bothwellhaugh Quad.
ML4: Bell 4B 126
Bothwellhaugh Rd.
ML1: Moth 6B 126
Bothwell Ho. ML3: Ham 4A 142
Bothwell La. *G12: Glas* *1C 82*
*(off Glasgow St.)*
G2: Glas 4E 83 (5B 4)
Bothwell Pk. Ind. Est.
G71: Udd 2E 125
Bothwellpark Pl. ML4: Bell 1H 125
Bothwellpark Rd. G71: Both 5F 125
Bothwell Pl. ML5: Coat 4B 90
PA2: Pais 5C 96
Bothwell Rd. G71: Udd 2D 124
ML3: Ham 2G 141
ML8: Carl 1E 165
Bothwell St. G2: Glas 4E 83 (5B 4)
G72: Camb 1G 121
ML3: Ham 4G 141
Bothwick Way PA2: Pais 5C 96
Boulevard, The G66: Len 2C 6
Bourhill Ct. ML2: Wis 1D 156
Bourne Ct. PA4: Inch 2H 57
Bourne Cres. PA4: Inch 2H 57
Bourne St. ML3: Ham 6B 142
Bourock Sq. G78: Barr 6F 115
Bourtree Rd. ML3: Ham 1C 152
Bouverie St. G14: Glas 3G 59
G73: Ruth 6B 104
Bowden Dr. G52: Glas 5B 80
Bowden Pk. G75: E Kil 3E 149
Bower St. G12: Glas 6C 62
Bowerwalls St. G78: Barr 3F 115
Bowes Cres. G69: Bail 1F 107
Bowfield Av. G52: Glas 5H 79
Bowfield Cres. G52: Glas 5H 79
Bowfield Dr. G52: Glas 5H 79
Bowfield Path G52: Glas 5H 79
Bowfield Pl. G52: Glas 5H 79
Bowhousebrae Rd.
ML6: Gart 1E 113
Bowhouse Dr. G45: Ruth 2C 120
Bowhouse Gdns. G45: Ruth 2C 120
Bowhouse Gro. G45: Glas 3C 120
Bowhouse Pl. G45: Glas 3C 120
Bowhouse Rd. ML6: Gart 6E 93
Bowie St. G82: Dumb 4E 17
BOWLING 5B 20
Bowling Grn. La. *G14: Glas* *6D 60*
*(off Westland Dr.)*
Bowling Grn. Rd. G14: Glas 6D 60
G32: Glas 1D 106
G44: Glas 2E 119
G69: Chry 1B 68
Bowling Grn. St. ML4: Bell 2D 126
Bowling Grn. Vw. G72: Flem 3F 123
Bowling Station (Rail) 5A 20
Bowling St. ML5: Coat 4B 90
Bowmanflat ML9: Lark 2E 161
Bowman St. G42: Glas 3E 103
Bowmont Gdns. G12: Glas 6A 62
Bowmont Hill G64: B'rig 3C 48
Bowmont Pl. G72: Camb 2D 122
G75: E Kil 4A 148
Bowmont Ter. G12: Glas 6A 62
Bowmore Gdns. G71: Tann 5C 108
G73: Ruth 4G 121
Bowmore Rd. G52: Glas 6E 81
Bowyer Vennel ML4: Bell 1B 126
Boyd Dr. ML1: Moth 2D 142
Boydstone Pl. G46: T'bnk 2G 117
Boydstone Rd.
G43: Glas, T'bnk 1E 117
G53: Glas 1E 117
Boyd St. G42: Glas 4F 103
Boylestone Rd. G78: Barr 3C 114
Boyle St. G81: Clyd 1F 59
Boyndie Path G34: Glas 3H 87
Boyndie St. G34: Glas 3H 87
Brabloch Cres. PA3: Pais 5B 78
Bracadale Dr. G69: Bail 1B 108
Bracadale Gdns. G69: Bail 1B 108
Bracadale Gro. G69: Bail 1A 108
Bracadale Rd. G69: Bail 1A 108
Brackenbrae Av. G64: B'rig 5A 48
Brackenbrae Rd. G64: B'rig 6B 48
Brackendene PA6: Hous 2D 74
Brackenhill Dr. ML3: Ham 4F 153
Brackenhill Rd. ML8: Law 5E 159
Brackenhirst Gdns. ML6: Glenm 3F 71
Brackenhirst Rd. ML6: Glenm 3F 71
Brackenhurst St. G82: Dumb 1H 17
Brackenrig Rd. G46: T'bnk 5E 117
Bracken St. G22: Glas 3F 63
ML1: New S 4A 128
Bracken Ter. G71: Both 4E 125
Bracken Way *ML9: Lark* *4G 161*
*(off Donaldson Rd.)*
Brackla Av. G81: Clyd 1G 59
Bradda Av. G73: Ruth 3E 121
Bradfield Av. G12: Glas 4A 62
Bradshaw Cres. ML3: Ham 6C 140
Brady Cres. G69: Mood 4E 53
BRAEDALE 3D 142
Braedale ML3: Ham 6E 141
Braedale Av. ML1: Moth 3D 142
ML6: Air 4B 92
Braedale Cres. ML2: Newm 4F 147
Braedale Pl. ML2: Newm 4G 147
Braeface Rd. G67: Cumb 3G 35
Braefield Dr. G46: T'bnk 4G 117
Braefoot Av. G62: Miln 5G 25
Braefoot Ct. ML8: Law 6D 158
Braefoot Cres. ML8: Law 1H 163
PA2: Pais 6B 98
BRAEHEAD 6H 135
Braehead G72: Blan 3B 140
Braehead Arena 6A 60
Braehead Av. G62: Miln 4F 25
G78: Neil 2D 130
G81: Dun 6C 22
ML5: Coat 2H 109
ML9: Lark 3C 160
Braehead Cres. G81: Dun 6C 22
Braehead Curling & Ice Rinks 6A 60
Braehead Dr. ML4: Bell 3B 126
Braehead Ind. Est. PA4: Renf 1H 79
Braehead Loan *ML8: Carl* *5H 165*
*(off Charles Cres.)*
Braehead Pl. ML4: Bell 3B 126
Braehead Quad. G78: Neil 2D 130
ML1: N'hill 3D 128
Braehead Rd. G67: Cumb 2B 36
G74: T'hall 6G 135
G81: Dun 6C 22
PA2: Pais 6G 97
Braehead Shop. Cen. G51: Glas 6A 60
Braehead St. G5: Glas 2H 103
G66: Kirk 4C 30
Braemar Av. G81: Clyd 3B 42
Braemar Ct. G44: Glas 3C 118
Braemar Cres. G61: Bear 5F 45
ML8: Carl 2G 165
PA2: Pais 4B 98
Braemar Dr. PA5: Eld 4H 95
Braemar Rd. G73: Ruth 4G 121
PA4: Inch 2H 57
Braemar St. G42: Glas 6D 102
ML3: Ham 3F 141
Braemar Vw. G81: Clyd 2B 42
Braemore Gdns. G22: Glas 5H 63
Braemount Av. PA2: Pais 6G 97
Braes Av. G81: Clyd 6F 43
Braesburn Ct. G67: Cumb 5F 15
Braesburn Pl. G67: Cumb 5F 15
Braesburn Rd. G67: Cumb 5F 15
Braeside Av. G62: Miln 5G 25
G69: Mood 5D 52
G73: Ruth 6E 105
Braeside Cres. G69: Barg 6D 88
G78: Barr 6G 115
Braeside Dr. G78: Barr 6F 115
G82: Dumb 2H 17
Braeside Gdns. ML3: Ham 3A 154
Braeside La. *ML9: Lark* *1F 161*
*(off Carrick Pl.)*
Braeside Pl. G72: Camb 3B 122
Braeside Rd. ML1: N'hill 3D 128
Braeside St. G20: Glas 5D 62
Braeside Way *ML9: Lark* *4F 161*
*(off Keir Hardie Rd.)*
Braes o'Yetts G66: Kirk 5G 31
Braeview Av. PA2: Pais 6F 97
Braeview Dr. PA2: Pais 6F 97
Braeview Gdns. PA2: Pais 6F 97
Brae Vw. Pl. G74: E Kil 5B 138
Braeview Rd. PA2: Pais 6F 97
Braid Av. ML1: Cle 6E 129
Braidbar Ct. G46: Giff 4A 118
Braidbar Farm Rd. G46: Giff 3B 118
(not continuous)
Braidbar Rd. G46: Giff 4A 118
Braidcraft Pl. G53: Glas 5C 100
Braidcraft Rd. G53: Glas 4C 100
Braidcraft Ter. G53: Glas 4D 100
BRAIDFAULD 2G 105
Braidfauld Gdns. G32: Glas 2H 105
Braidfauld Pl. G32: Glas 3H 105
Braidfauld St. G32: Glas 3H 105
Braidfield Gro. G81: Hard 2D 42
Braidfield Rd. G81: Hard 2D 42
Braidholm Cres. G46: Giff 4A 118
Braidholm Rd. G46: Giff 4A 118
Braidhurst Ind. Est.
ML1: Moth 6F 127
Braidhurst Sports Barn 6F 127
Braidhurst St. ML1: Moth 1G 143
Braidley Cres. G75: E Kil 6G 149
Braidpark Dr. G46: Giff 4B 118
Braids Circle PA2: Pais 4A 98
Braids Ct. PA2: Pais 4H 97
Braids Dr. G53: Glas 4H 99
Braids Ga. PA2: Pais 4H 97
Braid Sq. G4: Glas 1E 83 (1B 4)
Braids Rd. PA2: Pais 4A 98
Braid St. G4: Glas 1E 83
Braidwood Pl. PA3: Lin 5F 75
Braidwood St. ML2: Wis 2A 146
Bramah Av. G75: E Kil 4H 149
Bramble Ct. G66: Len 3E 7
Brambling Ct. ML2: Wis 2F 157
Bramley Pl. G66: Lenz 3E 51
ML6: Air 5E 93
Brampton G75: E Kil 5B 148
Branchalfield Dr. ML2: Wis 5C 146
Branchalmuir Cres.
ML2: Newm 3D 146
Branchal Rd. ML2: Wis 4B 146
Branchock Av. G72: Camb 3D 122
Brancumhall Rd. G74: E Kil 6D 138
Brandon Arc. ML1: Moth 3G 143
Brandon Ct. ML3: Ham 5G 141
Brandon Dr. G61: Bear 6E 25
Brandon Gdns. G72: Camb 2G 121
Brandon Ho. ML3: Ham 4A 142
Brandon Pde. E. ML1: Moth 2G 143
Brandon Pde. Sth. ML1: Moth 3G 143
Brandon Pl. ML4: Bell 4A 126
Brandon St. G31: Glas 5B 84
ML1: Moth 3H 143
ML3: Ham 6A 142
Brandon Way ML5: Coat 1H 109
Brand Pl. G51: Glas 5A 82
Brand St. G51: Glas 5A 82
Brankholm Brae ML3: Ham 5B 140
Branklyn Cl. G13: Glas 3D 60
Branklyn Ct. G13: Glas 3D 60
Branklyn Cres. G13: Glas 3D 60
Branklyn Gro. G13: Glas 3D 60
Branklyn Pl. G13: Glas 3D 60
BRANKUMHALL 6C 138
Brannock Av. ML1: N'hill 3D 128
Brannock Pl. ML1: N'hill 3D 128
Brannock Rd. ML1: N'hill 4D 128
Brassey St. G20: Glas 3C 62
Breadalbane Cres. ML1: Moth 6F 127
Breadalbane Gdns. G73: Ruth 3F 121
Breadalbane St. G3: Glas 3D 82
Breadie Dr. G62: Miln 5F 25
Breamish Pl. G75: E Kil 5B 148
Bream Pl. PA6: C'lee 3D 74
Brechin Rd. G64: B'rig 6E 49
Brechin St. G3: Glas 3C 82
Breck Av. PA2: Pais 6B 96
BREDILAND 4E 97
Brediland Rd. PA2: Pais 6C 96
PA3: Lin 5G 75
Bredin Way ML1: Moth 1D 142
Bredisholm Cres. G71: View 4G 109
Bredisholm Dr. G69: Bail 1A 108
Bredisholm Rd. G69: Bail 1A 108
(not continuous)
G69: Barg 1D 108
(not continuous)
Bredisholm Ter. G69: Bail 1A 108
Bredland Rd. PA2: Pais 3E 97
Bremners Cotts. G81: Dun 1B 42
Brenfield Av. G44: Glas 3D 118
Brenfield Dr. G44: Glas 3D 118
Brenfield Rd. G44: Glas 3D 118
G44: Neth 3D 118

**Brent Av.** G46: T'bnk . . . . . . . . . . .2F **117**
**Brent Ct.** G74: E Kil . . . . . . . . . . . .6G **137**
**Brent Cres.** PA6: C'lee . . . . . . . . . .3C **74**
**Brent Dr.** G46: T'bnk . . . . . . . . . . .2F **117**
**Brent Gdns.** G46: T'bnk . . . . . . . . .2F **117**
**Brent Rd.** G46: T'bnk . . . . . . . . . . .2F **117**
G74: E Kil . . . . . . . . . . . . . . .6G **137**
**Brent Way** G46: T'bnk . . . . . . . . . .2F **117**
**Brentwood Av.** G53: Glas . . . . . . .3A **116**
**Brentwood Dr.** G53: Glas . . . . . . .3B **116**
**Brentwood Sq.** G53: Glas . . . . . . .3B **116**
**Brereton St.** G42: Glas . . . . . . . . .4G **103**
**Bressay** G74: E Kil . . . . . . . . . . . .6G **137**
**Bressay Rd.** G33: Glas . . . . . . . . . .5E **87**
**Bressay Wynd** *ML2: Newm . . . . .3D **146***
*(off Tiree Cres.)*
**Breval Cres.** G81: Dun, Hard . . . . .6C **22**
**Brewery St.** PA5: John . . . . . . . . . .2F **95**
**Brewster Av.** PA3: Pais . . . . . . . . . .4C **78**
**Briar Bank** G66: Milt C . . . . . . . . . . .6B **8**
**Briarbush Way** G72: Blan . . . . . . .1A **140**
**Briarcroft Dr.** G33: Glas . . . . . . . . .2F **65**
**Briarcroft Pl.** G33: Glas . . . . . . . . .3G **65**
**Briarcroft Rd.** G33: Glas . . . . . . . . .3F **65**
**Briar Dr.** G81: Clyd . . . . . . . . . . . . .3D **42**
**Briar Gdns.** G43: Glas . . . . . . . . . .2B **118**
**Briar Gro.** G43: Glas . . . . . . . . . . .2B **118**
**Briarlea Dr.** G46: Giff . . . . . . . . . . .3A **118**
**Briar Neuk** G64: B'rig . . . . . . . . . . .1D **64**
**Briar Rd.** G43: Glas . . . . . . . . . . . .2B **118**
G66: Kirk . . . . . . . . . . . . . . . . .5F **31**
**Briar Wlk.** G66: Kirk . . . . . . . . . . . .5G **31**
**Briarwell La.** G62: Miln . . . . . . . . . .4H **25**
**Briarwell Rd.** G62: Miln . . . . . . . . . .4H **25**
**Briarwood Ct.** G32: Glas . . . . . . . .3E **107**
**Briarwood Gdns.** G32: Glas . . . . .3E **107**
**Briarwood Rd.** ML2: Wis . . . . . . .5E **145**
**Brick La.** PA3: Pais . . . . . . . . . . . . .6B **78**
**Bridgebar St.** G78: Barr . . . . . . . .3G **115**
**Bridgeburn Dr.** G69: Mood . . . . . . .5C **52**
**Bridgeford Av.** ML4: Bell . . . . . . . .6E **111**
**Bridgegait** G62: Miln . . . . . . . . . . . .5A **26**
**Bridgegate** G1: Glas . . . . . . . . . . . .5G **83**
**Bridgegate Path** *G1: Glas . . . . . . . .5H **83***
*(off Saltmarket)*
BRIDGEND . . . . . . . . . . . . . . . . . .4C **52**
**Bridgend** PA7: B'ton . . . . . . . . . . . .4G **39**
**Bridgend Cotts.** G66: Kirk . . . . . . . .6G **31**
**Bridgend Ct.** G68: C'cry . . . . . . . . .2F **15**
**Bridgend Cres.** G69: Mood . . . . . . .5C **52**
**Bridgend Pl.** G69: Mood . . . . . . . . .5C **52**
**Bridgend Rd.** PA5: Eld . . . . . . . . . .2A **96**
**Bridgend Vw.** ML8: Carl . . . . . . . .4F **165**
BRIDGE OF WEIR . . . . . . . . . . . . . .3F **73**
**Bridge of Weir Rd.** PA11: Bri W . . .4G **73**
PA3: Lin . . . . . . . . . . . . . . . . .6H **75**
PA5: Brkfld . . . . . . . . . . . . . . .6C **74**
PA6: Hous . . . . . . . . . . . . . . . .2A **74**
**Bridge Pl.** G62: Miln . . . . . . . . . . . .4G **25**
**Bridge St.** G5: Glas . . . . . . . . . . . . .5F **83**
G72: Camb . . . . . . . . . . . . . .1A **122**
G81: Clyd . . . . . . . . . . . . . . . .4A **42**
G82: Dumb . . . . . . . . . . . . . . .4E **17**
ML2: Wis . . . . . . . . . . . . . . .6E **145**
ML3: Ham . . . . . . . . . . . . . . .1G **153**
PA1: Pais . . . . . . . . . . . . . . . . .1A **98**
PA3: Lin . . . . . . . . . . . . . . . . . .5A **76**
Bridge Street Station (Und.) . . . . .6F **83**
BRIDGETON . . . . . . . . . . . . . . . .1B **104**
**Bridgeton Bus. Cen.** G40: Glas . . . .6B **84**
**Bridgeton Cross** G40: Glas . . . . . . .6B **84**
Bridgeton Station (Rail) . . . . . . .1B **104**
**Bridgewater Ind. Pk.**
PA8: Ersk . . . . . . . . . . . . . . . . .5F **41**
**Bridgewater Shop. Cen.**
PA8: Ersk . . . . . . . . . . . . . . . . .5F **41**
**Bridgeway Ct.** G66: Kirk . . . . . . . . .6F **31**
**Bridgeway Pl.** G66: Kirk . . . . . . . . .6F **31**
**Bridgeway Rd.** G66: Kirk . . . . . . . . .6F **31**
**Bridgeway Ter.** G66: Kirk . . . . . . . .6F **31**
**Bridie Ter.** G74: E Kil . . . . . . . . . .5C **138**
**Brierie Av.** PA6: C'lee . . . . . . . . . . .2B **74**
**Brierie Gdns.** PA6: C'lee . . . . . . . . .3B **74**
**Brierie Hill Ct.** PA6: C'lee . . . . . . . .3B **74**
**Brierie Hill Gro.** PA6: C'lee . . . . . .3B **74**
**Brierie Hill Rd.** PA6: C'lee . . . . . . .3A **74**
**Brierie La.** PA6: C'lee . . . . . . . . . . .3A **74**
**Brigbrae Av.** ML4: Bell . . . . . . . . .4E **127**
**Brigham Pl.** G23: Glas . . . . . . . . . . .1C **62**
**Brighton Pl.** G51: Glas . . . . . . . . . .5H **81**
**Brighton St.** G51: Glas . . . . . . . . . .5H **81**
**Brightside Av.** G71: Udd . . . . . . . .2D **124**
**Bright St.** G21: Glas . . . . . . . . . . . .2B **84**
**Brig o'Lea Ter.** G78: Neil . . . . . . .3D **130**
**Brigside Gdns.** ML3: Ham . . . . . .1C **154**
**Brisbane Ct.** G46: Giff . . . . . . . . .4B **118**
**Brisbane Rd.** PA7: B'ton . . . . . . . . .4H **39**
**Brisbane St.** G42: Glas . . . . . . . . .6E **103**
G81: Clyd . . . . . . . . . . . . . . . . .3H **41**
**Brisbane Ter.** G75: E Kil . . . . . . . .4E **149**

**Britannia Way** G81: Clyd . . . . . . . .5D **42**
PA4: Renf . . . . . . . . . . . . . . . . .2E **79**
**Briton St.** G51: Glas . . . . . . . . . . . .4H **81**
**Brittain Way** ML1: Holy . . . . . . . .6H **111**
**Broadcroft** G66: Kirk . . . . . . . . . . . .4C **30**
(not continuous)
**Broadcroft Rd.** G66: Kirk . . . . . . . .4C **30**
**Broadford St.** G4: Glas . . . . . . . . . .1G **83**
**Broadholm St.** G22: Glas . . . . . . . .3F **63**
**Broadleys Av.** G64: B'rig . . . . . . . .4B **48**
**Broadlie Ct.** G78: Neil . . . . . . . . .2D **130**
**Broadlie Dr.** G13: Glas . . . . . . . . . .3A **60**
**Broadlie Rd.** G78: Neil . . . . . . . . .2C **130**
**Broadloan** PA4: Renf . . . . . . . . . . . .1E **79**
**Broadmeadow Ind. Est.**
G82: Dumb . . . . . . . . . . . . . . .3F **17**
**Broadmoss Av.** G77: Newt M . . . .5A **134**
**Broad Sq.** G72: Blan . . . . . . . . . . .1A **140**
**Broad St.** G40: Glas . . . . . . . . . . . .6B **84**
**Broadway, The** ML2: Wis . . . . . . .5E **145**
**Broadwood Bus. Pk.**
G68: Cumb . . . . . . . . . . . . . . . .5B **34**
**Broadwood Dr.** G44: Glas . . . . . . .1F **119**
**BROADWOOD RDBT.** . . . . . . . . . . .5B **34**
Broadwood Stadium . . . . . . . . . . .4B **34**
**Brockburn Cres.** G53: Glas . . . . . .5B **100**
**Brockburn Rd.** G53: Glas . . . . . . .3A **100**
**Brockburn Ter.** G53: Glas . . . . . . .5C **100**
**Brocklinn Pk.** G75: E Kil . . . . . . . .4A **148**
**Brock Oval** G53: Glas . . . . . . . . . .1C **116**
**Brock Pl.** G53: Glas . . . . . . . . . . . .6C **100**
**Brock Rd.** G53: Glas . . . . . . . . . . .1B **116**
**Brock Ter.** G53: Glas . . . . . . . . . . .1C **116**
**Brockville St.** G32: Glas . . . . . . . . .5H **85**
**Brodick Av.** ML1: Moth . . . . . . . . .2D **142**
**Brodick Dr.** G74: E Kil . . . . . . . . . .6F **137**
**Brodick Pl.** G77: Newt M . . . . . . .5A **132**
**Brodick Sq.** G64: B'rig . . . . . . . . . . .1E **65**
**Brodick St.** G21: Glas . . . . . . . . . . .2C **84**
**Brodie Pk. Av.** PA2: Pais . . . . . . . . .3A **98**
**Brodie Pk. Cres.** PA2: Pais . . . . . . .3H **97**
**Brodie Pk. Gdns.** PA2: Pais . . . . . .3A **98**
**Brodie Pl.** G74: E Kil . . . . . . . . . . .6F **137**
**Brodie Rd.** G21: Glas . . . . . . . . . . .2F **65**
**Brogan Cres.** ML1: Moth . . . . . . .2D **142**
**Bromley Dr.** G46: Giff . . . . . . . . . .6A **118**
**Bromley La.** G46: Giff . . . . . . . . . .6A **118**
**Bron Way** G67: Cumb . . . . . . . . . . .4A **36**
**Brookbank Ter.** ML8: Carl . . . . . .4G **165**
BROOKFIELD . . . . . . . . . . . . . . . .6D **74**
**Brookfield Av.** G33: Glas . . . . . . . .2F **65**
**Brookfield Cnr.** G33: Glas . . . . . . .2F **65**
**Brookfield Dr.** G33: Glas . . . . . . . .2F **65**
**Brookfield Gdns.** G33: Glas . . . . . .2F **65**
**Brookfield Ga.** G33: Glas . . . . . . . .2F **65**
**Brookfield Pl.** G33: Glas . . . . . . . .2G **65**
**Brooklands** G74: E Kil . . . . . . . . .2C **148**
**Brooklands Av.** G71: Udd . . . . . . .6C **108**
**Brooklea Dr.** G46: Giff . . . . . . . . .2A **118**
**Brooklime Dr.** G74: E Kil . . . . . . . .5E **137**
**Brooklime Gdns.**
G74: E Kil . . . . . . . . . . . . . . .5E **137**
**Brooklyn Pl.** ML2: Over . . . . . . . .5H **157**
**Brookside St.** G40: Glas . . . . . . . . .6C **84**
**Brook St.** G40: Glas . . . . . . . . . . . .6B **84**
G81: Clyd . . . . . . . . . . . . . . . . .3B **42**
BROOM . . . . . . . . . . . . . . . . . . . .4H **133**
**Broom Av.** PA8: Ersk . . . . . . . . . . .2F **57**
**Broomburn Dr.** G77: Newt M . . . . .5F **133**
**Broom Cliff** G77: Newt M . . . . . . .6F **133**
**Broom Cres.** G75: E Kil . . . . . . . .6F **149**
G78: Barr . . . . . . . . . . . . . . . .2C **114**
**Broomcroft Rd.** G77: Newt M . . . .3G **133**
**Broom Dr.** G81: Clyd . . . . . . . . . . . .3C **42**
ML9: Lark . . . . . . . . . . . . . . .6A **156**
**Broomdyke Way** PA3: Pais . . . . . . .3H **77**
**Broomelton Rd.** ML3: Ham . . . . . .5A **160**
**Broomfauld Gdns.** G82: Dumb . . . .3G **17**
(not continuous)
**Broomfauld Ind. Est.**
G82: Dumb . . . . . . . . . . . . . . .4F **17**
**Broomfield** PA6: Hous . . . . . . . . . .2D **74**
**Broomfield Av.** G72: Camb . . . . . .6F **105**
G77: Newt M . . . . . . . . . . . . .6F **133**
**Broomfield Ct.** G21: Glas . . . . . . . .6E **65**
**Broomfield La.** G21: Glas . . . . . . . .4B **64**
**Broomfield Pl.** G21: Glas . . . . . . . .4B **64**
**Broomfield Rd.** G21: Glas . . . . . . . .4B **64**
G46: Giff . . . . . . . . . . . . . . . .3G **133**
ML9: Lark . . . . . . . . . . . . . . . .5F **161**
**Broomfield St.** ML6: Air . . . . . . . . .4B **92**
**Broomfield Ter.** G71: Tann . . . . . .4D **108**
**Broomfield Wlk.** G66: Kirk . . . . . . .5D **30**
**Broom Gdns.** G66: Lenz . . . . . . . . .1B **50**
BROOMHILL
Glasgow . . . . . . . . . . . . . . . . . .6F **61**
Kirkintilloch . . . . . . . . . . . . . . .3E **31**
**Broomhill Av.** G11: Glas . . . . . . . . .1F **81**
G32: Carm . . . . . . . . . . . . . . .5B **106**
G77: Newt M . . . . . . . . . . . . .5F **133**

**Broomhill Ct.** *G66: Kirk . . . . . . . . .4D **30***
*(off Eastside)*
ML9: Lark . . . . . . . . . . . . . . . .3E **161**
**Broomhill Cres.** ML4: Bell . . . . . .4B **126**
PA8: Ersk . . . . . . . . . . . . . . . . .2F **57**
**Broomhill Dr.** G11: Glas . . . . . . . . .6F **61**
G73: Ruth . . . . . . . . . . . . . . .2D **120**
G82: Dumb . . . . . . . . . . . . . . .2H **17**
**Broomhill Farm M.** G66: Kirk . . . . .4E **31**
**Broomhill Gdns.** G11: Glas . . . . . . .6F **61**
G77: Newt M . . . . . . . . . . . . .5F **133**
**Broomhill Ga.** ML9: Lark . . . . . . . .3E **161**
**Broomhill Ind. Est.** G66: Kirk . . . . .3E **31**
**Broomhill La.** G11: Glas . . . . . . . . .6F **61**
**Broomhill Path** *G11: Glas . . . . . . . .1F **81***
*(off Broomhill Dr.)*
**Broomhill Pl.** G11: Glas . . . . . . . . .1F **81**
**Broomhill Rd.** ML9: Lark . . . . . . .3D **160**
**Broomhill Ter.** G11: Glas . . . . . . . . .1F **81**
**Broomhill Vw.** ML9: Lark . . . . . . .3C **160**
BROOMHOUSE . . . . . . . . . . . . . .3H **107**
**Broomieknowe Dr.** G73: Ruth . . .1D **120**
**Broomieknowe Gdns.**
G73: Ruth . . . . . . . . . . . . . . .1C **120**
**Broomieknowe Rd.** G73: Ruth . . .1D **120**
**Broomielaw** G1: Glas . . . . . .5E **83** (6A **4**)
**Broomknoll St.** ML6: Air . . . . . . . . .4A **92**
**Broomknowe** G68: Cumb . . . . . . . .2F **35**
**Broomknowes Av.** G66: Lenz . . . . .3E **51**
**Broomknowes Rd.** G21: Glas . . . . .5C **64**
**Broomlands Av.** PA8: Ersk . . . . . . .1H **57**
**Broomlands Cres.** PA8: Ersk . . . . .1H **57**
**Broomlands Gdns.** PA8: Ersk . . . . .1H **57**
**Broomlands Rd.** G67: Cumb . . . . . .5A **36**
**Broomlands St.** PA1: Pais . . . . . . . .1F **97**
**Broomlands Way** PA8: Ersk . . . . . .1A **58**
**Broomlea Cres.** PA4: Inch . . . . . . .2G **57**
**Broomlee Rd.** G67: Cumb . . . . . . .1H **55**
**Broomloan Ct.** G51: Glas . . . . . . . .6G **81**
**Broomloan Pl.** G51: Glas . . . . . . . .5G **81**
**Broomloan Rd.** G51: Glas . . . . . . . .5G **81**
**Broompark Av.** G72: Blan . . . . . .3A **140**
**Broompark Cir.** G31: Glas . . . . . . . .4B **84**
**Broompark Cres.** ML6: Air . . . . . . .1A **92**
**Broompark Dr.** G31: Glas . . . . . . . .4B **84**
G77: Newt M . . . . . . . . . . . . .4G **133**
PA4: Inch . . . . . . . . . . . . . . . . .2H **57**
**Broompark La.** G31: Glas . . . . . . . .4B **84**
**Broompark Rd.** G72: Blan . . . . . .2A **140**
ML2: Wis . . . . . . . . . . . . . . .5D **144**
**Broompark St.** G31: Glas . . . . . . . .4B **84**
**Broom Path** G69: Bail . . . . . . . . .2F **107**
**Broom Pl.** G43: Glas . . . . . . . . . . .2B **118**
ML1: N'hill . . . . . . . . . . . . . . .3C **128**
ML5: Coat . . . . . . . . . . . . . . .2B **110**
PA11: Bri W . . . . . . . . . . . . . . .4G **73**
**Broom Rd.** G43: Glas . . . . . . . . . . .2B **118**
G67: Cumb . . . . . . . . . . . . . . . .6D **14**
G77: Newt M . . . . . . . . . . . . .3G **133**
**Broom Rd. E.** G77: Newt M . . . . . .6G **133**
**Broomside Cres.** ML1: Moth . . . .5G **143**
**Broomside St.** ML1: Moth . . . . . .5G **143**
**Broomstone Av.** G77: Newt M . . . .6F **133**
**Broom Ter.** PA5: John . . . . . . . . . . .4F **95**
**Broomton Rd.** G21: Glas . . . . . . . . .2E **65**
**Broomvale Dr.** G77: Newt M . . . . .4F **133**
**Broomward Dr.** PA5: John . . . . . . . .2H **95**
**Brora Cres.** ML3: Ham . . . . . . . .3D **152**
**Brora Dr.** G46: Giff . . . . . . . . . . . .5B **118**
G61: Bear . . . . . . . . . . . . . . . . .3H **45**
PA4: Renf . . . . . . . . . . . . . . . . .6G **59**
**Brora Gdns.** G64: B'rig . . . . . . . . . .6D **48**
**Brora Rd.** G64: B'rig . . . . . . . . . . . .6D **48**
**Brora St.** G33: Glas . . . . . . . . . . . .2F **85**
**Broughton** G75: E Kil . . . . . . . . .6G **149**
**Broughton Dr.** G23: Glas . . . . . . . . .1C **62**
**Broughton Gdns.** G23: Glas . . . . . .6D **46**
**Broughton Pl.** ML3: Ham . . . . . . .6E **141**
ML5: Coat . . . . . . . . . . . . . . .2D **110**
**Broughton Rd.** G23: Glas . . . . . . . . .1C **62**
**Brouster Ga.** G74: E Kil . . . . . . . .2G **149**
**Brouster Hill** G74: E Kil . . . . . . . .2G **149**
**Brouster Pl.** G74: E Kil . . . . . . . . .2G **149**
**Brown Av.** G81: Clyd . . . . . . . . . . . .1F **59**
G82: Dumb . . . . . . . . . . . . . . .1C **18**
**Brownhill Rd.** G43: Glas . . . . . . . .3H **117**
**Brownhill Vw.** ML2: Newm . . . . . .3H **147**
**Brownieside Pl.** ML6: Plain . . . . . .1G **93**
**Brownieside Rd.** ML6: Plain . . . . . .1H **93**
**Brownlee Rd.** ML8: Carl, Law . . .1D **162**
**Brownlie St.** G42: Glas . . . . . . . . .5F **103**
**Brown Pl.** G72: Camb . . . . . . . . . .1A **122**
**Brown Rd.** G67: Cumb . . . . . . . . . . .3H **35**
BROWNSBURN . . . . . . . . . . . . . .1C **112**
**Brownsburn Ind. Est.** ML6: Air . . .6B **92**
**Brownsburn Rd.** ML6: Air . . . . . . .1B **112**
**Brownsdale Rd.** G73: Ruth . . . . . .6B **104**
**Brownsfield Cres.** PA4: Inch . . . . . .4F **57**
**Brownsfield Rd.** PA4: Inch . . . . . . .4F **57**
**Brownshill Av.** ML5: Coat . . . . . . .1B **110**

**Brownside Av.** G72: Camb . . . . . .2G 1
G78: Barr . . . . . . . . . . . . . . . .2C 1
PA2: Pais . . . . . . . . . . . . . . . . .6G
**Brownside Cres.** G78: Barr . . . . . .2C 1
**Brownside Dr.** G13: Glas . . . . . . . .3H
G78: Barr . . . . . . . . . . . . . . . .2C 1
**Brownside Gro.** G78: Barr . . . . . .2C 1
**Brownside M.** G72: Camb . . . . . .2G 1
**Brownside Rd.** G73: Ruth . . . . . . .2F 1
**Brownsland Ct.** G69: G'csh . . . . . .3D
**Brown's La.** PA1: Pais . . . . . . . . . .1A
**Brown St.** G2: Glas . . . . . . . .4E **83** (6B
ML1: Moth . . . . . . . . . . . . . . .1H 1
ML2: Newm . . . . . . . . . . . . . . .5E 1
ML3: Ham . . . . . . . . . . . . . . . .1A 1
ML5: Coat . . . . . . . . . . . . . . . .6C
ML8: Carl . . . . . . . . . . . . . . . .2F 1
ML9: Lark . . . . . . . . . . . . . . . .1E 1
PA1: Pais . . . . . . . . . . . . . . . . .6G
PA4: Renf . . . . . . . . . . . . . . . . .1D
**Bruar Way** *ML2: Newm . . . . . . . .3D 1*
*(off Tiree Cre*
**Bruce Av.** ML1: Moth . . . . . . . . . .2F 1
PA3: Pais . . . . . . . . . . . . . . . . .4C
PA5: John . . . . . . . . . . . . . . . . .5E
**Bruce Ct.** ML6: Air . . . . . . . . . . . .3E
**Brucefield Pl.** G34: Glas . . . . . . . .3B
BRUCEHILL . . . . . . . . . . . . . . . . . .3C
**Brucehill Rd.** G82: Dumb . . . . . . . .3C
**Bruce Ho.** G67: Cumb . . . . . . . . . .2H
**Bruce Loan** ML2: Over . . . . . . . . .5A 1
**Bruce Pl.** G75: E Kil . . . . . . . . . . .4H 1
**Bruce Rd.** G41: Glas . . . . . . . . . . .1C 1
ML1: New S . . . . . . . . . . . . . . .5B 1
PA3: Pais . . . . . . . . . . . . . . . . .5C
PA4: Renf . . . . . . . . . . . . . . . . .2C
PA7: B'ton . . . . . . . . . . . . . . . .3G
**Bruce's Loan** *ML9: Lark . . . . . . . .3G 1*
*(off Keir Hardie R*
**Bruce St.** G81: Clyd . . . . . . . . . . . .6D
G82: Dumb . . . . . . . . . . . . . . . .5G
ML4: Bell . . . . . . . . . . . . . . . . .2D 1
ML5: Coat . . . . . . . . . . . . . . . . .3D
ML6: Plain . . . . . . . . . . . . . . . .1G
**Bruce Ter.** G72: Blan . . . . . . . . . . .6C 1
G75: E Kil . . . . . . . . . . . . . . . .4H 1
**Brunel Way** G75: E Kil . . . . . . . . .3H 1
**Brunstane Rd.** G34: Glas . . . . . . . .2G
**Brunswick Cen.** G21: Glas . . . . . . .4D
**Brunswick Ho.** G81: Clyd . . . . . . . .1H
**Brunswick La.** G1: Glas . . . .4G **83** (6F
**Brunswick St.** G1: Glas . . . .4G **83** (6F
**Brunton St.** G44: Glas . . . . . . . . . .2D 1
**Brunton Ter.** G44: Glas . . . . . . . . .3E 1
**Bruntsfield Av.** G53: Glas . . . . . . .4B 1
**Bruntsfield Gdns.** G53: Glas . . . . .4B 1
**Bryan St.** ML3: Ham . . . . . . . . . . .4F 1
**Bryce Gdns.** ML9: Lark . . . . . . . . .1E 1
**Bryce Pl.** G75: E Kil . . . . . . . . . . .5E 1
**Brydson Pl.** PA3: Lin . . . . . . . . . . .5H
**Bryson Ct.** ML3: Ham . . . . . . . . . .4H 1
**Bryson St.** G81: Faif . . . . . . . . . . .6G
**Buccleuch Av.** G52: Hill . . . . . . . . .3G
G76: Clar . . . . . . . . . . . . . . . . .2B 1
**Buccleuch Ct.** G61: Bear . . . . . . . . .6E
**Buccleuch Dr.** G61: Bear . . . . . . . . .6E
**Buccleuch La.** G3: Glas . . . .2E **83** (2B
**Buccleuch St.** G3: Glas . . . .2E **83** (2A
**Buchanan Av.** PA7: B'ton . . . . . . . .3H
**Buchanan Bus. Pk.** G33: Step . . . . .3F
**Buchanan Ct.** G33: Step . . . . . . . . .3E
(not continuou
**Buchanan Cres.** G64: B'rig . . . . . . .1E
ML3: Ham . . . . . . . . . . . . . . . .1F 1
**Buchanan Dr.** G61: Bear . . . . . . . . .3G
G64: B'rig . . . . . . . . . . . . . . . . .1E
G66: Lenz . . . . . . . . . . . . . . . . .4D
G72: Camb . . . . . . . . . . . . . . .1G 1
G73: Ruth . . . . . . . . . . . . . . . .1D 1
G77: Newt M . . . . . . . . . . . . . .2E 1
ML8: Law . . . . . . . . . . . . . . . . .5E 1
**Buchanan Galleries (Shop. Cen.)**
G1: Glas . . . . . . . . . . . .3G **83** (4E
**Buchanan Gro.** G69: Bail . . . . . . . .6H
**Buchanan Pl.** G64: Torr . . . . . . . . .4D
**Buchanan St.** G1: Glas . . . . .4F **83** (6D
G62: Miln . . . . . . . . . . . . . . . . .3H
G69: Bail . . . . . . . . . . . . . . . . .1H 1
G82: Dumb . . . . . . . . . . . . . . . .5G
ML5: Coat . . . . . . . . . . . . . . . . .5A
ML6: Air . . . . . . . . . . . . . . . . . .4A
PA5: John . . . . . . . . . . . . . . . . .3E
Buchanan Street Station (Und.)
. . . . . . . . . . . . . . . . . .3G **83** (4E
**Buchanan Way** PA5: John . . . . . . .3E
**Buchandyke Rd.** G74: E Kil . . . . . .5B 1
**Buchanen Gdns.** G32: Glas . . . . . . .3E 1
**Buchan Ga.** G74: E Kil . . . . . . . . . .6B 1
**Buchan Ho.** G67: Cumb . . . . . . . . .2H
**Buchan Rd.** ML1: New S . . . . . . . .4A 1

Buchan St.—Calderbank Vw.


uchan St. ML2: Wis 3H 145
ML3: Ham 3G 153
uchan Ter. G72: Camb 4G 121
uchlyvie Gdns. G64: B'rig 2B 64
uchlyvie Path G34: Glas 4H 87
uchlyvie Rd. PA1: Pais 6G 79
uchlyvie St. G34: Glas 4H 87
uckie PA8: Ersk 4E 41
uckie Wlk. ML4: Bell 1C 126
uckingham Ct. ML3: Ham 5C 140
uckingham Dr. G32: Carm 5B 106
G73: Ruth 6F 105
uckingham St. G12: Glas 6B 62
uckingham Ter. G12: Glas 6B 62
ucklaw Gdns. G52: Glas 1C 100
ucklaw Pl. G52: Glas 1C 100
ucklaw Ter. G52: Glas 1C 100
uckley St. G22: Glas 3H 63
ucksburn Rd. G21: Glas 5E 65
uckthorne Pl. G53: Glas 4B 116
uddon St. G40: Glas 1E 105
udhill Av. G32: Glas 6B 86
udshaw Av. ML6: Chap 3C 112
ulldale Ct. G14: Glas 4H 59
ulldale St. G14: Glas 3G 59
uller Cres. G72: Blan 5A 124
ullionslaw Dr. G73: Ruth 1F 121
ulloch Av. G46: Giff 5B 118
ull Rd. G76: Busby 3D 134
ullwood Av. G53: Glas 5H 99
ullwood Ct. G53: Glas 5H 99
ullwood Dr. G53: Glas 4H 99
ullwood Gdns. G53: Glas 4H 99
ullwood Pl. G53: Glas 4H 99
unbury Ter. G75: E Kil 3E 149
unessan St. G52: Glas 6F 81
unhouse Rd. G3: Glas 2A 82
urch Hall La. G11: Glas 1H 81
urghead Dr. G51: Glas 3E 81
urghead Pl. G51: Glas 3E 81
urgher St. G31: Glas 6E 85
urgh Hall St. G11: Glas 1H 81
urgh La. *G12: Glas 6B 62*
*(off Cresswell St.)*
urleigh Rd. G71: Both 4F 125
urleigh St. G51: Glas 3G 81
ML5: Coat 2D 110
urley Pl. G74: E Kil 1B 148
urlington Av. G12: Glas 3H 61
urmola St. G22: Glas 5F 63
urnacre Gdns. G71: Udd 6C 108
urnawn Ga. G33: Glas 2F 65
urnawn Gro. G33: Glas 2F 65
urnawn Pl. G33: Glas 2F 65
URNBANK 4E 141
urnbank Braes ML8: Carl 4F 165
urnbank Cen. ML3: Ham 4E 141
urnbank Dr. G78: Barr 6E 115
urnbank Gdns. G20: Glas 1D 82
*ML3: Ham 4E 141*
*(off Burnbank Rd.)*
urnbank La. G20: Glas 1D 82
urnbank M. G66: Lenz 3D 50
urnbank Pl. G20: Glas 1E 83
urnbank Quad. ML6: Air 3H 91
urnbank Rd. ML3: Ham 4E 141
urnbank St. ML5: Coat 3D 90
ML6: Air 3H 91
urnbank Ter. G20: Glas 1D 82
G65: Kils 2H 11
urnblea Gdns. ML3: Ham 1A 154
urnblea St. ML3: Ham 1H 153
urnbrae G65: Twe 2D 32
urn Brae G81: Dun 1C 42
urnbrae Av. G61: Bear 6G 25
G69: Mood 5D 52
PA3: Lin 6A 76
urnbrae Dr. G73: Ruth 2F 121
PA3: Lin 2B 96
urnbrae Gdns. G53: Glas 1D 116
urnbrae Pl. G74: E Kil 1E 149
urnbrae Rd. G66: Auch 5E 51
G66: Kirk 6H 31
G69: Chry, Lenz 3H 51
G72: Blan 2A 140
PA3: Lin 1H 95
urnbrae St. G21: Glas 5C 64
G81: Faif 5F 23
ML9: Lark 2D 160
urncleugh Av. G72: Camb 3A 122
urn Cres. ML1: New S 3A 128
ML6: Chap 3D 112
urncrooks Av. G61: Bear 6C 24
G74: E Kil 1E 149
urncrooks Ct. G81: Dun 1B 42
urndyke Ct. G51: Glas 4H 81
urndyke Sq. G51: Glas 4A 82
urnet Rose Ct. G74: E Kil 5E 137
urnet Rose Gdns.
G74: E Kil 5E 137

Burnet Rose Pl. G74: E Kil 5E 137
Burnett Rd. G33: Glas 4E 87
Burnfield Av. G46: Giff 3H 117
Burnfield Cotts. G46: Giff 3H 117
Burnfield Dr. G43: Glas 3H 117
Burnfield Gdns. G46: Giff 3A 118
Burnfield Rd. G43: Glas 2G 117
G46: Giff 3A 118
BURNFOOT 2G 91
Burnfoot Cres. G73: Ruth 2F 121
PA2: Pais 5G 97
Burnfoot Dr. G52: Glas 6B 80
Burnfoot Rd. ML6: Air 3G 91
Burngill Pl. *PA11: Bri W 3F 73*
*(off Kilmalcom Rd.)*
Burngreen G65: Kils 3H 11
Burngreen Ter. G67: Cumb 6B 14
Burnhall Pl. ML2: Wis 2B 158
Burnhall Rd. ML2: Wis 1A 158
Burnhall St. ML2: Wis 2B 158
Burnham Rd. G14: Glas 5A 60
Burnhaven PA8: Ersk 5E 41
BURNHEAD 2G 161
Burnhead Rd. G43: Glas 2C 118
G68: Cumb 3E 35
ML6: Air 1C 92
ML9: Lark 2F 161
Burnhead St. G71: View 5F 109
Burnhill Quad. G73: Ruth 5B 104
Burnhill Sports Cen.
5B 104
Burnhill St. G73: Ruth 5B 104
Burnhouse Brae G77: Newt M 6G 133
Burnhouse Cres. ML3: Ham 2F 153
Burnhouse Rd. ML3: Ham 2F 153
Burnhouse St. G20: Glas 3A 62
(not continuous)
Burniebrae ML6: Air 3G 91
Burniebrae Rd. ML6: Chap 2E 113
Burn La. ML1: New S 3A 128
Burnlea Cres. PA6: Hous 1A 74
Burnlip Rd. ML5: Glenb 5C 70
ML6: Glenm 5C 70
Burnmouth Ct. G33: Glas 5F 87
Burnmouth Pl. G61: Bear 2G 45
Burnmouth Rd. G33: Glas 5F 87
Burnock Pl. G75: E Kil 4A 148
Burnpark Av. G71: Udd 6B 108
Burn Pl. G72: Camb 6G 105
Burn Rd. ML8: Carl 2F 165
Burns Av. PA7: B'ton 4H 39
Burns Ct. G66: Kirk 4G 31
Burn's Cres. ML6: Air 5B 92
Burns Dr. G66: Kirk 3G 31
PA5: John 5E 95
Burns Gdns. G72: Blan 6A 124
Burns Gro. G46: T'bnk 5G 117
BURNSIDE 2E 121
Burnside G61: Bear 6C 24
Burnside Av. G66: Kirk 6B 30
G78: Barr 3D 114
ML4: Bell 3E 127
ML6: C'bnk 3B 112
PA5: Brkfld 6C 74
Burnside Ct. G61: Bear 1C 44
G73: Ruth 2E 121
G81: Clyd 3A 42
ML1: Moth 5B 144
*ML5: Coat 6B 90*
*(off Kirk St.)*
Burnside Cres. G72: Blan 3C 140
G81: Hard 6D 22
Burnside Gdns. G76: Clar 2B 134
PA10: Kilb 3B 94
Burnside Ga. G73: Ruth 2E 121
Burnside Gro. PA5: John 3E 95
Burnside Ind. Est.
G65: Kils 3G 11
Burnside La. ML3: Ham 1A 154
Burnside Pl. G82: Dumb 5H 17
ML9: Lark 2F 161
PA3: Pais 4E 77
(not continuous)
Burnside Quad. ML1: Holy 2A 128
Burnside Rd. G46: Giff 3H 133
G73: Ruth 2E 121
ML1: N'hill 3C 128
ML5: Coat 2E 91
PA5: Eld 4A 96
Burnside Station (Rail) 2E 121
Burnside St. G82: Dumb 5H 17
ML1: Moth 5B 144
Burnside Ter. *G82: Dumb 5H 17*
*(off Burnside Pl.)*
PA10: Kilb 3B 94
Burnside Twr. *ML1: Moth 5A 144*
*(off Burnside Ct.)*
Burnside Vw. ML5: Coat 6A 90
Burnside Wlk. ML5: Coat 6A 90
Burns La. ML6: Chap 2D 112

Burns Loan *ML9: Lark 1F 161*
*(off Carrick Pl.)*
Burns Pk. G74: E Kil 1A 150
Burns Path ML4: Bell 6D 110
Burns Rd. G66: Kirk 4F 31
G67: Cumb 3B 36
ML6: Chap 1D 112
Burns St. G4: Glas 1F 83
G81: Clyd 3A 42
ML3: Ham 1H 153
Burns Way ML1: N'hill 3C 128
Burntbroom Dr. G69: Bail 2F 107
Burntbroom Gdns. G69: Bail 2F 107
Burntbroom St. G33: Glas 3D 86
Burn Ter. G72: Camb 6G 105
Burnthills Ind. Est. *PA5: John 2F 95*
*(off High St.)*
Burntshields Rd. PA10: Kilb 2A 94
Burn Vw. G67: Cumb 2C 36
Burnwood Dr. ML6: Air 5G 93
Burra Gdns. G64: B'rig 5F 49
Burrell Collection Mus. 4H 101
Burrell Ct. G41: Glas 3A 102
Burrell's La. G4: Glas 4A 84 (5H 5)
Burrelton Rd. G43: Glas 1D 118
Burton La. G42: Glas 4E 103
ML8: Carl 3E 165
BUSBY 3D 134
Busby Equitation Cen. 5E 135
Busby Rd. G76: Clar 1C 134
G76: Crmck 3G 135
ML4: Bell 4B 126
Busby Station (Rail) 4E 135
Bush Cres. ML2: Wis 1A 158
Bushelhead Rd. ML8: Carl 6E 165
Bushes Av. PA2: Pais 4H 97
Busheyhill St. G72: Camb 2A 122
Bute G74: E Kil 2C 150
Bute Av. ML1: Moth 2E 143
PA4: Renf 2F 79
Bute Cres. G60: Old K 2G 41
G61: Bear 5F 45
PA2: Pais 6H 97
Bute Dr. G60: Old K 2G 41
PA5: John 4D 94
Bute Gdns. G12: Glas 1B 82
G44: Neth 3D 118
G60: Old K 1G 41
Bute La. G12: Glas 1B 82
PA3: Pais 4F 77
Bute Pl. G60: Old K 1G 41
Bute Rd. G66: Kirk 5H 31
PA3: Glas A 2G 77
Bute St. ML3: Ham 3F 141
ML5: Coat 1D 110
Bute Ter. G71: View 6F 109
G73: Ruth 2C 120
Bute Twr. G72: Camb 4G 121
Butler Wynd ML4: Bell 2B 126
Butterbiggins Rd. G42: Glas 2E 103
Butterburn Pk. St.
ML3: Ham 1H 153
Butterfield Pl. G41: Glas 2E 103
Buttermere G75: E Kil 6B 148
Byars Rd. G66: Kirk 5B 30
Byrebush Rd. G53: Glas 4C 100
Byres Av. PA3: Pais 5C 78
Byres Cres. PA3: Pais 5C 78
Byres Rd. G11: Glas 1A 82
ML1: N'hill 3E 129
PA5: Eld 3B 96
Byrestone Av. G77:
Newt M 5A 134
Byron Ct. G71: Both 5F 125
Byron St. G11: Glas 1E 81
G81: Clyd 3C 42
Byshot Path G22: Glas 5H 63
Byshot St. G22: Glas 5H 63


## C


Cable Dpt. Rd. G81: Clyd 5B 42
CADDER
Bishopbriggs 2D 48
Gilshochill 2D 62
Cadder Ct. G64: B'rig 2D 48
Cadder Gro. *G20: Glas 2C 62*
*(off Cadder Rd.)*
Cadder Pl. G20: Glas 2C 62
Cadder Rd. G20: Glas 1C 62
G23: Glas 1C 62
G64: B'rig 2D 48
Cadder Way G64: B'rig 2D 48
Cadell Gdns. G74: E Kil 4D 138
Cadger's Sheuch G65: Kils 3C 12
Cadoc St. G72: Camb 2B 122
Cadogan Sq. G2: Glas 4E 83 (6B 4)
Cadogan St. G2: Glas 4E 83 (5B 4)
Cadzow Av. G46: Giff 1H 133

Cadzow Bri. ML3: Ham 5A 142
Cadzow Castle 3C 154
Cadzow Cres. ML5: Coat 1A 110
Cadzow Dr. G72: Camb 2H 121
ML4: Bell 3F 127
Cadzow Grn. G74: E Kil 1F 149
Cadzow Ho. ML3: Ham 4A 142
Cadzow Ind. Est. ML3: Ham 3H 153
Cadzow La. ML3: Ham 5A 142
Cadzow Pk. ML3: Ham 5A 142
Cadzow St. G2: Glas 4E 83 (6A 4)
ML1: Moth 3F 143
ML3: Ham 5A 142
ML9: Lark 1E 161
Caerlaverock Pl. G72: Blan 3A 140
Caird Dr. G11: Glas 1H 81
Caird Gdns. ML3: Ham 4G 141
Caird Pk. ML3: Ham 4H 141
Caird St. ML3: Ham 4G 141
Caird Ter. *G61: Bear 6D 24*
*(off Grampian Way)*
Cairhill Trad. Est. ML6: Air 5A 92
Cairn Av. PA4: Renf 2G 79
Cairnbairn Ct. *ML8: Carl 2F 165*
*(off Carranbuie Rd.)*
Cairnban St. G51: Glas 5D 80
Cairnbrook Ind. Est.
G34: Glas 2A 88
Cairnbrook Rd. G34: Glas 3A 88
Cairn Ct. G74: E Kil 5G 137
ML1: Moth 4H 143
Cairncraig St. G40: Glas 1E 105
Cairndow Av. G44: Glas 3D 118
Cairndow Av. La. G44: Glas 3D 118
Cairndow Ct. G44: Glas 3D 118
Cairndow Pl. ML2: Wis 2H 157
Cairn Dr. PA3: Lin 5H 75
Cairndyke Cres. ML6: Air 5A 92
Cairneymount Rd. ML8: Carl 3F 165
Cairney Pl. ML2: Newm 3H 147
Cairngorm Cres. G61: Bear 1B 44
G78: Barr 6E 115
ML2: Wis 6F 145
PA2: Pais 4A 98
Cairngorm Gdns.
G68: Cumb 4D 34
Cairngorm Rd. G43: Glas 2A 118
CAIRNHILL 6H 91
Cairnhill Av. ML6: Air 6A 92
Cairnhill Cir. G52: Glas 2H 99
Cairnhill Ct. ML8: Carl 3F 165
Cairnhill Cres. ML5: Coat 2F 111
Cairnhill Dr. G52: Glas 2H 99
Cairnhill Pl. G52: Glas 2H 99
Cairnhill Rd. G61: Bear 6F 45
ML6: Air 6H 91
Cairnhope Av. ML6: Air 6H 91
Cairnlea Dr. G51: Glas 5H 81
Cairnlea Gdns. ML4: Bell 4D 126
Cairnlea Rd. G62: Miln 4E 25
Cairnmuir Rd. G73: Ruth 2H 137
G74: Roger 3F 137
G76: Crmck, Roger 4C 136
Cairnoch Hill G68: Cumb 3E 35
Cairn Pl. G74: E Kil 5G 137
Cairnryan G74: E Kil 6F 137
CAIRNS 3C 122
Cairns Av. G72: Camb 2B 122
Cairns Dr. G62: Miln 3G 25
Cairnsmore Dr. G61: Bear 6B 24
Cairnsmore Rd. G15: Glas 5G 43
Cairns Rd. G72: Camb 3B 122
PA7: B'ton 3G 39
Cairns St. ML1: Moth 3G 143
Cairn St. G21: Glas 3B 64
Cairnswell Av. G72: Camb 3C 122
Cairnswell Pl. G72: Camb 3C 122
Cairntoul Ct. G68: Cumb 4D 34
Cairntoul Dr. G14: Glas 3A 60
Cairntoul Pl. G14: Glas 4A 60
Cairn Vw. G66: Kirk 6H 31
ML6: Air 5H 91
Cairnview Rd. G66: Milt C 6B 8
Cairnwood Dr. ML6: Air 6H 91
Caithness Rd. G74: E Kil 6C 138
Caithness St. G20: Glas 5D 62
G4: Glas 1F 83
G72: Blan 3A 140
Cala Sona Ct. ML2: Wis 3E 157
Calcots Path G34: Glas 2A 88
Calcots Pl. G34: Glas 2A 88
Caldarvan St. G22: Glas 6F 63
Caldeen Rd. ML5: Coat 6D 90
Calder Av. G78: Barr 6E 115
ML2: Newm 3E 147
ML5: Coat 1D 110
CALDERBANK 3B 112
Calderbank Rd. ML6: Air 1A 112
Calderbank Ter. ML1: Moth 2H 143
Calderbank Vw. G69: Bail 1A 108

**Calderbankview Cotts.**
ML6: C'bnk 1B **112**
CALDERBRAES **5C 108**
**Calderbraes Av.** G71: Tann 4C **108**
**Calder Ct.** *ML5: Coat 1D* ***110***
*(off Whifflet St.)*
**Caldercuilt Rd.** G20: Glas 1A **62**
G23: Glas 1A **62**
**Calder Dr.** G72: Camb 2A **122**
ML4: Bell 3E **127**
**Calder Ga.** G64: B'rig 3B **48**
**Calderglen Av.** G72: Blan 4A **124**
Calderglen Country Pk. **6E 139**
Calderglen Country Pk. Vis. Cen. **5D 150**
**Calderglen Rd.** G74: E Kil 2C **150**
**Caldergrove** ML1: Moth 2G **143**
**Calderpark** G71: Udd 4H **107**
**Calderpark Av.** G71: Udd 3H **107**
**Calderpark Cres.** G71: Udd 3H **107**
**Calderpark Ter.** G71: Udd 3H **107**
**Calder Pl.** G69: Bail 1H **107**
**Calderrigg Pl.** ML6: Air 4E **93**
**Calder Rd.** G71: View 4H **109**
G72: Blan 2H **123**
ML4: Moss 2E **127**
PA3: Pais 6E **77**
**Calderside Gro.** G74: E Kil 5E **139**
**Calderside Rd.** G72: Blan 3D **150**
**Calder St.** G42: Glas 3E **103**
G72: Blan 1B **140**
ML5: Coat 1D **110**
ML6: C'bnk 3C **112**
**Calder Twr.** G74: E Kil 4B **150**
ML1: Moth 4G **143**
**Caldervale St.** ML6: Gart 1E **113**
**Calder Vw.** ML1: Moth 2H **143**
ML3: Ham 3F **153**
**Calderview Av.** ML5: Coat 1F **111**
CALDERWOOD **6B 138**
**Calderwood Av.** G69: Bail 2G **107**
**Calderwood Dr.** G69: Bail 2G **107**
G72: Blan 3B **140**
**Calderwood Gdns.** G69: Bail 2G **107**
G74: E Kil 5E **139**
**Calderwood Rd.** G43: Glas 1B **118**
G73: Ruth 6E **105**
G74: E Kil 2A **150**
**Calderwood Sq.** *G74: E Kil 6B* ***138***
*(off Pollock Pl.)*
**Caldwell Av.** G13: Glas 3A **60**
PA3: Lin 6F **75**
**Caldwell Gro.** ML4: Bell 5C **110**
**Caldwell Quad.** ML1: Moth 4E **143**
**Caldwell Rd.** ML8: Carl 5H **165**
**Caledonia Av.** G5: Glas 2G **103**
G73: Ruth 5D **104**
**Caledonia Ct.** PA3: Pais 5H **77**
**Caledonia Dr.** G69: Bail 2H **107**
ML1: N'hill 3E **129**
**Caledonia Gdns.** ML8: Carl 2E **165**
**Caledonian Av.** ML4: Bell 3B **126**
**Caledonian Ct.** G74: E Kil 3G **149**
**Caledonian Cres.** *G12: Glas 1C* ***82***
*(off Otago St.)*
**Caledonian Pk.** ML2: Wis 6D **144**
**Caledonian Rd.** ML2: Wis 2G **157**
ML9: Lark 2E **161**
**Caledonia Rd.** G5: Glas 1F **103**
G69: Bail 2G **107**
**Caledonia St.** G5: Glas 2G **103**
G81: Clyd 4B **42**
PA3: Pais 6H **77**
**Caledonia Ter.** G82: Dumb 4C **16**
**Caledonia Wlk.** *ML3: Ham 2A* ***154***
*(off Chatelherault Cres.)*
**Caledonia Way** PA3: Glas A 2H **77**
**Caledonia Way E.** PA3: Glas A 2A **78**
**Caledonia Way W.** PA3: Glas A 2H **77**
**Caledon La.** *G12: Glas 1A* ***82***
*(off Highburgh Rd.)*
**Caledon St.** G12: Glas 1A **82**
**Caley Brae** G71: Udd 1D **124**
**Calfhill Rd.** G53: Glas 2B **100**
**Calfmuir Rd.** G66: Kirk, Lenz 6G **31**
**Calgary Pk.** G75: E Kil 3F **149**
**Calgary Pl.** G75: E Kil 3F **149**
**Calgary St.** G4: Glas 2G **83** (2F **5**)
**Calico Way** G66: Len 2E **7**
**Callaghan Wynd** G72: Blan 6H **123**
**Callander Ct.** G68: Cumb 1H **35**
**Callander Rd.** G68: Cumb 1H **35**
ML6: Chap 4D **112**
**Callander St.** G20: Glas 6E **63**
**Callieburn Ct.** G64: B'rig 1C **64**
**Callieburn Rd.** G64: B'rig 1C **64**
**Callon St.** ML6: Air 4A **92**
**Cally Av.** G15: Glas 4A **44**
**Calside** PA2: Pais 3H **97**
**Calside Av.** PA2: Pais 2H **97**
**Calside Ct.** PA2: Pais 3A **98**
CALTON **5A 84**
**Calton Entry** *G40: Glas 5A* ***84***
*(off Stevenson St.)*
**Calvay Cres.** G33: Glas 4D **86**
**Calvay Pl.** G33: Glas 4E **87**
**Calvay Rd.** G33: Glas 4D **86**
**Cambourne Rd.** G69: Mood 4D **52**
**Cambridge Av.** G81: Clyd 4D **42**
**Cambridge Rd.** PA4: Renf 1E **79**
**Cambridge St.** G2: Glas 3F **83** (3C **4**)
G3: Glas 3F **83** (3C **4**)
**Camburn St.** G32: Glas 6H **85**
**Cambusdoon Rd.** G33: Glas 1C **86**
**Cambuskenneth Gdns.**
G32: Glas 6D **86**
**Cambuskenneth Pl.** G33: Glas 1C **86**
CAMBUSLANG **1A 122**
**Cambuslang Bri.** G32: Glas 6A **106**
**Cambuslang Ind. Pk.**
G32: Glas 5A **106**
**Cambuslang Investment Pk.**
G32: Glas 5A **106**
**Cambuslang Rd.** G32: Glas 5H **105**
G72: Camb 5G **105**
(Bogleshole Rd.)
G72: Camb 6F **105**
(Farmeloan Rd.)
G73: Ruth 4D **104**
Cambuslang Station (Rail) **1H 121**
**Cambusmore Pl.** G33: Glas 1C **86**
CAMBUSNETHAN **6C 146**
**Cambusnethan St.** ML2: Wis 5C **146**
**Cambus Pl.** G33: Glas 1C **86**
**Camden St.** G5: Glas 1G **103**
**Camden Ter.** G5: Glas 1G **103**
**Camellia Dr.** ML2: Wis 2E **157**
**Camelon Cres.** G72: Blan 2B **140**
**Camelon St.** G32: Glas 5H **85**
**Cameron Av.** PA7: B'ton 3H **39**
**Cameron Ct.** G52: Hill 4H **79**
G73: Ruth 6C **104**
G81: Clyd 1E **59**
ML6: Air 3E **93**
**Cameron Cres.** G76: Crmck 2A **136**
ML3: Ham 6F **141**
**Cameron Dr.** G61: Bear 4G **45**
G71: Tann 5E **109**
G77: Newt M 2E **133**
**Cameronian Dr.** ML8: Carl 4G **165**
**Cameronian Pl.** ML4: Bell 4B **126**
**Cameronian Way** ML9: Lark 4G **161**
**Cameron Path** *ML9: Lark 4G* ***161***
*(off Donaldson Rd.)*
**Cameron Rd.** ML8: Carl 5H **165**
**Cameron Sq.** G81: Hard 1E **43**
**Cameron St.** G52: Hill 4G **79**
G81: Clyd 1E **59**
ML1: Moth 3F **143**
ML5: Coat 3D **90**
**Cameron Way** G72: Blan 1B **140**
**Camie Ct.** G66: Kirk 5C **30**
CAMLACHIE **6D 84**
**Camlachie St.** G31: Glas 6D **84**
(not continuous)
**Campbell Av.** G62: Miln 4G **25**
G82: Dumb 1C **18**
PA7: B'ton 3H **39**
**Campbell Cres.** G71: Both 3E **125**
G77: Newt M 3E **133**
**Campbell Dr.** G61: Bear 2D **44**
G78: Barr 5E **115**
G82: Dumb 1C **18**
**Campbell Ho.** G67: Cumb 4G **35**
**Campbell La.** ML3: Ham 6A **142**
**Campbell Pl.** G64: Torr 4D **28**
G75: E Kil 4G **149**
**Campbell St.** G20: Glas 2B **62**
ML2: Wis 6H **145**
ML3: Ham 6A **142**
ML4: Bell 2C **126**
PA4: Renf 5F **59**
PA5: John 3F **95**
**Campbell Ter.** G82: Dumb 1C **18**
**Camphill** PA1: Pais 2H **97**
**Camphill Av.** G41: Glas 5C **102**
G66: Kirk 5C **30**
**Camphill Ct.** PA2: Pais 2H **97**
**Camphill Gdns.** PA7: B'ton 4A **40**
**Camphill Ho.** G41: Glas 4D **102**
**Campion Rd.** ML1: Moth 1G **143**
**Camp Rd.** G69: Bail 6H **87**
G73: Ruth 3B **104**
ML1: Moth 5G **143**
**Camps Cres.** PA4: Renf 1G **79**
**Campside Gdns.** G76: Clar 1A **134**
**Campsie Av.** G78: Barr 6E **115**
**Campsie Ct.** G66: Kirk 1C **50**
ML5: Coat 2E **111**
ML9: Lark 6H **155**
**Campsie Cres.** ML6: Air 3H **91**
**Campsie Dr.** G61: Bear 6D **24**
G62: Miln 3H **25**
G66: Len 5G **7**
PA2: Pais 5H **97**
PA3: Glas A 1A **78**
PA4: Renf 3C **78**
**Campsie Pl.** G69: Chry 1A **68**
Campsie Recreation Cen. **3G 7**
**Campsie Rd.** G64: Torr 4E **29**
G66: Kirk 4B **30**
G66: Len 5G **7**
(Rowantree Ter.)
G66: Len, Milt C 4H **7**
(MacCabe Gdns)
ML2: Wis 5E **145**
**Campsie St.** G21: Glas 4B **64**
**Campsie Vw.** G33: Step 5D **66**
G66: Kirk 5A **30**
G67: Cumb 2B **36**
G69: Barg 6D **88**
G69: Chry 1A **68**
G71: Tann 5E **109**
G72: Flem 4E **123**
ML3: Ham 1D **152**
**Campston Pl.** G33: Glas 2B **86**
**Camp St.** ML1: Moth 4G **143**
**Camstradden Dr. E.** G61: Bear 3C **44**
**Camstradden Dr. W.** G61: Bear 3C **44**
**Camus Pl.** G15: Glas 3H **43**
**Canal Av.** PA5: John 3G **95**
**Canal Bank** *G23: Glas 2E* ***63***
*(off Balmore Rd.)*
**Canal Gdns.** PA5: Eld 2B **96**
**Canal La.** G66: Kirk 4D **30**
PA4: Renf 5F **59**
**Canal Rd.** PA5: John 3F **95**
**Canal St.** G4: Glas 2G **83** (1F **5**)
G66: Kirk 4D **30**
G81: Clyd 1D **58**
PA1: Pais 1H **97**
PA4: Renf 5F **59**
PA5: Eld 2B **96**
PA5: John 2G **95**
**Canal Ter.** PA1: Pais 1A **98**
**Canberra Av.** G81: Clyd 3H **41**
**Canberra Ct.** G46: Giff 4C **118**
**Canberra Dr.** G75: E Kil 3E **149**
**Candermill & Marlage Rd.**
ML9: Ashg 6B **162**
**Cander Rigg** G64: B'rig 3C **48**
**Cander St.** ML9: Lark 5F **161**
**Candimilne Ct.** ML8: Carl 4H **165**
**Candleriggs** G1: Glas 4H **83** (6G **5**)
**Candren Rd.** PA3: Lin 6B **76**
PA3: Pais 1E **97**
(not continuous)
**Candren Way** PA3: Pais 6E **77**
**Caneluk Av.** ML8: Carl 5H **165**
**Canmore Pl.** G31: Glas 1F **105**
**Canmore St.** G31: Glas 1F **105**
**Cannerton Cres.** G66: Milt C 6B **8**
**Cannerton Pk.** G66: Milt C 6B **8**
**Cannich Dr.** PA2: Pais 4D **98**
**Cannich Pl.** ML2: Newm 3D **146**
**Canniesburn Rd.** G61: Bear 5C **44**
**Canniesburn Sq.** G61: Bear 5F **45**
**CANNIESBURN TOLL** **5F 45**
**Canniesbury Rd.** G61: Bear 4D **44**
**Canonbie Av.** G74: E Kil 5H **137**
**Canonbie St.** G34: Glas 2B **88**
**Canon Ct.** ML1: Carf 5D **128**
**Canongate** G74: E Kil 5D **138**
**Canterbury** G75: E Kil 5D **148**
**Cantieslaw Dr.** G74: E Kil 6A **138**
**Canting Way** G51: Glas 4A **82**
**Canyon Rd.** ML2: Wis 1D **156**
**Capel Av.** G77: Newt M 3F **133**
**Capel Gro.** G74: E Kil 6B **138**
**Capelridge Dr.** G74: E Kil 1B **150**
**Capelrig Dr.** G77: Newt M 1D **132**
**Capelrig La.** G77: Newt M 3D **132**
**Capelrig Rd.** G77: Newt M 1D **132**
**Capelrig St.** G46: T'bnk 3F **117**
Caper House Play Barn **5D 136**
**Caplaw Pl.** ML2: Wis 3F **157**
**Caplaw Rd.** PA2: Pais 6G **97**
**Caplaw Twr.** ML2: Wis 3F **157**
**Caplethill Rd.** PA2: Pais 6A **98**
**Caprington Pl.** G33: Glas 2A **86**
**Caprington St.** G33: Glas 2A **86**
**Cara Dr.** G51: Glas 3E **81**
**Caravelle Way** PA4: Renf 2F **79**
**Carbarns** ML2: Wis 2D **156**
**Carbarns E.** ML2: Wis 2D **156**
**Carbarns Rd.** ML2: Wis 3C **156**
**Carbarns W.** ML2: Wis 2D **156**
**Carberry Rd.** G41: Glas 3B **102**
**Carbeth Rd.** G62: Miln 4F **25**
**Carbeth St.** G22: Glas 5F **63**
**Carbisdale St.** G22: Glas 4A **6**
**Carbost St.** G23: Glas 6B **4**
**Carbrach Loan** *ML2: Newm 3D* ***14***
*(off Tiree Cres*
CARBRAIN **4A 3**
**Carbrain Ind. Est.**
G67: Cumb 4B **3**
**Carbrook St.** G21: Glas 2C **8**
PA1: Pais 1G **9**
**Cardarrach St.** G21: Glas 5C **6**
**Cardean Rd.** ML4: Moss 1G **12**
**Cardell Av.** PA2: Pais 2E **9**
**Cardell Cres.** ML6: Chap 3D **11**
**Cardell Dr.** PA2: Pais 2E **9**
**Cardell Rd.** PA2: Pais 2E **9**
CARDONALD **6B 8**
**Cardonald Dr.** G52: Glas 1A **10**
**Cardonald Gdns.** G52: Glas 1B **10**
**Cardonald Pk.** G51: Glas 4B **8**
**Cardonald Pl. Rd.**
G52: Glas 1B **10**
Cardonald Station (Rail) **5D 8**
**Cardowan Dr.** G33: Step 4D **6**
G68: Cumb 4A **3**
**Cardowan Pk.** G71: Tann 4F **10**
**Cardowan Rd.** G32: Glas 5H **8**
G33: Step 3E **6**
**Cardow Rd.** G21: Glas 5E **6**
**Cardrona St.** G33: Glas 6B **6**
**Cardross Ct.** G31: Glas 4B **8**
**Cardross Rd.** G82: Card, Dumb 2A **1**
G82: Dumb 3B **1**
**Cardross St.** G31: Glas 4B **8**
**Cardwell St.** G41: Glas 1E **10**
**Cardyke St.** G21: Glas 5C **6**
**Careston Pl.** G64: B'rig 6F **4**
**Carey Gdns.** ML1: Cle 6H **12**
CARFIN **5B 12**
**Carfin Ind. Est.** ML1: Carf 5B **12**
Carfin Lourdes Grotto **5D 12**
**Carfin Mill Rd.** ML1: Carf 6C **12**
**Carfin Rd.** ML1: N'hill 5D **12**
ML2: Wis 5C **14**
Carfin Station (Rail) **5D 12**
**Carfin St.** G42: Glas 3F **10**
ML1: New S 4A **12**
ML5: Coat 1D **11**
**Carfrae St.** G3: Glas 3A **8**
**Cargill Sq.** G64: B'rig 1E **6**
**Carham Cres.** G52: Glas 6C **8**
**Carham Dr.** G52: Glas 6C **8**
**Caribou Grn.** G75: E Kil 3D **14**
**Carillon Rd.** G51: Glas 6A **8**
**Carinthia Sq.** G81: Clyd 5D **4**
**Carisbrooke Cres.** G64: B'rig 3D **4**
**Carlaverock Rd.** G43: Glas 1B **11**
**Carleith Av.** G81: Dun 1B **4**
**Carleith Quad.** G51: Glas 4D **8**
**Carleith Ter.** G81: Dun 1B **4**
**Carleston St.** G21: Glas 5B **6**
**Carleton Ct.** G46: Giff 3A **11**
**Carleton Dr.** G46: Giff 3A **11**
**Carleton Ga.** G46: Giff 3A **11**
**Carlibar Av.** G13: Glas 3H **5**
**Carlibar Dr.** G78: Barr 4E **11**
**Carlibar Gdns.** G78: Barr 4E **11**
**Carlibar Rd.** G78: Barr 4D **11**
**Carlile Pl.** PA3: Pais 5A **7**
**Carlin La.** ML8: Carl 4H **16**
**Carlin's Pl.** G66: Len 3F
**Carlisle La.** ML6: Air 4C **9**
**Carlisle Rd.** ML1: N'hse 6G **11**
ML3: Fern, Ham 6B **14**
ML6: Air 5C **9**
ML9: Lark 5G **15**
(Lanark Rd. End
ML9: Lark 5F **16**
(Strutherhil
**Carlisle St.** G21: Glas 6H **6**
**Carlock Wlk.** G32: Glas 5C **8**
**Carlouk La.** ML8: Carl 4H **16**
**Carloway Ct.** G33: Glas 3B **8**
**Carlowrie Av.** G72: Blan 5A **12**
CARLSTON **3G 2**
**Carlton Ct.** G5: Glas 5F **8**
**Carlton Pl.** G5: Glas 5F **8**
CARLUKE **3F 16**
Carluke Leisure Cen. **3G 16**
**Carluke Station (Rail)**
**4D 16**
**Carlyle Av.** G52: Hill 3H **7**
**Carlyle Dr.** G74: E Kil 1A **15**
**Carlyle Ter.** G73: Ruth 4D **10**
G74: E Kil 1B **15**
**Carmaben Rd.** G33: Glas 3D **8**
**Carman Vw.** G82: Dumb 1G **1**
**Carment Dr.** G41: Glas 5B **10**
**Carmichael Path** *ML5: Glenb 3G* ***6***
*(off Oval, The*
**Carmichael Pl.** G42: Glas 6D **10**

Carmichael St.—Cemetery Rd.

armichael St. G51: Glas ... 5H 81
ML8: Law ... 6D 158
armichael Way ML8: Law ... 6D 158
RMUNNOCK ... 2H 135
armunnock By-Pass
G76: Crmck ... 6G 119
armunnock La. G44: Glas ... 2F 119
armunnock Rd. G44: Glas ... 6F 103
G45: Glas ... 6G 119
G74: E Kil ... 1F 149
G76: Busby ... 4E 135
G76: Crmck ... 6G 119
(Carmunnock By-Pass)
G76: Crmck ... 4C 136
(Kittochside Rd.)
ARMYLE ... 5C 106
armyle Av. G32: Carm, Glas ... 3B 106
ARMYLE AV. INTERCHANGE ... 4B 106
armyle Gdns. ML5: Coat ... 2A 110
armyle Station (Rail) ... 4B 106
arna Dr. G44: Glas ... 2G 119
arnarvon St. G3: Glas ... 2D 82 (1A 4)
arnbooth Ct. G45: Glas ... 5B 120
ARNBROE ... 1E 111
arnbroe Rd. ML4: Bell ... 6D 110
ML5: Coat ... 1F 111
arneddans Rd. G62: Miln ... 1C 24
arnegie Hill G75: E Kil ... 3F 149
arnegie Pl. G75: E Kil ... 3F 149
arnegie Rd. G52: Hill ... 4A 80
(not continuous)
arnoch St. G23: Glas ... 6B 46
arnock Cres. G78: Barr ... 6D 114
arnock Gdns. G62: Miln ... 3E 25
arnock Rd. G53: Glas ... 5C 100
arnoustie Ct. G71: Both ... 5D 124
arnoustie Cres. G64: B'rig ... 6E 49
G75: E Kil ... 5C 148
arnoustie Pl. G5: Glas ... 6D 82
ML4: Bell ... 6C 110
arnoustie St. G5: Glas ... 6D 82
arnoustie Way G68: Cumb ... 5H 13
ARNTYNE ... 4G 85
arntyne Gdns. G32: Glas ... 4G 85
arntynehall Rd. G32: Glas ... 4H 85
arntyne Ind. Est. G32: Glas ... 5G 85
arntyne Path G32: Glas ... 4F 85
arntyne Pl. G32: Glas ... 4F 85
arntyne Rd. G31: Glas ... 5E 85
G32: Glas ... 4F 85
arntyne Station (Rail) ... 5H 85
ARNWADRIC ... 3E 117
arnwadric Rd. G46: T'bnk ... 3E 117
arnwath Av. G43: Glas ... 1D 118
arnwath Rd. ML8: Carl ... 4F 165
aroline St. G31: Glas ... 6G 85
arolside Av. G76: Clar ... 2C 134
arolside Dr. G15: Glas ... 4B 44
arolside Gdns. G76: Clar ... 2C 134
arousel Cres. ML2: Wis ... 6A 146
arradale Cres. G68: Cumb ... 5B 34
arradale Gdns. G64: B'rig ... 6E 49
ML8: Carl ... 5G 165
arradale Pl. PA3: Lin ... 5G 75
arradale St. ML5: Coat ... 4B 90
(not continuous)
arranbuie Rd. ML8: Carl ... 2F 165
arrbridge Dr. G20: Glas ... 3B 62
arresbrook Av. G66: Kirk ... 1G 51
ARRIAGEHILL ... 4A 98
arriagehill Av. PA2: Pais ... 3A 98
arriagehill Dr. PA2: Pais ... 4A 98
arrickarden Rd. G61: Bear ... 4F 45
arrick Ct. G66: Kirk ... 3G 31
arrick Cres. G46: Giff ... 6A 118
ML2: Wis ... 5G 145
arrick Dr. G32: Glas ... 1E 107
G73: Ruth ... 2C 120
ML5: Coat ... 4H 89
arrick Gdns. G72: Blan ... 3B 140
ML3: Ham ... 1C 152
ML4: Bell ... 5C 110
ML8: Carl ... 5G 165
arrick Gro. G32: Glas ... 1E 107
arrick Pl. ML4: Bell ... 6D 110
ML5: Coat ... 4H 89
ML5: Glenb ... 3A 70
ML9: Lark ... 1F 161
arrick Rd. G64: B'rig ... 6E 49
G67: Cumb ... 1A 36
G73: Ruth ... 2B 120
G74: E Kil ... 6H 137
PA7: B'ton ... 5A 40
ARRICKSTONE ... 6G 13
arrickstone Rd. G68: Cumb ... 6G 13
ARRICKSTONE RDBT. ... 6G 13
arrickstone Vw. G68: Cumb ... 6H 13
arrick St. G2: Glas ... 4E 83 (6B 4)
ML9: Lark ... 3G 161
arrick Ter. G82: Dumb ... 3B 16
Carrick Vw. ML5: Glenb ... 3A 70
Carrick Way G71: Both ... 4E 125
Carriden Pl. G33: Glas ... 4E 87
Carrington St. G4: Glas ... 1D 82 (1A 4)
Carroglen Gdns. G32: Glas ... 6D 86
Carroglen Gro. G32: Glas ... 6D 86
Carroll Cres. ML1: Carf ... 5C 128
Carron Ct. *G72: Camb ... 2E 123*
*(off Mill Rd.)*
G72: Camb ... 2D 122
(Arnhem St.)
ML3: Ham ... 2F 153
Carron Cres. G22: Glas ... 4H 63
G61: Bear ... 4C 44
G64: B'rig ... 6D 48
G66: Lenz ... 3E 51
Carron Dr. PA7: B'ton ... 5A 40
Carron Ho. *G67: Cumb ... 3H 35*
*(in Cumbernauld Shop. Cen.)*
*G67: Cumb ... 4H 35*
*(off Town Cen.)*
Carron Pl. G22: Glas ... 4A 64
G75: E Kil ... 6H 149
ML5: Coat ... 2H 89
Carron St. G22: Glas ... 4A 64
ML2: Wis ... 2H 157
Carron Way *G67: Cumb ... 3H 35*
*(in Cumbernauld Shop. Cen.)*
ML1: N'hill ... 3C 128
PA3: Pais ... 4C 78
Carrour Gdns. G64: B'rig ... 5B 48
Carr Quad ML4: Moss ... 2F 127
Carruth Rd. PA11: Bri W ... 3E 73
Carsaig Dr. G52: Glas ... 6E 81
Carsaig Loan ML5: Glenb ... 3G 69
Carscallan Rd.
ML3: Ham, Quar ... 5H 153
Carsegreen Av. PA2: Pais ... 6F 97
Carsemeadow PA11: Q'riers ... 1A 72
Carse Vw. Dr. G61: Bear ... 1G 45
Carstairs St. G40: Glas ... 3B 104
Carswell Gdns. G41: Glas ... 3C 102
Carswell Rd. G77: Newt M ... 4B 132
Cartbank Gdns. G44: Glas ... 3E 119
Cartbank Gro. G44: Neth ... 3D 118
Cartbank Rd. G44: Glas ... 3D 118
Cartcraigs Rd. G43: Glas ... 1H 117
Cartha Cres. PA2: Pais ... 2C 98
Cartha St. G41: Glas ... 6C 102
Cartland Av. ML8: Carl ... 5F 165
Cart La. PA3: Pais ... 5A 78
Cartsbridge Rd. G76: Busby ... 3C 134
CARTSIDE ... 4D 94
Cartside Av. PA4: Inch ... 5F 57
PA5: John ... 4D 94
Cartside Dr. G76: Busby ... 3E 135
Cartside Pl. G76: Busby ... 4D 134
Cartside Quad. G42: Glas ... 6E 103
Cartside Rd. G76: Busby ... 4D 134
Cartside St. G42: Glas ... 6D 102
Cart St. G81: Clyd ... 1D 58
Cartvale La. PA3: Pais ... 5A 78
Cartvale Rd. G42: Glas ... 6D 102
Cartview Ct. G76: Busby ... 3D 134
Cart Wlk. PA1: Pais ... 1B 98
Cartyne Rd. G32: Glas ... 4B 86
Caskie Dr. G72: Blan ... 6C 124
Cassells St. ML1: Moth ... 1G 143
Cassels Gro. ML1: Moth ... 6E 127
Cassels St. ML1: Moth ... 1G 143
ML8: Carl ... 4F 165
Cassiltoun Gdns. G45: Glas ... 5H 119
Cassley Av. PA4: Renf ... 1H 79
Castburn Rd. G67: Cumb ... 5F 15
Castle Av. G71: Both, Udd ... 3C 124
ML1: Holy ... 1B 128
PA5: Eld ... 4H 95
Castle Bank Ct. G13: Glas ... 3E 61
Castlebank Dr. G11: Glas ... 2G 81
Castle Bank Gdns. G13: Glas ... 3E 61
Castlebank Pl. G11: Glas ... 2G 81
Castlebank St. G11: Glas ... 2F 81
(not continuous)
Castle Bank Vs. G13: Glas ... 3E 61
Castlebay Dr. G22: Glas ... 6G 47
Castlebay Pl. G22: Glas ... 1G 63
Castlebay St. G22: Glas ... 1G 63
Castlebrae G82: Dumb ... 2C 16
Castlebrae Gdns.
G44: Glas ... 1F 119
CASTLECARY ... 3E 15
Castle Cary ... 4F 15
Castlecary Rd.
G68: C'cry, Cumb ... 5C 14
Castle Chimmins Av.
G72: Camb ... 3D 122
Castle Chimmins Gdns.
G72: Camb ... 4D 122
Castle Chimmins Rd.
G72: Camb ... 4D 122
Castle Ct. G66: Kirk ... 5D 30
G68: C'cry ... 3F 15
Castle Cres. PA7: B'ton ... 5H 39
Castlecroft Gdns. G71: Udd ... 2D 124
Castle Dr. ML1: Holy ... 1B 128
Castlefern Rd. G73: Ruth ... 4D 120
Castlefield Ct. G33: Mille ... 5B 66
Castlefield Gdns. G75: E Kil ... 6D 148
Castle Gait G53: Glas ... 5A 100
PA1: Pais ... 2H 97
Castle Gdns. G69: Mood ... 5D 52
PA2: Pais ... 2E 97
Castle Ga. G71: Both ... 2C 124
G77: Newt M ... 6G 133
Castleglen Rd. G74: E Kil ... 5B 136
Castlegreen Cres. G82: Dumb ... 5H 17
Castlegreen Gdns.
G82: Dumb ... 5H 17
Castlegreen La. G82: Dumb ... 5G 17
Castlegreen St. G82: Dumb ... 5G 17
Castle Gro. G65: Kils ... 1G 11
CASTLEHEAD ... 2H 97
CASTLEHILL
Carluke ... 1E 165
Dumbarton ... 2C 16
Castlehill Cres. FK4: Bank ... 1E 15
Castle Hill Cres. ML3: Fern ... 2E 155
Castlehill Cres. ML3: Ham ... 1B 154
ML6: Chap ... 4F 113
ML8: Law ... 1A 164
PA4: Renf ... 5F 59
Castlehill Dr. G77: Newt M ... 5F 133
Castlehill Grn. G74: E Kil ... 5B 136
Castlehill Ind. Est. ML8: Carl ... 1E 165
Castlehill Quad. G82: Dumb ... 2C 16
Castlehill Rd. G61: Bear ... 1B 44
G82: Dumb ... 2C 16
ML2: Wis ... 3F 157
ML8: Carl ... 1E 165
Castlehill Vw. G65: Kils ... 1G 11
Castlelaw Gdns. G32: Glas ... 5B 86
Castlelaw St. G32: Glas ... 5B 86
Castle Mains Rd. G62: Miln ... 3D 24
CASTLEMILK ... 4A 120
Castlemilk Arc. G45: Glas ... 4A 120
Castlemilk Cres. G44: Glas ... 2A 120
Castlemilk Dr. G45: Glas ... 4A 120
Castlemilk Rd. G44: Glas ... 1A 120
(Croftend Av.)
G44: Glas ... 6A 104
(Curtis Av.)
Castlemilk Sports Cen. ... 4A 120
Castlemilk Swimming Pool ... 4A 120
Castlemount Av. G77: Newt M ... 6F 133
Castle Pl. G71: Udd ... 1C 124
Castle Quad. ML6: Air ... 4D 92
Castle Rd. G77: Newt M ... 5C 132
G82: Dumb ... 5G 17
ML6: Air ... 4D 92
PA11: Bri W ... 2F 73
PA5: Eld ... 2A 96
Castle Sq. G81: Clyd ... 4A 42
Castle St. G11: Glas ... 2A 82
G4: Glas ... 3A 84 (5H 5)
G69: Bail ... 2G 107
G73: Ruth ... 5C 104
G81: Clyd ... 4A 42
G82: Dumb ... 4F 17
ML3: Ham ... 5B 142
ML6: Chap ... 3D 112
PA1: Pais ... 1H 97
Castle Ter. G82: Dumb ... 4G 17
*PA11: Bri W ... 4G 73*
*(off Kilbarchan Rd.)*
Castleton Av. G64: B'rig ... 2A 64
G77: Newt M ... 6F 133
Castleton Ct. G45: Glas ... 5B 120
G77: Newt M ... 6F 133
Castleton Cres. G77: Newt M ... 6F 133
Castleton Dr. G77: Newt M ... 6F 133
Castleton Gro. G77: Newt M ... 6F 133
Castleview G66: Cam G ... 1B 6
Castle Vw. G66: Len ... 2C 6
Castleview G68: Cumb ... 3E 15
Castle Vw. G72: Blan ... 5A 124
G81: Clyd ... 4D 42
ML2: Newm ... 3E 147
Castleview Av. PA2: Pais ... 6E 97
Castleview Dr. PA2: Pais ... 6E 97
Castleview Pl. PA2: Pais ... 6E 97
Castleview Ter. FK4: Hag ... 1G 15
Castle Way G67: Cumb ... 1C 36
G69: Barg ... 6D 88
Castle Wynd G71: Both ... 5F 125
Cathay St. G22: Glas ... 1G 63
Cathburn Rd. ML2: Newm ... 5F 147
CATHCART ... 1E 119
Cathcart Castle ... 2F 119
Cathcart Cres. PA2: Pais ... 2C 98
Cathcart Pl. G73: Ruth ... 6B 104
Cathcart Rd. G42: Glas ... 3F 103
G73: Ruth ... 6B 104
Cathcart Station (Rail) ... 1E 119
Cathedral Sq. G4: Glas ... 4A 84
(not continuous)
Cathedral St. G1: Glas ... 3G 83 (4E 5)
Catherine St. G66: Kirk ... 5C 30
ML1: Moth ... 5G 143
Catherines Wlk. G72: Blan ... 3B 140
Catherine Way ML1: New S ... 4H 127
CATHKIN ... 5F 121
Cathkin Av. G72: Camb ... 1G 121
G73: Ruth ... 6E 105
Cathkin Braes Country Pk. ... 5D 120
Cathkin By-Pass G73: Ruth ... 4F 121
Cathkin Ct. G45: Glas ... 5B 120
Cathkin Cres. G68: Cumb ... 6G 13
Cathkin Gdns. G71: Tann ... 4C 108
Cathkin Pl. G72: Camb ... 1G 121
Cathkin Recreation Cen. ... 5F 103
Cathkin Rd. G42: Glas ... 6D 102
G71: Tann ... 4C 108
G73: Ruth ... 1B 136
G76: Crmck ... 1A 136
Cathkin Vw. G32: Carm ... 5B 106
Cathkinview Pl. G42: Glas ... 6F 103
Cathkinview Rd. G42: Glas ... 6E 103
Catrine G74: E Kil ... 1F 149
Catrine Av. *G81: Clyd ... 4F 43*
*(off Kirkoswald Dr.)*
Catrine Ct. G53: Glas ... 5A 100
Catrine Cres. ML1: Moth ... 6A 144
Catrine Gdns. G53: Glas ... 5A 100
Catrine Pl. G53: Glas ... 5A 100
Catrine Rd. G53: Glas ... 5A 100
Catrine St. ML9: Lark ... 3G 161
Catriona Way ML1: Holy ... 2B 128
Catter Gdns. G62: Miln ... 2E 25
Cauldstream Pl. G62: Miln ... 4E 25
Causewayside Cres.
G32: Glas ... 2A 106
Causewayside St. G32: Glas ... 3A 106
Causeyside St. PA1: Pais ... 1A 98
(Forbes Pl.)
PA1: Pais ... 2A 98
(Thompson Brae)
Causeystanes *G72: Blan ... 2B 140*
*(off Winton Cres.)*
Cavendish Ct. G5: Glas ... 1F 103
Cavendish Dr. G77: Newt M ... 3F 133
Cavendish Pl. G5: Glas ... 1F 103
Cavendish St. G5: Glas ... 1F 103
Cavin Dr. G45: Glas ... 3A 120
Cavin Rd. G45: Glas ... 3A 120
Cawder Ct. G68: Cumb ... 6F 13
Cawder Pl. G68: Cumb ... 6G 13
Cawder Rd. G68: Cumb ... 6G 13
Cawder Vw. G68: Cumb ... 6G 13
Cawder Way G68: Cumb ... 6G 13
Cawdor Cres. PA7: B'ton ... 5H 39
Cawdor Way G74: E Kil ... 6F 137
Cayton Gdns. G69: Bail ... 1F 107
Cecil St. G12: Glas ... 6B 62
G76: Clar ... 2C 134
ML5: Coat ... 6C 90
Cedar Av. G71: View ... 5F 109
G81: Clyd ... 3H 41
PA5: John ... 5F 95
Cedar Ct. G20: Glas ... 1E 83
G72: Flem ... 3E 123
G75: E Kil ... 6E 149
PA10: Kilb ... 2A 94
Cedar Cres. ML3: Ham ... 2A 154
Cedar Dr. G66: Lenz ... 2C 50
G71: View ... 5G 109
G75: E Kil ... 6E 149
Cedar Gdns. G73: Ruth ... 3E 121
ML1: N'hill ... 3C 128
ML8: Law ... 5D 158
Cedar La. ML1: Holy ... 3B 128
ML6: Air ... 4C 92
Cedar Pl. G72: Blan ... 6A 124
G75: E Kil ... 6E 149
G78: Barr ... 6F 115
Cedar Rd. FK4: Bank ... 1E 15
G64: B'rig ... 1D 64
G66: Milt C ... 6C 8
G67: Cumb ... 2D 36
Cedar St. G20: Glas ... 1E 83
Cedar Wlk. G64: B'rig ... 1D 64
Cedarwood Av.
G77: Newt M ... 5F 133
Cedric Pl. G13: Glas ... 2D 60
Cedric Rd. G13: Glas ... 2D 60
Celtic F.C. ... 6D 84
Celtic F.C. Vis. Cen. ... 1D 104
Celtic Pk. ... 6D 84
Celtic St. G20: Glas ... 2A 62
Cemetery Rd. G52: Glas ... 1D 100
G72: Blan ... 3A 140

Clifford Gdns.—Connor St.

lifford Gdns. G51: Glas . . . . . . . . .6H 81
ifford La. G51: Glas . . . . . . . . . . .6A 82
ifford Pl. *G51: Glas . . . . . . . . . . .6B 82*
*(off Clifford La.)*
ifford St. G51: Glas . . . . . . . . . . .6H 81
iff Rd. G3: Glas . . . . . . . . . . . . . .1D 82
iftonhill Stadium . . . . . . . . . . . .5E 91
ifton Pl. *G3: Glas . . . . . . . . . . . . .2C 82*
*(off Clifton St.)*
ML5: Coat . . . . . . . . . . . . . . . .5E 91
lifton Rd. G46: Giff . . . . . . . . . . .4H 117
ifton St. G3: Glas . . . . . . . . . . . . .2C 82
ifton Ter. G72: Camb . . . . . . . . .4G 121
*PA5: John . . . . . . . . . . . . . . . .3G 95*
*(off Auchenlodment Rd.)*
LIFTONVILLE . . . . . . . . . . . . . . .4E 91
liftonville Ct. *ML5: Coat . . . . . . . .5E 91*
*(off Clifton Pl.)*
LINCARTHILL . . . . . . . . . . . . . .6C 104
incarthill Rd. G73: Ruth . . . . . .6C 104
lincart Rd. G42: Glas . . . . . . . . .5F 103
LIPPENS . . . . . . . . . . . . . . . . . .5G 75
lippens Rd. PA3: Lin . . . . . . . . . .6H 75
PA6: Hous . . . . . . . . . . . . . . . .3E 75
loan Av. G15: Glas . . . . . . . . . . . .5B 44
loan Cres. G64: B'rig . . . . . . . . . .3D 48
lober Farm La. G62: Miln . . . . . . .2E 25
loberfield G62: Miln . . . . . . . . . . .1F 25
loberfield Gdns. G62: Miln . . . . . .2F 25
loberhill Rd. G13: Glas . . . . . . . . .6C 44
lober Rd. G62: Miln . . . . . . . . . . .2F 25
lochbar Av. G62: Miln . . . . . . . . . .2F 25
lochbar Gdns. G62: Miln . . . . . . . .3F 25
lochoderick Av. PA10: Kilb . . . . . .3B 94
loch St. G33: Glas . . . . . . . . . . . . .3A 86
lockerhill Pl. ML1: N'hill . . . . . . .3E 129
lock Sq. *G67: Cumb . . . . . . . . . . .4H 35*
*(in Cumbernauld Shop. Cen.)*
loister Av. ML6: Air . . . . . . . . . .1C 112
lonbeith St. G33: Glas . . . . . . . . .1E 87
loseburn St. G22: Glas . . . . . . . . .4G 63
loth St. G78: Barr . . . . . . . . . . . .5E 115
louden Rd. G67: Cumb . . . . . . . . . .3B 36
loudhowe Ter. G72: Blan . . . . . .6A 124
louston Ct. G20: Glas . . . . . . . . . .5C 62
louston La. G20: Glas . . . . . . . . . .5C 62
louston St. G20: Glas . . . . . . . . . .5B 62
lova Pl. G71: Udd . . . . . . . . . . . .1D 124
lova St. G46: T'bnk . . . . . . . . . . .3F 117
love Mill Wynd ML9: Lark . . . . .3C 160
lovend Dr. G73: Ruth . . . . . . . . .4D 120
loverbank St. G21: Glas . . . . . . . .2C 84
lovergate G64: B'rig . . . . . . . . . . .6A 48
loverhill Pl. G69: Chry . . . . . . . . .1A 68
loverhill Ter. G74: E Kil . . . . . . .2G 149
loverhill Vw. G74: E Kil . . . . . . . .2F 149
lunie Pl. ML2: Newm . . . . . . . . .3D 146
ML5: Coat . . . . . . . . . . . . . . .2D 110
lunie Rd. G52: Glas . . . . . . . . . .1E 101
luny Av. G61: Bear . . . . . . . . . . . .5G 45
G81: Hard . . . . . . . . . . . . . . . .6E 23
luny Dr. G61: Bear . . . . . . . . . . . .5G 45
G77: Newt M . . . . . . . . . . . .4B 132
PA3: Pais . . . . . . . . . . . . . . . .5C 78
luny Gdns. G14: Glas . . . . . . . . . .5E 61
G69: Bail . . . . . . . . . . . . . . .1G 107
luny Vs. G14: Glas . . . . . . . . . . . .5E 61
lutha Pl. G75: E Kil . . . . . . . . . .4C 148
lutha St. G51: Glas . . . . . . . . . . .5B 82
lyde Av. G64: Torr . . . . . . . . . . . .5D 28
G71: Both . . . . . . . . . . . . . . .6D 124
G78: Barr . . . . . . . . . . . . . . .6F 115
ML3: Fern . . . . . . . . . . . . . . .2E 155
LYDEBANK . . . . . . . . . . . . . . . .6D 42
lydebank Bus. Pk. G81: Clyd . . . .5C 42
lydebank Crematorium
G81: Dun . . . . . . . . . . . . . . . .1H 41
lydebank District Mus. . . . . . . . .6C 42
lydebank Ind. Est. G81: Clyd . . . .5H 41
lydebank Megabowl . . . . . . . . . . .6E 43
lydebank Station (Rail) . . . . . . .6D 42
lydebrae Dr. G71: Both . . . . . . . .1F 141
lydebrae St. G51: Glas . . . . . . . . .3H 81
lyde Bri. ML3: Ham . . . . . . . . . .4D 142
lydebuilt . . . . . . . . . . . . . . . . . .6A 60
lyde Ct. G81: Clyd . . . . . . . . . . . .2A 42
G82: Dumb . . . . . . . . . . . . . . . .3E 17
*ML5: Coat . . . . . . . . . . . . . . . . .5E 91*
*(off Clifton Pl.)*
lyde Dr. ML4: Bell . . . . . . . . . . .3E 127
lyde F.C. . . . . . . . . . . . . . . . . . .4B 34
lydeford Dr. G32: Glas . . . . . . . .2G 105
G71: Udd . . . . . . . . . . . . . . .6B 108
lydeford Rd. G32: Glas . . . . . . . .6A 106
G72: Camb . . . . . . . . . . . . . .1B 122
lydeholm Rd. G14: Glas . . . . . . . .1D 80
lydeholm Ter. G81: Clyd . . . . . . . .2F 59
lyde Ho. ML3: Ham . . . . . . . . . .4A 142
lyde La. ML1: New S . . . . . . . . .3A 128
lydeneuk Dr. G71: Udd . . . . . . . .6B 108
Clyde Pl. G5: Glas . . . . . . . . . . . . . .5E 83
G72: Camb . . . . . . . . . . . . . . .3D 122
ML1: New S . . . . . . . . . . . . . .3A 128
PA5: John . . . . . . . . . . . . . . . . .5C 94
Clyde Rd. PA3: Pais . . . . . . . . . . . .4D 78
CLYDESDALE . . . . . . . . . . . . . . .4H 127
Clydesdale Av. ML2: Wis . . . . . . .2D 156
ML3: Ham . . . . . . . . . . . . . . .5H 153
PA3: Pais . . . . . . . . . . . . . . . . .2C 78
Clydesdale Pl. ML3: Ham . . . . . .5H 153
Clydesdale St. ML3: Ham . . . . . .5G 141
ML4: Bell . . . . . . . . . . . . . . .3F 127
ML9: Lark . . . . . . . . . . . . . . .1E 161
Clyde Shop. Cen. G81: Clyd . . . . . .5D 42
Clydeshore Rd. G82: Dumb . . . . . .5E 17
Clydeside Expressway
G11: Glas . . . . . . . . . . . . . . . . .1F 81
G14: Glas . . . . . . . . . . . . . . . .6D 60
G3: Glas . . . . . . . . . . . . . . . . . .3B 82
Clydeside Ind. Est. G14: Glas . . . .1D 80
Clydeside Rd. G73: Ruth . . . . . . .3B 104
Clydesmill Dr. G32: Glas . . . . . .6A 106
Clydesmill Gro. G32: Glas . . . . . .6A 106
Clydesmill Pl. G32: Glas . . . . . . .5A 106
Clydesmill Rd. G32: Glas . . . . . . .5H 105
Clyde Sq. *G67: Cumb . . . . . . . . . . .4H 35*
*(in Cumbernauld Shop. Cen.)*
Clyde St. G1: Glas . . . . . . . . . . . . .5G 83
G81: Clyd . . . . . . . . . . . . . . . . .1E 59
ML5: Coat . . . . . . . . . . . . . . . . .4E 91
ML8: Carl . . . . . . . . . . . . . . .3D 164
PA4: Renf . . . . . . . . . . . . . . . . .4F 59
Clyde Ter. G71: Both . . . . . . . . . .6E 125
ML1: Moth . . . . . . . . . . . . . . .1C 156
Clyde Twr. G74: E Kil . . . . . . . . .4B 150
*ML1: Moth . . . . . . . . . . . . . . .4G 143*
*(off Airbles Rd.)*
Clyde Tunnel G51: Glas . . . . . . . . . .2E 81
Clydevale G71: Both . . . . . . . . . . .6F 125
Clyde Valley Av. ML1: Moth . . . . .5G 143
Clydeview G71: Both . . . . . . . . . .6G 125
Clyde Vw. G82: Dumb . . . . . . . . . . .5E 17
ML3: Ham . . . . . . . . . . . . . . .2F 153
ML9: Ashg . . . . . . . . . . . . . . .5C 162
PA2: Pais . . . . . . . . . . . . . . . . .3D 98
Clyde Vw. Ct. G60: Bowl . . . . . . . . .5A 20
Clydeview La. G11: Glas . . . . . . . . .1F 81
Clydeview Shop. Cen. G72: Blan
. . . . . . . . . . . . . . . . . . . . . . . .2C 140
Clydeview Ter. G32: Carm . . . . . .5C 106
Clyde Wlk. *G67: Cumb . . . . . . . . . .4H 35*
*(in Cumbernauld Shop. Cen.)*
ML2: Newm . . . . . . . . . . . . . .3E 147
Clyde Walkway G3: Glas . . . . . . . . . .6A 4
Clyde Way *G67: Cumb . . . . . . . . . .4H 35*
*(in Cumbernauld Shop. Cen.)*
PA3: Pais . . . . . . . . . . . . . . . . .4D 78
Clydeway Ind. Est. *G3: Glas . . . . . . .3C 82*
*(off Finnieston Sq.)*
Clyde Workshops G32: Glas . . . . .4H 105
Clynder St. G51: Glas . . . . . . . . . . .5H 81
Clyth Dr. G46: Giff . . . . . . . . . . .5B 118
Coach Cl. G65: Kils . . . . . . . . . . . .3C 12
Coach Pl. G65: Kils . . . . . . . . . . . .4A 12
Coach Rd. G65: Kils . . . . . . . . . . . .4B 12
Coalburn Rd. G71: Both . . . . . . . .2F 125
Coalhall Av. ML1: Carf . . . . . . . .6A 128
Coalhill St. G31: Glas . . . . . . . . . .6D 84
Coatbank St. ML5: Coat . . . . . . . . .6D 90
Coatbank Way ML5: Coat . . . . . . . .5D 90
COATBRIDGE . . . . . . . . . . . . . . . .4C 90
Coatbridge Central Station (Rail)
. . . . . . . . . . . . . . . . . . . . . . . . .4B 90
Coatbridge College Sports Cen.
. . . . . . . . . . . . . . . . . . . . . . . . .4D 90
Coatbridge Indoor Bowling Club
. . . . . . . . . . . . . . . . . . . . . . . . .4F 91
Coatbridge Ind. Est. ML5: Coat . . .2C 90
Coatbridge Outdoor Sports Complex
. . . . . . . . . . . . . . . . . . . . . . . . .6B 90
Coatbridge Rd. G69: Bail . . . . . . . .6B 88
G69: Barg . . . . . . . . . . . . . . . . .5D 88
G69: G'csh . . . . . . . . . . . . . . . .5E 69
ML5: Coat . . . . . . . . . . . . . . . . .2D 90
ML5: Glenb . . . . . . . . . . . . . . . .4B 70
ML6: Glenm . . . . . . . . . . . . . . .2D 90
Coatbridge Sunnyside Station (Rail)
. . . . . . . . . . . . . . . . . . . . . . . . .3C 90
COATDYKE . . . . . . . . . . . . . . . . . .5F 91
Coatdyke Station (Rail) . . . . . . . . .4F 91
Coathill St. ML5: Coat . . . . . . . .1C 110
Coats Cres. G69: Bail . . . . . . . . . . .6G 87
Coats Dr. PA2: Pais . . . . . . . . . . . .2F 97
COATSHILL . . . . . . . . . . . . . . . .6A 124
Coatshill Av. G72: Blan . . . . . . . .6A 124
Coats Observatory . . . . . . . . . . . .6H 77
Coats St. ML5: Coat . . . . . . . . . . . .5D 90
Cobbett Rd. ML1: Moth . . . . . . . .4D 142
Cobblerigg Way G71: Udd . . . . . .2C 124
Cobbleton Rd. ML1: New S . . . . .5H 127
Cobden Rd. G21: Glas . . . . . . . . . .1B 84
Cobington Pl. G33: Glas . . . . . . . . .2B 86
Cobinshaw St. G32: Glas . . . . . . . .5A 86
Coburg St. G5: Glas . . . . . . . . . . . .6F 83
(Kilbarchan St.)
G5: Glas . . . . . . . . . . . . . . . . . .5F 83
(Norfolk St.)
Cochno Rd. G81: Faif . . . . . . . . . . .5F 23
G81: Hard . . . . . . . . . . . . . . . .6D 22
Cochno St. G81: Clyd . . . . . . . . . .1E 59
COCHRANE CASTLE . . . . . . . . . .5E 95
Cochrane Ct. G62: Miln . . . . . . . . .5A 26
Cochranemill Rd. PA5: John . . . . .4C 94
Cochrane Sq. PA3: Lin . . . . . . . . . .5H 75
Cochrane St. G1: Glas . . . . .4G 83 (5F 5)
G78: Barr . . . . . . . . . . . . . . .5D 114
Cochrane St. ML4: Bell . . . . . . . .2B 126
Cochran St. PA1: Pais . . . . . . . . . .1B 98
Cockburn Pl. ML5: Coat . . . . . . .1B 110
Cockels Loan PA4: Renf . . . . . . . . .2D 78
Cockenzie St. G32: Glas . . . . . . . . .6A 86
Cockerhill Rd. G52: Glas . . . . . . .4D 100
Cockhill Way ML4: Bell . . . . . . . .1H 125
Cockmuir St. G21: Glas . . . . . . . . .5C 64
Coddington Cres. ML1: Holy . . . .6H 111
Cogan Pl. G78: Barr . . . . . . . . . .5D 114
Cogan Rd. G43: Glas . . . . . . . . . .1A 118
Cogan St. G43: Glas . . . . . . . . . .6A 102
G78: Barr . . . . . . . . . . . . . . .5D 114
Colbert St. G40: Glas . . . . . . . . .1B 104
Colbreggan Ct. G81: Hard . . . . . . .1E 43
Colbreggan Gdns. G81: Hard . . . . .1E 43
Colbreggan Pl. G81: Hard . . . . . . . .1E 43
Colchester Dr. G12: Glas . . . . . . . .3G 61
Coldingham Av. G14: Glas . . . . . . .3G 59
Coldstream Cres. ML2: Wis . . . . .4A 146
Coldstream Dr. G73: Ruth . . . . . . .6F 105
PA2: Pais . . . . . . . . . . . . . . . . .4E 97
Coldstream Pl. G21: Glas . . . . . . . .6G 63
Coldstream Rd. G81: Clyd . . . . . . .6D 42
Coldstream St. G72: Blan . . . . . . .2B 140
Cole G74: E Kil . . . . . . . . . . . . . .3C 150
Colebrooke Pl. G12: Glas . . . . . . . .6C 62
Colebrooke St. G12: Glas . . . . . . . .6C 62
Colebrooke Ter. G12: Glas . . . . . . .6C 62
Colebrook St. G72: Camb . . . . . . .1A 122
Coleridge G75: E Kil . . . . . . . . . .4C 148
Coleridge Av. G71: Both . . . . . . . .4F 125
Colfin St. G34: Glas . . . . . . . . . . . .2A 88
Colgrain St. G20: Glas . . . . . . . . . .3E 63
Colgrave Cres. G32: Glas . . . . . . .2H 105
Colinbar Circ. G78: Barr . . . . . . .6D 114
Colinslee Av. PA2: Pais . . . . . . . . .4B 98
Colinslee Cres. PA2: Pais . . . . . . . .4B 98
Colinslee Dr. PA2: Pais . . . . . . . . .4B 98
Colinslie Rd. G53: Glas . . . . . . . .5D 100
Colinton Pl. G32: Glas . . . . . . . . . .4B 86
Colintraive Av. G33: Glas . . . . . . .6G 65
Colintraive Cres. G33: Glas . . . . . .6G 65
Collace Av. PA11: Bri W . . . . . . . . .4F 73
Colla Gdns. G64: B'rig . . . . . . . . . .5F 49
Coll Av. PA4: Renf . . . . . . . . . . . . .2F 79
Coll Dr. ML5: Coat . . . . . . . . . . .1H 109
College Ga. G61: Bear . . . . . . . . . .1C 44
College La. G1: Glas . . . . . .4H 83 (6H 5)
COLLEGE MILTON . . . . . . . . . . .6D 136
College St. G1: Glas . . . . . .4H 83 (6G 5)
G82: Dumb . . . . . . . . . . . . . . . .3F 17
Coll. Way Shop. Cen. G82: Dumb .4F 17
Collessie Dr. G33: Glas . . . . . . . . .1C 86
Collier St. PA5: John . . . . . . . . . . .2F 95
Colliertree Rd. ML6: Air . . . . . . . . .3D 92
Collina St. G20: Glas . . . . . . . . . . .3A 62
Collins Gallery . . . . . . . . .4H 83 (5G 5)
Collins St. G4: Glas . . . . . . .4A 84 (5H 5)
G81: Faif . . . . . . . . . . . . . . . . . .1E 43
Coll Lea ML3: Ham . . . . . . . . . . .2D 152
Coll Pl. G21: Glas . . . . . . . . . . . . .1D 84
ML6: Air . . . . . . . . . . . . . . . . . .6C 92
Collree Gdns. G34: Glas . . . . . . . . .4A 88
Coll St. G21: Glas . . . . . . . . . . . . .1D 84
ML2: Newm . . . . . . . . . . . . . .3D 146
Collylinn Rd. G61: Bear . . . . . . . . .3E 45
Colmonell Av. G13: Glas . . . . . . . .2H 59
Colonsay G74: E Kil . . . . . . . . . . .4B 150
Colonsay Av. PA4: Renf . . . . . . . . .2E 79
Colonsay Cres. ML5: Coat . . . . . .1H 109
Colonsay Dr. G77: Newt M . . . . . .4B 132
Colonsay Rd. G52: Glas . . . . . . . . .6E 81
PA2: Pais . . . . . . . . . . . . . . . . .6H 97
Colquhoun Av. G52: Hill . . . . . . . . .4A 80
Colquhoun Ct. G41: Glas . . . . . . .1A 102
Colquhoun Dr. G61: Bear . . . . . . . .2D 44
Colquhoun Pk. *G52: Hill . . . . . . . . .4B 80*
*(off Hepburn Rd.)*
Colquhoun Rd. G82: Milt . . . . . . . . .4E 19
Colquhoun St. G82: Dumb . . . . . . . .3G 17
Colson Pl. ML4: Bell . . . . . . . . . .4E 127
COLSTON . . . . . . . . . . . . . . . . . . .2A 64
Colston Av. G64: B'rig . . . . . . . . . .2B 64
Colston Dr. G64: B'rig . . . . . . . . . .2B 64
Colston Gdns. G64: B'rig . . . . . . . .2A 64
ML6: Air . . . . . . . . . . . . . . . . . .4C 92
Colston Gro. G64: B'rig . . . . . . . . .2B 64
Colston Path G64: B'rig . . . . . . . . .2A 64
Colston Pl. G64: B'rig . . . . . . . . . .2A 64
ML6: Air . . . . . . . . . . . . . . . . . .4C 92
Colston Rd. G64: B'rig . . . . . . . . . .2A 64
ML6: Air . . . . . . . . . . . . . . . . . .4C 92
Colston Ter. ML6: Air . . . . . . . . . .4C 92
Colt Av. ML5: Coat . . . . . . . . . . . .3A 90
Coltmuir Cres. G64: B'rig . . . . . . .1A 64
Coltmuir Dr. G64: B'rig . . . . . . . . .1A 64
Coltmuir Gdns. G64: B'rig . . . . . . .1A 64
Coltmuir St. G22: Glas . . . . . . . . . .3F 63
COLTNESS . . . . . . . . . . . . . . . . .3A 146
Coltness Dr. ML4: Bell . . . . . . . . .3D 126
Coltness La. G33: Glas . . . . . . . . . .4C 86
Coltness Rd. ML2: Wis . . . . . . . .3A 146
Coltness St. G33: Glas . . . . . . . . . .3C 86
Coltpark Av. G64: B'rig . . . . . . . . .1A 64
Coltpark La. G64: B'rig . . . . . . . . .1B 64
Colt Pl. ML5: Coat . . . . . . . . . . . . .3C 90
Coltsfoot Dr. G53: Glas . . . . . . . .4B 116
Coltswood Ct. ML5: Coat . . . . . . . .3C 90
Coltswood Rd. ML5: Coat . . . . . . . .2C 90
Colt Ter. ML5: Coat . . . . . . . . . . . .3C 90
Columba G81: Clyd . . . . . . . . . . . . .5F 43
Columba Cres. ML1: Moth . . . . . .5F 127
Columba Path G72: Blan . . . . . . . .1A 140
Columba Sports Complex
. . . . . . . . . . . . . . . . . . . . . . . .1C 110
Columba St. G51: Glas . . . . . . . . . .4H 81
Columbia Pl. G75: E Kil . . . . . . . .3D 148
Columbia Way G75: E Kil . . . . . . .3D 148
Columbine Way ML8: Carl . . . . . .5F 165
Colvend La. G40: Glas . . . . . . . . .2B 104
Colvend St. G40: Glas . . . . . . . . .2B 104
Colville Dr. G73: Ruth . . . . . . . . .1F 121
Colvilles Pl. G75: E Kil . . . . . . . .5B 150
Colvilles Rd. G75: E Kil . . . . . . . .6A 150
Colwood Av. G53: Glas . . . . . . . . .3A 116
Colwood Gdns. G53: Glas . . . . . . .4A 116
Colwood Path G53: Glas . . . . . . . .3A 116
Colwood Pl. G53: Glas . . . . . . . . .4A 116
Colwood Sq. G53: Glas . . . . . . . . .4A 116
Colwyn Ct. ML6: Air . . . . . . . . . . . .2A 92
COLZIUM . . . . . . . . . . . . . . . . . . .1C 12
Colzium Vw. G65: Kils . . . . . . . . . .3A 12
Combe Quad. ML4: Bell . . . . . . . .4A 126
Comedie Rd. G33: Step . . . . . . . . . .5E 67
Comely Bank ML3: Ham . . . . . . . .6D 140
Comelybank La. G82: Dumb . . . . . .3D 16
Comelybank Rd. G82: Dumb . . . . . .3D 16
Comelypark Pl. *G31: Glas . . . . . . .5C 84*
*(off Comelypark St.)*
Comelypark St. G31: Glas . . . . . . . .5B 84
Commerce St. G5: Glas . . . . . . . . . .6F 83
Commercial Ct. G5: Glas . . . . . . . . .6H 83
Commercial Rd. G78: Barr . . . . . .4E 115
Common Grn. ML3: Ham . . . . . . .5A 142
Commonhead Av. ML6: Air . . . . . .2H 91
Commonhead La. ML6: Air . . . . . .2H 91
Commonhead Rd. G34: Glas . . . . . .3B 88
Commonhead St. ML6: Air . . . . . . .2H 91
Commonside St. ML6: Air . . . . . . . .2H 91
Commore Av. G78: Barr . . . . . . . .6F 115
Commore Dr. G13: Glas . . . . . . . . .2A 60
Commore Pl. G78: Neil . . . . . . . . .3C 130
Community Av. ML4: Bell . . . . . . .5C 126
Community Pl. ML4: Bell . . . . . . .4D 126
Community Rd. ML4: Bell . . . . . . .4B 126
Comrie Cres. ML3: Ham . . . . . . . .6B 140
Comrie Rd. G33: Step . . . . . . . . . . .4C 66
Comrie St. G32: Glas . . . . . . . . . .2B 106
Conan Ct. G72: Camb . . . . . . . . . .2D 122
Cona St. G46: T'bnk . . . . . . . . . .3E 117
Condor Glen ML1: Holy . . . . . . . .6G 111
CONDORRAT . . . . . . . . . . . . . . . . .6C 34
CONDORRAT INTERCHANGE . . . .5D 34
Condorrat Ring Rd.
G67: Cumb . . . . . . . . . . . . . . . .6D 34
Condorrat Rd. G67: Cumb . . . . . . . .4D 54
ML6: Glenm . . . . . . . . . . . . . . .1F 71
Coneypark Cres. FK4: Bank . . . . . .1C 14
Coneypark Pl. FK4: Bank . . . . . . . .1C 14
Congress Rd. G3: Glas . . . . . . . . . .4B 82
Congress Way G3: Glas . . . . . . . . .4C 82
Conifer Pl. G66: Lenz . . . . . . . . . . .1B 50
Conisborough Path G34: Glas . . . . .1F 87
Conisborough Rd. G34: Glas . . . . . .1F 87
Coniston G75: E Kil . . . . . . . . . . .6B 148
Coniston Cres. ML3: Ham . . . . . . .5G 153
Coniston Dr. ML4: Bell . . . . . . . . .4D 126
Conistone Cres. G69: Bail . . . . . . .1F 107
Connal St. G40: Glas . . . . . . . . . .2D 104
Connell Cres. G62: Miln . . . . . . . . .4A 26
Conniston St. G32: Glas . . . . . . . . .4G 85
Connor Rd. G78: Barr . . . . . . . . . .4D 114
Connor St. ML6: Air . . . . . . . . . . . .2E 93

# Conolly's Land—Craigton Ind. Est.

Conolly's Land G81: Hard . . . . . . . .1C 42
(off Dumbarton Rd.)
Conon Av. G61: Bear . . . . . . . . . . .4C 44
Conservation Pl. ML2: Wis . . . . .1H 157
Consett La. G33: Glas . . . . . . . . . .3C 86
Consett St. G33: Glas . . . . . . . . . .3C 86
Constarry Rd. G65: Croy . . . . . . . .6A 12
Contin Pl. G20: Glas . . . . . . . . . . .4B 62
Convair Way PA4: Renf . . . . . . . .2F 79
Conval Way PA3: Pais . . . . . . . . .3H 77
Cook St. G5: Glas . . . . . . . . . . . . .6E 83
Coolgardie Grn. G75: E Kil . . . . .4E 149
Coolgardie Pl. G75: E Kil . . . . . .4E 149
Cooperage Pl. G3: Glas . . . . . . . .3A 82
Co-operative Ter. PA5: John . . . .2G 95
Cooper Av. ML8: Carl . . . . . . . . .2E 165
Cooper's Well St. G11: Glas . . . . .2A 82
Copenhagen Av. G75: E Kil . . . . .5G 149
Copland Pl. G51: Glas . . . . . . . . .5H 81
Copland Quad. G51: Glas . . . . . .5H 81
Copland Rd. G51: Glas . . . . . . . . .6H 81
Coplaw Ct. G42: Glas . . . . . . . . .2E 103
Coplaw St. G42: Glas . . . . . . . . .2E 103
Copperfield La. G71: Tann . . . . . .6E 109
Coral Mt. Gdns. G66: Kirk . . . . . .6E 31
Corbett Ct. G32: Glas . . . . . . . . .2H 105
Corbett St. G32: Glas . . . . . . . . .2H 105
Corbie Pl. G62: Miln . . . . . . . . . .3D 24
Corbiston Way G67: Cumb . . . . . .3B 36
Cordiner St. G44: Glas . . . . . . . . .6F 103
CORKERHILL . . . . . . . . . . . . . . .3D 100
Corkerhill Gdns. G52: Glas . . . . .1E 101
Corkerhill Pl. G52: Glas . . . . . . . .3D 100
Corkerhill Rd. G52: Glas . . . . . . .2D 100
Corkerhill Station (Rail) . . . . . . . .3D 100
Corlaich Av. G42: Glas . . . . . . . . .6A 104
Corlaich Dr. G42: Glas . . . . . . . . .6A 104
Cormack Av. G64: Torr . . . . . . . . .4E 29
Cormorant Av. PA6: C'lee . . . . . .3D 74
Cornaig Rd. G53: Glas . . . . . . . . .5B 100
Cornalee Gdns. G53: Glas . . . . . .5A 100
Cornalee Pl. G53: Glas . . . . . . . . .5A 100
(not continuous)
Cornalee Rd. G53: Glas . . . . . . . .5B 100
Cornelian Ter. ML4: Bell . . . . . . .3C 126
Cornelia St. ML1: Moth . . . . . . . .6D 126
Cornhill Dr. ML5: Coat . . . . . . . . .3A 90
Cornhill St. G21: Glas . . . . . . . . .4C 64
Cornish Ct. ML5: Coat . . . . . . . . .3B 90
Cornock Cres. G81: Clyd . . . . . . .4D 42
Cornock St. G81: Clyd . . . . . . . . .4D 42
Cornsilloch Brae ML9: Lark . . . . .2B 162
Corn St. G4: Glas . . . . . . . .1F 83 (1C 4)
Cornwall Av. G73: Ruth . . . . . . . .2F 121
Cornwall Ct. G74: E Kil . . . . . . . .2H 149
Cornwall St. G41: Glas . . . . . . . . .6B 82
G74: E Kil . . . . . . . . . . . . . . . .2F 149
Cornwall St. Sth. G41: Glas . . . . .6B 82
Cornwall Way G74: E Kil . . . . . . .2H 149
Coronation Av. ML9: Lark . . . . . .5E 161
Coronation Cres. ML9: Lark . . . . .5E 161
Coronation Pl. G69: G'csh . . . . . .2C 68
ML9: Lark . . . . . . . . . . . . . . .5F 161
Coronation Rd. ML1: New S . . . .3H 127
Coronation Rd. E.
ML1: New S . . . . . . . . . . . . .4H 127
Coronation St. ML2: Wis . . . . . . .6B 146
Coronation Way G61: Bear . . . . . .5F 45
Corpach Pl. G34: Glas . . . . . . . . .2B 88
Corporation Yd. G15: Glas . . . . . .4H 43
Corra Linn ML3: Ham . . . . . . . . .6E 141
Corran Av. G77: Newt M . . . . . . .3C 132
Corran St. G33: Glas . . . . . . . . . .3H 85
Correen Gdns. G61: Bear . . . . . . .6B 24
Corrie Brae G65: Kils . . . . . . . . . .2G 11
Corrie Ct. ML3: Ham . . . . . . . . .1D 152
Corrie Dr. ML1: Moth . . . . . . . . .2D 142
PA1: Pais . . . . . . . . . . . . . . . .1G 99
Corrie Gro. G44: Neth . . . . . . . . .3D 118
Corrie Pl. G66: Lenz . . . . . . . . . .3E 51
Corrie Rd. G65: Kils . . . . . . . . . . .2G 11
Corrie Vw. G68: Cumb . . . . . . . . .5B 34
Corrie Vw. Cotts. G65: Twe . . . . .1C 32
Corrie Way ML9: Lark . . . . . . . . .3F 161
Corrour Rd. G43: Glas . . . . . . . . .6B 102
G77: Newt M . . . . . . . . . . . .3C 132
Corsebar Av. PA2: Pais . . . . . . . .3G 97
Corsebar Cres. PA2: Pais . . . . . .4G 97
Corsebar Dr. PA2: Pais . . . . . . . .3G 97
Corsebar La. PA2: Pais . . . . . . . .4F 97
Corsebar Rd. PA2: Pais . . . . . . . .4F 97
Corsebar Way PA2: Pais . . . . . . .2G 97
CORSEFORD . . . . . . . . . . . . . . . .6B 94
Corseford Av. PA5: John . . . . . . .5C 94
Corsehill Path G34: Glas . . . . . . .3A 88
Corsehill Pl. G34: Glas . . . . . . . . .3A 88
Corsehill St. G34: Glas . . . . . . . . .3A 88
Corselet Rd. G53: Glas . . . . . . . .4A 116
G78: Barr . . . . . . . . . . . . . . .1A 132
Corse Rd. G52: Glas . . . . . . . . . . .5G 79

Corsewall Av. G32: Glas . . . . . . .2E 107
Corsewall St. ML5: Coat . . . . . . .4A 90
Corsford Dr. G53: Glas . . . . . . . .1C 116
Corsock Av. ML3: Ham . . . . . . . .1C 152
Corston St. G33: Glas . . . . . . . . . .3F 85
Cortachy Pl. G64: B'rig . . . . . . . . .6F 49
Coruisk Dr. G76: Clar . . . . . . . . .1B 134
Coruisk Way PA2: Pais . . . . . . . .5C 96
Corunna Ct. ML8: Carl . . . . . . . .4H 165
Corunna St. G3: Glas . . . . . . . . . .3C 82
Coshneuk Rd. G33: Mille . . . . . . .4B 66
Cosy Neuk ML9: Lark . . . . . . . . .4G 161
Cottar St. G20: Glas . . . . . . . . . . .2C 62
Cotton Av. PA3: Lin . . . . . . . . . . .6H 75
Cotton St. G40: Glas . . . . . . . . . .3C 104
PA1: Pais . . . . . . . . . . . . . . . .1B 98
Cotton St. Ent. Pk. G40: Glas . . .3B 104
Cotton Va. ML1: Cle . . . . . . . . . .1E 145
Coulin Gdns. G22: Glas . . . . . . . .5H 63
Coulter Av. ML2: Wis . . . . . . . . .2A 146
ML5: Coat . . . . . . . . . . . . . . .3A 90
Countess Way G69: Barg . . . . . . .6E 89
(off Princess Dr.)
County Av. G72: Camb . . . . . . . . .6F 105
County Pl. PA1: Pais . . . . . . . . . . .6A 78
County Sq. PA1: Pais . . . . . . . . . .6A 78
Couper Pl. G4: Glas . . . . . .2H 83 (2G 5)
Couper St. G4: Glas . . . . . .2H 83 (2G 5)
Coursington Cres. ML1: Moth . . . .2A 144
Coursington Gdns.
ML1: Moth . . . . . . . . . . . . . .2H 143
Coursington Pl. ML1: Moth . . . . .2H 143
Coursington Rd. ML1: Moth . . . . .2H 143
(not continuous)
Coursington Twr. ML1: Moth . . . .2H 143
(off Coursington Rd.)
Courthill G61: Bear . . . . . . . . . . .1D 44
Court Hill G65: Kils . . . . . . . . . . . .3A 12
Courthill Av. G44: Glas . . . . . . . .2F 119
Courthill Cres. G65: Kils . . . . . . . .3A 12
Coustonholm Rd. G43: Glas . . . . .6B 102
Couther Quad. ML6: Air . . . . . . . .1A 92
Covanburn Av. ML3: Ham . . . . . .2B 154
Covenant Cres. ML9: Lark . . . . . .3F 161
Covenanters Way
ML2: Over . . . . . . . . . . . . . . .5A 158
Covenany Pl. ML2: Wis . . . . . . . .1C 156
Coventry Dr. G31: Glas . . . . . . . .3D 84
Cowal Cres. G66: Kirk . . . . . . . . .4H 31
Cowal Dr. PA3: Lin . . . . . . . . . . . .6G 75
Cowal St. G20: Glas . . . . . . . . . . .2A 62
Cowal Vw. G81: Clyd . . . . . . . . . .4D 42
Cowan Cres. G78: Barr . . . . . . . .4F 115
Cowan La. G12: Glas . . . . . . . . . .1C 82
(off Glasgow St.)
Cowan Rd. G68: Cumb . . . . . . . . .3D 34
Cowan St. G12: Glas . . . . . . . . . . .1C 82
Cowan Wilson Av. G72: Blan . . . .1B 140
Cowan Wynd G71: Tann . . . . . . . .5E 109
ML2: Over . . . . . . . . . . . . . . .4A 158
COWCADDENS . . . . . . . .2F 83 (1E 5)
Cowcaddens Rd.
G4: Glas . . . . . . . . . . . . .2F 83 (2C 4)
Cowcaddens Station (Und.)
. . . . . . . . . . . . . . . . . .2F 83 (2C 4)
Cowden Dr. G64: B'rig . . . . . . . . .4C 48
Cowdenhill Cir. G13: Glas . . . . . .1D 60
Cowdenhill Pl. G13: Glas . . . . . . .1D 60
Cowdenhill Rd. G13: Glas . . . . . .1D 60
Cowden St. G51: Glas . . . . . . . . .4D 80
Cowdray Cres. PA4: Renf . . . . . . .6F 59
Cowgate G66: Kirk . . . . . . . . . . . .4C 30
Cowglen Rd. G53: Glas . . . . . . . .6C 100
COWLAIRS . . . . . . . . . . . . . . . . .5A 64
Cowlairs Ind. Est. G21: Glas . . . .5H 63
Cowlairs Rd. G21: Glas . . . . . . . . .5A 64
(off Kemp St.)
G21: Glas . . . . . . . . . . . . . . . .5A 64
(Millarbank St.)
Coxdale Av. G66: Kirk . . . . . . . . .5B 30
Coxhill St. G21: Glas . . . . . . . . . .6H 63
Coxton Pl. G33: Glas . . . . . . . . . .2D 86
Coylton Cres. ML3: Ham . . . . . . .2C 152
Coylton Rd. G43: Glas . . . . . . . . .2C 118
Crabb Quad. ML1: Moth . . . . . . .6E 127
Cragdale G74: E Kil . . . . . . . . . . .6E 137
Craggan Dr. G14: Glas . . . . . . . . .3H 59
Crags Av. PA2: Pais . . . . . . . . . . .4B 98
Crags Cres. PA2: Pais . . . . . . . . .3B 98
Crags Rd. PA2: Pais . . . . . . . . . . .4B 98
Cragwell Pk. G76: Crmck . . . . . . .2A 136
Craigallan Av. G72: Camb . . . . . .3D 122
Craiganour La. G43: Glas . . . . . . .1A 118
Craiganour Pl. G43: Glas . . . . . . .1A 118
Craigard Pl. G73: Ruth . . . . . . . . .4F 121
Craigash Quad. G62: Miln . . . . . .2E 25
Craigash Rd. G62: Miln . . . . . . . .3E 25
Craigbank Dr. G53: Glas . . . . . . .1A 116

Craigbank Rd. ML9: Lark . . . . . . .5E 161
Craigbank St. ML9: Lark . . . . . . .4E 161
Craigbanzo St. G81: Faif . . . . . . .5F 23
Craigbarnet Av. G64: Torr . . . . . . .5C 28
Craigbarnet Cres. G33: Mille . . . .5B 66
Craigbarnet Rd. G62: Miln . . . . . .3D 24
Craigbet Av. PA11: Q'riers . . . . . .1A 72
Craigbet Cres. PA11: Q'riers . . . .1A 72
Craigbet Pl. PA11: Q'riers . . . . . .1A 72
Craigbo Av. G23: Glas . . . . . . . . .6B 46
Craigbo Ct. G23: Glas . . . . . . . . .1B 62
Craigbo Dr. G23: Glas . . . . . . . . .6B 46
Craigbog Av. PA5: John . . . . . . . .4D 94
Craigbog Rd. PA5: John . . . . . . . .5F 95
Craigbo Pl. G23: Glas . . . . . . . . .1B 62
Craigbo Rd. G23: Glas . . . . . . . . .1B 62
Craigbo St. G23: Glas . . . . . . . . .6B 46
Craigburn Av. PA6: C'lee . . . . . . .3D 74
Craigburn Ct. ML9: Ashg . . . . . . .4B 162
Craigburn Cres. PA6: C'lee . . . . .4D 74
Craigburn Pl. PA6: C'lee . . . . . . .4D 74
Craigburn St. ML3: Ham . . . . . . .3H 153
Craig Cres. G66: Kirk . . . . . . . . . .6H 31
(off Bk. o'Dykes Rd.)
Craigdhu Av. G62: Miln . . . . . . . .4F 25
ML6: Air . . . . . . . . . . . . . . . .4E 93
Craigdhu Farm Cotts. G62: Miln . .4E 25
Craigdhu Rd. G61: Bear . . . . . . . .5D 24
(not continuous)
Craigdonald Pl. PA5: John . . . . . .2F 95
Craigellan Rd. G43: Glas . . . . . . .1B 118
Craigelvan Av. G67: Cumb . . . . . .1B 54
Craigelvan Ct. G67: Cumb . . . . . .1B 54
Craigelvan Dr. G67: Cumb . . . . . .1B 54
Craigelvan Gdns. G67: Cumb . . . .1B 54
Craigelvan Gro. G67: Cumb . . . . .1B 54
Craigelvan Pl. G67: Cumb . . . . . .1B 54
Craigelvan Vw. G67: Cumb . . . . .1B 54
Craigenbay Cres. G66: Lenz . . . . .2E 51
Craigenbay Rd. G66: Lenz . . . . . .3D 50
Craigenbay St. G21: Glas . . . . . . .5D 64
Craigencart Ct. G81: Dun . . . . . . .1B 42
CRAIGEND . . . . . . . . . . . . . . . . . .6C 66
Craigend Cres. G62: Miln . . . . . . .3F 25
Craigend Dr. ML5: Coat . . . . . . . .1G 109
Craigend Dr. W. G62: Miln . . . . . .3E 25
Craigend Ho. G82: Dumb . . . . . . .3C 16
CRAIGENDMUIR . . . . . . . . . . . . .5E 67
Craigendmuir Cvn. Site
G33: Step . . . . . . . . . . . . . . .5E 67
Craigendmuir Rd. G33: Step . . . . .5E 67
Craigendmuir St. G33: Glas . . . . .1F 85
Craigendon Oval PA2: Pais . . . . .6G 97
Craigendon Rd. PA2: Pais . . . . . .6G 97
Craigend Pl. G13: Glas . . . . . . . . .3E 61
Craigend Rd. G67: Cumb . . . . . . .2B 54
CRAIGENDS . . . . . . . . . . . . . . . .3D 74
Craigends Av. PA11: Q'riers . . . . .1A 72
Craigends Dr. PA10: Kilb . . . . . . .2A 94
Craigends Pl. PA11: Q'riers . . . . .1A 72
Craigends Rd. PA6: C'lee, Hous . .4D 74
Craigend St. G13: Glas . . . . . . . . .3E 61
Craigend Vw. G67: Cumb . . . . . . .2B 54
Craigenfeoch Av. PA5: John . . . . .4D 94
Craigens Rd. ML6: Gart . . . . . . . .6F 93
Craigfaulds Av. PA2: Pais . . . . . .3F 97
Craigfell Ct. ML3: Ham . . . . . . . .1C 152
Craigflower Av. G53: Glas . . . . . .3A 116
Craigflower Gdns. G53: Glas . . . .3A 116
Craigflower Rd. G53: Glas . . . . . .4A 116
Craig Gdns. G77: Newt M . . . . . .5C 132
Craighalbert Rd. G68: Cumb . . . . .2E 35
(not continuous)
CRAIGHALBERT RDBT. . . . . . . . .1E 35
Craighalbert Way G68: Cumb . . . .1E 35
Craighall Quad. G78: Neil . . . . . .3D 130
Craighall Rd. G4: Glas . . . . .1F 83 (1D 4)
Craighaw St. G81: Faif . . . . . . . . .5F 23
CRAIGHEAD . . . . . . . . . . . . . . . .1E 141
Craighead Av. G33: Glas . . . . . . .6F 65
G66: Milt C . . . . . . . . . . . . . .5C 8
Craighead Dr. G62: Miln . . . . . . . .3D 24
Craighead Rd. G66: Milt C . . . . . .5C 8
PA7: B'ton . . . . . . . . . . . . . . .5H 39
Craighead St. G78: Barr . . . . . . . .5D 114
ML6: Air . . . . . . . . . . . . . . . .3E 93
Craighead Way G78: Barr . . . . . . .5D 114
(not continuous)
Craig Hill G75: E Kil . . . . . . . . . . .4E 149
Craighill Dr. G76: Clar . . . . . . . . .3B 134
Craighill Gro. G76: Clar . . . . . . . .3B 134
Craigholme PA6: Hous . . . . . . . . .1D 74
Craighouse St. G33: Glas . . . . . . .2A 86
Craighton Gdns. G66: Len . . . . . .3H 7
Craighurst Dr. G81: Dun, Hard . . .6C 22
Craighurst Rd. G62: Miln . . . . . . .3D 24
Craigiebar Dr. PA2: Pais . . . . . . . .5G 97
Craigieburn Gdns. G20: Glas . . . .1H 61
Craigieburn Rd. G67: Cumb . . . . .4H 35
Craigie Dr. G77: Newt M . . . . . . .6E 133

Craigiehall Av. PA8: Ersk . . . . . . .2E 5
Craigiehall Cres. PA8: Ersk . . . . .2E 5
Craigiehall Pl. G51: Glas . . . . . . .5B 82
Craigiehall St. G51: Glas . . . . . . .5C 82
Craigiehall Way PA8: Ersk . . . . . .2E 5
Craigie La. ML9: Lark . . . . . . . . . .1F 16
(off Duncan Graham St.)
Craigielea Ct. PA4: Renf . . . . . . . .5E 59
Craigielea Cres. G62: Miln . . . . . .3E 25
Craigielea Dr. PA3: Pais . . . . . . . .5F 7
Craigielea Pk. PA4: Renf . . . . . . .6E 59
Craigielea Rd. G81: Dun . . . . . . . .6A 22
PA4: Renf . . . . . . . . . . . . . . .6E 5
Craigielinn Av. PA2: Pais . . . . . . .6F 9
Craigie Pk. G66: Lenz . . . . . . . . . .2E 5
Craigie St. G42: Glas . . . . . . . . . .3E 103
Craigievar Pl. G77: Newt M . . . . .4B 132
Craigievar St. G33: Glas . . . . . . . .1E 87
Craiglea Pl. ML6: Air . . . . . . . . . .3C 9
Craiglea Ter. ML6: Plain . . . . . . . .1F 93
Craiglee G75: E Kil . . . . . . . . . . .6G 149
Craigleith St. G32: Glas . . . . . . . .5G 85
CRAIGLINN . . . . . . . . . . . . . . . . . .4B 3
Craiglinn Pk. Rd. G68: Cumb . . . .4C 34
CRAIGLINN RDBT. . . . . . . . . . . . .4C 34
Craiglockhart St. G33: Glas . . . . .1D 80
Craigmaddie Gdns. G64: Torr . . . .5C 28
Craigmaddie Rd.
G62: Balder, Bard . . . . . . . . .3D 20
Craigmaddie Ter. La. G3: Glas . . .2C 8
(off Derby St.)
CRAIGMARLOCH . . . . . . . . . . . . .1E 35
Craigmarloch Av. G64: Torr . . . . .5D 2
CRAIGMARLOCH RDBT. . . . . . . .2E 35
Craigmillar Av. G62: Miln . . . . . . .3H 25
Craigmillar Rd. G42: Glas . . . . . .6E 103
Craigmochan Av. ML6: Air . . . . . .1H 91
Craigmont Dr. G20: Glas . . . . . . .3C 62
Craigmont St. G20: Glas . . . . . . .3C 62
Craigmore Pl. ML5: Coat . . . . . . .2A 110
Craigmore Rd. G61: Bear . . . . . . .6B 24
Craigmore St. G31: Glas . . . . . . .5E 85
Craigmore Wynd ML9: Lark . . . . .1F 16
(off Carrick Pl.)
Craigmount Av. PA2: Pais . . . . . . .6G 97
Craigmount St. G66: Kirk . . . . . . .6D 30
Craigmuir Cres. G52: Glas . . . . . .5H 79
Craigmuir Gdns. G72: Blan . . . . . .3H 139
Craigmuir Pl. G52: Glas . . . . . . . .5G 79
Craigmuir Rd. G52: Glas . . . . . . .5G 79
G72: Blan . . . . . . . . . . . . . . .3H 139
Craigneil St. G33: Glas . . . . . . . . .1E 87
Craigneith Castle (Ruins) . . . . . . .6E 139
Craigneith Ct. G74: E Kil . . . . . . .5E 139
Craignethan Rd. G46: Giff . . . . . .2G 133
ML8: Carl . . . . . . . . . . . . . . .2E 165
CRAIGNEUK
Airdrie . . . . . . . . . . . . . . . . . . .4D 92
Wishaw . . . . . . . . . . . . . . . . .5D 144
Craigneuk Av. ML6: Air . . . . . . . .5C 92
Craigneuk St. ML1: Moth . . . . . . .4B 144
ML2: Wis . . . . . . . . . . . . . . .4B 144
Craignure Cres. ML6: Air . . . . . . .4E 93
Craignure Rd. G73: Ruth . . . . . . .4D 120
Craigpark G31: Glas . . . . . . . . . . .4C 84
Craigpark Dr. G31: Glas . . . . . . . .4C 84
Craigpark St. G81: Faif . . . . . . . . .6F 23
Craigpark Ter. G31: Glas . . . . . . .4C 84
(off Craigpark)
Craigpark Way G71: Tann . . . . . . .6E 109
Craig Pl. G77: Newt M . . . . . . . . .1D 130
Craig Rd. G44: Glas . . . . . . . . . . .2E 119
G78: Neil . . . . . . . . . . . . . . . .3D 130
PA3: Lin . . . . . . . . . . . . . . . . .4F 75
Craigs Av. G81: Faif, Hard . . . . . .1E 43
Craigsheen Av. G76: Crmck . . . . .2H 135
Craigside Ct. G68: Cumb . . . . . . .6B 34
Craigside Pl. G68: Cumb . . . . . . .6B 34
Craigside Rd. G68: Cumb . . . . . . .6B 34
Craigson Pl. ML6: Air . . . . . . . . . .5F 93
Craigstone Vw. G65: Kils . . . . . . .3B 12
Craigston Pl. PA5: John . . . . . . . .3F 95
Craigston Rd. PA5: John . . . . . . .3E 95
Craig St. G72: Blan . . . . . . . . . . .3C 140
ML5: Coat . . . . . . . . . . . . . . .1B 110
ML6: Air . . . . . . . . . . . . . . . .4H 91
Craigthornhill Rd. ML3: Ham . . . .6A 160
CRAIGTON . . . . . . . . . . . . . . . . .6D 80
Craigton Av. G62: Miln . . . . . . . . .3F 25
G78: Barr . . . . . . . . . . . . . . .6G 115
Craigton Cl. G77: Newt M . . . . . .6C 83
Craigton Cotts. G62: Miln . . . . . . .1C 24
Craigton Crematorium
G52: Glas . . . . . . . . . . . . . . .6D 80
Craigton Dr. G51: Glas . . . . . . . . .5F 81
G77: Newt M . . . . . . . . . . . .4C 132
G78: Barr . . . . . . . . . . . . . . .6G 115
Craigton Gdns. G62: Miln . . . . . . .2E 25
Craigton Ind. Est. G52: Glas . . . . .6D 80

Culzean Dr.—Deerdykes Vw.


Culzean Dr. G32: Glas 1D 106
G74: E Kil 6F 137
ML1: Carf 4C 128
Culzean Pl. G74: E Kil 6F 137
Cumberland Pl. G5: Glas 1G 103
ML5: Coat 6G 89
Cumberland St. G5: Glas 6F 83
(not continuous)
CUMBERNAULD 4H 35
Cumbernauld Mus. 4H 35
Cumbernauld Rd.
FK4: C'cry, Longc 1F 15
G31: Glas 4D 84
G33: Glas 4D 84
G33: Mille, Step 5A 66
G33: Step 2G 67
G67: Mollin 3H 53
G68: Mollin 1C 68
G69: Chry 2G 67
G69: Mood 1C 68
G69: Muirh 2A 68
CUMBERNAULD RD. INTERCHANGE 1G 85
Cumbernauld Shop. Cen., The
G67: Cumb 3H 35
Cumbernauld Station (Rail) 5A 36
Cumbernauld Theatre 1B 36
CUMBERNAULD VILLAGE 6B 14
Cumbrae G74: E Kil 2C 150
Cumbrae Ct. G81: Clyd 5D 42
Cumbrae Cres. ML5: Coat 6G 91
Cumbrae Cres. Nth.
G82: Dumb 2C 16
Cumbrae Cres. Sth. G82: Dumb 2B 16
Cumbrae Dr. ML1: Moth 1E 143
Cumbrae Pl. ML5: Coat 1G 111
Cumbrae Rd. PA2: Pais 6A 98
PA4: Renf 2F 79
Cumbrae St. G33: Glas 3A 86
Cumlodden Dr. G20: Glas 2A 62
Cumming Dr. G42: Glas 5F 103
Cummock Dr. G78: Barr 6F 115
Cumnock Dr. ML3: Ham 2B 152
ML6: Air 1A 112
Cumnock Rd. G33: Glas 3G 65
Cumroch Rd. G66: Len 2E 7
Cunard Ct. G81: Clyd 1D 58
Cunard St. G81: Clyd 1D 58
Cunningair Dr. ML1: Moth 5G 143
Cunningham Dr. G46: Giff 4C 118
G81: Dun 1B 42
Cunninghame Rd. G73: Ruth 5E 105
G74: E Kil 2G 149
PA10: Kilb 2B 94
Cunningham Gdns. PA6: C'lee 2D 74
Cunningham Rd. G52: Hill 3H 79
Cunningham St. ML1: Moth 3F 143
Cuparhead Av. ML5: Coat 1H 109
Curfew Rd. G13: Glas 6D 44
Curle St. G14: Glas 1D 80
(not continuous)
Curlew Pl. PA5: John 6C 94
Curling Cres. G44: Glas 6G 103
Curlinghaugh Cres. ML2: Wis 6A 146
Curlingmire G75: E Kil 5G 149
Curran Av. ML2: Wis 2E 157
Currie Ct. *PA5: John 4E 95*
*(off Tannahill Cres.)*
Currie Pl. G20: Glas 3C 62
Currie St. G20: Glas 3C 62
Curtis Av. G44: Glas 5G 103
Curzon St. G20: Glas 3C 62
Cuthbertson St. G42: Glas 2E 103
Cuthbert St. G71: View 6F 109
Cuthelton Dr. G31: Glas 1G 105
Cuthelton St. G31: Glas 1F 105
Cuthelton Ter. G31: Glas 1F 105
Cut, The G71: Udd 2D 124
Cypress Av. G71: View 5F 109
G72: Blan 6A 124
Cypress Ct. G66: Lenz 1B 50
G75: E Kil 6E 149
ML3: Ham 1A 154
Cypress Cres. G75: E Kil 6E 149
Cypress Pl. G75: E Kil 6E 149
Cypress St. G22: Glas 4H 63
Cypress Way G72: Flem 3F 123
Cyprus Av. PA5: Eld 3H 95
Cyril St. PA1: Pais 1C 98

## D

Daer Av. PA4: Renf 2G 79
Daer Wlk. ML9: Lark 5E 161
Daer Way ML3: Ham 6E 141
Daffodil Way ML1: Moth 1G 143
Dairsie Ct. G44: Glas 3D 118
Dairsie Gdns. G64: B'rig 1F 65
Dairsie St. G44: Glas 3D 118
Daisy St. G42: Glas 4F 103
Dakala Ct. ML2: Wis 1G 157
Dakota Way PA4: Renf 2F 79
Dalbeattie Braes ML6: Chap 4E 113
DALBETH 3G 105
Dalbeth Pl. G32: Glas 3H 105
Dalbeth Rd. G32: Glas 3H 105
Dalcharn Path *G34: Glas 3G 87*
*(off Kildermorie Rd.)*
Dalcharn Pl. G34: Glas 3G 87
Dalcraig Cres. G72: Blan 5A 124
Dalcross Pass *G11: Glas 1A 82*
*(off Dalcross St.)*
Dalcross St. G11: Glas 1A 82
Dalcruin Gdns. G69: Mood 3E 53
Daldowie Av. G32: Glas 2D 106
Daldowie Complex, The (Land Services)
G71: Udd 5G 107
Daldowie Crematorium
G71: Udd 5H 107
DALDOWIE INTERCHANGE 4H 107
Daldowie Rd. G71: Udd 3G 107
Daldowie St. ML5: Coat 2A 110
(not continuous)
Dale Av. G75: E Kil 4E 149
Dale Ct. ML2: Wis 1C 156
Dale Dr. ML1: New S 3A 128
Dale Path *G40: Glas 1B 104*
*(off Main St.)*
Dale St. G40: Glas 1B 104
(not continuous)
Daleview Av. G12: Glas 3H 61
Daleview Dr. G76: Clar 3B 134
Daleview Gro. G76: Clar 3B 134
Dale Way G73: Ruth 3D 120
Dalfoil Ct. PA1: Pais 1H 99
Dalgarroch Av. G81: Clyd 1G 59
Dalgleish Av. G81: Dun 1A 42
Dalhousie Gdns. G64: B'rig 5B 48
Dalhousie La. G3: Glas 2E 83 (2B 4)
Dalhousie Rd. PA10: Kilb 3B 94
Dalhousie St. G3: Glas 3E 83 (3B 4)
(not continuous)
Dalilea Dr. G34: Glas 2B 88
Dalilea Path *G34: Glas 2B 88*
*(off Dalilea Dr.)*
Dalilea Pl. G34: Glas 2B 88
Dalintober St. G5: Glas 5E 83
Dalkeith Av. G41: Glas 1H 101
G64: B'rig 4D 48
Dalkeith Rd. G64: B'rig 3D 48
Dalmacoulter Rd. ML6: Air 1B 92
Dalmahoy Cres. PA11: Bri W 5D 72
Dalmahoy St. G32: Glas 4G 85
Dalmally St. G20: Glas 6D 62
DALMARNOCK 2D 104
Dalmarnock Bri. G73: Ruth 3D 104
Dalmarnock Ct. G40: Glas 2D 104
Dalmarnock Dr. G40: Glas 1B 104
Dalmarnock Rd. G40: Glas 1B 104
G73: Ruth 3D 104
Dalmarnock Rd. Ind. Est.
G73: Ruth 4D 104
Dalmarnock Station (Rail) 2C 104
Dalmary Dr. PA1: Pais 5D 78
Dalmellington Ct. *G74: E Kil 1F 149*
*(off Dalmellington Dr.)*
ML3: Ham 2B 152
Dalmellington Dr. G53: Glas 5A 100
G74: E Kil 1F 149
Dalmellington Rd. G53: Glas 4A 100
Dalmeny Av. G46: Giff 4A 118
Dalmeny Dr. G78: Barr 5C 114
Dalmeny Rd. ML3: Ham 1H 153
Dalmeny St. G5: Glas 3A 104
Dalmoor Dr. ML6: Air 5A 92
DALMUIR 4A 42
Dalmuir Ct. G81: Clyd 4A 42
Dalmuir Station (Rail) 4A 42
Dalnair Pl. G62: Miln 3D 24
Dalnair St. G3: Glas 2A 82
Dalness Pas. *G32: Glas 1A 106*
*(off Ochil St.)*
Dalness St. G32: Glas 2A 106
Dalnottar Av. G60: Old K 1F 41
Dalnottar Dr. G60: Old K 2F 41
Dalnottar Gdns. G60: Old K 2F 41
Dalnottar Hill Rd. G60: Old K 1F 41
Dalnottar Ter. G60: Old K 1F 41
DALREOCH 3D 16
Dalreoch Av. G69: Bail 6A 88
Dalreoch Ct. G82: Dumb 3D 16
Dalreoch Ho. *G82: Dumb 3D 16*
*(off School La.)*
Dalreoch Path G69: Bail 6A 88
Dalreoch Station (Rail) 3E 17
Dalriada Cres. ML1: Moth 5F 127
Dalriada Dr. G64: Torr 5E 29
Dalriada St. G40: Glas 1E 105
Dalry Gdns. ML3: Ham 1B 152
Dalrymple Ct. G66: Kirk 6D 30
Dalrymple Dr. G74: E Kil 6G 137
G77: Newt M 5G 133
ML5: Coat 6B 90
Dalry Pl. ML6: Chap 5D 112
Dalry Rd. G71: View 6F 109
Dalry St. G32: Glas 1B 106
DALSERF 3D 162
Dalserf Ct. G31: Glas 6D 84
Dalserf Cres. G46: Giff 6H 117
Dalserf Gdns. G31: Glas 6D 84
Dalserf Path *ML9: Lark 4G 161*
*(off Bannockburn Dr.)*
Dalserf St. G31: Glas 6D 84
Dalsetter Av. G15: Glas 5H 43
Dalsetter Pl. G15: Glas 5A 44
DALSHANNON 1B 54
Dalshannon Pl. G67: Cumb 6C 34
Dalshannon Rd. G67: Cumb 6D 34
Dalshannon Vw. G67: Cumb 6C 34
Dalshannon Way G67: Cumb 6C 34
Dalsholm Av. G20: Glas 1H 61
Dalsholm Ind. Est. G20: Glas 2H 61
Dalsholm Rd. G20: Glas 2H 61
Dalskeith Av. PA3: Pais 6E 77
Dalskeith Cres. PA3: Pais 6E 77
Dalskeith Rd. PA3: Pais 1E 97
Dalswinton Path G34: Glas 3B 88
Dalswinton St. G34: Glas 3A 88
Dalton Av. G81: Clyd 6G 43
Dalton Cotts. G72: Flem 5F 123
Dalton Hill ML3: Ham 1C 152
Dalton St. G31: Glas 6G 85
Dalveen Ct. G78: Barr 6E 115
Dalveen Dr. G71: Tann 5C 108
Dalveen Quad. ML5: Coat 6F 91
Dalveen St. G32: Glas 6H 85
Dalveen Way G73: Ruth 4E 121
Dalwhinnie Av. G72: Blan 5A 124
Daly Gdns. G72: Blan 6C 124
Dalzell Av. ML1: Moth 5A 144
Dalzell Country Pk. 6H 143
Dalzell Dr. ML1: Moth 5A 144
Dalziel Dr. G41: Glas 2A 102
Dalziel Quad. G41: Glas 2A 102
Dalziel Rd. G52: Hill 3H 79
Dalziel St. ML1: Moth 2H 143
ML3: Ham 4F 141
Dalziel Twr. ML1: Moth 6B 144
Damshot Cres. G53: Glas 5D 100
Damshot Rd. G53: Glas 6D 100
Danby Rd. G69: Bail 1F 107
Danes Av. G14: Glas 5C 60
Danes Cres. G14: Glas 4B 60
Danes Dr. G14: Glas 4B 60
Danes La. Nth. G14: Glas 5C 60
Danes La. Sth. G14: Glas 5C 60
Daniel McLaughlin Pl.
G66: Kirk 4E 31
Dargarvel Av. G41: Glas 1H 101
Dargavel Av. PA7: B'ton 4H 39
Dargavel Path *G41: Glas 2C 101*
*(off Dumbreck Pl.)*
Dargavel Rd. PA7: B'ton 6A 40
(not continuous)
Darkwood Ct. PA3: Pais 5F 77
Darkwood Cres. PA3: Pais 5F 77
Darkwood Dr. PA3: Pais 5F 77
Darleith St. G32: Glas 6H 85
Darley Pl. ML3: Ham 3F 153
Darley Rd. G68: Cumb 6G 13
Darluith Pk. La. PA5: Brkfld 5C 74
Darluith Rd. PA6: C'lee 5E 75
Darnaway Av. G33: Glas 1D 86
Darnaway Dr. G33: Glas 1D 86
Darnaway St. G33: Glas 1D 86
Darngavel Ct. *ML6: Air 3F 91*
*(off Monkscourt Av.)*
Darnick St. G21: Glas 6C 64
Darnley Cres. G64: B'rig 4B 48
Darnley Gdns. G41: Glas 3C 102
Darnley Ind. Est. G53: Glas 3B 116
Darnley Mains Rd. G53: Glas 4C 116
Darnley Path G46: T'bnk 2E 117
Darnley Pl. G41: Glas 3C 102
Darnley Rd. G41: Glas 3C 102
G78: Barr 4F 115
Darnley St. G41: Glas 3D 102
Darragh Grn. ML2: Newm 3E 147
Darroch Dr. PA8: Ersk 4D 40
Darroch Way G67: Cumb 2A 36
Dartford St. G22: Glas 6F 63
Darvel Cres. PA1: Pais 1F 99
Darvel Dr. G77: Newt M 4G 133
Darwin Pl. G81: Clyd 3H 41
Darwin Rd. G75: E Kil 3E 149
Davaar G74: E Kil 2C 150
Davaar Dr. ML1: Moth 5E 127
ML5: Coat 4H 89
PA2: Pais 6A 98
Davaar Pl. G77: Newt M 3C 132
Davaar Rd. PA4: Renf 2F 79
Davaar St. G40: Glas 1D 104
Davan Loan *ML2: Newm 3D 146*
*(off Isla Av.)*
Dava St. G51: Glas 4G 81
Dave Barrie Av. ML9: Lark 6H 155
Daventry Dr. G12: Glas 4G 61
David Donnely Pl. G66: Kirk 4C 30
David Gray Dr. G66: Kirk 4G 31
David Livingstone Cen. 5C 124
David Lloyd Leisure 2D 78
David Pl. G69: Bail 1F 107
PA3: Pais 4D 78
Davidson Cres. G65: Twe 2D 32
Davidson Gdns. *G14: Glas 5E 61*
*(off Westland Dr.)*
Davidson La. G14: Glas 5E 61
*ML8: Carl 4H 165*
*(off Ramage Rd.)*
Davidson Pl. G32: Glas 5C 86
Davidson Quad. G81: Dun 1C 42
Davidson St. G40: Glas 3C 104
G81: Clyd 1G 59
ML5: Coat 1D 110
ML6: Air 3H 91
Davidston Pl. G66: Lenz 3F 51
David St. G40: Glas 6C 84
ML5: Coat 4E 91
David Way PA3: Pais 4D 78
Davieland Rd. G46: Giff 6G 117
Davie's Acre G74: E Kil 5B 136
Davies Quad. ML1: Moth 5F 127
Davie's Sq. G81: Dun 1C 42
Davington Dr. ML3: Ham 1B 152
Daviot St. G51: Glas 5D 80
Davlea G51: Glas 4E 81
Dawson Av. G75: E Kil 2D 148
Dawson Pl. G4: Glas 6F 63
Dawson Rd. G4: Glas 6F 63
Deaconsbank Av. G46: T'bnk 6D 116
Deaconsbank Cres.
G46: T'bnk 6D 116
Deaconsbank Gdns.
G46: T'bnk 6E 117
Deaconsbank Gro. G46: T'bnk 6D 116
Deaconsbank Pl. G46: T'bnk 6E 117
Deacons Rd. G65: Kils 3A 12
Dealston Rd. G78: Barr 3D 114
Deanbrae St. G71: Udd 1D 124
Dean Cres. G69: Chry 6B 52
ML3: Ham 2G 153
Deanfield Quad. G52: Glas 5H 79
DEAN PARK 1G 79
Dean Pk. Av. G71: Both 5E 125
Dean Pk. Dr. G72: Camb 3D 122
Dean Pk. Rd. PA4: Renf 1G 79
Deans Av. G72: Camb 3D 122
Deanside Rd. G52: Hill 3A 80
Deanside Transit Dpt.
G52: Hill 2A 80
Deanston Av. G78: Barr 6D 114
Deanston Dr. G41: Glas 5B 102
Deanstone Pl. ML5: Coat 2F 111
Deanston Gdns G78: Barr 6D 114
Deanston Gro. ML5: Coat 2A 110
Deanston Pk. G78: Barr 6D 114
Dean St. G81: Clyd 6E 43
ML4: Bell 2D 126
Deanwood Av. G44: Neth 4D 118
Deanwood Rd. G44: Neth 4D 118
Dechmont G75: E Kil 6F 149
Dechmont Av. G72: Camb 4D 122
ML1: Moth 2E 143
Dechmont Cotts. G72: Flem 4F 123
Dechmont Gdns. G71: Tann 4C 108
G72: Blan 6A 124
Dechmont Pl. G72: Camb 4D 122
Dechmont Rd. G71: Tann 4C 108
Dechmont St. G31: Glas 1E 105
ML3: Ham 1G 153
Dechmont Vw. G71: Tann 6E 109
ML4: Bell 4B 126
Dee Av. PA2: Pais 3D 96
PA4: Renf 6G 59
Deedes St. ML6: Air 5F 91
Dee Dr. PA2: Pais 4D 96
Dee Path ML1: Holy 2B 128
ML9: Lark 5E 161
Deep Dale G74: E Kil 6E 137
Deepdene Rd. G61: Bear 4D 44
G69: Mood 5D 52
Dee Pl. G75: E Kil 4A 148
PA5: John 5C 94
Deerdykes Ct. Nth. G68: Cumb 1A 54
Deerdykes Ct. Sth. G68: Cumb 2A 54
Deerdykes Pl. G68: Cumb 1A 54
Deerdykes Rd. G68: Cumb 1A 54
DEERDYKES RDBT. 2H 53
Deerdykes Vw. G68: Cumb 2H 53

Deer Pk. Ct.—Drummond Av.


eer Pk. Ct. ML3: Ham 4H 153
eer Pk. Pl. ML3: Ham 4A 154
eeside Dr. ML8: Carl 2G 165
eeside Pl. ML5: Coat 1F 111
ee St. G33: Glas 2F 85
ML5: Coat 1H 89
ee Ter. ML3: Ham 3F 153
elhi Av. G81: Clyd 3G 41
ellburn St. ML1: Moth 4A 144
ellburn Trad. Est. ML1: Moth 4A 144
ell, The G77: Newt M 4H 133
ML4: Bell 4F 127
elny Pl. G33: Glas 4E 87
elvin Rd. G44: Glas 1E 119
empsey Rd. ML4: Bell 4B 126
enbak Av. ML3: Ham 1E 153
enbeck St. G32: Glas 6H 85
enbrae St. G32: Glas 6H 85
ene Wlk. G64: B'rig 1E 65
enewood Av. PA2: Pais 5H 97
enham St. G22: Glas 6F 63
enholm Cres. G75: E Kil 3G 149
enholm Dr. G46: Giff 6A 118
ML2: Wis 3A 146
enholm Grn. G75: E Kil 3H 149
enholm Ter. ML3: Ham 6C 140
enmark St. G22: Glas 5G 63
enmark St. Ind. Cen.
G22: Glas 4G 63
enmilne Gdns. G34: Glas 4A 88
enmilne Path G34: Glas 4A 88
enmilne Rd. G69: Barg 4B 88
enmilne St. G34: Glas 4A 88
ENNISTOUN 4C 84
ennistoun St. ML4: Bell 2C 126
ennystoun Forge G82: Dumb 3E 17
ENNYSTOWN 3D 16
entdale G74: E Kil 6E 137
eramore Av. G46: Giff 2G 133
erby St. G3: Glas 3C 82
erby Ter. La. *G3: Glas 3C 82*
*(off Derby St.)*
erby Wynd ML1: Carf 6B 128
errywood Rd. G66: Milt C 5C 8
erwent Dr. ML5: Coat 1G 89
erwent St. G22: Glas 5F 63
erwentwater G75: E Kil 5B 148
espard Av. G32: Glas 1D 106
espard Gdns. G32: Glas 1E 107
everon Av. G46: Giff 5B 118
everon Cres. ML3: Ham 5B 140
everon Rd. G61: Bear 5C 44
G74: E Kil 2A 150
ML1: Holy 1B 128
everon St. G33: Glas 2F 85
ML5: Coat 2G 89
everon Way *G67: Cumb 4H 35*
*(in Cumbernauld Shop. Cen.)*
PA2: Pais 4D 96
evine Ct. ML2: Wis 6H 145
evine Gro. ML2: Newm 2E 147
evlin Gro. G72: Blan 2C 140
evol Cres. G53: Glas 5B 100
evondale Av. G72: Blan 6A 124
evon Dr. PA7: B'ton 4A 40
evon Gdns. G64: B'rig 4B 48
ML8: Carl 3E 165
evonhill Av. ML3: Ham 4H 153
evon Pl. G41: Glas 1F 103
evonport Pk. G75: E Kil 4C 148
evonshire Gdns. G12: Glas 5H 61
evonshire Gdns. La.
G12: Glas 5H 61
evonshire Ter. G12: Glas 5H 61
evonshire Ter. La. G12: Glas 5H 61
evon St. G5: Glas 1F 103
evonview Pl. ML6: Air 5H 91
evonview St. ML6: Air 4H 91
evon Wlk. G68: Cumb 5A 34
evon Way ML1: Moth 3D 142
ewar Cl. G71: Tann 4E 109
ewar Dr. G15: Glas 4A 44
ewar Ga. G15: Glas 4A 44
iamond St. ML4: Bell 3C 126
iana Av. G13: Glas 1B 60
iana Quad. ML1: Holy 2A 128
ickens Av. G81: Clyd 3B 42
ickens Gro. ML1: Carf 5D 128
ickson Sq. ML1: Cle 6H 129
ickson St. ML9: Lark 4G 161
icks Pk. G75: E Kil 3F 149
ick St. G20: Glas 6D 62
iffer Av. G65: Twe 3D 32
ilwara Av. G14: Glas 1E 81
imity St. PA5: John 3F 95
IMSDALE 2A 158
imsdale Cres. ML2: Wis 2A 158
imsdale Rd. ML2: Wis 2A 158
inard Dr. G46: Giff 3A 118
inart St. G33: Glas 2F 85
Dinduff St. G34: Glas 2A 88
Dinmont Av. PA2: Pais 4D 96
Dinmont Cres. ML1: Moth 5E 127
Dinmont Pl. *G41: Glas 4C 102*
*(off Dinmont Rd.)*
Dinmont Rd. G41: Glas 4B 102
Dinmont Way PA2: Pais 4C 96
Dinnet Way *ML2: Newm 3D 146*
*(off Isla Av.)*
Dinwiddie St. G21: Glas 1E 85
Dinyra Pl. ML5: Glenb 3G 69
Dipple Pl. G15: Glas 5B 44
Dirleton Dr. G41: Glas 5C 102
PA2: Pais 4E 97
Dirleton Ga. G61: Bear 4D 44
Dirleton Pl. G41: Glas 5C 102
Divernia Way G78: Barr 6E 115
Dixon Av. G42: Glas 3E 103
G82: Dumb 4E 17
Dixon Dr. G82: Dumb 5D 16
Dixon Pl. G74: E Kil 6D 136
Dixon Rd. G42: Glas 4F 103
Dixons Blazes Ind. Est.
G5: Glas 2G 103
Dixon St. G1: Glas 5F 83
ML3: Ham 6H 141
ML5: Coat 1D 110
PA1: Pais 1B 98
Dobbies Ct. ML8: Law 5E 159
Dobbie's Loan G4: Glas 2F 83 (1D 4)
DOBBIES LOAN INTERCHANGE
2G 83 (1E 5)
Dobbie's Loan Pl.
G4: Glas 3H 83 (3G 5)
Dochart Av. PA4: Renf 2G 79
Dochart Dr. G68: Cumb 6E 13
ML5: Coat 1G 89
Dochart St. G33: Glas 1G 85
Dock St. G81: Clyd 2F 59
Dodhill Pl. G13: Glas 3B 60
Dodside Gdns. G32: Glas 1C 106
Dodside Pl. G32: Glas 1C 106
Dodside St. G32: Glas 1C 106
Dolan St. G69: Bail 6H 87
Dollan Aqua Cen. 2G 149
Dollar Pk. ML1: Moth 6B 144
Dollar Ter. *G20: Glas 1A 62*
*(off Crosbie St.)*
Dolley Rd. ML2: Wis 6G 145
Dolphin Rd. G41: Glas 3B 102
Dominica Grn. G75: E Kil 2C 148
Donald Dewar Leisure Cen.
4A 44
Donaldfield Rd.
PA11: Bri W 4D 72
Donaldson Av. G65: Kils 4H 11
Donaldson Cres. G66: Kirk 6C 30
Donaldson Dr. PA4: Renf 6E 59
Donaldson Grn. G71: Tann 5E 109
Donaldson Pl. G66: Kirk 5D 30
Donaldson Rd. ML9: Lark 4G 161
Donaldson St. G66: Kirk 6C 30
ML3: Ham 4E 141
Donaldswood Pk. PA2: Pais 5G 97
Donaldswood Rd. PA2: Pais 5G 97
Donald Ter. ML3: Ham 2G 153
Donald Way G71: Tann 6E 109
Don Av. PA4: Renf 1G 79
Doncaster St. G20: Glas 6E 63
Don Ct. ML3: Ham 3E 153
Don Dr. PA2: Pais 4D 96
Donnelly Way ML2: Wis 5C 144
Donnies Brae G78: Barr 1F 131
Donohoe Ct. G64: B'rig 6C 48
Don Path ML9: Lark 5E 161
Don Pl. PA5: John 5C 94
Don St. G33: Glas 3F 85
Doon Cres. G61: Bear 4D 44
Doonfoot Ct. G74: E Kil 1F 149
Doonfoot Gdns. G74: E Kil 1F 149
Doonfoot Rd. G43: Glas 1B 118
Doon Pl. G66: Kirk 3F 31
Doon Rd. G66: Kirk 4F 31
Doonside G67: Cumb 3B 36
Doonside Twr. ML1: Moth 5B 144
Doon St. G81: Clyd 4F 43
ML1: Moth 5A 144
ML9: Lark 3G 161
Doon Way G66: Kirk 4G 31
Dorain Rd. ML1: N'hill 4D 128
Dora St. G40: Glas 2C 104
Dorchester Av. G12: Glas 3G 61
Dorchester Ct. G12: Glas 3G 61
Dorchester Pl. G12: Glas 3G 61
Dorian Dr. G76: Clar 1H 133
Dorlin Rd. G33: Step 4E 67
Dormanside Ct. G53: Glas 2B 100
Dormanside Ga. G53: Glas 2B 100
Dormanside Gro. G53: Glas 2B 100
Dormanside Pl. G53: Glas 4C 100
Dormanside Rd. G53: Glas 2B 100
(not continuous)
Dornal Av. G13: Glas 2G 59
Dornford Av. G32: Glas 3D 106
Dornford Rd. G32: Glas 3D 106
Dornie Dr. G32: Carm 5B 106
Dornie Path *ML2: Newm 3D 146*
*(off Isla Av.)*
Dornoch Av. G46: Giff 6A 118
Dornoch Ct. ML4: Bell 1C 126
Dornoch Pl. G64: B'rig 5F 49
G69: Chry 6B 52
G74: E Kil 1E 149
Dornoch Rd. G61: Bear 5D 44
ML1: Holy 3B 128
Dornoch St. G40: Glas 6B 84
Dornoch Way G68: Cumb 6A 14
ML6: Air 6H 91
Dorset Sq. *G3: Glas 3D 82*
*(off Dorset St.)*
Dorset St. G3: Glas 3D 82
Dosk Av. G13: Glas 1H 59
Dosk Pl. G13: Glas 1H 59
Double Hedges Rd. G78: Neil 3D 130
Dougalston Av. G62: Miln 4H 25
Dougalston Cres. G62: Miln 4H 25
Dougalston Gdns. Nth.
G62: Miln 4H 25
Dougalston Gdns. Sth.
G62: Miln 4H 25
Dougalston Rd. G23: Glas 1C 62
Douglas Av. G32: Carm 4B 106
G46: Giff 6A 118
G66: Lenz 2D 50
G73: Ruth 2E 121
PA5: Eld 3H 95
Douglas Ct. G66: Lenz 2D 50
Douglas Cres. G71: Tann 5F 109
ML3: Ham 5H 153
ML6: Air 5A 92
PA8: Ersk 4D 40
Douglasdale G74: E Kil 1F 149
Douglas Dr. G15: Glas 6H 43
G69: Bail 6F 87
G71: Both 6E 125
G72: Camb 2H 121
G75: E Kil 4A 148
G77: Newt M 3E 133
ML4: Bell 3E 127
ML9: Ashg 5B 162
Douglas Dr. La. G45: Glas 4H 119
Douglas Gdns. G46: Giff 6A 118
G61: Bear 3F 45
G66: Lenz 2D 50
G71: Udd 2D 124
Douglas Ga. G72: Camb 2H 121
Douglas Ho. G67: Cumb 3H 35
G82: Dumb 1H 17
Douglas La. G2: Glas 4B 4
Douglas Muir Dr. G62: Miln 2C 24
Douglas Muir Gdns. G62: Miln 2C 24
Douglas Muir Pl. G62: Miln 2C 24
Douglas Muir Rd. G62: Miln 3D 24
G81: Faif 6F 23
Douglas Pk. Cres. G61: Bear 1G 45
Douglas Pk. La. ML3: Ham 5G 141
Douglas Pl. G61: Bear 2E 45
G66: Lenz 2D 50
ML3: Ham 5H 153
ML5: Coat 5B 90
Douglas Rd. G82: Dumb 4H 17
PA4: Renf 3C 78
Douglas St. G2: Glas 4E 83 (6B 4)
G62: Miln 4G 25
G66: Miln 4G 25
G71: Tann 5F 109
G72: Blan 3A 140
ML1: Moth 2F 143
ML2: Over 4B 158
ML3: Ham 4G 141
(not continuous)
ML6: Air 5A 92
ML8: Carl 3E 165
ML9: Lark 1E 161
PA1: Pais 6G 77
Douglas Ter. G41: Glas 3D 102
Douglas Twr. G71: Both 3B 124
Douglas Vw. ML5: Coat 2B 110
Dougray Pl. G78: Barr 5E 115
Dougrie Dr. G45: Glas 4H 119
Dougrie Gdns. G45: Glas 5H 119
Dougrie Pl. G45: Glas 4A 120
Dougrie Rd. G45: Glas 5G 119
Dougrie St. G45: Glas 4A 120
Dougrie Ter. G45: Glas 4H 119
Doune Cres. G64: B'rig 3D 48
G77: Newt M 4F 133
ML6: Chap 4D 112
Doune Gdns. G20: Glas 6C 62
Doune Gdns. La. G20: Glas 6C 62
Doune Pk. Way ML5: Coat 1B 110
Doune Quad. G20: Glas 6C 62
Doune Ter. ML5: Coat 2H 89
Dovecot G43: Glas 5A 102
Dovecotehall St. G78: Barr 4F 115
Dovecote Vw. G66: Kirk 6F 31
DOVECOTHALL 3G 115
DOVECOTWOOD 2H 11
Dovecotwood G65: Kils 2H 11
Doveholm G82: Dumb 2G 17
Doveholm Av. G82: Dumb 2H 17
Dove Pl. G75: E Kil 5B 148
Dover St. G3: Glas 3C 82
ML5: Coat 1H 89
G53: Glas 2A 116
Dove Wynd ML4: Bell 6A 110
Dowanfield Rd. G67: Cumb 4F 35
DOWANHILL 6A 62
Dowanhill St. G11: Glas 1A 82
Dowan Rd.
G62: Balder, Bard, Miln 6C 26
Dowanside La. G12: Glas 6B 62
Dowanside Rd. G12: Glas 6A 62
Downcraig Dr. G45: Glas 5H 119
Downcraig Gro. G45: Glas 5G 119
Downcraig Rd. G45: Glas 6G 119
Downcraig Ter. G45: Glas 5H 119
Downfield Dr. ML3: Ham 4F 153
Downfield Gdns. G71: Both 5D 124
Downfield St. G32: Glas 2G 105
Downiebrae Rd. G73: Ruth 3D 104
Downie Cl. G71: Tann 5F 109
Downie St. ML3: Ham 2H 153
Downs St. G21: Glas 4B 64
Dowrie Cres. G53: Glas 4B 100
Draffen Ct. ML1: Moth 2H 143
Draffen St. ML1: Moth 2H 143
Draffen Twr. ML1: Moth 2H 143
Drakemire Av. G45: Glas 3G 119
Drakemire Dr. G45: Glas 5F 119
Drake St. G40: Glas 6A 84
Dreghorn St. G31: Glas 4E 85
Drimmin Rd. G33: Step 4F 67
Drive Rd. G51: Glas 3E 81
Drochil St. G34: Glas 2G 87
Dromore St. G66: Kirk 6D 30
Drove Hill G68: Cumb 2D 34
Drumaling Ter. G66: Len 3H 7
Drumbathie Rd. ML6: Air 3B 92
Drumbathie Ter. ML6: Air 3C 92
Drumbeg Dr. G53: Glas 1A 116
Drumbeg Pl. G53: Glas 1A 116
Drumbeg Ter. G62: Miln 3D 24
Drumbottie Rd. G21: Glas 4C 64
Drumby Cres. G76: Clar 6B 118
Drumby Dr. G76: Clar 1B 134
Drumcarn Dr. G62: Miln 4F 25
Drumcavel Rd. G69: Muirh 2B 68
Drumchapel Gdns. G15: Glas 5A 44
Drumchapel Pl. G15: Glas 5B 44
Drumchapel Rd. G15: Glas 5A 44
Drumchapel Shop. Cen.
G15: Glas 4H 43
Drumchapel Sports Cen. 5H 43
Drumchapel Station (Rail) 6A 44
Drumchapel Swimming Pool
5H 43
Drumclair Pl. ML6: Air 4D 92
Drumclog Av. G62: Miln 1G 25
Drumclog Gdns. G33: Glas 3H 65
Drumcross Rd. G53: Glas 4C 100
PA7: B'ton 4B 40
Drumduff G75: E Kil 6F 149
DRUMGELLOCH 3D 92
Drumgelloch Station (Rail) 4D 92
Drumgelloch St. ML6: Air 2D 92
Drumglass Vw. G65: Croy 1B 34
DRUMGREW 4F 33
DRUMGREW RDBT. 4F 33
Drumhead Pl. G32: Glas 4H 105
Drumhead Rd. G32: Glas 4H 105
Drumhill G66: Kirk 3H 31
Drumilaw Cres. G73: Ruth 2C 120
Drumilaw Rd. G73: Ruth 2C 120
Drumilaw Way G73: Ruth 2C 120
Drumlaken Av. *G23: Glas 6A 46*
*(off Drumlaken St.)*
Drumlaken Ct. G23: Glas 6B 46
Drumlaken Path *G23: Glas 6B 46*
*(off Littleton St.)*
Drumlaken Pl. *G23: Glas 6B 46*
*(off Drumlaken Ct.)*
Drumlaken St. G23: Glas 6A 46
Drumlanrig Av. G34: Glas 2A 88
Drumlanrig Pl. G34: Glas 3B 88
Drumlin Dr. G62: Miln 5F 25
Drumloch Gdns. G75: E Kil 6G 149
Drumlochy Rd. G33: Glas 2A 86
Drum Mains Pk. G68: Cumb 6G 33
Drummond Av. G73: Ruth 5B 104

Drummond Dr.—Duntocher Rd.

Drummond Dr. ML2: Wis .1H 157
PA1: Pais .1F 99
Drummond Hill G74: E Kil .6B 138
Drummond Ho. G67: Cumb .2A 36
Drummond Pl. G74: E Kil .6B 138
Drummond Way G77: Newt M .4A 132
Drummore Av. ML5: Coat .2F 111
Drummore Rd. G15: Glas .2A 44
Drumnessie Ct. G68: Cumb .5B 34
Drumnessie Rd. G68: Cumb .5B 34
Drumnessie Vw. G68: Cumb .5B 34
Drumore Av. ML6: Chap .4D 112
Drumover Dr. G31: Glas .1G 105
DRUMOYNE .5E 81
Drumoyne Av. G51: Glas .4E 81
Drumoyne Cir. G51: Glas .5E 81
Drumoyne Dr. G51: Glas .4E 81
Drumoyne Pl. G51: Glas .5E 81
Drumoyne Quad. G51: Glas .5E 81
Drumoyne Rd. G51: Glas .5E 81
Drumoyne Sq. G51: Glas .4E 81
Drumpark St. G46: T'bnk .3F 117
ML5: Coat .1F 109
DRUMPELLIER .4H 89
Drumpellier Av. G67: Cumb .1E 55
G69: Bail .2H 107
ML5: Coat .4G 89
Drumpellier Butterfly House .3F 89
Drumpellier Country Pk. .3F 89
Drumpellier Country Pk. Vis. Cen. .2E 89
Drumpellier Ct. G67: Cumb .6E 35
Drumpellier Cres. ML5: Coat .5H 89
Drumpellier Gdns. G67: Cumb .6E 35
Drumpellier Gro. G67: Cumb .6E 35
Drumpellier Pl. G67: Cumb .6E 35
G69: Bail .1H 107
Drumpellier Rd. G69: Bail .2G 107
Drumpellier St. G33: Glas .1F 85
Drumreoch Dr. G42: Glas .5A 104
Drumreoch Pl. G42: Glas .5A 104
DRUMRY .4E 43
Drumry Pl. G15: Glas .5G 43
Drumry Rd. G81: Clyd .4E 43
Drumry Rd. E. G15: Glas .5G 43
Drumry Station (Rail) .5F 43
Drumsack Av. G69: Chry .1A 68
Drumsargard Rd. G73: Ruth .2F 121
Drums Av. PA3: Pais .5G 77
Drums Cres. PA3: Pais .6G 77
Drumshangie Pl. ML6: Air .1A 92
Drumshangie St. ML6: Air .1A 92
Drumshaw Dr. G32: Carm .5C 106
Drums Rd. G53: Glas .2A 100
Drumtrocher St. G65: Kils .3H 11
Drumvale Dr. G69: Mood .5C 52
Drury La. Ct. G74: E Kil .5C 138 (off Bosworth Rd.)
Drury St. G2: Glas .4F 83 (5D 4)
Dryad St. G46: T'bnk .2E 117
Dryburgh Av. G73: Ruth .6D 104
PA2: Pais .4E 97
Dryburgh Gdns. G20: Glas .6D 62
Dryburgh Hill G74: E Kil .2F 149
Dryburgh La. G74: E Kil .2F 149
Dryburgh Pl. G66: Kirk .5F 31
ML5: Coat .4B 90
Dryburgh Rd. G61: Bear .1C 44
ML2: Wis .6G 145
Dryburgh St. ML3: Ham .3F 141
Dryburgh Wlk. G69: Mood .4E 53
Dryburgh Way G72: Blan .2B 140 (off Winton Cres.)
Dryburn Av. G52: Glas .6A 80
Dryden St. ML3: Ham .3F 141
Drygait PA9: How .6A 94
Drygate G4: Glas .4A 84
Drygate St. ML9: Lark .1E 161
Drygrange Rd. G33: Glas .1C 86
Drymen Pl. G66: Lenz .4D 50
Drymen Rd. G61: Bear .1D 44
Drymen St. G52: Glas .6E 81
Drymen Wynd G61: Bear .4F 45
Drynoch Pl. G22: Glas .2F 63
Drysdale St. G14: Glas .4H 59 (not continuous)
Duart Dr. G74: E Kil .6F 137
G77: Newt M .4G 133
PA5: Eld .4H 95
Duart St. G20: Glas .1A 62
Dubs Rd. G78: Barr .4G 115
Dubton Path G34: Glas .2H 87
Dubton St. G34: Glas .2H 87
Duchall Pl. G14: Glas .5B 60
Duchess Ct. ML3: Ham .1C 154
Duchess Pl. G73: Ruth .5E 105
Duchess Rd. G73: Ruth .4E 105
Duchess Way G69: Barg .6D 88 (off Park Rd.)
Duchray Dr. PA1: Pais .2G 99
Duchray La. G33: Glas .2F 85
Duchray St. G33: Glas .2F 85
Dudhope St. G33: Glas .1D 86
Dudley Dr. G12: Glas .6G 61
ML5: Coat .1G 89
Dudley La. G12: Glas .6G 61
Duffus Pl. G32: Carm .5C 106
Duffus St. G34: Glas .2G 87
Duffus Ter. G32: Carm .5C 106
Duich Gdns. G23: Glas .5C 46
Duisdale Rd. G32: Carm .5C 106
Duke's Ct. ML9: Lark .1E 161
Dukes Ga. G71: Both .3C 124
Dukes Pl. ML3: Ham .5H 153
Dukes Rd. G69: Barg .6D 88
Duke's Rd. G72: Camb .1G 121
G73: Ruth .2E 121
Duke St. G31: Glas .5D 84
G4: Glas .4A 84 (5H 5)
ML1: Moth .1G 143
ML2: Newm .3D 146
ML3: Ham .6A 142
ML9: Lark .1E 161
PA2: Pais .3A 98
Duke Street Station (Rail) .4D 84
DULLATUR .5F 13
Dullatur Rd. G68: Dull .5F 13
DULLATUR RDBT. .6H 13
Dulnain St. G72: Camb .2D 122
Dulsie Rd. G21: Glas .3E 65
DUMBARTON .4F 17
Dumbarton Castle .6G 17
Dumbarton Central Station (Rail) .3F 17
Dumbarton East Station (Rail) .4H 17
Dumbarton Rd. G11: Glas .1F 81
G14: Glas .3G 59
G60: Bowl, Old K .5G 19
G81: Clyd .3G 41
G81: Dun, Hard .1B 42
G82: Milt .4E 19
DUMBRECK .2A 102
Dumbreck Av. G41: Glas .1G 101
Dumbreck Ct. G41: Glas .2G 101
Dumbreck Path G41: Glas .2G 101 (off Dumbreck Pl.)
Dumbreck Pl. G41: Glas .2G 101
G66: Lenz .3E 51
Dumbreck Rd. G41: Glas .6G 81
DUMBRECK RD. INTERCHANGE .6H 81
Dumbreck Sq. G41: Glas .1G 101
Dumbreck Station (Rail) .1A 102
Dumbreck Ter. G65: Queen .3D 10
Dumbrock Rd. G62: Miln .3D 24
DUMBUCK .4E 19
Dumbuck Cres. G82: Dumb .5H 17
Dumbuck Gdns. G82: Dumb .5H 17
Dumbuck Rd. G82: Dumb .3H 17 (Overwood Dr., not continuous)
G82: Dumb .2H 17 (Stirling Rd.)
Dumbuie Av. G82: Dumb .3H 17
Dumfries Cres. ML6: Air .6H 91
Dumgoyne Av. G62: Miln .4F 25
Dumgoyne Ct. ML6: Air .1B 92 (off Thrushbush Rd.)
Dumgoyne Dr. G61: Bear .6D 24
Dumgoyne Gdns. G62: Miln .4F 25
Dumgoyne Pl. G76: Clar .2A 134
Dunagoil Gdns. G45: Glas .5A 120
Dunagoil Pl. G45: Glas .6A 120
Dunagoil Rd. G45: Glas .5H 119
Dunagoil St. G45: Glas .5A 120
Dunalastair Dr. G33: Mille .4B 66
Dunan Pl. G33: Glas .4E 87
Dunard Ct. ML8: Carl .2F 165 (off Carranbute Rd.)
Dunard Rd. G73: Ruth .6D 104
Dunard St. G20: Glas .5D 62
Dunard Way PA3: Pais .4H 77
Dunaskin St. G11: Glas .2A 82
Dunavon Pl. ML5: Coat .1F 111
Dunbar Av. G73: Ruth .6E 105
ML5: Coat .1H 109
PA5: John .5E 95
Dunbar Dr. ML1: Moth .5A 144
Dunbar Hill G74: E Kil .2E 149
Dunbar La. ML1: New S .5A 128
Dunbar Pl. G74: E Kil .2E 149
Dunbar Rd. PA2: Pais .4E 97
Dunbar St. ML3: Ham .4F 141
Dunbeath Av. G77: Newt M .4F 133
Dunbeith Pl. G20: Glas .4B 62
DUNBETH .4D 90
Dunbeth Av. ML5: Coat .4D 90
Dunbeth Ct. ML5: Coat .4D 90
Dunbeth Rd. ML5: Coat .3D 90
Dunblane Dr. G74: E Kil .6H 137
Dunblane Pl. G74: E Kil .1H 149
ML5: Coat .1B 110
Dunblane St. G4: Glas .2F 83 (1D 4) (not continuous)
Dunbrach Rd. G68: Cumb .2D 34
Dunbritton Rd. G82: Dumb .2C 18
Duncan Av. G14: Glas .6C 60
Duncan Ct. ML1: Moth .6F 127
Duncan Graham St. ML9: Lark .1F 161
Duncan La. G14: Glas .6C 60 (off Gleneagles La. Nth.)
Duncan La. Nth. G14: Glas .5C 60 (off Norse La. Nth.)
Duncan McIntosh Rd. G68: Cumb .4B 14
Dun Cann PA8: Ersk .2G 57
Duncannon La. Nth. G14: Glas .5C 60 (off Earlbank Av.)
Duncanrig Sports Cen. .3D 148
Duncansby Rd. G33: Glas .5D 86
Duncarnock Av. G78: Neil .2E 131
Duncarnock Cres. G78: Neil .2E 131
Dunchattan Pl. G31: Glas .4B 84
Dunchattan St. G31: Glas .4B 84
Dunchurch Rd. PA1: Pais .6F 79
Dunclutha Dr. G71: Both .6E 125
Dunclutha St. G40: Glas .3D 104
Duncolm Pl. G62: Miln .3D 24
Duncombe Av. G81: Hard .6D 22
Duncombe St. G20: Glas .2B 62
Duncombe Vw. G81: Clyd .4F 43
Duncraig Cres. PA5: John .5D 94
Duncrub Dr. G64: B'rig .6A 48
Duncruin St. G20: Glas .2A 62
Duncruin Ter. G20: Glas .2B 62
Duncryne Av. G32: Glas .1D 106
Duncryne Gdns. G32: Glas .1E 107
Duncryne Pl. G64: B'rig .1A 64
Dundaff Hill G68: Cumb .3E 35
Dundas Av. G64: Torr .5D 28
Dundas Cotts. FK4: Alla .1G 15
Dundas Ct. G74: E Kil .1G 149
Dundashill G4: Glas .1F 83 (1D 4)
Dundas La. G1: Glas .3G 83 (4E 5)
Dundas Pl. G74: E Kil .1G 149
Dundas St. G1: Glas .3G 83 (4E 5) (not continuous)
Dundasvale Ct. G4: Glas .2F 83 (1D 4)
Dundee Dr. G52: Glas .1B 100
Dundee Path G52: Glas .2C 100
Dundonald Av. PA5: John .4D 94
Dundonald Cres. G77: Newt M .5G 133
Dundonald Dr. ML3: Ham .4H 153
Dundonald Pl. G78: Neil .2D 130
Dundonald Rd. G12: Glas .6A 62
PA3: Pais .4C 78
Dundonald St. G72: Blan .1A 140
Dundrennan Rd. G42: Glas .6D 102
DUNDYVAN .6B 90
Dundyvan Gdns. ML5: Coat .6C 90
Dundyvan Ga. ML5: Coat .6C 90
Dundyvan Ind. Est. ML5: Coat .6B 90
Dundyvan La. ML2: Wis .1G 157
Dundyvan Rd. ML5: Coat .5B 90
Dundyvan St. ML2: Wis .1G 157
Dundyvan Way ML5: Coat .6B 90
Dunearn Pl. PA2: Pais .2C 98
Dunearn St. G4: Glas .1D 82
Duneaton Wynd ML9: Lark .5F 161
Dunedin Ct. G75: E Kil .3C 148
Dunedin Dr. G75: E Kil .2C 148
Dunedin Rd. ML9: Lark .4F 161
Dunedin Ter. G81: Clyd .1E 59
Dunellan Av. G69: Mood .5E 53
Dunellan Ct. G69: Mood .5E 53
Dunellan Cres. G69: Mood .5E 53
Dunellan Dr. G81: Hard .6D 22
Dunellan Gdns. G69: Mood .5E 53
Dunellan Rd. G62: Miln .3C 24
Dunellan St. G52: Glas .6E 81
Dungavel Gdns. ML3: Ham .3A 154
Dungavel La. ML8: Carl .4H 165 (off Kelso Dr.)
Dungeonhill Rd. G34: Glas .3B 88
Dunglass Av. G14: Glas .5C 60
G74: E Kil .6H 137
Dunglass La. G14: Glas .5C 60 (off Norse La. Sth.)
Dunglass La. Nth. G14: Glas .5C 60 (off Danes La. Sth.)
Dunglass Pl. G62: Miln .2E 25
G77: Newt M .4A 132
Dunglass Rd. PA7: B'ton .5A 40
Dunglass Sq. G74: E Kil .1H 149
Dungoil Av. G68: Cumb .2D 34
Dungoil Rd. G66: Lenz .3E 51
Dungoyne St. G20: Glas .1A 62
Dunholme Pk. G81: Clyd .4H 41
Dunira St. G32: Glas .2H 105
Duniston Rd. ML6: Air .1H 113
Dunivaig Rd. G33: Glas .4D 86
Dunkeld Av. G73: Ruth .6D 10
Dunkeld Dr. G61: Bear .3H 4
Dunkeld Gdns. G64: B'rig .5D 4
Dunkeld La. G69: Mood .5E 5
Dunkeld Pl. G77: Newt M .5H 13
ML3: Ham .6C 14
ML5: Coat .1B 11
Dunkeld St. G31: Glas .1E 10
Dunkenny Pl. G15: Glas .3H 4
Dunkenny Rd. G15: Glas .4H 4
Dunkenny Sq. G15: Glas .4H 4
Dunlin G12: Glas .3G 6
G74: E Kil .5G 13
Dunlin Ct. ML4: Bell .5A 11
Dunlin Cres. PA6: C'lee .2C 7
Dunlop Ct. ML3: Ham .4A 15
Dunlop Cres. G71: Both .6F 12
PA4: Renf .5F 5
Dunlop Gro. G71: Tann .4E 10
Dunlop Pl. G62: Miln .2F 2
ML9: Ashg .5C 16
Dunlop St. G1: Glas .5G 8 (not continuous)
G72: Camb .1E 12
PA3: Lin .5A 7
PA4: Renf .5F 5 (off Dunlop Cres.)
Dunlop Twr. G75: E Kil .3G 14 (off Denholm Cres.)
Dunmore Dr. G62: Miln .5A 2
Dunmore St. G81: Clyd .1E 5
Dunnachie Dr. ML5: Coat .1F 10
Dunnachie Pl. ML5: Coat .1G 10
Dunnet Av. ML6: Glenm .4H 71
Dunnet Dr. PA6: C'lee .2B 74
Dunnichen Gdns. G64: B'rig .6F 49
Dunnikier Wlk. G68: Cumb .4A 34
Dunnolly St. G21: Glas .2C 84
Dunnotar Wlk. ML2: Newm .3D 14 (off Tiree Cres.)
Dunnottar Ct. G74: E Kil .6E 137
Dunnottar Cres. G74: E Kil .6E 137
Dunnottar St. G33: Glas .1B 86
G64: B'rig .5F 49
Dunn Sq. PA1: Pais .1A 98
Dunn St. G40: Glas .2B 104
G81: Clyd .4A 42
G81: Dun .1B 42
PA1: Pais .6C 78
Dunns Wood Rd. G67: Cumb .5D 14
Dunolly Dr. G77: Newt M .4F 133
Dunottar Av. ML5: Coat .3D 110
Dunottar Pl. ML5: Coat .2D 110
Dun Pk. G66: Kirk .5D 30
Dunphail Dr. G34: Glas .3B 88
Dunphail Rd. G34: Glas .3B 88
Dunragit St. G31: Glas .4E 85
DUNROBIN .4E 93
Dunrobin Av. PA5: Eld .4A 96
Dunrobin Ct. G74: E Kil .6F 137
G81: Clyd .5C 42
Dunrobin Cres. G74: E Kil .6F 137
Dunrobin Dr. G74: E Kil .6F 137
Dunrobin Gdns. ML6: Air .5E 93
Dunrobin Pl. ML5: Coat .4B 90
Dunrobin Rd. ML6: Air .4E 93
Dunrobin St. G31: Glas .5D 84
Dunrod Hill G74: E Kil .6H 137
Dunrod St. G32: Glas .1B 106
Dunscore Brae ML3: Ham .1C 152
Duns Cres. ML2: Wis .3A 146
Dunside Dr. G53: Glas .1A 116
Dunskaith Pl. G34: Glas .4B 88
Dunskaith St. G34: Glas .4B 88
Dunsmore Rd. PA7: B'ton .3G 39
Dunsmuir St. G51: Glas .4H 81
Duns Path ML5: Coat .2F 111
Dunster Gdns. G64: B'rig .3D 48
Dunswin Av. G81: Clyd .4A 42
Dunswin Ct. G81: Clyd .4A 42
Dunsyre Pl. G23: Glas .6C 46
Dunsyre St. G33: Glas .3G 85
Duntarvie Av. G34: Glas .3A 88
Duntarvie Cl. G34: Glas .3A 88
Duntarvie Cres. G34: Glas .3A 88
Duntarvie Dr. G34: Glas .3H 87
Duntarvie Gdns. G34: Glas .3A 88
Duntarvie Pl. G34: Glas .3H 87
Duntarvie Rd. G34: Glas .3H 87
Dunterlie Av. G13: Glas .3A 60
Dunterlie Ct. G78: Barr .4E 115
DUNTIBLAE .6G 31
Duntiblae Rd. G66: Kirk .6G 31
Duntiglennan Rd. G81: Dun .1C 42
DUNTOCHER .1C 42
Duntocher Rd. G61: Bear .1A 44
G81: Clyd .4A 42
G81: Dun .2C 42
G81: Faif .6G 23

Duntreath Av.—Ellangowan Ct.


**ntreath Av.** G13: Glas 1G 59
G15: Glas 6H 43
**ntreath Dr.** G15: Glas 6H 43
**ntreath Gdns.** G15: Glas 5H 43
**ntreath Gro.** G15: Glas 6H 43
**ntreath Ter.** G65: Kils 3H 11
**ntroon Pl.** *ML4: Bell 4D 126*
*(off Glencalder Cres.)*
**ntroon St.** G31: Glas 3D 84
**nure Dr.** G73: Ruth 2B 120
G77: Newt M 4G 133
ML3: Ham 1B 152
**nure Pl.** G77: Newt M 5G 133
ML5: Coat 2A 110
**nure St.** G20: Glas 2B 62
ML5: Coat 2A 110
**nvegan** ML6: Glenm 5G 71
**nvegan Av.** ML5: Coat 2H 89
PA5: Eld 4H 95
**nvegan Ct.** G13: Glas 3B 60
**nvegan Dr.** G64: B'rig 3C 48
G77: Newt M 4G 133
**nvegan Pl.** G71: Tann 5B 108
G74: E Kil 6F 137
**nvegan Quad.** PA4: Renf 5D 58
**nwan Av.** G13: Glas 2H 59
**nwan Pl.** G13: Glas 2H 59
**rban Av.** G81: Clyd 3G 41
**rham St.** G41: Glas 6B 82
**risdeer Dr.** ML3: Ham 2C 152
**rness Av.** G61: Bear 2H 45
**rno Path** G33: Glas 4E 87
**ror St.** G32: Glas 6A 86
**rris Gdns.** G32: Glas 2D 106
**rrockstock Cres.** PA2: Pais 6D 96
**rrockstock Rd.** PA2: Pais 6D 96
**rrockstock Way** PA2: Pais 6D 96
**rward** G74: E Kil 5E 139
**rward Av.** G41: Glas 4B 102
**rward Ct.** G41: Glas 4B 102
ML1: Moth 5F 127
**rward Cres.** PA2: Pais 4D 96
**rward Way** PA2: Pais 4D 96
**thie Pk. Gdns.** G13: Glas 3D 60
**thie Pk. Pl.** G13: Glas 3D 60
**thil St.** G51: Glas 5D 80
**ce Av.** ML6: Air 1G 111
**ce La.** G11: Glas 1G 81
**er's La.** G1: Glas 5H 83
**er's Wynd** PA1: Pais 6A 78
**frig St.** G72: Blan 1A 140
**KEBAR** 4D 98
**kebar Av.** G13: Glas 3B 60
**kebar Cres.** PA2: Pais 3D 98
**kehead Cres.** ML6: Air 1H 91
**kehead La.** G33: Glas 4D 86
**kehead Rd.** G65: Queen 2C 10
G68: Dull 5E 13
G69: Barg 6D 88
ML6: Air 1H 91
**kehead Sq.** ML3: Ham 6D 140
**kehead St.** G33: Glas 4D 86
**kemuir Pl.** G21: Glas 5D 64
**kemuir Quad.** G21: Glas 5C 64
**kemuir St.** G21: Glas 5C 64
**ke Rd.** G13: Glas 2A 60
G14: Glas 4H 59
**ke St.** G69: Bail 6A 88
ML5: Coat 1F 109
**sart Ct.** G68: Cumb 4A 34
**sart Way** ML6: Air 5G 93

## E

**agle Cres.** G61: Bear 1B 44
**agle Hgts.** G21: Glas 1H 83
**aglesham Ct.** G51: Glas 5C 82
**aglesham Path** ML5: Glenb 3G 69
**aglesham Pl.** G51: Glas 5C 82
**aglesham Rd.** G75: E Kil 3A 148
G76: Clar 6B 134
G77: Newt M 5D 132
**agle St.** G4: Glas 1G 83
**arlbank Av.** G14: Glas 5C 60
**arlbank La. Nth.** *G14: Glas 5C 60*
*(off Verona Av.)*
*G14: Glas 5C 60*
*(off Earlbank Av.)*
**arlbank La. Sth.** G14: Glas 5C 60
**arl Haig Rd.** G52: Hill 4H 79
**arl La.** G14: Glas 6C 60
(not continuous)
**arl Pl.** G14: Glas 5C 60
PA11: Bri W 5F 73
**arlsburn Rd.** G66: Lenz 3E 51
**arlscourt** G69: Mood 6D 52
**arl's Ga.** G71: Both 4C 124
**arlsgate** PA6: C'lee 2B 74
**arl's Hill** G68: Cumb 3D 34
**Earlspark Av.** G43: Glas 1D 118
**Earlston Av.** G21: Glas 2B 84
**Earlston Cres.** ML5: Coat 2F 111
**Earlston Pl.** G21: Glas 2B 84
**Earlston St.** ML2: Wis 3A 146
**Earl St.** G14: Glas 5A 60
**Earl Vw.** ML1: New S 4A 128
**Earlybraes Gdns.** G33: Glas 5D 86
**Earn Av.** G61: Bear 3H 45
ML4: Bell 1A 126
PA4: Renf 1G 79
**Earn Cres.** ML2: Wis 2H 157
**Earn Gdns.** ML9: Lark 5E 161
**Earn La.** *ML1: Holy 2A 128*
*(off Howden Pl.)*
**EARNOCK** 1C 152
**Earnock Av.** ML1: Moth 3E 143
**Earnock Gdns.** ML3: Ham 2D 152
**Earnock Rd.** ML3: Ham 1B 152
**Earnock St.** G33: Glas 5F 65
ML3: Ham 5E 141
**Earn Rd.** G77: Newt M 2D 132
**Earnside St.** G32: Glas 6B 86
**Earn St.** G33: Glas 2G 85
**Easdale** G74: E Kil 4B 150
**Easdale Dr.** G32: Glas 1A 106
**Easdale Path** ML5: Coat 1F 111
ML5: Glenb 3G 69
**Easdale Pl.** G77: Newt M 4B 132
**Easdale Ri.** ML3: Ham 6C 140
**E. Academy St.** ML2: Wis 1H 157
**East Av.** G71: View 1G 125
G72: Blan 4B 140
ML1: New S 5A 128
ML6: Plain 1G 93
ML8: Carl 3D 164
PA4: Renf 6F 59
**EAST BALGROCHAN** 3E 29
**Eastbank Dr.** G32: Glas 6C 86
**Eastbank Pl.** G32: Glas 6C 86
**Eastbank Ri** G32: Glas 6C 86
**E. Barns St.** G81: Clyd 1F 59
**E. Bath La.** G2: Glas 3G 83 (4E 5)
**E. Buchanan M.** *PA1: Pais 6B 78*
*(off E. Buchanan St.)*
**E. Buchanan St.** PA1: Pais 6B 78
**Eastburn Cres.** G21: Glas 3D 64
**Eastburn Pl.** G21: Glas 3D 64
**Eastburn Rd.** G21: Glas 4D 64
**E. Burnside St.** G65: Kils 3H 11
**E. Campbell St.** G40: Glas 5A 84
**Eastcote Av.** G14: Glas 5E 61
**EAST CRAIGEND** 6D 40
**EAST CRINDLEDYKE** 3E 147
**Eastcroft** G73: Ruth 5D 104
**Eastcroft Ter.** G21: Glas 5C 64
**E. Dean St.** ML4: Bell 2D 126
**Eastend Av.** ML1: Carf 6B 128
**Easterbrae** ML1: Moth 5F 143
**Easter Cadder Cotts.** G66: Kirk 6H 29
**Easter Craigs** G31: Glas 3D 84
**Easter Cres.** ML2: Wis 5C 146
**Easter Garngaber Rd.**
G66: Lenz 2E 51
**Eastergreens Av.** G66: Kirk 6C 30
**Easterhill Pl.** G32: Glas 2H 105
**Easterhill St.** G32: Glas 2H 105
**EASTERHOUSE** 3G 87
**Easterhouse Pl.** G34: Glas 3A 88
**Easterhouse Rd.** G34: Glas 3A 88
G69: Bail 6H 87
**EASTERHOUSE ROAD INTERCHANGE**
4A 88
Easterhouse Sports Cen. 2F 87
**Easterhouse Station (Rail)** 5A 88
Easterhouse Swimming Pool 3G 87
**Easterhouse Township Cen.**
G34: Glas 2G 87
**Eastermains** G66: Kirk 3H 31
**Easter M.** G71: Udd 2C 124
**Easter Queenslie Rd.** G33: Glas 3E 87
**Easter Rd.** G76: Busby 3E 135
**Easterton Av.** G76: Busby 4E 135
**Easterton Cotts.** G64: Torr 3E 29
**Easter Wood Cres.** G71: View 4H 109
**EASTFIELD** 6F 105
**Eastfield Av.** G72: Camb 1G 121
**Eastfield Cres.** G82: Dumb 5H 17
**Eastfield Pl.** G82: Dumb 5H 17
**Eastfield Rd.** G21: Glas 5A 64
G68: Cumb 3C 34
ML8: Carl 4G 165
**Eastfield Ter.** ML4: Bell 3F 127
**EAST FULTON** 5F 75
**Eastgate** G69: G'csh 4E 69
**East Ga.** ML2: Wis 6B 146
ML5: Glenb 2H 69
**E. George St.** ML5: Coat 3D 90
**E. Glebe Ter.** ML3: Ham 1H 153
**E. Greenlees Av.** G72: Camb 4C 122
**E. Greenlees Cres.**
G72: Camb 4B 122
**E. Greenlees Dr.** G72: Camb 4C 122
**East Greenlees Gro.**
G72: Camb 4H 121
**E. Greenlees Rd.** G72: Camb 4A 122
**E. Hallhill Road** G69: Bail 5G 87
**Easthall Pl.** G33: Glas 4F 87
**E. Hamilton St.** ML2: Wis 1H 157
**E. High St.** ML6: Air 3A 92
**EAST KILBRIDE** 2H 149
East Kilbride Arts Cen. 6H 137
East Kilbride Ice Rink 3H 149
**East Kilbride Station (Rail)**
1G 149
**E. Kilbride Rd.** G73: Ruth 2E 121
G76: Busby 3E 135
**East Kilbride Rd.** G76: Crmck 5G 135
East Kilbride Sports Cen. 5C 150
East Kilbride Village Theatre
1H 149
**East La.** PA1: Pais 1C 98
**Eastlea Pl.** ML6: Air 5B 92
**E. Machan St.** ML9: Lark 4F 161
**EAST MAINS** 1A 150
**E. Mains Rd.** G74: E Kil 1G 149
**E. Milton Gro.** G75: E Kil 2D 148
**Eastmuir St.** G32: Glas 6B 86
ML2: Wis 5C 146
**Easton Pl.** ML5: Coat 6D 90
**East Rd.** ML1: New S 3A 128
PA10: Kilb 1A 94
**E. Scott Ter.** ML3: Ham 2H 153
**EAST SHAWHEAD** 3E 111
**Eastside** G66: Kirk 4D 30
**Eastside Ind. Est.** *G66: Kirk 4D 30*
*(off Kilsyth Rd.)*
**E. Springfield Ter.** G64: B'rig 1D 64
**E. Station Ind. Est.** ML9: Lark 1F 161
**E. Stewart Pl.** ML5: Coat 4E 91
**E. Stewart St.** ML5: Coat 5E 91
**E. Thomson St.** G81: Clyd 4D 42
**E. Thornlie St.** ML2: Wis 1H 157
**Eastvale Pl.** G3: Glas 3A 82
**E. Wellbrae Cres.** ML3: Ham 2F 153
**E. Wellington St.** G31: Glas 6F 85
**E. Whitby St.** G31: Glas 1E 105
**Eastwood Av.** G41: Glas 5B 102
G46: Giff 4A 118
Eastwood Butterfly Kingdom 5F 117
**Eastwood Cres.** G46: T'bnk 3F 117
**Eastwood Dr.** ML2: Newm 3E 147
**Eastwoodmains Rd.** G46: Giff 6H 117
G76: Clar 6H 117
Eastwood Recreation Cen. 5H 117
**Eastwood Rd.** G69: Mood 5D 52
**Eastwood Toll** G46: Giff 6H 117
**Eastwood Vw.** G72: Camb 1E 123
**Eastwood Way** *ML9: Lark 1F 161*
*(off Antrim La.)*
**Easwald Bank** PA10: Kilb 3B 94
**Ebroch Dr.** G65: Kils 3A 12
**Ebroch Pk.** G65: Kils 3A 12
**Eccles St.** G22: Glas 4A 64
**Eckford St.** G32: Glas 1A 106
**Eck Path** *ML1: Holy 2A 128*
*(off Howden Pl.)*
**Eday St.** G22: Glas 3H 63
**Edderton Pl.** G34: Glas 4G 87
**Edderton Way** G34: Glas 4G 87
**Eddington Dr.** G77: Newt M 6C 132
**Eddleston Pl.** G72: Camb 2D 122
**EDDLEWOOD** 4H 153
**Eddlewood Ct.** G33: Glas 4G 87
**Eddlewood Path** G33: Glas 4F 87
**Eddlewood Pl.** G33: Glas 4F 87
**Eddlewood Rd.** G33: Glas 4F 87
Eddlewood Sports Barn 4H 153
**Eden Dr.** G75: E Kil 5B 148
**Eden Gdns.** G75: E Kil 4B 148
**Eden Gro.** G75: E Kil 4B 148
**Eden La.** G33: Glas 2F 85
**Eden Pk.** G71: Both 5D 124
**Eden Pl.** G72: Camb 2D 122
PA4: Renf 1G 79
**Edenside** G68: Cumb 4B 14
**Eden St.** G33: Glas 2F 85
**Edenwood St.** G31: Glas 6G 85
**Edgam Dr.** G52: Glas 6C 80
**Edgefauld Av.** G21: Glas 6B 64
**Edgefauld Dr.** G21: Glas 5B 64
**Edgefauld Pl.** G21: Glas 4B 64
**Edgefauld Rd.** G21: Glas 5B 64
**Edgehill La.** G11: Glas 5G 61
**Edgehill Rd.** G11: Glas 5F 61
G61: Bear 1E 45
**Edgemont Pk.** ML3: Ham 3G 153
**Edgemont St.** G41: Glas 5C 102
**Edinbeg Av.** G42: Glas 5A 104
**Edinbeg Pl.** G42: Glas 5A 104
**Edinburgh Rd.** G33: Glas 4F 85
G69: Bail 5G 87
ML1: N'hse 1C 128
**Edington Gdns.** G69: Mood 4D 52
**Edington St.** G4: Glas 1F 83 (1C 4)
**Edison St.** G52: Hill 3G 79
(not continuous)
**Edmiston Dr.** G51: Glas 5F 81
PA3: Lin 5F 75
**Edmonstone Ct.** G81: Clyd 2F 59
**Edmonstone Dr.** G65: Kils 4H 11
**Edmonton Ter.** G75: E Kil 3E 149
**Edmund Kean** G74: E Kil 4C 138
**Edrick Ct.** *ML5: Coat 5B 90*
*(off Kirk St.)*
**Edrom Ct.** G32: Glas 6H 85
**Edrom Path** G32: Glas 6H 85
**Edrom St.** G32: Glas 6H 85
(not continuous)
**Edward Av.** PA4: Renf 5G 59
**Edward St.** G65: Kils 2H 11
G69: Barg 6D 88
G81: Clyd 2F 59
ML1: Moth 4H 143
ML3: Ham 1H 153
**Edwin St.** G51: Glas 6B 82
**Edzell Ct.** G14: Glas 1D 80
**Edzell Dr.** G77: Newt M 5E 133
PA5: Eld 3B 96
**Edzell Gdns.** G64: B'rig 1E 65
ML2: Wis 1G 157
**Edzell Pl.** G14: Glas 6D 60
**Edzell St.** G14: Glas 1D 80
ML5: Coat 1H 109
**Egidia Av.** G46: Giff 5A 118
**Egilsay Cres.** G22: Glas 1G 63
**Egilsay Pl.** G22: Glas 1G 63
**Egilsay St.** G22: Glas 1G 63
**Egilsay Ter.** G22: Glas 1G 63
**Eglinton Ct.** G5: Glas 6F 83
**Eglinton Dr.** G46: Giff 5A 118
**Eglinton St.** G41: Glas 1E 103
ML5: Coat 3D 90
**Egmont Pk.** G75: E Kil 4C 148
**Eider** G12: Glas 2G 61
**Eider Av.** G75: E Kil 6C 148
**Eider Gro.** G75: E Kil 6C 148
**Eider Pl.** G75: E Kil 6C 148
**Eighth St.** G71: Tann 4C 108
**Eildon Cres.** ML6: Chap 4F 113
**Eildon Dr.** G78: Barr 6E 115
**Eildon Rd.** G66: Kirk 5F 31
**Eileen Gdns.** G64: B'rig 5D 48
**Eilt Wlk.** *ML2: Newm 3D 146*
*(off Islay Av.)*
**Elcho St.** G40: Glas 5B 84
**Elderbank** G61: Bear 4E 45
**Elder Cres.** G72: Flem 3E 123
**Elder Gro.** G51: Glas 4D 80
G71: View 5F 109
**Elder Gro. Ct.** G51: Glas 4D 80
**Elderpark Gdns.** G51: Glas 4F 81
**Elderpark Gro.** G51: Glas 4F 81
**Elderpark St.** G51: Glas 4F 81
**Elderslea Rd.** ML8: Carl 5G 165
**ELDERSLIE** 2A 96
Elderslie Leisure Cen. 2B 96
**Elderslie St.** G3: Glas 2D 82
**Elder St.** G51: Glas 4F 81
(not continuous)
**Elders Way** ML2: Wis 6B 146
**Eldin Pl.** PA11: Bri W 5G 73
PA5: Eld 3H 95
**Eldon Ct.** G11: Glas 1H 81
**Eldon Gdns.** G64: B'rig 6A 48
**Eldon St.** G3: Glas 1C 82
**Elgin Av.** G74: E Kil 6H 137
**Elgin Gdns.** G76: Clar 1D 134
**Elgin Pl.** G65: Kils 2H 11
G74: E Kil 6H 137
ML5: Coat 2D 110
ML6: Air 6G 91
**Elgin Rd.** G61: Bear 6F 25
**Elgin Ter.** ML3: Ham 5C 140
**Elgin Way** ML4: Bell 1C 126
**Elibank St.** G33: Glas 2A 86
**Elie Ct.** G68: Cumb 6H 13
**Elie St.** G11: Glas 1A 82
**Eliot Cres.** ML3: Ham 2H 153
**Eliot Ter.** ML3: Ham 1H 153
**Elison Ct.** ML1: Moth 5B 144
**Elizabethan Way** PA4: Renf 2E 79
**Elizabeth Av.** G66: Milt C 5B 8
**Elizabeth Ct.** G74: E Kil 1H 149
**Elizabeth Cres.** G46: T'bnk 4G 117
**Elizabeth Quad.** ML1: Holy 2A 128
**Elizabeth St.** G51: Glas 6A 82
**Elizabeth Wynd** ML3: Ham 4H 153
**Ella Gdns.** ML4: Bell 3E 127
**Ellangowan Ct.** G62: Miln 3G 25

Ellangowan Rd.—Fennsbank Av.

**Ellangowan Rd.** G41: Glas . . . . . .5A **102**
G62: Miln . . . . . . . . . . . . . . . .3G **25**
**Ellergreen Rd.** G61: Bear . . . . . . . .3E **45**
**Ellerslie St.** PA5: John . . . . . . . . .2G **95**
**Ellesmere St.** G22: Glas . . . . . . . . .6E **63**
**Ellinger Ct.** G81: Clyd . . . . . . . . . .3H **41**
**Elliot Av.** G46: Giff . . . . . . . . . . .5A **118**
PA2: Pais . . . . . . . . . . . . . . . .6C **96**
**Elliot Ct.** ML1: Moth . . . . . . . . . .6F **127**
**Elliot Cres.** G74: E Kil . . . . . . . . .1B **150**
**Elliot Dr.** G46: Giff . . . . . . . . . . .4A **118**
**Elliot Pl.** G3: Glas . . . . . . . . . . . . .4C **82**
**Elliot St.** G3: Glas . . . . . . . . . . . . .4C **82**
(not continuous)
**Ellisland** G66: Kirk . . . . . . . . . . . .3H **31**
G74: E Kil . . . . . . . . . . . . . . .6D **138**
**Ellisland Av.** G81: Clyd . . . . . . . . .4E **43**
**Ellisland Cres.** G73: Ruth . . . . . . .2B **120**
**Ellisland Dr.** G66: Kirk . . . . . . . . . .3G **31**
G72: Blan . . . . . . . . . . . . . . .3H **139**
**Ellisland Rd.** G43: Glas . . . . . . . .1B **118**
G67: Cumb . . . . . . . . . . . . . . .3B **36**
G76: Busby . . . . . . . . . . . . . .4C **134**
**Ellisland Wynd** ML1: N'hill . . . . . .4C **128**
**Ellismuir Farm Rd.** G69: Bail . . . .1B **108**
**Ellismuir Pl.** G69: Bail . . . . . . . . .1A **108**
**Ellismuir Rd.** G69: Bail . . . . . . . . .1A **108**
**Ellismuir St.** ML5: Coat . . . . . . . .2H **109**
(not continuous)
**Ellismuir Way** G71: Tann . . . . . . .4E **109**
**Ellis St.** ML5: Coat . . . . . . . . . . . .4C **90**
**Elliston Av.** G53: Glas . . . . . . . . .2C **116**
**Elliston Cres.** G53: Glas . . . . . . . .2C **116**
**Elliston Dr.** G53: Glas . . . . . . . . . .2C **116**
**Ellis Way** ML1: Moth . . . . . . . . . .4H **143**
**Ellon Dr.** PA3: Lin . . . . . . . . . . . . .6G **75**
**Ellon Gro.** PA3: Pais . . . . . . . . . . .4B **78**
**Ellon Way** PA3: Pais . . . . . . . . . . .4B **78**
**Ellrig** G75: E Kil . . . . . . . . . . . . . .6F **149**
**Elm Av.** G66: Lenz . . . . . . . . . . . . .1C **50**
PA4: Renf . . . . . . . . . . . . . . . . .5E **59**
**Elm Bank** G64: B'rig . . . . . . . . . . .6D **48**
G66: Kirk . . . . . . . . . . . . . . . . .4D **30**
**Elmbank Av.** G71: View . . . . . . . . .6F **109**
**Elmbank Cres.** G2: Glas . . . .3E **83** (3A **4**)
ML3: Ham . . . . . . . . . . . . . . .5E **141**
**Elmbank Dr.** ML9: Lark . . . . . . . . .4G **161**
**Elmbank St.** G2: Glas . . . . . .3E **83** (4A **4**)
ML4: Bell . . . . . . . . . . . . . . . .2C **126**
ML8: Carl . . . . . . . . . . . . . . . .5G **165**
**Elmbank St. La.** G2: Glas . . . . . . . . .4A **4**
**Elm Cres.** G71: View . . . . . . . . . . .6H **109**
**Elm Dr.** G67: Cumb . . . . . . . . . . . .1F **37**
G72: Camb . . . . . . . . . . . . . . .2C **122**
PA5: John . . . . . . . . . . . . . . . . .5F **95**
**Elmfoot St.** G5: Glas . . . . . . . . . . .3H **103**
**Elm Gdns.** G61: Bear . . . . . . . . . . . .1E **45**
**Elmhurst** ML1: Moth . . . . . . . . . . .5F **143**
**Elmira Rd.** G69: Muirh . . . . . . . . . .2B **68**
**Elm La. W.** *G14: Glas* . . . . . . . . . . .*6D* ***60***
*(off Lime St.)*
**Elm Lea** PA5: John . . . . . . . . . . . . .3H **95**
**Elmore Av.** G44: Glas . . . . . . . . . .2F **119**
**Elmore La.** G44: Glas . . . . . . . . . .2F **119**
**Elm Pl.** G75: E Kil . . . . . . . . . . . . .5E **149**
**Elm Quad.** ML6: Air . . . . . . . . . . . .4D **92**
**Elm Rd.** G73: Ruth . . . . . . . . . . . .3D **120**
G81: Clyd . . . . . . . . . . . . . . . . .2C **42**
G82: Dumb . . . . . . . . . . . . . . . .3F **17**
ML1: Holy . . . . . . . . . . . . . . . .2B **128**
ML1: New S . . . . . . . . . . . . . .5A **128**
PA11: Bri W . . . . . . . . . . . . . . .2G **73**
PA2: Pais . . . . . . . . . . . . . . . . .4C **98**
**Elmslie Ct.** G69: Bail . . . . . . . . . . .1A **108**
**Elms, The** G44: Glas . . . . . . . . . . .3E **119**
**Elm St.** G14: Glas . . . . . . . . . . . . . .6D **60**
G66: Len . . . . . . . . . . . . . . . . . .3G **7**
G72: Blan . . . . . . . . . . . . . . . . .2C **140**
G76: Busby . . . . . . . . . . . . . . .3D **134**
ML1: Moth . . . . . . . . . . . . . . . .2F **143**
ML5: Coat . . . . . . . . . . . . . . . .6E **91**
**Elm St. E.** *G14: Glas* . . . . . . . . . . . .*6D* ***60***
*(off Elm St.)*
**Elmtree Gdns.** G45: Glas . . . . . . .3B **120**
**Elmvale Row** G21: Glas . . . . . . . . .4A **64**
**Elmvale St.** G21: Glas . . . . . . . . . . .4A **64**
**Elm Vw. Ct.** ML4: Bell . . . . . . . . . .3F **127**
**Elm Wlk.** G61: Bear . . . . . . . . . . . . .1E **45**
**Elm Way** G72: Flem . . . . . . . . . . .3E **123**
ML9: Lark . . . . . . . . . . . . . . . .6A **156**
**Elmwood** ML2: Wis . . . . . . . . . . . .2E **157**
**Elmwood Av.** G11: Glas . . . . . . . . . .5F **61**
G77: Newt M . . . . . . . . . . . . .3F **133**
**Elmwood Ct.** G71: Both . . . . . . . . .5E **125**
**Elmwood Gdns.** G66: Lenz . . . . . . .2A **50**
**Elmwood La.** G11: Glas . . . . . . . . . .5F **61**
**Elphinstone Cres.** G75: E Kil . . . .4H **149**
**Elphinstone Pl.** G51: Glas . . . . . . . .4A **82**
**Elphinstone Rd.** G46: Giff . . . . . . .2G **133**
**Elphin St.** G23: Glas . . . . . . . . . . . .6B **46**
**Elrig Rd.** G44: Glas . . . . . . . . . . . .2D **118**
**Elsinore Path** G75: E Kil . . . . . . . .6G **149**
**Elspeth Gdns.** G64: B'rig . . . . . . . . .5E **49**
**Eltham St.** G22: Glas . . . . . . . . . . . .6F **63**
**Elvan Ct.** ML1: Moth . . . . . . . . . . .3F **143**
**Elvan Pl.** G75: E Kil . . . . . . . . . . . .4A **148**
**Elvan St.** G32: Glas . . . . . . . . . . . . .6H **85**
ML1: Moth . . . . . . . . . . . . . . .2F **143**
**Elvan Twr.** ML1: Moth . . . . . . . . . .4G **143**
**Embo Dr.** G13: Glas . . . . . . . . . . . .3B **60**
**Emerald Ter.** ML4: Bell . . . . . . . . .3C **126**
**Emerson Rd.** G64: B'rig . . . . . . . . .6C **48**
**Emerson Rd. W.** G64: B'rig . . . . . .6C **48**
**Emily Dr.** ML1: Moth . . . . . . . . . . .5G **143**
**Emma Jay Rd.** ML4: Bell . . . . . . . .2D **126**
**Empire Way** ML1: Moth . . . . . . . . .6E **127**
**Endfield Av.** G12: Glas . . . . . . . . . .3H **61**
**Endrick Bank** G64: B'rig . . . . . . . . .3C **48**
**Endrick Dr.** G61: Bear . . . . . . . . . . .4F **45**
PA1: Pais . . . . . . . . . . . . . . . . .5D **78**
**Endrick Gdns.** G62: Miln . . . . . . . . .3E **25**
**Endrick Ho.** G82: Dumb . . . . . . . . . .1H **17**
**Endrick St.** G21: Glas . . . . . . . . . . .6H **63**
**English Row** ML6: C'bnk . . . . . . . .3C **112**
**English St.** ML2: Wis . . . . . . . . . . .6D **144**
**Ennerdale** G75: E Kil . . . . . . . . . . .5B **148**
**Ennisfree Rd.** G72: Blan . . . . . . . .1B **140**
**Ensay St.** G22: Glas . . . . . . . . . . . .2H **63**
**Enterkin St.** G32: Glas . . . . . . . . .1H **105**
**Eriboll Pl.** G22: Glas . . . . . . . . . . . .2F **63**
**Eriboll St.** G22: Glas . . . . . . . . . . . .2F **63**
**Eribol Wlk.** ML1: N'hill . . . . . . . . .4D **128**
**Ericht Rd.** G43: Glas . . . . . . . . . . .2A **118**
**Eriska Av.** G14: Glas . . . . . . . . . . . .4A **60**
**Eriskay Av.** G77: Newt M . . . . . . .4B **132**
ML3: Ham . . . . . . . . . . . . . . .1D **152**
**Eriskay Cres.** G77: Newt M . . . . . .4B **132**
**Eriskay Dr.** G60: Old K . . . . . . . . . . .1G **41**
**Eriskay Pl.** G60: Old K . . . . . . . . . . .1G **41**
**Erradale St.** G22: Glas . . . . . . . . . . .2E **63**
**Errogie St.** G34: Glas . . . . . . . . . . . .3H **87**
**Errol Gdns.** G5: Glas . . . . . . . . . . .1G **103**
ERSKINE . . . . . . . . . . . . . . . . . . . .6F **41**
**Erskine Av.** G41: Glas . . . . . . . . . .1H **101**
**Erskine Bri.** G60: Old K . . . . . . . . . . .2E **41**
PA7: B'ton . . . . . . . . . . . . . . . . .3D **40**
**Erskine Ct.** *ML6: Air* . . . . . . . . . . .*3E* ***93***
*(off Katherine St.)*
**Erskine Cres.** ML6: Air . . . . . . . . . . .6H **91**
**Erskinefauld Rd.** PA3: Lin . . . . . . .5G **75**
**Erskine Ferry Rd.** G60: Old K . . . . .2F **41**
**Erskine Rd.** G46: Giff . . . . . . . . . .3H **133**
**Erskine Sq.** G52: Hill . . . . . . . . . . .4H **79**
Erskine Swimming Pool . . . . . . . .5F **41**
**Erskine Vw.** G60: Old K . . . . . . . . . . .1E **41**
G81: Clyd . . . . . . . . . . . . . . . . .4D **42**
**Ervie St.** G34: Glas . . . . . . . . . . . . .4A **88**
**Escart Rd.** ML8: Carl . . . . . . . . . . .2F **165**
**Esdaile Ct.** ML1: New S . . . . . . . . .4A **128**
**Esk Av.** PA4: Renf . . . . . . . . . . . . . .1G **79**
**Eskbank St.** G32: Glas . . . . . . . . . .5A **86**
**Eskdale** G74: E Kil . . . . . . . . . . . . .6E **137**
G77: Newt M . . . . . . . . . . . . .4H **133**
**Eskdale Dr.** G73: Ruth . . . . . . . . . .6F **105**
**Eskdale Rd.** G61: Bear . . . . . . . . . . .5D **44**
**Eskdale St.** G42: Glas . . . . . . . . . .4F **103**
**Esk Dr.** PA2: Pais . . . . . . . . . . . . . .4C **96**
**Esk St.** G14: Glas . . . . . . . . . . . . . .4H **59**
**Esk Wlk.** *G67: Cumb* . . . . . . . . . . .*4H* ***35***
*(in Cumbernauld Shop. Cen.)*
**Esk Way** PA2: Pais . . . . . . . . . . . . .4C **96**
**Esmond St.** G3: Glas . . . . . . . . . . . .2A **82**
**Espedair St.** PA2: Pais . . . . . . . . . .2A **98**
**Espieside Cres.** ML5: Coat . . . . . . .3H **89**
Esporta Health & Fitness Club
Finnieston . . . . . . . . . . . . . .3C **82**
Hamilton . . . . . . . . . . . . . . .4B **142**
Esporta Health & Racquets
. . . . . . . . . . . . . . . . . . . . . .2B **26**
**Essenside Av.** G15: Glas . . . . . . . . .5B **44**
**Essex Dr.** G14: Glas . . . . . . . . . . . . .5D **60**
**Essex La.** G14: Glas . . . . . . . . . . . . .5D **60**
(not continuous)
**Esslemont Av.** G14: Glas . . . . . . . . .4B **60**
**Esslemont La.** G14: Glas . . . . . . . . .4C **60**
**Estate Quad.** G32: Carm . . . . . . . .5C **106**
**Estate Rd.** G32: Carm . . . . . . . . . .5C **106**
**Etive Av.** G61: Bear . . . . . . . . . . . . .3H **45**
ML3: Ham . . . . . . . . . . . . . . .2E **153**
**Etive Ct.** G67: Cumb . . . . . . . . . . . .1D **54**
G81: Hard . . . . . . . . . . . . . . . .2E **43**
ML5: Coat . . . . . . . . . . . . . . .2D **110**
**Etive Cres.** G64: B'rig . . . . . . . . . . .6D **48**
G67: Cumb . . . . . . . . . . . . . . . .1D **54**
ML2: Wis . . . . . . . . . . . . . . . .3H **157**
**Etive Dr.** G46: Giff . . . . . . . . . . . .6B **118**
G67: Cumb . . . . . . . . . . . . . . . .1D **54**
ML6: Air . . . . . . . . . . . . . . . . . .6C **92**
PA7: B'ton . . . . . . . . . . . . . . . . .5A **40**
**Etive Pl.** G67: Cumb . . . . . . . . . . . .1E **55**
**Etive St.** G32: Glas . . . . . . . . . . . . .6A **86**
ML2: Wis . . . . . . . . . . . . . . . .2H **157**
**Etna Ind. Est.** ML2: Wis . . . . . . . .5C **144**
**Etna St.** ML2: Wis . . . . . . . . . . . . .5C **144**
**Eton La.** *G12: Glas* . . . . . . . . . . . .*1C* ***82***
*(off Gt. George St.)*
**Etrick Av.** ML4: Bell . . . . . . . . . . . .6C **110**
**Etterick Wynd** *G72: Blan* . . . . . . . .*2A* ***140***
*(off Cheviot St.)*
**Ettrick Av.** PA4: Renf . . . . . . . . . . . .1H **79**
**Ettrick Ct.** G72: Camb . . . . . . . . . .2D **122**
ML5: Coat . . . . . . . . . . . . . . . .2E **111**
**Ettrick Cres.** G73: Ruth . . . . . . . . .6E **105**
**Ettrick Dr.** G61: Bear . . . . . . . . . . . .6C **24**
PA7: B'ton . . . . . . . . . . . . . . . . .5A **40**
**Ettrick Hill** G74: E Kil . . . . . . . . . .6A **138**
**Ettrick Oval** PA2: Pais . . . . . . . . . . .5C **96**
**Ettrick Pl.** G43: Glas . . . . . . . . . . .6B **102**
**Ettrick Sq.** *G67: Cumb* . . . . . . . . . .*4H* ***35***
*(in Cumbernauld Shop. Cen.)*
**Ettrick St.** ML2: Wis . . . . . . . . . . .4G **145**
**Ettrick Ter.** PA5: John . . . . . . . . . . .5C **94**
**Ettrick Wlk.** *G67: Cumb* . . . . . . . . .*4H* ***35***
*(in Cumbernauld Shop. Cen.)*
**Ettrick Way** *G67: Cumb* . . . . . . . . .*4H* ***35***
*(in Cumbernauld Shop. Cen.)*
PA4: Renf . . . . . . . . . . . . . . . . .1H **79**
**Eurocentral** ML1: Holy . . . . . . . . .5H **111**
**Eurocentral Ind. Est.**
ML1: Holy . . . . . . . . . . . . . . .6H **111**
**EUROCENTRAL JUNC.** . . . . . . . . .4H **111**
**Evan Cres.** G46: Giff . . . . . . . . . . .5B **118**
**Evan Dr.** G46: Giff . . . . . . . . . . . . .5B **118**
**Evanton Dr.** G46: T'bnk . . . . . . . . .4E **117**
**Evanton Pl.** G46: T'bnk . . . . . . . . .4E **117**
**Everall Dr.** ML2: Newm . . . . . . . . .4E **147**
**Everard Ct.** G21: Glas . . . . . . . . . . .2A **64**
**Everard Dr.** G21: Glas . . . . . . . . . . .3A **64**
**Everard Pl.** G21: Glas . . . . . . . . . . .2A **64**
**Everard Quad.** G21: Glas . . . . . . . .2A **64**
**Everglades, The** G69: Chry . . . . . .1H **67**
**Eversley St.** G32: Glas . . . . . . . . .2A **106**
**Everton Rd.** G53: Glas . . . . . . . . .3C **100**
Ewan Mundy Fine Art Gallery
. . . . . . . . . . . . . . . . . . . . . . .4C **4**
**Ewart Cres.** ML3: Ham . . . . . . . . .1E **153**
**Ewart Ter.** ML3: Ham . . . . . . . . . .1F **153**
**Ewing Ct.** ML3: Ham . . . . . . . . . . .4G **153**
**Ewing Pl.** G31: Glas . . . . . . . . . . . . .6E **85**
**Ewing St.** G73: Ruth . . . . . . . . . . .6C **104**
PA10: Kilb . . . . . . . . . . . . . . . .2A **94**
**Ewing Wlk.** G62: Miln . . . . . . . . . . .4A **26**
**Excelsior Pk.** ML2: Wis . . . . . . . . .1D **156**
**Excelsior St.** ML2: Wis . . . . . . . . .1C **156**
**Exchange Pl.** G1: Glas . . . . . . . . . . . .5E **5**
ML5: Coat . . . . . . . . . . . . . . . . .5C **90**
**Exeter Dr.** G11: Glas . . . . . . . . . . . .1G **81**
**Exeter La.** *G11: Glas* . . . . . . . . . . . .*1G* ***81***
*(off Dumbarton Rd.)*
**Exeter St.** ML5: Coat . . . . . . . . . . . .6C **90**
Exhibition Centre Station (Rail)
. . . . . . . . . . . . . . . . . . . . . . .3C **82**
**Eynort St.** G22: Glas . . . . . . . . . . . .2E **63**
**Eyrepoint Ct.** G33: Glas . . . . . . . . .3A **86**

## F

**Factory Rd.** ML1: Moth . . . . . . . .4G **143**
**Fagan Ct.** G72: Blan . . . . . . . . . . .6C **124**
FAIFLEY . . . . . . . . . . . . . . . . . . . .6E **23**
**Faifley Rd.** G81: Faif, Hard . . . . . . .6F **23**
**Fairbairn Cres.** G46: T'bnk . . . . . .5G **117**
**Fairbairn Path** *G40: Glas* . . . . . . .*1C* ***104***
*(off Ruby St.)*
**Fairbairn St.** G40: Glas . . . . . . . . .1C **104**
**Fairburn St.** G32: Glas . . . . . . . . .1H **105**
**Fairfax Av.** G44: Glas . . . . . . . . . .2G **119**
**Fairfield Ct.** G76: Busby . . . . . . . .4C **134**
**Fairfield Dr.** G76: Busby . . . . . . . .4C **134**
PA4: Renf . . . . . . . . . . . . . . . . .2F **79**
**Fairfield Gdns.** G51: Glas . . . . . . . .3F **81**
**Fairfield Pl.** G51: Glas . . . . . . . . . . .3F **81**
G71: Both . . . . . . . . . . . . . . .5F **125**
G74: E Kil . . . . . . . . . . . . . . . .1D **148**
ML3: Ham . . . . . . . . . . . . . . .2A **154**
**Fairfield St.** G51: Glas . . . . . . . . . . .3F **81**
**Fairford Dr.** G67: Cumb . . . . . . . . . .6F **35**
**Fairhaven Av.** ML6: Air . . . . . . . . . .5E **93**
**Fairhaven Rd.** G23: Glas . . . . . . . . .1C **62**
FAIRHILL . . . . . . . . . . . . . . . . . .3G **153**
**Fairhill Av.** G53: Glas . . . . . . . . . .6C **100**
ML3: Ham . . . . . . . . . . . . . . .2G **153**
**Fairhill Cres.** ML3: Ham . . . . . . . .2G **153**
**Fairhill Pl.** ML3: Ham . . . . . . . . . .4F **153**
**Fairholm Av.** ML3: Fern . . . . . . . .2E **155**
**Fairholm St.** G32: Glas . . . . . . . . .1H **105**
ML9: Lark . . . . . . . . . . . . . . .1D **160**
**Fairley St.** G51: Glas . . . . . . . . . . . .5H **81**
**Fairlie** G74: E Kil . . . . . . . . . . . . . .6F **137**
**Fairlie Pk. Dr.** G11: Glas . . . . . . . . .1G
**Fair Oaks** G76: Crmck . . . . . . . . . .1A **13**
**Fairview Ct.** *G62: Miln* . . . . . . . . . .*4G*
*(off Main S*
**Fairway** G61: Bear . . . . . . . . . . . . .2B **4**
**Fairway Av.** PA2: Pais . . . . . . . . . . .5H **9**
**Fairways** ML9: Lark . . . . . . . . . . . .2G **16**
**Fairways, The** G44: Neth . . . . . . .5D **11**
PA5: John . . . . . . . . . . . . . . . . .6D **9**
**Fairways Vw.** G81: Hard . . . . . . . . .1F **4**
**Fairweather Pl.**
G77: Newt M . . . . . . . . . . . . . .5C **13**
**Fairyknowe Gdns.** G71: Both . . . .5F **12**
**Faith Av.** PA11: Q'riers . . . . . . . . . .1A **7**
**Falconbridge Rd.** G74: E Kil . . . . .5C **13**
**Falcon Cres.** PA3: Pais . . . . . . . . . .5F **7**
**Falconer Ter.** ML3: Ham . . . . . . . .2G **15**
**Falcon Ho.** PA3: Pais . . . . . . . . . . .4A **7**
**Falcon Rd.** PA5: John . . . . . . . . . . .6D **9**
**Falcon Ter.** G20: Glas . . . . . . . . . . .1A **6**
**Falcon Ter. La.** *G20: Glas* . . . . . . . .*1A* ***6***
*(off Caldercuilt Rd*
**Falfield St.** G5: Glas . . . . . . . . . . .1E **10**
**Falkland Av.** G77: Newt M . . . . . .4G **13**
**Falkland Cres.** G64: B'rig . . . . . . . .1F **6**
**Falkland Dr.** G74: E Kil . . . . . . . . .2E **14**
**Falkland La.** G12: Glas . . . . . . . . . .6H **6**
**Falkland Pk.** G74: E Kil . . . . . . . . .2F **14**
**Falkland Pl.** G74: E Kil . . . . . . . . .2F **14**
ML5: Coat . . . . . . . . . . . . . . . .2D **11**
**Falkland St.** G12: Glas . . . . . . . . . .6H **6**
**Falloch Rd.** G42: Glas . . . . . . . . . .6E **10**
G61: Bear . . . . . . . . . . . . . . . . .5C **4**
G62: Miln . . . . . . . . . . . . . . . . .3D **2**
FALLSIDE . . . . . . . . . . . . . . . . . .1G **12**
**Fallside Av.** G71: View . . . . . . . . .1G **12**
**Fallside Rd.** G71: Both . . . . . . . . .5E **12**
**Falside Av.** PA2: Pais . . . . . . . . . . .4A **9**
**Falside Rd.** G32: Glas . . . . . . . . . .3A **10**
PA2: Pais . . . . . . . . . . . . . . . . .4H **9**
**Falstaff** G74: E Kil . . . . . . . . . . . . .4C **13**
**Faraday Av.** ML2: Wis . . . . . . . . . .6A **14**
**Faraday Retail Pk.**
ML5: Coat . . . . . . . . . . . . . . . . .5C **9**
**Fara St.** G23: Glas . . . . . . . . . . . . .1D **6**
**Farie St.** G73: Ruth . . . . . . . . . . . .5B **10**
**Farm Ct.** G71: Both . . . . . . . . . . . .3F **12**
**Farm Cres.** ML1: N'hill . . . . . . . . .3F **12**
**Farme Castle Ct.** G73: Ruth . . . . .4E **10**
**Farme Castle Est.** G73: Ruth . . . .4E **10**
FARME CROSS . . . . . . . . . . . . . .4E **10**
**Farme Cross** G73: Ruth . . . . . . . .4D **10**
**Farmeloan Rd.** G73: Ruth . . . . . .5D **10**
**Farmgate Sq.** ML4: Bell . . . . . . . .3B **12**
**Farmington Av.** G32: Glas . . . . . . .6D **8**
**Farmington Gdns.** G32: Glas . . . . .6D **8**
**Farmington Ga.** G32: Glas . . . . . .1D **10**
**Farmington Gro.** G32: Glas . . . . . .6D **8**
**Farm La.** G71: Udd . . . . . . . . . . . .2E **12**
ML4: Bell . . . . . . . . . . . . . . . . .4B **12**
**Farm Pk.** G66: Lenz . . . . . . . . . . . .3D **5**
**Farm Rd.** G41: Glas . . . . . . . . . . . .6H **8**
G72: Blan . . . . . . . . . . . . . . . . .6B **12**
G81: Clyd . . . . . . . . . . . . . . . . .4H **4**
G81: Dun, Hard . . . . . . . . . . . .6C **2**
ML3: Ham . . . . . . . . . . . . . . . .5D **14**
**Farm St.** ML1: Moth . . . . . . . . . . .2F **14**
**Farm Ter.** ML3: Ham . . . . . . . . . . .5D **14**
**Farndale** G74: E Kil . . . . . . . . . . . .6E **13**
**Farne Dr.** G44: Glas . . . . . . . . . . . .3F **11**
**Farnell St.** G4: Glas . . . . . . . . . . . .1F **8**
**Farrier Ct.** PA5: John . . . . . . . . . . .2F **9**
**Faskally Av.** G64: B'rig . . . . . . . . . .4A **4**
**Faskally Wlk.** ML2: Newm . . . . . .3D **14**
**Faskin Cres.** G53: Glas . . . . . . . . . .6H **9**
**Faskine Av.** ML6: Air . . . . . . . . . . .5H **9**
ML6: C'bnk . . . . . . . . . . . . . . .3B **11**
**Faskine Cres.** ML6: Air . . . . . . . . . .5H **9**
**Faskin Pl.** G53: Glas . . . . . . . . . . . .6H **9**
**Faskin Rd.** G53: Glas . . . . . . . . . . .6H **9**
**Fasque Pl.** G15: Glas . . . . . . . . . . .3G **4**
**Fastnet St.** G33: Glas . . . . . . . . . . .3A **8**
FAULDHEAD . . . . . . . . . . . . . . . . .1H **5**
**Fauldhouse St.** G5: Glas . . . . . . . .2H **10**
**Faulds** G69: Bail . . . . . . . . . . . . . .6A **8**
**Faulds Gdns.** G69: Bail . . . . . . . . .6A **8**
**Fauldshead Rd.** PA4: Renf . . . . . . .6E **5**
**Faulds La.** ML5: Coat . . . . . . . . . .2B **11**
**Fauldspark Cres.** G69: Bail . . . . . .5A **8**
**Faulds St.** ML5: Coat . . . . . . . . . .2A **11**
**Fauldswood Cres.** PA2: Pais . . . . .3F **9**
**Fauldswood Dr.** PA2: Pais . . . . . . .3F **9**
**Faulkner Gro.** ML1: Cle . . . . . . . .1F **14**
**Fearnmore Rd.** G20: Glas . . . . . . .2B **6**
**Fells, The** G66: Len . . . . . . . . . . . .3G
**Fellsview Av.** G66: Kirk . . . . . . . . .4F **3**
**Felton Pl.** G13: Glas . . . . . . . . . . . .2H **5**
**Fendoch St.** G32: Glas . . . . . . . . .1A **10**
**Fenella St.** G32: Glas . . . . . . . . . . .6B **8**
**Fennsbank Av.** G73: Ruth . . . . . . .4F **12**

Fenwick Dr.—Fotheringay La.

nwick Dr. G78: Barr 6E 115
ML3: Ham 4A 154
nwick Pl. G46: Giff 6H 117
nwick Rd. G46: Giff 6H 117
rclay St. G81: Faif 6F 23
reneze Av. G76: Clar 1A 134
G78: Barr 4D 114
PA4: Renf 3C 78
reneze Cres. G13: Glas 3A 60
ML3: Ham 6D 140
reneze Dr. PA2: Pais 5F 97
eneze Gro. G78: Barr 4D 114
reneze Rd. G78: Neil 2A 130
rgus Av. PA3: Pais 6E 77
rgus Ct. G20: Glas 5C 62
rgus Dr. G20: Glas 5C 62
PA3: Pais 6E 77
rgus Gdns. ML3: Ham 1B 154
rgus La. G20: Glas 5D 62
rguslie PA1: Pais 2D 96
RGUSLIE PARK 5E 77
rguslie Pk. Av. PA3: Pais 6E 77
rguslie Pk. Cres. PA3: Pais 1E 97
rguslie Park Sports & Recreation Cen. 5E 77
rguslie Wlk. PA1: Pais 1F 97
(not continuous)
rguson Av. G62: Miln 3F 25
PA4: Renf 6F 59
rguson Dr. ML1: Moth 6G 143
rguson St. PA4: Renf 5F 59
PA5: John 2E 95
rguson Way ML6: Air 1B 92
rgusson Pl. G74: E Kil 4D 138
rgusson Rd. G67: Cumb 3H 35
rgusson Ter. G66: Milt C 5C 8
rguston Rd. G61: Bear 3F 45
rnan St. G32: Glas 6H 85
rn Av. G64: B'rig 1D 64
G66: Lenz 3C 50
PA8: Ersk 2F 57
rnbank Av. G72: Camb 3C 122
rnbank St. G21: Glas 4A 64
G22: Glas 4A 64
rnbrae Av. G73: Ruth 4D 120
rnbrae Way G73: Ruth 4D 120
rn Cotts. G13: Glas 4F 61
rncroft Dr. G44: Glas 2H 119
rndale ML9: Lark 4E 161
rndale Ct. G23: Glas 1B 62
rndale Dr. G23: Glas 1B 62
rndale Gdns. G23: Glas 1B 62
rndale Pl. G23: Glas 1B 62
rn Dr. G78: Barr 3D 114
rness Oval G21: Glas 2E 65
rness Pl. G21: Glas 2E 65
rness Rd. G21: Glas 3E 65
rn Gro. G69: G'csh 3E 69
rngrove Av. G12: Glas 3H 61
RNHILL 4D 120
rnhill Grange G71: Both 6E 125
rnhill Rd. G73: Ruth 2C 120
RNIEGAIR 2D 154
rnie Gdns. G20: Glas 2C 62
rn La. G12: Glas 4F 61
G13: Glas 4F 61
G66: Len 2E 7
rnlea G61: Bear 4E 45
rnleigh Pl. G69: Mood 5D 52
rnleigh Rd. G43: Glas 2B 118
rnside Wlk. ML3: Ham 2A 154
rnslea Av. G72: Blan 1A 140
rn St. ML1: Moth 5A 144
rryden Ct. G14: Glas 1E 81
rryden St. G11: Glas 1E 81
G14: Glas 1E 81
rry Rd. G3: Glas 3H 81
G71: Both 5E 125
G71: Udd 1C 124
rry Rd. PA4: Renf 5F 59
PA7: B'ton 4G 39
rsit Ct. G43: Glas 1A 118
rsit St. G43: Glas 1A 118
tlar Dr. G44: Glas 2G 119
tlar Rd. PA11: Bri W 3E 73
ttercairn Av. G15: Glas 4G 43
ttercairn Gdns.
G64: B'rig 6E 49
ttes St. G33: Glas 3H 85
ddoch Ct. ML2: Newm 2D 146
dra St. G33: Glas 3H 85
elden Pl. G40: Glas 6C 84
elden St. G40: Glas 6C 84
eld Gro. G76: Busby 4D 134
eldhead Dr. G43: Glas 2G 117
eldhead Sq. G43: Glas 2G 117
eld Rd. G76: Busby 4D 134
G81: Faif 5F 23
ML9: Lark 3F 161
elds La. PA6: Hous 1B 74
Field St. ML3: Ham 2H 153
Fife Av. G52: Glas 1B 100
ML6: Air 6A 92
Fife Ct. G71: Both 6E 125
Fife Cres. G71: Both 6E 125
Fife Dr. ML1: Moth 5F 127
Fife Way G64: B'rig 1F 65
Fifth Av. G12: Glas 4F 61
G33: Mille 4B 66
G72: Blan 4C 140
ML6: Air 3C 92
PA4: Renf 1E 79
Fifty Pitches Pl. G51: Glas 4B 80
Fifty Pitches Rd. G51: Glas 4B 80
Finart Dr. PA2: Pais 4D 98
Finaven Gdns. G61: Bear 5B 24
Finch Dr. G13: Glas 1H 59
Finch Pl. PA5: John 6D 94
Findhorn PA8: Ersk 4E 41
Findhorn Av. PA2: Pais 4D 96
PA4: Renf 6G 59
Findhorn Ct. G75: E Kil 3A 148
Findhorn Pl. G75: E Kil 3A 148
Findhorn St. G33: Glas 3F 85
Findlay Ct. *ML1: Moth 1F 143*
*(off Roman Rd.)*
Findlay St. G65: Kils 3H 11
ML1: Moth 4H 143
Findochty PA8: Ersk 4E 41
Findochty St. G33: Glas 2D 86
Fingal La. G20: Glas 2A 62
Fingal St. G20: Glas 2B 62
Fingalton Rd. G77: Newt M 4A 132
Fingask St. G32: Glas 1C 106
Finglas Av. PA2: Pais 4D 98
Finglen Gdns. G62: Miln 3E 25
Finglen Pl. G53: Glas 3B 116
Fingleton Av. G78: Barr 6F 115
Finhaven St. G32: Glas 2G 105
Finlarig St. G34: Glas 4A 88
Finlas Pl. G21: Glas 4H 63
Finlas St. G22: Glas 5H 63
Finlay Dr. G31: Glas 4C 84
PA3: Lin 6F 75
Finlay Ri. G62: Miln 5H 25
Finlayson Dr. ML6: Air 4E 93
Finlayson Quad. ML6: Air 4E 93
Finlaystone St. ML5: Coat 4A 90
Finnart Sq. G40: Glas 2B 104
Finnart St. G40: Glas 2B 104
FINNIESTON 3C 82
Finnieston Crane 4C 82
Finnieston Sq. G3: Glas 3C 82
Finnieston St. G3: Glas 4C 82
Finnie Wynd ML1: Moth 5B 144
Finsbay St. G51: Glas 5D 80
Fintaig La. ML2: Wis 6C 146
Fintrie Ter. ML3: Ham 5C 140
Fintry Av. PA2: Pais 5A 98
Fintry Ct. ML5: Coat 2E 111
Fintry Cres. G64: B'rig 6E 49
G78: Barr 6E 115
Fintry Dr. G44: Glas 6G 103
Fintry Gdns. G61: Bear 5C 24
Firbank Av. G64: Torr 5D 28
Fir Bank Av. ML9: Lark 3F 161
Firbank Quad. ML6: Chap 2E 113
Firbank Ter. G78: Barr 6G 115
Fir Ct. G72: Flem 3E 123
ML5: Coat 1A 110
Firdon Cres. G15: Glas 6A 44
Fir Dr. G75: E Kil 6D 148
Fir Gro. G71: View 5F 109
ML1: New S 5A 128
FIRHILL 5E 63
Firhill Av. ML6: Air 5H 91
Firhill Pk. 5E 63
Firhill Rd. G20: Glas 5D 62
Firhill St. G20: Glas 5E 63
Firlee G75: E Kil 3B 148
Fir Pk. 5H 143
Firpark Rd. G64: B'rig 1D 64
Firpark St. G31: Glas 3B 84
Fir Pk. St. ML1: Moth 5H 143
Firpark Ter. G31: Glas 4B 84
Fir Pl. G69: Bail 2G 107
G72: Camb 1C 122
ML1: Cle 6H 129
PA5: John 4G 95
First Av. G33: Mille 4B 66
G44: Neth 5D 118
G61: Bear 4G 45
G66: Auch 6D 50
G71: Tann 5C 108
G82: Dumb 3C 18
PA4: Renf 1E 79
First Gdns. G41: Glas 1G 101
Firs, The G44: Glas 2F 119
First Rd. G72: Blan 4C 140
First St. G71: Tann 5D 108
First Ter. G81: Clyd 4C 42
Firthview Ter. G82: Dumb 4C 16
Firtree Pl. ML2: Newm 3F 147
Firtree Rd. ML2: Newm 3F 147
Fir Vw. ML6: C'bnk 3B 112
Firwood Courts G77: Newt M 5E 133
Firwood Dr. G44: Glas 1G 119
Firwood Rd. G77: Newt M 4E 133
Fischer Gdns. PA1: Pais 1D 96
Fisher Av. G65: Kils 3H 11
PA1: Pais 1D 96
Fisher Ct. G31: Glas 4B 84
Fisher Cres. G81: Hard 1D 42
Fisher Dr. PA1: Pais 1D 96
Fishers Rd. PA4: Renf 3E 59
Fisher St. ML9: Lark 4F 161
Fisher Way PA1: Pais 1D 96
Fishescoates Av. G73: Ruth 3E 121
(not continuous)
Fishescoates Gdns. G73: Ruth 2F 121
Fitness First Health Club 3F 103
Fitzalan Dr. PA3: Pais 5C 78
Fitzalan Rd. PA4: Renf 2C 78
Fitzroy La. G3: Glas 3C 82
Fitzroy Pl. *G3: Glas 3C 82*
*(off Royal Cres.)*
Flakefield G74: E Kil 1D 148
Flanders St. G81: Hard 6E 23
Flaxford Gro. ML1: Moth 5F 127
Flaxmill Av. ML2: Wis 5D 144
Flax Rd. G71: Udd 2E 125
Fleet Av. PA4: Renf 2G 79
Fleet St. G32: Glas 1B 106
Fleming Av. G69: Chry 1A 68
G81: Clyd 1F 59
Fleming Ct. G81: Clyd 5D 42
ML1: Moth 5A 144
ML3: Ham 5C 140
ML8: Carl 4E 165
Fleming Pl. G75: E Kil 3G 149
Fleming Rd. G67: Cumb 3H 35
ML4: Bell 1D 126
PA6: Hous 1A 74
PA7: B'ton 4H 39
Fleming St. G31: Glas 5D 84
PA3: Pais 4A 78
FLEMINGTON
Cambuslang 3E 123
Motherwell 5B 144
Flemington Ind. Est.
G72: Flem 3E 123
Flemington Ind. Pk.
ML1: Moth 4C 144
Flemington Rd. G72: Camb 2E 139
Flemington St. G21: Glas 6A 64
ML1: Moth 4A 144
Fleming Way ML3: Ham 5B 140
Flenders Av. G76: Clar 3A 134
Flenders Rd. G76: Clar 3A 134
Fleurs Av. G41: Glas 1H 101
Fleurs Rd. G41: Glas 1H 101
Flinders Pl. G75: E Kil 3D 148
Flloyd St. ML5: Coat 4B 90
Floorsburn Cres. PA5: John 3E 95
Floors St. PA5: John 3E 95
Floors St. Ind. Est. PA5: John 3F 95
Flora Gdns. G64: B'rig 5E 49
Florence Dr. G46: Giff 5A 118
Florence Gdns. G73: Ruth 3E 121
Florence St. *G5: Glas 1G 103*
*(off Caledonia Rd.)*
G5: Glas 6G 83
(Ballater St.)
Florida Av. G42: Glas 5F 103
Florida Cres. G42: Glas 5F 103
Florida Dr. G42: Glas 5E 103
Florida Gdns. G69: Bail 6G 87
Florida Sq. G42: Glas 5F 103
Florida St. G42: Glas 5F 103
Florish Rd. PA8: Ersk 1H 57
Flowerdale Pl. G53: Glas 4B 116
Flowerhill Ind. Est.
ML6: Air 3B 92
Flowerhill St. ML6: Air 3B 92
FLUCHTER 3E 27
Fluchter Rd. G62: Balm, Bard 4E 27
G64: Balm 3F 27
Flures Av. PA8: Ersk 1A 58
Flures Cres. PA8: Ersk 1A 58
Flures Dr. PA8: Ersk 1A 58
Flures Pl. PA8: Ersk 1A 58
Fochabers Dr. G52: Glas 5C 80
Fogo Pl. G20: Glas 3B 62
Foinhaven Dr. G46: T'bnk 2F 117
Foinhaven Gdns. G46: T'bnk 1F 117
Foinhaven Way G46: T'bnk 1G 117
Footfield Rd. ML4: Bell 3B 126
Forbes Dr. G40: Glas 6B 84
ML1: Moth 5D 126
Forbes Pl. PA1: Pais 1A 98
Forbes St. G40: Glas 5B 84
Fordneuk St. G40: Glas 6C 84
Fordoun St. G34: Glas 3B 88
Ford Rd. G12: Glas 5B 62
G77: Newt M 6D 132
Fordyce Ct. G77: Newt M 5D 132
Fordyce St. G11: Glas 1H 81
Foremount Ter. La. *G12: Glas 6A 62*
*(off Hyndland Rd.)*
Fore Row ML3: Ham 5A 142
Forest Av. ML3: Ham 5H 153
Forestburn Ct. *ML6: Air 4F 91*
*(off Monkscourt Av.)*
Forest Dr. G71: Both 4E 125
ML4: Bell 4E 127
Forest Gdns. G66: Lenz 3A 50
Foresthall Cres. G21: Glas 6C 64
Foresthall Dr. G21: Glas 6C 64
(not continuous)
Forest Kirk ML8: Carl 5H 165
Forest La. ML3: Ham 5H 153
Forestlea Rd. ML8: Carl 5G 165
Forest Pk. ML2: Wis 4B 146
Forest Pl. G66: Lenz 3A 50
PA2: Pais 3A 98
Fore St. G14: Glas 6C 60
Forest Rd. G67: Cumb 5D 14
ML9: Lark 3F 161
Forest Vw. G67: Cumb 2C 36
Forfar Av. G52: Glas 1B 100
Forfar Cres. G64: B'rig 1E 65
Forgan Gdns. G64: B'rig 1F 65
Forge Dr. ML5: Coat 4B 90
Forge Pl. G21: Glas 1D 84
Forge Rd. ML6: Air 5F 93
Forge Row ML6: C'bnk 2C 112
Forge Shop. Cen., The
G31: Glas 6E 85
Forge St. G21: Glas 1D 84
Forge, The G46: Giff 4B 118
FORGEWOOD 6F 127
Forgewood Path ML6: Air 5F 93
Forgewood Rd. ML1: Moth 5E 127
Forglen St. G34: Glas 2H 87
Formakin Estate Country Pk. 5B 38
Formby Dr. G23: Glas 6B 46
Forres Av. G46: Giff 4A 118
Forres Cres. ML4: Bell 1C 126
Forres Ga. G46: Giff 5B 118
Forres Quad. ML2: Wis 4H 145
Forres St. G23: Glas 6C 46
G72: Blan 3A 140
Forrest Dr. G61: Bear 4B 24
Forrester Ct. G64: B'rig 1B 64
Forrestfield Cres.
G77: Newt M 4E 133
Forrestfield Gdns.
G77: Newt M 4D 132
Forrestfield St. G21: Glas 2C 84
Forrest Ga. G71: Tann 4F 109
ML3: Ham 2F 153
Forrest St. G40: Glas 6C 84
G72: Blan 2D 140
ML6: Air 3C 92
(not continuous)
Forsyth St. ML6: Air 3B 92
Fort Antonine Theatre 6B 48
Forteviot Av. G69: Bail 6A 88
Forteviot Pl. G69: Bail 6A 88
Forth Av. PA2: Pais 4D 96
Forth Ct. G75: E Kil 4A 148
Forth Cres. G75: E Kil 3A 148
Forth Gro. G75: E Kil 4A 148
Forth Pl. ML9: Lark 5F 161
PA5: John 5C 94
Forth Rd. G61: Bear 5D 44
G64: Torr 5D 28
Forth St. G41: Glas 2D 102
G81: Clyd 1E 59
Forth Ter. ML3: Ham 3F 153
Forth Wlk. *G67: Cumb 4H 35*
*(in Cumbernauld Shop. Cen.)*
Forth Way *G67: Cumb 4H 35*
*(in Cumbernauld Shop. Cen.)*
Forties Ct. G46: T'bnk 2F 117
Forties Cres. G46: T'bnk 2G 117
Forties Gdns. G46: T'bnk 2G 117
Forties Rd. PA6: C'lee 3C 74
Forties Way G46: T'bnk 2G 117
Fortieth Av. G75: E Kil 6H 149
Fortingale Av. G12: Glas 3A 62
Fortingall Pl. G12: Glas 3A 62
Fortingall Rd. G72: Blan 4D 140
Fortrose St. G11: Glas 1H 81
Fort St. ML1: Moth 1D 142
Forum Pl. ML1: Moth 6E 127
Fossil Gro. G66: Kirk 4G 31
Fossil Ho. 6D 60
Foswell Pl. G15: Glas 2H 43
Fotheringay La. G41: Glas 3B 102

Fotheringay Rd.—Gear Ter.


Fotheringay Rd. G41: Glas . . . . . .3B 102
Foulis La. G13: Glas . . . . . . . . . . .3F 61
Foulis St. G13: Glas . . . . . . . . . . .3F 61
FOULSYKES . . . . . . . . . . . . . . .5C 146
Foulsykes Rd. ML2: Wis . . . . . . . .5C 146
Foundry La. G78: Barr . . . . . . . . .5E 115
Foundry Rd. ML1: Cle . . . . . . . . .5H 129
Fountain Av. PA4: Inch . . . . . . . . . .5F 57
Fountain Cres. PA4: Inch . . . . . . . .4F 57
Fountain Dr. PA4: Inch . . . . . . . . .5G 57
Fountainwell Av. G21: Glas . . . . . .1H 83
Fountainwell Dr. G21: Glas . . . . . .1H 83
Fountainwell Path G21: Glas . . . . .6H 63
Fountainwell Pl. G21: Glas . . . . . .1H 83
Fountainwell Rd. G21: Glas . . . . . .1H 83
Fountainwell Sq. G21: Glas . . . . . .1A 84
Fountainwell Ter. G21: Glas . . . . . .1A 84
Fourth Av. G33: Mille . . . . . . . . . . .4B 66
G66: Auch . . . . . . . . . . . . . . . .6D 50
G82: Dumb . . . . . . . . . . . . . . . .3C 18
PA4: Renf . . . . . . . . . . . . . . . . .1E 79
Fourth Gdns. G41: Glas . . . . . . . .1G 101
Fourth Rd. G72: Blan . . . . . . . . . .4C 140
Fourth St. G71: Tann . . . . . . . . . .4D 108
Four Windings PA6: Hous . . . . . . .1B 74
Fowlis Dr. G77: Newt M . . . . . . . .3C 132
FOXBAR . . . . . . . . . . . . . . . . . .4D 96
Foxbar Cres. PA2: Pais . . . . . . . . . .6C 96
Foxbar Dr. G13: Glas . . . . . . . . . . .3B 60
PA2: Pais . . . . . . . . . . . . . . . . .6C 96
Foxbar Rd. PA2: Pais . . . . . . . . . . .6B 96
PA5: Eld . . . . . . . . . . . . . . . . . .6B 96
Foxes Gro. G66: Lenz . . . . . . . . . . .2E 51
Foxglove Pl. G53: Glas . . . . . . . . .4B 116
Fox Gro. ML1: Moth . . . . . . . . . . .2D 142
Foxhills Pl. G23: Glas . . . . . . . . . . .6C 46
FOXLEY . . . . . . . . . . . . . . . . . .3C 106
Foxley St. G32: Carm . . . . . . . . . .4C 106
Fox St. G1: Glas . . . . . . . . . . . . . . .5F 83
Foyers Ter. G21: Glas . . . . . . . . . .5C 64
Foyes Ct. G13: Glas . . . . . . . . . . . .3B 60
Francis St. G5: Glas . . . . . . . . . . .1E 103
Franconia Sq. G81: Clyd . . . . . . . . .6D 42
Frankfield Rd. G33: Step . . . . . . . .4E 67
Frankfield St. G33: Glas . . . . . . . . .1F 85
Frankfort St. G41: Glas . . . . . . . . .4C 102
Franklin Pl. G75: E Kil . . . . . . . . .2D 148
Franklin St. G40: Glas . . . . . . . . .2B 104
Fraser Av. G73: Ruth . . . . . . . . . .5E 105
G77: Newt M . . . . . . . . . . . . . .3E 133
G82: Dumb . . . . . . . . . . . . . . . .1C 18
PA5: John . . . . . . . . . . . . . . . . .3G 95
PA7: B'ton . . . . . . . . . . . . . . . .3H 39
Fraser Ct. ML3: Ham . . . . . . . . . .1F 153
*ML6: Air . . . . . . . . . . . . . . . . . .3E 93*
*(off Katherine St.)*
Fraser Cres. ML3: Ham . . . . . . . . .1F 153
Fraser Gdns. G66: Kirk . . . . . . . . . .5B 30
Fraser St. G72: Camb . . . . . . . . . .1G 121
ML1: Cle . . . . . . . . . . . . . . . . .5H 129
Frazer River Twr. G75: E Kil . . . . .3F 149
Frazer St. G40: Glas . . . . . . . . . . . .6C 84
Frederick St. ML5: Coat . . . . . . . . .3A 90
FREELAND . . . . . . . . . . . . . . . . .2F 57
Freeland Brae *G75: E Kil . . . . . . .3H 149*
*(off Telford Rd.)*
Freeland Ct. G53: Glas . . . . . . . . .1C 116
Freeland Cres. G53: Glas . . . . . . .1B 116
Freeland Dr. G53: Glas . . . . . . . . .1B 116
PA11: Bri W . . . . . . . . . . . . . . . .2F 73
PA4: Inch . . . . . . . . . . . . . . . . .3G 57
Freeland La. *G75: E Kil . . . . . . . .3H 149*
*(off Telford Rd.)*
Freeland Pl. G66: Kirk . . . . . . . . . .5D 30
Freeland Rd. PA8: Ersk . . . . . . . . . .2F 57
Freelands Ct. G60: Old K . . . . . . . .3G 41
Freelands Cres. G60: Old K . . . . . .2G 41
Freelands Pl. G60: Old K . . . . . . . .3G 41
Freelands Rd. G60: Old K . . . . . . .2G 41
Freesia Ct. ML1: Moth . . . . . . . . .4G 143
French St. G40: Glas . . . . . . . . . .2B 104
G81: Clyd . . . . . . . . . . . . . . . . .4A 42
ML2: Wis . . . . . . . . . . . . . . . .6H 145
PA4: Renf . . . . . . . . . . . . . . . . .1D 78
Freuchie St. G34: Glas . . . . . . . . . .4H 87
Frew St. ML6: Air . . . . . . . . . . . . .3A 92
Friar Av. G64: B'rig . . . . . . . . . . . .4D 48
Friarscourt Av. G13: Glas . . . . . . . .6D 44
Friarscourt La. *G13: Glas . . . . . . .1D 60*
*(off Knightscliffe Av.)*
Friarscourt Rd. G69: Chry . . . . . . .6H 51
Friars Cft. G66: Kirk . . . . . . . . . . .5E 31
Friars Pl. G13: Glas . . . . . . . . . . . .1D 60
Friars Way ML6: Air . . . . . . . . . .1C 112
Friarton Rd. G43: Glas . . . . . . . . .2D 118
Friendship Way PA4: Renf . . . . . . . .2F 79
Frood St. ML1: Moth . . . . . . . . . .6E 127
Fruin Av. G77: Newt M . . . . . . . .3E 133
Fruin Dr. ML2: Wis . . . . . . . . . . .6C 146
Fruin Ho. G82: Dumb . . . . . . . . . . .1H 17
Fruin Pl. G22: Glas . . . . . . . . . . . . .5G 63
Fruin Ri. ML3: Ham . . . . . . . . . . .1C 152
Fruin Rd. G15: Glas . . . . . . . . . . . .6H 43
Fruin St. G22: Glas . . . . . . . . . . . . .5G 63
Fulbar Av. PA4: Renf . . . . . . . . . . .5E 59
Fulbar Ct. PA4: Renf . . . . . . . . . . . .5F 59
Fulbar Cres. PA2: Pais . . . . . . . . . .3D 96
Fulbar Gdns. PA2: Pais . . . . . . . . .3D 96
Fulbar La. PA4: Renf . . . . . . . . . . . .5F 59
Fulbar Path G51: Glas . . . . . . . . . .4C 80
Fulbar Rd. G51: Glas . . . . . . . . . . .4C 80
PA2: Pais . . . . . . . . . . . . . . . . .3D 96
Fulbar St. PA4: Renf . . . . . . . . . . . .5F 59
FULLARTON . . . . . . . . . . . . . . .3A 106
Fullarton Av. G32: Glas . . . . . . . .3A 106
Fullarton Dr. G32: Glas . . . . . . . .4A 106
Fullarton La. G32: Glas . . . . . . . .3A 106
Fullarton Pl. ML5: Coat . . . . . . . .2H 109
Fullarton Rd. G32: Glas . . . . . . . .5H 105
G68: Cumb . . . . . . . . . . . . . . . .6G 13
FULLARTON ROAD INTERCHANGE
. . . . . . . . . . . . . . . . . . . .4A 106
Fullarton St. ML5: Coat . . . . . . . .2A 110
Fullers Ga. G81: Faif . . . . . . . . . . .6E 23
Fullerton St. PA3: Pais . . . . . . . . . .4H 77
Fullerton Ter. PA3: Pais . . . . . . . . .4A 78
Fullwood Ind. Est. ML3: Ham . . . .5F 141
Fulmar Ct. G64: B'rig . . . . . . . . . . .1B 64
Fulmar Pk. G74: E Kil . . . . . . . . .6F 137
Fulmar Pl. PA5: John . . . . . . . . . . .6C 94
Fulton Cres. PA10: Kilb . . . . . . . . .2A 94
Fulton Dr. PA6: C'lee . . . . . . . . . . .3E 75
Fulton Gdns. PA6: C'lee . . . . . . . . .3E 75
Fulton Rd. G62: Miln . . . . . . . . . . .4H 25
Fulton St. G13: Glas . . . . . . . . . . .2D 60
Fulwood Av. G13: Glas . . . . . . . . .2H 59
PA3: Lin . . . . . . . . . . . . . . . . . .5H 75
Fulwood Pl. G13: Glas . . . . . . . . . .2H 59
Furlongs, The ML3: Ham . . . . . . .4A 142
Fyneart St. ML2: Wis . . . . . . . . .5C 146
Fyne Av. ML4: Bell . . . . . . . . . . .6A 110
Fyne Ct. ML3: Ham . . . . . . . . . . .2E 153
Fyne Cres. ML9: Lark . . . . . . . . .6H 155
Fyne Way *ML1: Holy . . . . . . . . . .2A 128*
*(off Howden Pl.)*
Fynloch Pl. G81: Dun . . . . . . . . . . .6A 22
Fyvie Av. G43: Glas . . . . . . . . . . .2G 117
Fyvie Cres. ML6: Air . . . . . . . . . . . .4F 93

## G

Gadie Av. PA4: Renf . . . . . . . . . . . .1G 79
Gadie St. G33: Glas . . . . . . . . . . . . .3F 85
Gadloch Av. G66: Auch . . . . . . . . . .5D 50
Gadloch Gdns. G66: Lenz . . . . . . . .4D 50
Gadloch St. G22: Glas . . . . . . . . . .3G 63
Gadloch Vw. G66: Auch . . . . . . . . .5D 50
Gadsburn Ct. G21: Glas . . . . . . . . .3E 65
Gadshill St. G21: Glas . . . . . . . . . .2B 84
Gailes Pk. G71: Both . . . . . . . . . .5D 124
Gailes Rd. G68: Cumb . . . . . . . . . .6H 13
Gailes St. G40: Glas . . . . . . . . . .1D 104
Gain & Shankburn Rd.
G67: Cumb . . . . . . . . . . . . . . . .6D 54
Gainburn Ct. G67: Cumb . . . . . . . .1B 54
Gainburn Cres. G67: Cumb . . . . . .2B 54
Gainburn Gdns. G67: Cumb . . . . . .2B 54
Gainburn Pl. G67: Cumb . . . . . . . .1B 54
Gainburn Vw. G67: Cumb . . . . . . . .1C 54
Gain Rd. G67: Cumb . . . . . . . . . . . .6B 54
ML5: Glenb . . . . . . . . . . . . . . . .6B 54
Gainside Rd. ML5: Glenb . . . . . . . .3G 69
Gairbraid Av. G20: Glas . . . . . . . . .3A 62
Gairbraid Ct. G20: Glas . . . . . . . . .3A 62
Gairbraid Pl. G20: Glas . . . . . . . . .3B 62
Gairbraid Ter. G69: Barg . . . . . . . . .6E 89
Gair Cres. ML2: Wis . . . . . . . . . . .2H 157
ML8: Carl . . . . . . . . . . . . . . . .2G 165
Gairloch Gdns. G66: Kirk . . . . . . . .4H 31
Gair Rd. ML8: Carl . . . . . . . . . . .1G 165
Gala Av. PA4: Renf . . . . . . . . . . . .1G 79
Gala Cres. ML2: Wis . . . . . . . . . .4G 145
Gala St. G33: Glas . . . . . . . . . . . . .1G 85
Galbraith Cres. ML8: Law . . . . . . .5E 159
Galbraith Dr. G51: Glas . . . . . . . . .3D 80
G62: Miln . . . . . . . . . . . . . . . . .5F 25
Galdenoch St. G33: Glas . . . . . . . . .1B 86
Gallacher Av. PA2: Pais . . . . . . . . .4E 97
Gallacher Ct. ML1: Moth . . . . . . .6B 144
PA1: Pais . . . . . . . . . . . . . . . . .6G 77
Gallan Av. G23: Glas . . . . . . . . . . .6C 46
Gallery of Modern Art . . . . . . . . . .5E 5
Galloway Av. ML3: Ham . . . . . . . .4G 153
Galloway Dr. G73: Ruth . . . . . . . .4D 120
Galloway Rd. G74: E Kil . . . . . . . .6C 138
ML6: Air . . . . . . . . . . . . . . . . . .6H 91
Galloway St. G21: Glas . . . . . . . . .3B 64
GALLOWFLAT . . . . . . . . . . . . . .6E 105
Gallowflat St. G73: Ruth . . . . . . .5D 104
GALLOWGATE . . . . . . . . . . . . . . .6C 84
Gallowgate G1: Glas . . . . . . . . . . . .5H 83
GALLOWHILL . . . . . . . . . . . . . . .4D 78
Gallowhill ML9: Lark . . . . . . . . . .3E 161
Gallowhill Av. G66: Lenz . . . . . . . .1C 50
Gallowhill Ct. PA3: Pais . . . . . . . . .3C 78
Gallowhill Gro. G66: Kirk . . . . . . . .6C 30
Gallowhill Rd. G66: Kirk, Lenz . . . .1C 50
G76: Crmck . . . . . . . . . . . . . . .1H 135
PA3: Pais . . . . . . . . . . . . . . . . .5B 78
Galston Av. G77: Newt M . . . . . . .4G 133
Galston Ct. ML3: Ham . . . . . . . . .4A 154
Galston St. G53: Glas . . . . . . . . .1H 115
Galt Pl. G75: E Kil . . . . . . . . . . . .4F 149
Gamrie Dr. G53: Glas . . . . . . . . .6A 100
Gamrie Gdns. G53: Glas . . . . . . .6A 100
Gamrie Rd. G53: Glas . . . . . . . . .5A 100
Gannochy Dr. G64: B'rig . . . . . . . . .6E 49
Gantock Cres. G33: Glas . . . . . . . . .4B 86
GARDENHALL . . . . . . . . . . . . . .4A 148
Gardenhall G75: E Kil . . . . . . . . .3A 148
Gardenhall Ct. G75: E Kil . . . . . . .3A 148
Gardenside ML4: Bell . . . . . . . . . .3C 126
Gardenside Av. G32: Carm . . . . . .5B 106
G71: Udd . . . . . . . . . . . . . . . .1C 124
Gardenside Cres. G32: Carm . . . .5B 106
Gardenside Gro. G32: Carm . . . . .5B 106
Gardenside Pl. G32: Carm . . . . . .5B 106
Gardenside Rd. ML3: Ham . . . . . .1H 153
Gardenside St. G71: Udd . . . . . . .1C 124
Garden Sq. Wlk. ML6: Air . . . . . . . .3F 91
Garden Veteran's Cotts.
PA7: B'ton . . . . . . . . . . . . . . . .2D 40
Gardner Gro. G71: Tann . . . . . . . .5E 109
Gardner St. G11: Glas . . . . . . . . . .1H 81
Gardyne St. G34: Glas . . . . . . . . . .2G 87
Gareloch Av. ML6: Air . . . . . . . . . .1H 91
PA2: Pais . . . . . . . . . . . . . . . . .3E 97
Garfield Av. ML4: Bell . . . . . . . . .2E 127
Garfield Dr. ML4: Bell . . . . . . . . .3E 127
Garfield St. G31: Glas . . . . . . . . . .5C 84
Garforth Rd. G69: Bail . . . . . . . . .1F 107
Gargrave Av. G69: Bail . . . . . . . . .1F 107
Garion Dr. G13: Glas . . . . . . . . . . .4B 60
Garlieston Rd. G33: Glas . . . . . . . .5F 87
Garmouth Ct. G51: Glas . . . . . . . . .3G 81
Garmouth Gdns. G51: Glas . . . . . . .3G 81
Garmouth St. G51: Glas . . . . . . . . .3F 81
GARNETHILL . . . . . . . . .2E 83 (2C 4)
Garnethill St. G3: Glas . . . . .2E 83 (2B 4)
Garnet St. G3: Glas . . . . . .2E 83 (3A 4)
Garngaber Av. G66: Lenz . . . . . . . .2D 50
Garngaber Ct. G66: Lenz . . . . . . . .2E 51
Garngrew Rd. FK4: Hag . . . . . . . . .1F 15
Garnhall Farm Rd. G68: Cumb . . . .3E 15
Garnie Av. PA8: Ersk . . . . . . . . . . .6H 41
Garnie Cres. PA8: Ersk . . . . . . . . .6H 41
Garnieland Rd. PA8: Ersk . . . . . . . .6H 41
Garnie La. PA8: Ersk . . . . . . . . . . .1H 57
Garnie Oval PA8: Ersk . . . . . . . . . .6H 41
Garnie Pl. PA8: Ersk . . . . . . . . . . .6H 41
GARNKIRK . . . . . . . . . . . . . . . . . .3G 67
Garnkirk La. G33: Step . . . . . . . . .4E 67
Garnock Pl. G74: E Kil . . . . . . . .2B 150
Garnock St. G21: Glas . . . . . . . . . .2B 84
GARNQUEEN . . . . . . . . . . . . . . . .4H 69
Garrell Av. G65: Kils . . . . . . . . . . .2H 11
Garrell Gro. G65: Kils . . . . . . . . . .1H 11
Garrell Pl. G65: Kils . . . . . . . . . . .3G 11
Garrell Rd. G65: Kils . . . . . . . . . . .4G 11
Garrell Way G65: Kils . . . . . . . . . .3G 11
G67: Cumb . . . . . . . . . . . . . . . .3G 35
Garrioch Cres. G20: Glas . . . . . . . .4B 62
Garrioch Dr. G20: Glas . . . . . . . . .4B 62
Garrioch Ga. G20: Glas . . . . . . . . .4B 62
Garriochmill Rd. G20: Glas . . . . . .5B 62
(not continuous)
Garrioch Quad. G20: Glas . . . . . . .4B 62
Garrioch Rd. G20: Glas . . . . . . . . .5B 62
Garrion Bus. Pk. ML2: Wis . . . . .3H 157
Garrion Pl. ML9: Ashg . . . . . . . . .4B 162
Garrion St. ML2: Over . . . . . . . . .5A 158
Garrochmill Way *G20: Glas . . . . . .6D 62*
*(off Henderson St.)*
GARROWHILL . . . . . . . . . . . . . . .6G 87
Garrowhill Dr. G69: Bail . . . . . . . . .6F 87
Garrowhill Station (Rail) . . . . . . . .6F 87
Garry Av. G61: Bear . . . . . . . . . . .5H 45
Garry Dr. PA2: Pais . . . . . . . . . . . .3E 97
Garry St. G44: Glas . . . . . . . . . . .6E 103
Garscadden Rd. Sth. G13: Glas . . .1A 60
*G15: Glas . . . . . . . . . . . . . . . . .1H 59*
*(off Gt. Western Rd.)*
Garscadden Station (Rail) . . . . . . .3A 60
Garscadden Vw. G81: Clyd . . . . . . .4F 43
Garscube Rd. G20: Glas . . . . . . . . .6E 63
G4: Glas . . . . . . . . . . . . .2F 83 (1C 4)
Garshake Av. G82: Dumb . . . . . . . .1C 18
Garshake Rd. G82: Dumb . . . . . . . .3H 17
Garshake Ter. G82: Dumb . . . . . . . .1C 18
Gartartan Rd. PA1: Pais . . . . . . . . .6H
Gartcarron Hill G68: Cumb . . . . . . .2E
Gartcloss Rd. ML5: Coat . . . . . . . .1G
Gartconnell Dr. G61: Bear . . . . . . .1E
Gartconnell Gdns. G61: Bear . . . . .1E
Gartconnell Rd. G61: Bear . . . . . . .1E
Gartconner Av. G66: Kirk . . . . . . . .5H
GARTCOSH . . . . . . . . . . . . . . . . .4D
Gartcosh Rd. G69: Barg . . . . . . . . .5D
(Coatbridge R
G69: Barg . . . . . . . . . . . . . . . . .3E
(Cuilhill R
G69: G'csh . . . . . . . . . . . . . . . .1E
Gartcosh Wlk. ML4: Bell . . . . . . . .2B 1
Gartcraig Path *G33: Glas . . . . . . . .2H*
*(off Gartcraig R*
Gartcraig Pl. G33: Glas . . . . . . . . .2H
Gartferry Av. G69: Mood . . . . . . . .5D
Gartferry Rd. G68: Mollin . . . . . . . .5C
G69: Chry . . . . . . . . . . . . . . . . .5B
G69: Mood . . . . . . . . . . . . . . . .5C
Gartferry St. G21: Glas . . . . . . . . .5C
Gartfield St. ML6: Air . . . . . . . . . .5B
Gartgill Rd. ML5: Coat . . . . . . . . .1A
GARTHAMLOCK . . . . . . . . . . . . . .1E
Garthland Dr. G31: Glas . . . . . . . . .4C
Garthland La. PA1: Pais . . . . . . . . .6B
Garth St. G1: Glas . . . . . . . .4G 83 (6F
GARTLEA . . . . . . . . . . . . . . . . . .5B
Gartlea Av. ML6: Air . . . . . . . . . . .4A
Gartlea Gdns. ML6: Air . . . . . . . . .4B
Gartleahill ML6: Air . . . . . . . . . . .5A
Gartlea Rd. ML6: Air . . . . . . . . . . .4A
Gartliston Rd. ML5: Coat . . . . . . . .6B
Gartliston Ter. G69: Barg . . . . . . . .6E
Gartloch Rd. G33: G'csh, Glas . . . .2C
G33: Glas . . . . . . . . . . . . . . . . .1H
G69: G'csh . . . . . . . . . . . . . . . .6H
Gartly St. G44: Glas . . . . . . . . . . .3D 1
Gartmore Gdns. G71: Tann . . . . . .5C 1
Gartmore La. G69: Mood . . . . . . . .5E
Gartmore Rd. PA1: Pais . . . . . . . . .1D
Gartmore Ter. G72: Camb . . . . . . .4G 1
GARTNESS . . . . . . . . . . . . . . . . .6E
Gartness Dr. ML6: Gart . . . . . . . . .6E
Gartness Rd. ML6: Air . . . . . . . . . .2G 1
Gartocher Dr. G32: Glas . . . . . . . . .6C
Gartocher Rd. G32: Glas . . . . . . . .6C
Gartocher Ter. G32: Glas . . . . . . . .6C
Gartons Rd. G21: Glas . . . . . . . . . .4E
GARTSHERRIE . . . . . . . . . . . . . . .2B
Gartsherrie Av. ML5: Glenb . . . . . .4B
Gartsherrie Ind. Est. ML5: Coat . . .2B
Gartsherrie Rd. ML5: Coat . . . . . . .3A
Gartshore Cres. G65: Twe . . . . . . .3D
Gartshore Gdns. G68: Cumb . . . . .4A
Garturk St. G42: Glas . . . . . . . . . .3F 1
ML5: Coat . . . . . . . . . . . . . . . .1D 1
Garvald Ct. G40: Glas . . . . . . . . . .2D 1
Garvald St. G40: Glas . . . . . . . . . .2D 1
Garve Av. G44: Glas . . . . . . . . . . .3E 1
Garvel Cres. G33: Glas . . . . . . . . .5E
Garvel Pl. G62: Miln . . . . . . . . . . .3D
Garvel Rd. G33: Glas . . . . . . . . . .5E
G62: Miln . . . . . . . . . . . . . . . . .3D
Garvin Lea ML4: Bell . . . . . . . . . .5C 1
Garvock Dr. G43: Glas . . . . . . . . .2H 1
Garwhitter Dr. G62: Miln . . . . . . . .3H
Gascoyne G75: E Kil . . . . . . . . . . .4E 1
Gaskin Path G33: Step . . . . . . . . . .4E
Gask Pl. G13: Glas . . . . . . . . . . . .1H
Gas St. PA5: John . . . . . . . . . . . . .2G
Gasworks Rd. ML8: Carl . . . . . . . .2C 1
Gatehouse St. G32: Glas . . . . . . . .6B
GATESIDE . . . . . . . . . . . . . . . . .6B 1
Gateside Av. G65: Kils . . . . . . . . . .3F 1
G72: Camb . . . . . . . . . . . . . . . .2D 1
Gateside Cres. G78: Barr . . . . . . . .6C 1
ML6: Air . . . . . . . . . . . . . . . . . .3A
Gateside Pk. G65: Kils . . . . . . . . . .2F 1
Gateside Pl. PA10: Kilb . . . . . . . . .2A
Gateside Rd. G78: Barr . . . . . . . . .6B 1
ML2: Wis . . . . . . . . . . . . . . . . .5E 1
Gateside St. G31: Glas . . . . . . . . .5D
ML3: Ham . . . . . . . . . . . . . . . .1A 1
Gateway, The G74: E Kil . . . . . . . .5A 1
Gaughan Quad. ML1: Moth . . . . . .4F 1
Gauldry Av. G52: Glas . . . . . . . . . .2C 1
Gauze St. PA1: Pais . . . . . . . . . . . .6A
Gavell Rd. G65: Queen . . . . . . . . .4D 1
Gavinburn Gdns. G60: Old K . . . . .6D
Gavinburn Pl. G60: Old K . . . . . . .6E
Gavinburn St. G60: Old K . . . . . . .6E
Gavin's Mill Rd. G62: Miln . . . . . . .4G
Gavins Rd. G81: Hard . . . . . . . . . .2D
Gavin St. ML1: Moth . . . . . . . . . . .4G 1
Gavinton St. G44: Glas . . . . . . . . .2D 1
Gayne Dr. ML5: Glenb . . . . . . . . . .3G
Gean Ct. G67: Cumb . . . . . . . . . . .1F
Gear Ter. G40: Glas . . . . . . . . . . . .3D 1

Geary St.—Glendevon Sq.

**ary St.** G23: Glas . . . . . . . . . . .6B **46**
**ddes Hill** G74: E Kil . . . . . . . .5B **138**
**ddes Rd.** G21: Glas . . . . . . . . . .2E **65**
**elong Gdns.** G66: Len . . . . . . . . .2F **7**
**ils Av.** G82: Dumb . . . . . . . . . .2C **18**
**ils Quad.** G82: Dumb . . . . . . . .2C **18**
**iston St.** G32: Glas . . . . . . . . .1B **106**
**mini Gro.** ML1: Holy . . . . . . . .2B **128**
**mmel Pl.** G77: Newt M . . . . . .5B **132**
**nerals Ga.** G71: Udd . . . . . . .1C **124**
**ntle Row** G81: Dun . . . . . . . . . .1B **42**
**orge Av.** G81: Clyd . . . . . . . . . .4E **43**
**orge V Bri.** G5: Glas . . . . . . . . .5F **83**
**orge Cl.** ML2: Wis . . . . . . . . .1E **157**
**orge Ct.** ML3: Ham . . . . . . . . .4E **141**
PA1: Pais . . . . . . . . . . . . . . . .1H **97**
**orge Cres.** G81: Clyd . . . . . . . .4E **43**
**orge Gray St.** G73: Ruth . . . . . .5E **105**
**orge La.** PA1: Pais . . . . . . . . . .1A **98**
**orge Mann Ter.** G73: Ruth . . . .3C **120**
**orge Pl.** PA1: Pais . . . . . . . . . .1A **98**
**orge Reith Av.** G12: Glas . . . . . .4F **61**
**orge Sq.** G2: Glas . . . . . .4G **83** (5E **5**)
**orge St.** G1: Glas . . . . . .4G **83** (5F **5**)
G69: Bail . . . . . . . . . . . . . . .1H **107**
G78: Barr . . . . . . . . . . . . . . .4D **114**
ML1: Moth . . . . . . . . . . . . . .5G **143**
ML1: New S . . . . . . . . . . . . .3B **128**
ML3: Ham . . . . . . . . . . . . . .4E **141**
ML4: Bell . . . . . . . . . . . . . . .2B **126**
ML6: Air . . . . . . . . . . . . . . . . .4G **91**
ML6: Chap . . . . . . . . . . . . . .2D **112**
PA1: Pais . . . . . . . . . . . . . . . .1G **97**
(Broomlands St.)
PA1: Pais . . . . . . . . . . . . . . . .1H **97**
(George Ct.)
**orge St.** PA5: John . . . . . . . . . .2F **95**
**orge Way** *ML9: Lark . . . . . . . . .1F* ***161***
*(off Duncan Graham St.)*
**rard Pl.** ML4: Bell . . . . . . . . . .6D **110**
RMISTON . . . . . . . . . . . . . . .1D 84
**rtrude Pl.** G78: Barr . . . . . . . .5C **114**
**llies La.** ML1: Moth . . . . . . . .6E **127**
**bon Cres.** G74: E Kil . . . . . . . .6C **138**
**b St.** ML1: Cle . . . . . . . . . . . .6H **129**
ML6: Chap . . . . . . . . . . . . . . .2D **112**
**bson Av.** G82: Dumb . . . . . . . . .3H **17**
**bson Cres.** PA5: John . . . . . . . .3E **95**
**bson Hgts.** *G4: Glas . . . . . . . . .4A* ***84***
*(off Drygate)*
**bson Quad.** ML1: Moth . . . . . . .6E **127**
**bson Rd.** PA4: Renf . . . . . . . . . .3D **78**
**bson St.** G12: Glas . . . . . . . . . .1B **82**
G40: Glas . . . . . . . . . . . . . . . .5A **84**
G82: Dumb . . . . . . . . . . . . . . .3G **17**
FNOCK . . . . . . . . . . . . . . . .4A **118**
**fnock Pk. Av.** G46: Giff . . . . . .3A **118**
**fnock Station (Rail)** . . . . . . . . .4A **118**
fnock Tennis Squash & Hockey Club . . . . . . . . . . . . . . . . . . . .6A 118
**ford Dr.** G52: Glas . . . . . . . . . . .6A **80**
**ford Wynd** PA2: Pais . . . . . . . . .3D **96**
**gha Gdns.** ML8: Carl . . . . . . . .5G **165**
**gha Quad.** ML2: Wis . . . . . . . .2E **157**
**bank La.** *ML9: Lark . . . . . . . . .3G* ***161***
*(off Shawrigg Rd.)*
**bertfield Path** G33: Glas . . . . . . .1B **86**
**bertfield Pl.** G33: Glas . . . . . . . .1B **86**
**bertfield Rd.**
G72: Camb, Flem . . . . . . . . . .4C **122**
**bertfield St.** G33: Glas . . . . . . . .1B **86**
**bert St.** G3: Glas . . . . . . . . . . . .3A **82**
**christ Ct.** *PA5: John . . . . . . . . . .4E* ***95***
*(off Tannahill Cres.)*
**christ Gdns.** G71: Both . . . . . . .6F **125**
**christ St.** ML5: Coat . . . . . . . . . .3D **90**
**christ Way** ML2: Wis . . . . . . . .2A **158**
**derdale** G74: E Kil . . . . . . . . . .1E **149**
**fillan Pl.** ML2: Over . . . . . . . . .4A **158**
**fillan Way** PA2: Pais . . . . . . . . . .5C **96**
**hill St.** G20: Glas . . . . . . . . . . .2B **62**
**lbank Av.** ML8: Carl . . . . . . . . .3D **164**
**lburn St.** ML2: Over . . . . . . . . .5A **158**
**lies Cres.** G74: E Kil . . . . . . . . .4D **138**
**lies La.** G69: Bail . . . . . . . . . . .1A **108**
**l Rd.** ML2: Over . . . . . . . . . . .4A **158**
(not continuous)
**martin Rd.** PA3: Lin . . . . . . . . . .5E **75**
**merton St.** G32: Glas . . . . . . . .1A **106**
**mour Av.** G74: T'hall . . . . . . . .6F **135**
G81: Hard . . . . . . . . . . . . . . . .2D **42**
**mour Cres.** G73: Ruth . . . . . . .5B **104**
**mour Dr.** ML3: Ham . . . . . . . . .1D **152**
**mour Pl.** G5: Glas . . . . . . . . . .1G **103**
ML4: Bell . . . . . . . . . . . . . . . .2A **126**
ML5: Coat . . . . . . . . . . . . . . . .3B **90**
**mour St.** G81: Clyd . . . . . . . . . .3E **43**
PA1: Pais . . . . . . . . . . . . . . . . .6A **78**
**mourton Cres.**
G77: Newt M . . . . . . . . . . . . .6D **132**
GILSHOCHILL . . . . . . . . . . . . . . . .2B **62**
Gilshochill Station (Rail) . . . . . . . . . . . . . . . . . . . . . . .2C **62**
**Gimmerscroft Cres.** ML6: Air . . . . .5F **93**
**Girthon St.** G32: Glas . . . . . . . . . .1C **106**
**Girvan Cres.** ML6: Chap . . . . . . . .4D **112**
**Girvan St.** G33: Glas . . . . . . . . . . . .2F **85**
**Glade, The** ML9: Lark . . . . . . . . . .3F **161**
**Gladney Av.** G13: Glas . . . . . . . . . .1G **59**
**Gladsmuir Rd.** G52: Glas . . . . . . . .5A **80**
GLADSTONE . . . . . . . . . . . . . . . .6H **39**
**Gladstone Av.** G78: Barr . . . . . . . .5D **114**
PA5: John . . . . . . . . . . . . . . . .6D **94**
**Gladstone Ct.** ML3: Ham . . . . . . .4E **141**
**Gladstone St.** G4: Glas . . . .1E **83** (1A **4**)
G81: Clyd . . . . . . . . . . . . . . . .5B **42**
ML4: Bell . . . . . . . . . . . . . . . .2D **126**
**Glaive Rd.** G13: Glas . . . . . . . . . . .6D **44**
**Glamis Av.** G77: Newt M . . . . . . .4F **133**
ML8: Carl . . . . . . . . . . . . . . . .3F **165**
PA5: Eld . . . . . . . . . . . . . . . . .4H **95**
**Glamis Ct.** ML1: Carf . . . . . . . . . .5C **128**
**Glamis Dr.** G74: E Kil . . . . . . . . . .6H **137**
**Glamis Gdns.** G64: B'rig . . . . . . . . .3D **48**
**Glamis Rd.** G31: Glas . . . . . . . . . .1F **105**
**Glanderston Av.** G77: Newt M . . .3B **132**
**Glanderston Ct.** G13: Glas . . . . . .1A **60**
**Glanderston Dr.** G13: Glas . . . . . . .2A **60**
**Glanderston Ga.** G77: Newt M . . .3B **132**
**Glanderston Rd.**
G78: Neil, Newt M . . . . . . . . .3H **131**
**Glandston Av.** G78: Barr . . . . . . .5G **115**
GLASGOW . . . . . . . . . . . . .4G **83** (5F **5**)
Glasgow Academical Athletic Ground . . . . . . . . . . . . . . . . . . . . . .3D 60
**Glasgow Airport** PA3: Glas A . . . . .1H **77**
**GLASGOW AIRPORT INTERCHANGE** . . . . . . . . . . . . . . . . . . . . .3H **77**
**Glasgow & Edinburgh Rd.**
G69: Bail . . . . . . . . . . . . . . . . .6B **88**
G69: Barg . . . . . . . . . . . . . . . .1D **108**
ML1: Holy . . . . . . . . . . . . . . . .4A **112**
ML1: N'hse . . . . . . . . . . . . . . .5E **113**
ML4: Bell . . . . . . . . . . . . . . . .4G **111**
ML5: Coat . . . . . . . . . . . . . . .1D **108**
Glasgow Botanic Gardens . . . . . . . . . . . . . . . . . . . . . .5B 62
**Glasgow Bri.** G5: Glas . . . . . . . . . .5F **83**
**Glasgow Bri. Cotts.** *G66: Kirk . . . .6G* ***29***
*(off Kirkintilloch Rd.)*
**Glasgow Crematorium**
G23: Glas . . . . . . . . . . . . . . . .1D **62**
Glasgow Film Theatre . . . .3F 83 (3C 4)
**Glasgow Fish Mkt.** G21: Glas . . . . .2D **84**
**Glasgow Fort Shop. Cen.**
G34: Glas . . . . . . . . . . . . . . . .2E **87**
**Glasgow Fruit Mkt.** G21: Glas . . . .2C **84**
Glasgow Golf Course . . . . . . . . .4A 46
Glasgow Green Football Cen. . . .1A 104
**Glasgow Harbour Terraces**
G11: Glas . . . . . . . . . . . . . . . .2G **81**
Glasgow Hawks R.U.F.C. . . . . . . .3E 61
**Glasgow Necropolis** G31: Glas . . . .4A **84**
**Glasgow Rd.** G62: Miln . . . . . . . . .5G **25**
G65: Kils . . . . . . . . . . . . . . . . .3E **11**
G66: Kirk . . . . . . . . . . . . . . . .6H **29**
G67: Cumb . . . . . . . . . . . . . . . .5E **35**
(Condorrat Ring Rd.)
G67: Cumb . . . . . . . . . . . . . . . .1B **36**
(Old Glasgow Rd.)
G69: Bail . . . . . . . . . . . . . . . .1F **107**
G69: Barg, Coat . . . . . . . . . . . .5F **89**
G71: Tann, Udd . . . . . . . . . . .4A **108**
G72: Blan . . . . . . . . . . . . . . . .6H **123**
G72: Camb . . . . . . . . . . . . . . .6G **105**
(Duke's Rd.)
G72: Camb . . . . . . . . . . . . . . .6H **121**
(E. Kilbride Rd.)
G73: Ruth . . . . . . . . . . . . . . . .5H **121**
(E. Kilbride Rd.)
G73: Ruth . . . . . . . . . . . . . . . .3B **104**
(Shawfield Rd.)
G74: Ners . . . . . . . . . . . . . . . .2A **138**
G76: Water . . . . . . . . . . . . . . .6B **134**
G78: Barr . . . . . . . . . . . . . . . .3F **115**
G81: Clyd . . . . . . . . . . . . . . . .1D **58**
G81: Hard . . . . . . . . . . . . . . . .1D **42**
G82: Dumb, Milt . . . . . . . . . . . .3E **17**
ML2: Wis . . . . . . . . . . . . . . . .6D **144**
ML3: Ham . . . . . . . . . . . . . . . .4E **141**
ML5: Barg, Coat . . . . . . . . . . . .5F **89**
PA1: Pais . . . . . . . . . . . . . . . . .6B **78**
PA4: Renf . . . . . . . . . . . . . . . .6G **59**
Glasgow Rowing Club . . . . . . . . . .6A 84
Glasgow Royal Concert Hall . . . . . . . . . . . . . . . . . . . .3G 83 (3E 5)
Glasgow School of Art . . . .3E 83 (3B 4)
Glasgow Science Cen. . . . . . . . . .4B 82
Glasgow's Grand Ole Opry . . . . . .5C 82
Glasgow Ski Cen. . . . . . . . . . . . .1G 101
**Glasgow Southern Orbital**
G74: E Kil . . . . . . . . . . . . . . .2A **148**
G74: E Kil . . . . . . . . . . . . . . .6A **136**
**Glasgow St.** G12: Glas . . . . . . . . . .6C **62**
**Glassel Rd.** G34: Glas . . . . . . . . . .2B **88**
**Glasserton Pl.** G43: Glas . . . . . . .2D **118**
**Glasserton Rd.** G43: Glas . . . . . . .2D **118**
**Glassford St.** G1: Glas . . . . .4G **83** (6F **5**)
G62: Miln . . . . . . . . . . . . . . . . .3H **25**
ML1: Moth . . . . . . . . . . . . . . .5A **144**
**Glassford Twr.** *ML1: Moth . . . . . .5A* ***144***
*(off Burnside Ct.)*
**Glaudhall Av.** G69: G'csh . . . . . . . .2C **68**
**Glazert Dr.** G66: Len . . . . . . . . . . . .1C **6**
**Glazert Mdw.** G66: Len . . . . . . . . . .4G **7**
**Glazert Pk. Dr.** G66: Len . . . . . . . . .4G **7**
**Glazert Pl.** G66: Milt C . . . . . . . . . .6B **8**
**Glebe Av.** G71: Both . . . . . . . . . .5F **125**
G76: Crmck . . . . . . . . . . . . . .2H **135**
ML5: Coat . . . . . . . . . . . . . . .1H **109**
**Glebe Ct.** G4: Glas . . . . . . . .3H **83** (3H **5**)
**Glebe Cres.** G74: E Kil . . . . . . . . .2H **149**
ML3: Ham . . . . . . . . . . . . . . .1G **153**
ML6: Air . . . . . . . . . . . . . . . . .3D **92**
**Glebe Gdns.** PA6: Hous . . . . . . . . .1B **74**
**Glebe Hollow** G71: Both . . . . . . . .5F **125**
**Glebe La.** G77: Newt M . . . . . . . .5D **132**
**Glebe Pk.** G82: Dumb . . . . . . . . . . .2H **17**
**Glebe Pl.** G72: Camb . . . . . . . . . .2B **122**
G73: Ruth . . . . . . . . . . . . . . . .5B **104**
**Glebe Rd.** G77: Newt M . . . . . . . .5D **132**
**Glebe St.** G4: Glas . . . . . . . .2H **83** (2H **5**)
(Kennedy St.)
G4: Glas . . . . . . . . . . . .3A **84** (3H **5**)
(McAslin St., not continuous)
G74: E Kil . . . . . . . . . . . . . . . .1H **149**
ML3: Ham . . . . . . . . . . . . . . . .1G **153**
ML4: Bell . . . . . . . . . . . . . . . .2B **126**
PA4: Renf . . . . . . . . . . . . . . . . .6F **59**
**Glebe, The** G71: Both . . . . . . . . . .5F **125**
**Glebe Wynd** G71: Both . . . . . . . . .5F **125**
**Gleddoch Rd.** G52: Glas . . . . . . . . .5G **79**
**Gledstane Rd.** PA7: B'ton . . . . . . . .5H **39**
**Glenacre Cres.** G71: Tann . . . . . .5C **108**
**Glenacre Dr.** G45: Glas . . . . . . . . .4H **119**
ML6: Air . . . . . . . . . . . . . . . . .5D **92**
**Glenacre Gro.** G45: Glas . . . . . . . .3A **120**
**Glenacre Quad.** G45: Glas . . . . . . .4H **119**
**Glenacre Rd.** G67: Cumb . . . . . . . .5H **35**
**Glenacre St.** G45: Glas . . . . . . . . .4H **119**
**Glenacre Ter.** G45: Glas . . . . . . . .4H **119**
**Glenafeoch Rd.** ML8: Carl . . . . . . .4F **165**
**Glen Affric** G74: E Kil . . . . . . . . . .2B **150**
**Glen Affric Av.** G53: Glas . . . . . . .3D **116**
**Glen Affric Way** *ML6: Chap . . . . .4D* ***112***
*(off Glen Avon Dr.)*
**Glenafton Vw.** ML3: Ham . . . . . . .3F **153**
**Glen Alby Pl.** G53: Glas . . . . . . . .3C **116**
**Glenallan Ter.** ML1: Moth . . . . . . .6F **127**
**Glenallan Way** PA2: Pais . . . . . . . .6B **96**
**Glen Almond** G74: E Kil . . . . . . . .1D **150**
**Glenalmond Rd.** G73: Ruth . . . . . .4F **121**
**Glenalmond St.** G32: Glas . . . . . . .1A **106**
**Glenalva Ct.** G65: Kils . . . . . . . . . .2H **11**
**Glenapp Av.** PA2: Pais . . . . . . . . . .4D **98**
**Glenapp Pl.** G69: Mood . . . . . . . . .4D **52**
**Glenapp Rd.** PA2: Pais . . . . . . . . . .4D **98**
**Glenapp St.** G41: Glas . . . . . . . . .2D **102**
**Glenarklet Dr.** PA2: Pais . . . . . . . .4C **98**
**Glen Arroch** G74: E Kil . . . . . . . . .2B **150**
**Glenartney** PA6: Hous . . . . . . . . . .1A **74**
**Glenartney Rd.** G69: Chry . . . . . . .6A **52**
**Glenashdale Way**
PA2: Pais . . . . . . . . . . . . . . . . .4C **98**
**Glen Av.** G32: Glas . . . . . . . . . . . .5B **86**
G69: Mood . . . . . . . . . . . . . . . .5D **52**
G78: Neil . . . . . . . . . . . . . . . .2E **131**
ML9: Lark . . . . . . . . . . . . . . . .5D **160**
**Glenavon Ct.** ML3: Ham . . . . . . . .2F **153**
**Glen Avon Dr.** ML6: Chap . . . . . .4D **112**
**Glenavon Rd.** G20: Glas . . . . . . . . .2B **62**
**Glenbank Av.** G66: Lenz . . . . . . . . .3D **50**
**Glenbank Dr.** G46: T'bnk . . . . . . . .5F **117**
**Glenbank Rd.** G66: Lenz . . . . . . . . .3D **50**
**Glenbarr St.** G21: Glas . . . . . . . . . .2B **84**
**Glen Bervie** G74: E Kil . . . . . . . . .1B **150**
**Glenbervie Cres.** G68: Cumb . . . . .1H **35**
**Glenbervie Pl.** G23: Glas . . . . . . . .6B **46**
G77: Newt M . . . . . . . . . . . . .4A **132**
GLENBOIG . . . . . . . . . . . . . . . . . . .3A **70**
**Glenboig Farm Rd.**
ML5: Glenb . . . . . . . . . . . . . . . .3A **70**
**Glenboig New Rd.** ML5: Glenb . . . .3B **70**
**Glenboig Rd.** G69: G'csh . . . . . . . .1F **69**
**Glen Brae** PA11: Bri W . . . . . . . . .3E **73**
**Glenbrittle Dr.** PA2: Pais . . . . . . . .4C **98**
**Glenbrittle Way** PA2: Pais . . . . . . .4C **98**
**Glenbuck Av.** G33: Glas . . . . . . . . .3H **65**
**Glenbuck Dr.** G33: Glas . . . . . . . . .3H **65**
GLENBURN . . . . . . . . . . . . . . . . . .5H **97**
**Glenburn Av.** G69: Bail . . . . . . . . . .6A **88**
G69: Mood . . . . . . . . . . . . . . . .5D **52**
G72: Camb . . . . . . . . . . . . . . .2F **121**
ML1: N'hill . . . . . . . . . . . . . . .3C **128**
**Glenburn Ct.** *G66: Kirk . . . . . . . . . .5D* ***30***
*(off Willowbank Gdns.)*
G74: E Kil . . . . . . . . . . . . . . . .6C **136**
**Glenburn Cres.** G66: Milt C . . . . . . .6C **8**
G71: View . . . . . . . . . . . . . . . .5G **109**
PA2: Pais . . . . . . . . . . . . . . . . .5H **97**
**Glenburn Gdns.** G64: B'rig . . . . . . .5B **48**
ML5: Glenb . . . . . . . . . . . . . . .3G **69**
**Glenburnie Pl.** G34: Glas . . . . . . . .4F **87**
**Glenburn La.** G20: Glas . . . . . . . . .2C **62**
**Glenburn Rd.** G46: Giff . . . . . . . .6H **117**
G61: Bear . . . . . . . . . . . . . . . . .2D **44**
G74: E Kil . . . . . . . . . . . . . . . .6C **136**
ML3: Ham . . . . . . . . . . . . . . . .6F **141**
PA2: Pais . . . . . . . . . . . . . . . . .5F **97**
**Glenburn St.** G20: Glas . . . . . . . . . .2C **62**
**Glenburn Ter.** ML1: Carf . . . . . . . .6C **128**
ML8: Carl . . . . . . . . . . . . . . . .5E **165**
**Glenburn Wlk.** G69: Bail . . . . . . . . .6A **88**
**Glenburn Way** G74: E Kil . . . . . . .6B **136**
**Glenburn Wynd** *ML9: Lark . . . . . .1F* ***161***
*(off Muirshot Rd.)*
**Glencairn Av.** ML2: Wis . . . . . . . .5D **144**
**Glencairn Ct.** *PA3: Pais . . . . . . . . .3D* ***78***
*(off Montgomery Rd.)*
**Glencairn Dr.** G41: Glas . . . . . . . .3B **102**
G69: Mood . . . . . . . . . . . . . . . .5C **52**
G73: Ruth . . . . . . . . . . . . . . . .5B **104**
**Glencairn Gdns.** G41: Glas . . . . . .3C **102**
G72: Camb . . . . . . . . . . . . . . .2D **122**
**Glencairn La.** G41: Glas . . . . . . . .3C **102**
**Glencairn Path** *G32: Glas . . . . . . . .5C* ***86***
*(off Mansionhouse Dr.)*
**Glencairn Rd.** G67: Cumb . . . . . . .3C **36**
G82: Dumb . . . . . . . . . . . . . . . .4C **16**
PA3: Pais . . . . . . . . . . . . . . . . .4C **78**
**Glencairn St.** G66: Kirk . . . . . . . . .6D **30**
ML1: Moth . . . . . . . . . . . . . . .4G **143**
**Glencairn Twr.** ML1: Moth . . . . . .4G **143**
**Glen Calder Ct.** ML6: Air . . . . . . . .6D **92**
**Glencalder Cres.** ML4: Bell . . . . .4D **126**
**Glen Cally** G74: E Kil . . . . . . . . . .1B **150**
**Glencally Av.** PA2: Pais . . . . . . . . .4D **98**
**Glen Cannich** G74: E Kil . . . . . . . .2B **150**
**Glen Carron** G74: E Kil . . . . . . . . .2B **150**
**Glencart Gro.** PA10: John . . . . . . . .4C **94**
**Glencleland Rd.** ML2: Wis . . . . . .5D **144**
**Glenclora Dr.** PA2: Pais . . . . . . . . .4C **98**
**Glencloy St.** G20: Glas . . . . . . . . .2A **62**
**Glen Clunie** G74: E Kil . . . . . . . . .1D **150**
**Glen Clunie Dr.** G53: Glas . . . . . . .3C **116**
**Glen Clunie Pl.** G53: Glas . . . . . . .3C **116**
**Glencoats Dr.** PA3: Pais . . . . . . . . .6E **77**
**Glencoe Dr.** ML1: Holy . . . . . . . .2A **128**
**Glencoe Pl.** G13: Glas . . . . . . . . . .2F **61**
ML3: Ham . . . . . . . . . . . . . . . .3F **153**
**Glencoe Rd.** G73: Ruth . . . . . . . . .4F **121**
ML8: Carl . . . . . . . . . . . . . . . .5G **165**
**Glencoe St.** G13: Glas . . . . . . . . . .2F **61**
**Glen Cona Dr.** G53: Glas . . . . . . .2C **116**
**Glenconner Way** G66: Kirk . . . . . . .4G **31**
**Glencorse Rd.** PA2: Pais . . . . . . . . .3G **97**
**Glencorse St.** G32: Glas . . . . . . . . .4G **85**
**Glen Ct.** ML1: Moth . . . . . . . . . .5B **144**
ML5: Coat . . . . . . . . . . . . . . . .6H **89**
**Glen Cova** G74: E Kil . . . . . . . . . .1B **150**
**Glen Cova Dr.** G68: Cumb . . . . . . . .1E **35**
**Glencraig St.** ML6: Air . . . . . . . . . .4G **91**
**Glen Creran Cres.** G78: Neil . . . . .3C **130**
**Glen Cres.** G13: Glas . . . . . . . . . .2G **59**
**Glencroft Av.** G71: Tann . . . . . . . .5C **108**
**Glencroft Rd.** G44: Glas . . . . . . . .2H **119**
**Glencryan Rd.** G67: Cumb . . . . . . .5A **36**
**Glendale Av.** ML6: Air . . . . . . . . . .5D **92**
**Glendale Cres.** G64: B'rig . . . . . . . .1E **65**
**Glendale Dr.** G64: B'rig . . . . . . . . .1E **65**
**Glendale Gro.** ML5: Coat . . . . . . .2A **110**
**Glendale Pl.** G31: Glas . . . . . . . . . .5D **84**
G64: B'rig . . . . . . . . . . . . . . . .2E **65**
**Glendale St.** G31: Glas . . . . . . . . . .5D **84**
**Glendaruel Av.** G61: Bear . . . . . . . .3H **45**
**Glendaruel Rd.** G73: Ruth . . . . . .5G **121**
**Glendarvel Gdns.** G22: Glas . . . . . .5H **63**
**Glendee Gdns.** PA4: Renf . . . . . . . .1F **79**
**Glendee Rd.** PA4: Renf . . . . . . . . . .1F **79**
**Glen Dene Way** G53: Glas . . . . . .3C **116**
**Glendentan Rd.** PA11: Bri W . . . . .4E **73**
**Glendermott Ct.** ML8: Carl . . . . . .2F **165**
**Glen Derry** G74: E Kil . . . . . . . . .6D **138**
**Glen Dessary** G74: E Kil . . . . . . . .3B **150**
**Glendeveron Way** ML1: Carf . . . .5A **128**
**Glen Devon** G74: E Kil . . . . . . . . .2D **150**
**Glendevon Cotts.** G81: Clyd . . . . . .4B **42**
**Glendevon Pl.** G81: Clyd . . . . . . . .4B **42**
ML3: Ham . . . . . . . . . . . . . . . .3F **153**
**Glendevon Sq.** G33: Glas . . . . . . . . .1B **86**

## Glen Dewar Pl.—Grahamston Ct.


Glen Dewar Pl. G53: Glas 3C 116
Glendinning Rd. G13: Glas 6E 45
Glendoick Pl. G77: Newt M 4A 132
Glen Doll G74: E Kil 1B 150
Glen Doll Rd. G78: Neil 4B 130
Glendorch Av. ML2: Wis 2A 146
Glendore St. G14: Glas 1E 81
Glen Douglas Dr. G68: Cumb 1E 35
Glendoune Rd. G76: Clar 4C 134
Glendower Way PA2: Pais 5C 96
Glen Dr. ML1: Holy 2B 128
Glenduffhill Rd. G69: Bail 6F 87
Glen Dye G74: E Kil 1B 150
Glen Eagles G74: E Kil 2C 150
Gleneagles Av. G68: Cumb 6A 14
Gleneagles Ct. *G64: B'rig 4C 48*
*(off Hilton Rd.)*
Gleneagles Dr. G64: B'rig 4C 48
G77: Newt M 5H 133
Gleneagles Gdns. G64: B'rig 4B 48
Gleneagles Ga. G77: Newt M 5H 133
Gleneagles La. Nth. G14: Glas 5C 60
Gleneagles La. Sth. G14: Glas 6C 60
Gleneagles Pk. G71: Both 5D 124
Glenelg Cres. G66: Kirk 4G 31
Glenelg Path ML5: Glenb 3G 69
Glenelg Quad. G34: Glas 2B 88
Glenelm Pl. ML4: Bell 1C 126
Glen Esk G74: E Kil 1C 150
Glen Esk Cres. G53: Glas 3C 116
Glen Esk Dr. G53: Glas 3C 116
Glen Esk Pl. G53: Glas 3C 116
Glen Etive Pl. G73: Ruth 5G 121
Glen Falloch G74: E Kil 2C 150
Glen Falloch Cres. G78: Neil 4D 130
Glen Farg G74: E Kil 2D 150
Glenfarg Ct. ML3: Ham 3F 153
Glenfarg Cres. G61: Bear 3H 45
Glenfarg Rd. G73: Ruth 3D 120
Glenfarg St. G20: Glas 1E 83
Glenfarm Rd. ML1: N'hill 3E 129
Glen Farrar G74: E Kil 2B 150
Glen Feshie G74: E Kil 3B 150
Glenfield Av. PA2: Pais 6H 97
Glenfield Cres. PA2: Pais 6H 97
Glenfield Gdns. PA2: Pais 6H 97
Glenfield Grange PA2: Pais 1A 114
Glenfield Gro. PA2: Pais 6H 97
Glenfield Rd. G75: E Kil 5A 150
PA2: Pais 6G 97
Glen Finlet Cres. G78: Neil 4C 130
Glenfinnan Dr. G20: Glas 3B 62
G61: Bear 4H 45
Glenfinnan Gro. ML4: Bell 3F 127
Glenfinnan Pl. *G20: Glas 3B 62*
*(off Glenfinnan Rd.)*
Glenfinnan Rd. G20: Glas 3B 62
Glenfruin Cres. PA2: Pais 4D 98
Glen Fruin Dr. ML9: Lark 4G 161
Glen Fruin Pl. *ML6: Chap 3D 112*
*(off Glen Rannoch Dr.)*
Glenfruin Rd. G72: Blan 1A 140
Glen Fyne Rd. G68: Cumb 1D 34
Glen Gairn G74: E Kil 1D 150
Glen Gairn Cres. G78: Neil 3C 130
Glen Gdns. PA5: Eld 2A 96
Glen Garrell Pl. G65: Kils 2F 11
Glengarriff Rd. ML4: Bell 5D 110
Glen Garry G74: E Kil 3B 150
Glengarry Dr. G52: Glas 6C 80
Glengavel Cres. G33: Glas 3H 65
Glengavel Gdns. ML2: Wis 2A 146
Glengonnar St. ML9: Lark 5E 161
GLENGOWAN 2C 160
Glengowan Rd. PA11: Bri W 3E 73
Glen Gro. G65: Kils 1H 11
G75: E Kil 4F 149
Glengyre St. G34: Glas 2A 88
Glenhead Cres. G22: Glas 3G 63
G81: Dun, Hard 6C 22
Glenhead Dr. ML1: Moth 5F 143
Glenhead Rd. G66: Lenz 3D 50
G81: Clyd 2B 42
Glenhead St. G22: Glas 3G 63
Glenholme Av. PA2: Pais 4F 97
Glenhove Rd. G67: Cumb 3A 36
Gleniffer Av. G13: Glas 3A 60
Gleniffer Braes Country Pk. 1A 114
Gleniffer Ct. PA2: Pais 6F 97
Gleniffer Cres. PA5: Eld 4A 96
Gleniffer Dr. G78: Barr 2C 114
Gleniffer Rd. PA2: Pais 6D 96
PA4: Renf 3D 78
Gleniffer Vw. G78: Neil 1D 130
G81: Clyd 4F 43
Glen Isla G74: E Kil 1C 150
Glenisla Av. G69: Mood 3E 53
Glen Isla Av. G78: Neil 4C 130
Glenisla St. G31: Glas 2F 105
Glenkirk Dr. G15: Glas 5B 44
Glen Kyle Dr. G53: Glas 3C 116
Glen La. PA3: Pais 6A 78
Glen Lednock Dr. G68: Cumb 1D 34
Glen Lee G74: E Kil 1C 150
Glenlee St. ML3: Ham 4D 140
Glen Lethnot G74: E Kil 1C 150
Glen Livet Pl. G53: Glas 3C 116
Glenlivet Rd. G78: Neil 3C 130
Glen Lochay Gdns. G68: Cumb 1D 34
Glenlora Dr. G53: Glas 6A 100
Glenlora Ter. G53: Glas 6B 100
Glen Loy Pl. G53: Glas 3C 116
Glenluce Dr. G32: Glas 2D 106
Glenluce Gdns. G69: Mood 4E 53
Glenluce Ter. G74: E Kil 1E 149
Glenluggie Rd. G66: Kirk 6G 31
Glenlui Av. G73: Ruth 2D 120
Glen Luss Gdns. G68: Cumb 1D 34
Glen Luss Pl. G53: Glas 3C 116
ML5: Coat 6F 91
Glen Lyon G74: E Kil 2C 150
Glen Lyon Ct. G68: Cumb 1D 34
Glenlyon Ct. ML3: Ham 3F 153
Glenlyon Pl. G73: Ruth 4E 121
Glen Lyon Rd. G78: Neil 3C 130
Glen Mallie G74: E Kil 2C 150
Glenmalloch Pl. PA5: Eld 2A 96
Glenmanor Av. G69: Mood 5C 52
Glenmanor Rd. G69: Mood 5C 52
Glenmare Av. G66: Kirk 6G 31
Glen Mark G74: E Kil 1C 150
Glen Mark Rd. G78: Neil 3C 130
GLENMAVIS 5G 71
Glenmavis Ct. ML8: Carl 4G 165
Glenmavis Cres. ML8: Carl 4G 165
Glenmavis Rd. ML6: Glenm 6G 71
Glenmavis St. G4: Glas 2F 83 (1D 4)
Glen More G74: E Kil 2A 150
Glenmore Av. G42: Glas 5A 104
ML4: Bell 4D 126
Glenmore Rd. ML1: N'hill 4C 128
Glen Moriston G74: E Kil 2C 150
Glen Moriston Rd.
G53: Glas 4C 116
G68: Cumb 1D 34
Glenmoss Av. PA8: Ersk 6D 40
Glen Moy G74: E Kil 2B 150
Glenmuir Dr. G53: Glas 2B 116
Glen Muir Rd. G78: Neil 3C 130
Glen Nevis G74: E Kil 3B 150
Glen Nevis Pl. G73: Ruth 5E 121
Glen Noble ML1: Cle 1G 145
Glen Ochil Rd. ML6: Chap 4D 112
Glen Ogilvie G74: E Kil 1C 150
Glenogle St. G32: Glas 1D 106
Glenoran La. ML9: Lark 1F 161
Glenorchard Rd. G64: Balm 3H 27
Glen Orchy Ct. G68: Cumb 6D 12
Glen Orchy Dr. G53: Glas 3C 116
G68: Cumb 1D 34
Glen Orchy Gro. G53: Glas 3D 116
Glen Orchy Pl. G53: Glas 4D 116
G68: Cumb 1D 34
*ML6: Chap 4D 112*
*(off Glen Rannoch Dr.)*
Glen Orchy Way G53: Glas 4C 116
Glen Orrin Way G78: Neil 3C 130
Glenpark ML6: Air 5E 93
Glenpark Av. G46: T'bnk 5F 117
Glenpark Gdns. G72: Camb 6G 105
Glenpark Ind. Est. G31: Glas 5D 84
Glenpark Rd. G31: Glas 5D 84
Glenpark St. G31: Glas 5D 84
ML2: Wis 5G 145
Glenpark Ter. G72: Camb 6G 105
Glenpath G82: Dumb 2C 18
Glenpatrick Rd. PA5: Eld 5A 96
Glen Pl. G76: Clar 2C 134
Glen Prosen G74: E Kil 1C 150
Glen Quoich G74: E Kil 6D 138
Glenraith Path G33: Glas 6B 66
Glenraith Rd. G33: Glas 6B 66
Glenraith Sq. G33: Glas 6B 66
Glenraith Wlk. G33: Glas 6C 66
Glen Rannoch Dr. ML6: Chap 4D 112
Glen Rinnes Dr. G78: Neil 4D 130
Glen Rd. G32: Glas 4B 86
G60: Old K 1F 41
G66: Cam G, Len 1C 6
G68: Dull 4F 13
G74: E Kil 5B 136
(not continuous)
ML1: N'hse 6D 112
ML2: Wis 5G 145
ML6: Air 5E 93
PA7: B'ton 3G 39
Glen Rosa Gdns. G68: Cumb 1D 34
Glen Roy Dr. G78: Neil 3C 130
Glen Sannox Vw. G68: Cumb 1D 34
Glen Sannox Way G68: Cumb 1D 34
Glen Sannox Wynd G68: Cumb 1E 35
Glen Sax Dr. PA4: Renf 2G 79
Glen Shee G74: E Kil 1C 150
Glen Shee Av. G78: Neil 3C 130
Glenshee Ct. G31: Glas 1F 105
Glen Shee Cres. ML6: Chap 4D 112
Glenshee Gdns. G31: Glas 1G 105
Glenshee St. G31: Glas 1F 105
Glenshee Ter. ML3: Ham 3F 153
Glenshiel Av. PA2: Pais 4C 98
Glenshira Av. PA2: Pais 4C 98
Glen Shirva Rd. G65: Twe 1D 32
Glenside Av. G53: Glas 3B 100
Glenside Cotts. *PA11: Bri W 3F 73*
*(off Mill of Gryffe Rd.)*
Glenside Dr. G73: Ruth 1F 121
Glenside Rd. G82: Dumb 1H 17
Glen Spean Pl. ML5: Coat 6F 91
Glenspean St. G43: Glas 1A 118
Glen St. G72: Camb 3D 122
G78: Barr 5E 115
ML1: Moth 6G 127
ML1: N'hill 3D 128
PA3: Pais 6H 77
Glentanar Ct. PA1: Pais 1C 98
Glentanar Dr. G69: Mood 5E 53
Glentanar Pl. G22: Glas 2F 63
Glentanar Rd. G22: Glas 2F 63
Glen Tanner G74: E Kil 1D 150
Glentarbert Rd. G73: Ruth 4F 121
Glen Tarbet Dr. G78: Neil 3C 130
Glen Tennet G74: E Kil 1C 150
Glentore Quad. ML6: Air 1A 92
Glen Twr. *ML1: Moth 5B 144*
*(off Glen Ct.)*
Glentrool Gdns. G22: Glas 5H 63
G69: Mood 4E 53
Glen Turret G74: E Kil 1C 150
Glenturret St. G32: Glas 1A 106
Glentyan Av. PA10: Kilb 1A 94
Glentyan Dr. G53: Glas 6A 100
Glen Urquhart G74: E Kil 2B 150
Glenview G66: Kirk 5D 30
Glen Vw. G67: Cumb 2C 36
ML3: Ham 5H 153
Glenview ML6: Air 5D 92
ML9: Lark 1D 160
Glenview Av. FK4: Bank 1E 15
Glenview Cres. G69: Mood 4D 52
Glenview Pl. G72: Blan 6B 124
Glenview St. ML6: Glenm 5G 71
Glenville Av. G46: Giff 4H 117
Glenville Ga. G76: Busby 4E 135
Glenville Ter. G76: Busby 4E 135
Glenward Av. G66: Len 3G 7
Glenwell St. ML6: Glenm 6G 71
Glenwood Av. ML6: Air 1C 112
Glenwood Bus. Cen.
G45: Glas 4A 120
Glenwood Ct. G66: Lenz 2A 50
Glenwood Dr. G46: T'bnk 5F 117
Glenwood Gdns. G66: Lenz 2A 50
Glenwood Path G45: Glas 4A 120
Glenwood Pl. G45: Glas 4A 120
G66: Lenz 2A 50
Glenwood Rd. G66: Lenz 2A 50
Glidden Ct. ML2: Over 4A 158
Globe Ct. G74: E Kil 4D 138
Glorat Av. G66: Len 3G 7
Gloucester Av. G73: Ruth 2F 121
G76: Clar 2B 134
Gloucester St. G5: Glas 6E 83
Goals (Five a Side Football Cen.)
4F 43
Goals Football Cen. 4D 102
GOCKSTON 3H 77
Gockston Rd. PA3: Pais 4H 77
Goddard Pl. ML2: Newm 4F 147
Gogar Pl. G33: Glas 3G 85
Gogar St. G33: Glas 3G 85
Goil Av. ML4: Bell 1H 125
Goil Way *ML1: Holy 2A 128*
*(off Howden Pl.)*
Goldberry Av. G14: Glas 4B 60
Goldberry La. *G14: Glas 4B 60*
*(off Esslemont Av.)*
Goldenhill Ct. G81: Hard 1D 42
Goldenlee Vw. PA6: C'lee 3A 74
Goldie Rd. G71: Udd 3E 125
Golf Av. ML4: Bell 4C 126
Golf Course Rd. G64: Balm 5A 28
PA11: Bri W 3D 72
Golf Ct. G44: Neth 5C 118
Golf Dr. G15: Glas 6H 43
PA1: Pais 1E 99
Golf Gdns. ML9: Lark 3G 161
GOLFHILL 1H 91
Golfhill Dr. G31: Glas 3C 84
Golfhill Quad. ML6: Air 1A 92
Golfhill Rd. ML2: Wis 5D 144
Golf Pl. ML4: Bell 4D 1
Golf Rd. G73: Ruth 3D 1
G76: Clar 2B 1
Golfview G61: Bear 2B
Golf Vw. G81: Clyd 3B
Golfview Dr. ML5: Coat 4G
Golfview Pl. ML5: Coat 5G
Golspie Av. ML6: Air 1G 1
Golspie St. G51: Glas 3G
Goodview Gdns.
ML9: Lark 3G 1
Goosedubs *G1: Glas 5G*
*(off Bridgega*
Gooseholm Cres. G82: Dumb 2G
Gooseholm Rd. G82: Dumb 2G
Gopher Av. G71: View 5F 1
GORBALS 1G 1
Gorbals Cross G5: Glas 6G
ML9: Lark 2E 1
Gorbals Leisure Cen. 6G
Gorbals St. G5: Glas 6F
Gordon Av. G44: Neth 5C 1
G52: Hill 4G
G69: Bail 6F
PA7: B'ton 3G
Gordon Ct. ML6: Air 3E
Gordon Cres. G77: Newt M 3E 1
Gordon Dr. G44: Neth 5C 1
G74: E Kil 6B 1
Gordon La. G1: Glas 4F 83 (5D
Gordon Pl. ML4: Bell 4B 1
Gordon Rd. G44: Neth 5C 1
ML3: Ham 5D 1
Gordon Sq. PA5: John 3F
Gordon St. G1: Glas 4F 83 (5D
PA1: Pais 1A
Gordon Ter. G72: Blan 5A 1
ML3: Ham 6D 1
Gorebridge St. G32: Glas 4G
Goremire Rd. ML8: Carl 6G 1
Gorget Av. G13: Glas 6C
Gorget Pl. G13: Glas 6C
Gorget Quad. G13: Glas 6B
Gorse Cres. PA11: Bri W 4G
Gorse Dr. G78: Barr 3D 1
Gorsehall St. ML1: Cle 5H 1
Gorse Pl. G71: View 5F 1
Gorsewood G64: B'rig 6A
Gorstan Path G23: Glas 1B
Gorstan Pl. G20: Glas 4A
Gorstan St. G23: Glas 1B
Gosford La. G14: Glas 5A
Gotter Bank PA11: Q'riers 1A
Goudie St. PA3: Pais 4H
Gough La. *G33: Glas 3F*
*(off Gough*
Gough St. G33: Glas 3F
Gourlay G74: E Kil 4D 1
Gourlay Dr. ML2: Over 5A 1
Gourlay St. G21: Glas 6H
(not continuo
Gourock St. G41: Glas 1E 1
GOVAN 3G
GOVANHILL 3F 1
Govanhill St. G42: Glas 3F 1
(not continuo
Govanhill Swimming Pool 3E 1
Govan Rd. G51: Glas 2D
Govan Station (Und.) 3G
Gowanbank Gdns. PA5: John 3E
Gowanbrae G66: Lenz 1C
Gowanlea Av. G15: Glas 6A
Gowanlea Dr. G46: Giff 3B 1
Gowanlea Ter. G71: View 6F 1
Gowanside Pl. ML8: Carl 3D 1
Gower St. G41: Glas 1A 1
Gower Ter. G41: Glas 6A
Gowkhall Av. ML1: N'hill 4F 1
GOWKTHRAPPLE 3G 1
Goyle Av. G15: Glas 4C
Grace Av. G69: Barg 6D
Grace St. G3: Glas 4D
Graeme Ct. ML1: Moth 5F 1
Graffham Av. G46: Giff 4B 1
Grafton Pl. G1: Glas 3G 83 (3F
Graham Av. G72: Camb 2D 1
G74: E Kil 1G 1
G81: Clyd 4D
ML3: Ham 3H 1
(not continuo
Graham Dr. G62: Miln 3E
Graham Ho. G67: Cumb 3G
Graham Pl. G65: Kils 1G
ML9: Ashg 4B 1
Graham Rd. G82: Dumb 3D
Grahamsdyke Rd. G66: Kirk 4E
Grahamshill Av. ML6: Air 3D
Grahamshill St. ML6: Air 3C
Graham Sq. G40: Glas 5B
Grahamston Ct. PA2: Pais 5E

## H

Hamilton Cres.—Herndon Ct.

**Hamilton Cres.** ML5: Coat 6C 90
PA4: Renf 4F 59
PA7: B'ton 4F 39
**Hamilton Dr.** G12: Glas 6C 62
G46: Giff 5B 118
G71: Both 6F 125
G72: Blan 4H 139
G72: Camb 2A 122
ML1: Moth 5H 143
ML6: Air 2B 92
PA8: Ersk 4D 40
**Hamilton Farm** G73: Ruth 5G 105
HAMILTONHILL 5F 63
**Hamiltonhill Cres.** G22: Glas 5F 63
**Hamiltonhill Rd.** G22: Glas 6F 63
**HAMILTON INTERCHANGE** 5C 142
**Hamilton Intl. Tech. Pk.**
G72: Blan 4A 140
(Technology Av.)
G72: Blan 5A 140
(Watt Pl.)
Hamilton Mausoleum 4B 142
**Hamilton Pk. Av.** G12: Glas 6C 62
**Hamilton Pk. Nth.** ML3: Ham 3H 141
Hamilton Pk. Racecourse 3H 141
**Hamilton Pk. Sth.** ML3: Ham 3H 141
**Hamilton Pl.** G75: E Kil 4G 149
G78: Neil 2F 131
ML1: N'hill 3C 128
ML1: New S 3B 128
ML3: Ham 5H 153
**Hamilton Retail Pk.** ML3: Ham 4G 141
**Hamilton Rd.** G32: Glas 2B 106
G71: Both 6F 125
G71: Udd 3F 107
G72: Blan 4F 139
G72: Camb, Flem 1A 122
G73: Ruth 5D 104
G74: E Kil 4C 138
ML1: Moth 4D 142
ML4: Bell 4B 126
ML9: Lark 6H 155
**Hamilton St.** G42: Glas 4G 103
G81: Clyd 2F 59
G82: Dumb 3G 17
ML8: Carl 4F 165
ML9: Lark 1E 161
PA3: Pais 6B 78
**Hamilton Ter.** G81: Clyd 2F 59
**Hamilton Twr.** G71: Both 3B 124
**Hamilton Vw.** G71: Tann 6E 109
Hamilton Water Palace 5H 141
**Hamilton West Station (Rail)** 5G 141
**Hamlet** G74: E Kil 4C 138
**Hampden Dr.** G42: Glas 6F 103
**Hampden La.** G42: Glas 5F 103
Hampden Pk. 6F 103
**Hampden Ter.** G42: Glas 5F 103
**Hampden Way** PA4: Renf 2F 79
**Handel Pl.** G5: Glas 1G 103
HANGINGSHAW 5G 103
**Hangingshaw Pl.** G42: Glas 5G 103
**Hannay St.** *PA1: Pais 6G 77*
*(off Well St.)*
**Hanover Cl.** G42: Glas 5E 103
**Hanover Ct.** G1: Glas 3G 83 (4F 5)
G11: Glas 1G 81
PA1: Pais 6C 78
PA5: John 2F 95
**Hanover Gdns.** G64: B'rig 6C 48
*PA1: Pais 1G 97*
*(off Wilson St.)*
**Hanover Pl.** G11: Glas 1G 81
**Hanover St.** G1: Glas 4G 83 (5E 5)
**Hanson Pk.** G31: Glas 3B 84
**Hanson St.** G31: Glas 4B 84
**Hapland Av.** G53: Glas 3C 100
**Hapland Rd.** G53: Glas 3C 100
**Harbour La.** PA3: Pais 6A 78
**Harbour Pl.** G11: Kils 2G 11
**Harbour Rd.** PA3: Pais 4A 78
**Harburn Pl.** G23: Glas 6C 46
**Harbury Pl.** G14: Glas 3H 59
**Harcourt Dr.** G31: Glas 3D 84
HARDGATE 1E 43
**Hardgate Dr.** G51: Glas 3C 80
**Hardgate Gdns.** G51: Glas 3C 80
**Hardgate Path** G51: Glas 3C 80
**Hardgate Pl.** G51: Glas 3C 80
**Hardgate Rd.** G51: Glas 3C 80
**Hardie Av.** G73: Ruth 5E 105
**Hardie St.** G72: Blan 2B 140
ML1: Moth 1G 143
ML3: Ham 1F 153
**Hardmoor Gdns.** G66: Kirk 4E 31
**Hardmoor Rd.** G66: Kirk 4E 31
**Hardridge Av.** G52: Glas 3E 101
**Hardridge Pl.** G52: Glas 3E 101
**Hardridge Rd.** G52: Glas 3D 100
**Harefield Dr.** G14: Glas 4B 60
**Harelaw Av.** G44: Glas 3C 118
G78: Barr 6F 115
G78: Neil 3D 130
**Harelaw Cres.** PA2: Pais 6G 97
HARELEESHILL 3F 161
**Hareleeshill Rd.** ML9: Lark 3F 161
Hareleeshill Sports Barn 4G 161
HARESTANES 4H 31
**Harestanes Gdns.** G66: Kirk 4G 31
**Harestone Cres.** ML2: Wis 1A 158
**Harestone Rd.** ML2: Wis 1A 158
**Harhill St.** G51: Glas 4F 81
**Harkins Av.** G72: Blan 2A 140
**Harkness Av.** G66: Milt C 6B 8
**Harland Cotts.** G14: Glas 6C 60
**Harland St.** G14: Glas 6C 60
**Harlaw Gdns.** G64: B'rig 5F 49
**Harley St.** G51: Glas 5A 82
**Harmetray St.** G22: Glas 3H 63
**Harmony Pl.** G51: Glas 4G 81
**Harmony Row** G51: Glas 4G 81
(not continuous)
**Harmony Sq.** G51: Glas 4G 81
**Harmsworth St.** G11: Glas 1E 81
**Harper Cres.** ML2: Wis 5C 146
**Harport St.** G46: T'bnk 2E 117
**Harriet Pl.** G43: Glas 1H 117
**Harriet St.** G73: Ruth 6C 104
**Harrington Rd.** G74: E Kil 2G 149
**Harris Cl.** G77: Newt M 3B 132
**Harris Cres.** G60: Old K 2F 41
**Harris Dr.** G60: Old K 2F 41
**Harris Gdns.** G60: Old K 2G 41
**Harrison Dr.** G51: Glas 5H 81
**Harrison Quad.** ML2: Wis 4C 146
**Harris Rd.** G23: Glas 6C 46
G60: Old K 2F 41
**Harrow Ct.** G15: Glas 4H 43
**Harrow Pl.** G15: Glas 4H 43
**Hartfield Ct.** G82: Dumb 3G 17
**Hartfield Cres.** G78: Neil 2E 131
**Hartfield Gdns.** G82: Dumb 3G 17
**Hartfield Ter.** PA2: Pais 3B 98
**Hartlaw Cres.** G52: Glas 5A 80
**Hartree Av.** G13: Glas 1G 59
**Hartstone Pl.** G53: Glas 6B 100
**Hartstone Rd.** G53: Glas 6B 100
**Hartstone Ter.** G53: Glas 6B 100
**Hart St.** G31: Glas 6G 85
G81: Faif 6F 23
PA3: Lin 6H 75
**Harvest Dr.** ML1: Moth 5F 143
**Harvey St.** G4: Glas 1G 83
**Harvey Way** ML4: Bell 6E 111
**Harvie Av.** G77: Newt M 4C 132
**Harvie St.** G51: Glas 5B 82
**Harwood Gdns.** G69: Mood 4E 53
**Harwood St.** G32: Glas 4G 85
**Hastie St.** G3: Glas 2B 82
**Hastings** G75: E Kil 4D 148
**Hatfield Dr.** G12: Glas 4F 61
**Hathaway Dr.** G46: Giff 5H 117
**Hathaway La.** G20: Glas 4C 62
**Hathaway St.** G20: Glas 4C 62
**Hathersage Av.** G69: Bail 6H 87
**Hathersage Dr.** G69: Bail 6H 87
**Hathersage Gdns.** G69: Bail 6H 87
**Hatton Gdns.** G52: Glas 1A 100
**Hattonhill** ML1: Carf 5C 128
**Hatton Path** *G52: Glas 1A 100*
*(off Hatton Gdns.)*
**Hatton Pl.** ML1: Carf 5C 128
**Hattonrigg** ML4: Bell 1D 126
**Hattonrigg Rd.** ML4: Bell 1D 126
**Hatton Ter.** ML1: Carf 5C 128
**Haughburn Pl.** G53: Glas 6B 100
**Haughburn Rd.** G53: Glas 6B 100
**Haughburn Ter.** G53: Glas 6C 100
HAUGHHEAD 1C 6
**Haughhead Bri.** G71: Udd 5A 108
**Haugh Pl.** ML3: Ham 2A 154
**Haugh Rd.** G3: Glas 3B 82
G65: Kils 3G 11
**Haughton Av.** G65: Kils 3A 12
**Haughview Rd.** ML1: Moth 3D 142
**Havelock La.** G11: Glas 1A 82
**Havelock Pk.** G75: E Kil 2C 148
**Havelock St.** G11: Glas 1A 82
**Haven Pl.** G75: E Kil 5B 148
**Havoc Rd.** G82: Dumb 4B 16
**Hawbank Rd.** G74: E Kil 6C 136
**HAWBANK RDBT.** 1D 148
**Hawick Av.** PA2: Pais 4F 97
**Hawick Cres.** ML9: Lark 3E 161
**Hawick Dr.** ML5: Coat 2F 111
**Hawick St.** G13: Glas 3G 59
ML2: Wis 4A 146
HAWKHEAD 3E 99
**Hawkhead Av.** PA2: Pais 3D 98
**Hawkhead Rd.** PA1: Pais 1D 98
Hawkhead Station (Rail) 1D 98
**Hawksland Wlk.** ML3: Ham 2A 154
**Hawkwood** G75: E Kil 6F 149
**Hawkwood Rd.** ML6: Glenm 5H 71
**Hawthorn Av.** G61: Bear 6G 25
G64: B'rig 1D 64
G66: Lenz 2C 50
G82: Dumb 2B 16
ML2: Newm 3G 147
PA5: John 4G 95
PA8: Ersk 1A 58
**Hawthorn Ct.** G22: Glas 4G 63
G76: Busby 3C 134
**Hawthorn Cres.** PA8: Ersk 1A 58
**Hawthornden Gdns.** G23: Glas 5C 46
**Hawthorn Dr.** FK4: Bank 1E 15
G78: Barr 6F 115
ML1: New S 4B 128
ML2: Wis 1A 158
ML5: Coat 6F 91
ML6: Air 4D 92
**Hawthorn Gdns.** G72: Flem 3E 123
G76: Busby 3C 134
ML4: Bell 3E 127
ML9: Lark 3G 161
**Hawthorn Gro.** ML8: Law 5D 158
**Hawthorn Hill** ML3: Ham 2A 154
**Hawthornhill Rd.** G82: Dumb 2B 16
**Hawthorn Pl.** G72: Blan 2C 140
**Hawthorn Quad.** G22: Glas 4G 63
**Hawthorn Rd.** G67: Cumb 1F 37
G76: Busby 3C 134
PA8: Ersk 1A 58
**Hawthorn St.** G22: Glas 4G 63
G64: Torr 4E 29
G81: Clyd 3C 42
**Hawthorn Ter.** G71: View 6F 109
G75: E Kil 5D 148
**Hawthorn Wlk.** G72: Camb 2F 121
**Hawthorn Way** G66: Milt C 6C 8
G82: Dumb 3B 16
PA8: Ersk 1A 58
**Hay Av.** PA7: B'ton 4A 40
**Hayburn Cres.** G11: Glas 6G 61
**Hayburn Ga.** G11: Glas 1H 81
**Hayburn La.** G12: Glas 6G 61
**Hayburn St.** G11: Glas 2G 81
**Hay Dr.** PA5: John 2H 95
**Hayfield Ct.** G5: Glas 1H 103
**Hayfield St.** G5: Glas 1H 103
**Hayle Gdns.** G69: Mood 4D 52
**Haylynn St.** G14: Glas 1E 81
**Haymarket St.** G32: Glas 4G 85
**Haystack Pl.** G66: Lenz 3D 50
HAYSTON 5A 30
**Hayston Cres.** G22: Glas 4F 63
**Hayston Rd.** G66: Kirk 5A 30
G68: Cumb 1G 35
**Hayston St.** G22: Glas 4F 63
**Haywood St.** G22: Glas 3F 63
**Hazel Av.** G44: Glas 3D 118
G61: Bear 6G 25
G66: Lenz 1D 50
G82: Dumb 2B 16
**Hazel Av.** PA5: John 4G 95
**Hazel Bank** G66: Milt C 1B 30
**Hazelbank** ML1: Holy 2B 128
**Hazelbank Wlk.** ML6: Air 3F 91
**Hazeldean Cres.** ML2: Wis 4A 146
**Hazel Dene** G64: B'rig 6D 48
**Hazeldene La.** *ML9: Lark 4G 161*
*(off Keir Hardie Rd.)*
**Hazelden Gdns.** G44: Glas 3C 118
**Hazelden Pk.** G44: Glas 3C 118
**Hazelfield Gro.** ML6: Chap 4E 113
**Hazel Gdns.** ML1: Moth 6G 143
**Hazel Gro.** G66: Lenz 1D 50
ML8: Law 5D 158
**Hazelhead** G74: E Kil 1B 150
**Hazellea Dr.** G46: Giff 3C 118
**Hazel Pk.** ML3: Ham 1A 154
**Hazel Path** ML1: Cle 6H 129
**Hazel Rd.** FK4: Bank 1E 15
G67: Cumb 2D 36
**Hazel Ter.** G71: View 6F 109
**Hazelton** ML1: Moth 4F 143
**Hazel Wood** ML2: Wis 4B 146
**Hazelwood Av.** G77: Newt M 5E 133
PA11: Bri W 4F 73
PA2: Pais 6C 96
**Hazelwood Dr.** G72: Blan 1A 140
**Hazelwood Gdns.** G73: Ruth 3E 121
**Hazelwood La.** PA11: Bri W 4F 73
**Hazelwood Rd.** G41: Glas 1A 102
PA11: Bri W 4F 73
**Hazlitt Gdns.** G20: Glas 3E 63
**Hazlitt Pl.** G20: Glas 3E 63
**Hazlitt St.** G20: Glas 3F 63
**Headhouse Ct.** G75: E Kil 3F 149
**Headhouse Grn.** G75: E Kil 3G 149
**Headsmuir Av.** ML8: Carl 3D 1
**Heath Av.** G64: B'rig 1D
G66: Lenz 3C
**Heathcliffe Av.** G72: Blan 6A 1
**Heathcot Av.** G15: Glas 5G
**Heathcot Pl.** G15: Glas 5F
**Heather Av.** G61: Bear 5D
G78: Barr 2C 1
G81: Hard 6C
ML1: Holy 2A 1
Heatherbank Mus. of Social Work
1C
**Heatherbank Wlk.** ML6: Air 3F
HEATHERBELL 6H
**Heatherbrae** G64: B'rig 6A
**Heather Dr.** G66: Lenz 3A
**Heather Gdns.** G66: Lenz 3A
**Heather Gro.** *G75: E Kil 4G 1*
*(off Heathery Kno*
**Heatherlea Pl.** ML5: Coat 2F 1
**Heather Pl.** G66: Lenz 2A
PA5: John 3G
**Heather Row** ML8: Carl 1E 1
**Heather Vw.** G66: Len 2
**Heather Way** ML1: New S 3A 1
**Heathery Knowe** G75: E Kil 4G 1
**Heatheryknowe Rd.**
G69: Barg 4C
(not continuo
**Heathery Rd.** ML2: Wis 6F 1
**Heathfield** ML2: Wis 4G 1
**Heathfield Av.** G69: Mood 5D
**Heathfield Dr.** G62: Miln 2H
**Heathfield St.** G33: Glas 3C
**Heath Rd.** ML9: Lark 2F 1
**Heathside Rd.** G46: Giff 4B 1
**Heathwood Dr.** G46: T'bnk 4G 1
**Hecla Av.** G15: Glas 4H
**Hecla Pl.** G15: Glas 4H
**Hecla Sq.** G15: Glas 5H
**Hector Rd.** G41: Glas 5B 1
**Helena Pl.** G76: Clar 1C 1
**Helena Ter.** G81: Dun 1C
**Helensburgh Dr.** G13: Glas 3D
**Helenslea** G72: Camb 3D 1
**Helenslea Pl.** ML4: Bell 3B 1
**Helenslee Ct.** G82: Dumb 4D
**Helenslee Cres.** G82: Dumb 4E
**Helenslee Rd.** G82: Dumb 4D
**Helen St.** G51: Glas 6F
G52: Glas 6F
**HELEN ST. INTERCHANGE** 6F
**Helenvale Ct.** G31: Glas 6F
**Helenvale St.** G31: Glas 1E 1
**Helen Wynd** ML9: Lark 3E 1
**Helmsdale Av.** G72: Blan 4A 1
**Helmsdale Ct.** G72: Camb 2D 1
**Helmsdale Dr.** PA2: Pais 3D
**Hemlock St.** G13: Glas 2F
**Henderland Dr.** G61: Bear 5E
**Henderland Rd.** G61: Bear 5E
**Henderson Av.** G72: Camb 1D 1
**Henderson St.** G20: Glas 6D
G81: Clyd 1G
ML5: Coat 5B
ML6: Air 3B
PA1: Pais 6H
**Henrietta St.** G14: Glas 6C
**Henry Bell Grn.** *G75: E Kil 3H 1*
*(off Muirhouse L*
**Henry St.** G78: Barr 4D 1
Henry Wood Hall, The 3C
**Hepburn Hill** ML3: Ham 3F 1
**Hepburn Rd.** G52: Hill 4B
**Herald Av.** G13: Glas 6D
**Herald Gro.** ML1: Moth 5F 1
**Herald Way** PA4: Renf 2E
**Herbertson Gro.** G72: Blan 6A 1
**Herbertson St.** G5: Glas 6F
G72: Blan 2C 1
**Herbert St.** G20: Glas 6D
**Herbison Ct.** ML9: Lark 1F 1
**Hercules Way** PA4: Renf 2F
**Heriot Av.** PA2: Pais 5C
**Heriot Ct.** PA2: Pais 5D
**Heriot Cres.** G64: B'rig 4C
**Heriot Rd.** G66: Lenz 4C
**Heritage Ct.** G77: Newt M 4E 1
**Heritage Vw.** ML5: Coat 3B
**Heritage Way** ML5: Coat 4B
**Herma St.** G23: Glas 1C
**Hermes Way** ML4: Moss 2H 1
**Hermiston Av.** G32: Glas 5C
**Hermiston Pl.** G32: Glas 5C
*ML1: Holy 2A 1*
*(off Windsor R*
**Hermiston Rd.** G32: Glas 4B
**Hermitage Av.** G13: Glas 2C
**Hermitage Cres.** ML5: Coat 2D 1
**Herndon Ct.** G77: Newt M 3G 1

Heron Ct.—Hope St.


ron Ct. G81: Hard . . . . . . . . . . . .2D 42
ron Pl. PA5: John . . . . . . . . . . . .6D 94
ron St. G40: Glas . . . . . . . . . . .1B 104
ron Way PA4: Renf . . . . . . . . . . .2E 79
rries Rd. G41: Glas . . . . . . . . . .4A 102
rriet St. G41: Glas . . . . . . . . . .2D 102
rriot St. ML5: Coat . . . . . . . . . . .3A 90
rschell St. G13: Glas . . . . . . . . . .3F 61
rtford Av. G12: Glas . . . . . . . . . .3H 61
wett Cres. PA6: C'lee . . . . . . . . .2C 74
xham Gdns. G41: Glas . . . . . . .4B 102
ys St. G78: Barr . . . . . . . . . . . .5E 115
kman St. G42: Glas . . . . . . . . .4F 103
kman Ter. G42: Glas . . . . . . . .3G 103
kory Cres. G71: View . . . . . . .4G 109
kory St. G22: Glas . . . . . . . . . . .4A 64
h Avon St. ML9: Lark . . . . . . .1D 160
H BALMALLOCH . . . . . . . . . . .2G 11
h Barholm PA10: Kilb . . . . . . . .2A 94
h Barrwood Rd. G65: Kils . . . . .3A 12
h Beeches G76: Crmck . . . . . .1A 136
H BLANTYRE . . . . . . . . . . . .4A 140
h Blantyre Rd. ML3: Ham . . . .4D 140
hburgh Dr. G73: Ruth . . . . . . .2D 120
hburgh Rd. G12: Glas . . . . . . . .6A 62
H BURNSIDE . . . . . . . . . . . .3E 121
h Burnside Av. ML5: Coat . . . . .6A 90
h Calside PA2: Pais . . . . . . . . . .2H 97
h Coats ML5: Coat . . . . . . . . . .4D 90
h Comn. Rd. G75: E Kil . . . . . .4B 150
hcraig Av. PA5: John . . . . . . . . .4D 94
h Craigends G65: Kils . . . . . . . .3H 11
h Craighall Rd. G4: Glas . . . . . .1F 83
hcroft Av. G44: Glas . . . . . . . .2H 119
hcross Av. ML5: Coat . . . . . . .1H 109
H CROSSHILL . . . . . . . . . . . .2D 120
herness Way ML5: Coat . . . . .2A 110
hfield Av. G66: Kirk . . . . . . . . . .4E 31
PA2: Pais . . . . . . . . . . . . . . . .6H 97
hfield Ct. G66: Kirk . . . . . . . . . .5F 31
hfield Cres. ML1: Moth . . . . . .1A 144
PA2: Pais . . . . . . . . . . . . . . . .6H 97
hfield Dr. G12: Glas . . . . . . . . .3H 61
G73: Ruth . . . . . . . . . . . . . . .4E 121
G76: Clar . . . . . . . . . . . . . . .2B 134
hfield Gro. G66: Kirk . . . . . . . . .4E 31
hfield Pl. G12: Glas . . . . . . . . . .3H 61
G74: E Kil . . . . . . . . . . . . . . .6H 137
hfield Rd. G66: Kirk . . . . . . . . .4E 31
ML9: Lark . . . . . . . . . . . . . . .2F 161
h Flender Rd. G76: Clar . . . . .3A 134
H GALLOWHILL . . . . . . . . . . . .2B 50
hgrove Ct. PA4: Renf . . . . . . . .6G 59
hgrove Rd. PA4: Renf . . . . . . . .6G 59
h Kirk Vw. PA5: John . . . . . . . .3F 95
H KNIGHTSWOOD . . . . . . . . .1D 60
hland Av. G72: Blan . . . . . . . .1A 140
hland La. G51: Glas . . . . . . . . .3A 82
HLAND PARK . . . . . . . . . . . .1G 11
hland Pk. G65: Kils . . . . . . . . .2G 11
hland Pl. G65: Kils . . . . . . . . .1G 11
hland Rd. G62: Miln . . . . . . . . .3G 25
h Mains Av. G82: Dumb . . . . . .2C 18
h Mair PA4: Renf . . . . . . . . . . . .1E 79
h Mdw. ML8: Carl . . . . . . . . . .5H 165
(not continuous)
h Mill Rd. ML8: Carl . . . . . . . .3G 165
h Murray Gro. G72: Camb . . . .2C 122
h Parksail PA8: Ersk . . . . . . . . .1G 57
h Parks Cres. ML3: Ham . . . . .5H 153
h Patrick St. ML3: Ham . . . . . .1A 154
h Pleasance ML9: Lark . . . . . .2E 161
h Rd. ML1: Moth . . . . . . . . . . .2F 143
PA2: Pais . . . . . . . . . . . . . . . .2G 97
h Row Cotts. G64: B'rig . . . . . .2D 48
hstonehall Rd.
ML3: Ham . . . . . . . . . . . . . .4C 152
h St. G1: Glas . . . . . . . .5H 83 (6G 5)
G66: Kirk . . . . . . . . . . . . . . . .4C 30
G73: Ruth . . . . . . . . . . . . . . .5C 104
G78: Neil . . . . . . . . . . . . . . .2D 130
G82: Dumb . . . . . . . . . . . . . . .4E 17
ML1: N'hill . . . . . . . . . . . . . .3E 129
ML6: Air . . . . . . . . . . . . . . . . .3H 91
ML8: Carl . . . . . . . . . . . . . . .3F 165
PA1: Pais . . . . . . . . . . . . . . . .1H 97
PA4: Renf . . . . . . . . . . . . . . . .5F 59
PA5: John . . . . . . . . . . . . . . . .2E 95
h Street Station (Rail)
. . . . . . . . . . . . . . . . .4H 83 (6H 5)
h Whitehills Rd.
G75: E Kil . . . . . . . . . . . . . .6F 149
ary Dr. G69: Bail . . . . . . . . . . . .6F 87
da Cres. G33: Glas . . . . . . . . . .5G 65
lary Av. G73: Ruth . . . . . . . . .1F 121
l Av. G77: Newt M . . . . . . . . .5C 132
lbrae St. G51: Glas . . . . . . . . . .5D 80
l Cres. G76: Busby . . . . . . . . .3C 134
lcrest G69: Chry . . . . . . . . . . . .1B 68
G76: Crmck . . . . . . . . . . . . . .1H 135

Hillcrest Av. G32: Carm . . . . . . . .5B 106
G44: Glas . . . . . . . . . . . . . . . .3C 118
G67: Cumb . . . . . . . . . . . . . . . .5G 35
G81: Dun . . . . . . . . . . . . . . . . .6C 22
ML2: Wis . . . . . . . . . . . . . . . .6E 145
ML5: Coat . . . . . . . . . . . . . . . . .5E 91
PA2: Pais . . . . . . . . . . . . . . . . .6G 97
Hillcrest Ct. G67: Cumb . . . . . . . . .4H 35
Hillcrest Dr. G77: Newt M . . . . . .4G 133
Hillcrest Rd. G32: Carm . . . . . . . .4C 106
G61: Bear . . . . . . . . . . . . . . . . .3F 45
G65: Queen . . . . . . . . . . . . . . .3C 10
G71: Tann . . . . . . . . . . . . . . . .6E 109
Hillcrest St. G62: Miln . . . . . . . . . .3G 25
Hillcrest Ter. G71: Both . . . . . . . .4F 125
Hillcrest Vw. ML9: Lark . . . . . . . .3F 161
Hillcroft Ter. G64: B'rig . . . . . . . . . .1B 64
Hillend Cotts. G66: Lenz . . . . . . . . .1C 50
Hillend Cres. G76: Clar . . . . . . . .3A 134
G81: Dun . . . . . . . . . . . . . . . . .1B 42
Hillend Rd. G22: Glas . . . . . . . . . . .2E 63
G73: Ruth . . . . . . . . . . . . . . .2D 120
G76: Clar . . . . . . . . . . . . . . .3A 134
Hillfoot PA6: C'lee . . . . . . . . . . . . .3D 74
Hillfoot Av. G61: Bear . . . . . . . . . . .2F 45
G73: Ruth . . . . . . . . . . . . . . .6C 104
G82: Dumb . . . . . . . . . . . . . . . .1C 18
ML2: Wis . . . . . . . . . . . . . . . .2B 146
Hillfoot Cres. ML2: Wis . . . . . . . .2B 146
Hillfoot Dr. G61: Bear . . . . . . . . . . .2F 45
ML2: Wis . . . . . . . . . . . . . . . .2B 146
ML5: Coat . . . . . . . . . . . . . . . . .5H 89
Hillfoot Gdns. G71: Tann . . . . . . .5C 108
ML2: Wis . . . . . . . . . . . . . . . .2B 146
Hillfoot Rd. ML6: Air . . . . . . . . . . . .5A 92
Hillfoot Station (Rail) . . . . . . . . . .2G 45
Hillfoot St. G31: Glas . . . . . . . . . . .4C 84
Hillfoot Ter. ML8: Carl . . . . . . . . .4G 165
HILLHEAD
Glasgow . . . . . . . . . . . . . . . . . . .6B 62
Kirkintilloch . . . . . . . . . . . . . . .4D 30
Hillhead Av. FK4: Bank . . . . . . . . . .1E 15
G69: Mood . . . . . . . . . . . . . . . . .5D 52
G73: Ruth . . . . . . . . . . . . . . .3D 120
ML1: Carf . . . . . . . . . . . . . . . .5A 128
ML8: Carl . . . . . . . . . . . . . . . .3G 165
Hillhead Cres. ML1: Carf . . . . . . .5A 128
ML3: Ham . . . . . . . . . . . . . . . .6C 140
Hillhead Dr. ML1: Carf . . . . . . . . .6A 128
ML6: Air . . . . . . . . . . . . . . . . . .5A 92
Hillhead Pl. G73: Ruth . . . . . . . .3D 120
Hillhead Rd. G21: Glas . . . . . . . . . .2F 65
G66: Kirk . . . . . . . . . . . . . . . . .4D 30
Hillhead Station (Und.) . . . . . . . . .6B 62
Hillhead St. G12: Glas . . . . . . . . . . .1B 82
G62: Miln . . . . . . . . . . . . . . . . .3G 25
Hillhead Ter. ML3: Ham . . . . . . . .6C 140
HILLHOUSE . . . . . . . . . . . . . . . .6D 140
Hillhouse Cres. ML3: Ham . . . . . .6D 140
Hillhouse Ga. ML8: Carl . . . . . . . .5H 165
Hillhouse Pk. Ind. Est.
ML3: Ham . . . . . . . . . . . . . . . .5E 141
Hillhouse Rd. G72: Blan . . . . . . . .4H 139
ML3: Ham . . . . . . . . . . . . . . . .5C 140
Hillhouse St. G21: Glas . . . . . . . . . .5C 64
Hillhouse Ter. ML3: Ham . . . . . . .6D 140
HILLINGTON . . . . . . . . . . . . . . . . .6A 80
Hillington East Station (Rail) . . . .5B 80
Hillington Gdns. G52: Glas . . . . . .1C 100
HILLINGTON INDUSTRIAL ESTATE
. . . . . . . . . . . . . . . . . . . . . . . . .3H 79
HILLINGTON INTERCHANGE . . . . .2H 79
Hillington Pk. Cir. G52: Glas . . . . .6C 80
Hillington Quad. G52: Glas . . . . . . .6A 80
Hillington Rd. G52: Hill . . . . . . . . . .2H 79
(not continuous)
Hillington Rd. Sth. G52: Glas . . . . .5A 80
Hillington Shop. Cen. G52: Hill . . .3H 79
Hillington Ter. G52: Glas . . . . . . . . .6A 80
Hillington West Station (Rail) . . . .4H 79
Hillkirk Pl. G21: Glas . . . . . . . . . . .5B 64
Hillkirk St. G21: Glas . . . . . . . . . . .5B 64
Hillkirk St. La. *G21: Glas . . . . . . . .5B 64*
*(off Hillkirk St.)*
Hillneuk Av. G61: Bear . . . . . . . . . .2F 45
Hillneuk Dr. G61: Bear . . . . . . . . . .2G 45
Hillpark Av. PA2: Pais . . . . . . . . . . .4H 97
Hillpark Dr. G43: Glas . . . . . . . . .1H 117
Hill Pl. ML1: Carf . . . . . . . . . . . . .5C 128
ML4: Bell . . . . . . . . . . . . . . . .4B 126
Hillrigg Av. ML6: Air . . . . . . . . . . . .3C 92
Hill Rd. G65: Kils . . . . . . . . . . . . . .1H 11
G67: Cumb . . . . . . . . . . . . . . . .3G 35
Hillsborough Rd. G69: Bail . . . . . . .6F 87
HILLSIDE . . . . . . . . . . . . . . . . . .5B 114
Hillside G65: Croy . . . . . . . . . . . . .6B 12
PA6: C'lee . . . . . . . . . . . . . . . . .3D 74
Hillside Av. G61: Bear . . . . . . . . . .2F 45
G76: Clar . . . . . . . . . . . . . . . .2B 134
Hillside Cotts. ML5: Glenb . . . . . . .3A 70

Hillside Ct. G46: T'bnk . . . . . . . . .4F 117
Hillside Cres. G78: Neil . . . . . . . .2D 130
ML1: N'hill . . . . . . . . . . . . . . .3D 128
ML3: Ham . . . . . . . . . . . . . . . .1H 153
ML5: Coat . . . . . . . . . . . . . . .1B 110
Hillside Dr. G61: Bear . . . . . . . . . .2G 45
G64: B'rig . . . . . . . . . . . . . . . . .5C 48
G78: Barr . . . . . . . . . . . . . . . .4C 114
Hillside Gdns. La. *G11: Glas . . . . .6H 61*
*(off Nth. Gardner St.)*
Hillside Gro. G78: Barr . . . . . . . . .5C 114
Hillside La. ML3: Ham . . . . . . . . .1G 153
Hillside Pk. G81: Hard . . . . . . . . . .1D 42
Hillside Pl. ML1: N'hill . . . . . . . . .4D 128
Hillside Quad. G43: Glas . . . . . . .2H 117
Hillside Rd. G43: Glas . . . . . . . . .2H 117
G78: Barr . . . . . . . . . . . . . . . .5B 114
G78: Neil . . . . . . . . . . . . . . . .2D 130
PA2: Pais . . . . . . . . . . . . . . . . .3C 98
Hillside Ter. G60: Old K . . . . . . . . .1F 41
G66: Milt C . . . . . . . . . . . . . . . . .6B 8
ML3: Ham . . . . . . . . . . . . . . . .1G 153
Hill St. G3: Glas . . . . . . . . . .2E 83 (2A 4)
G82: Dumb . . . . . . . . . . . . . . . .4D 16
ML2: Wis . . . . . . . . . . . . . . . .1G 157
ML3: Ham . . . . . . . . . . . . . . . .6D 140
ML6: Chap . . . . . . . . . . . . . . .3D 112
ML9: Lark . . . . . . . . . . . . . . . .3E 161
Hillsview G69: Chry . . . . . . . . . . . .1H 67
Hillswick Cres. G22: Glas . . . . . . . .1F 63
Hill Ter. ML1: Carf . . . . . . . . . . . .5C 128
Hilltop Av. ML4: Bell . . . . . . . . . . .6C 110
Hilltop Ter. G69: Mood . . . . . . . . . .5D 52
Hill Vw. G75: E Kil . . . . . . . . . . .3G 149
G82: Milt . . . . . . . . . . . . . . . . . .4F 19
Hillview Av. G65: Kils . . . . . . . . . . .4H 11
G66: Len . . . . . . . . . . . . . . . . . .3G 7
Hillview Cotts. G65: Twe . . . . . . . .1D 32
Hillview Cres. G71: Tann . . . . . . .5C 108
ML4: Bell . . . . . . . . . . . . . . . .5C 110
ML9: Lark . . . . . . . . . . . . . . . .3F 161
Hillview Dr. G72: Blan . . . . . . . . .5A 124
G76: Clar . . . . . . . . . . . . . . . .2B 134
Hill Vw. Gdns.
G64: B'rig . . . . . . . . . . . . . . . . .1E 65
Hillview Pl. G76: Clar . . . . . . . . .2C 134
G77: Newt M . . . . . . . . . . . . .5D 132
Hillview Rd. PA11: Bri W . . . . . . . .4G 73
PA5: Eld . . . . . . . . . . . . . . . . . .3H 95
Hillview St. G32: Glas . . . . . . . . . .6H 85
Hillview Ter. G60: Old K . . . . . . . . .2F 41
Hiltonbank St. ML3: Ham . . . . . . .5F 141
Hilton Ct. G64: B'rig . . . . . . . . . . . .4C 48
Hilton Gdns. G13: Glas . . . . . . . . . .2F 61
Hilton Gdns. La. G13: Glas . . . . . . .2F 61
Hilton Pk. G64: B'rig . . . . . . . . . . .3B 48
Hilton Rd. G62: Miln . . . . . . . . . . . .3E 25
G64: B'rig . . . . . . . . . . . . . . . . .4B 48
Hilton Ter. G13: Glas . . . . . . . . . . .2E 61
G64: B'rig . . . . . . . . . . . . . . . . .3B 48
G72: Camb . . . . . . . . . . . . . . .4G 121
Hindsland Rd. ML9: Lark . . . . . . .4F 161
Hinshaw St. G20: Glas . . . . . . . . . .6E 63
Hinshelwood Dr. G51: Glas . . . . . .5G 81
Hinshelwood Pl. G51: Glas . . . . . .6H 81
Hirsel Pl. G71: Both . . . . . . . . . .5F 125
Hobart Cres. G81: Clyd . . . . . . . . .2H 41
Hobart Quad. ML2: Wis . . . . . . . .6C 146
Hobart Rd. G75: E Kil . . . . . . . . .4E 149
Hobart St. G22: Glas . . . . . . . . . . .5F 63
Hobden St. G21: Glas . . . . . . . . . . .6C 64
Hoddam Av. G45: Glas . . . . . . . . .4B 120
Hoddam Ter. G45: Glas . . . . . . . .4C 120
Hodge Ct. G22: Glas . . . . . . . . . . . .3F 63
Hoey Dr. ML2: Over . . . . . . . . . . .4A 158
Hogan Ct. G81: Dun . . . . . . . . . . . .1B 42
Hogan Way ML1: Cle . . . . . . . . . .6E 129
Hogarth Av. G32: Glas . . . . . . . . . .4F 85
Hogarth Cres. G32: Glas . . . . . . . . .4F 85
Hogarth Dr. G32: Glas . . . . . . . . . . .4F 85
Hogarth Gdns. G32: Glas . . . . . . . .4F 85
HOGGANFIELD . . . . . . . . . . . . . . .1A 86
Hogganfield St. G33: Glas . . . . . . .1F 85
Hogg Av. PA5: John . . . . . . . . . . . .4E 95
Hogg Rd. ML6: Chap . . . . . . . . . .1D 112
Hogg St. ML6: Air . . . . . . . . . . . . .4A 92
Holeburn La. G43: Glas . . . . . . . .1A 118
Holeburn Rd. G43: Glas . . . . . . . .1A 118
HOLEHILLS . . . . . . . . . . . . . . . . .2B 92
Holehills Dr. ML6: Air . . . . . . . . . . .1B 92
Holehills Pl. ML6: Air . . . . . . . . . . .1B 92
HOLEHOUSE . . . . . . . . . . . . . . . .2C 130
Holehouse Brae G78: Neil . . . . . . .2C 130
Holehouse Dr. G13: Glas . . . . . . . . .3A 60
Holehouse Ter. G78: Neil . . . . . . .2C 130
Hollandbush Av. FK4: Bank . . . . . . .1E 15
Hollandbush Cres. FK4: Bank . . . . .1F 15
Hollandbush Gro. ML3: Ham . . . .3H 153
Hollandhurst Rd. ML5: Coat . . . . . .2B 90
Holland St. G2: Glas . . . . . .3E 83 (4A 4)

Hollinwell Rd. G23: Glas . . . . . . . .1B 62
Hollowglen Rd. G32: Glas . . . . . . .5B 86
Hollows Av. PA2: Pais . . . . . . . . . .6D 96
Hollows Cres. PA2: Pais . . . . . . . .6D 96
Hollows, The *G46: Giff . . . . . . . . .6H 117*
*(off Ayr Rd.)*
Holly Av. G66: Milt C . . . . . . . . . . . .6B 8
Hollybank Pl. G72: Camb . . . . . . .3B 122
Hollybank St. G21: Glas . . . . . . . . .2C 84
Hollybrook Pl. *G42: Glas . . . . . . . .3F 103*
*(off Jamieson St.)*
Hollybrook St. G42: Glas . . . . . . .3F 103
(not continuous)
Hollybush Av. PA2: Pais . . . . . . . . .6F 97
Hollybush Rd. G52: Glas . . . . . . . .6H 79
Holly Dr. G21: Glas . . . . . . . . . . . . .6C 64
G82: Dumb . . . . . . . . . . . . . . . . .2B 16
Holly Gro. FK4: Bank . . . . . . . . . . .1F 15
ML4: Moss . . . . . . . . . . . . . . .2H 127
Hollymount G61: Bear . . . . . . . . . .5F 45
Holly Pl. PA5: John . . . . . . . . . . . .5G 95
Holly St. G81: Clyd . . . . . . . . . . . . .3C 42
ML6: Air . . . . . . . . . . . . . . . . . .4C 92
Hollytree Gdns. G66: Len . . . . . . . . .3E 7
Hollywood Bowl . . . . . . . . . . . . .1F 109
Holm Av. G71: Udd . . . . . . . . . . . .6C 108
PA2: Pais . . . . . . . . . . . . . . . . . .3B 98
Holmbank Av. G41: Glas . . . . . . . .6B 102
Holmbrae Av. G71: Tann . . . . . . .6D 108
Holmbrae Rd. G71: Tann . . . . . . .6D 108
Holmbyre Ct. G45: Glas . . . . . . . .6F 119
Holmbyre Rd. G45: Glas . . . . . . . .6F 119
Holmbyre Ter. G45: Glas . . . . . . .5G 119
Holmes Av. PA4: Renf . . . . . . . . . . .2E 79
Holmes Quad. ML4: Bell . . . . . . . .4C 126
Holmfauldhead Pl. G51: Glas . . . . .3E 81
Holmfauld Rd. G51: Glas . . . . . . . .3E 81
Holmfield G66: Kirk . . . . . . . . . . . .6E 31
Holm Gdns. ML4: Bell . . . . . . . . .3E 127
Holmhead Cres. G44: Glas . . . . . .1E 119
Holmhead Pl. G44: Glas . . . . . . . .1E 119
Holmhead Rd. G44: Glas . . . . . . . .2E 119
Holmhill Av. G72: Camb . . . . . . . .3A 122
Holmhills Dr. G72: Camb . . . . . . .4H 121
Holmhills Gdns. G72: Camb . . . . .3H 121
Holmhills Gro. G72: Camb . . . . . .3H 121
Holmhills Pl. G72: Camb . . . . . . .3H 121
Holmhills Rd. G72: Camb . . . . . . .3H 121
Holmhills Ter. G72: Camb . . . . . . .3H 121
Holm La. G74: E Kil . . . . . . . . . . .2G 149
Holmlea Rd. G42: Glas . . . . . . . . .6E 103
G44: Glas . . . . . . . . . . . . . . . .1E 119
HOLMPARK . . . . . . . . . . . . . . . . .4H 39
Holmpark PA7: B'ton . . . . . . . . . . .4G 39
Holm Pl. ML9: Lark . . . . . . . . . . .3C 160
PA3: Lin . . . . . . . . . . . . . . . . . .4H 75
Holms Cres. PA8: Ersk . . . . . . . . . .5D 40
Holms Pl. G69: G'csh . . . . . . . . . . .2C 68
Holm St. G2: Glas . . . . . . . .4E 83 (6B 4)
ML1: New S . . . . . . . . . . . . . . .4A 128
ML8: Carl . . . . . . . . . . . . . . . .3E 165
Holmswood Av. G72: Blan . . . . . .1B 140
Holmwood Av. G71: Udd . . . . . . .6D 108
Holmwood Gdns. G71: Udd . . . . .6D 108
Holyknowe Cres. G66: Len . . . . . . . .3G 7
Holyknowe Rd. G66: Len . . . . . . . . .4G 7
Holyrood Cres. G4: Glas . . . . . . . . .1D 82
Holyrood Quad. *G20: Glas . . . . . . . .1D 82*
*(off Holyrood Cres.)*
Holyrood Sports Cen.
. . . . . . . . . . . . . . . . . . . . . . . .4G 103
Holyrood St. ML3: Ham . . . . . . . .4E 141
HOLYTOWN . . . . . . . . . . . . . . . .2A 128
Holytown Rd. ML4: Moss . . . . . . .2G 127
Holytown Station (Rail)
. . . . . . . . . . . . . . . . . . . . . . . .4A 128
Holywell St. G31: Glas . . . . . . . . . .6D 84
Homeblair Ho. G46: Giff . . . . . . . .2A 118
Homefield Pl. G51: Glas . . . . . . . . .3E 81
Homer Pl. ML4: Moss . . . . . . . . .2G 127
Homeston Av. G71: Both . . . . . . .4E 125
Honeybank Cres. ML8: Carl . . . . .2F 165
Honeybog Rd. G52: Glas . . . . . . . .5G 79
Honeywell Cres. ML6: Chap . . . . .4E 113
Hood St. G81: Clyd . . . . . . . . . . . .5E 43
Hope Av. PA11: Q'riers . . . . . . . . . .1A 72
Hope Cres. ML9: Lark . . . . . . . . . .2F 161
Hopefield Av. G12: Glas . . . . . . . . .4A 62
Hopehill Gdns. G20: Glas . . . . . . . .6E 63
Hopehill Rd. G20: Glas . . . . . . . . . .6E 63
(not continuous)
Hopeman PA8: Ersk . . . . . . . . . . . .4E 41
Hopeman Av. G46: T'bnk . . . . . . .3E 117
Hopeman Dr. G46: T'bnk . . . . . . .3E 117
Hopeman Path G46: T'bnk . . . . . .2E 117
Hopeman Rd. G46: T'bnk . . . . . . .3E 117
Hopeman St. G46: T'bnk . . . . . . . .3E 117
Hope St. G2: Glas . . . . . . . . .4F 83 (6C 4)
ML1: Moth . . . . . . . . . . . . . . . .2G 143
ML2: Newm . . . . . . . . . . . . . . .5E 147

Kingston St.—Ladymuir Cres.


ngston St. G5: Glas 5E 83
ng St. G1: Glas 5G 83
G65: Kils 3H 11
G73: Ruth 5C 104
G81: Clyd 1H 109
ML2: Newm 4D 146
ML2: Wis 1H 157
ML3: Ham 4D 140
ML5: Coat 5A 90
ML9: Lark 2E 161
PA3: Pais 6G 77
ng St. La. G65: Kils 3H 11
G73: Ruth 5C 104
ng's Vw. G68: Cumb 5H 13
ngs Vw. G73: Ruth 6B 104
ngsway G14: Glas 4A 60
G65: Kils 2H 11
G66: Kirk 3H 31
G74: E Kil 4A 138
ng's Way G82: Dumb 2C 16
ngsway Ct. G14: Glas 4A 60
ngswood Dr. G44: Glas 1G 119
ngswood Rd. PA7: B'ton 3F 39
ngussie Dr. G44: Glas 1G 119
niver Dr. G15: Glas 6A 44
nkell Gdns. G66: Kirk 4H 31
nloch Av. G72: Camb 3B 122
PA3: Lin 6G 75
nloch Dr. ML1: Moth 5F 127
nloch Rd. G77: Newt M 3C 132
PA4: Renf 3D 78
nloch St. G40: Glas 1E 105
nloss Pl. G74: E Kil 1H 149
nmount Av. G44: Glas 6F 103
nmount La. G44: Glas 6G 103
nnaird Av. G77: Newt M 4G 133
nnaird Cres. G61: Bear 3H 45
nnaird Dr. PA3: Lin 5H 75
nnaird Pl. G64: B'rig 2D 64
nnear Rd. G40: Glas 2C 104
nneil Ho. ML3: Ham 4A 142
nneil Pl. ML3: Ham 1D 152
nnell Av. G52: Glas 2C 100
nnell Cres. G52: Glas 2C 100
nnell Path G52: Glas 2C 100
nnell Pl. G52: Glas 2D 100
nnell Sq. G52: Glas 2C 100
NNING PARK 1C 102
nning Pk. Ind. Est. G5: Glas 6D 82
nning Park Station (Und.) 6B 82
nning St. G5: Glas 6E 83
nnoul Gdns. G61: Bear 6D 24
nnoul La. G12: Glas 6A 62
nnoull Pl. G72: Blan 2B 140
npurnie Rd. PA1: Pais 6F 79
nross Av. G52: Glas 1B 100
nross Pk. G74: E Kil 6D 138
nsail Dr. G52: Glas 5H 79
nstone Av. G14: Glas 4A 60
ntail Gdns. G66: Kirk 4H 31
ntessack Pl. G64: B'rig 5F 49
ntillo Dr. G13: Glas 3B 60
ntore Pk. ML3: Ham 4F 153
ntore Rd. G43: Glas 1D 118
ntore Twr. G72: Camb 4G 121
ntra St. G51: Glas 5H 81
(not continuous)
ntyre Av. PA3: Lin 1G 95
ntyre Cres. G77: Newt M 3C 132
ML6: Plain 1F 93
ntyre Gdns. G66: Kirk 4H 31
ntyre Rd. G72: Blan 1A 140
ntyre St. G21: Glas 2C 84
ntyre Wynd ML8: Carl 2F 165
pland Wlk. ML5: Coat 6F 91
ppen Dr. G76: Busby 4E 135
ppen St. G22: Glas 3H 63
ML6: Air 5F 91
pperoch Rd. G82: Dumb 1B 16
ppford Pl. ML6: Chap 4F 113
ppford St. G32: Glas 1C 106
pps Av. ML6: Air 3G 91
ppsbyre Ct. *ML6: Air* 4F 91
(off Monkscourt Av.)
rkaig Av. PA4: Renf 1H 79
rk Bean Av. G73: Ruth 3C 120
rkburn Av. G72: Camb 3A 122
rkcaldy Rd. G41: Glas 3B 102
rkconnel Av. G13: Glas 3H 59
G68: Cumb 4A 34
rkconnel Dr. G73: Ruth 2B 120
rk Cres. G60: Old K 6E 21
rkcudbright Pl. G74: E Kil 6D 138
rkdale Dr. G52: Glas 1E 101
rkdene Av. G77: Newt M 4H 133
rkdene Bank G77: Newt M 4H 133
rkdene Cres. G77: Newt M 4H 133
rkdene Gro. G77: Newt M 5H 133
rkdene Pl. G77: Newt M 4H 133
rkfieldbank Way ML3: Ham 6E 141
Kirkfield Rd. G71: Both 4E 125
Kirkford Rd. G69: Mood 5C 52
Kirkgate ML2: Newm 5D 146
Kirk Glebe G78: Neil 2E 131
Kirkhall Rd. ML1: N'hill 3D 128
KIRKHILL
Cambuslang 2B 122
Newton Mearns 4G 133
Kirkhill Av. G72: Camb 4A 122
Kirkhill Bowling Club 3H 121
Kirkhill Cres. G78: Neil 1E 131
Kirkhill Dr. G20: Glas 4B 62
Kirkhill Gdns. G72: Camb 4A 122
Kirkhill Ga. G77: Newt M 5H 133
Kirkhill Gro. G72: Camb 4A 122
Kirkhill Pl. G20: Glas 4B 62
ML2: Wis 1C 156
Kirkhill Rd. G69: G'csh 4D 68
G71: Tann 5C 108
G77: Newt M 4G 133
ML2: Wis 2B 156
Kirkhill Station (Rail) 2A 122
Kirkhill St. ML2: Wis 2D 156
Kirkhill Ter. G72: Camb 4A 122
Kirkhope Dr. G15: Glas 6B 44
Kirkinner Pl. *PA11: Bri W* 3F 73
(off Main Rd.)
Kirkinner Rd. G32: Glas 2D 106
KIRKINTILLOCH 4C 30
Kirkintilloch Ind. Est.
G66: Kirk 3C 30
Kirkintilloch Rd. G64: B'rig 2B 64
G64: B'rig, Kirk 1F 49
G66: Kirk 2H 29
(Campsie Rd.)
G66: Kirk 1G 49
(Torrence Rd.)
G66: Lenz 2C 50
Kirkland Gro. PA5: John 2F 95
KIRKLANDNEUK 5D 58
Kirklandneuk Cres. PA4: Renf 5C 58
Kirklandneuk Rd. PA4: Renf 5C 58
Kirklands Cres. G65: Kils 4H 11
G71: Both 4E 125
Kirklands Dr. G77: Newt M 6D 132
Kirklands Pl. G77: Newt M 6D 132
Kirkland St. G20: Glas 6D 62
ML1: Moth 2F 143
Kirk La. G43: Glas 6A 102
G61: Bear 2E 45
Kirklea Gdns. PA3: Pais 6E 77
Kirkle Dr. G77: Newt M 4H 133
Kirklee Cir. G12: Glas 5A 62
Kirklee Gdns. G12: Glas 4B 62
Kirklee Gdns. La. G12: Glas 4B 62
Kirklee Ga. G12: Glas 4B 62
Kirklee Pl. G12: Glas 5B 62
Kirklee Quad. G12: Glas 5B 62
Kirklee Quad. La. G12: Glas 5B 62
Kirklee Rd. G12: Glas 5A 62
ML1: New S 6G 127
ML4: Bell 3F 127
Kirklee Ter. G12: Glas 5A 62
Kirklee Ter. La. G12: Glas 5B 62
Kirklee Ter. Rd. G12: Glas 5A 62
Kirkliston St. G32: Glas 5H 85
Kirk M. *G72: Camb* 2A 122
(off Greenlees Rd.)
Kirkmichael Av. G11: Glas 6G 61
Kirkmichael Gdns.
G11: Glas 6G 61
Kirkmuir Dr. G73: Ruth 4D 120
Kirkness St. ML6: Air 3A 92
Kirknethan ML2: Wis 2C 156
Kirknewton St. G32: Glas 5B 86
Kirkoswald G74: E Kil 6D 138
Kirkoswald Dr. G81: Clyd 4E 43
Kirkoswald Rd. G43: Glas 1B 118
ML1: N'hill 3E 129
Kirkpatrick Dr. G33: Step 4E 67
Kirkpatrick St. G40: Glas 6C 84
Kirk Pl. G61: Bear 2E 45
G67: Cumb 6C 34
G71: Udd 2C 124
Kirkriggs Av. G73: Ruth 2D 120
Kirkriggs Gdns. G73: Ruth 2D 120
Kirkriggs Vw. G73: Ruth 2D 120
Kirkriggs Way *G73: Ruth* 2D 120
(off Kirkriggs Gdns.)
Kirk Rd. G61: Bear 2E 45
G76: Crmck 2H 135
ML1: N'hse 6D 112
ML2: Wis 6H 145
ML8: Carl 3E 165
ML9: Dals 3D 162
PA6: Hous 1B 74
Kirkshaw Ct. *PA5: John* 2F 95
(off Walkinshaw St.)
KIRKSHAWS 2A 110
Kirkshaws Av. ML5: Coat 2A 110
Kirkshaws Pl. ML5: Coat 2B 110
Kirkshaws Rd. ML5: Coat 2H 109
Kirkstall Gdns. G64: B'rig 3D 48
Kirkstone G77: Newt M 4H 133
Kirkstone Cl. G75: E Kil 5B 148
Kirk St. G62: Miln 3E 25
ML1: Moth 2G 143
ML5: Coat 5B 90
(not continuous)
ML8: Carl 3E 165
Kirkstyle Av. ML8: Carl 4E 165
Kirkstyle Cres. G78: Neil 2D 130
ML6: Air 1H 91
Kirkstyle La. G78: Neil 2E 131
Kirkstyle Pl. ML6: Glenm 5F 71
Kirksyde Av. G66: Kirk 6D 30
KIRKTON 3E 131
Kirkton G60: Old K 6E 21
PA8: Ersk 4E 41
Kirkton Av. G13: Glas 3A 60
G72: Blan 4A 140
G78: Barr 5D 114
ML8: Carl 3E 165
Kirkton Ct. ML8: Carl 4E 165
Kirkton Cres. G13: Glas 3A 60
G66: Milt C 6C 8
ML5: Coat 2F 111
Kirktonfield Dr. G78: Neil 2F 131
Kirktonfield Rd. G78: Neil 2E 131
Kirkton Ga. G74: E Kil 1G 149
KIRKTONHILL 4D 16
Kirktonholme Cres. G74: E Kil 1F 149
Kirktonholme Rd. G74: E Kil 1D 148
Kirkton Ho. G72: Blan 3B 140
Kirkton Pk. G74: E Kil 1H 149
Kirkton Pl. G72: Blan 3B 140
G74: E Kil 1H 149
(not continuous)
ML5: Coat 1F 111
Kirkton Rd. G72: Camb 2B 122
G78: Neil 3D 130
G82: Dumb 4D 16
Kirkton Side G78: Barr 6D 114
Kirkton St. ML8: Carl 4F 165
Kirkton Ter. G66: Cam G 1B 6
Kirkvale Ct. G77: Newt M 4H 133
Kirkvale Cres. G77: Newt M 4H 133
Kirkvale Dr. G77: Newt M 4H 133
Kirkview G67: Cumb 1C 54
Kirkview Ct. G67: Cumb 1C 54
Kirkview Cres. G77: Newt M 6E 133
Kirkview Gdns. G71: Tann 5D 108
Kirkville Pl. G15: Glas 6B 44
Kirkwall G67: Cumb 6A 14
Kirkwall Av. G72: Blan 5A 124
Kirkwell Rd. G44: Glas 2F 119
KIRKWOOD 1G 109
Kirkwood Av. G33: Step 4G 67
G81: Clyd 6F 43
Kirkwood Pl. ML5: Coat 6A 90
Kirkwood Quad. G81: Clyd 6F 43
Kirkwood Rd. G71: Tann 5D 108
Kirkwood Sports Barn 1F 109
Kirkwood Station (Rail) 6H 89
Kirkwood St. G51: Glas 6A 82
G73: Ruth 5C 104
ML5: Coat 5A 90
Kirn St. G20: Glas 1A 62
Kirriemuir G74: E Kil 4D 138
Kirriemuir Av. G52: Glas 2C 100
Kirriemuir Gdns. G64: B'rig 5E 49
Kirriemuir Pl. *G52: Glas* 1C 100
(off Bucklaw Gdns.)
Kirriemuir Rd. G64: B'rig 6E 49
Kirtle Dr. PA4: Renf 1G 79
Kirtle Pl. G75: E Kil 4A 148
Kishorn Pl. G33: Glas 2C 86
Kitchener St. ML2: Wis 6G 145
Kittoch Pl. G74: E Kil 1H 149
KITTOCHSIDE 5C 136
Kittochside Rd. G76: Crmck 2A 136
Kittoch St. G74: E Kil 1G 149
Klondike Ct. ML1: New S 4B 128
Knapdale St. G22: Glas 2E 63
Knightsbridge St. G13: Glas 2D 60
Knightscliffe Av. G13: Glas 1D 60
Knights Ga. G71: Both 2C 124
KNIGHTSWOOD 2D 60
Knightswood Ct. G13: Glas 3D 60
Knightswood Cross G13: Glas 2D 60
Knightswood Rd. G13: Glas 6C 44
Knightswood Swimming Pool 3B 60
Knightswood Ter. G72: Blan 6C 124
Knivysbridge Pl. ML4: Bell 4B 126
Knockburnie Rd. G71: Both 3E 125
Knockhall St. G33: Glas 1D 86
Knockhill Dr. G44: Glas 6F 103
Knockhill La. G44: Glas 6F 103
Knockhill Rd. PA4: Renf 2D 78
Knockside Av. PA2: Pais 6H 97
Knock Way PA3: Pais 4C 78
Knollpark Dr. G76: Clar 2B 134
Knowe Cres. ML1: N'hill 3D 128
Knowehead Dr. G71: Udd 1C 124
Knowehead Gdns. G41: Glas 2C 102
G71: Udd 1C 124
Knowehead Rd. ML2: Wis 1A 158
Knowehead Ter. G41: Glas 2C 102
Knowenoble St. ML1: Cle 5H 129
Knowe Rd. G69: Chry 1A 68
PA3: Pais 4D 78
Knowes Av. G77: Newt M 4E 133
Knowes Rd. G77: Newt M 4F 133
Knowe St. G62: Miln 3F 25
Knowetap St. G20: Glas 2C 62
KNOWETOP 5H 143
Knowetop Av. ML1: Moth 4H 143
Knowetop Cres. G82: Dumb 2C 16
KNOWNOBLE 5H 129
Knox Av. PA11: Bri W 4E 73
Knoxland Sq. G82: Dumb 5G 17
Knoxland St. G82: Dumb 5G 17
Knox Pl. G77: Newt M 5B 132
Knox St. ML6: Air 3B 92
PA1: Pais 1F 97
Koko's 4C 90
Kronberg Way G75: E Kil 6F 149
Kyleakin Dr. G72: Blan 5H 123
Kyleakin Rd. G46: T'bnk 4D 116
Kyleakin Ter. G46: T'bnk 4D 116
Kyle Ct. G72: Camb 1A 122
Kyle Dr. G46: Giff 4C 118
Kyle Gro. ML1: New S 4A 128
Kylemore Cres. ML1: Moth 5F 127
KYLEPARK 6B 108
Kylepark Av. G71: Udd 1B 124
Kylepark Cres. G71: Udd 6B 108
Kylepark Dr. G71: Udd 6B 108
Kyle Quad. ML1: N'hill 3C 128
ML2: Wis 2E 157
Kylerhea Rd. G46: T'bnk 4D 116
Kyle Rd. G67: Cumb 2B 36
Kyle Sq. G73: Ruth 2B 120
Kyle St. G4: Glas 2G 83 (2F 5)
ML1: Moth 2D 142
Kyle Ter. G82: Dumb 2B 16


## L


La Belle Allee *G3: Glas* 2C 82
(off Claremont St.)
La Belle Pl. G3: Glas 2C 82
Laberge Gdns. ML1: New S 4B 128
Laburnum Av. G75: E Kil 5E 149
Laburnum Ct. G75: E Kil 5E 149
Laburnum Cres. ML2: Wis 4H 145
Laburnum Dr. G66: Milt C 6B 8
Laburnum Gdns. G66: Lenz 2B 50
Laburnum Gro. G66: Lenz 2B 50
ML5: Coat 6D 90
Laburnum Lea ML3: Ham 2A 154
Laburnum Pl. PA5: John 5G 95
Laburnum Rd. FK4: Bank 1E 15
G41: Glas 1A 102
G67: Cumb 3D 36
G71: View 4G 109
Lachlan Cres. PA8: Ersk 6C 40
La Crusse Ter. G12: Glas 6C 62
Lacy St. PA1: Pais 6C 78
Ladeside Cl. G77: Newt M 3C 132
Ladeside Dr. G65: Kils 2B 12
PA5: John 3D 94
Lade Ter. G52: Glas 1A 100
Ladhope Pl. G13: Glas 1G 59
Ladyacres PA4: Inch 3H 57
Ladyacres Way PA4: Inch 3H 57
Lady Ann Cres. ML6: Air 5C 92
Lady Anne St. G14: Glas 4H 59
Ladybank G68: Cumb 5H 13
Ladybank Ct. G74: E Kil 1G 149
Ladybank Dr. G52: Glas 1E 101
Ladybank Gdns. G74: E Kil 1G 149
Ladybank Pl. G74: E Kil 1G 149
Ladyburn St. PA1: Pais 1C 98
Ladyhill Dr. G69: Bail 1G 107
Lady Isle Cres. G71: Udd 1C 124
Lady Jane Ga. G71: Both 3B 124
Ladykirk Cres. G52: Glas 5B 80
PA2: Pais 2B 98
Ladykirk Dr. G52: Glas 5B 80
Lady La. PA1: Pais 1H 97
Ladyloan Av. G15: Glas 3G 43
Ladyloan Ct. G15: Glas 3H 43
Ladyloan Gdns. G15: Glas 3H 43
Ladyloan Gro. G15: Glas 3H 43
Ladyloan Pl. G15: Glas 3G 43
Lady Mary Wlk. ML3: Ham 2A 154
Ladymuir Circ. PA8: Ersk 6D 40
Ladymuir Cres. G53: Glas 3C 100

Ladysmith Av.—Ledaig Pl.

Ladysmith Av. PA10: Kilb 3B 94
Ladysmith St. ML2: Wis 5C 144
Lady Watson Gdns. ML3: Ham 1E 153
Ladywell Rd. ML1: Moth 3D 142
Ladywell St. G4: Glas 4A 84
Lady Wilson St. ML6: Air 5B 92
Ladywood G62: Miln 3H 25
Lagan Rd. ML8: Carl 4F 165
Laggan Quad. ML6: Air 2G 91
Laggan Rd. G43: Glas 2C 118
G64: B'rig 6D 48
G77: Newt M 2D 132
ML6: Air 2H 91
Laggan Ter. PA4: Renf 5D 58
Laggan Way ML2: Newm 2D 146
Lagholm Dr. PA3: Lin 6A 76
Lagoon Leisure Cen. 1B 98
Laidlaw Av. ML1: New S 4H 127
Laidlaw Gdns. G71: Tann 4D 108
Laidlaw St. G5: Glas 6E 83
(not continuous)
Laidon Rd. ML6: Air 2H 91
Laidon Wlk. *ML2: Newm 3D 146*
*(off Murdostoun Vw.)*
Laighcartside St. PA5: John 2G 95
Laighlands Rd. G71: Both 5F 125
Laighmuir St. G71: Udd 2D 124
LAIGH PARK 5A 78
Laighpark Av. PA7: B'ton 4H 39
Laighpark Vw. PA3: Pais 4A 78
Laigh Rd. G77: Newt M 4H 133
LAIGHSTONEHALL 1F 153
Laighstonehall Rd. ML3: Ham 1F 153
Laightoun Ct. G67: Cumb 1C 54
Laightoun Dr. G67: Cumb 1C 54
Laightoun Gdns. G67: Cumb 1C 54
Lainshaw Dr. G45: Glas 5E 119
Laird Gro. G71: Tann 5E 109
Laird Pl. G40: Glas 1B 104
Lairds Ga. G71: Both 2B 124
Lairds Hill G67: Cumb 3G 35
Laird's Hill Ct. G65: Kils 3E 11
Laird's Hill Pl. G65: Kils 3E 11
Lairdsland Rd. G66: Kirk 5D 30
Laird St. ML5: Coat 4D 90
Lairg Dr. G72: Blan 5A 124
Lairhills Rd. G75: E Kil 4G 149
Lamberton Dr. G52: Glas 5B 80
LAMBHILL 2E 63
Lambhill Quad. G41: Glas 6C 82
Lambhill St. G41: Glas 6B 82
Lambie Cres. G77: Newt M 4C 132
Lamb St. G22: Glas 3F 63
ML3: Ham 6A 142
Lamerton Rd. G67: Cumb 3C 36
Lamington Rd. G52: Glas 1B 100
Lamlash Cres. G33: Glas 3B 86
Lamlash Pl. G33: Glas 3B 86
ML1: Moth 2E 143
Lamlash Sq. G33: Glas 3C 86
Lammermoor G74: E Kil 5E 139
Lammermoor Av. G52: Glas 1C 100
Lammermoor Cres. G66: Kirk 5F 31
Lammermoor Dr. G67: Cumb 6G 35
Lammermoor Gdns.
G66: Kirk 5F 31
Lammermoor Rd. G66: Kirk 5F 31
Lammermoor Ter. ML2: Wis 6H 145
Lammermuir Ct. PA2: Pais 5A 98
Lammermuir Dr. PA2: Pais 5H 97
Lammermuir Gdns. G61: Bear 6C 24
Lammermuir Pl. *ML1: Holy 3B 128*
*(off Cherry Pl.)*
Lammermuir Way ML6: Chap 4F 113
Lammermuir Wynd ML9: Lark 6H 155
Lammer Wynd *ML9: Lark 4G 161*
*(off Pitlochry Dr.)*
Lamont Av. PA7: B'ton 4A 40
Lamont Rd. G21: Glas 3D 64
Lanark Av. ML6: Air 1H 111
Lanark Rd. ML8: Carl 4F 165
ML8: Crsfd, Rose 4E 163
ML9: Dals, Lark 4G 155
Lanark Rd. End ML9: Lark 4G 155
Lanarkshire Ice Rink 4A 142
Lanark St. G1: Glas 5H 83
Lancaster Av. ML6: Chap 4D 112
Lancaster Cres. G12: Glas 5A 62
Lancaster Cres. La. G12: Glas 5A 62
Lancaster Rd. G64: B'rig 3D 48
Lancaster Ter. G12: Glas 5A 62
Lancaster Ter. La. G12: Glas 5A 62
Lancaster Way PA4: Renf 2E 79
Lancefield Quay G3: Glas 4C 82
Lancefield St. G3: Glas 4D 82
Landemer Ct. G73: Ruth 1C 120
Landemer Dr. G73: Ruth 1B 120
Landressy Pl. G40: Glas 1B 104
Landressy St. G40: Glas 6B 84
Landsdowne Gdns. ML3: Ham 6B 142
Landsdowne Rd. ML9: Lark 3G 161
Lane, The G68: Dull 5F 13
Lanfine Rd. PA1: Pais 1D 98
Langa Gro. *G20: Glas 2C 62*
*(off Lochburn Cres.)*
Langa St. G20: Glas 2C 62
Lang Av. PA4: Renf 1E 79
PA7: B'ton 4A 40
Langbank St. G5: Glas 6F 83
Langbar Cres. G33: Glas 4E 87
Langbar Gdns. G33: Glas 4F 87
Langbar Path *G33: Glas 4D 86*
*(off Langbar Cres.)*
Langcraigs G82: Dumb 2G 17
Langcraigs Ct. PA2: Pais 5G 97
Langcraigs Dr. PA2: Pais 6G 97
Langcraigs Ter. PA2: Pais 6G 97
Langcroft Dr. G72: Camb 3C 122
Langcroft Pl. G51: Glas 4C 80
Langcroft Rd. G51: Glas 4C 80
Langcroft Ter. G51: Glas 4D 80
Langdale G74: E Kil 6E 137
G77: Newt M 4H 133
Langdale Av. G33: Glas 6G 65
Langdale Rd. G69: Mood 5D 52
Langdales Av. G68: Cumb 3F 35
Langdale St. G33: Glas 6G 65
Langfaulds Cres. G81: Faif 6F 23
Langford Dr. G53: Glas 4A 116
Langford Pl. G53: Glas 4B 116
Langhaul Av. G53: Glas 4H 99
Langhaul Ct. G53: Glas 4H 99
Langhaul Pl. G53: Glas 4H 99
Langhaul Rd. G53: Glas 4H 99
Langhill Dr. G68: Cumb 2F 35
Langholm G75: E Kil 5B 148
Langholm Ct. G69: Mood 5D 52
Langholm Cres. ML2: Wis 3H 145
Langholm Path G72: Blan 2A 140
Langlands Av. G51: Glas 4D 80
G75: E Kil 6H 149
Langlands Ct. G51: Glas 3F 81
Langlands Dr. G51: Glas 3C 80
G75: E Kil 6H 149
Langlands Path *G51: Glas 4E 81*
*(off Langlands Rd.)*
Langlands Rd. G51: Glas 4D 80
LANGLANDS-SEAFAR INTERCHANGE
5G 35
Langlands Ter. G82: Dumb 1H 17
Langlea Av. G72: Camb 3F 121
Langlea Ct. G72: Camb 3G 121
Langlea Dr. G72: Camb 2G 121
Langlea Gdns. G72: Camb 2G 121
Langlea Rd. G72: Camb 3G 121
Langlea Way G72: Camb 2G 121
Langlees Av. G77: Newt M 4H 133
Langley Av. G13: Glas 1B 60
Langley Gro. G72: Camb 3G 121
LANGLOAN 6A 90
Langloan Cres. ML5: Coat 6A 90
Langloan Pl. ML5: Coat 5A 90
Langloan St. ML5: Coat 6A 90
Langlook Cres. G53: Glas 5H 99
Langlook Pl. G53: Glas 5H 99
Langlook Rd. G53: Glas 5H 99
LANGMUIR 4H 31
Langmuir Av. G66: Kirk 4E 31
Langmuirhead Rd. G66: Auch 1H 65
Langmuir Rd. G66: Kirk 4G 31
G69: Barg 6E 89
Langmuir Way G69: Barg 6E 89
Langness Rd. G33: Glas 3B 86
Langoreth Av. ML3: Ham 1D 152
Lang Pl. PA5: John 2F 95
Langrig Rd. G21: Glas 4C 64
G77: Newt M 6C 132
Langshaw Cres. ML8: Carl 3F 165
Langshot St. G51: Glas 6B 82
LANGSIDE 5D 102
Langside Av. G41: Glas 4C 102
G71: View 1G 125
Langside Ct. G71: Both 6F 125
Langside Dr. G43: Glas 3C 118
PA10: Kilb 3A 94
Langside Gdns. G42: Glas 6E 103
Langside La. G42: Glas 4E 103
Langside Pk. PA10: Kilb 3A 94
Langside Pl. G41: Glas 5D 102
Langside Rd. G42: Glas 5D 102
G71: Both 6F 125
Langside Station (Rail) 1C 118
Langside St. G81: Faif 1G 43
Langstile Pl. G52: Glas 6H 79
Langstile Rd. G52: Glas 6H 79
Lang St. PA1: Pais 1C 98
Langton Cres. G53: Glas 4C 100
G78: Barr 6F 115
Langton Gdns. G69: Bail 1F 107
Langton Ga. G77: Newt M 4C 132
Langton Pl. G77: Newt M 4C 132
Langton Rd. G53: Glas 4C 100
Langtree Av. G46: Giff 6G 117
LANRIGG 6A 52
Lanrig Pl. G69: Chry 1A 68
Lanrig Rd. G69: Chry 6A 52
Lansbury Gdns. PA3: Pais 4H 77
Lansbury Ter. ML9: Lark 4G 161
Lansdowne Cres. G20: Glas 1D 82
Lansdowne Cres. La.
*G20: Glas 1D 82*
*(off Holyrood Cres.)*
Lansdowne Dr. G68: Cumb 6H 13
Lantana Gro. ML1: Moth 1F 143
Lanton Dr. G52: Glas 6B 80
Lanton Rd. G43: Glas 2C 118
Lappin St. G81: Clyd 1F 59
Larbert St. G4: Glas 2F 83 (2D 4)
Larch Av. G64: B'rig 1D 64
G66: Lenz 1C 50
Larch Ct. G67: Cumb 1D 36
G72: Blan 1A 140
G75: E Kil 6D 148
Larch Cres. G66: Lenz 1C 50
Larch Dr. FK4: Bank 1E 15
G75: E Kil 6D 148
Larches, The G69: Mood 3E 53
Larchfield Av. G14: Glas 5B 60
G77: Newt M 5E 133
Larchfield Ct. G77: Newt M 5D 132
Larchfield Cres. ML2: Wis 3A 146
Larchfield Dr. G73: Ruth 3D 120
Larchfield Gdns. ML2: Wis 3B 146
Larchfield Gro. ML2: Wis 2B 146
Larchfield Pl. G14: Glas 5B 60
ML2: Wis 3B 146
Larchfield Rd. G61: Bear 6F 45
Larch Gro. G66: Milt C 6B 8
G67: Cumb 1D 36
ML1: Holy 2B 128
ML3: Ham 1A 154
Larchgrove Av. G32: Glas 5C 86
Larchgrove Pl. G32: Glas 4C 86
Larchgrove Rd. G32: Glas 4C 86
Larch Pl. G71: View 5H 109
G75: E Kil 6D 148
PA5: John 5G 95
Larch Rd. G41: Glas 1H 101
G67: Cumb 1D 36
Larchwood Ter. G78: Barr 6F 115
Largie Rd. G43: Glas 2D 118
Largo Pl. G51: Glas 4E 81
Larkfield Ct. G72: Blan 3A 140
Larkfield Dr. G72: Blan 3B 140
Larkfield Rd. G66: Lenz 1E 51
Larkfield St. G42: Glas 2F 103
LARKHALL 2E 161
Larkhall Ind. Est. ML9: Lark 5G 161
LARKHALL INTERCHANGE
5A 156
Larkhall Leisure Cen.
3E 161
Larkin Gdns. PA3: Pais 4H 77
Larkin Way ML4: Bell 6B 110
Larksfield Dr. ML8: Carl 5G 165
Larkspur Dr. G74: E Kil 5E 137
Larkspur Way ML8: Carl 5F 165
Lark Way ML4: Bell 5B 110
Lashley Gro. ML2: Over 4A 158
Lasswade St. G14: Glas 3G 59
Latherton Dr. G20: Glas 4B 62
Latimer Gdns. G52: Glas 1A 100
Latimer Path *G52: Glas 1A 100*
*(off Hatton Gdns.)*
Latta St. G82: Dumb 3G 17
Lauchlin Pl. G66: Kirk 6H 31
Lauchope Rd. ML1: N'hse 6D 112
Lauchope St. ML6: Chap 3E 113
Lauder Cres. ML2: Wis 3H 145
Lauderdale Dr. G77: Newt M 6C 132
Lauderdale Gdns.
G12: Glas 6H 61
Lauderdale La. G12: Glas 6H 61
Lauder Dr. G73: Ruth 1F 121
PA3: Lin 6H 75
Lauder Gdns. G72: Blan 5A 124
ML5: Coat 2F 111
Lauder Grn. G74: E Kil 5B 138
Lauder La. ML3: Ham 6C 140
Lauder St. G5: Glas 1E 103
Laughland Dr. ML1: N'hill 4D 128
Laundry La. G33: Step 4C 66
Lauranne Pl. ML4: Bell 2A 126
Laurel Av. G66: Lenz 1D 50
G81: Clyd 3H 41
Laurel Bank ML3: Ham 3G 153
Laurelbank ML5: Coat 3C 90
Laurelbank Rd. G32: Carm 5C 106
G69: Chry 2H 67
Laurel Cl. G75: E Kil 6F 149
Laurel Dr. G75: E Kil 6E 1
ML2: Wis 5D 1
ML9: Lark 3G 1
Laurel Gdns. G71: Tann 5D 1
ML6: Chap 3E 1
Laurel La. *ML9: Lark 4G 1*
*(off Donaldson R*
Laurel Pk. Gdns. G13: Glas 3C
Laurel Pk. Sports Club 3D
Laurel Pl. G11: Glas 1G
G75: E Kil 6F 14
Laurel Sq. FK4: Bank 1E 1
Laurels, The G77: Newt M 4D 1
ML1: Carf 5B 1
Laurel St. G11: Glas 1G
Laurel Wlk. G73: Ruth 4E 1
Laurel Way G78: Barr 4D 1
Laurence Ct. G15: Glas 4G
Laurence Dr. G15: Glas 4G
G61: Bear 1D
Laurence Gdns. G15: Glas 4G
Laurenstone Ter. *G74: E Kil 1B 1*
*(off Capelrig D*
Lauren Vw. ML6: Air 4H
Lauren Way PA2: Pais 4D
Laurie Ct. G71: Tann 6E 1
LAURIESTON 6F
Laurieston Rd. G5: Glas 1F 1
Laurieston Way G73: Ruth 3D 1
Lauriston Gro. G77: Newt M 4B 1
Lavelle Dr. ML5: Coat 4E
Lavender Dr. G75: E Kil 6F 14
Lavender La. ML8: Carl 5E 1
Laverock Av. ML3: Ham 1C 1
Laverockhall St. G21: Glas 6B
Laverock Rd. ML6: Air 1B
Laverock Ter. G69: Mood 6D
LAW 6D 1
Law Dr. ML1: N'hill 3C 1
Lawers Dr. G61: Bear 1C
Lawers La. ML1: N'hill 3C 1
Lawers Rd. G43: Glas 2H 1
PA4: Renf 2E
Lawfield Av. G77: Newt M 4H 1
LAW HILL 1A 1
Lawhill Av. G45: Glas 3H 1
Lawhill Rd. ML8: Carl, Law 6D 1
Lawhope Mill Rd. ML6: Chap 2F 1
Lawmarnock Cres.
PA11: Bri W 4E
Lawmarnock Rd.
PA11: Bri W 5E
Lawmoor Av. G5: Glas 3G 1
Lawmoor Pl. G5: Glas 3G 1
Lawmoor Rd. G5: Glas 2G 1
Lawmoor St. G5: Glas 2G 1
Lawmuir Cres. G81: Faif 6G
Lawmuir Pl. ML4: Bell 5C 1
Lawmuir Rd. ML4: Bell 4C 1
ML8: Law 6D 1
LAWN PARK 4A
Lawn Pk. G62: Miln 4A
Lawn St. PA1: Pais 6B
LAW OF MAULDSLIE 1H 1
Law Pl. G74: E Kil 5G 1
Lawrence Av. G46: Giff 6A 1
Lawrence St. G11: Glas 1A
Lawrie St. G11: Glas 1H
ML2: Newm 4D 1
Lawrie Way ML9: Lark 4G 1
LAW RDBT. 5G 1
Lawson Av. ML1: Moth 6G 1
Law St. G40: Glas 6C
Law Vw. ML2: Over 5A 1
Laxford Av. G44: Glas 3E 1
Laxford Pl. ML5: Coat 6F
Laxford Rd. PA8: Ersk 6C
Laxford Way ML1: N'hill 3C 1
Laxton Dr. G66: Lenz 3E
Lea Av. G78: Neil 2D 1
Leabank Av. PA2: Pais 5A
Leadburn Rd. G21: Glas 5E
Leadburn St. G32: Glas 4G
Leader St. G33: Glas 2F
Leaend Rd. ML6: Air 2G
Leander Cres. ML4: Moss 2G 1
PA4: Renf 1G
Learigg Rd. ML6: Plain 1H
Learmouth Pl. G62: Miln 3F
Leathem Pl. ML2: Wis 2C 1
Leathen Pl. PA8: Ersk 6C
Leckethill Av. G68: Cumb 6B
Leckethill Ct. G68: Cumb 6B
Leckethill Pl. G68: Cumb 6A
Leckethill Vw. G68: Cumb 6B
Leckie Ct. *ML3: Ham 5G 1*
*(off Leckie D*
Leckie Dr. ML3: Ham 5G 1
Leckie St. G43: Glas 5A 1
Ledaig Pl. G31: Glas 4E

Ledaig St.—Lismore Gdns.


daig St. G31: Glas 4E 85
dard Rd. G42: Glas 5D 102
dcameroch Cres. G61: Bear 3D 44
dcameroch Pk. G61: Bear 3D 44
dcameroch Rd. G61: Bear 3D 44
dgate G66: Kirk 4D 30
dgowan Pl. G20: Glas 1B 62
di Dr. G61: Bear 6B 24
di Path ML1: N'hill 4C 128
di Rd. G43: Glas 2A 118
dmore Dr. G15: Glas 3H 43
dnock Rd. G33: Step 4C 66
G52: Glas 6A 80
e Av. G33: Glas 2G 85
ebank Dr. G44: Neth 6D 118
eburn Av. PA6: Hous 2C 74
eburn Gdns. PA6: Hous 2C 74
echlee Rd. ML3: Ham 6A 142
e Cres. G64: B'rig 1C 64
efield Dr. G44: Neth 5D 118
ehill Rd. G21: Glas 2A 64
e Pl. ML4: Bell 3F 127
esburn Pl. G74: E Kil 5H 137
e's Ct. ML5: Coat 6C 90
eside Rd. G21: Glas 2A 64
esland G71: Tann 5E 109
eward Circ. G75: E Kil 2C 148
ewood Dr. G44: Neth 5E 119
Froy Gdns. G75: E Kil 3E 149
Froy La. G75: E Kil 3E 149
froy St. ML5: Coat 4A 90
gbrannock Av. ML1: N'hse 6D 112
gbrannock Cres. ML1: N'hill 3D 128
gbrannock Rd. ML1: N'hse 1E 129
ggatson Rd. G53: Glas 4C 116
glen Wood Cres. G21: Glas 3F 65
glen Wood Dr. G21: Glas 3F 65
glen Wood Gdns. G21: Glas 3F 65
glen Wood Pl. G21: Glas 3G 65
glen Wood Rd. G21: Glas 3F 65
icester Av. G12: Glas 4H 61
ighton St. G20: Glas 3C 62
ML2: Wis 1H 157
isuredome Bishopbriggs Sports Cen. 3A 48
itchland Rd. PA2: Pais 5B 96
PA5: Eld 5B 96
eithington Rd. G46: Giff 2G 133
eithland Av. G53: Glas 4B 100
eithland Rd. G53: Glas 4B 100
eith St. G33: Glas 3F 85
eman Dr. PA6: C'lee 3D 74
eman Gro. PA6: C'lee 3D 74
embert Dr. G76: Clar 1B 134
endale La. G64: B'rig 3C 48
endalfoot Gdns. ML3: Ham 1B 152
endal Pl. G75: E Kil 5A 148
endel Pl. G51: Glas 5B 82
enihall Dr. G45: Glas 5A 120
enihall Ter. G45: Glas 5A 120
ennox Av. G14: Glas 6C 60
G62: Miln 4G 25
ML5: Coat 4A 90
PA7: B'ton 4H 39
ennox Ct. *G66: Kirk* 5E 31
*(off Highfield Rd.)*
ennox Cres. G64: B'rig 1B 64
ennox Dr. G61: Bear 1F 45
G81: Faif 6E 23
ennox Gdns. G14: Glas 5D 60
ennox Ho. G67: Cumb 3H 35
ennox La. E. G14: Glas 6D 60
ennox La. W. *G14: Glas* 6C 60
*(off Earlbank Av.)*
*G14: Glas* 5D 60
*(off Norse La. Nth.)*
ennox Pl. G66: Len 3F 7
G81: Clyd 4A 42
ennox Rd. G66: Len 2E 7
G67: Cumb 3H 35
G82: Dumb 4H 17
G82: Milt 4E 19
ennox Sq. *G66: Len* 3F 7
*(off Service St.)*
ennox St. G20: Glas 2A 62
G82: Dumb 4G 17
ML2: Wis 5C 146
ennox Ter. PA3: Pais 3C 78
ENNOXTOWN 3F 7
ennox Vw. G81: Clyd 4D 42
entran St. G34: Glas 4A 88
eny St. G20: Glas 5D 62
ENZIE 2C 50
ENZIEMILL 5A 36
enziemill Rd. G67: Cumb 6H 35
enzie Pl. G21: Glas 3B 64
enzie Rd. G33: Step 2D 66
G66: Kirk 6D 30
enzie Station (Rail) 3C 50
enzie St. G21: Glas 4B 64
Lenzie Ter. G21: Glas 3A 64
Lenzie Way G21: Glas 3A 64
Lesley Quad. ML4: Bell 5B 126
Leslie Av. G77: Newt M 2E 133
PA7: B'ton 4H 39
Leslie Rd. G41: Glas 3C 102
Leslie St. G41: Glas 2D 102
ML1: Moth 2H 143
Lesmuir Dr. G14: Glas 4H 59
Lesmuir Pl. G14: Glas 4H 59
Letham Ct. G43: Glas 2C 118
Letham Dr. G43: Glas 2C 118
G64: B'rig 1E 65
Letham Grange G68: Cumb 1H 35
Lethamhill Cres. G33: Glas 2H 85
Lethamhill Pl. G33: Glas 2G 85
Lethamhill Rd. G33: Glas 2G 85
Letham Oval G64: B'rig 1F 65
Lethbridge Pl. G75: E Kil 3E 149
Letherby Dr. G44: Glas 6F 103
Letheron Dr. ML2: Wis 4H 145
Lethington Av. G41: Glas 5C 102
Lethington Pl. G41: Glas 5D 102
Letterfearn Dr. G23: Glas 6C 46
Letterickhills Cres. G72: Flem 4E 123
Lettoch St. G51: Glas 4G 81
Leven Av. G64: B'rig 6D 48
Leven Ct. G78: Barr 2D 114
G82: Dumb 3E 17
Leven Dr. G61: Bear 3F 45
ML3: Ham 3F 153
Levenford Ter. G82: Dumb 4E 17
Levengrove Ct. G82: Dumb 4E 17
Levengrove Ter. G82: Dumb 4E 17
Leven Path *ML1: Holy* 2A 128
*(off Graham St.)*
Leven Pl. PA8: Ersk 6C 40
Leven Quad. ML6: Air 1H 91
Leven Rd. ML5: Coat 2G 89
Leven Sq. PA4: Renf 5D 58
Leven St. G41: Glas 2D 102
G82: Dumb 4G 17
ML1: Moth 4G 143
Leven Ter. ML1: Carf 5C 128
Leven Valley Ent. Cen.
G82: Dumb 3D 16
Leven Vw. G81: Clyd 4D 42
Leven Way *G67: Cumb* 4H 35
*(in Cumbernauld Shop. Cen.)*
G75: E Kil 5B 148
PA2: Pais 4C 96
Levernbridge Ct. G53: Glas 6H 99
Levernbridge Gro. G53: Glas 6H 99
Levernbridge Pl. G53: Glas 1H 115
Levernbridge Rd. G53: Glas 1H 115
Levernbridge Way G53: Glas 1H 115
Levern Cres. G78: Barr 5D 114
Leverndale Ct. G53: Glas 4H 99
Levern Gdns. G78: Barr 4D 114
Leverngrove Ct. G53: Glas 1H 115
Levern Rd. G53: Glas 1G 115
Levernside Av. G53: Glas 5C 100
G78: Barr 5C 114
Levernside Cres. G53: Glas 4B 100
Levernside Rd. G53: Glas 4C 100
Lewis Av. ML2: Wis 4C 146
PA4: Renf 2F 79
Lewis Cres. G60: Old K 2G 41
PA10: Kilb 3C 94
Lewis Dr. G60: Old K 2F 41
Lewis Gdns. G60: Old K 2G 41
G61: Bear 1B 44
Lewis Gro. G60: Old K 2G 41
Lewis Pl. G60: Old K 2G 41
G77: Newt M 3B 132
ML6: Air 5D 92
Lewiston Dr. *G23: Glas* 6B 46
*(off Lewiston Rd.)*
Lewiston Pl. *G23: Glas* 6B 46
*(off Lewiston Rd.)*
Lewiston Rd. G23: Glas 6B 46
Lexwell Av. PA5: Eld 2B 96
Leyden Ct. G20: Glas 4C 62
Leyden Gdns. G20: Glas 4D 62
Leyden St. G20: Glas 4C 62
Leys Pk. ML3: Ham 5E 141
Leys, The G64: B'rig 6C 48
Libberton Way ML3: Ham 6E 141
Liberton St. G33: Glas 3F 85
Liberty Av. G69: Barg 6E 89
Liberty Path G72: Blan 2B 140
Liberty Rd. ML4: Bell 3C 126
Libo Av. G53: Glas 4D 100
Libo Pl. PA8: Ersk 5C 40
Library Gdns. G72: Camb 1H 121
Library La. G46: T'bnk 4F 117
Library Rd. ML2: Wis 6H 145
Lickprivick Rd. G75: E Kil 6D 148
Liddell Gro. G75: E Kil 4F 149
Liddells Ct. G64: B'rig 2C 64
Liddell St. G32: Carm 4C 106
Liddel Rd. G67: Cumb 4G 35
(Seafar Rd.)
G67: Cumb 4A 36
(Torbrex Rd.)
Liddesdale Pl. G22: Glas 2A 64
Liddesdale Rd. G22: Glas 2F 63
Liddesdale Sq. G22: Glas 2H 63
Liddesdale Ter. G22: Glas 2A 64
Liddlesdale Pas. G22: Glas 2G 63
Liddoch Way G73: Ruth 5B 104
Liff Gdns. G64: B'rig 1F 65
Liff Pl. G34: Glas 2A 88
LIGHTBURN
Cambuslang 4E 123
Glasgow 4A 86
Lightburn Pl. G32: Glas 4B 86
Lightburn Rd. G31: Glas 5E 85
G72: Camb, Flem 3D 122
Lighthouse, The 6D 4
Lilac Av. G67: Cumb 6E 15
G81: Clyd 2H 41
Lilac Ct. G67: Cumb 6E 15
Lilac Cres. G71: View 5F 109
Lilac Gdns. G64: B'rig 1D 64
Lilac Hill G67: Cumb 6F 15
ML3: Ham 1B 154
Lilac Pl. G67: Cumb 6F 15
Lilac Way ML1: Holy 2B 128
Lilac Wynd G72: Flem 3E 123
Lillie Art Gallery 3H 25
Lillyburn Pl. G15: Glas 3G 43
Lilybank Av. G69: Muirh 2A 68
G72: Camb 3B 122
ML6: Air 1B 92
Lilybank Gdns. G12: Glas 1B 82
Lilybank Gdns. La.
*G12: Glas* 1B 82
*(off Lilybank Gdns.)*
Lilybank La. *G12: Glas* 1B 82
*(off Lilybank Gdns.)*
Lilybank St. ML3: Ham 5G 141
Lilybank Ter. G12: Glas 1B 82
Lilybank Ter. La. *G12: Glas* 1B 82
*(off Gt. George St.)*
Lily St. G40: Glas 2D 104
Limecraigs Av. PA2: Pais 6G 97
Limecraigs Cres. PA2: Pais 6G 97
Limecraigs Rd. PA2: Pais 6F 97
Lime Cres. G67: Cumb 2E 37
ML6: Air 4C 92
Lime Gro. G66: Lenz 2D 50
G72: Blan 6A 124
ML1: Moth 5G 143
Limegrove St. ML4: Bell 6C 110
Limekilns Rd. G67: Cumb 1H 55
Limekilns St. G81: Faif 6F 23
Lime La. G14: Glas 6D 60
Lime Loan ML1: Holy 3B 128
Lime Rd. G82: Dumb 3F 17
Limeside Av. G73: Ruth 6D 104
Limeside Gdns. G73: Ruth 6E 105
Limes, The G44: Glas 3F 119
Lime St. G14: Glas 6D 60
Limetree Av. G71: View 5F 109
Limetree Ct. ML3: Ham 4E 141
Limetree Cres. G77: Newt M 5D 132
Limetree Dr. G81: Clyd 3C 42
Limetree Quad. G71: View 5G 109
Limetree Wlk. G66: Milt C 1B 30
Limeview Av. PA2: Pais 6F 97
Limeview Cres. PA2: Pais 6F 97
Limeview Rd. PA2: Pais 6F 97
Limeview Way PA2: Pais 6F 97
Linacre Dr. G32: Glas 6C 86
Linacre Gdns. G32: Glas 6D 86
LINBURN 6D 40
Linburn Pl. G52: Glas 5A 80
Linburn Rd. G52: Glas 4G 79
PA8: Ersk 6C 40
LINCLIVE INTERCHANGE 6B 76
Linclive Spur PA3: Lin 6B 76
Linclive Ter. PA3: Lin 6B 76
Lincluden Path G41: Glas 1D 102
Lincoln Av. G13: Glas 2C 60
G71: Tann 4D 108
Lincuan Av. G46: Giff 6A 118
Lindams G71: Udd 2D 124
Lindcres Av. G73: Ruth 6D 104
Linden Av. ML2: Wis 3A 146
Linden Ct. G81: Hard 1C 42
Linden Dr. FK4: Bank 1E 15
G81: Hard 1C 42
Linden Lea G66: Milt C 6B 8
ML3: Ham 5F 141
Linden Pl. G13: Glas 2F 61
Linden St. G13: Glas 2F 61
Linden Way G13: Glas 2F 61
Lindores Dr. G74: E Kil 2E 149
Lindores Pl. G74: E Kil 2E 149
Lindores St. G42: Glas 5F 103
Lindrick Dr. G23: Glas 6C 46
Lindsaybeg Ct. G69: Chry 1A 68
Lindsaybeg Rd. G66: Lenz 3D 50
G69: Chry 5H 51
G69: Lenz 4G 51
Lindsay Dr. G12: Glas 3H 61
Lindsayfield Av. G75: E Kil 6D 148
Lindsayfield Rd. G75: E Kil 6D 148
Lindsay Gro. G74: E Kil 1H 149
Lindsay Pl. G12: Glas 3H 61
G66: Lenz 4D 50
G74: E Kil 2A 150
*PA5: John* 2G 95
*(off John Lang St.)*
Lindsay Rd. G74: E Kil 2H 149
Lindsay Ter. G66: Len 3G 7
Lindum Cres. ML1: Moth 1D 142
Lindum St. ML1: Moth 1D 142
Linfern Rd. G12: Glas 6A 62
Linghope Pl. ML2: Wis 3F 157
Lingley Av. ML6: Air 5A 92
Linhope Pl. G75: E Kil 4A 148
Links Rd. G32: Glas 2D 106
G44: Glas 3G 119
Links, The G68: Cumb 5B 14
Links Vw. ML9: Lark 3G 161
Linksview Rd. ML1: Carf 6B 128
Linkwood Av. G15: Glas 4H 43
Linkwood Cres. G15: Glas 4A 44
Linkwood Dr. G15: Glas 4H 43
Linkwood Gdns. G15: Glas 4B 44
Linkwood Pl. G15: Glas 4H 43
Linlithgow Gdns. G32: Glas 6D 86
Linn Crematorium G45: Glas 5E 119
Linn Cres. PA2: Pais 6G 97
Linndale Dr. G45: Glas 6G 119
Linndale Gdns. G45: Glas 6G 119
Linndale Gro. G45: Glas 6G 119
Linndale Rd. G45: Glas 6G 119
Linn Dr. G44: Neth 4D 118
Linnet Av. PA5: John 6C 94
Linnet Pl. G13: Glas 2H 59
Linnet Rd. ML4: Bell 3D 126
Linnet Way ML4: Bell 5B 110
Linn Gdns. G68: Cumb 3B 34
Linn Glen G66: Len 3H 7
Linnhead Dr. G53: Glas 1B 116
Linnhead Pl. G14: Glas 5B 60
Linnhe Av. G44: Glas 3E 119
G64: B'rig 6D 48
ML3: Ham 2E 153
Linnhe Ct. ML9: Lark 6H 155
Linnhe Cres. ML2: Wis 2H 157
Linnhe Dr. G78: Barr 2D 114
Linnhe Pl. G72: Blan 5A 124
PA8: Ersk 6C 40
Linnpark Av. G44: Neth 5D 118
Linnpark Ct. G44: Neth 4D 118
Linn Pk. Gdns. PA5: John 3G 95
Linnpark Ind. Est. G45: Glas 4G 119
Linnvale Way G68: Dull 5E 13
Linn Valley Dr. G45: Glas 4H 119
Linside Av. PA1: Pais 1C 98
Lint Butts G72: Blan 2A 140
Lintfield Loan *G71: Udd* 2E 125
*(off Bellshill Rd.)*
Linthaugh Rd. G53: Glas 3A 100
Linthaugh Ter. G53: Glas 4D 100
LINTHOUSE 3E 81
Linthouse Bldgs. G51: Glas 3E 81
Linthouse Rd. G51: Glas 2E 81
Lintie Rd. ML1: N'hill 3C 128
Lintlaw G72: Blan 5B 124
Lintlaw Dr. G52: Glas 5B 80
Lintmill Ter. G78: Neil 3C 130
Linton Pl. ML5: Coat 2A 110
Linton St. G33: Glas 3G 85
Lintwhite Ct. *PA11: Bri W* 4G 73
*(off Lintwhite Cres.)*
Lintwhite Cres. PA11: Bri W 3G 73
LINVALE 6G 43
Linwell Cres. PA2: Pais 6H 97
LINWOOD 6A 76
Linwood Av. G74: E Kil 1B 148
G76: Busby 2D 134
Linwood Ct. G44: Glas 2E 119
Linwood Ind. Est. PA3: Lin 1H 95
Linwood Rd. PA1: Pais 6B 76
PA3: Pais 6B 76
Linwood Sports Complex 4G 75
Linwood Ter. ML3: Ham 5F 141
Lion Bank G66: Kirk 4D 30
Lismore G74: E Kil 3C 150
Lismore Av. ML1: Moth 1D 142
PA4: Renf 2F 79
Lismore Dr. ML5: Coat 1H 109
PA2: Pais 6H 97
PA3: Lin 6F 75
Lismore Gdns. PA10: Kilb 3C 94

Lismore Hill—Loudon Ter.


Lismore Hill ML3: Ham 6B 140
Lismore Pl. G69: Mood 4E 53
G77: Newt M 4B 132
Lismore Rd. G12: Glas 4H 61
Lister Gdns. G76: Busby 4E 135
Lister Hgts. *G4: Glas 4A 84*
*(off Drygate)*
Lister Pl. G52: Hill 4A 80
Lister Rd. G52: Hill 4H 79
(not continuous)
Lister St. G4: Glas 2H 83 (2H 5)
Lister Twr. *G75: E Kil 3H 149*
*(off Sinclair Pl.)*
Lister Wlk. ML4: Bell 6E 111
Lithgow Av. G66: Kirk 6E 31
Lithgow Cres. PA2: Pais 3C 98
Lithgow Dr. ML1: Cle 6H 129
Lithgow Pl. G74: E Kil 1D 148
Lit. Dovehill G1: Glas 5H 83
Lit. Drum Rd. G68: Cumb 5F 33
LITTLE EARNOCK 2E 153
Littlehill St. G21: Glas 5C 64
Littleholm Pl. G81: Clyd 3A 42
Lit. John Gdns. ML2: Newm 5D 146
Littlemill Av. G68: Cumb 4A 34
Littlemill Cres. G53: Glas 5A 100
Littlemill Dr. G53: Glas 5A 100
Littlemill Gdns. G53: Glas 5A 100
Littlemill La. G60: Bowl 5A 20
Lit. Mill Way ML1: Carf 6B 128
Littlesdale Av. PA2: Pais 6B 96
Littleston Gdns. PA8: Ersk 6D 40
Little St. G3: Glas 4D 82
Littleton Dr. *G23: Glas 6B 46*
*(off Littleton St.)*
Littleton St. G23: Glas 6B 46
Lively Pl. *G72: Blan 2A 140*
*(off Burnbrae Rd.)*
Livery Wlk. *PA11: Bri W 3F 73*
*(off Main St.)*
Livingston Dr. ML6: Plain 1G 93
Livingstone Av. G52: Hill 3A 80
Livingstone Blvd. G72: Blan 4A 140
Livingstone Cl. G75: E Kil 4F 149
Livingstone Cres. G72: Blan 6B 124
Livingstone Dr. G75: E Kil 3F 149
Livingstone Gdns. ML9: Lark 2F 161
Livingstone La. G71: Both 4E 125
Livingstone Pk. G65: Kils 1F 11
Livingstone Pl. ML6: Air 4B 92
Livingstone St. G81: Clyd 6E 43
ML3: Ham 5D 140
Lloyd Av. G32: Glas 3A 106
Lloyd Dr. ML1: Carf 6A 128
Lloyds St. ML5: Coat 6C 90
Lloyd St. G31: Glas 3C 84
G73: Ruth 4D 104
ML1: Carf 6A 128
Loanbank Pl. G51: Glas 4G 81
Loanbank Quad. G51: Glas 4F 81
Loancroft Av. G69: Bail 2A 108
Loancroft Gdns. G71: Udd 2C 124
Loancroft Ga. G71: Udd 2C 124
Loancroft Ho. G69: Bail 2H 107
Loancroft Pl. G69: Bail 2H 107
Loanend Cotts. G72: Flem 6F 123
Loanfoot Av. G13: Glas 2A 60
G78: Neil 3D 130
Loanfoot Rd. G72: Blan 4B 140
LOANHEAD 1E 79
Loanhead Av. ML1: N'hill 4D 128
PA3: Lin 5G 75
PA4: Renf 6F 59
Loanhead Cres. ML1: N'hill 4D 128
Loanhead La. PA3: Lin 5G 75
Loanhead Rd. ML1: N'hill 4C 128
PA3: Lin 5G 75
Loanhead St. G32: Glas 4H 85
ML5: Coat 2A 110
Loaning *ML9: Lark 3G 161*
*(off Hareleeshill Rd.)*
Loaninghead Dr.
G82: Dumb 1H 17
Loaning, The G46: Giff 1G 133
G61: Bear 2E 45
G66: Kirk 6C 30
ML1: Moth 2E 143
Loan Lea Cres. ML9: Lark 4F 161
Loan, The G62: Miln 1C 24
Lobnitz Av. PA4: Renf 6F 59
Lochaber Dr. G73: Ruth 3F 121
Lochaber Path G72: Blan 2B 140
Lochaber Pl. G74: E Kil 6H 137
Lochaber Rd. G61: Bear 5G 45
Lochaber Wlk. G66: Milt C 4C 8
Lochachray Gdns. G32: Glas 1C 106
Lochachray St. G32: Glas 1C 106
Lochaline Av. PA2: Pais 3E 97
Lochaline Dr. G44: Glas 3E 119
Lochalsh Cres. G66: Milt C 5C 8
Lochalsh Dr. PA2: Pais 3E 97
Lochalsh Pl. G72: Blan 5H 123
Lochar Cres. G53: Glas 3D 100
Lochard Dr. PA2: Pais 4E 97
Lochar Pl. G75: E Kil 4A 148
Loch Assynt G74: E Kil 3B 150
Loch Awe G74: E Kil 3A 150
Loch Awe Pl. ML5: Coat 5B 90
Lochay St. G32: Glas 1C 106
Lochbrae Dr. G73: Ruth 3E 121
Lochbridge Rd. G34: Glas 4G 87
Lochbroom Dr. G77: Newt M 3F 133
PA2: Pais 3E 97
Loch Brora Cres. ML5: Coat 5A 90
Lochbrown Ct. G77: Newt M 3F 133
Lochbuie La. ML6: Glenm 5G 71
Lochburn Cres. G20: Glas 2C 62
Lochburn Gro. *G20: Glas 2C 62*
*(off Lochburn Cres.)*
Lochburn Pas. G20: Glas 2C 62
Lochburn Rd. G20: Glas 3B 62
Lochdochart Path *G34: Glas 4B 88*
*(off Lentran St.)*
Lochdochart Rd. G34: Glas 3A 88
Lochearn Cres. ML6: Air 1H 91
PA2: Pais 3E 97
Lochearnhead Rd. G33: Step 4B 66
Lochend Av. G69: G'csh 2C 68
Lochend Cres. G61: Bear 2A 44
Lochend Dr. G61: Bear 4D 44
Lochend Path G34: Glas 2H 87
Lochend Rd. G34: Glas 2H 87
G61: Bear 4E 45
G69: G'csh 2B 88
(Easterhouse)
G69: G'csh 2D 68
(Mount Ellen)
Lochend St. ML1: Moth 3H 143
Locher Av. PA6: C'lee 2E 75
Locherburn Av. PA6: C'lee 3D 74
Locherburn Gro. PA6: C'lee 3D 74
Locherburn Pl. PA6: C'lee 3D 74
Locher Cres. PA6: C'lee 3E 75
Locher Gait PA6: C'lee 3E 75
Locher Gdns. PA6: C'lee 3E 75
Locher Pl. ML5: Coat 2F 111
Locher Rd. PA11: Bri W 6H 73
Locher Way PA6: C'lee 3E 75
Lochfauld Rd. G23: Glas 5E 47
LOCHFIELD 4B 98
Lochfield Cres. PA2: Pais 4B 98
Lochfield Dr. PA2: Pais 4C 98
Lochfield Gdns. G34: Glas 2B 88
Lochfield Rd. PA2: Pais 4A 98
Lochgarry Way ML5: Coat 1H 109
Lochgilp St. G20: Glas 2A 62
Loch Goil G74: E Kil 2A 150
Lochgoin Av. G15: Glas 3G 43
Lochgoin Gdns. G15: Glas 3G 43
Lochgreen Pl. ML3: Ham 3F 153
ML5: Coat 1G 89
Lochgreen St. G33: Glas 6F 65
Lochhead Av. PA3: Lin 6H 75
Lochiel Ct. *ML6: Air 4F 91*
*(off Monkscourt Av.)*
Lochiel Dr. G66: Milt C 5C 8
Lochiel La. G73: Ruth 3F 121
Lochiel Rd. G46: T'bnk 3F 117
Lochinch Pl. G77: Newt M 4A 132
Lochinvar Rd. G67: Cumb 6F 35
Lochinver Cres. PA2: Pais 3E 97
Lochinver Dr. G44: Glas 3E 119
Lochinver Gro. G72: Camb 2B 122
Loch Laidon Ct. G32: Glas 1C 106
Loch Laidon St. G32: Glas 1D 106
Loch Laxford G74: E Kil 3B 150
Loch Lea G66: Kirk 3F 31
Lochlea G74: E Kil 5D 138
Lochlea Av. G81: Clyd 4E 43
Lochlea Loan *ML9: Lark 3G 161*
*(off Catrine St.)*
Lochlea Rd. G43: Glas 1B 118
G67: Cumb 2B 36
G73: Ruth 2G 121
(Burnside)
G73: Ruth 2B 120
(Spittal)
G76: Busby 4C 134
Lochlea Way ML1: N'hill 3E 129
Lochleven La. G42: Glas 6E 103
Lochleven Rd. G42: Glas 6E 103
LOCHLIBO 6C 114
Lochlibo Av. G13: Glas 3H 59
Lochlibo Cres. G78: Barr 6C 114
Lochlibo Rd. G78: Neil 3A 130
Lochlibo Ter. G78: Barr 6C 114
Loch Long G74: E Kil 3A 150
Loch Loyal G74: E Kil 3B 150
Lochmaben Rd. G52: Glas 1H 99
Lochmaddy Av. G44: Glas 3E 119
Loch Maree G74: E Kil 3B 150
Loch Meadie G74: E Kil 3B 150
Lochnagar Dr. G61: Bear 6B 24
Lochnagar Way *ML9: Lark 3G 161*
*(off Keir Hardie Way)*
Loch Naver G74: E Kil 3B 150
Lochore Av. PA3: Pais 4B 78
Loch Pk. ML2: Wis 6A 146
Loch Pk. Av. ML8: Carl 5E 165
Loch Pk. Pl. ML9: Lark 4E 161
Lochpark Stadium 5F 165
Loch Pl. PA11: Bri W 3F 73
Lochranza Ct. ML1: Carf 5B 128
Lochranza Dr. G75: E Kil 6D 148
Lochranza La. G75: E Kil 6E 149
Loch Rd. G33: Step 4D 66
G62: Miln 2H 25
G66: Kirk 6D 30
ML6: Chap 3D 112
PA11: Bri W 3F 73
Loch Shin G74: E Kil 3B 150
Lochside G61: Bear 4F 45
G69: G'csh 3D 68
Lochside St. G41: Glas 4C 102
Lochsloy Ct. G22: Glas 5H 63
Loch St. ML6: C'bnk 3B 112
Loch Striven G74: E Kil 2A 150
Loch Torridon G74: E Kil 3B 150
Loch Vw. ML6: C'bnk 3B 112
Lochview Cres. G33: Glas 6H 65
Lochview Dr. G33: Glas 6H 65
Lochview Gdns. G33: Glas 6H 65
Lochview Pl. G33: Glas 6H 65
Lochview Quad. ML4: Bell 4B 126
Lochview Rd. G61: Bear 4E 45
ML5: Coat 2G 89
Lochview Ter. G69: G'csh 4D 68
Loch Voil St. G32: Glas 1D 106
Lochwood Loan G69: Mood 4E 53
Lochwood St. G33: Glas 1G 85
Lochy Av. PA4: Renf 2H 79
Lochy Gdns. G64: B'rig 6D 48
Lochy Pl. PA8: Ersk 6C 40
Lochy St. ML2: Wis 2G 157
Locke Gro. ML1: Cle 6F 129
Lockerbie Av. G43: Glas 1D 118
Locket Yett Vw. ML4: Bell 2A 126
Lockhart Av. G72: Camb 1D 122
Lockhart Dr. G72: Camb 1D 122
G77: Newt M 6D 132
Lockhart Pl. ML2: Wis 5C 146
Lockhart St. G21: Glas 1D 84
ML3: Ham 5G 153
ML8: Carl 3F 165
Lockhart Ter. G74: E Kil 1B 150
Locksley Av. G13: Glas 1C 60
G67: Cumb 1G 55
Locksley Ct. G67: Cumb 1G 55
Locksley Cres. G67: Cumb 1G 55
Locksley Pl. G67: Cumb 1G 55
Locksley Rd. G67: Cumb 1G 55
PA2: Pais 4D 96
Locksley Way PA2: Pais 4D 96
Locks St. ML5: Coat 5F 91
Lodge Twr. *ML1: Moth 5A 144*
*(off Glassford St.)*
Logan Av. G77: Newt M 3C 132
Logandale Av. ML2: Newm 3D 146
Logan Dr. G68: Cumb 2F 35
PA3: Pais 5G 77
Logan Gdns. ML1: Cle 1H 145
Loganlea Dr. ML1: Carf 6A 128
Logans Rd. ML1: Moth 2D 142
Logan St. G5: Glas 3H 103
G72: Blan 2C 140
Loganswell Dr. G46: T'bnk 5E 117
Loganswell Gdns.
G46: T'bnk 5E 117
Loganswell Pl. G46: T'bnk 5E 117
Loganswell Rd. G46: T'bnk 5E 117
Logan Twr. G72: Camb 3E 123
Logie Pk. G74: E Kil 6A 138
Logie Sq. G74: E Kil 6A 138
Lomax St. G33: Glas 3F 85
Lomond G75: E Kil 6G 149
Lomond Av. PA4: Renf 2D 78
Lomond Ct. G67: Cumb 6E 35
G78: Barr 5E 115
G82: Dumb 3E 17
Lomond Cres. G67: Cumb 6E 35
PA11: Bri W 3E 73
PA2: Pais 5H 97
Lomond Dr. G64: B'rig 4B 48
G67: Cumb 6D 34
G71: Both 4F 125
G77: Newt M 2D 132
G78: Barr 3D 114
G82: Dumb 1H 17
ML2: Wis 1G 157
ML6: Air 2G 91
Lomond Gdns. PA5: Eld 3A
Lomond Gro. G67: Cumb 6E 3
Lomond Pl. G33: Step 5D 6
G67: Cumb 6D 3
ML5: Coat 2A 9
PA8: Ersk 6C 4
(not continuou
Lomond Rd. G61: Bear 5E 4
G66: Lenz 2D 5
G71: Tann 4D 10
ML5: Coat 1G 8
Lomondside Av. G76: Clar 1A 13
Lomond St. G22: Glas 4F 6
Lomondveiw Ind. Est.
*PA5: John 2F 9*
*(off High S*
Lomond Vw. G67: Cumb 6E 3
*G81: Clyd 4D 4*
*(off Church S*
ML3: Ham 1D 15
Lomond Wlk. ML1: N'hill 3C 12
*ML9: Lark 1F 16*
*(off Ashburn Loa*
Lomond Way *ML1: Holy 2A 12*
*(off Graham S*
London Dr. G32: Glas 3E 10
London La. *G1: Glas 5H 8*
*(off St Andrews S*
London Rd. G1: Glas 5H 8
G32: Glas 4A 10
G40: Glas 1D 10
London St. ML9: Lark 1E 16
PA4: Renf 4F 5
London Way G1: Glas 5H 8
Lonend PA1: Pais 1B 9
Longay Pl. G22: Glas 1G 6
Longay St. G22: Glas 1G 6
Long Calderwood Cotts.
*G74: E Kil 5C 13*
*(off Maxwellton Rd*
Long Crags Vw. G82: Dumb 1H 1
LONGCROFT 1G 1
Longcroft Dr. PA4: Renf 5E 5
Longden St. G81: Clyd 1F 5
Long Dr. G75: E Kil 4A 15
Longford St. G33: Glas 3F 8
Longlee G69: Bail 1H 10
Longmeadow PA5: John 4D 9
Longmorn Pl. ML1: Carf 6B 12
Long Row G66: Kirk 6H 3
G69: Bail 5A 8
Longstone Pl. G33: Glas 3B 8
Longstone Rd. G33: Glas 3B 8
Longwill Ter. G67: Cumb 1B 3
Lonsdale Av. G46: Giff 4A 11
Loom Wlk. PA10: Kilb 2A 9
(not continuou
Lora Dr. G52: Glas 1E 10
Lord Way G69: Barg 6D 8
Loretto Pl. G33: Glas 3H 8
Loretto St. G33: Glas 3H 8
Lorimer Cres. G75: E Kil 4F 14
Lorn Av. G69: Chry 1B 6
Lorne Ct. *G20: Glas 1E 8*
*(off Cedar S*
Lorne Cres. G64: B'rig 5F 4
Lorne Dr. ML1: Moth 5F 12
PA3: Lin 6G 7
Lorne Pl. ML5: Coat 6F 9
Lorne Rd. G52: Hill 3H 7
Lorne St. G51: Glas 5B 8
ML3: Ham 5G 14
Lorne Ter. G72: Camb 4H 12
Lorn Pl. G66: Kirk 4A 3
Lorraine Gdns. G12: Glas 5A 6
Lorraine Gdns. La. *G12: Glas 5A 6*
*(off Lorraine Gdns*
Lorraine Rd. G12: Glas 5A 6
Loskin Dr. G22: Glas 2F 6
Lossie Cres. PA4: Renf 1H 7
Lossie St. G33: Glas 2F 8
Lothian Cres. PA2: Pais 4H 9
Lothian Dr. G76: Clar 1B 13
Lothian Gdns. G20: Glas 6C 6
Lothian St. G52: Hill 3G 7
(not continuous
Lothian Way G74: E Kil 6C 13
Louden Hill Dr. G33: Glas 3G 6
Louden Hill Gdns. G33: Glas 3G 6
Louden Hill Pl. G33: Glas 3G 6
Louden Hill Rd. G33: Glas 3G 6
Louden Hill Way G33: Glas 3G 6
Louden St. ML6: Air 4A 9
Loudon G75: E Kil 6G 14
Loudon Gdns. PA5: John 2G 9
Loudonhill Av. ML3: Ham 3A 15
Loudon Rd. G33: Mille 5B 6
Loudon St. ML2: Wis 3H 14
Loudon Ter. *G61: Bear 6D 2*
*(off Grampian Wa*

Louise Gdns.—Main St.


)uise Gdns. ML1: Holy ... 2H 127
ouisville Av. ML2: Wis ... 4B 146
OUNSDALE ... 3E 97
)unsdale Av. PA2: Pais ... 2F 97
)unsdale Cres. PA2: Pais ... 3E 97
)unsdale Dr. PA2: Pais ... 3F 97
ounsdale Gro. PA2: Pais ... 2F 97
ounsdale Ho. PA2: Pais ... 4D 96
ounsdale Pl. G14: Glas ... 5B 60
ounsdale Rd. PA2: Pais ... 3F 97
)unsdale Way PA2: Pais ... 2F 97
ourdes Av. G52: Glas ... 1D 100
ourdes Ct. G52: Glas ... 1D 100
ovat Av. G61: Bear ... 6E 25
ovat Dr. G66: Kirk ... 5B 30
)vat Path *ML9: Lark ... 3G 161*
*(off Shawrigg Rd.)*
ovat Pl. G52: Hill ... 4G 79
G73: Ruth ... 3F 121
ove Av. PA11: Q'riers ... 1A 72
)ve St. PA3: Pais ... 5A 78
ow Barholm PA10: Kilb ... 3B 94
OW BLANTYRE ... 6C 124
ow Broadlie Rd. G78: Neil ... 1D 130
ow Craigends G65: Kils ... 3A 12
)w Cres. G81: Clyd ... 1G 59
wr. Admiralty Rd. G60: Old K ... 2F 41
wr. Auchingramont Rd.
ML3: Ham ... 5A 142
wr. Bourtree Dr. G73: Ruth ... 3E 121
ower Millgate G71: Udd ... 1D 124
wr. Mill Rd. G76: Busby ... 3D 134
ow Flender Rd. G76: Clar ... 4B 134
ow Moss Ind. Est. G64: B'rig ... 3E 49
owndes St. G78: Barr ... 5E 115
ow Parksail PA8: Ersk ... 1G 57
ow Parks Mus. ... 5A 142
ow Patrick St. ML3: Ham ... 6B 142
ow Pleasance ML9: Lark ... 2F 161
ow Quarry Gdns. ML3: Ham ... 1H 153
ow Rd. PA2: Pais ... 2G 97
owther Av. G61: Bear ... 6C 24
owther Ter. G12: Glas ... 5A 62
OW WATERS ... 2A 154
ow Waters Rd. ML3: Ham ... 3H 153
oyal Av. PA8: Ersk ... 6D 40
oyal Gdns. G61: Bear ... 6B 24
oyal Pl. PA8: Ersk ... 6D 40
oyne Dr. PA4: Renf ... 1H 79
uath St. G51: Glas ... 3G 81
ubas Av. G42: Glas ... 6H 103
ubas Pl. G42: Glas ... 6H 103
ubnaig Dr. PA8: Ersk ... 6D 40
ubnaig Gdns. G61: Bear ... 6C 24
ubnaig Pl. ML6: Air ... 1G 91
ubnaig Rd. G43: Glas ... 2C 118
ubnaig Wlk. ML1: Holy ... 2A 128
uckiesfauld G78: Neil ... 3D 130
uckingsford Av. PA4: Inch ... 2H 57
uckingsford Dr. PA4: Inch ... 2G 57
uckingsford Rd. PA4: Inch ... 2G 57
ucy Brae G71: Tann ... 5C 108
udovic Sq. PA5: John ... 2F 95
uffness Gdns. G32: Glas ... 3B 106
ugar Dr. G52: Glas ... 1E 101
ugar Pl. G44: Glas ... 2B 120
ugar St. ML5: Coat ... 3D 90
uggiebank Pl. G69: Barg ... 1E 109
uggiebank Rd. G66: Kirk ... 5D 30
(not continuous)
uggie Gro. G66: Kirk ... 6G 31
uggie Rd. ML8: Carl ... 3D 164
uggie Vw. G67: Cumb ... 6C 34
uing ML6: Air ... 5E 93
uing Rd. G52: Glas ... 6E 81
uma Gdns. G51: Glas ... 4C 80
UMLOCH ... 1G 65
umloch St. G21: Glas ... 5C 64
umsden La. *G3: Glas ... 2B 82*
*(off Lumsden St.)*
umsden St. G3: Glas ... 3B 82
unan Dr. G64: B'rig ... 1E 65
unan Pl. G51: Glas ... 4E 81
unar Path ML6: Chap ... 4D 112
uncarty Pl. G32: Glas ... 2A 106
uncarty St. G32: Glas ... 2A 106
underston Cl. G53: Glas ... 1B 116
underston Dr. G53: Glas ... 6A 100
underston Gdns. G53: Glas ... 1B 116
undie Gdns. G64: B'rig ... 1F 65
undie St. G32: Glas ... 2G 105
uss Brae ML3: Ham ... 1C 152
usset Glen G60: Old K ... 1F 41
ussett Rd. G60: Old K ... 1F 41
usset Vw. G81: Clyd ... 4D 42
usshill Ter. G71: Udd ... 3H 107
uss Rd. G51: Glas ... 4F 81
ybster Cres. G73: Ruth ... 4F 121
ye Brae G67: Cumb ... 3B 36
yell Gro. G74: E Kil ... 6G 137
Lyell Pl. G74: E Kil ... 6G 137
Lyle Cres. PA7: B'ton ... 3F 39
Lyle Pl. PA2: Pais ... 3B 98
Lyle Rd. ML6: Air ... 4F 93
Lyle's Land PA6: Hous ... 1B 74
Lylesland Ct. PA2: Pais ... 3A 98
Lyle Sq. G62: Miln ... 3E 25
(Hilton Rd.)
G62: Miln ... 3E 25
(Kelvin Rd.)
Lyman Dr. ML2: Wis ... 2A 146
Lymburn St. G3: Glas ... 3B 82
Lymekilns Rd. G74: E Kil ... 1F 149
Lyndale Pl. G20: Glas ... 1B 62
Lyndale Rd. G20: Glas ... 1B 62
Lyndhurst Gdns. G20: Glas ... 6D 62
Lyndhurst Gdns. La. *G20: Glas ... 6C 62*
*(off Lothian Gdns.)*
Lyne Cft. G64: B'rig ... 3C 48
Lynedoch Cres. G3: Glas ... 2D 82
Lynedoch Cres. La. *G3: Glas ... 2D 82*
*(off Woodlands Rd.)*
Lynedoch Pl. G3: Glas ... 2D 82
Lynedoch St. G3: Glas ... 2D 82
Lynedoch Ter. G3: Glas ... 2D 82
Lyne St. ML2: Wis ... 4G 145
Lynnburn Av. ML4: Bell ... 1C 126
Lynn Ct. ML9: Lark ... 3E 161
Lynn Dr. G62: Miln ... 3A 26
Lynne Dr. G23: Glas ... 6C 46
Lynnhurst G71: Tann ... 6D 108
Lynn Wlk. *G71: Udd ... 2E 125*
*(off Bellshill Rd.)*
Lynton Av. G46: Giff ... 6G 117
Lynwood Rd. ML2: Newm ... 3G 147
Lyoncross Av. G78: Barr ... 5F 115
Lyoncross Cres. G78: Barr ... 4F 115
Lyoncross Rd. G53: Glas ... 2B 100
Lyon Rd. PA2: Pais ... 4D 96
PA3: Lin ... 1H 95
PA8: Ersk ... 6C 40
Lyons Quad. ML2: Wis ... 5D 144
Lysander Way PA4: Renf ... 2F 79
Lysa Va. Pl. ML4: Bell ... 2A 126
Lytham Dr. G23: Glas ... 6C 46
Lytham Mdws. G71: Both ... 5C 124
Lyttelton G75: E Kil ... 5D 148


## M


Mabel St. ML1: Moth ... 4G 143
Macadam Gdns. ML4: Bell ... 1C 126
Macadam Pl. G75: E Kil ... 3G 14
Maleny Gro. G77: Newt M ... 6B 132
McAllister Av. ML6: Air ... 3D 92
McAlpine St. G2: Glas ... 4E 83 (6A 4)
ML2: Wis ... 1H 157
McArdle Av. ML1: Moth ... 2D 142
McArron Way *G67: Cumb ... 4H 35*
*(in Cumbernauld Shop. Cen.)*
Macarthur Av. ML6: Glenm ... 6F 71
Macarthur Ct. G74: E Kil ... 6E 137
Macarthur Cres. G74: E Kil ... 5E 137
(not continuous)
Macarthur Dr. G74: E Kil ... 6E 137
Macarthur Gdns. G74: E Kil ... 6E 137
McArthur Pk. G66: Kirk ... 6C 30
McArthur St. G43: Glas ... 6A 102
Macarthur Wynd G72: Camb ... 2C 122
McAslin Ct. G4: Glas ... 3H 83 (3H 5)
McAslin St. G4: Glas ... 3A 84 (3H 5)
Macbeth G74: E Kil ... 4B 138
Macbeth Pl. G31: Glas ... 1F 105
Macbeth St. G31: Glas ... 1F 105
McBride Av. G66: Kirk ... 6C 30
MacCabe Gdns. G66: Len ... 4H 7
McCallum Av. G73: Ruth ... 6D 104
McCallum Ct. G74: E Kil ... 5D 136
Maccallum Dr. G72: Camb ... 2C 122
McCallum Gdns. ML4: Bell ... 5B 126
McCallum Gro. G74: E Kil ... 5D 136
McCallum Pl. G74: E Kil ... 5D 136
McCallum Rd. ML9: Lark ... 4F 161
McCarrison Rd. ML2: Newm ... 3E 147
McCash Pl. G66: Kirk ... 6C 30
McCloy Gdns. G53: Glas ... 2H 115
McClue Av. PA4: Renf ... 6D 58
McClue Rd. PA4: Renf ... 5E 59
McClurg Ct. ML1: Moth ... 4G 143
McCormack Gdns. ML1: N'hill ... 3E 129
McCourt Gdns. *ML4: Moss ... 2E 127*
*(off Main St.)*
McCracken Av. PA4: Renf ... 1D 78
McCracken Dr. G71: View ... 5G 109
McCreery St. G81: Clyd ... 1F 59
Maccrimmon Pk. G74: E Kil ... 5D 136
McCrorie Pl. PA10: Kilb ... 2A 94
McCulloch Av. G71: View ... 1G 125
McCulloch St. G41: Glas ... 1D 102
McCulloch Way G78: Neil ... 2D 130
McCulloghs Wlk. G66: Len ... 3F 7
Macdairmid Dr. ML3: Ham ... 4F 153
Macdonald Av. G74: E Kil ... 5C 136
McDonald Av. PA5: John ... 4E 95
Macdonald Cres. G65: Twe ... 2D 32
McDonald Cres. G81: Clyd ... 1F 59
MacDonald Gro. ML4: Bell ... 5B 126
McDonald Pl. G78: Neil ... 2E 131
ML1: Holy ... 2A 128
Macdonald St. G73: Ruth ... 6C 104
ML1: Moth ... 4H 143
Macdougal Dr. G72: Camb ... 2C 122
Macdougall St. G43: Glas ... 6A 102
Macdougal Quad. ML4: Bell ... 5B 126
Macdowall St. PA3: Pais ... 5H 77
PA5: John ... 2F 95
Macduff PA8: Ersk ... 5E 41
Macduff Pl. G31: Glas ... 1F 105
Macduff St. G31: Glas ... 1F 105
Macedonian Gro. ML1: N'hill ... 3C 128
Mace Rd. G13: Glas ... 6C 44
McEwan Gdns. G74: E Kil ... 5C 136
Macfarlane Cres. G72: Camb ... 2C 122
Macfarlane Rd. G61: Bear ... 4G 45
McFarlane St. G40: Glas ... 5A 84
PA3: Pais ... 4G 77
Macfie Pl. G74: E Kil ... 5D 136
McGhee St. G81: Clyd ... 3D 42
McGowan Pl. ML3: Ham ... 4E 141
McGown St. PA3: Pais ... 5H 77
McGregor Av. ML6: Air ... 3D 92
PA4: Renf ... 1D 78
Macgregor Ct. G72: Camb ... 2C 122
McGregor Dr. G82: Dumb ... 1C 18
McGregor Path ML5: Glenb ... 3G 69
McGregor Rd. G67: Cumb ... 4G 35
McGregor St. G51: Glas ... 5F 81
G81: Clyd ... 1F 59
ML2: Wis ... 5D 144
McGrigor Rd. G62: Miln ... 2F 25
MACHAN ... 4F 161
Machan Av. ML9: Lark ... 2E 161
Machanhill ML9: Lark ... 2F 161
Machanhill Vw. ML9: Lark ... 3F 161
Machan Rd. ML9: Lark ... 3E 161
Machrie Dr. G45: Glas ... 3B 120
G77: Newt M ... 3E 133
Machrie Rd. G45: Glas ... 3A 120
Machrie St. G45: Glas ... 4A 120
ML1: Moth ... 2D 142
McInnes Ct. ML2: Wis ... 1H 157
McInnes Pl. ML2: Over ... 4H 157
McIntosh Ct. *G31: Glas ... 4B 84*
*(off McIntosh St.)*
McIntosh Pl. G31: Glas ... 4B 84
Macintosh Pl. G75: E Kil ... 4E 149
McIntosh Quad. ML4: Bell ... 5B 126
McIntosh St. G31: Glas ... 4B 84
McIntosh Way ML1: Moth ... 4E 143
McIntyre Pl. PA2: Pais ... 3A 98
Macintyre St. G3: Glas ... 4D 82
McIntyre Ter. G72: Camb ... 1A 122
McIver St. G72: Camb ... 1D 122
Macivor Cres. G74: E Kil ... 5C 136
McKay Ct. G77: Newt M ... 5C 132
McKay Cres. PA5: John ... 3G 95
McKay Gro. ML4: Bell ... 2B 126
McKay Pl. G74: E Kil ... 5C 136
G77: Newt M ... 5C 132
MacKean St. PA3: Pais ... 5G 77
McKechnie St. G51: Glas ... 3G 81
MacKeith St. G40: Glas ... 1B 104
McKenna Dr. ML6: Air ... 4G 91
McKenzie Av. G81: Clyd ... 3D 42
Mackenzie Dr. PA10: Kilb ... 4B 94
Mackenzie Gdns. G74: E Kil ... 5C 136
McKenzie St. PA3: Pais ... 6G 77
Mackenzie Ter. ML4: Bell ... 6C 110
McKeown Gdns. ML4: Bell ... 3F 127
McKerrell St. PA1: Pais ... 6C 78
Mackie's Mill Rd. PA5: Eld ... 5B 96
MacKinlay Pl. G77: Newt M ... 5D 132
Mackinlay St. G5: Glas ... 1F 103
MacKinnon Mills ML5: Coat ... 2C 110
Mack St. ML6: Air ... 3A 92
McLaren Ct. G46: Giff ... 6H 117
McLaren Cres. G20: Glas ... 2C 62
McLaren Dr. ML4: Bell ... 3F 127
McLaren Gro. G74: E Kil ... 5C 136
McLaren Pl. G44: Neth ... 5D 118
McLaurin Cres. PA5: John ... 4D 94
Maclay Av. PA10: Kilb ... 3A 94
McLean Av. PA4: Renf ... 2E 79
Maclean Ct. G74: E Kil ... 5D 136
McLean Dr. ML4: Bell ... 5B 126
Maclean Gro. G74: E Kil ... 5D 136
Maclean Pl. *G67: Cumb ... 6C 34*
*(off Airdrie Rd.)*
McLean Pl. PA3: Pais ... 4H 77
Maclean Rd. G74: E Kil ... 5D 136
G78: Neil ... 3E 131
Maclean Sq. G51: Glas ... 5B 82
Maclean St. G51: Glas ... 5B 82
Mclean St. *G81: Clyd ... 1G 59*
*(off Wood Quad.)*
McLees La. ML1: Moth ... 2D 142
Maclehose Rd. G67: Cumb ... 2C 36
McLelland Dr. ML6: Plain ... 1H 93
Maclellan St. G41: Glas ... 6B 82
Mclennan Galleries ... 3F 83 (3C 4)
McLennan St. G42: Glas ... 5F 103
Macleod Pl. G74: E Kil ... 6B 138
McLeod Rd. G82: Dumb ... 1C 18
Macleod St. G4: Glas ... 4A 84 (5H 5)
Macleod Way G72: Camb ... 2C 122
McMahon Dr. ML2: Newm ... 3E 147
McMahon Gro. ML4: Bell ... 1D 126
Macmillan Gdns. G71: Tann ... 5E 109
McMillan Rd. ML2: Wis ... 1D 156
Macmillan St. ML9: Lark ... 3D 160
McMillan Way ML8: Law ... 6D 158
McNair St. G32: Glas ... 6A 86
McNeil Av. G81: Clyd ... 6G 43
McNeil Dr. ML1: Holy ... 6G 111
McNeil Gdns. G5: Glas ... 1H 103
Macneill Dr. G74: E Kil ... 5D 136
Macneill Gdns. G74: E Kil ... 5D 136
Macneill St. ML9: Lark ... 2D 160
McNeil Pl. ML2: Over ... 4A 158
McNeil St. G5: Glas ... 1H 103
Macneish Way G74: E Kil ... 5D 136
Macnicol Ct. G74: E Kil ... 5C 136
Macnicol Pk. G74: E Kil ... 5C 136
Macnicol Pl. G74: E Kil ... 5C 136
McPhail St. G40: Glas ... 1A 104
McPhater St. G4: Glas ... 2F 83 (2D 4)
McPherson Cres. ML6: Chap ... 4E 113
McPherson Dr. G71: Both ... 4F 125
Macpherson Pk. G74: E Kil ... 6E 137
McPherson St. G1: Glas ... 5H 83 (6G 5)
ML4: Moss ... 2F 127
Macphie Rd. G82: Dumb ... 1C 18
Macquisten Bri. G41: Glas ... 6B 102
Macrae Ct. *PA5: John ... 4E 95*
*(off Tannahill Cres.)*
Macrae Gdns. G74: E Kil ... 6E 137
Macrimmon Pl. G75: E Kil ... 3G 149
McShannon Gro. ML4: Bell ... 4C 126
McSparran Rd. G65: Croy ... 1B 34
MacTaggart Rd. G67: Cumb ... 5G 35
Madison Av. G44: Glas ... 2F 119
Madison La. G44: Glas ... 2F 119
Madison Pl. G72: Blan ... 2B 140
Madras Pl. G40: Glas ... 2B 104
G78: Neil ... 2E 131
Madras St. G40: Glas ... 2B 104
Mafeking St. G51: Glas ... 5H 81
ML2: Wis ... 5D 144
Mafeking Ter. G78: Neil ... 2C 130
Magdalen Way PA2: Pais ... 6B 96
Magna St. ML1: Moth ... 1D 142
Magnolia Dr. G72: Flem ... 4F 123
Magnolia Gdns. ML1: N'hill ... 4C 128
Magnolia Pl. G71: View ... 5G 109
Magnolia St. ML2: Wis ... 4H 145
Magnus Cres. G44: Glas ... 3F 119
Magnus Rd. PA6: C'lee ... 3C 74
Mahon Ct. G69: Mood ... 6D 52
Maidens G74: E Kil ... 6F 137
Maidens Av. G77: Newt M ... 4G 133
Maidland Rd. G53: Glas ... 5C 100
Mailerbeg Gdns. G69: Mood ... 4D 52
Mailie Wlk. ML1: N'hill ... 4C 128
Mailing Av. G64: B'rig ... 5D 48
Mainhead Ter. G67: Cumb ... 6B 14
Mainhill Av. G69: Bail ... 6B 88
Mainhill Dr. G69: Bail ... 6A 88
Mainhill Pl. G69: Bail ... 5B 88
Mainhill Rd. G69: Barg ... 6C 88
Main Rd. G67: Cumb ... 2B 54
PA2: Pais ... 1H 97
PA5: Eld ... 3H 95
Mains Av. G46: Giff ... 6H 117
Mains Castle ... 4F 137
Mainscroft PA8: Ersk ... 6G 41
Mains Dr. PA8: Ersk ... 6G 41
Mains Hill PA8: Ersk ... 6F 41
Mainshill Av. PA8: Ersk ... 6F 41
Mainshill Gdns. PA8: Ersk ... 6F 41
Mains Pl. ML4: Bell ... 4C 126
Mains River PA8: Ersk ... 6G 41
Mains Rd. G74: E Kil ... 6G 137
G74: E Kil, Ners ... 4G 137
Main St. G40: Glas ... 2B 104
G46: T'bnk ... 4F 117
G62: Miln ... 4G 25
(not continuous)
G64: Torr ... 5D 28
G65: Kils ... 2H 11

Main St. —Maybole Pl.


**Main St.** G65: Twe 1D 32
G66: Len 3F 7
G67: Cumb 6B 14
G69: Bail 1H 107
G69: Chry 1A 68
G71: Both 5E 125
G71: Udd 1D 124
G72: Blan 3H 139
G72: Camb 1A 122
G73: Ruth 5C 104
G74: E Kil 1H 149
G76: Busby 3D 134
G78: Barr 5D 114
G78: Neil 2D 130
ML1: Cle 1H 145
ML1: Holy 2A 128
ML2: Newm 6E 147
ML2: Over 5A 158
ML2: Wis 5F 145
ML4: Bell 2B 126
ML5: Coat 4C 90
(not continuous)
ML5: Glenb 3H 69
ML6: C'bnk 2C 112
ML6: Chap 2E 113
ML6: Plain 1G 93
PA11: Bri W 3F 73
PA6: Hous 1A 74
**Mains Wood** PA8: Ersk 6H 41
**Mair St.** G51: Glas 5C 82
**Maitland Bank** ML9: Lark 2G 161
**Maitland Dr.** G64: Torr 4D 28
**Maitland Pl.** PA4: Renf 1D 78
**Maitland St.** G4: Glas 2F 83 (1D 4)
**Malcolm Gdns.** G74: E Kil 1E 149
**Malcolm St.** ML1: Moth 3E 143
**Maleny Gro.** G77: Newt M 6B 132
**Mal Fleming's Brae**
G65: Kils 4B 12
**Malin Pl.** G33: Glas 3H 85
**Mallaig Path** *G51: Glas 4D 80*
*(off Mallaig Rd.)*
**Mallaig Pl.** G51: Glas 4D 80
**Mallaig Rd.** G51: Glas 4D 80
**Mallard Cres.** G75: E Kil 6C 148
**Mallard La.** G71: Both 4E 125
**Mallard Pl.** G75: E Kil 6C 148
**Mallard Rd.** G81: Hard 2D 42
**Mallard Ter.** G75: E Kil 6C 148
**Mallard Way** ML4: Bell 4B 110
**Malleable Gdns.** ML1: Moth 5E 127
**MALLETSHEUGH** 5B 132
**Malletsheugh Rd.**
G77: Newt M 6A 132
(not continuous)
**Malloch Cres.** PA5: Eld 3H 95
**Malloch Pl.** G74: E Kil 1B 150
**Malloch St.** G20: Glas 4C 62
**Mallotts Vw.** G77: Newt M 6B 132
**Malov Ct.** G75: E Kil 6G 149
**Malplaquet Ct.** ML8: Carl 4H 165
**Malta Ter.** G5: Glas 1F 103
**Maltbarns St.** G20: Glas 6E 63
**Malvaig La.** G72: Blan 3A 140
**Malvern Ct.** G31: Glas 5C 84
**Malvern Way** PA3: Pais 3H 77
**Mambeg Dr.** G51: Glas 3E 81
**Mamore Pl.** G43: Glas 1A 118
**Mamore St.** G43: Glas 1A 118
**Manchester Dr.** G12: Glas 3G 61
**M & D's Theme Pk.**
6A 126
**Mandora Ct.** ML8: Carl 4H 165
**Manitoba Cres.** G75: E Kil 2D 148
**Mannering** G74: E Kil 5D 138
**Mannering Ct.** G41: Glas 5A 102
**Mannering Rd.** G41: Glas 5A 102
PA2: Pais 6C 96
**Mannering Way** PA2: Pais 5C 96
**Mannoch Pl.** ML5: Coat 2F 111
**Mannofield** G61: Bear 3D 44
**Manor Dr.** ML6: Air 3G 91
**Manor Ga.** G77: Newt M 6F 133
**Manor Pk.** ML3: Ham 1H 153
**Manor Pk. Av.** PA2: Pais 4F 97
**Manor Rd.** G14: Glas 5E 61
G15: Glas 6H 43
G69: G'csh 4D 68
PA2: Pais 4D 96
**Manor Vw.** ML6: C'bnk 3B 112
ML9: Lark 3G 161
**Manor Way** G73: Ruth 3E 121
**Manresa Pl.** G4: Glas 1F 83
**Manse Av.** G61: Bear 2F 45
G71: Both 5E 125
ML5: Coat 1H 109
**Manse Brae** G44: Glas 1F 119
G72: Flem 5F 123
ML9: Ashg, Dals 6D 162
**Manse Bri.** ML8: Carl 4G 165
**Manse Ct.** G65: Kils 4H 11
G78: Barr 4F 115
ML8: Law 1A 164
**Manse Cres.** PA6: Hous 1B 74
**Mansefield Av.** G72: Camb 3A 122
**Mansefield Cres.** G60: Old K 6E 21
G76: Clar 3B 134
**Mansefield Dr.** G71: Udd 1D 124
**Mansefield Rd.** G76: Clar 3C 134
ML3: Ham 5H 153
**Manse Gdns.** G32: Glas 1D 106
**Manse La.** G74: E Kil 6H 137
**Mansel St.** G21: Glas 4B 64
**Manse Pl.** ML6: Air 4A 92
**Manse Rd.** G32: Glas 1D 106
G60: Bowl 5B 20
G61: Bear 2E 45
G65: Kils 4H 11
G69: Barg 5C 88
G76: Crmck 2H 135
G78: Neil 2D 130
ML1: Moth 1G 155
ML2: Newm 5D 146
**Manse Rd. Gdns.** G61: Bear 2F 45
**Manse St.** ML5: Coat 5B 90
PA4: Renf 5F 59
**Manse Vw.** ML1: N'hill 3F 129
ML9: Lark 3F 161
**MANSEWOOD** 2A 118
**Mansewood Dr.** G82: Dumb 2H 17
**Mansewood Rd.** G43: Glas 1H 117
**Mansfield Rd.** G52: Hill 4H 79
ML4: Bell 3B 126
**Mansfield St.** G11: Glas 1A 82
**Mansion Ct.** G72: Camb 1A 122
**Mansionhouse Av.** G32: Carm 5C 106
**Mansionhouse Dr.** G32: Glas 5C 86
**Mansionhouse Gdns.**
G41: Glas 6C 102
**Mansionhouse Gro.** G32: Glas 2E 107
**Mansionhouse Rd.** G32: Glas 1E 107
G41: Glas 6C 102
PA1: Pais 6C 78
**Mansion St.** G22: Glas 4G 63
G72: Camb 1A 122
**Manson Pl.** G75: E Kil 6B 150
**Manus Duddy Ct.** G72: Blan 1B 140
**Maple Av.** G66: Milt C 6B 8
G77: Newt M 5D 132
G82: Dumb 2B 16
**Maple Bank** ML3: Ham 1B 154
**Maple Ct.** G67: Cumb 6F 15
*ML5: Coat 1B 110*
*(off Ailsa Rd.)*
**Maple Cres.** G72: Flem 4F 123
**Maple Dr.** G66: Lenz 2A 50
G78: Barr 6F 115
G81: Clyd 2B 42
ML9: Lark 6A 156
PA5: John 5F 95
**Maple Gro.** G75: E Kil 6D 148
**Maple Pl.** FK4: Bank 1E 15
G71: View 5H 109
G75: E Kil 5D 148
PA5: John 5G 95
**Maple Quad.** ML6: Air 5D 92
**Maple Rd.** G41: Glas 1H 101
G67: Cumb 6F 15
ML1: Holy 2B 128
**Maple Ter.** G75: E Kil 5D 148
**Maple Wlk.** G66: Milt C 6B 8
**Maple Way** G72: Blan 2A 140
**Maplewood** ML2: Wis 2D 156
**Mar Av.** PA7: B'ton 4H 39
**Marchbank Gdns.** PA1: Pais 1F 99
**Marchfield** G64: B'rig 4A 48
**Marchfield Av.** PA3: Pais 3H 77
**Marchglen Pl.** G51: Glas 4D 80
**Marchmont Gdns.** G64: B'rig 4B 48
**Marchmont Ter.** *G12: Glas 6A 62*
*(off Observatory Rd.)*
**March St.** G41: Glas 3D 102
**Mardale** G74: E Kil 6E 137
**Mar Dr.** G61: Bear 6F 25
**Maree Dr.** G52: Glas 1E 101
G67: Cumb 6D 34
**Maree Gdns.** G64: B'rig 6D 48
**Maree Rd.** PA2: Pais 3E 97
**Maree Wlk.** *ML2: Newm 3D 146*
*(off Banavie Rd.)*
**Maree Way** G72: Blan 1B 140
**Marfield St.** G32: Glas 4G 85
**Mar Gdns.** G73: Ruth 3F 121
**Margaret Av.** FK4: Hag 1G 15
**Margaret Pl.** ML4: Bell 2A 126
**Margaret Rd.** ML3: Ham 3F 141
**Margaret's Pl.** ML9: Lark 2E 161
**Margaret St.** ML5: Coat 1C 110
**Margaretta Bldgs.** G44: Glas 1E 119
**Margaretvale Dr.** ML9: Lark 3E 161
**Marguerite Av.** G66: Lenz 1C 50
**Marguerite Dr.** G66: Lenz 1C 50
**Marguerite Gdns.** G66: Lenz 1C 50
G71: Both 5F 125
**Marguerite Gro.** G66: Lenz 1C 50
**Marguerite Pl.** G66: Milt C 5B 8
**Marian Dr.** ML1: Carf 5C 128
**Maric La.** ML6: Plain 1G 93
**Marigold Av.** ML1: Moth 1G 143
**Marigold Way** ML8: Carl 5F 165
**Marina Ct.** ML4: Bell 4B 126
**Marine Cres.** G51: Glas 5C 82
**Marine Gdns.** G51: Glas 5C 82
**Mariner Ct.** G81: Clyd 5C 42
**Marion St.** ML4: Moss 2F 127
**Mariscat Rd.** G41: Glas 3C 102
**Marjory Dr.** PA3: Pais 4C 78
**Marjory Rd.** PA4: Renf 2C 78
**Markdow Av.** G53: Glas 4A 100
**Market Cl.** G65: Kils 3H 11
**Market Ct.** *G65: Kils 3H 11*
*(off Market St.)*
**Markethill Rd.** G74: E Kil, Roger 3F 137
(not continuous)
**MARKETHILL RDBT.** 6G 137
**Market Pl.** G65: Kils 3H 11
G71: View 6G 109
ML8: Carl 3F 165
**Market Rd.** G66: Kirk 6G 31
G71: View 6G 109
ML8: Carl 3F 165
**Market Sq.** G65: Kils 3H 11
**Market St.** G65: Kils 3H 11
G71: View 6G 109
ML6: Air 4A 92
**Marlach Pl.** G53: Glas 5A 100
**Marlborough Av.** G11: Glas 6F 61
**Marlborough La. Nth.** G11: Glas 6F 61
**Marlborough La. Sth.** *G11: Glas 6F 61*
*(off Broomhill Dr.)*
*G52: Hill 4B 80*
*(off Nasmyth Rd. Nth.)*
**Marlborough Pk.** G75: E Kil 4C 148
**Marldon La.** G11: Glas 6F 61
**Marley Way** G66: Milt C 5B 8
**Marlfield Gdns.** ML4: Bell 6C 110
**Marlow St.** G41: Glas 1C 102
**Marlow Ter.** G41: Glas 1C 102
**Marmion Ct.** PA2: Pais 5D 96
**Marmion Cres.** ML1: Moth 5F 127
**Marmion Dr.** G66: Kirk 5F 31
**Marmion Pl.** G67: Cumb 6G 35
**Marmion Rd.** G67: Cumb 6G 35
PA2: Pais 5C 96
**Marne St.** G31: Glas 4D 84
**Marnoch Dr.** ML5: Glenb 2H 69
**Marnoch Way** G69: Mood 5D 52
**MARNOCK** 3G 69
**Marnock Ter.** PA2: Pais 2C 98
**Marquis Ga.** G71: Both 2C 124
**Marrswood Grn.** ML3: Ham 5E 141
**Marshall Gro.** ML3: Ham 6F 141
**Marshall La.** ML2: Wis 6G 145
**Marshall's La.** PA1: Pais 1A 98
**Marshall St.** ML2: Wis 1F 157
ML9: Lark 2E 161
**Martha Pl.** ML9: Lark 3F 161
**Martha St.** G1: Glas 3G 83 (4F 5)
**Martin Ct.** ML3: Ham 6G 141
**Martin Cres.** G69: Bail 6A 88
**Martin Pl.** ML1: N'hill 4C 128
**Martinside** G75: E Kil 6G 149
**Martin St.** G40: Glas 2B 104
ML5: Coat 4F 91
**Martlet Dr.** PA5: John 6C 94
**Mart St.** G1: Glas 5G 83
(not continuous)
**Martyn St.** ML6: Air 4G 91
**Martyrs Pl.** G64: B'rig 1C 64
**Marwick St.** G31: Glas 4D 84
**Mary Dr.** ML4: Bell 4A 126
**Mary Fisher Cres.** G82: Dumb 3C 18
**Mary Glen** ML2: Wis 4B 146
**MARYHILL** 1A 62
**Maryhill Rd.** G20: Glas 3B 62 (1A 4)
G61: Bear 5F 45
**Maryhill Shop. Cen.** G20: Glas 4C 62
**Maryhill Station (Rail)** 1A 62
**Maryknowe Rd.** ML1: Carf 5C 128
**Maryland Dr.** G52: Glas 6E 81
**Maryland Gdns.** G52: Glas 6E 81
**Maryland Rd.** G82: Dumb 1H 17
**Mary Rae Rd.** ML4: Bell 4A 126
**Mary Sq.** G69: Barg 6D 88
**Maryston St.** G33: Glas 1F 85
**Mary St.** ML3: Ham 1G 153
PA2: Pais 3A 98
PA5: John 2G 95
**Maryville Av.** G46: Giff 5A 118
**Maryville Gdns.** G46: Giff 5A 118
**MARYVILLE INTERCHANGE** 5A 1
**Maryville La.** G71: Tann 5B 10
**Maryville Vw.** G71: Tann 4B 10
**Marywood Sq.** G41: Glas 3D 10
**Mary Young Pl.** G76: Busby 3D 13
**Masonfield Av.** G68: Cumb 3F 3
**Mason La.** ML1: Moth 3G 14
(not continuou
**Mason St.** ML1: Moth 3G 14
ML9: Lark 4G 16
**Masterton Pl.** G21: Glas 6G 6
**Masterton Way** G71: Tann 4F 10
**Matherton Av.** G77: Newt M 4H 13
**Mathieson Rd.** G73: Ruth 4E 10
**Mathieson St.** PA1: Pais 6D 7
**Matilda Rd.** G41: Glas 2C 10
**Matthew McWhirter Pl.**
ML9: Lark 1F 16
**Mauchline** G74: E Kil 6D 13
**Mauchline Av.** G66: Kirk 3G 3
**Mauchline Ct.** G66: Kirk 3G 3
ML3: Ham 1B 15
**Mauchline St.** G5: Glas 1E 10
**Maukinfauld Ct.** G32: Glas 2F 10
**Maukinfauld Gdns.** G31: Glas 1G 10
**Maukinfauld Rd.** G32: Glas 2G 10
**Mauldslie Dr.** ML8: Law 5D 15
**Mauldslie Pl.** ML9: Ashg 5B 16
**Mauldslie Rd.** ML8: Carl 2F 16
**Mauldslie St.** G40: Glas 1D 10
ML4: Bell 3C 12
ML5: Coat 6C 9
**Maule Dr.** G11: Glas 1G 8
**Mausoleum Dr.** ML3: Ham 4A 14
**Mavis Bank** G64: B'rig 1B 6
G72: Blan 2A 14
**Mavisbank Gdns.** G51: Glas 5C 8
ML4: Bell 1C 12
**Mavisbank Rd.** G51: Glas 4B 8
**Mavisbank St.** ML2: Newm 4G 14
ML6: Air 3G 9
**Mavisbank Ter.** PA1: Pais 2B 9
PA5: John 3F 9
**Mavis Valley Rd.**
G64: B'rig 3A 4
**Mavor Av.** G74: E Kil 5H 13
**MAVOR RDBT.** 5H 13
**Maxton Av.** G78: Barr 4C 11
**Maxton Cres.** ML2: Wis 3A 14
**Maxton Gro.** G78: Barr 5C 11
**Maxton Ter.** G72: Camb 4H 12
**Maxwell Av.** G41: Glas 1C 10
G61: Bear 4E 4
G69: Bail 1G 10
**Maxwell Ct.** G41: Glas 1C 10
**Maxwell Cres.** G72: Blan 3B 14
**Maxwell Dr.** G41: Glas 1A 10
G69: Bail 6F 8
G74: E Kil 1H 14
PA8: Ersk 4D 4
**Maxwell Gdns.** G41: Glas 1B 10
**Maxwell Gro.** G41: Glas 1B 10
**Maxwell La.** G41: Glas 1C 10
**Maxwell Oval** G41: Glas 1D 10
**Maxwell Park Station (Rail)**
3B 10
**Maxwell Path** *ML9: Lark 3G 16*
*(off Keir Hardie Rd.)*
**Maxwell Pl.** G41: Glas 2E 10
G65: Kils 2H 1
G71: Udd 1E 12
ML5: Coat 6B 9
PA11: Bri W 3F 7
**Maxwell Rd.** G41: Glas 1D 10
PA7: B'ton 4H 3
**Maxwell St.** G1: Glas 4G 83 (6E 5
(Argyle St
G1: Glas 5G 8
(Broomielaw
G69: Bail 1H 10
G81: Clyd 3B 4
PA3: Pais 6A 7
**Maxwell Ter.** G41: Glas 1C 10
**Maxwellton Av.** G74: E Kil 1A 15
**Maxwellton Ct.** PA1: Pais 1G 9
**Maxwellton Pl.** G74: E Kil 6B 13
**Maxwellton Rd.** G74: E Kil 6B 13
PA1: Pais 1F 9
**Maxwellton St.** PA1: Pais 1G 9
**Maxwelton Rd.** G33: Glas 1F 8
**Maybank La.** G42: Glas 4E 10
**Maybank St.** G42: Glas 4E 10
**Mayberry Cres.** G32: Glas 6D 8
**Mayberry Gdns.** G32: Glas 6D 8
**Mayberry Gro.** G32: Glas 6D 8
**Mayberry Pl.** G72: Blan 1B 14
**Maybole Cres.** G77: Newt M 5G 13
**Maybole Gdns.** ML3: Ham 1B 15
**Maybole Gro.** G77: Newt M 5G 13
**Maybole Pl.** ML5: Coat 2F 11

Maybole St.—Millgate Rd.

aybole St. G53: Glas 1H 115
ayfield Av. G76: Clar 2C 134
ayfield Gdns. ML8: Carl 6G 165
ayfield Pl. ML5: Coat 2C 110
ML8: Carl 6G 165
ayfield Rd. ML3: Ham 5D 140
ayfield St. G20: Glas 4D 62
ay Gdns. ML3: Ham 4G 141
ay Rd. PA2: Pais 6A 98
ay St. ML3: Ham 4H 141
ay Ter. G42: Glas 5F 103
G46: Giff 4A 118
eadow Av. G72: Blan 3B 140
eadowbank La. G71: Udd 1C 124
eadowbank Pl.
G77: Newt M 4D 132
eadowbank St. G82: Dumb 3E 17
(not continuous)
eadowburn G64: B'rig 3C 48
eadowburn Av. G66: Lenz 2E 51
G77: Newt M 4D 132
eadowburn Rd. ML2: Wis 6A 146
eadow Ct. G82: Dumb 2F 17
eadowfield Pl. ML2: Newm 3G 147
eadowhead Av. G69: Mood 5D 52
eadowhead Rd. ML2: Wis 5C 144
(not continuous)
eadowhead Rd. ML6: Plain 1F 93
EADOWHILL 2F 161
eadowhill G77: Newt M 4D 132
eadowhill St. ML9: Lark 2F 161
eadow La. G71: Both 5F 125
PA4: Renf 4F 59
eadowpark St. G31: Glas 4D 84
(not continuous)
eadow Path ML6: Chap 4D 112
eadow Rd. G11: Glas 1G 81
G82: Dumb 3F 17
ML1: Moth 4H 143
eadows Av. ML9: Lark 2F 161
PA8: Ersk 6G 41
eadows Dr. PA8: Ersk 6G 41
eadow Side ML3: Ham 5H 153
eadowside Av. PA5: Eld 3B 96
eadowside Gdns. ML6: Air 4D 92
eadowside Ind. Est.
PA4: Renf 3F 59
eadowside Pl. ML6: Air 4D 92
eadowside Quay Sq.
G11: Kils 2G 81
eadowside Quay Wlk.
G11: Glas 2F 81
eadowside Rd. G65: Queen 3C 10
eadowside St. G11: Glas 2G 81
PA4: Renf 4F 59
eadow Sports Cen. 3F 17
eadows, The PA6: Hous 2D 74
eadow St. ML5: Coat 1D 110
eadow Vw. G67: Cumb 1C 36
ML6: Plain 1G 93
eadow Wlk. ML5: Coat 5D 90
eadow Way G77: Newt M 4D 132
eadowwell St. G32: Glas 6B 86
eadside Av. PA10: Kilb 1A 94
eadside Rd. PA10: Kilb 1A 94
ealkirk St. G81: Faif 6E 23
EARNS 6E 133
EARNS CASTLE 6G 133
earns Castle 6G 133
earns Ct. ML3: Ham 4A 154
earnscroft Gdns.
G77: Newt M 6F 133
earnscroft Rd. G77: Newt M 6F 133
earnskirk Rd. G77: Newt M 6D 132
earns Rd. G76: Clar 3H 133
earns Rd. G77: Newt M 6E 133
ML1: Moth 1E 143
earns Way G64: B'rig 5F 49
edlar Ct. G72: Flem 4F 123
edlar Rd. G67: Cumb 3D 36
edrox Gdns. G67: Cumb 2B 54
edwin Ct. G75: E Kil 4A 148
edwin Gdns. G75: E Kil 4A 148
edwin St. G72: Camb 2D 122
edwyn St. G14: Glas 6D 60
(not continuous)
eek Pl. G72: Camb 2B 122
eetinghouse La. PA1: Pais 6A 78
egan Ga. G40: Glas 1B 104
egan St. G40: Glas 1B 104
eigle Rd. ML6: Air 1H 111
eikle Av. PA4: Renf 1E 79
eikle Bin Brae G66: Len 3G 7
eikle Cres. ML3: Ham 4G 153
EIKLE EARNOCK 4G 153
eikle Earnock Rd.
ML3: Ham 5D 152
eiklehill Ct. G66: Kirk 4E 31
(not continuous)
eiklehill Rd. G66: Kirk 4E 31
Meiklem St. ML4: Moss 2E 127
Meiklerig Cres. G53: Glas 3C 100
MEIKLERIGGS 3F 97
Meikleriggs Ct. PA2: Pais 3F 97
Meikleriggs Dr. PA2: Pais 4E 97
Meikle Rd. G53: Glas 5C 100
Meiklewood Rd. G51: Glas 5D 80
(not continuous)
Melbourne Av. G75: E Kil 4E 149
G81: Clyd 2H 41
Melbourne Ct. G46: Giff 4B 118
Melbourne Grn. G75: E Kil 3E 149
Melbourne St. G31: Glas 5B 84
Meldon Pl. G51: Glas 4D 80
Meldrum Gdns. G41: Glas 3B 102
Meldrum Mains ML6: Glenm 5G 71
Meldrum St. G81: Clyd 1F 59
Melford Av. G46: Giff 5B 118
G66: Kirk 5B 30
Melford Ct. G81: Clyd 5E 43
Melford Rd. ML4: Bell 1H 125
Melford Way PA3: Pais 3D 78
Melfort Av. G41: Glas 1H 101
G81: Clyd 4D 42
Melfort Gdns. PA10: John 4C 94
Melfort Path ML2: Newm 2D 146
(off Kildonan Ct.)
Melfort Quad. ML1: N'hill 4D 128
(off Glenmore Rd.)
Melfort Rd. ML3: Ham 6C 140
Mellerstain Dr. G14: Glas 3G 59
Mellerstain Gro. G14: Glas 3H 59
Melness Pl. G51: Glas 4D 80
Melrose Av. G69: Barg 6D 88
G73: Ruth 6D 104
ML1: Holy 1B 128
ML6: Chap 3D 112
PA2: Pais 4E 97
PA3: Lin 6H 75
Melrose Ct. G73: Ruth 6D 104
(off Dunard Rd.)
Melrose Cres. ML2: Wis 4G 145
Melrose Gdns. G20: Glas 6D 62
G65: Twe 1C 32
(off Glen Shirva Rd.)
G71: Tann 4D 108
Melrose Pl. G72: Blan 6A 124
ML5: Coat 4B 90
ML9: Lark 4E 161
Melrose Rd. G67: Cumb 6G 35
Melrose St. G4: Glas 1A 4
ML3: Ham 4F 141
Melrose Ter. G74: E Kil 6H 137
ML3: Ham 3F 141
Melvaig Pl. G20: Glas 4B 62
Melvick Pl. G51: Glas 4D 80
Melville Ct. G1: Glas 6F 5
Melville Cres. ML1: Moth 3H 143
Melville Dr. ML1: Moth 3G 143
Melville Gdns. G64: B'rig 5C 48
Melville Pk. G74: E Kil 6B 138
Melville Pl. ML8: Carl 3E 165
Melville St. G41: Glas 2D 102
Memel St. G21: Glas 4A 64
Memus Av. G52: Glas 1C 100
Mennock Ct. ML3: Ham 1C 152
Mennock Dr. G64: B'rig 3C 48
Mennock St. ML1: Cle 5H 129
Menock Rd. G44: Glas 1F 119
Menteith Av. G64: B'rig 6D 48
Menteith Dr. G73: Ruth 5F 121
Menteith Gdns. G61: Bear 5C 24
Menteith Loan ML1: Holy 2A 128
Menteith Pl. G73: Ruth 5F 121
Menteith Rd. ML1: Moth 2G 143
Menzies Dr. G21: Glas 4C 64
Menzies Pl. G21: Glas 4C 64
Menzies Rd. G21: Glas 3D 64
Merchant La. G1: Glas 5G 83
Merchants Cl. PA10: Kilb 2A 94
Merchants Ho. 5E 5
Merchiston Av. PA3: Lin 6F 75
Merchiston Dr. PA5: Brkfld 6D 74
Merchiston St. G32: Glas 4G 85
Merkins Av. G82: Dumb 1H 17
MERKLAND 4G 31
Merkland Ct. G11: Glas 2H 81
G66: Kirk 4F 31
Merkland Dr. G66: Kirk 4G 31
Merkland Pl. G66: Kirk 4F 31
Merkland Rd. ML5: Coat 1G 89
Merkland St. G11: Glas 1H 81
Merksworth Way PA3: Pais 4A 78
(off Mosslands Rd.)
Merlewood Av. G71: Both 3F 125
Merlin Av. ML4: Bell 6C 110
Merlinford Av. PA4: Renf 6G 59
Merlinford Cres.
PA4: Renf 6G 59
Merlinford Dr. PA4: Renf 6G 59
Merlinford Way PA4: Renf 6G 59
Merlin Way PA3: Pais 4D 78
Merrick Ct. ML6: Air 1B 92
Merrick Gdns. G51: Glas 6H 81
G61: Bear 6C 24
Merrick Path G51: Glas 6H 81
(off Merrick Gdns.)
Merrick Ter. G71: View 6F 109
Merrick Way G73: Ruth 4D 120
Merryburn Av. G46: Giff 2B 118
Merrycrest Av. G46: Giff 3A 118
Merrycroft Av. G46: Giff 3B 118
Merryflats G65: Twe 1D 32
Merryland Pl. G51: Glas 4H 81
Merryland St. G51: Glas 4H 81
(not continuous)
MERRYLEE 3B 118
Merrylee Cres. G46: Giff 2A 118
Merrylee Pk. Av. G46: Giff 3A 118
Merrylee Pk. M. G46: Giff 2A 118
Merrylee Rd. G43: Glas 2B 118
G44: Glas 2D 118
Merrylees Rd. G72: Blan 2A 140
Merryston Ct. ML5: Coat 5A 90
Merrystone St. ML5: Coat 4B 90
Merry St. ML1: Carf 6B 128
ML1: Moth 2G 143
(not continuous)
Merryton Av. G15: Glas 4B 44
G46: Giff 3A 118
Merryton Gdns. G15: Glas 4B 44
Merryton Rd. ML1: Moth 1B 156
ML9: Lark 5H 155
Merryton St. ML9: Lark 6H 155
Merryton Twr. ML1: Moth 1B 156
Merryvale Av. G46: Giff 2B 118
Merryvale Pl. G46: Giff 2A 118
Merton Dr. G52: Glas 6A 80
Meryon Gdns. G32: Glas 3D 106
Meryon Rd. G32: Glas 2D 106
Methil St. G14: Glas 6C 60
Methlan Pk. G82: Dumb 5E 17
Methlick Av. ML6: Air 1G 111
Methuen Rd. PA3: Pais 2B 78
Methven Av. G61: Bear 2H 45
Methven Pl. G74: E Kil 1E 149
Methven Rd. G46: Giff 3G 133
Methven St. G31: Glas 2F 105
G81: Clyd 3B 42
Methven Ter. ML5: Coat 2D 90
Metropole La. G1: Glas 5G 83
Mews La. PA3: Pais 4B 78
Mey Ct. G77: Newt M 5A 132
Mey Pl. G77: Newt M 5A 132
M8 Food Pk. G21: Glas 1H 83
Michael McParland Dr.
G64: Torr 5D 28
Michael Ter. ML6: Chap 4D 112
Micklehouse Oval G69: Bail 5H 87
Micklehouse Pl. G69: Bail 5H 87
Micklehouse Rd. G69: Bail 5H 87
Micklehouse Wynd G69: Bail 5H 87
Midas Pl. ML4: Moss 2G 127
Mid Barrwood Rd. G65: Kils 4A 12
Mid Carbarns ML2: Wis 2D 156
Midcroft G64: B'rig 4A 48
Midcroft Av. G44: Glas 2H 119
Middlefield G75: E Kil 6G 149
Middlehouse Ct. ML8: Carl 3D 164
Middlemuir Av. G66: Lenz 2D 50
Middlemuir Rd. G66: Lenz 1D 50
Middlerigg Rd. G68: Cumb 3F 35
Middlesex Gdns G41: Glas 5C 82
Middlesex St. G41: Glas 6C 82
Middleton Av. ML9: Lark 5F 161
Middleton Dr. G62: Miln 3H 25
Middleton Rd. PA3: Lin 5A 76
PA3: Pais 5F 77
Middleton St. G51: Glas 5A 82
Middleward St. G81: Faif 6F 23
Midfaulds Av. PA4: Renf 1G 79
Midland St. G1: Glas 4F 83 (6C 4)
Midlem Dr. G52: Glas 6C 80
Midlem Oval G52: Glas 6C 80
Midlock St. G51: Glas 6A 82
Midlothian Dr. G41: Glas 4B 102
Mid Park G75: E Kil 3G 149
Mid Rd. G67: Cumb 1H 55
Midton Rd. PA9: How 6B 94
Midton St. G21: Glas 6B 64
Mid Wharf St. G4: Glas 1G 83 (1F 5)
Migvie Pl. G20: Glas 4B 62
Milford G75: E Kil 4D 148
Milford St. G33: Glas 3A 86
Millands Av. G72: Blan 6A 124
Millarbank St. G21: Glas 5A 64
Millar Gro. ML3: Ham 5E 141
Millar Pk. ML3: Ham 5F 141
Millars Pl. G66: Lenz 3D 50
MILLARSTON 1E 97
Millarston Av. PA1: Pais 1E 97
Millarston Ct. PA1: Pais 1F 97
Millarston Dr. PA1: Pais 1E 97
Millarston Ind. Est.
PA1: Pais 2E 97
Millar St. PA1: Pais 6B 78
Millar Ter. G73: Ruth 4D 104
Millbank Av. ML4: Bell 4D 126
Millbank Rd. ML2: Wis 1F 157
Millbeg Cres. G33: Glas 5E 87
Millbeg Pl. G33: Glas 6E 87
Mill Brae PA11: Bri W 3F 73
Millbrae Av. G69: Chry 1B 68
Millbrae Ct. G42: Glas 6D 102
ML5: Coat 6H 89
Millbrae Cres. G42: Glas 6C 102
G81: Clyd 2F 59
Millbrae Gdns. G42: Glas 6D 102
Millbrae Rd. G43: Glas 6C 102
Millbrix Av. G14: Glas 4A 60
Millbrook G74: E Kil 1D 148
Millburn Av. G73: Ruth 1C 120
G81: Clyd 1G 59
PA4: Renf 6F 59
Millburn Ct. G75: E Kil 4A 148
Millburn Cres. G82: Dumb 4H 17
Millburn Dr. PA4: Renf 6G 59
Millburn Gdns. G75: E Kil 4A 148
Millburn La. ML9: Lark 3G 161
Millburn Pl. ML9: Lark 5F 161
Millburn Rd. G82: Dumb 4H 17
ML9: Ashg 4B 162
PA4: Renf 6F 59
Millburn St. G21: Glas 2C 84
G66: Len 3F 7
ML1: Moth 2G 143
Millburn Way G75: E Kil 4A 148
PA4: Renf 6G 59
Mill Ct. G73: Ruth 5C 104
ML3: Ham 1G 153
Mill Cres. G40: Glas 2B 104
G64: Torr 4E 29
Millcroft Rd. G67: Cumb 4B 36
(Sth. Carbrain Rd.)
G67: Cumb 3G 55
(Summerhill & Garngibbock Rd)
G73: Ruth 3B 104
Milldam Rd. G81: Faif 6E 23
Millennium Ct. G34: Glas 3A 88
Millennium Gdns. G34: Glas 4A 88
Millennium Pk. 2D 82
(off Ashley St.)
Miller Cl. G64: B'rig 1F 65
Miller Ct. G82: Dumb 3H 17
Miller Dr. G64: B'rig 1F 65
Millerfield Pl. G40: Glas 2D 104
ML3: Ham 6B 142
Millerfield Rd. G40: Glas 2D 104
Miller Gdns. G64: B'rig 1F 65
Miller Pl. G64: B'rig 1F 65
Millerslea G82: Milt 4F 19
(off Colquhoun Rd.)
MILLERSNEUK 3E 51
Millersneuk Av. G66: Lenz 3D 50
Millersneuk Ct. G66: Lenz 3D 50
Millersneuk Cres. G33: Mille 4A 66
Millersneuk Dr. G66: Lenz 3D 50
Millersneuk Rd. G66: Lenz 3D 50
(not continuous)
Miller's Pl. ML6: Air 4B 92
MILLERSTON 5C 134
Millerston St. G40: Glas 5C 84
Miller St. G1: Glas 4G 83 (6E 5)
G69: Bail 1H 107
G81: Clyd 6D 42
G82: Dumb 3H 17
ML2: Wis 6G 145
ML3: Ham 6B 142
ML5: Coat 6D 90
ML8: Carl 3F 165
ML9: Lark 2E 161
PA5: John 2H 95
Miller Wlk. G64: B'rig 1F 65
Millfield Av. ML1: Moth 1H 143
PA8: Ersk 6D 40
Millfield Cres. PA8: Ersk 6E 41
Millfield Dr. PA8: Ersk 1E 57
Millfield Gdns. PA8: Ersk 6E 41
Millfield Hill PA8: Ersk 6D 40
Millfield La. PA8: Ersk 6D 40
Millfield Mdw. PA8: Ersk 6D 40
Millfield Pl. PA8: Ersk 6D 40
Millfield Vw. PA8: Ersk 6D 40
Millfield Wlk. PA8: Ersk 1E 57
Millfield Wynd PA8: Ersk 6D 40
Millford Dr. PA3: Lin 6H 75
Millgate G71: Tann 5D 108
Millgate Av. G71: Tann 5D 108
Millgate Ct. G71: Udd 6D 108
Millgate Rd. ML3: Ham 2G 153

Mill Gro.—Morrison Quad.


Mill Gro. ML3: Ham 1G 153
MILLHEUGH 3C 160
Millheugh Brae ML9: Lark 3C 160
Millheugh Pl. G72: Blan 3A 140
Millheugh Rd. ML3: Ham 6C 160
ML9: Lark 3C 160
Millholm Rd. G44: Glas 3F 119
Millhouse Cres. G20: Glas 2A 62
Millhouse Dr. G20: Glas 2H 61
Millichen Rd. G23: Glas 3B 46
Milliken Dr. PA10: Kilb 3C 94
MILLIKENPARK 4C 94
Millikenpark Station (Rail) 5C 94
Milliken Pk. Rd. PA10: Kilb 4C 94
Milliken Pl. *PA10: Kilb* 3C 94
(off Easwald Bank)
Milliken Rd. PA10: Kilb 3C 94
Mill Loan ML6: Air 3A 92
Mill of Gryffe Rd.
PA11: Bri W 3F 73
Mill Pk. ML3: Ham 1G 153
Mill Pl. PA3: Lin 5G 75
Millport Av. G44: Glas 6G 103
Millrig G75: E Kil 6F 149
Mill Ri. G66: Lenz 3D 50
Mill Rd. G65: Queen 4C 10
G71: Both 6E 125
G72: Camb 3D 122
(Hamilton Rd.)
G72: Camb 1C 122
(Westburn Rd.)
G78: Barr 4D 114
G81: Clyd 2F 59
ML1: Moth 2H 143
ML2: Newm 6G 147
ML6: Air 2A 92
ML8: Carl 4E 165
Millroad Dr. G40: Glas 5A 84
Millroad Gdns. *G40: Glas* 5B 84
(off Millroad Dr.)
Millroad St. G40: Glas 5A 84
(not continuous)
Millstream Ct. PA1: Pais 1B 98
Mill St. G40: Glas 2B 104
G73: Ruth 6C 104
(not continuous)
PA1: Pais 1B 98
Mill St. Ind. Est. ML6: Air 3A 92
Mill Vennel PA4: Renf 6F 59
Millview G78: Barr 4F 115
Millview Mdws. G78: Neil 2C 130
Millview Pl. G53: Glas 3B 116
Millview Ter. G78: Neil 2C 130
Mill Way G66: Kirk 6G 31
Millwood St. G41: Glas 5C 102
MILNBANK 3C 84
Milnbank St. G31: Glas 3C 84
Milncroft Pl. G33: Glas 2A 86
Milncroft Rd. G33: Glas 2A 86
Milner La. G13: Glas 4E 61
Milner Rd. G13: Glas 4E 61
MILNGAVIE 3H 25
Milngavie Station (Rail) 4H 25
Milngavie Rd. G61: Bear 4F 45
Milnpark Gdns. G41: Glas 6B 82
Milnpark St. G41: Glas 6C 82
MILNWOOD 3E 127
Milnwood Dr. ML1: Moth 5E 127
ML4: Bell 3E 127
Milovaig Av. G23: Glas 6B 46
Milovaig St. G23: Glas 6B 46
Milrig Rd. G73: Ruth 6B 104
Milroy Gdns. ML4: Bell 5C 110
MILTON
Dumbarton 4F 19
Glasgow 1G 63
Milton Av. G72: Camb 2G 121
Milton Brae G82: Milt 1F 19
Milton Ct. *G66: Kirk* 5E 31
(off Highfield Rd.)
G82: Milt 3F 19
ML6: Air 3A 92
Milton Cres. ML8: Carl 4F 165
Milton Douglas Rd.
G81: Dun, Hard 2C 42
Milton Dr. G64: B'rig 2B 64
Milton Gdns. G71: Tann 5C 108
Milton Hill G82: Milt 4F 19
Milton Mains Rd. G81: Clyd 2C 42
MILTON OF CAMPSIE 5C 8
Milton Rd. G66: Kirk 3C 30
G66: Len 4G 7
G74: E Kil 1C 148
ML8: Carl 5B 164
Milton St. G4: Glas 2F 83 (2D 4)
ML1: Moth 1G 143
ML3: Ham 5E 141
ML6: Air 3A 92
ML8: Carl 3E 165
Milton Ter. ML3: Ham 4E 141
Milverton Av. G61: Bear 1C 44
Milverton Rd. G46: Giff 6G 117
Mimosa Rd. PA11: Bri W 3F 73
Mimosas, The *PA11: Bri W* 3F 73
(off Mimosa Rd.)
Minard Rd. G41: Glas 4C 102
Minard Way G71: Tann 6E 109
Mincher Cres. ML1: Moth 5G 143
Minch Way ML6: Air 6C 92
Minella Gdns. ML4: Bell 5C 110
Minerva Ct. *G3: Glas* 3C 82
(off Houldsworth St.)
Minerva St. G3: Glas 3C 82
Minerva Way G3: Glas 3B 82
Mingarry La. G20: Glas 5C 62
Mingarry St. G20: Glas 5C 62
Mingulay Cres. G22: Glas 1H 63
Mingulay Pl. G22: Glas 1A 64
Mingulay St. G22: Glas 1H 63
Minister's Pk. G74: E Kil 5B 136
Minmoir Rd. G53: Glas 6H 99
Minster Wlk. G69: Barg 6D 88
Minstrel Rd. G13: Glas 6D 44
Minto Av. G73: Ruth 3F 121
Minto Cres. G52: Glas 6F 81
Minto Pk. ML2: Wis 3A 146
Minto St. G52: Glas 6F 81
Mireton St. G22: Glas 4F 63
Mirren Ct. PA3: Pais 4B 78
Mirren Dr. G81: Dun 6B 22
Mirrlees Dr. G12: Glas 5A 62
Mirrlees La. G12: Glas 5A 62
Mitchell Arc. G73: Ruth 5D 104
Mitchell Av. G72: Camb 1E 123
PA4: Renf 1D 78
Mitchell Ct. G74: E Kil 1E 149
Mitchell Dr. G62: Miln 4A 26
G73: Ruth 1D 120
Mitchell Gro. G74: E Kil 1E 149
Mitchell Hill Rd. G45: Glas 5B 120
Mitchell La. G1: Glas 4F 83 (5D 4)
Mitchell Rd. G67: Cumb 3A 36
Mitchell St. G1: Glas 4F 83 (6D 4)
ML5: Coat 1F 109
ML6: Air 3H 91
Mitchell Theatre, The 3D 82
Mitchison Rd. G67: Cumb 2A 36
Mitre Ct. G11: Glas 5F 61
Mitre Ga. G11: Glas 6F 61
Mitre La. G14: Glas 5E 61
Mitre La. W. G14: Glas 5D 60
Mitre Rd. G11: Glas 5F 61
G14: Glas 5D 60
Moat Av. G13: Glas 2C 60
Mochrum Rd. G43: Glas 1C 118
Moffat Ct. G75: E Kil 4A 148
Moffat Gdns. G75: E Kil 4A 148
Moffathill ML6: Gart 6E 93
MOFFAT MILLS 5F 93
Moffat Pl. G72: Blan 6B 124
G75: E Kil 4A 148
ML5: Coat 1F 111
ML6: Air 3F 93
Moffat Rd. ML6: Air 4F 93
Moffat St. G5: Glas 1H 103
Moffat Vw. ML6: Plain 1G 93
Mogarth Av. PA2: Pais 5D 96
Moidart Av. PA4: Renf 5D 58
Moidart Ct. G78: Barr 3D 114
Moidart Cres. G52: Glas 6F 81
Moidart Gdns. G66: Kirk 4H 31
G77: Newt M 3E 133
Moidart Pl. G52: Glas 6F 81
Moidart Rd. G52: Glas 6E 81
Moir St. G1: Glas 5H 83
Molendinar St. G1: Glas 5H 83
Molendinar Ter. G78: Neil 3C 130
MOLLINSBURN 3H 53
MOLLINSBURN JUNC. 4G 53
Mollinsburn Rd. G67: Cumb 3A 54
ML5: Anna 6B 54
Mollinsburn St. G21: Glas 6A 64
Mollins Ct. G68: Cumb 2H 53
Mollins Rd. G68: Cumb 1G 53
MOLLINS RDBT. 3H 53
Monach Rd. G33: Glas 3C 86
Monar Dr. G22: Glas 6F 63
Monar Pl. G22: Glas 6F 63
Monar St. G22: Glas 6F 63
Monart Pl. G20: Glas 4D 62
Monar Way *ML2: Newm* 3D 146
(off Murdostoun Vw.)
Moncrieff Av. G66: Lenz 2C 50
Moncrieffe Rd. ML6: Chap 1D 112
Moncrieff Gdns. G66: Lenz 2D 50
Moncrieff St. PA3: Pais 6A 78
Moncur St. G40: Glas 5A 84
(not continuous)
Moness Dr. G52: Glas 1E 101
Money Gro. ML1: Moth 5B 144
Monieburgh Cres. G65: Kils 2A 12
Monieburgh Rd. G65: Kils 2A 12
Monifieth Av. G52: Glas 2D 100
Monikie Gdns. G64: B'rig 6F 49
Monkcastle Dr. G72: Camb 1A 122
Monkdyke Ho. PA4: Renf 6F 59
Monkland Av. G66: Kirk, Lenz 6D 30
Monkland La. ML5: Coat 1A 110
Monklands Ind. Est.
ML5: Coat 3B 110
Monkland St. ML6: Air 4B 92
Monkland Ter. ML5: Glenb 3H 69
Monkland Vw. G71: Tann 4E 109
ML6: C'bnk 3B 112
Monkland Vw. Cres.
G69: Barg 1D 108
Monksbridge Av. G13: Glas 6C 44
Monkscourt Av. ML6: Air 3G 91
Monkscroft Av. G11: Glas 6G 61
Monkscroft Ct. G11: Glas 1G 81
Monkscroft Gdns. G11: Glas 6G 61
Monks Rd. ML6: Air 6C 92
Monkton Dr. G15: Glas 5B 44
Monkton Gdns. G77: Newt M 5G 133
Monmouth Av. G12: Glas 3G 61
Monreith Av. G61: Bear 5D 44
Monreith Rd. G43: Glas 1B 118
Monreith Rd. E. G44: Glas 2E 119
Monroe Dr. G71: Tann 4D 108
Monroe Pl. G71: Tann 4D 108
Montague La. G12: Glas 5H 61
Montague St. G4: Glas 1D 82
Montalto Av. ML1: Carf 6A 128
Montclair Pl. PA3: Lin 5H 75
Montego Grn. G75: E Kil 2C 148
Monteith Dr. G76: Clar 1D 134
Monteith Gdns. G76: Clar 1D 134
Monteith Pl. G40: Glas 6A 84
G72: Blan 1C 140
Monteith Row G40: Glas 5H 83
Montford Av. G44: Glas 6H 103
G73: Ruth 6A 104
Montgarrie St. G51: Glas 5D 80
Montgomery Av. ML5: Coat 4B 90
PA3: Pais 4D 78
Montgomery Ct. PA3: Pais 4D 78
Montgomery Cres. ML2: Wis 2E 157
Montgomery Dr. G46: Giff 6A 118
PA10: Kilb 1A 94
Montgomery Pl. G74: E Kil 1H 149
ML9: Lark 3F 161
Montgomery Rd. PA3: Pais 3C 78
Montgomery St. G72: Camb 2D 122
G74: E Kil 1H 149
ML9: Lark 1E 161
Montgomery Ter. G40: Glas 1C 104
G66: Milt C 6B 8
Montgomery Wynd *G74: E Kil* 1H 149
(off Montgomery St.)
Montraive St. G73: Ruth 4E 105
Montrave Path G52: Glas 1D 100
Montrave St. G52: Glas 1D 100
Montreal Ho. G81: Clyd 1H 41
Montreal Pk. G75: E Kil 2E 149
Montrose Av. G32: Carm 4B 106
G52: Hill 3G 79
Montrose Ct. PA2: Pais 5D 96
Montrose Cres. ML3: Ham 5H 141
Montrose Dr. G61: Bear 6E 25
Montrose Gdns. G62: Miln 2H 25
G65: Kils 2G 11
G72: Blan 5A 124
Montrose La. ML3: Ham 5G 141
Montrose Pl. PA3: Lin 5G 75
Montrose Rd. PA2: Pais 5D 96
Montrose St. G1: Glas 4H 83 (5G 5)
G81: Clyd 5D 42
ML1: Moth 6F 127
Montrose Ter. G64: B'rig 2E 65
PA11: Bri W 4F 73
Montrose Way PA2: Pais 5D 96
Monument Dr. G33: Glas 4G 65
Monymusk Gdns. G64: B'rig 5F 49
Monymusk Pl. G15: Glas 2G 43
MOODIESBURN 5D 52
Moodiesburn St. G33: Glas 1F 85
Moorburn Av. G46: Giff 4H 117
Moorburn Pl. PA3: Lin 5E 75
Moorcroft Dr. ML6: Air 4E 93
Moorcroft Rd. G77: Newt M 6C 132
Moore Dr. G61: Bear 4F 45
Moore Gdns. ML3: Ham 4A 154
Moore St. G31: Glas 5B 84
ML1: New S 4A 128
Moorfield Cres. ML6: Air 4F 93
Moorfield Rd. G72: Blan 3A 140
Moorfoot G64: B'rig 5E 49
Moorfoot Av. G46: T'bnk 4G 117
PA2: Pais 4H 97
Moorfoot Dr. ML2: Wis 6F 145
Moorfoot Path PA2: Pais 5H 9
Moorfoot St. G32: Glas 5G 8
Moorfoot Way G61: Bear 5B 2
Moorhill Cres. G77: Newt M 6C 13
Moorhill Rd. G77: Newt M 5C 13
Moorhouse Av. G13: Glas 3H 5
PA2: Pais 3F 9
Moorhouse St. G78: Barr 5E 11
Moorings, The PA2: Pais 2F 9
Moorland Dr. ML6: Air 4F 9
MOORPARK 1D 7
Moorpark Av. G52: Glas 5H 7
G69: Muirh 2A 6
ML6: Air 4E 9
Moorpark Ct. PA4: Renf 1D 7
Moorpark Pl. G52: Glas 5H 7
Moorpark Sq. PA4: Renf 1D 7
Moor Rd. G62: Miln 3H 2
Moorside St. ML8: Carl 3G 16
Morag Av. G72: Blan 6A 12
Moraine Av. G15: Glas 6A 4
Moraine Cir. G15: Glas 6A 4
Moraine Dr. G15: Glas 6A 4
G76: Clar 1B 13
Moraine Pl. G15: Glas 6B 4
Morar Av. G81: Clyd 3D 4
Morar Ct. G67: Cumb 5D 3
G81: Clyd 3D 4
ML3: Ham 2E 15
ML9: Lark 6H 15
Morar Cres. G64: B'rig 5B 4
G81: Clyd 3D 4
ML5: Coat 2H 8
ML6: Air 1G 9
PA7: B'ton 5A 4
Morar Dr. G61: Bear 4H 4
G67: Cumb 6D 3
G73: Ruth 4D 12
G81: Clyd 3D 4
PA2: Pais 3D 9
PA3: Lin 6G 7
Morar Pl. G74: E Kil 6H 13
G77: Newt M 2D 13
G81: Clyd 3D 4
PA4: Renf 5D 5
Morar Rd. G52: Glas 6E 8
G81: Clyd 3D 4
Morar St. ML2: Wis 2G 15
Morar Ter. G71: View 6F 10
G73: Ruth 4F 12
Morar Way ML1: N'hill 4C 12
Moravia Av. G71: Both 4E 12
Moray Av. ML6: Air 6A 9
Moray Ct. G73: Ruth 5C 10
Moray Dr. G64: Torr 4D 2
G76: Clar 2D 13
Moray Gdns. G68: Cumb 6H 1
G71: Tann 5D 10
G76: Clar 1D 13
Moray Ga. G71: Both 3C 12
Moray Pl. G41: Glas 3C 10
G64: B'rig 6E 4
G66: Kirk 4G 3
G69: Chry 1B 6
G72: Blan 3A 14
PA3: Lin 5G 7
Moray Quad. ML4: Bell 2C 12
Moray Way ML1: Holy 2A 12
Mordaunt St. G40: Glas 2C 10
Moredun Cres. G32: Glas 4C 8
Moredun Dr. PA2: Pais 4F 9
Moredun Rd. PA2: Pais 4F 9
Moredun St. G32: Glas 4C 8
Morefield Rd. G51: Glas 4D 8
Morgan M. G42: Glas 2F 10
Morgan St. ML3: Ham 1H 15
ML9: Lark 2D 16
Morina Gdns. G53: Glas 4C 11
Morion Rd. G13: Glas 1D 6
Morison Ho. *G67: Cumb* 3A 3
(off Burns Rd
Moriston Ct. ML2: Newm 3D 14
Morland G74: E Kil 4D 13
Morley St. G42: Glas 6E 10
Morna La. *G14: Glas* 1E 8
(off Glendore St
MORNINGSIDE 6G 14
Morningside Rd.
ML2: Newm 4E 14
Morningside St. G33: Glas 3F 8
Morrin Path G21: Glas 6A 6
Morrin St. G21: Glas 5A 6
Morris Cres. G72: Blan 2B 14
ML1: Cle 6E 12
Morrishall Rd. G74: E Kil 5C 13
Morrison Dr. G66: Len 4G
Morrison Gdns. G64: Torr 5E 2
Morrison Pl. *PA11: Bri W* 3F 7
(off Main St
Morrison Quad. G81: Clyd 6G 4

Morrison St.—Nagle Gdns.


**Morrison St.** G5: Glas ... 5E **83**
G81: Dun ... 1B **42**
**Morris St.** ML3: Ham ... 2H **153**
ML9: Lark ... 4G **161**
**Morriston Cres.** PA4: Renf ... 2H **79**
**Morriston Pk. Dr.** G72: Camb ... 1A **122**
**Morriston St.** G72: Camb ... 1A **122**
**Morton Gdns.** G41: Glas ... 4A **102**
**Morton St.** ML1: Moth ... 1G **143**
**Morton Ter.** *PA11: Bri W ... 3E **73***
*(off Horsewood Rd.)*
**Morvan St.** G52: Glas ... 6E **81**
**Morven Av.** G64: B'rig ... 6E **49**
G72: Blan ... 6A **124**
PA2: Pais ... 5H **97**
**Morven Dr.** G76: Clar ... 1B **134**
PA3: Lin ... 6G **75**
**Morven Gait** PA8: Ersk ... 1A **58**
**Morven Gdns.** G71: Tann ... 5D **108**
**Morven La.** G72: Blan ... 6A **124**
**Morven Rd.** G61: Bear ... 1E **45**
G72: Camb ... 4H **121**
**Morven St.** ML5: Coat ... 3C **90**
**Morven Way** G66: Kirk ... 5H **31**
G71: Both ... 4F **125**
**Mosesfield St.** G21: Glas ... 4B **64**
**Mosque Av.** G5: Glas ... 6G **83**
**Mossacre Rd.** ML2: Wis ... 5A **146**
**Moss Av.** PA3: Lin ... 5H **75**
**Mossbank** G72: Blan ... 3B **140**
G75: E Kil ... 3B **148**
**Mossbank Av.** G33: Glas ... 5H **65**
**Mossbank Cres.** ML1: N'hill ... 3F **129**
**Mossbank Dr.** G33: Glas ... 5H **65**
**Mossbank Rd.** ML2: Wis ... 5A **146**
**Mossbell Rd.** ML4: Bell ... 1A **126**
**Mossblown St.** ML9: Lark ... 2D **160**
**Mossburn Rd.** ML2: Wis ... 6B **146**
**Mossburn St.** ML2: Wis ... 2B **158**
**Mosscastle Rd.** G33: Glas ... 1C **86**
**Mossdale** G74: E Kil ... 6E **137**
**Mossdale Ct.** ML4: Bell ... 2F **127**
**Mossdale Gdns.** ML3: Ham ... 1C **152**
**Moss Dr.** G78: Barr ... 2C **114**
PA8: Ersk ... 2F **57**
**Mossedge Ind. Est.** PA3: Lin ... 5A **76**
MOSSEND ... **2E 127**
**Mossend La.** G33: Glas ... 3D **86**
**Mossend St.** G33: Glas ... 3D **86**
**Mossgiel** G75: E Kil ... 4D **148**
**Mossgiel Av.** G73: Ruth ... 2C **120**
**Mossgiel Cres.** G76: Busby ... 4D **134**
**Mossgiel Dr.** G81: Clyd ... 4E **43**
**Mossgiel Gdns.** G66: Kirk ... 4F **31**
G71: Tann ... 5C **108**
**Mossgiel La.** *ML9: Lark ... 4G **161***
*(off Keir Hardie La.)*
**Mossgiel Pl.** G73: Ruth ... 2C **120**
**Mossgiel Rd.** G43: Glas ... 1B **118**
(Doonfoot Rd., not continuous)
G43: Glas ... 6B **102**
(Newlands Rd.)
G67: Cumb ... 2B **36**
(not continuous)
**Mossgiel Ter.** G72: Blan ... 5A **124**
**Mossgiel Way** ML1: N'hill ... 3C **128**
**Mosshall Gro.** ML1: N'hill ... 3F **129**
**Mosshall Rd.** ML1: N'hse ... 6D **112**
**Mosshall St.** ML1: N'hill ... 3F **129**
**Mosshead Rd.** G61: Bear ... 6F **25**
**Moss Hgts. Av.** G52: Glas ... 6D **80**
**Mosshill Rd.** ML4: Bell ... 5D **110**
**Moss Knowe** G67: Cumb ... 3C **36**
**Mossland Dr.** ML2: Wis ... 5A **146**
**Mossland Rd.** G52: Hill ... 3F **79**
PA4: Renf ... 2H **79**
**Mosslands Rd.** PA3: Pais ... 3H **77**
**Mosslingal** G75: E Kil ... 6G **149**
**Mossmulloch** G75: E Kil ... 6G **149**
MOSSNEUK ... **4B 148**
**Mossneuk Av.** G75: E Kil ... 3A **148**
**Mossneuk Cres.** ML2: Wis ... 5B **146**
**Mossneuk Dr.** G75: E Kil ... 4B **148**
ML2: Wis ... 5A **146**
PA2: Pais ... 5G **97**
**Mossneuk Pk.** ML2: Wis ... 5A **146**
**Mossneuk Rd.** G75: E Kil ... 3B **148**
**Mossneuk St.** ML5: Coat ... 2B **110**
MOSSPARK ... **2E 101**
**Mosspark Av.** G52: Glas ... 2F **101**
G62: Miln ... 2G **25**
**Mosspark Blvd.** G52: Glas ... 1E **101**
**Mosspark Dr.** G52: Glas ... 1C **100**
**Mosspark La.** G52: Glas ... 2E **101**
**Mosspark Oval** G52: Glas ... 2E **101**
**Mosspark Rd.** G62: Miln ... 2G **25**
ML5: Coat ... 3H **89**
**Mosspark Sq.** G52: Glas ... 2E **101**
Mosspark Station (Rail) ... **2C 100**
**Moss Path** G69: Bail ... 2F **107**
**Moss Rd.** G51: Glas ... 3D **80**
G66: Kirk ... 6H **31**
G66: Lenz ... 1B **50**
G67: Cumb ... 2E **37**
G69: Muirh ... 2A **68**
ML2: Wis ... 6C **146**
ML6: Air ... 5A **92**
PA11: Bri W ... 3G **73**
PA6: Hous ... 1H **75**
**Moss Side Av.** ML6: Air ... 3G **91**
ML8: Carl ... 3D **164**
**Mossside Rd.** G41: Glas ... 4B **102**
**Moss St.** PA1: Pais ... 6A **78**
**Mossvale Cres.** G33: Glas ... 1C **86**
**Mossvale La.** PA3: Pais ... 5H **77**
**Mossvale Path** G33: Glas ... 6C **66**
**Mossvale Rd.** G33: Glas ... 6B **66**
**Mossvale Sq.** G33: Glas ... 1B **86**
PA3: Pais ... 5H **77**
**Mossvale St.** PA3: Pais ... 4H **77**
**Mossvale Ter.** G69: Mood ... 4E **53**
**Mossvale Wlk.** G33: Glas ... 1C **86**
**Mossvale Way** G33: Glas ... 1C **86**
**Mossview Cres.** ML6: Air ... 5A **92**
**Mossview La.** G52: Glas ... 6C **80**
**Mossview Quad.** G52: Glas ... 6D **80**
**Mossview Rd.** G33: Step ... 4E **67**
**Mosswell Rd.** G62: Miln ... 2H **25**
**Mossywood Ct.** G68: Cumb ... 6B **34**
**Mossywood Pl.** G68: Cumb ... 6B **34**
**Mossywood Rd.** G68: Cumb ... 6B **34**
**Mote Hill** ML3: Ham ... 5A **142**
**Motehill Rd.** PA3: Pais ... 5C **78**
MOTHERWELL ... **3G 143**
**Motherwell Bus. Cen.**
ML1: Moth ... 2H **143**
Motherwell Concert Hall &
Theatre Complex ... **4H 143**
Motherwell F.C. ... **5H 143**
*Motherwell Heritage Cen. ... 3F 143*
*(off High Rd.)*
**Motherwell Rd.** ML1: Carf ... 6C **128**
ML1: N'hse ... 2G **129**
ML3: Ham ... 5C **142**
ML4: Bell ... 2C **126**
Motherwell Station (Rail) ... **2G 143**
**Motherwell St.** ML6: Air ... 2C **92**
**Moulin Cir.** G52: Glas ... 1A **100**
**Moulin Pl.** G52: Glas ... 1A **100**
**Moulin Rd.** G52: Glas ... 1A **100**
**Moulin Ter.** G52: Glas ... 1A **100**
**Mountainblue St.** G31: Glas ... 6C **84**
**Mt. Annan Dr.** G44: Glas ... 6F **103**
MOUNTBLOW ... **2G 41**
**Mountblow Rd.** G81: Clyd, Dun ... 1H **41**
**Mt. Cameron Dr. Nth.**
G74: E Kil ... 3A **150**
**Mt. Cameron Dr. Sth.**
G74: E Kil ... 3A **150**
MOUNT ELLEN ... **2C 68**
MOUNT FLORIDA ... **5F 103**
Mount Florida Station (Rail) ... **5E 103**
**Mountgarrie Path** G51: Glas ... 4D **80**
**Mountgarrie Rd.** G51: Glas ... 4D **80**
**Mt. Harriet Av.** G33: Step ... 3E **67**
**Mt. Harriet Dr.** G33: Step ... 3D **66**
**Mountherrick** G75: E Kil ... 6G **149**
**Mt. Lockhart** G71: Udd ... 3H **107**
**Mt. Lockhart Gdns.** G71: Udd ... 3H **107**
**Mt. Lockhart Pl.** G71: Udd ... 3H **107**
**Mt. Pleasant Cres.** G66: Milt C ... 5B **8**
**Mt. Pleasant Ho.** G60: Old K ... 1E **41**
**Mt. Pleasant Pl.** *G60: Old K ... 1F **41***
*(off Station Rd.)*
*G60: Old K ... 1F **41***
*(off Mt. Pleasant Rd.)*
**Mt. Pleasant Rd.** G60: Old K ... 6F **21**
**Mt. Stewart St.** ML8: Carl ... 3E **165**
**Mount St.** G20: Glas ... 6D **62**
**Mt. Stuart St.** G41: Glas ... 5C **102**
**Mount, The** ML1: Moth ... 3F **143**
MOUNT VERNON ... **3D 106**
**Mt. Vernon Av.** G32: Glas ... 3E **107**
ML5: Coat ... 4A **90**
Mount Vernon Station (Rail) ... **3F 107**
**Mournian Way** ML3: Ham ... 2H **153**
**Mowbray** G74: E Kil ... 5C **138**
**Mowbray Av.** G69: G'csh ... 4D **68**
**Moyne Rd.** G53: Glas ... 3A **100**
**Moy Path** *ML2: Newm ... 3D **146***
*(off Murdostoun Vw.)*
**Muckcroft Rd.** G66: Kirk, Lenz ... 3H **51**
G69: Chry, Lenz ... 3H **51**
**Mugdock Rd.** G62: Miln ... 3G **25**
**Mugdock Rd. S.** G62: Miln ... 3G **25**
**Muirbank Av.** G73: Ruth ... 6B **104**
**Muirbank Gdns.** G73: Ruth ... 6B **104**
**Muirbrae Rd.** G73: Ruth ... 3D **120**
**Muirbrae Way** G73: Ruth ... 3D **120**
**Muirburn Av.** G44: Glas ... 3C **118**
**Muir Ct.** G44: Neth ... 5C **118**
(not continuous)
**Muircroft Dr.** ML1: Cle ... 5H **129**
**Muirdrum Av.** G52: Glas ... 2D **100**
**Muirdyke Rd.** ML5: Coat ... 3H **89**
ML5: Glenb ... 5B **70**
**Muirdykes Av.** G52: Glas ... 6A **80**
**Muirdykes Rd.** G52: Glas ... 6A **80**
PA3: Pais ... 4F **77**
**Muiredge Ct.** G71: Udd ... 1D **124**
**Muiredge Ter.** G69: Bail ... 1H **107**
MUIREND ... **3D 118**
**Muirend Av.** G44: Glas ... 3D **118**
**Muirend Rd.** G44: Glas ... 3C **118**
Muirend Station (Rail) ... **3D 118**
**Muirfield Ct.** G44: Glas ... 3D **118**
**Muirfield Cres.** G23: Glas ... 6C **46**
**Muirfield Mdws.** G71: Both ... 5C **124**
**Muirfield Rd.** G68: Cumb ... 6A **14**
MUIRHEAD
Glasgow ... **1H 107**
North Lanarkshire ... **2A 68**
**MUIRHEAD-BRAEHEAD INTERCHANGE**
... **3A 36**
**Muirhead Cotts.** G66: Kirk ... 6H **31**
**Muirhead Ct.** G69: Bail ... 1A **108**
**Muirhead Dr.** ML1: N'hill ... 3F **129**
ML8: Law ... 5E **159**
PA3: Lin ... 6G **75**
**Muirhead Gdns.** G69: Bail ... 1A **108**
**Muirhead Ga.** G71: Tann ... 5F **109**
**Muirhead Gro.** G69: Bail ... 1A **108**
**Muirhead Rd.** G69: Bail ... 2H **107**
G78: Neil ... 4A **130**
**MUIRHEAD RDBT.** ... **2B 36**
**Muirhead St.** G66: Kirk ... 6C **30**
**Muirhead Ter.** ML1: Moth ... 5G **143**
**Muirhead Way** G64: B'rig ... 6F **49**
**Muirhill Av.** G44: Glas ... 3C **118**
**Muirhill Cres.** G13: Glas ... 2A **60**
MUIRHOUSE ... **1B 156**
**Muirhouse Av.** ML1: Moth ... 6B **144**
ML2: Newm ... 3F **147**
**Muirhouse Dr.** ML1: Moth ... 1B **156**
**Muirhouse La.** G75: E Kil ... 3H **149**
**Muirhouse Pk.** G61: Bear ... 5D **24**
**Muirhouse Rd.** ML1: Moth ... 1B **156**
**Muirhouse St.** G41: Glas ... 2E **103**
**Muirhouse Twr.** ML1: Moth ... 6B **144**
**Muirhouse Works** G41: Glas ... 2E **103**
**Muirkirk Dr.** G13: Glas ... 2F **61**
ML3: Ham ... 1B **152**
**Muirlee Rd.** ML8: Carl ... 4H **165**
**Muirlees Cres.** G62: Miln ... 3E **25**
**Muirmadkin Rd.** ML4: Bell ... 2D **126**
**Muirpark Av.** PA4: Renf ... 1E **79**
**Muirpark Dr.** G52: Glas ... 5A **80**
G64: B'rig ... 1C **64**
**Muirpark St.** G11: Glas ... 1H **81**
**Muirpark Ter.** G64: B'rig ... 1B **64**
**Muir Rd.** G82: Dumb ... 1H **17**
**Muirshiel Av.** G53: Glas ... 1C **116**
**Muirshiel Ct.** G53: Glas ... 2C **116**
**Muirshiel Cres.** G53: Glas ... 1C **116**
**Muirshot Rd.** ML9: Lark ... 1F **161**
**Muirside Av.** G32: Glas ... 2E **107**
G66: Kirk ... 5G **31**
**Muirside Pl.** ML2: Newm ... 3D **146**
**Muirside Rd.** G69: Bail ... 1H **107**
PA3: Pais ... 4F **77**
**Muirside St.** G69: Bail ... 1H **107**
**Muirskeith Cres.** G43: Glas ... 1D **118**
**Muirskeith Pl.** G43: Glas ... 1D **118**
**Muirskeith Rd.** G43: Glas ... 1D **118**
**Muir St.** G64: B'rig ... 6C **48**
G72: Blan ... 3B **140**
ML1: Moth ... 1F **143**
ML3: Ham ... 5H **141**
ML5: Coat ... 4A **90**
ML8: Law ... 5D **158**
ML9: Lark ... 2E **161**
PA4: Renf ... 5F **59**
**Muir Ter.** PA3: Pais ... 4C **78**
**Muirton Dr.** G64: B'rig ... 4B **48**
**Muiryfauld Dr.** G31: Glas ... 1G **105**
**Muiryhall St.** ML5: Coat ... 4C **90**
**Muiryhall St. E.** ML5: Coat ... 4D **90**
**Mulben Cres.** G53: Glas ... 6H **99**
**Mulben Pl.** G53: Glas ... 6H **99**
**Mulben Ter.** G53: Glas ... 5H **99**
**Mulberry Cres.** ML6: Chap ... 2E **113**
**Mulberry Dr.** G75: E Kil ... 6E **149**
**Mulberry Rd.** G43: Glas ... 2B **118**
G71: View ... 4G **109**
**Mulberry Way** G75: E Kil ... 6E **149**
**Mulberry Wynd** G72: Flem ... 4F **123**
**Mull** G74: E Kil ... 3C **150**
ML6: Air ... 6D **92**
**Mullardoch St.** *G23: Glas ... 6B **46***
*(off Rothes Dr.)*
**Mull Av.** PA2: Pais ... 6A **98**
PA4: Renf ... 2E **79**
**Mull Ct.** ML3: Ham ... 2D **152**
**Mullen Ct.** G33: Step ... 4F **67**
**Mull Quad.** ML2: Wis ... 4C **146**
**Mull St.** G21: Glas ... 1D **84**
**Mulvey Cres.** ML6: Air ... 4G **91**
**Mungo Pk.** G75: E Kil ... 3F **149**
**Mungo Pl.** G71: Tann ... 4E **109**
**Munlochy Rd.** G51: Glas ... 4D **80**
**Munro Ct.** G81: Dun ... 1B **42**
**Munro Dr.** G66: Milt C ... 6B **8**
**Munro La.** G13: Glas ... 4E **61**
**Munro La. E.** G13: Glas ... 4E **61**
**Munro Pl.** G13: Glas ... 2E **61**
G74: E Kil ... 6B **138**
**Munro Rd.** G13: Glas ... 4E **61**
**Murano St.** G20: Glas ... 4D **62**
**Murchison** G12: Glas ... 3G **61**
**Murchison Dr.** G75: E Kil ... 4D **148**
**Murchison Rd.** PA6: C'lee ... 2C **74**
**Murdoch Ct.** *PA5: John ... 4E **95***
*(off Tannahill Cres.)*
**Murdoch Dr.** G62: Miln ... 5B **26**
**Murdoch Pl.** ML1: New S ... 4H **127**
**Murdoch Sq.** ML4: Bell ... 6E **111**
**Murdock Rd.** G75: E Kil ... 3G **149**
**Murdostoun Gdns.** ML2: Wis ... 4H **145**
**Murdostoun Rd.** ML2: Newm ... 1G **147**
**Murdostoun Vw.** ML2: Newm ... 3D **146**
**Muriel La.** G78: Barr ... 4E **115**
**Muriel St.** G78: Barr ... 4E **115**
**Murray Av.** G65: Kils ... 4H **11**
**Murray Business Area**
PA3: Pais ... 5G **77**
**Murray Bus. Area** PA3: Pais ... 5H **77**
**Murray Cres.** ML2: Newm ... 2E **147**
**Murrayfield** G64: B'rig ... 4C **48**
**Murrayfield Dr.** G61: Bear ... 6E **45**
**Murrayfield St.** G32: Glas ... 4G **85**
**Murray Gdns.** G66: Milt C ... 5C **8**
**Murray Gro.** G61: Bear ... 5B **24**
**Murrayhill** G75: E Kil ... 3F **149**
**Murray Path** G71: Udd ... 1C **124**
**Murray Pl.** G78: Barr ... 3F **115**
G82: Dumb ... 1C **18**
ML4: Bell ... 6A **110**
**Murray Rd.** G71: Both ... 4E **125**
ML8: Law ... 1H **163**
**Murray Rd., The** G75: E Kil ... 3E **149**
**MURRAY RDBT., THE** ... **3H 149**
**Murray Sq., The** G75: E Kil ... 4G **149**
**Murray St.** PA3: Pais ... 5G **77**
PA4: Renf ... 6E **59**
**Murray Ter.** ML1: Moth ... 2D **142**
MURRAY, THE ... **4G 149**
**Murrin Av.** G64: B'rig ... 6F **49**
**Murroch Av.** G82: Dumb ... 1H **17**
**Murroes Rd.** G51: Glas ... 4D **80**
Mus. of 602 (City of Glasgow)
Squadron ... **4G 79**
Mus. of Piping ... **2D 4**
Mus. of Scottish Country Life
... **5B 136**
**Musgrove Pl.** G75: E Kil ... 3E **149**
**Muslin St.** G40: Glas ... 1B **104**
**Muttonhole Rd.** ML3: Ham ... 3H **151**
M.V. Gipsy Princess ... **5H 11**
**Mybole Dr.** ML6: Air ... 1A **112**
**Mybster Pl.** G51: Glas ... 4D **80**
**Myers Cres.** G71: Udd ... 2E **125**
**Myreside Pl.** G32: Glas ... 5F **85**
**Myreside St.** G32: Glas ... 5F **85**
**Myres Rd.** G53: Glas ... 5D **100**
**Myrie Gdns.** G64: B'rig ... 5D **48**
**Myroch Pl.** G34: Glas ... 2A **88**
**Myrtle Av.** G66: Lenz ... 2C **50**
**Myrtle Dr.** ML1: Holy ... 2B **128**
ML2: Wis ... 5D **144**
**Myrtle Hill La.** G42: Glas ... 5G **103**
**Myrtle La.** ML9: Lark ... 4F **161**
**Myrtle Pk.** G42: Glas ... 4F **103**
**Myrtle Pl.** G42: Glas ... 4G **103**
**Myrtle Rd.** G71: View ... 5F **109**
G81: Clyd ... 3H **41**
**Myrtle Sq.** G64: B'rig ... 1C **64**
**Myrtle St.** G72: Blan ... 6B **124**
**Myrtle Vw. Rd.** G42: Glas ... 5G **103**
**Myrtle Wlk.** G72: Camb ... 1H **121**
**Myvot Av.** G67: Cumb ... 1D **54**
**Myvot Rd.** G67: Cumb ... 1D **54**
(Condorrat)
G67: Cumb ... 3A **54**
(Mollinsburn)


## N


**Naburn Ga.** G5: Glas ... 1G **103**
**Nagle Gdns.** ML1: Cle ... 1F **145**

Nairn Av. G72: Blan . . . . . . . . . . .5A **124**
  ML4: Bell . . . . . . . . . . . . . .1C **126**
Nairn Cres. ML6: Air . . . . . . . . .6A **92**
Nairn Pl. G74: E Kil . . . . . . . . . .6C **138**
  G81: Clyd . . . . . . . . . . . . . . .4B **42**
Nairn Quad. ML2: Wis . . . . . . .4H **145**
Nairnside Rd. G21: Glas . . . . . .2E **65**
Nairn St. G3: Glas . . . . . . . . . . .2B **82**
  G72: Blan . . . . . . . . . . . . . . .3A **140**
  G81: Clyd . . . . . . . . . . . . . . .4B **42**
  ML9: Lark . . . . . . . . . . . . . .3D **160**
Nairn Way G68: Cumb . . . . . . .6A **14**
Naismith St. G32: Carm . . . . . .5C **106**
Naismith Wlk. ML4: Bell . . . . . .6E **111**
Nansen St. G20: Glas . . . . . . . .6E **63**
Napier Ct. G60: Old K . . . . . . . .2G **41**
  G68: Cumb . . . . . . . . . . . . . .3D **14**
Napier Cres. G82: Dumb . . . . . .4C **16**
Napier Dr. G51: Glas . . . . . . . . .3H **81**
Napier Gdns. PA3: Lin . . . . . . . .5A **76**
Napier Hill G75: E Kil . . . . . . . .3G **149**
Napier La. G75: E Kil . . . . . . . . .3G **149**
Napier Pk. G68: Cumb . . . . . . . .4C **14**
Napier Pl. G51: Glas . . . . . . . . .3H **81**
  G60: Old K . . . . . . . . . . . . . .2G **41**
  G68: Cumb . . . . . . . . . . . . . .3C **14**
Napier Rd. G51: Glas . . . . . . . . .3H **81**
  G52: Hill . . . . . . . . . . . . . . . .4A **80**
  G68: Cumb . . . . . . . . . . . . . .4C **14**
Napiershall La. *G20: Glas* . . . . . .*1D **82***
  *(off Napiershall St.)*
Napiershall Pl. G20: Glas . . . . . .1D **82**
Napiershall St. G20: Glas . . . . . .1D **82**
Napier Sq. ML4: Bell . . . . . . . . .6D **110**
Napier St. G51: Glas . . . . . . . . .3H **81**
  G81: Clyd . . . . . . . . . . . . . . .2E **59**
  PA3: Lin . . . . . . . . . . . . . . . .5A **76**
  PA5: John . . . . . . . . . . . . . .2E **95**
Napier Ter. G51: Glas . . . . . . . .3H **81**
Napier Way G68: Cumb . . . . . . .4C **14**
Naproch Pl. G77: Newt M . . . . . .4A **134**
Naseby Av. G11: Glas . . . . . . . . .6F **61**
Naseby La. G11: Glas . . . . . . . . .6F **61**
Nasmyth Av. G61: Bear . . . . . . .5B **24**
  G75: E Kil . . . . . . . . . . . . . .4H **149**
Nasmyth Bank G75: E Kil . . . . .4H **149**
Nasmyth Rd. G52: Hill . . . . . . . .4A **80**
Nasmyth Rd. Nth. G52: Hill . . . .4A **80**
  *(not continuous)*
Nasmyth Rd. Sth. G52: Hill . . . .4A **80**
Nassau Pl. G75: E Kil . . . . . . . .2C **148**
National Bank La.
  G1: Glas . . . . . . . . .4F **83** (5D **4**)
Navar Pl. PA2: Pais . . . . . . . . . .3C **98**
Naver St. G33: Glas . . . . . . . . . .2G **85**
Naylor La. ML6: Air . . . . . . . . . .3B **92**
Needle Grn. ML8: Carl . . . . . . . .3F **165**
Neidpath G69: Bail . . . . . . . . . .1G **107**
Neidpath Av. ML5: Coat . . . . . . .2D **110**
Neidpath E. G74: E Kil . . . . . . . .1F **149**
Neidpath Pl. ML5: Coat . . . . . . .2C **110**
Neidpath Rd. ML8: Carl . . . . . . .2E **165**
Neidpath Rd. E. G46: Giff . . . . . .3G **133**
Neidpath Rd. W. G46: Giff . . . . . .2G **133**
Neidpath W. G74: E Kil . . . . . . . .1F **149**
Neilsland Dr. ML1: Moth . . . . . . .3D **142**
  ML3: Ham . . . . . . . . . . . . . .4G **153**
Neilsland Oval G53: Glas . . . . . .5D **100**
Neilsland Rd. ML3: Ham . . . . . . .2F **153**
Neilsland Sq. G53: Glas . . . . . . .4D **100**
  ML3: Ham . . . . . . . . . . . . . .2G **153**
Neilsland St. ML3: Ham . . . . . . .2G **153**
Neilson Ct. ML3: Ham . . . . . . . . .1A **154**
Neilson St. ML4: Bell . . . . . . . . .2C **126**
NEILSTON . . . . . . . . . . . . . . . . .2E **131**
Neilston Av. G53: Glas . . . . . . . .2C **116**
Neilston Ct. G53: Glas . . . . . . . .2C **116**
Neilston Leisure Cen. . . . . . . .2E **131**
Neilston Pl. G65: Kils . . . . . . . . .2F **11**
Neilston Rd. G78: Neil . . . . . . . .1E **131**
  PA2: Pais . . . . . . . . . . . . . . .2A **98**
Neilston Station (Rail) . . . . . . .2D **130**
Neilston Wlk G65: Kils . . . . . . . .2F **11**
  *(not continuous)*
Neil St. PA4: Renf . . . . . . . . . . .4F **59**
Neilvaig Dr. G73: Ruth . . . . . . . .4D **120**
Neistpoint Dr. G33: Glas . . . . . . .3A **86**
Nelson Av. ML5: Coat . . . . . . . . .1A **110**
Nelson Cres. ML1: Moth . . . . . . .5B **144**
Nelson Mandela Pl.
  G2: Glas . . . . . . . . .3G **83** (4E **5**)
Nelson Pl. G69: Bail . . . . . . . . . .1H **107**
Nelson St. G5: Glas . . . . . . . . . .5E **83**
  G69: Bail . . . . . . . . . . . . . . .1H **107**
Nelson Ter. G74: E Kil . . . . . . . .3A **150**
Neptune St. G51: Glas . . . . . . . .4H **81**
Neptune Way ML4: Moss . . . . . .2G **127**
NERSTON . . . . . . . . . . . . . . . . .3A **138**
Nerston Rd. G74: Ners, Roger . .3G **137**
Ness Av. PA5: John . . . . . . . . . .5C **94**

Ness Dr. G72: Blan . . . . . . . . . .6C **124**
  G74: E Kil . . . . . . . . . . . . . .2B **150**
Ness Gdns. G64: B'rig . . . . . . . .6D **48**
  ML9: Lark . . . . . . . . . . . . . .5E **161**
Ness Rd. PA4: Renf . . . . . . . . . .5D **58**
Ness St. G33: Glas . . . . . . . . . . .2G **85**
  ML2: Wis . . . . . . . . . . . . . . .3H **157**
Ness Ter. ML3: Ham . . . . . . . . . .2E **153**
Ness Way ML1: Holy . . . . . . . . .2A **128**
Nethan Av. ML2: Wis . . . . . . . . .1C **156**
Nethan Ga. ML3: Ham . . . . . . . .6G **141**
Nethan Path ML9: Lark . . . . . . .5E **161**
Nethan Pl. ML3: Ham . . . . . . . . .5H **153**
Nethan St. G51: Glas . . . . . . . . .3G **81**
  ML1: Moth . . . . . . . . . . . . . .5E **127**
Nether Auldhouse Rd.
  G43: Glas . . . . . . . . . . . . . .1H **117**
Netherbank Rd. ML2: Wis . . . . .1D **156**
Netherbog Av. G82: Dumb . . . . .3H **17**
Netherbog Rd. G82: Dumb . . . . .3H **17**
Netherburn Av. G44: Neth . . . . .5D **118**
  PA6: C'lee . . . . . . . . . . . . . . .3E **75**
Netherburn Gdns. PA6: C'lee . . .3E **75**
Netherburn Rd. ML9: Ashg . . . . .5C **162**
Netherby Dr. G41: Glas . . . . . . .1B **102**
Nethercairn Pl. G77: Newt M . . .4A **134**
Nethercairn Rd. G43: Glas . . . . .3A **118**
Nethercliffe Av. G44: Neth . . . . .5D **118**
Nethercommon Ind. Est.
  PA3: Pais . . . . . . . . . . . . . . .3A **78**
  *(not continuous)*
Nethercraigs Ct. PA2: Pais . . . . .6F **97**
Nethercraigs Dr. PA2: Pais . . . . .5G **97**
Nethercraigs Rd. PA2: Pais . . . . .6F **97**
Nethercroy Rd. G65: Croy . . . . . .6A **12**
Netherdale G77: Newt M . . . . . .4H **133**
Netherdale Cres. ML2: Wis . . . . .1C **156**
Netherdale Dr. PA1: Pais . . . . . .1H **99**
Netherdale Rd. ML2: Wis . . . . . .1E **157**
Nethergreen Cres. PA4: Renf . . .6D **58**
Nethergreen Wynd
  PA4: Renf . . . . . . . . . . . . . . .6D **58**
Netherhall Rd. ML2: Wis . . . . . .1D **156**
Netherhill Av. G44: Neth . . . . . . .6D **118**
Netherhill Cotts. *PA3: Pais* . . . . . .*4C **78***
  *(off Netherhill Rd.)*
Netherhill Cres. PA3: Pais . . . . .5C **78**
Netherhill Rd. G69: Mood . . . . . .6D **52**
  PA3: Pais . . . . . . . . . . . . . . .5B **78**
Netherhill Way PA3: Pais . . . . . .4D **78**
Netherhouse Av. G66: Lenz . . . . .3E **51**
  ML5: Coat . . . . . . . . . . . . . .2B **110**
Netherhouse Pl. G34: Glas . . . . .3C **88**
Netherhouse Rd. G34: Glas . . . .4B **88**
  G69: Barg . . . . . . . . . . . . . .4B **88**
NETHER KIRKTON . . . . . . . . . .1F **131**
NETHERLEE . . . . . . . . . . . . . . .5D **118**
Netherlee Pl. G44: Glas . . . . . . .3E **119**
Netherlee Rd. G44: Glas . . . . . . .2E **119**
Nethermains Rd. G62: Miln . . . . .5G **25**
Netherpark Av. G44: Neth . . . . . .6D **118**
Netherplace . . . . . . . . . . . . . . .5A **132**
Netherplace Cres.
  G77: Newt M . . . . . . . . . . . .5C **132**
Netherplace Rd. G53: Glas . . . . .5B **100**
  G77: Newt M . . . . . . . . . . . .5A **132**
Netherpool Cres. G53: Glas . . . .5B **100**
NETHERTON
  Glasgow . . . . . . . . . . . . . . .1E **61**
  Wishaw . . . . . . . . . . . . . . .2E **157**
Netherton Av. G13: Glas . . . . . . .2E **61**
Netherton Ct. G45: Glas . . . . . . .5B **120**
  G77: Newt M . . . . . . . . . . . .3F **133**
Netherton Dr. G78: Barr . . . . . . .5F **115**
Netherton Farm La. G61: Glas . .1F **61**
Netherton Hill G66: Len . . . . . . .3C **6**
Netherton Ind. Est. ML2: Wis . . .1E **157**
Netherton Oval G66: Len . . . . . .3D **6**
Netherton Rd. G13: Glas . . . . . . .1E **61**
  G75: E Kil . . . . . . . . . . . . . .6C **148**
  *(Mallard Cres.)*
  G75: E Kil . . . . . . . . . . . . . .5E **149**
  *(Owen Av.)*
  G77: Newt M . . . . . . . . . . . .3F **133**
  ML2: Wis . . . . . . . . . . . . . . .1C **156**
Netherton St. ML2: Wis . . . . . . .1F **157**
Nethervale Av. G44: Neth . . . . . .6D **118**
Netherview Rd. G44: Neth . . . . . .6E **118**
Netherway G44: Neth . . . . . . . . .6D **118**
Netherwood Av. G68: Cumb . . . .5C **34**
Netherwood Ct. G68: Cumb . . . .5C **34**
  *ML1: Moth* . . . . . . . . . . . . . .*1B **156***
  *(off Muirhouse Rd.)*
Netherwood Gro. G68: Cumb . . . .5B **34**
Netherwood Pl. G68: Cumb . . . .5B **34**
Netherwood Rd. G68: Cumb . . . .5B **34**
  ML1: Moth . . . . . . . . . . . . . .6B **144**
Netherwood Twr. ML1: Moth . . . .1B **156**
Netherwood Way G68: Cumb . . .5C **34**
Nethy Way PA4: Renf . . . . . . . . .2H **79**

Neuk Av. G69: Muirh . . . . . . . . .2A **68**
  PA6: Hous . . . . . . . . . . . . . .2C **74**
Neuk Cres. PA6: Hous . . . . . . . .1C **74**
Neuk, The ML2: Wis . . . . . . . . . .6E **145**
Neuk Way G32: Carm . . . . . . . . .5C **106**
  PA6: Hous . . . . . . . . . . . . . .2C **74**
Neva Pl. *PA11: Bri W* . . . . . . . . . .*3F **73***
  *(off Main St.)*
Neville G74: E Kil . . . . . . . . . . .4C **138**
Nevis Av. ML3: Ham . . . . . . . . . .1E **153**
Nevis Ct. G78: Barr . . . . . . . . . .6E **115**
  ML1: Moth . . . . . . . . . . . . . .5G **143**
  ML5: Coat . . . . . . . . . . . . . .2E **111**
Nevis Dr. G64: Torr . . . . . . . . . . .4D **28**
Nevison St. ML9: Lark . . . . . . . .3F **161**
Nevis Rd. G43: Glas . . . . . . . . . .2H **117**
  G61: Bear . . . . . . . . . . . . . . .6B **24**
  PA4: Renf . . . . . . . . . . . . . . .2D **78**
Nevis Way PA3: Glas A . . . . . . . .2A **78**
Newark Dr. G41: Glas . . . . . . . . .2B **102**
  ML2: Wis . . . . . . . . . . . . . . .3A **146**
  PA2: Pais . . . . . . . . . . . . . . .5G **97**
Newark Pl. ML2: Wis . . . . . . . . .3B **146**
NEWARTHILL . . . . . . . . . . . . . .3F **129**
Newarthill Rd. ML1: Carf . . . . . .5C **128**
New Ashtree St. ML2: Wis . . . . .6E **145**
Newbank Ct. G31: Glas . . . . . . . .1G **105**
Newbank Gdns. G31: Glas . . . . . .1F **105**
Newbank Rd. G31: Glas . . . . . . .1G **105**
Newbarns St. ML8: Carl . . . . . . .2F **165**
Newbattle Av. ML6: C'bnk . . . . . .3B **112**
Newbattle Ct. G32: Glas . . . . . . .3B **106**
Newbattle Gdns. G32: Glas . . . . .3B **106**
Newbattle Pl. G32: Glas . . . . . . .3B **106**
Newbattle Rd. G32: Glas . . . . . . .3A **106**
Newbold Av. G21: Glas . . . . . . . .2A **64**
NEWBRIDGE END . . . . . . . . . . .5F **165**
New Broomfield Stadium . . . . . .5C **92**
Newburgh PA8: Ersk . . . . . . . . .4E **41**
Newburgh St. G43: Glas . . . . . . .6B **102**
Newcastleton Dr. G23: Glas . . . .6C **46**
New City Rd. G4: Glas . . . . .1E **83** (1B **4**)
  *(not continuous)*
Newcraigs Dr. G76: Crmck . . . . .2H **135**
Newcroft Dr. G44: Glas . . . . . . . .2H **119**
New Cross *ML6: Air* . . . . . . . . . . .*4A **92***
  *(off Stirling St.)*
New Cross Cen. ML3: Ham . . . . .6A **142**
Newdyke Av. G66: Kirk . . . . . . . .5E **31**
Newdyke Rd. G66: Kirk . . . . . . . .5E **31**
New Edinburgh Rd.
  G71: Tann, View . . . . . . . . . .6C **108**
  ML4: Bell . . . . . . . . . . . . . . .2A **126**
Newfield Cres. ML3: Ham . . . . . .5F **141**
Newfield La. G71: Both . . . . . . . .4F **125**
Newfield Pl. G46: T'bnk . . . . . . .5F **117**
  G73: Ruth . . . . . . . . . . . . . . .6A **104**
Newfield Sq. G53: Glas . . . . . . . .1A **116**
Newford Gro. G76: Busby . . . . . .4D **134**
Newgrove Gdns. G72: Camb . . . .1A **122**
Newhall St. G40: Glas . . . . . . . . .2B **104**
Newhaven Rd. G33: Glas . . . . . . .3B **86**
Newhaven St. G32: Glas . . . . . . .4A **86**
Newhills Rd. G33: Glas . . . . . . . .4E **87**
NEWHOUSE . . . . . . . . . . . . . . .5H **113**
Newhouse Ind. Est.
  ML1: N'hse . . . . . . . . . . . . . .6C **112**
  *(Greenside Rd.)*
  ML1: N'hse . . . . . . . . . . . . . .5D **112**
  *(York Rd.)*
NEWHOUSE INTERCHANGE
  . . . . . . . . . . . . . . . . . . . . . . . . .5G **113**
Newhousemill Rd.
  G72: Blan . . . . . . . . . . . . . . .4F **151**
Newhousemill Rd. G74: E Kil . . .4C **150**
  ML3: Ham . . . . . . . . . . . . . .3H **151**
Newhut Rd. ML1: Moth . . . . . . . .1F **143**
New Inchinnan Rd. PA3: Pais . . .4A **78**
Newington St. G32: Glas . . . . . . .5H **85**
New Kirk Rd. G61: Bear . . . . . . .2E **45**
New Lairdsland Rd. G66: Kirk . . .4C **30**
NEWLANDS . . . . . . . . . . . . . . .2C **118**
Newlands Dr. ML3: Ham . . . . . . .3H **153**
Newlandsfield Rd. G43: Glas . . . .6B **102**
Newlands Gdns. PA5: Eld . . . . . .4A **96**
NEWLANDSMUIR . . . . . . . . . . . .6B **148**
Newlandsmuir Rd. G75: E Kil . . .5B **148**
Newlands Pl. G74: E Kil . . . . . . .2G **149**
Newlands Rd. G43: Glas . . . . . . .6B **102**
  G71: Tann . . . . . . . . . . . . . . .5D **108**
  G75: E Kil . . . . . . . . . . . . . .6A **148**
  *(Newlandsmuir)*
  G75: E Kil . . . . . . . . . . . . . .4C **148**
  *(Westwood)*
Newlands Squash & Tennis Club
  . . . . . . . . . . . . . . . . . . . . . . . . .1D **118**
Newlands St. ML5: Coat . . . . . . .1C **110**
Newlands Ter. G66: Milt C . . . . . .5C **8**
  ML8: Carl . . . . . . . . . . . . . . .3F **165**
New La. ML6: C'bnk . . . . . . . . . .3B **112**

New Line Pend *G74: E Kil* . . . . . .*1H **14***
  *(off Kittoch Pl.)*
New Luce Dr. G32: Glas . . . . . . .2D **10?**
NEWMAINS
  Renfrew . . . . . . . . . . . . . . .2E **79**
  Wishaw . . . . . . . . . . . . . . .5E **147**
Newmains Av. PA4: Inch . . . . . . .4F **57**
Newmains Rd. PA4: Renf . . . . . .1D **78**
Newmill Rd. G21: Glas . . . . . . . .4E **65**
Newmilns St. G53: Glas . . . . . . .1H **115**
NEW MONKLAND . . . . . . . . . . . .5G **71**
Newnham Rd. PA1: Pais . . . . . . .1G **99**
Newpark Cres. G72: Camb . . . . .6A **106**
New Pk. St. ML3: Ham . . . . . . . .4G **141**
New Plymouth G75: E Kil . . . . . .3E **123**
New Rd. G72: Camb . . . . . . . . . .3E **123**
Newrose Av. ML4: Bell . . . . . . . .6D **110**
Newshot Ct. *G81: Clyd* . . . . . . . . .*2F **59***
  *(off Clydeholm Ter.)*
Newshot Dr. PA8: Ersk . . . . . . . .5F **41**
New Sneddon St. PA3: Pais . . . . .5A **78**
  *(not continuous)*
Newstead Gdns. G23: Glas . . . . .6C **48**
NEW STEVENSTON . . . . . . . . . .3C **128**
New Stevenston Rd.
  ML1: Carf . . . . . . . . . . . . . . .5B **128**
  *(not continuous)*
New St. G72: Blan . . . . . . . . . . .2A **140**
  G81: Dun . . . . . . . . . . . . . . .1C **42**
  PA1: Pais . . . . . . . . . . . . . . .1A **98**
  PA10: Kilb . . . . . . . . . . . . . .2A **94**
NEWTON . . . . . . . . . . . . . . . . .1G **123**
Newton Av. G72: Camb . . . . . . . .1D **122**
  G78: Barr . . . . . . . . . . . . . . .6F **115**
  PA3: Pais . . . . . . . . . . . . . . .4D **78**
  PA5: Eld . . . . . . . . . . . . . . . .2C **96**
Newton Brae G72: Newt . . . . . . .1F **123**
Newton Ct. G77: Newt M . . . . . . .6E **133**
Newton Dr. G71: Tann . . . . . . . . .6E **109**
  ML2: Newm . . . . . . . . . . . . .4E **147**
  PA5: Eld . . . . . . . . . . . . . . . .2C **96**
Newton Farm Rd. G72: Newt . . . .6F **107**
Newtongrange Av. G32: Glas . . . .2B **106**
Newtongrange Gdns.
  G32: Glas . . . . . . . . . . . . . .3B **106**
Newton Gro. G77: Newt M . . . . . .6D **132**
Newtonlea Av. G77: Newt M . . . . .5E **133**
NEWTON MEARNS . . . . . . . . . . .5D **132**
Newton Pl. G3: Glas . . . . . . . . . .2D **82**
  G77: Newt M . . . . . . . . . . . .6E **133**
  PA7: B'ton . . . . . . . . . . . . . . .4F **39**
Newton Station (Rail) . . . . . . . .2E **123**
Newton Sta. Rd.
  G72: Flem, Newt . . . . . . . . . .3E **123**
Newton St. G3: Glas . . . . . .3E **83** (3A **4**)
  ML5: Coat . . . . . . . . . . . . . .1A **110**
  PA1: Pais . . . . . . . . . . . . . . .1G **97**
Newton Ter. *G3: Glas* . . . . . . . . .*3D **82***
  *(off Sauchiehall St.)*
  PA1: Pais . . . . . . . . . . . . . . .2D **96**
Newton Ter. La. *G3: Glas* . . . . . . .*3D **82***
  *(off Elderslie St.)*
Newton Way PA3: Pais . . . . . . . .4D **78**
Newtown St. G65: Kils . . . . . . . .3H **11**
Newtyle Dr. G53: Glas . . . . . . . .4H **99**
  G64: B'rig . . . . . . . . . . . . . . .6F **49**
Newtyle Pl. G53: Glas . . . . . . . .4H **99**
Newtyle Rd. PA1: Pais . . . . . . . .1D **98**
New Vw. Cres. ML4: Bell . . . . . . .4C **126**
New Vw. Dr. ML4: Bell . . . . . . . .4C **126**
New Vw. Pl. ML4: Bell . . . . . . . .4C **126**
New Wynd G1: Glas . . . . . . .5G **83** (6F **5**)
Next Generation Health Club . . .1F **61**
Niamh Ct. PA4: Inch . . . . . . . . . .2G **57**
Nicholas St. G1: Glas . . . . .4H **83** (5H **5**)
Nicholson St. G5: Glas . . . . . . . .6F **83**
Nicklaus Way ML1: N'hse . . . . . .6E **113**
Nicolson Ct. G33: Step . . . . . . . .4D **66**
Nicol St. ML6: Air . . . . . . . . . . . .3B **92**
Niddrie Rd. G42: Glas . . . . . . . . .3D **102**
Niddrie Sq. G42: Glas . . . . . . . . .3D **102**
Niddry St. PA3: Pais . . . . . . . . . .6B **78**
Nigel Gdns. G41: Glas . . . . . . . .4B **102**
Nigel St. ML1: Moth . . . . . . . . . .3F **143**
Nigg Pl. G34: Glas . . . . . . . . . . .3G **87**
Nightingale Pl. PA5: John . . . . . .6D **94**
Nikitas Av. ML9: Lark . . . . . . . . .6F **161**
Nimmo Dr. G51: Glas . . . . . . . . .4E **81**
Nimmo Pl. ML2: Wis . . . . . . . . . .6A **146**
  ML8: Carl . . . . . . . . . . . . . . .3F **165**
Ninian Av. PA6: C'lee . . . . . . . . .3C **74**
Ninian Rd. ML6: Air . . . . . . . . . .6B **92**
Ninian's Ri. G66: Kirk . . . . . . . . .6F **31**
Nisbet St. G31: Glas . . . . . . . . . .6F **85**
Nisbett Pl. ML6: Chap . . . . . . . . .2E **113**
Nisbett St. ML6: Chap . . . . . . . .3E **113**
Nissen Pl. G53: Glas . . . . . . . . . .4H **99**
Nith Dr. ML3: Ham . . . . . . . . . . .3E **153**
  PA4: Renf . . . . . . . . . . . . . . .1G **79**

Nith La.—Orchard Gro.


ith La. ML2: Newm 3D 146
(off King St.)
ith Path ML1: Cle 5H 129
.th Pl. PA5: John 5C 94
ith Quad. ML1: N'hill 4C 128
ithsdale G74: E Kil 6D 138
'thsdale Cres. G61: Bear 1C 44
thsdale Dr. G41: Glas 3D 102
.thsdale Pl. G41: Glas 2D 102
ithsdale Rd. G41: Glas 1H 101
(Dumbreck Rd.)
G41: Glas 3D 102
(Pollokshaws Rd.)
thsdale St. G41: Glas 3D 102
ith St. G33: Glas 2F 85
ith Way PA4: Renf 1G 79
ITSHILL 2A 116
itshill Rd. G53: Glas, T'bnk 1H 115
itshill Station (Rail) 2A 116
iven St. G20: Glas 3A 62
oble Rd. ML4: Bell 2C 126
obles Pl. ML4: Bell 3B 126
obles Vw. ML4: Bell 3B 126
oldrum Av. G32: Carm 5C 106
oldrum Gdns. G32: Carm 5C 106
orbreck Dr. G46: Giff 3A 118
orby Rd. G11: Glas 6F 61
oremac Way ML4: Bell 6B 110
orfield Dr. G44: Glas 6F 103
orfolk Ct. G5: Glas 6F 83
orfolk Cres. G64: B'rig 4A 48
orfolk St. G5: Glas 6F 83
orham St. G41: Glas 4C 102
orman St. G40: Glas 2B 104
orse La. Nth. G14: Glas 5C 60
orse La. Sth. G14: Glas 5C 60
orse Pl. G14: Glas 5C 60
orse Rd. G14: Glas 5C 60
orthall Quad. ML1: Carf 6A 128
orthampton Dr. G12: Glas 3H 61
orthampton La. *G12: Glas* *3H 61*
*(off Northampton Dr.)*
orth & South Rd. ML1: Cle 1C 146
orth Av. G72: Camb 1H 121
G81: Clyd 4C 42
ML1: New S 5A 128
ML8: Carl 3D 164
orth Bank *PA6: Hous* *1B 74*
*(off North St.)*
orthbank Av. G66: Kirk 5C 30
G72: Camb 1D 122
th. Bank Pl. G81: Clyd 1E 59
orthbank Rd. G66: Kirk 5C 30
orthbank St. G72: Camb 1D 122
th. Bank St. G81: Clyd 1E 59
ORTH BARR 4E 41
th. Barr Av. PA8: Ersk 4E 41
ORTH BARRWOOD 3A 12
th. Berwick Av. G68: Cumb 6H 13
th. Berwick Cres. G75: E Kil 5C 148
th. Berwick Gdns. G68: Cumb 6H 13
th. Biggar Rd. ML6: Air 3B 92
th. Birbiston Rd. G66: Len 3F 7
orthbrae Pl. G13: Glas 3B 60
orth Bri. St. ML6: Air 3H 91
th. British Rd. G71: Udd 1D 124
orthburn Av. ML6: Air 2B 92
orthburn Pl. ML6: Air 1B 92
orthburn Rd. ML5: Coat 2E 91
orthburn St. ML6: Plain 1H 93
th. Bute St. ML5: Coat 1D 110
th. Caldeen Rd. ML5: Coat 6E 91
th. Calder Dr. ML6: Air 5D 92
th. Calder Gro. G71: Udd 3H 107
th. Calder Pl. G71: Udd 3G 107
th. Calder Rd. G71: View 4G 109
th. Campbell Av. G62: Miln 4F 25
th. Canal Bank G4: Glas 1G 83
th. Canal Bank St.
G4: Glas 1G 83 (1E 5)
th. Carbrain Rd. G67: Cumb 5G 35
ORTH CARDONALD 4B 80
th. Claremont La. G62: Miln 3G 25
th. Claremont St. G3: Glas 2C 82
th. Corsebar Rd. PA2: Pais 3G 97
orth Ct. G1: Glas 4G 83 (5E 5)
orth Ct. La. G1: Glas 4G 83 (5E 5)
orthcroft Rd. G69: Mood 5C 52
th. Croft St. PA3: Pais 6B 78
th. Dean Pk. Av. G71: Both 4E 125
th. Douglas St. G81: Clyd 1E 59
orth Dr. G1: Glas 4F 83 (6D 4)
PA3: Lin 5H 75
th. Dryburgh Rd. ML2: Wis 4G 145
th. Dumgoyne Av. G62: Miln 2F 25
th. Elgin Pl. G81: Clyd 2E 59
th. Elgin St. G81: Clyd 2E 59
th. Erskine Pk. G61: Bear 2D 44
ORTHFIELD 2F 11
orthfield G75: E Kil 4B 148
Northfield Rd. G65: Kils 2F 11
Northfield St. ML1: Moth 1G 143
Nth. Frederick St. G1: Glas 4G 83 (5F 5)
Nth. Gardinar St. G11: Glas 1H 81
Northgate Quad. G21: Glas 2E 65
Northgate Rd. G21: Glas 2E 65
Nth. Gower St. G51: Glas 6A 82
Nth. Grange Rd. G61: Bear 1E 45
Nth. Hanover St. G1: Glas 3G 83 (5F 5)
Northinch Ct. G14: Glas 1D 80
Northinch St. G14: Glas 1D 80
Nth. Iverton Pk. Rd. PA5: John 2G 95
NORTH KELVIN 6C 62
Nth. Kilmeny Cres. ML2: Wis 3A 146
Northland Av. G14: Glas 4C 60
Northland Dr. G14: Glas 4C 60
Northland Gdns. G14: Glas 4C 60
Northland La. G14: Glas 5C 60
North La. PA3: Lin 5A 76
NORTH LODGE 5F 143
Nth. Lodge Av. ML1: Moth 5G 143
Nth. Lodge Rd. PA4: Renf 5E 59
Nth. Moraine La. G15: Glas 5C 44
NORTH MOTHERWELL 2D 142
Northmuir Dr. ML2: Wis 5B 146
Northmuir Rd. G15: Glas 3B 44
Nth. Orchard St. ML1: Moth 2F 143
Nth. Park Av. G46: T'bnk 3F 117
Northpark St. G20: Glas 5D 62
North Pk. Vs. G46: T'bnk 4F 117
Nth. Portland St.
G1: Glas 4H 83 (5G 5)
North Rd. G68: Cumb 5C 34
ML4: Bell 2C 126
PA5: John 3E 95
North Sq. ML5: Coat 3A 90
North St. G3: Glas 2D 82 (2A 4)
ML1: Moth 1H 143
ML9: Lark 1E 161
PA3: Pais 5A 78
PA6: Hous 1A 74
Northumberland St. G20: Glas 5C 62
North Vw. G61: Bear 5D 44
North Vw. Rd. PA11: Bri W 5H 73
Nth. Wallace St.
G4: Glas 2H 83 (2G 5)
Northway G72: Blan 6A 124
Northwood Dr. ML2: Newm 3E 147
Nth. Woodside Leisure Cen. 1E 83
Nth. Woodside Rd. G20: Glas 6D 62
(not continuous)
Norval St. G11: Glas 1G 81
Norwich Dr. G12: Glas 4H 61
Norwood Av. G66: Kirk 5B 30
Norwood Dr. G46: Giff 6G 117
Norwood Pk. G61: Bear 4F 45
Norwood Ter. G71: Tann 6E 109
Nottingham Av. G12: Glas 3H 61
Nottingham La. *G12: Glas* *3H 61*
*(off Northampton Dr.)*
Novar Dr. G12: Glas 5G 61
Novar Gdns. G64: B'rig 5A 48
Novar St. ML3: Ham 1H 153
Nuneaton St. G40: Glas 2C 104
Nuneaton St. Ind. Est.
G40: Glas 2C 104
Nurseries Rd. G69: Bail 5F 87
Nursery Av. PA7: B'ton 3C 40
Nursery Ct. ML8: Carl 2E 165
Nursery Dr. ML9: Ashg 5C 162
Nursery La. G41: Glas 3D 102
Nursery Pk. ML8: Carl 3E 165
Nursery Pl. G72: Blan 3B 140
Nursery St. G41: Glas 2E 103
Nutberry Ct. G42: Glas 4F 103


## O


Oak Av. G61: Bear 6F 25
G75: E Kil 5D 148
Oakbank Av. ML2: Wis 2E 157
Oakbank Dr. G78: Barr 6F 115
Oakbank Ind. Est. G20: Glas 6F 63
Oakbank St. ML6: Air 4D 92
Oakburn Av. G62: Miln 4F 25
Oakburn Cres. G62: Miln 3F 25
Oak Cres. G69: Bail 1G 107
Oakdene Av. G71: Tann 6F 109
ML4: Bell 6C 110
Oakdene Cres. ML1: N'hill 4C 128
Oak Dr. G66: Lenz 2B 50
G72: Camb 3C 122
Oak Fern Dr. G74: E Kil 5F 137
Oak Fern Gro. G74: E Kil 5F 137
Oakfield Av. G12: Glas 1C 82
Oakfield Dr. ML1: Moth 3G 143
Oakfield La. *G12: Glas* *1C 82*
*(off Gibson St.)*
Oakfield Rd. ML1: Moth 3G 143
Oakfield Twr. ML1: Moth 4G 143
Oak Gro. ML6: Chap 2E 113
Oakhill Av. G69: Bail 2F 107
Oak Lea ML3: Ham 1B 154
Oaklea Cres. G72: Blan 1A 140
Oakley Dr. G44: Neth 4D 118
Oakley Ter. G31: Glas 4B 84
Oak Pk. G64: B'rig 6D 48
ML1: Moth 5F 143
Oak Pl. G71: View 6G 109
G75: E Kil 5D 148
ML5: Coat 6E 91
Oakridge Cres. PA3: Pais 6F 77
Oak Rd. G67: Cumb 1E 37
G81: Clyd 2B 42
PA2: Pais 4C 98
Oakshaw Brae PA1: Pais 6H 77
Oakshawhead PA1: Pais 6H 77
Oakshaw St. E. PA1: Pais 6H 77
Oakshaw St. W. PA1: Pais 6H 77
Oakside Pl. ML3: Ham 4H 153
Oaks, The G44: Glas 3F 119
PA5: John 3E 95
Oak St. G2: Glas 4E 83 (5A 4)
Oaktree Gdns. G45: Glas 3B 120
G82: Dumb 3C 18
Oakwood Av. PA2: Pais 4F 97
Oakwood Cres. G34: Glas 2B 88
Oakwood Dr. G34: Glas 2B 88
G77: Newt M 5F 133
ML5: Coat 6H 89
Oakwood Vw. ML1: Holy 2B 128
Oak Wynd G72: Flem 4F 123
Oates Gdns. ML1: Moth 5B 144
Oatfield St. G21: Glas 5D 64
OATLANDS 3H 103
Oban Ct. G20: Glas 5C 62
Oban Dr. G20: Glas 5C 62
Oban La. G20: Glas 5C 62
Oban Pass G20: Glas 5C 62
Observatory La. G12: Glas 6B 62
Observatory Rd. G12: Glas 6A 62
Ochel Path ML6: Chap 4F 113
Ochil Dr. G78: Barr 6D 114
PA2: Pais 5H 97
Ochil Pl. G32: Glas 1A 106
Ochil Rd. G61: Bear 6B 24
G64: B'rig 6E 49
PA4: Renf 2D 78
Ochil St. G32: Glas 1A 106
ML2: Wis 5F 145
Ochiltree Av. G13: Glas 2F 61
Ochiltree Dr. ML3: Ham 2C 152
Ochil Vw. G71: Tann 5E 109
Odense Ct. G75: E Kil 5G 149
Odeon Cinema 5D 82
Ogilvie Athletic Ground 5A 66
Ogilvie Ct. *ML6: Air* *3E 93*
*(off Katherine St.)*
Ogilvie Pl. G31: Glas 1F 105
Ogilvie St. G31: Glas 1F 105
Old Aisle Rd. G66: Kirk 6F 31
Old Albert St. ML5: Coat 4C 90
Old Avon Rd. ML3: Ham 1C 154
OLD BALORNOCK 4D 64
Old Bore Rd. ML6: Air 3E 93
Old Bothwell Rd. G71: Both 6F 125
Old Bridgend ML8: Carl 4F 165
Old Bridge of Weir Rd.
PA6: Hous 1A 74
Old Castle Gdns. G44: Glas 1F 119
Old Castle Rd. G44: Glas 1E 119
Old Chu. Gdns. G69: Barg 6E 89
Old Coach Rd. G74: E Kil 6H 137
Old Cross ML6: Air 3A 92
Old Dalmarnock Rd.
G40: Glas 1B 104
Old Dalnottar Rd. G60: Old K 2F 41
Old Dullatur Rd. G68: Dull 5F 13
Old Dumbarton Rd. G3: Glas 2A 82
Old Edinburgh Rd. G71: Tann 4B 108
ML4: Bell 1A 126
Old Farm La. G61: Glas 1F 61
Old Farm Rd. PA2: Pais 4F 99
Old Ferry Rd. PA8: Ersk 3D 40
Old Gartloch Rd. G69: G'csh 5D 68
Old Glasgow Rd. G67: Cumb 1H 35
G71: Udd 6B 108
(not continuous)
Old Govan Rd. PA4: Renf 6H 59
Old Greenock Rd. PA4: Inch 6C 40
(East Craigend)
PA4: Inch 2G 57
(Inchinnan)
PA7: B'ton 2A 38
PA8: Ersk 6C 40
Oldhall Rd. PA1: Pais 6E 79
OLDHILL 6G 79
Old Howwood Rd. PA9: How 6C 94
Old Humbie Rd. G77: Newt M 6E 133
OLD INNS INTERCHANGE
5B 14
OLD INNS RDBT. 5B 14
OLD KILPATRICK 1E 41
Old Lanark Rd. ML8: Carl 4F 165
(not continuous)
Old Manse Rd. G32: Glas 1D 106
ML2: Wis 3E 157
Old Mill Ga. *G73: Ruth* *1C 120*
*(off Mill St.)*
Old Mill Pk. Ind. Est.
G66: Kirk 4C 30
Old Mill Rd. G71: Both 6E 125
G71: Udd 1D 124
(Lwr. Millgate)
G71: Udd 2D 124
(Bellshill Rd.)
G72: Camb 2D 122
G74: E Kil 1H 149
G81: Dun, Hard 1C 42
PA2: Pais 2F 97
Old Mill Vw. G65: Croy 1B 34
OLD MONKLAND 1A 110
Old Monkland Rd. ML5: Coat 2H 109
Old Playfield Rd. G76: Crmck 1H 135
Old Quarry Rd. G68: Cumb 2H 53
Old Rd. PA5: Eld 2H 95
Old Rutherglen Rd. G5: Glas 6G 83
Old School Ct. ML5: Coat 1C 110
Old Schoolhouse La.
PA6: Hous 1B 74
Old Shettleston Rd. G32: Glas 6H 85
Old Sneddon St. PA3: Pais 6A 78
Old Stable Row ML5: Coat 4D 90
Old St. G81: Dun 1B 42
Old Union St. ML6: Air 4B 92
Old Vic Ct. *G74: E Kil* *5B 138*
*(off Bosworth Rd.)*
Old Wishaw Rd. ML8: Carl 2E 165
ML8: Law 6G 159
Old Wood Rd. G69: Bail 2G 107
Old Wynd G1: Glas 5G 83 (6F 5)
Olifard Av. G71: Both 4F 125
Oliphant Ct. PA2: Pais 5D 96
Oliphant Cres. G76: Busby 4C 134
PA2: Pais 5C 96
Oliphant Oval PA2: Pais 5C 96
Olive Bank G71: View 4G 109
Olive Ct. *ML1: Holy* *2B 128*
*(off Elm Rd.)*
Olive St. G33: Glas 5F 65
Ollach PA8: Ersk 2G 57
Olympia G74: E Kil 2H 149
Olympia Arc. *G74: E Kil* *3H 149*
*(off Olympia Ct.)*
Olympia Ct. G74: E Kil 2H 149
Olympia St. G40: Glas 6B 84
Olympia, The *G74: E Kil* *3H 149*
*(off Olympia Ct.)*
Olympia Way G74: E Kil 2H 149
Omoa Rd. ML1: Cle 6G 129
O'Neill Av. G64: B'rig 1D 64
Onslow G75: E Kil 4E 149
Onslow Dr. G31: Glas 4C 84
Onslow Rd. G81: Clyd 5E 43
Onslow Sq. G31: Glas 4C 84
Ontario Pk. G75: E Kil 2D 148
Ontario Pl. G75: E Kil 2D 148
Onyx St. ML4: Bell 3C 126
Oran Gdns. G20: Glas 4C 62
Oran Ga. G20: Glas 4C 62
Oran Pl. G20: Glas 5C 62
Oran St. G20: Glas 4C 62
ORBISTON 3C 126
Orbiston Ct. ML1: Moth 4A 144
Orbiston Dr. G81: Faif 6F 23
ML4: Bell 4D 126
Orbiston Gdns. G32: Glas 6A 86
Orbiston Pl. G81: Faif 6F 23
Orbiston Rd. ML4: Bell 5D 126
(Community Rd.)
ML4: Bell 3B 126
(Crofthead Cres.)
Orbiston Sq. ML4: Bell 4B 126
Orbiston St. ML1: Moth 3H 143
Orcades Dr. G44: Glas 3F 119
Orchard Av. G71: Both 6F 125
Orchard Brae G66: Lenz 3E 51
Orchard Ct. G32: Carm 5B 106
G46: T'bnk 4G 117
Orchard Dr. G46: Giff 4H 117
(not continuous)
G72: Blan 1A 140
G73: Ruth 5B 104
Orchard Fld. G66: Lenz 3E 51
Orchard Ga. ML9: Lark 3E 161
Orchard Grn. G74: E Kil 5B 138
Orchard Gro. G46: Giff 3H 117
ML5: Coat 5D 90

Orchard Park—Pavilion Theatre

ORCHARD PARK
Lenzie .4E 51
Thornliebank .4H 117
**Orchard Pk.** G46: Giff .4A **118**
**Orchard Pk. Av.** G46: T'bnk .3G **117**
**Orchard Pl.** G66: Kirk .6G **31**
ML3: Ham .6H **141**
ML4: Bell .4B **126**
**Orchard St.** G69: Bail .2F **107**
ML1: Moth .2F **143**
ML2: Over .5H **157**
ML3: Ham .6H **141**
ML8: Carl .4F **165**
PA1: Pais .1A **98**
PA4: Renf .5F **59**
**Orchardton Rd.** G68: Cumb .1G **53**
(Mollins Rd.)
G68: Cumb .2H **53**
(Old Quarry Rd.)
**Orchardton Woods Ind. Pk.**
G68: Cumb .5G **33**
**Orchid Pl.** G66: Len .3E **7**
**Orchy Av.** G76: Clar .6D **118**
**Orchy Ct.** G81: Hard .2E **43**
**Orchy Cres.** G61: Bear .5D **44**
ML6: Air .6C **92**
PA2: Pais .4D **96**
**Orchy Dr.** G76: Clar .6D **118**
**Orchy Gdns.** G76: Clar .6D **118**
**Orchy St.** G44: Glas .1E **119**
**Orchy Ter.** G74: E Kil .2B **150**
**Orefield Pl.** G74: E Kil .6G **137**
**Oregon Pl.** G5: Glas .1G **103**
**Orion Pl.** ML4: Moss .2G **127**
**Orion Way** G72: Camb .1A **122**
ML8: Carl .3D **164**
**Orkney Pl.** G51: Glas .4H **81**
**Orkney Quad.** ML2: Wis .5B **146**
**Orkney St.** G51: Glas .4H **81**
**Orlando** G74: E Kil .4C **138**
**Orleans Av.** G14: Glas .6E **61**
**Orleans La.** *G14: Glas .6E **61***
*(off Victoria Pk. Dr. Nth.)*
**Orlington Ct.** ML5: Coat .3B **90**
**Ormiston Av.** G14: Glas .5C **60**
**Ormiston Dr.** ML3: Ham .3G **153**
**Ormiston La.** *G14: Glas .5C **60***
*(off Norse La. Sth.)*
**Ormiston La. Nth.** *G14: Glas .5C **60***
*(off Norse La. Nth.)*
**Ormonde Av.** G44: Neth .4D **118**
**Ormonde Ct.** G44: Neth .4C **118**
**Ormonde Cres.** G44: Neth .4D **118**
**Ormonde Dr.** G44: Neth .4D **118**
**Ornsay St.** G22: Glas .2H **63**
**Oronsay Ct.** G60: Old K .1G **41**
**Oronsay Cres.** G60: Old K .1G **41**
G61: Bear .4H **45**
**Oronsay Gdns.** G60: Old K .1G **41**
**Oronsay Pl.** G60: Old K .1G **41**
**Oronsay Sq.** G60: Old K .1G **41**
**Orr Church Sq.** PA1: Pais .6H **77**
**Orr Sq.** PA1: Pais .6A **78**
**Orr St.** G40: Glas .6B **84**
(not continuous)
PA1: Pais .6A **78**
PA2: Pais .2A **98**
**Orr Ter.** G78: Neil .3C **130**
**Orton Pl.** G51: Glas .5G **81**
**Osborne Cres.** G74: T'hall .6F **135**
**Osborne St.** G1: Glas .5G **83** (6E **5**)
G81: Clyd .4C **42**
**Oskaig** PA8: Ersk .2G **57**
**Osprey Cres.** ML2: Wis .5G **145**
**Osprey Dr.** G71: Tann .6E **109**
**Osprey Ho.** PA3: Pais .3A **78**
**Ossian Av.** PA1: Pais .6H **79**
**Ossian Rd.** G43: Glas .1C **118**
**Oswald St.** G1: Glas .5F **83** (6C **4**)
**Oswald Wlk.** G62: Miln .5A **26**
**Otago La.** G12: Glas .1C **82**
**Otago La. Nth.** *G12: Glas .1C **82***
*(off Otago St.)*
**Otago Pk.** G75: E Kil .2C **148**
**Otago St.** G12: Glas .1C **82**
**Othello** G74: E Kil .5B **138**
**Ottawa Cres.** G81: Clyd .3H **41**
**Otterburn Dr.** G46: Giff .6A **118**
**Otterswick Pl.** G33: Glas .1C **86**
**Oudenarde Ct.** ML8: Carl .4H **165**
Our Lady of Good Aid R.C. Cathedral
.2G 143
**Oval Path** G52: Glas .2E **101**
**Oval, The** G76: Clar .6D **118**
ML5: Glenb .3G **69**
**Overbrae Pl.** G15: Glas .2H **43**
**Overburn Av.** G82: Dumb .3F **17**
**Overburn Cres.** G82: Dumb .2F **17**
**Overburn Ter.** G82: Dumb .2G **17**
**Overcroy Rd.** G65: Croy .1B **34**
**Overdale Av.** G42: Glas .5D **102**
**Overdale Gdns.** G42: Glas .5D **102**
**Overdale Pl.** ML2: Over .5A **158**
**Overdale St.** G42: Glas .5D **102**
**Overjohnstone Dr.** ML2: Wis .5D **144**
**Overlea Av.** G73: Ruth .1F **121**
**Overlee Rd.** G76: Busby .2D **134**
**Overnewton Pl.** G3: Glas .3B **82**
**Overnewton Sq.** G3: Glas .2B **82**
**Overnewton St.** G3: Glas .2B **82**
**Overton Cres.** PA5: John .2H **95**
**Overton Rd.**
G72: Camb, Flem .3D **122**
PA5: John .3G **95**
**Overton St.** G72: Camb .3D **122**
**Overtoun Av.** G82: Dumb .4H **17**
**Overtoun Dr.** G73: Ruth .6C **104**
G81: Clyd .3B **42**
**Overtoun Rd.** G81: Clyd .3A **42**
OVERTOWN .5A 158
**Overtown Av.** G53: Glas .1A **116**
**Overtown Ct.** G81: Clyd .4A **42**
**Overtown Rd.** ML2: Wis .4B **158**
**Overtown St.** G40: Glas .6C **84**
**Overwood Dr.** G44: Glas .1G **119**
G82: Dumb .3H **17**
**Overwood Gro.** G82: Dumb .3H **17**
**Owen Av.** G75: E Kil .4E **149**
**Owendale Av.** ML4: Bell .6D **110**
**Owen Pk.** G75: E Kil .4F **149**
**Owen St.** ML1: Moth .1G **143**
**O'Wood Av.** ML1: Holy .1B **128**
**Oxford Dr.** PA3: Lin .5H **75**
**Oxford La.** G5: Glas .6F **83**
PA4: Renf .6E **59**
**Oxford Rd.** PA4: Renf .6E **59**
**Oxford St.** G5: Glas .5F **83**
G66: Kirk .5C **30**
ML5: Coat .5B **90**
OXGANG .6F 31
**Oxgang Pl.** G66: Kirk .6E **31**
**Oxhill Pl.** G82: Dumb .4D **16**
**Oxhill Rd.** G82: Dumb .3D **16**
**Oxton Dr.** G52: Glas .6B **80**

P

**Pacific Dr.** G51: Glas .5A **82**
**Paddock St.** ML5: Coat .1F **111**
**Paddock, The** G76: Busby .4E **135**
**Paidmyre Cres.** G77: Newt M .6D **132**
**Paidmyre Gdns.** G77: Newt M .6D **132**
**Paidmyre Rd.** G77: Newt M .6C **132**
PAISLEY .1H 97
Paisley Arts Cen. .1A 98
Paisley Canal Station (Rail) .2A 98
**Paisley Cen., The** PA1: Pais .1A **98**
Paisley Gilmour Street Station (Rail)
.6A 78
Paisley Mus. & Art Gallery .6H 77
**Paisley Rd.** G5: Glas .5D **82**
G78: Barr .2D **114**
PA4: Renf .3C **78**
**Paisley Rd. W.** G51: Glas .6A **82**
(not continuous)
G52: Glas .1H **99**
Paisley St James Station (Rail)
.5G 77
**Palacecraig St.** ML5: Coat .2C **110**
**Palace Gdns. Retail Pk.**
ML3: Ham .5B **142**
**Palace Grounds Rd.**
ML3: Ham .5B **142**
Palace of Art .6G 81
Palace of Paisley, The .1B 98
Palacerigg Country Pk. .6E 37
**Paladin Av.** G13: Glas .1B **60**
**Palermo St.** G21: Glas .5A **64**
**Palladium Pl.** G14: Glas .6D **60**
**Palmer Av.** G13: Glas .6D **44**
**Palmerston** G75: E Kil .4C **148**
**Palmerston Pl.** G3: Glas .3B **82**
PA5: John .5C **94**
**Palm Pl.** G71: View .4F **109**
**Pandora Way** G71: Tann .6E **109**
**Pankhurst Pl.** G74: E Kil .1H **149**
**Panmure Cl.** G22: Glas .5E **63**
**Panmure Pl.** G22: Glas .4E **63**
**Panmure St.** G20: Glas .5E **63**
**Parkandarroch Cres.**
ML8: Carl .4G **165**
**Park Av.** G3: Glas .1D **82**
G62: Miln .4G **25**
G64: B'rig .4C **48**
G65: Twe .1D **32**
G66: Kirk .5C **30**
G78: Barr .6D **114**
G82: Dumb .4H **17**
ML1: Holy .2A **128**
**Park Av.** ML8: Carl .2F **165**
PA2: Pais .4G **97**
PA5: Eld .3A **96**
**Park Bank** PA8: Ersk .6F **41**
**Park Brae** PA8: Ersk .1G **57**
**Parkbrae Av.** G20: Glas .3E **63**
**Parkbrae Dr.** G20: Glas .3E **63**
**Parkbrae Gdns.** G20: Glas .3E **63**
**Parkbrae Ga.** G20: Glas .3E **63**
**Parkbrae La.** G20: Glas .3E **63**
**Parkburn Av.** G66: Kirk .1C **50**
**Park Burn Ct.** ML3: Ham .3D **140**
**Park Burn Ind. Est.**
ML3: Ham .3E **141**
**Parkburn Rd.** G65: Kils .2H **11**
**Park Cir.** G3: Glas .2C **82**
ML8: Carl .2F **165**
**Park Cir. La.** G3: Glas .2C **82**
**Park Cir. Pl.** G3: Glas .2D **82**
**Park Ct.** G46: Giff .4H **117**
G64: B'rig .4D **48**
G81: Clyd .3A **42**
**Park Cres.** G61: Bear .2B **44**
G64: B'rig .5C **48**
G64: Torr .4E **29**
G72: Blan .3A **140**
G82: Dumb .2F **17**
ML6: Air .3G **91**
PA4: Inch .2G **57**
**Park Dr.** G3: Glas .1C **82**
G73: Ruth .6C **104**
G74: T'hall .6G **135**
ML2: Newm .4E **147**
ML3: Fern .2E **155**
PA8: Ersk .1F **57**
**Parker Pl.** G65: Kils .3H **11**
ML9: Lark .2F **161**
**Parkfield** G75: E Kil .6G **149**
**Parkfoot St.** G65: Kils .2H **11**
**Park Gdns.** G3: Glas .2C **82**
PA10: Kilb .1B **94**
**Park Gdns. La.** *G3: Glas .2C **82***
*(off Clifton St.)*
**Park Ga.** G3: Glas .2C **82**
PA8: Ersk .1F **57**
**Park Ga. Pl.** ML4: Bell .2B **126**
**Park Glade** PA8: Ersk .1F **57**
**Park Grn.** PA8: Ersk .1F **57**
**Park Gro.** PA8: Ersk .1G **57**
**Parkgrove Av.** G46: Giff .3B **118**
**Parkgrove Ter.** G3: Glas .2C **82**
**Parkgrove Ter. La.**
*G3: Glas .2C **82***
*(off Derby St.)*
PARKHALL .2B 42
**Parkhall Rd.** G81: Clyd .3B **42**
**Parkhall St.** G74: E Kil .1H **149**
**Parkhall Ter.** G81: Clyd .2B **42**
PARKHEAD .6F 85
**Parkhead Cross** G31: Glas .6F **85**
**Parkhead La.** ML6: Air .3A **92**
**Parkhead St.** ML1: Moth .4H **143**
ML6: Air .3A **92**
**Park Hill** PA8: Ersk .6F **41**
**Parkhill Dr.** G73: Ruth .6C **104**
**Parkhill Rd.** G43: Glas .5B **102**
**Parkholm La.** G5: Glas .5D **82**
PARKHOUSE .3H 115
**Park Ho.** ML3: Ham .4H **141**
**Parkhouse Path**
G53: Glas .3B **116**
**Parkhouse Rd.** G53: Glas .3H **115**
G78: Barr .3H **115**
**Parkinch** PA8: Ersk .1G **57**
**Parklands Oval** G53: Glas .3H **99**
**Parklands Rd.** G44: Neth .4D **118**
**Parklands Vw.** G53: Glas .4H **99**
**Park La.** G40: Glas .6B **84**
G65: Kils .3H **11**
G72: Blan .1B **140**
ML8: Carl .4E **165**
**Parklea** G64: B'rig .4A **48**
**Parklee Dr.** G76: Crmck .2A **136**
PARK MAINS .2G 57
**Park Moor** PA8: Ersk .1F **57**
PARKNEUK .1G 151
**Parkneuk Rd.** G43: Glas .3H **117**
G72: Blan .1G **151**
**Parkneuk St.** ML1: Moth .1F **143**
**Parknook Way** *ML9: Lark .2F **161***
*(off Muirshot Rd.)*
**Park Pl.** G74: T'hall .6G **135**
ML4: Bell .4A **126**
ML5: Coat .1F **111**
PA3: Lin .5A **76**
PA5: John .3F **95**
**Park Quad.** G3: Glas .2C **82**
ML2: Wis .2E **157**
**Park Rd** G4: Glas .1C **82**
**Park Ridge** PA8: Ersk .1F **57**
**Park Rd.** G32: Carm .5C **10**
G46: Giff .5A **11**
G62: Miln .4G **2**
G64: B'rig .5C **4**
G69: Barg .6D **8**
G69: Chry .1A **6**
G81: Clyd .4B **4**
ML1: New S .4A **12**
ML3: Ham .6H **14**
ML4: Bell .3C **12**
ML6: C'bnk .3B **11**
PA11: Bri W .2F **7**
PA2: Pais .5H **9**
PA4: Inch .2H **5**
PA5: John .3F **9**
**Parksail** PA8: Ersk .2G **5**
**Parksail Dr.** PA8: Ersk .1G **5**
**Parkside Gdns.** G20: Glas .3E **6**
**Parkside Pl.** G20: Glas .3E **6**
**Parkside Rd.** ML1: Moth .3D **14**
**Park St.** G66: Kirk .6H **3**
G82: Dumb .4G **1**
ML1: Cle .4H **12**
ML1: Moth .2G **14**
ML1: New S .4A **12**
ML5: Coat .3D **9**
ML6: Air .3G **9**
ML8: Carl .4F **16**
**Park St. Sth.** G3: Glas .2C **8**
**Parks Vw.** ML3: Ham .5H **15**
**Park Ter.** G3: Glas .2C **8**
G46: Giff .5A **11**
G74: E Kil .2G **14**
**Park Ter. E. La.** G3: Glas .2D **8**
**Park Ter. La.** G3: Glas .2C **8**
**Park Top** PA8: Ersk .6G **4**
**Parkvale Cres.** PA8: Ersk .1H **5**
**Parkvale Dr.** PA8: Ersk .1H **5**
**Parkvale Gdns.** PA8: Ersk .1H **5**
**Parkvale Pl.** PA8: Ersk .1H **5**
**Parkvale Way** PA8: Ersk .1H **5**
**Parkview** G82: Milt .3F **1**
**Park Vw.** ML9: Lark .3F **16**
PA10: Kilb .1A **9**
PA2: Pais .3H **9**
**Parkview Av.** G66: Kirk .6D **3**
**Parkview Ct.** G66: Kirk .6D **3**
**Parkview Cres.** ML2: Newm .5E **14**
**Parkview Dr.** G33: Step .3E **6**
ML5: Coat .4A **9**
**Parkville Dr.** G72: Blan .3C **14**
(not continuous
**Parkville Rd.** ML4: Bell .6E **11**
**Parkway** G32: Carm .5C **10**
**Park Way** G67: Cumb .1B **3**
**Parkway** PA8: Ersk .1F **5**
**Parkway Ct.** G69: Bail .4H **8**
ML5: Coat .5A **9**
**Parkway Pl.** ML5: Coat .6A **9**
**Park Winding** PA8: Ersk .1G **5**
**Park Wood** PA8: Ersk .6G **4**
**Parlbrae Pl.** G20: Glas .3E **6**
**Parnell St.** ML6: Air .6H **9**
**Parnie St.** G1: Glas .5G **8**
**Parry Ter.** G75: E Kil .2D **14**
**Parsonage Row**
G1: Glas .4H **83** (6H **5**
**Parsonage Sq.** G1: Glas .4H **83** (6H **5**
(not continuous
**Parson St.** G4: Glas .3A **84** (3H **5**)
PARTICK .1H 81
**Partick Bri. St.** G11: Glas .2A **82**
PARTICKHILL .1H 81
**Partickhill Av.** G11: Glas .6H **61**
**Partickhill Ct.** G11: Glas .6H **61**
**Partickhill Rd.** G11: Glas .6H **61**
Partick Station (Rail, Und.) .1H 81
**Partick St.** ML5: Coat .6E **91**
Partick Thistle F.C. .5E 63
**Patchy Pk.** ML9: Lark .5E **161**
**Paterson Pl.** G61: Bear .5C **24**
**Paterson's Laun** G64: Balm .6A **28**
**Paterson St.** G5: Glas .6E **83**
(not continuous)
ML1: Moth .2G **143**
**Paterson Ter.** G75: E Kil .4F **149**
**Pathead Gdns.** G33: Glas .3H **65**
**Pather St.** ML2: Wis .1H **157**
**Pathhead Rd.** G76: Crmck .2H **135**
**Patna Ct.** ML3: Ham .2C **152**
**Patna St.** G40: Glas .2D **104**
PATNER .2H 157
**Paton St.** G31: Glas .4D **84**
**Patrick St.** PA2: Pais .2B **98**
**Patterson Dr.** ML8: Law .5E **159**
PATTERTON .1D 132
**Patterton Dr.** G78: Barr .6F **115**
Patterton Station (Rail) .1D 132
**Pattison St.** G81: Clyd .4A **42**
Pavilion Theatre .3D 4

Paxton Ct.—Primrose Ct.


axton Ct. G74: E Kil .... 5H 137
(off Paxton Cres.)
axton Cres. G74: E Kil .... 5H 137
ayne St. G4: Glas .... 1G 83 (1E 5)
eace Av. PA11: Q'riers .... 1B 72
eacock Av. PA2: Pais .... 3D 96
eacock Cross ML3: Ham .... 5G 141
eacock Cross Ind. Est.
ML3: Ham .... 5G 141
eacock Dr. ML3: Ham .... 5G 141
PA2: Pais .... 3D 96
eacock Loan ML8: Carl .... 2F 165
(off Carranbute Rd.)
earce La. G51: Glas .... 3G 81
earce St. G51: Glas .... 3G 81
earl St. ML4: Bell .... 4D 126
earson Dr. PA4: Renf .... 1F 79
earson Pl. PA3: Lin .... 6H 75
eathill Av. G69: Chry .... 6H 51
eathill St. G21: Glas .... 6G 63
eat Pl. G53: Glas .... 2A 116
eat Rd. G53: Glas .... 2A 116
PA11: Bri W .... 4G 73
edmyre La. G76: Crmck .... 2G 135
eebles Dr. G73: Ruth .... 6F 105
eebles Path ML5: Coat .... 2F 111
eel Av. ML1: Moth .... 5G 143
eel Brae G66: Kirk .... 4C 30
eel Ct. G72: Camb .... 1A 122
eel Glen Gdns. G15: Glas .... 2A 44
eel Glen Rd. G15: Glas .... 3A 44
eel La. G11: Glas .... 1H 81
EEL PARK .... 1A 148
eel Pk. Ind. Est. G74: E Kil .... 1A 148
eel Pk. Pl. G74: E Kil .... 2B 148
eel Pl. G71: Both .... 4E 125
ML5: Coat .... 6H 89
eel Rd. G74: T'hall .... 6F 135
eel St. G11: Glas .... 1H 81
eel Vw. G81: Clyd .... 4F 43
egasus Av. ML8: Carl .... 3E 165
PA1: Pais .... 6B 76
egasus Rd. ML4: Moss .... 2G 127
einchorran PA8: Ersk .... 2G 57
eiter Pl. G72: Blan .... 2A 140
(off Burnbrae Rd.)
embroke G74: E Kil .... 5D 138
embroke St. G3: Glas .... 3D 82
encaitland Dr. G32: Glas .... 2A 106
encaitland Gro. G32: Glas .... 3A 106
encaitland Pl. G23: Glas .... 6C 46
endale Ri. G45: Glas .... 4H 119
end Cl. PA5: John .... 4F 95
endeen Cres. G33: Glas .... 6E 87
endeen Pl. G33: Glas .... 5F 87
endeen Rd. G33: Glas .... 6E 87
endicle Cres. G61: Bear .... 4D 44
endicle Rd. G61: Bear .... 4D 44
endle Ct. G69: G'csh .... 3D 68
enfold Cres. G75: E Kil .... 3F 149
enicuik St. G32: Glas .... 5F 85
ENILEE .... 5G 79
enilee Rd. G52: Hill .... 3F 79
enilee Ter. G52: Glas .... 4G 79
eninver Dr. G51: Glas .... 3E 81
enman Av. G73: Ruth .... 5B 104
ennan PA8: Ersk .... 5E 41
ennan Pl. G14: Glas .... 4A 60
enneld Rd. G52: Glas .... 6H 79
enniecroft Av. G82: Dumb .... 2H 17
ennine Gro. ML6: Chap .... 4F 113
ennyroyal Ct. G74: E Kil .... 5F 137
enrith Av. G46: Giff .... 4A 118
enrith Dr. G12: Glas .... 3G 61
enrith Pl. G75: E Kil .... 5B 148
enryn Gdns. G32: Glas .... 2D 106
enston Rd. G33: Glas .... 3D 86
entland Av. PA3: Lin .... 6G 75
entland Ct. G78: Barr .... 6D 114
ML5: Coat .... 2E 111
ML6: Air .... 1B 92
entland Cres. ML9: Lark .... 6G 155
PA2: Pais .... 5H 97
entland Dr. G64: B'rig .... 5F 49
G78: Barr .... 6D 114
PA4: Renf .... 3D 78
entland Pl. G61: Bear .... 6B 24
entland Rd. G43: Glas .... 2A 118
G69: Chry .... 1B 68
ML2: Wis .... 5E 145
enzance Way G69: Mood .... 4C 52
eockland Gdns. PA5: John .... 2G 95
eockland Pl. PA5: John .... 2G 95
eople's Palace (Museum) .... 6A 84
eploe Dr. G74: E Kil .... 4D 138
erchy Vw. ML2: Wis .... 2A 158
ercy Dr. G46: Giff .... 6A 118
ercy Rd. PA4: Renf .... 3C 78
ercy St. G51: Glas .... 6B 82
ML9: Lark .... 1E 161
Perran Gdns. G69: Mood .... 5C 52
Perray Av. G82: Dumb .... 2B 16
Perrays Cres. G82: Dumb .... 2A 16
Perrays Dr. G82: Dumb .... 3A 16
Perrays Way G82: Dumb .... 2A 16
Perth Av. ML6: Air .... 1A 112
Perth Cres. G81: Clyd .... 2H 41
Perth St. G3: Glas .... 4D 82
(not continuous)
Peter Coats Bldg. PA2: Pais .... 2A 98
Peter Dr. G66: Kirk .... 4D 30
PETERSBURN .... 5E 93
Petersburn Pl. ML6: Air .... 5D 92
Petersburn Rd. ML6: Air .... 6C 92
PETERSHILL .... 6D 64
Petershill Ct. G21: Glas .... 6D 64
Petershill Dr. G21: Glas .... 5D 64
Petershill Pl. G21: Glas .... 5D 64
Petershill Rd. G21: Glas .... 6B 64
Peterson Dr. G13: Glas .... 1G 59
Peterson Gdns. G13: Glas .... 1G 59
Petition Pl. G71: Udd .... 2E 125
Pettigrew St. G32: Glas .... 6A 86
Peveril Av. G41: Glas .... 4B 102
G73: Ruth .... 2E 121
Peveril Ct. G73: Ruth .... 3E 121
Pharonhill St. G31: Glas .... 6G 85
Philip Murray Rd. ML4: Bell .... 1H 125
PHILIPSHILL .... 5A 136
Philipshill Ga. G74: E Kil .... 5A 136
Philipshill Rd. G76: Crmck .... 6A 136
Phoenix Bus. Pk., The
PA1: Pais .... 6C 76
Phoenix Ct. G74: E Kil .... 4D 138
(off Bosworth Rd.)
Phoenix Cres. ML4: Bell .... 5A 110
Phoenix Ind. Est. PA3: Glas A .... 3A 78
Phoenix Pl. ML1: New S .... 4A 128
PA5: Eld .... 2B 96
Phoenix Retail Pk., The
PA1: Pais .... 1D 96
Phoenix Rd. G4: Glas .... 1E 83 (1A 4)
ML4: Moss .... 2G 127
Phyliss Jane Ct. ML2: Wis .... 2H 157
Piazza Shop. Cen. PA1: Pais .... 6A 78
Picadilly St. G3: Glas .... 4D 82 (6A 4)
PICKERSTONHILL .... 2F 129
Pickerstonhill ML1: N'hill .... 3E 129
Picketlaw Dr. G76: Crmck .... 2H 135
Picketlaw Farm Rd. G76: Crmck .... 2G 135
Piershill St. G32: Glas .... 4H 85
Pikeman Rd. G13: Glas .... 3C 60
Pillans Ct. ML3: Ham .... 3E 141
Pilmuir Av. G44: Glas .... 3D 118
Pilrig St. G32: Glas .... 4G 85
Pilton Rd. G15: Glas .... 3A 44
Pine Av. G72: Flem .... 4F 123
Pine Cl. G67: Cumb .... 1E 37
Pine Ct. G67: Cumb .... 1E 37
G75: E Kil .... 6D 148
ML5: Coat .... 1A 110
(off Ailsa Rd.)
Pine Cres. G67: Cumb .... 1E 37
G75: E Kil .... 6D 148
PA5: John .... 4G 95
Pine Gro. G67: Cumb .... 1E 37
G71: View .... 5F 109
ML1: Holy .... 2B 128
ML6: C'bnk .... 3B 112
Pinelands G64: B'rig .... 3C 48
Pine Lawn ML2: Wis .... 4B 146
Pine Pk. ML3: Ham .... 2A 154
Pine Pl. G5: Glas .... 1G 103
G67: Cumb .... 1E 37
Pine Quad. ML6: Chap .... 2E 113
Pine Rd. G67: Cumb .... 6E 15
G81: Clyd .... 3H 41
G82: Dumb .... 3F 17
Pines, The G44: Glas .... 3F 119
Pine St. G66: Len .... 3G 7
ML6: Air .... 4D 92
PA2: Pais .... 3C 98
Pinewood Av. G66: Lenz .... 2A 50
Pinewood Ct. G66: Lenz .... 2A 50
G82: Dumb .... 2H 17
Pinewood Pl. G66: Lenz .... 2A 50
Pinewood Sq. G15: Glas .... 4B 44
Pinkerton Av. G73: Ruth .... 5A 104
Pinkston Dr. G21: Glas .... 1H 83 (1H 5)
Pinkston Rd. G21: Glas .... 6H 63 (1H 5)
G4: Glas .... 1H 83
Pinmore Pl. G53: Glas .... 2H 115
Pinmore St. G53: Glas .... 2H 115
Pinwherry Dr. G33: Glas .... 3H 65
Pinwherry Pl. G71: Both .... 4E 125
Piper Av. PA6: C'lee .... 3C 74
Piper Rd. ML6: Air .... 6C 92
PA6: C'lee .... 3C 74
Pirnie Pl. G65: Kils .... 3H 11
Pirnmill Av. ML1: Moth .... 2D 142
Pitcairn Cres. G75: E Kil .... 3B 148
Pitcairn Gro. G75: E Kil .... 3C 148
Pitcairn Pl. G75: E Kil .... 3B 148
Pitcairn St. G31: Glas .... 1G 105
Pitcairn Ter. ML3: Ham .... 5E 141
Pitcaple Dr. G43: Glas .... 1H 117
Pitlochry Dr. G52: Glas .... 1B 100
ML9: Lark .... 4G 161
Pitmedden Rd. G64: B'rig .... 5F 49
Pitmilly Rd. G15: Glas .... 3C 44
Pitreavie Ct. ML3: Ham .... 3F 153
Pitreavie Pl. G33: Glas .... 2C 86
Pit Rd. G66: Kirk .... 6A 32
ML4: Bell .... 1B 126
Pitt St. G2: Glas .... 4E 83 (5B 4)
Pladda Rd. PA4: Renf .... 2F 79
Pladda St. ML1: Moth .... 2D 142
PLAINS .... 1G 93
Plaintrees Ct. PA2: Pais .... 4A 98
Plane Pl. G71: View .... 4G 109
Planetree Pl. PA5: John .... 4G 95
Planetree Rd. G81: Clyd .... 2C 42
PLANTATION .... 5B 82
Plantation Av. ML1: Holy .... 1B 128
Plantation Pk. Gdns. G51: Glas .... 6B 82
(not continuous)
PLANTATION RD. INTERCHANGE
.... 6B 82
Plantation Sq. G51: Glas .... 5C 82
Plant St. G31: Glas .... 5E 85
Platthorn Dr. G74: E Kil .... 2H 149
Platthorn Rd. G74: E Kil .... 2H 149
Play Drome, The .... 6D 42
Playfair St. G40: Glas .... 2C 104
Plaza, The G74: E Kil .... 2G 149
Pleaknowe Cres. G69: Mood .... 5C 52
Pleamuir Pl. G68: Cumb .... 4E 35
Plean St. G14: Glas .... 4A 60
Pleasance St. G43: Glas .... 5A 102
Pleasance Way G43: Glas .... 6B 102
Plotcock Castle (Remains of) .... 4A 160
Plotcock Rd. ML3: Ham .... 4A 160
Plover Dr. G75: E Kil .... 6C 148
Plover Pl. PA5: John .... 6C 94
Plusgarten Loan ML2: Newm .... 2D 146
Pochard Way ML4: Bell .... 5B 110
Poet's Vw. G66: Kirk .... 6F 31
Poindfauld Ter. G82: Dumb .... 3G 17
Pointhouse Rd. G3: Glas .... 3A 82
Pollock Av. ML3: Ham .... 6D 140
Pollock Rd. G61: Bear .... 4G 45
G77: Newt M .... 5C 132
Pollock St. ML1: Moth .... 2G 143
ML4: Bell .... 2E 127
POLLOK .... 6C 100
Pollok Av. G43: Glas .... 5H 101
Pollok Country Pk. .... 4G 101
Pollok Dr. G64: B'rig .... 5A 48
Pollok Ho. .... 5F 101
Pollok La. G74: E Kil .... 6B 138
Pollok Leisure Pool .... 6C 100
Pollok Pl. G74: E Kil .... 6B 138
POLLOKSHAWS .... 6A 102
Pollokshaws East Station (Rail)
.... 6B 102
Pollokshaws Rd. G41: Glas .... 4C 102
G43: Glas .... 6H 101
Pollokshaws Sports Cen. .... 5A 102
(off Ashtree Rd.)
Pollokshaws West Station (Rail)
.... 6H 101
POLLOKSHIELDS .... 2C 102
Pollokshields East Station (Rail)
.... 2E 103
Pollokshields Sq. G41: Glas .... 3C 102
Pollokshields West Station (Rail)
.... 3D 102
Pollok Township Cen.
G53: Glas .... 6C 100
POLMADIE .... 3H 103
Polmadie Av. G5: Glas .... 3H 103
Polmadie Ind. Est. G5: Glas .... 3A 104
Polmadie Rd. G42: Glas .... 4G 103
Polmadie St. G42: Glas .... 4G 103
Polnoon Av. G13: Glas .... 3A 60
Polquhap Cl. G53: Glas .... 5A 100
Polquhap Gdns. G53: Glas .... 5A 100
Polquhap Pl. G53: Glas .... 5A 100
Polquhap Rd. G53: Glas .... 5A 100
Polson Dr. PA5: John .... 3E 95
Polsons Cres. PA2: Pais .... 3H 97
Polwarth La. G12: Glas .... 6H 61
Polwarth St. G12: Glas .... 6H 61
Pomona Pl. ML3: Ham .... 1D 152
Poplar Av. G11: Glas .... 5F 61
G77: Newt M .... 6D 132
PA5: John .... 4G 95
PA7: B'ton .... 5H 39
Poplar Ct. ML5: Coat .... 1A 110
Poplar Cres. PA7: B'ton .... 5H 39
Poplar Dr. G66: Lenz .... 2A 50
G66: Milt C .... 6C 8
G81: Clyd .... 2B 42
Poplar Gdns. G75: E Kil .... 6E 149
Poplar Pl. G71: View .... 5H 109
G72: Blan .... 6A 124
ML1: Holy .... 3B 128
Poplar Rd. G82: Dumb .... 3F 17
Poplars, The G61: Bear .... 5D 24
Poplar St. ML6: Air .... 4D 92
Poplar Way G72: Flem .... 4F 123
Poplin St. G40: Glas .... 2B 104
Porchester St. G33: Glas .... 1D 86
Portal Rd. G13: Glas .... 1C 60
PORT DUNDAS .... 1G 83
Port Dundas Ind. Est. G4: Glas .... 1G 83
Port Dundas Pl.
G2: Glas .... 3G 83 (3E 5)
Port Dundas Rd.
G4: Glas .... 2F 83 (1D 4)
PORT EGLINGTON .... 1E 103
PORTERFIELD .... 1D 78
Porterfield Rd. PA4: Renf .... 6D 58
Porters La. ML6: Chap .... 3D 112
Porter St. G51: Glas .... 6A 82
Porters Well G71: Udd .... 2C 124
Portessie PA8: Ersk .... 5E 41
Portland Pk. ML3: Ham .... 1A 154
Portland Pl. ML3: Ham .... 1A 154
Portland Rd. G68: Cumb .... 6H 13
PA2: Pais .... 2D 98
Portland Sq. ML3: Ham .... 1A 154
Portland St. ML5: Coat .... 3D 90
Portland Wynd ML9: Lark .... 1F 161
(off Muirshot Rd.)
Portlethen PA8: Ersk .... 5E 41
Portman St. G41: Glas .... 6C 82
Portmarnock Dr. G23: Glas .... 1C 62
Porton Pl. PA7: B'ton .... 4G 39
Portpatrick Rd. G60: Old K .... 6D 20
Portreath Rd. G69: Mood .... 4D 52
Portree Av. ML5: Coat .... 1A 110
Portree Pl. G15: Glas .... 3G 43
Portsoy PA8: Ersk .... 5E 41
Portsoy Av. G13: Glas .... 1H 59
Portsoy Pl. G13: Glas .... 1G 59
Port St. G3: Glas .... 4D 82
Portugal St. G5: Glas .... 6F 83
Portwell ML3: Ham .... 5A 142
POSSIL PARK .... 4G 63
Possilpark & Parkhouse Station (Rail)
.... 3F 63
Possil Pk. Millennium Cen. .... 5F 63
Possil Pk. Trad. Cen. G22: Glas .... 4G 63
Possil Rd. G4: Glas .... 1F 83
Postgate ML3: Ham .... 5A 142
Potassels Rd. G69: Muirh .... 2A 68
Potrail Pl. ML3: Ham .... 6E 141
Potter Cl. G32: Glas .... 2G 105
Potter Gro. G32: Glas .... 2G 105
POTTERHILL .... 4H 97
Potterhill Av. PA2: Pais .... 5A 98
Potterhill Rd. G53: Glas .... 3A 100
Potter Path G32: Glas .... 2G 105
Potter Pl. G32: Glas .... 2G 105
Potter St. G32: Glas .... 2G 105
Potts Way ML1: Moth .... 6E 127
Powbrone G75: E Kil .... 6G 149
POWBURN .... 5C 108
Powburn Cres. G71: Udd .... 6B 108
Powerdrome Bowl .... 5E 91
Powerleague Soccer Cen.
Glasgow .... 3A 84 (2H 5)
Hamilton .... 3G 141
Paisley .... 2C 98
Powfoot St. G31: Glas .... 6F 85
Powforth Cl. ML9: Lark .... 2C 160
Powrie St. G33: Glas .... 6C 66
Prentice La. G71: Tann .... 5E 109
Prentice Rd. ML1: Moth .... 4D 142
Prestonfield G62: Miln .... 4E 25
Preston Pl. G42: Glas .... 3F 103
Preston St. G42: Glas .... 3F 103
Prestwick Ct. G68: Cumb .... 1H 35
Prestwick Pl. G77: Newt M .... 5G 133
Prestwick St. G53: Glas .... 1A 116
Priestfield Ind. Est. G72: Blan .... 4B 140
Priestfield St. G72: Blan .... 3A 140
PRIESTHILL .... 1A 116
Priesthill & Darnley Station (Rail)
.... 2C 116
Priesthill Av. G53: Glas .... 1C 116
Priesthill Cres. G53: Glas .... 1C 116
Priesthill Gdns. G53: Glas .... 2C 116
Priesthill Rd. G53: Glas .... 1B 116
PRIESTKNOWE RDBT. .... 2H 149
Prieston Rd. PA11: Bri W .... 4E 73
Primrose Av. ML4: Bell .... 6C 110
ML9: Lark .... 5E 161
Primrose Ct. G14: Glas .... 6D 60

Primrose Cres.—Redburn Pl.

**Primrose Cres.** ML1: Moth . . . . . 4G 143
**Primrose Pl.** G67: Cumb . . . . . . . 6D 34
G71: View . . . . . . . . . . . . . . 5G 109
**Primrose St.** G14: Glas . . . . . . . . . 6C 60
**Primrose Way** G66: Len . . . . . . . . . 4G 7
ML8: Carl . . . . . . . . . . . . . . . 5E 165
**Prince Albert Rd.** G12: Glas . . . . . 6H 61
**Prince Edward St.** G42: Glas . . . . 3E 103
**Prince of Wales Gdns.**
G20: Glas . . . . . . . . . . . . . . . 1A 62
**Prince Pl.** ML2: Newm . . . . . . . . 3E 147
**Prince's Gdns.** G12: Glas . . . . . . . 6H 61
**Prince's Gdns. La.** G12: Glas . . . . 6H 61
**Princes Ga.** G71: Both . . . . . . . . 3C 124
G73: Ruth . . . . . . . . . . . . . . 5C 104
**Princes Mall** *G74: E Kil . . . . . . . 2G 149*
*(off Olympia)*
**Princes Pk.** PA7: B'ton . . . . . . . . . 3C 40
**Prince's Pl.** G12: Glas . . . . . . . . . 6A 62
**Princess Anne Quad.** *ML1: Holy . 2H 127*
*(off Sherry Av.)*
**Princess Cres.** PA1: Pais . . . . . . . 6D 78
**Princess Dr.** G69: Barg . . . . . . . . . 6E 89
**Princes Sq.** G74: E Kil . . . . . . . . 2G 149
**Princes Sq. Shop. Cen.**
G1: Glas . . . . . . . . . . . . . . . . . 6E 5
**Princess Rd.** ML1: New S . . . . . 3H 127
**Princess Sq.** G78: Barr . . . . . . . . 4F 115
ML2: Newm . . . . . . . . . . . . . 4D 146
**Princes St.** G73: Ruth . . . . . . . . . 5C 104
ML1: Moth . . . . . . . . . . . . . . 1G 143
**Prince's Ter.** G12: Glas . . . . . . . . . 6A 62
**Prince's Ter. La.** G12: Glas . . . . . . 6A 62
**Printers Land** G76: Busby . . . . . . 3E 135
**Printers Lea** G66: Len . . . . . . . . . . 3E 7
Priorscroft Bowling Club . . . . . . . *1B 98*
*(off Cochran St.)*
**Priorwood Ct.** G13: Glas . . . . . . . . 3D 60
**Priorwood Gdns.** G13: Glas . . . . . 3D 60
**Priorwood Ga.** G77: Newt M . . . . 5A 132
**Priorwood Pl.** G13: Glas . . . . . . . . 3D 60
**Priorwood Rd.** G77: Newt M . . . . 5A 132
**Priorwood Way** G77: Newt M . . . . 5A 132
**Priory Av.** PA3: Pais . . . . . . . . . . 4C 78
**Priory Dr.** G71: Udd . . . . . . . . . . 6B 108
**Priory Ga.** ML2: Over . . . . . . . . . 4H 157
**Priory Pl.** G13: Glas . . . . . . . . . . . 2D 60
G68: Cumb . . . . . . . . . . . . . . . 4A 34
**Priory Rd.** G13: Glas . . . . . . . . . . 2D 60
**Priory St.** G72: Blan . . . . . . . . . . 1B 140
**Priory Ter.** ML2: Wis . . . . . . . . . . 1C 156
Pro Bowl . . . . . . . . . . . . . . . . . . 4D 30
**Procession Rd.** PA2: Pais . . . . . . . 1A 114
**Professors Sq.** G12: Glas . . . . . . . . 1B 82
Pro Lane Bowl . . . . . . . . . . . . . 5A 150
Pro Life Fitness Cen. . . . . . . . . . . 5A 78
**Prosen St.** G32: Glas . . . . . . . . . 2G 105
**Prospect Av.** G71: Udd . . . . . . . . 1C 124
G72: Camb . . . . . . . . . . . . . . 1H 121
**Prospect Ct.** G72: Blan . . . . . . . . 4B 140
**Prospect Dr.** ML9: Ashg . . . . . . . 5B 162
**Prospecthill Cir.** G42: Glas . . . . . 4H 103
**Prospecthill Cres.** G42: Glas . . . . 5A 104
**Prospect Hill Dr.** G42: Glas . . . . . 5G 103
**Prospecthill Gro.** G42: Glas . . . . . 5E 103
**Prospecthill Pl.** G42: Glas . . . . . . 5A 104
**Prospecthill Rd.** G42: Glas . . . . . . 5E 103
**Prospecthill Sq.** G42: Glas . . . . . . 4H 103
**Prospecthill Way** *G42: Glas . . . . . 6E 103*
*(off Prospecthill Gro.)*
**Prospect Rd.** G43: Glas . . . . . . . . 5B 102
G68: Dull . . . . . . . . . . . . . . . . 5E 13
**Provandhall Cres.** G69: Bail . . . . 2H 107
Provand's Lordship . . . . . . . . . . . 4H 5
Provan Hall . . . . . . . . . . . . . . . . 2F 87
**Provanhill St.** G21: Glas . . . . . . . . 2B 84
**PROVAN INTERCHANGE** . . . . . . . 2E 85
PROVANMILL . . . . . . . . . . . . . . . 6G 65
**Provanmill Pl.** *G33: Glas . . . . . . . 6F 65*
*(off Provanmill Rd.)*
**Provanmill Rd.** G33: Glas . . . . . . . 6F 65
**Provan Rd.** G33: Glas . . . . . . . . . . 2E 85
**Provan Wlk.** G34: Glas . . . . . . . . . 2E 87
**Provost Cl.** PA5: John . . . . . . . . . . 2F 95
**Provost Dr. Ct.** PA4: Renf . . . . . . . 1F 79
**Provost Ga.** ML9: Lark . . . . . . . . 2E 161
P.S. Waverley . . . . . . . . . . . . . . 5D 82
**Purdie** G74: E Kil . . . . . . . . . . . . 4D 138
**Purdie St.** ML3: Ham . . . . . . . . . 4E 141
**Purdon St.** G11: Glas . . . . . . . . . . 1H 81
**Pyatshaw Rd.** ML9: Lark . . . . . . . 4F 161

## Q

**Quadrant Rd.** G43: Glas . . . . . . . 1C 118
**Quadrant Shop. Cen.**
ML5: Coat . . . . . . . . . . . . . . . . 4C 90
**Quadrant, The** G76: Clar . . . . . . . 1C 134
QUARRELTON . . . . . . . . . . . . . . . 3E 95
**Quarrelton Gro.** PA5: John . . . . . . . 4F 95
**Quarrelton Rd.** PA5: John . . . . . . . 3E 95
QUARRIER'S VILLAGE . . . . . . . . . 1A 72
**Quarry Av.** G72: Camb . . . . . . . . 4D 122
**Quarrybank** PA10: Kilb . . . . . . . . . 3C 94
**Quarrybrae Av.** G76: Clar . . . . . . 2B 134
**Quarrybrae Gdns.** G71: View . . . . 1G 125
**Quarrybrae St.** G31: Glas . . . . . . . 6F 85
**Quarry Dr.** G66: Kirk . . . . . . . . . . . 5F 31
**Quarryknowe** G73: Ruth . . . . . . . 6B 104
**Quarry Knowe** G82: Dumb . . . . . . . 2D 16
**Quarry Knowe Pl.** ML4: Bell . . . . 4B 126
**Quarryknowe St.** G31: Glas . . . . . . 6G 85
G81: Faif . . . . . . . . . . . . . . . . . 6F 23
**Quarry La.** G66: Len . . . . . . . . . . . . 2F 7
G82: Dumb . . . . . . . . . . . . . . . . 4E 17
**Quarry Pk.** G75: E Kil . . . . . . . . . 3G 149
**Quarry Pl.** G72: Camb . . . . . . . . . 1G 121
G82: Dumb . . . . . . . . . . . . . . . . 2D 16
ML3: Ham . . . . . . . . . . . . . . . 6A 142
**Quarry Rd.** G75: E Kil . . . . . . . . . 6F 149
G78: Barr . . . . . . . . . . . . . . . 3D 114
ML6: Air . . . . . . . . . . . . . . . . . . 2H 91
ML8: Carl . . . . . . . . . . . . . . . 3H 163
ML9: Lark . . . . . . . . . . . . . . . 3E 161
PA2: Pais . . . . . . . . . . . . . . . . . 4B 98
**Quarryside St.** ML6: Glenm . . . . . . 5G 71
**Quarry St.** ML1: New S . . . . . . . . 3A 128
ML2: Wis . . . . . . . . . . . . . . . . 6G 145
ML3: Ham . . . . . . . . . . . . . . . 6A 142
ML5: Coat . . . . . . . . . . . . . . . . . 5F 91
ML9: Lark . . . . . . . . . . . . . . . 4F 161
PA5: John . . . . . . . . . . . . . . . . . 2F 95
**Quarrywood Av.** G21: Glas . . . . . . 5E 65
**Quarrywood Rd.** G21: Glas . . . . . . 5E 65
**Quay Pend** G82: Dumb . . . . . . . . . 4E 17
**Quay Rd.** G73: Ruth . . . . . . . . . . 4C 104
**Quay Rd. Nth.** G73: Ruth . . . . . . . 4C 104
**Quay St.** G82: Dumb . . . . . . . . . . . 4F 17
**Quay, The** G5: Glas . . . . . . . . . . . . 5D 82
**Quebec Dr.** G75: E Kil . . . . . . . . . 3E 149
**Quebec Grn.** G75: E Kil . . . . . . . . 2E 149
**Quebec Ho.** G81: Clyd . . . . . . . . . . 1H 41
**Quebec Wynd** G32: Carm . . . . . . . 5C 106
**Queen Elizabeth Av.** G52: Hill . . . . 4G 79
**Queen Elizabeth Ct.** G81: Clyd . . . 4C 42
ML1: Moth . . . . . . . . . . . . . . . 2F 143
**Queen Elizabeth Gdns.**
G5: Glas . . . . . . . . . . . . . . . . 1G 103
**Queen Margaret Ct.** *G20: Glas . . . . 5C 62*
*(off Fergus Dr.)*
**Queen Margaret Dr.** G12: Glas . . . . 6B 62
**Queen Margaret Rd.** G20: Glas . . . 5C 62
**Queen Mary Av.** G42: Glas . . . . . . 4E 103
G81: Clyd . . . . . . . . . . . . . . . . 5F 43
**Queen Mary Gdns.** G81: Clyd . . . . 4C 42
**Queen Mary St.** G40: Glas . . . . . . 1C 104
**Queen's Av.** G72: Camb . . . . . . . . 1B 122
**Queensbank Av.** G69: G'csh . . . . . . 2C 68
**Queensberry Av.** G61: Bear . . . . . . 6E 25
G76: Clar . . . . . . . . . . . . . . . 2C 134
**Queensborough Gdns.**
G12: Glas . . . . . . . . . . . . . . . . 5G 61
**Queensby Av.** G69: Bail . . . . . . . . . 6H 87
**Queensby Dr.** G69: Bail . . . . . . . . . 5H 87
**Queensby Pl.** G69: Bail . . . . . . . . . 5A 88
**Queensby Rd.** G69: Bail . . . . . . . . . 5H 87
**Queen's Ct.** G62: Miln . . . . . . . . . . 5G 25
**Queen's Cres.** G4: Glas . . . . 1D 82 (1A 4)
G69: Barg . . . . . . . . . . . . . . . . . 6D 88
**Queens Cres.** ML1: New S . . . . . . 4H 127
**Queen's Cres.** ML4: Bell . . . . . . . 3B 126
ML6: Chap . . . . . . . . . . . . . . . 2D 112
ML8: Carl . . . . . . . . . . . . . . . 3G 165
**Queensdale Av.** ML9: Lark . . . . . . 5F 161
**Queensdale Rd.** ML9: Lark . . . . . . 5F 161
**Queen's Dr.** G42: Glas . . . . . . . . 3D 102
G68: Cumb . . . . . . . . . . . . . . . . 5H 13
**Queens Dr.** ML3: Ham . . . . . . . . 5H 153
PA7: B'ton . . . . . . . . . . . . . . . . 4H 39
**Queen's Dr. La.** G42: Glas . . . . . . 4E 103
**Queensferry St.** G5: Glas . . . . . . 3A 104
**Queen's Gdns.** G12: Glas . . . . . . . . 6A 62
**Queen's Ga.** G76: Clar . . . . . . . . 1C 134
**Queen's Ga. La.** G12: Glas . . . . . . . 6A 62
**Queens Gro.** G66: Lenz . . . . . . . . . 3C 50
**Queenside Cres.** PA8: Ersk . . . . . . 6D 40
**Queensland Ct.** G52: Glas . . . . . . . 5C 80
**Queensland Dr.** G52: Glas . . . . . . . 5C 80
**Queensland Gdns.** G52: Glas . . . . . 5C 80
**Queensland La. E.** G52: Glas . . . . 5C 80
**Queensland La. W.** G52: Glas . . . . 5C 80
**Queenslie Ind. Est.** G33: Glas . . . . 3D 86
**Queenslie St.** G33: Glas . . . . . . . . 1F 85
**Queen's Pk. Av.** G42: Glas . . . . . . 4F 103
Queen's Pk. F.C. . . . . . . . . . . . . 6F 103
Queen's Park Station (Rail) . . . . 3E 103
**Queens Pl.** G12: Glas . . . . . . . . . . 6A 62
**Queen Sq.** G41: Glas . . . . . . . . . 3D 102
**Queen's Rd.** PA5: Eld . . . . . . . . . . 3A 96
**Queen's St.** ML1: Cle . . . . . . . . . 5H 129
**Queen St.** G1: Glas . . . . . . . 4G 83 (6E 5)
G66: Kirk . . . . . . . . . . . . . . . . . 5C 30
G73: Ruth . . . . . . . . . . . . . . . 5C 104
ML1: Moth . . . . . . . . . . . . . . . 2G 143
ML2: Newm . . . . . . . . . . . . . 3D 146
ML3: Ham . . . . . . . . . . . . . . . 4E 141
PA1: Pais . . . . . . . . . . . . . . . . 1G 97
PA4: Renf . . . . . . . . . . . . . . . . . 6F 59
Queen Street Station (Rail)
. . . . . . . . . . . . . . . . 3G 83 (4E 5)
**Queens Way** G64: Torr . . . . . . . . . 5D 28
**Queensway** G74: E Kil . . . . . . . . . 6B 136
**Queen Victoria Ct.** G14: Glas . . . . 5C 60
**Queen Victoria Dr.** G13: Glas . . . . 5C 60
G14: Glas . . . . . . . . . . . . . . . . 5C 60
**Queen Victoria Ga.** G13: Glas . . . . 4C 60
**Queen Victoria St.** ML6: Air . . . . . 4H 91
QUEENZIEBURN . . . . . . . . . . . . . . 3C 10
**Queenzieburn Ind. Est.**
G65: Queen . . . . . . . . . . . . . . . 4D 10
**Quendale Dr.** G32: Glas . . . . . . . . 2H 105
**Quentin St.** G41: Glas . . . . . . . . . 4C 102
**Quinton Gdns.** G69: Bail . . . . . . . . 6G 87

## R

**Raasay Cres.** ML6: Air . . . . . . . . . . 5E 93
**Raasay Dr.** PA2: Pais . . . . . . . . . . 6H 97
**Raasay Gdns.** G77: Newt M . . . . . 4B 132
**Raasay Pl.** G22: Glas . . . . . . . . . . 1G 63
**Raasay St.** G22: Glas . . . . . . . . . . 1G 63
**Racecourse Vw.** ML3: Ham . . . . . 4A 142
RADNOR PARK . . . . . . . . . . . . . . . 3C 42
**Radnor St.** G3: Glas . . . . . . . . . . . 2B 82
G81: Clyd . . . . . . . . . . . . . . . . 4C 42
(not continuous)
**Raeberry St.** G20: Glas . . . . . . . . . 6D 62
**Raebog Cres.** ML6: Air . . . . . . . . . 1H 91
**Raebog Rd.** ML6: Glenm . . . . . . . . 5G 71
**Raeburn Av.** G74: E Kil . . . . . . . . 5B 138
PA1: Pais . . . . . . . . . . . . . . . . 1B 98
**Raeburn Cres.** ML3: Ham . . . . . . 6C 140
**Raeburn Pl.** G74: E Kil . . . . . . . . 5B 138
**Raeburn Wlk.** ML4: Bell . . . . . . . 6D 110
**Raeside Av.** G77: Newt M . . . . . . 6D 132
**Raes Rd.** ML8: Carl . . . . . . . . . . 5B 164
**Raeswood Dr.** G53: Glas . . . . . . . . 5H 99
**Raeswood Gdns.** G53: Glas . . . . . . 5H 99
**Raeswood Pl.** G53: Glas . . . . . . . . 5H 99
**Raeswood Rd.** G53: Glas . . . . . . . . 5H 99
**Raewell Cres.** ML4: Bell . . . . . . . 4B 126
**Rafford St.** G51: Glas . . . . . . . . . . 4G 81
**Raglan St.** G4: Glas . . . . . . . . . . . 1E 83
**Railway Rd.** ML6: Air . . . . . . . . . . 4F 91
**Raith Av.** G45: Glas . . . . . . . . . . 3H 119
**Raithburn Av.** G45: Glas . . . . . . . 3G 119
**Raithburn Rd.** G45: Glas . . . . . . . 4G 119
Raith Cottage Vis. Cen.
. . . . . . . . . . . . . . . . . . . . . . 6H 125
**Raith Dr.** G68: Cumb . . . . . . . . . . 4H 33
ML4: Bell . . . . . . . . . . . . . . . 3D 126
**RAITH INTERCHANGE** . . . . . . . . 5G 125
RALSTON . . . . . . . . . . . . . . . . . . 1F 99
**Ralston Av.** PA1: Pais . . . . . . . . . . 2H 99
**Ralston Cotts.** PA1: Pais . . . . . . . . 1F 99
**Ralston Ct.** G52: Glas . . . . . . . . . . 1H 99
**Ralston Dr.** G52: Glas . . . . . . . . . . 1H 99
**Ralston Path** G52: Glas . . . . . . . . . 1H 99
**Ralston Pl.** G52: Glas . . . . . . . . . . 1H 99
**Ralston Rd.** G61: Bear . . . . . . . . . . 2E 45
G78: Barr . . . . . . . . . . . . . . . 5E 115
**Ralston St.** ML6: Air . . . . . . . . . . . 4G 91
PA1: Pais . . . . . . . . . . . . . . . . 1C 98
**Ramage Rd.** ML8: Carl . . . . . . . . 5H 165
**Ramillies Ct.** G81: Clyd . . . . . . . . . 5E 43
ML8: Carl . . . . . . . . . . . . . . . 4G 165
**Rampart Av.** G13: Glas . . . . . . . . . 1A 60
**Ramsay Av.** PA5: John . . . . . . . . . . 4E 95
**Ramsay Ct.** G77: Newt M . . . . . . . 6E 133
**Ramsay Cres.** PA10: Kilb . . . . . . . . 3B 94
**Ramsay Hill** G74: E Kil . . . . . . . . 6A 138
**Ramsay Ind. Est.** G66: Kirk . . . . . . 4B 30
**Ramsay Pl.** ML5: Coat . . . . . . . . . . 6G 89
PA5: John . . . . . . . . . . . . . . . . . 4E 95
**Ramsay St.** G81: Clyd . . . . . . . . . . 4B 42
**Ramsey Wynd** ML4: Bell . . . . . . . 6D 110
**Ram St.** G32: Glas . . . . . . . . . . . . 6H 85
**Ranaldard Gdns.** G73: Ruth . . . . . 4F 121
**Randolph Av.** G76: Clar . . . . . . . . 6E 119
**Randolph Dr.** G76: Clar . . . . . . . . 6D 118
**Randolph Gdns.** G76: Clar . . . . . . 6D 118
**Randolph Ga.** G11: Glas . . . . . . . . . 5F 61
**Randolph La.** G11: Glas . . . . . . . . . 6F 61
**Randolph Rd.** G11: Glas . . . . . . . . . 5F 61
RANFURLY . . . . . . . . . . . . . . . . . 5G 73
**Ranfurly Ct.** PA11: Bri W . . . . . . . 4F 73
**Ranfurly Dr.** G68: Cumb . . . . . . . . 1G 35
**Ranfurly Pl.** PA11: Bri W . . . . . . . 4F 73
**Ranfurly Rd.** G52: Glas . . . . . . . . . . 6H 7
PA11: Bri W . . . . . . . . . . . . . . . 5F 7
**Range Av.** ML1: Moth . . . . . . . . . 5C 14
**Range Pl.** ML3: Ham . . . . . . . . . . 2A 15
Rangers F.C. . . . . . . . . . . . . . . . . 5G 8
Rangers F.C. Training Cen. &
Youth Academy . . . . . . . . . . 5A 2
**Rangerhouse Rd.** G75: E Kil . . . . . 6H 14
**Range Rd.** ML1: Moth . . . . . . . . . 5B 14
**Range Rd. Ind. Est.** ML1: Moth . . 6C 14
(Range Av
ML1: Moth . . . . . . . . . . . . . . . 5B 14
(Range Rd
**Range St.** ML1: Moth . . . . . . . . . . 5B 14
**Rankin Dr.** G77: Newt M . . . . . . . . 3C 13
**Rankine Av.** G75: E Kil . . . . . . . . . 4A 15
**Rankine Pl.** G75: E Kil . . . . . . . . . 4A 15
PA5: John . . . . . . . . . . . . . . . . . 2F 9
**Rankine St.** PA5: John . . . . . . . . . . 2F 9
**Rankin Gait Cen.** *ML8: Carl . . . . . 3F 16*
*(off High St*
**Rankin Rd.** ML2: Wis . . . . . . . . . . 5C 14
**Rankin St.** ML8: Carl . . . . . . . . . . 3F 16
**Rankin Way** G78: Barr . . . . . . . . . 4G 11
**Rannoch Av.** G64: B'rig . . . . . . . . . 6D 4
G77: Newt M . . . . . . . . . . . . . 2D 13
ML3: Ham . . . . . . . . . . . . . . . 2E 15
ML5: Coat . . . . . . . . . . . . . . . . 2H 8
**Rannoch Ct.** G67: Cumb . . . . . . . . . 1D 5
G72: Blan . . . . . . . . . . . . . . . 4D 14
**Rannoch Dr.** G61: Bear . . . . . . . . . . 2H 4
G66: Kirk . . . . . . . . . . . . . . . . . 4H 3
G67: Cumb . . . . . . . . . . . . . . . . 1D 5
ML2: Wis . . . . . . . . . . . . . . . . 2H 15
PA4: Renf . . . . . . . . . . . . . . . . . 5E 5
**Rannoch Gdns.** G64: B'rig . . . . . . . 6E 4
**Rannoch Grn.** G74: E Kil . . . . . . . 6H 13
**Rannoch La.** G69: Mood . . . . . . . . . 5E 5
**Rannoch Pl.** PA2: Pais . . . . . . . . . . 2C 9
**Rannoch Rd.** G71: Tann . . . . . . . . 4C 10
ML6: Air . . . . . . . . . . . . . . . . . . 2H 9
PA5: John . . . . . . . . . . . . . . . . . 4E 9
**Rannoch St.** G44: Glas . . . . . . . . . 1E 11
**Rannoch Ter.** ML9: Lark . . . . . . . 4G 16
**Rannoch Way** G71: Both . . . . . . . . 4E 12
RAPLOCH . . . . . . . . . . . . . . . . . 2D 16
**Raploch Av.** G14: Glas . . . . . . . . . 5B 6
**Raploch Cres.** G81: Faif . . . . . . . . . 6F 2
**Raploch La.** G14: Glas . . . . . . . . . . 5B 6
**Raploch Rd.** ML9: Lark . . . . . . . . 2D 16
**Raploch St.** ML9: Lark . . . . . . . . . 2D 16
RASHIEBURN . . . . . . . . . . . . . . . . 5E 4
**Rashieburn** PA8: Ersk . . . . . . . . . . . . 5
41
**Rashieglen** PA8: Ersk . . . . . . . . . . . 5E 4
**Rashiehill** PA8: Ersk . . . . . . . . . . . 5E 4
**Rashielee Rd.** PA8: Ersk . . . . . . . . 5E 4
**Rashiewood** PA8: Ersk . . . . . . . . . . 5F 4
**Rashilee Av.** PA8: Ersk . . . . . . . . . 5F 4
**Rathlin St.** G51: Glas . . . . . . . . . . 3G 8
**Rathlin Ter.** G82: Dumb . . . . . . . . 2C 1
**Ratho Dr.** G21: Glas . . . . . . . . . . . 5A 6
G68: Cumb . . . . . . . . . . . . . . . . 6F 1
**Ratho Pk.** ML3: Ham . . . . . . . . . . 4F 15
**Rattray** PA8: Ersk . . . . . . . . . . . . . 4E 4
**Rattray St.** G32: Glas . . . . . . . . . . 2G 10
**Ravel Row** G31: Glas . . . . . . . . . . . 6F 8
**Ravelston Rd.** G61: Bear . . . . . . . . 5E 4
(not continuous
**Ravelston St.** G32: Glas . . . . . . . . . 5F 8
**Ravel Wynd** G71: Tann . . . . . . . . . 5F 10
**Ravenscliffe Dr.** G46: Giff . . . . . . 4H 11
**Ravens Ct.** G64: B'rig . . . . . . . . . . 1B 6
**Ravenscourt** G74: T'hall . . . . . . . . 6G 13
**Ravenscraig Av.** PA2: Pais . . . . . . 4G 9
**Ravenscraig Ct.** ML4: Bell . . . . . . 2D 12
**Ravenscraig Dr.** G53: Glas . . . . . . 1B 11
**Ravenscraig Ter.** G53: Glas . . . . . 2C 11
**Ravenshall** ML1: Cle . . . . . . . . . . 1H 14
**Ravenshall Rd.** G41: Glas . . . . . . 5A 10
**Ravenshill Dr.** ML1: Cle . . . . . . . . 6H 12
**Ravenstone Dr.** G46: Giff . . . . . . 2A 11
**Ravenswood Av.** PA2: Pais . . . . . . 6C 9
**Ravenswood Dr.** G41: Glas . . . . . . 4B 10
**Ravenswood Rd.** G69: Bail . . . . . . 6A 8
**Raven Wynd** ML2: Wis . . . . . . . . . 5H 14
RAWYARDS . . . . . . . . . . . . . . . . . 2C 9
**Rawyards Av.** ML6: Air . . . . . . . . . 1B 9
**Raymond Pl.** G75: E Kil . . . . . . . . 2E 14
**Rayne Pl.** G15: Glas . . . . . . . . . . . 3B 4
**Ream Av.** ML6: Air . . . . . . . . . . . . 5F 9
**Reay Av.** G74: E Kil . . . . . . . . . . . 1D 14
**Reay Gdns.** G74: E Kil . . . . . . . . . 1D 14
**Rebrae Pl.** G66: Kirk . . . . . . . . . . . 4E 3
**Redan St.** G40: Glas . . . . . . . . . . . 6B 8
**Redbrae Rd.** G66: Kirk . . . . . . . . . 4D 3
**Red Bri. Ct.** ML5: Coat . . . . . . . . . 3C 9
**Redburn Av.** G46: Giff . . . . . . . . . 1H 13
**Redburn Ct.** G67: Cumb . . . . . . . . . 5F 1
**Redburn Pl.** G67: Cumb . . . . . . . . . 6F 1

Redburn Rd.—Ross Cres.


dburn Rd. G67: Cumb .5F 15
dcastle Sq. G33: Glas .2E 87
dcliffe Dr. G75: E Kil .3D 148
d Deer Rd. G75: E Kil .3E 149
derech Cres. ML3: Ham .1D 152
dford St. G33: Glas .3F 85
dgate Pl. G14: Glas .5B 60
dgrave G74: E Kil .4C 138
dhill Rd. G68: Cumb .2F 35
dhills Vw. G66: Len .4G 7
dholme *ML9: Lark .4F 161*
*(off Keir Hardie Rd.)*
dhouse La. ML8: Carl .2F 165
dhurst Cres. PA2: Pais .6F 97
dhurst La. PA2: Pais .6G 97
dhurst Way PA2: Pais .6F 97
dlands La. G12: Glas .5A 62
dlands Rd. G12: Glas .5A 62
dlands Ter. G12: Glas .5A 62
dlands Ter. La. G12: Glas .5A 62
dlawood Pl. G72: Newt .1G 123
dlawood Rd. G72: Newt .1G 123
dmoss Rd. G66: Milt C .6B 8
G81: Dun .1B 42
dmoss St. G22: Glas .4F 63
dnock St. G22: Glas .5G 63
dpath Dr. G52: Glas .5B 80
d Rd. G21: Glas .5D 64
d Rd. Ct. G21: Glas .6D 64
d Road Recreation Cen. .6E 65
dwing Gdns. ML2: Wis .2F 157
dwood Av. G74: E Kil .2A 148
dwood Ct. G74: E Kil .2A 148
dwood Cres. G71: View .5G 109
G72: Flem .3F 123
G74: E Kil .6A 136
PA7: B'ton .4A 40
dwood Dr. G21: Glas .6C 64
G74: E Kil .3A 148
dwood Gro. ML5: Coat .5D 90
dwood Pl. G66: Lenz .2B 50
G71: View .5G 109
G74: E Kil .1A 148
dwood Rd. G67: Cumb .3D 36
ML1: Holy .2C 128
dwood Way G72: Flem .4F 123
elick Av. G13: Glas .1G 59
elick Quad. G13: Glas .1G 59
ema Rd. ML4: Bell .1D 126
en Pl. G71: Both .3F 125
gency Ct. ML3: Ham .1C 154
gency M. G69: Bail .1A 108
gency Way ML1: New S .3H 127
gent Dr. G73: Ruth .5C 104
gent Moray St. G3: Glas .2B 82
gent Pk. Sq. G41: Glas .3D 102
gent Pl. G81: Clyd .3A 42
gents Ga. G71: Both .3B 124
gent Shop. Cen. G66: Kirk .5C 30
gent Sq. G66: Lenz .3C 50
gent St. G66: Kirk .5C 30
G81: Clyd .3A 42
PA1: Pais .6D 78
egent Way ML3: Ham .6A 142
gister Av. ML4: Bell .4C 126
gister Rd. G65: Kils .3A 12
gwood St. G41: Glas .5B 102
eid Av. G61: Bear .1G 45
PA3: Lin .6H 75
id Gro. ML1: Moth .5B 144
id Pl. G40: Glas .1B 104
id St. G40: Glas .2B 104
G73: Ruth .5D 104
ML3: Ham .4D 140
ML5: Coat .3C 90
ML6: Air .2B 92
idvale St. G31: Glas .5B 84
eilly Rd. PA6: Hous .6B 38
eith Dr. G75: E Kil .4F 149
emus Pl. ML4: Moss .2G 127
enfield La. G2: Glas .4F 83 (5D 4)
enfield St. G2: Glas .4F 83 (5D 4)
PA4: Renf .5F 59
ENFREW .5F 59
enfrew Community Mus. .5F 59
enfrew Ct. *G1: Glas .3G 5*
*(off St Mungo Av.)*
G2: Glas .3G 83 (3E 5)
enfrew La. G2: Glas .3F 83 (3D 4)
enfrew Pl. ML5: Coat .1G 109
enfrew Rd. G51: Glas .3B 80
PA3: Pais .5B 78
PA4: Renf .1A 80
enfrew St. G3: Glas .2E 83 (2A 4)
ML5: Coat .1G 109
ennie Pl. G74: E Kil .6C 136
ennie Rd. G65: Kils .2F 11
enshaw Dr. G52: Glas .5B 80
enshaw Rd. PA5: Eld .4A 96
PA7: B'ton .4H 39
Renton Rd. G82: Dumb .1D 16
Renton St. G4: Glas .2G 83 (1E 5)
Resipol Rd. G33: Step .4E 67
Reston Dr. G52: Glas .5B 80
Reuther Av. G73: Ruth .6D 104
Revoch Dr. G13: Glas .2A 60
Reynolds Av. G75: E Kil .4A 150
Reynolds Dr. G33: Step .4F 67
Reynolds Path ML2: Wis .2B 158
Rhannan Rd. G44: Glas .2E 119
Rhannan Ter. G44: Glas .2E 119
Rhindhouse Pl. G69: Bail .6B 88
Rhindhouse Rd. G69: Bail .6B 88
Rhindmuir Av. G69: Bail .6A 88
Rhindmuir Ct. G69: Bail .5A 88
Rhindmuir Cres. G69: Bail .5B 88
Rhindmuir Dr. G69: Bail .5A 88
Rhindmuir Gdns. G69: Bail .5A 88
Rhindmuir Gro. G69: Bail .5B 88
Rhindmuir Path G69: Bail .5B 88
Rhindmuir Pl. G69: Bail .5A 88
Rhindmuir Rd. G69: Bail .5A 88
Rhindmuir Vw. G69: Bail .5B 88
Rhindmuir Wynd G69: Bail .5B 88
Rhinds St. ML5: Coat .1F 109
Rhinsdale Cres. G69: Bail .6A 88
Rhumhor Gdns. PA10: Kilb .3C 94
Rhu Quad. ML2: Over .5A 158
Rhymer St. G21: Glas .2A 84
Rhymie Rd. G32: Glas .2D 106
Rhynie Dr. G51: Glas .6H 81
Riach Gdns. ML1: Moth .6E 127
Ribblesdale G74: E Kil .6E 137
Riccarton G75: E Kil .4D 148
Riccarton St. G42: Glas .3G 103
Riccartsbar Av. PA2: Pais .2G 97
Rice Way ML1: Moth .5B 144
Richmond Av. G76: Clar .2C 134
Richmond Ct. G73: Ruth .5E 105
Richmond Dr. G64: B'rig .3D 48
G72: Camb .2G 121
G73: Ruth .6E 105
PA3: Lin .4G 75
Richmond Gdns. G69: Chry .1H 67
Richmond Gro. G73: Ruth .6E 105
Richmond Pl. G73: Ruth .5E 105
Richmond Rd. G73: Ruth .6F 105
Richmond St. G1: Glas .4H 83 (5G 5)
G81: Clyd .6E 43
Riddell St. G81: Clyd .4D 42
ML5: Coat .4E 91
Riddon Av. G13: Glas .1G 59
Riddon Pl. G13: Glas .1G 59
RIDDRIE .2F 85
Riddrie Cres. G33: Glas .3G 85
RIDDRIE KNOWES .3G 85
Riddrie Knowes G33: Glas .3G 85
Riddrievale Ct. G33: Glas .2G 85
Riddrievale St. G33: Glas .2G 85
Rigby St. G31: Glas .6G 85
Rigghead Av. G67: Cumb .6B 14
Rigg Pl. G33: Glas .4E 87
Riggside Rd. G33: Glas .1C 86
Riggs, The G62: Miln .2G 25
Righead Ga. *G74: E Kil .2G 149*
*(off Princess Sq.)*
Righead Ind. Est. ML4: Bell .6A 110
RIGHEAD RDBT. .2F 149
Riglands Way PA4: Renf .6E 59
Riglaw Pl. G13: Glas .2A 60
Rigmuir Rd. G51: Glas .4C 80
Rimsdale St. G40: Glas .6C 84
Ringford St. G21: Glas .6B 64
Ripon Dr. G12: Glas .3G 61
Risk St. G81: Clyd .3B 42
G82: Dumb .4E 17
Ristol Rd. G13: Glas .4B 60
Ritchie Cres. PA5: Eld .2A 96
Ritchie Pk. PA5: John .2H 95
Ritchie Pl. G77: Newt M .5C 132
Ritchie St. G5: Glas .1E 103
ML2: Wis .6D 144
Riverbank Dr. ML4: Bell .4E 127
Riverbank St. G43: Glas .6A 102
River Ct. G76: Busby .3D 134
Riverdale Gdns. ML3: Ham .2A 154
Riverford Rd. G43: Glas .6A 102
G73: Ruth .4E 105
River Rd. G32: Carm .6B 106
Riversdale La. G14: Glas .4A 60
Riverside G62: Miln .3G 25
G66: Len .1C 6
PA6: Hous .2D 74
Riverside Ct. G44: Neth .4D 118
Riverside Gdns. G76: Busby .4D 134
Riverside La. G82: Dumb .4E 17
Riverside Pk. G44: Neth .5E 119
Riverside Pl. G72: Camb .1E 123
Riverside Rd. G43: Glas .6C 102
ML9: Lark .5E 161
Riverside Ter. G76: Busby .4D 134
Riverside Wlk. ML1: Moth .1H 143
Riverton Dr. G75: E Kil .3D 148
Riverview Dr. G5: Glas .5E 83
Riverview Gdns. G5: Glas .5E 83
Riverview Pl. G5: Glas .5E 83
R.N.I.B. Springfield Cen.
G64: B'rig .6D 48
Roaden Av. PA2: Pais .6D 96
Roaden Rd. PA2: Pais .6D 96
Roadside G67: Cumb .6A 14
Robb Ter. G66: Kirk .1G 51
Robert Burns Av. G81: Clyd .4E 43
ML1: N'hill .3E 129
Robert Burns Quad. ML4: Bell .2B 126
Robert Dr. G51: Glas .4G 81
Roberton St. ML6: Chap .2E 113
Robert Smillie Cres.
ML9: Lark .4E 161
Robertson Av. G41: Glas .3A 102
PA4: Renf .6D 58
Robertson Cl. PA4: Renf .6E 59
Robertson Cres. G78: Neil .2D 130
Robertson Dr. G74: E Kil .1B 150
ML4: Bell .3C 126
Robertson La. G2: Glas .6B 4
Robertson St. G1: Glas .5F 83 (6C 4)
G78: Barr .5D 114
ML3: Ham .4D 140
ML6: Air .4G 91
Robertson Ter. G69: Bail .6A 88
Roberts Quad. ML4: Bell .4D 126
Roberts St. G81: Clyd .4A 42
ML2: Wis .6G 145
Robert St. G51: Glas .4G 81
Robert Templeton Dr.
G72: Camb .2B 122
Robert Wynd ML2: Newm .3E 147
Robet Gilson Gdns. ML5: Coat .6D 90
Robin Pl. ML2: Wis .6H 145
Robin Way G32: Carm .5C 106
ROBROYSTON .3G 65
Robroyston Av. G33: Glas .6G 65
ROBROYSTON INTERCHANGE
.4H 65
Robroyston Rd. G33: Glas .4F 65
G64: B'rig .6H 49
G66: Auch .6H 49
Robshill Ct. G77: Newt M .5D 132
Robslee Dr. G46: Giff .4H 117
Robslee Rd. G46: Giff, T'bnk .5G 117
Robson Gro. G42: Glas .2F 103
Rochdale Pl. G66: Kirk .5C 30
Rochsoles Cres. ML6: Air .1A 92
Rochsoles Dr. ML6: Air .1H 91
Rochsolloch Farm Cotts.
ML6: Air .4G 91
Rochsolloch Rd. ML6: Air .5F 91
Rockall Dr. G44: Glas .3F 119
Rockbank Pl. G40: Glas .6C 84
G81: Hard .1E 43
Rockbank St. G40: Glas .6C 84
Rockburn Cres. ML4: Bell .6C 110
Rockburn Dr. G76: Clar .1A 134
Rockcliffe St. G40: Glas .2B 104
Rock Dr. PA10: Kilb .3B 94
Rockfield Pl. G21: Glas .4E 65
Rockfield Rd. G21: Glas .4E 65
Rockhampton Av. G75: E Kil .4D 148
Rockmount Av. G46: T'bnk .3G 117
G78: Barr .6F 115
Rock St. G4: Glas .6F 63
Rockwell Av. PA2: Pais .5G 97
Roddinghead Rd. G46: Giff .3G 133
Rodger Av. G77: Newt M .4C 132
Rodger Dr. G73: Ruth .1C 120
Rodger Pl. G73: Ruth .1C 120
Rodil Av. G44: Glas .3G 119
Rodney St. G4: Glas .1F 83
Roebank Dr. G78: Barr .6E 115
Roebank St. G31: Glas .3D 84
(not continuous)
Roffey Pk. Rd. PA1: Pais .6F 79
Rogart St. G40: Glas .6B 84
(not continuous)
Rogerfield Rd. G69: Barg .4A 88
ROGERTON .3F 137
Roland Cres. G77: Newt M .6F 133
Roman Av. G15: Glas .6A 44
G61: Bear .2F 45
Roman Bath House .2F 45
Roman Ct. G61: Bear .2F 45
Roman Cres. G60: Old K .6D 20
Roman Dr. G61: Bear .2F 45
ML4: Bell .3D 126
Roman Gdns. G61: Bear .2F 45
Roman Hill Rd. G81: Hard .6D 22
Roman Pl. ML4: Bell .4A 126
Roman Rd. G61: Bear .2E 45
G66: Kirk .5B 30
Roman Rd. G81: Hard .1C 42
ML1: Moth .1F 143
(not continuous)
Roman Way G71: View .1G 125
Romney Av. G44: Glas .2G 119
Romulus Ct. ML1: Moth .6E 127
Ronaldsay Dr. G64: B'rig .5F 49
Ronaldsay Pas. G22: Glas .2H 63
Ronaldsay Pl. G67: Cumb .5F 35
Ronaldsay St. G22: Glas .2G 63
Ronald St. ML5: Coat .3C 90
Rona St. G21: Glas .1D 84
Rona Ter. G72: Camb .4H 121
Ronay St. G22: Glas .2H 63
ML2: Wis .4C 146
Rooksdell Av. PA2: Pais .4G 97
Ropework La. G1: Glas .5G 83
Rorison Pl. ML9: Ashg .4B 162
Rosa Burn Av. G75: E Kil .6D 148
ROSEBANK
Carluke .5E 163
Glasgow .5G 31
Rosebank PA5: John .3F 95
Rosebank Av. G66: Kirk .4E 31
G72: Blan .6C 124
Rosebank Dr. G71: View .6G 109
G72: Camb .3C 122
Rosebank Gdns. G71: Udd .3H 107
Rosebank La. G71: Both .4F 125
Rosebank Pl. G68: Dull .5E 13
G71: Udd .3H 107
ML3: Ham .6E 141
Rosebank Rd. ML2: Over .5A 158
ML4: Bell .5D 110
Rosebank St. ML6: Air .3E 93
Rosebank Ter. G69: Barg .1D 108
Rosebank Twr. *G72: Camb .1A 122*
*(off Main St.)*
Roseberry La. ML6: Chap .2E 113
Roseberry Pl. ML3: Ham .5E 141
Roseberry Rd. ML6: Chap .1D 112
Roseberry St. G5: Glas .2A 104
Roseburn Ct. G67: Cumb .5F 15
Rose Cres. ML3: Ham .5D 140
Rose Dale G64: B'rig .1D 64
Rosedale G74: E Kil .6E 137
Rosedale Av. PA2: Pais .6B 96
Rosedale Dr. G69: Bail .1G 107
Rosedale Gdns. G20: Glas .1A 62
Rosedene Ter. ML4: Bell .1C 126
Rosefield Gdns. G71: Udd .6C 108
Rosegreen Cres. ML4: Bell .5C 110
ROSEHALL .2D 110
Rosehall Av. ML5: Coat .1D 110
Rosehall Ind. Est. ML5: Coat .2C 110
Rosehall Rd. ML4: Bell .1B 126
Rosehall Ter. ML2: Wis .2E 157
Rosehill Dr. G67: Cumb .1C 54
Rosehill Pl. G67: Cumb .1C 54
Rosehill Rd. G64: Torr .5D 28
Rose Knowe Rd. G42: Glas .5H 103
Roselea Dr. G62: Miln .2H 25
Roselea Gdns. G13: Glas .2F 61
Roselea Pl. G72: Blan .6A 124
Roselea Rd. G71: Tann .5C 108
Roselea St. ML9: Lark .1F 161
Rosemary Cres. G74: E Kil .5F 137
Rosemary Pl. G74: E Kil .5F 137
Rosemount G68: Cumb .6H 13
Rose Mt. Ct. ML6: Air .3C 92
Rosemount Gdns. ML6: Air .4A 92
Rosemount La. *ML9: Lark .4G 161*
*(off Dickson St.)*
PA11: Bri W .5D 72
Rosemount Mdws. G71: Both .5D 124
Rosemount St. G21: Glas .2B 84
Rosendale Way G72: Blan .2C 140
Roseneath Ga. G74: E Kil .1E 149
Roseness Pl. G33: Glas .3A 86
Rosepark Av. G71: View .1G 125
Rosepark Cotts. ML5: Coat .2B 110
Rose St. G3: Glas .3F 83 (3C 4)
G66: Kirk .5D 30
G67: Cumb .6D 34
ML1: Moth .4A 144
Rosevale Cres. ML4: Bell .3E 127
Rosevale Gdns. ML3: Ham .1F 153
Rosevale Rd. G61: Bear .3E 45
Rosevale St. G11: Glas .1G 81
Rosewood Av. ML4: Bell .6D 110
PA2: Pais .4F 97
Rosewood Path ML4: Bell .2A 126
Rosewood St. G13: Glas .2E 61
Roslea Dr. G31: Glas .4C 84
Roslin Twr. G72: Camb .4G 121
Roslyn Dr. G69: Barg .6D 88
Rosneath St. G51: Glas .3G 81
Ross Av. G66: Kirk .5F 31
PA4: Renf .2C 78
Ross Cres. ML1: Moth .4E 143

St Mirren Pk.—Shawfield Cres.


Mirren Pk. . . . . . . . . . . . . . . . .5A 78
Mirren R.C. Cathedral . . . . . . .6B 78
Mirren Sports & Leisure Complex
. . . . . . . . . . . . . . . . . . . .5A 78
Mirren's Rd. G65: Kils . . . . . . . .3A 12
Mirren St. PA1: Pais . . . . . . . . . .1A 98
Monance St. G21: Glas . . . . . . .4B 64
Monicas Way ML5: Coat . . . . .1H 109
Mungo Av. G4: Glas . . . . .3G 83 (3F 5)
Mungo Ct. PA11: Bri W . . . . . . .3G 73
Mungo Mus. of Religious Life & Art
. . . . . . . . . . . . . . . . . . . .3A 84
Mungo Pl. G4: Glas . . . . .3H 83 (3H 5)
ML3: Ham . . . . . . . . . . . . . .5B 140
Mungo's Cathedral . . . . . . . . .3A 84
Mungo's Cres. ML1: Carf . . . . .5B 128
Mungo's Rd. G67: Cumb . . . . . .4H 35
Mungo St. G64: B'rig . . . . . . . . .1B 64
Mungo's Wlk. G67: Cumb . . . . .3H 35
(in Cumbernauld Shop. Cen.)
Ninian's Cres. PA2: Pais . . . . . .3B 98
Ninians Gro. ML2: Wis . . . . . . .3B 146
Ninian's Pl. ML3: Ham . . . . . . .6D 140
Ninian's Rd. ML3: Ham . . . . . .6D 140
PA2: Pais . . . . . . . . . . . . . . . . .3B 98
Ninian Ter. G5: Glas . . . . . . . . . .6G 83
Peters La. G2: Glas . . . . .4E 83 (5B 4)
Peter's Path G4: Glas . . . . . . . . .1E 83
(off St Peter's St.)
Peter's St. G4: Glas . . . . .1E 83 (1B 4)
Roberts Gdns. G53: Glas . . . . . .2C 116
Rollox Brae G21: Glas . . . . . . . .1A 84
Rollox Bus. & Retail Pk.
G21: Glas . . . . . . . . . . . . . . . .1B 84
Ronan's Dr. G41: Glas . . . . . . .4B 102
Ronans Dr. G73: Ruth . . . . . . .1E 121
Ronan's Dr. ML3: Ham . . . . . . .3G 153
Stephen's Av. G73: Ruth . . . . . .4F 121
Stephen's Cres. G73: Ruth . . .4G 121
Valentine Ter. G5: Glas . . . . . .1H 103
Vigean's Av. G77: Newt M . . . .6B 132
Vigeans Pl. G77: Newt M . . . . .6C 132
Vincent Cres. G3: Glas . . . . . . . .3B 82
Vincent Cres. La. G3: Glas . . . . .3B 82
Vincent La. G2: Glas . . . .3E 83 (4B 4)
Vincent Pl. G1: Glas . . . .4G 83 (5E 5)
G75: E Kil . . . . . . . . . . . . . . . .3C 148
ML1: Moth . . . . . . . . . . . . . . .2G 143
Vincent St. G2: Glas . . . .3E 83 (4A 4)
G3: Glas . . . . . . . . . . . .3D 82 (4A 4)
Vincent Ter. G3: Glas . . .3D 82 (4A 4)
Winifred's Way ML2: Wis . . . .5G 145
alamanca St. G31: Glas . . . . . . . .6F 85
(not continuous)
alasaig Ct. G33: Glas . . . . . . . . .4A 86
alen St. G52: Glas . . . . . . . . . . . .6F 81
alford Pl. G66: Kirk . . . . . . . . . . .4C 30
(off Glasgow Rd.)
aline St. ML6: Air . . . . . . . . . . . .5F 91
alisbury G74: E Kil . . . . . . . . . .5D 138
alisbury Cres. ML1: Moth . . . . .1D 142
alisbury Pl. G81: Clyd . . . . . . . . .2H 41
alisbury St. G5: Glas . . . . . . . .1F 103
alkeld St. G5: Glas . . . . . . . . . .1E 103
almona St. G22: Glas . . . . . . . . . .5F 63
altaire Av. G71: Udd . . . . . . . . .2E 125
alterland Rd. G53: Glas . . . . . . .2G 115
altire Cres. ML9: Lark . . . . . . . .3G 161
altmarket G1: Glas . . . . . . . . . . .5G 83
altmarket Pl. G1: Glas . . . . . . . . .5G 83
altoun La. G12: Glas . . . . . . . . . .6B 62
altoun St. G12: Glas . . . . . . . . . .6A 62
alvia St. G72: Camb . . . . . . . . . .1H 121
amson Cres. ML8: Carl . . . . . . . .5H 165
andaig Rd. G33: Glas . . . . . . . . . .6E 87
andale Path G72: Blan . . . . . . . .3A 140
andalwood Av. G74: E Kil . . . . . .5F 137
andalwood Ct. G74: E Kil . . . . . .5F 137
anda St. G20: Glas . . . . . . . . . . . .5C 62
andbank Av. G20: Glas . . . . . . . .2B 62
andbank Cres. G20: Glas . . . . . . .3B 62
andbank Dr. G20: Glas . . . . . . . .2B 62
andbank St. G20: Glas . . . . . . . .1B 62
andbank Ter. G20: Glas . . . . . . . .2B 62
andend PA8: Ersk . . . . . . . . . . . .4E 41
andend Rd. G53: Glas . . . . . . . .6A 100
anderling Pl. G75: E Kil . . . . . . .6C 148
PA5: John . . . . . . . . . . . . . . . . .6D 94
anderling Rd. PA3: Glas A . . . . . .3H 77
anderson Av. G71: View . . . . . .1H 125
andfield Av. G62: Miln . . . . . . . . .2G 25
andfield St. G20: Glas . . . . . . . . .4C 62
andford Gdns. G69: Bail . . . . . . .6H 87
andgate Av. G32: Glas . . . . . . . .2D 106
andhaven Pl. G53: Glas . . . . . . .6A 100
andhaven Rd. G53: Glas . . . . . . .6A 100
andhead Cres. ML6: Chap . . . . .4E 113
andholes Rd. PA5: Brkfld . . . . . . .6C 74
andholes St. PA1: Pais . . . . . . . .1G 97
andholm Pl. G14: Glas . . . . . . . .4H 59
Sandholm Ter. G14: Glas . . . . . . . .4H 59
Sandiefield Rd. G5: Glas . . . . . . .1G 103
Sandielands Av. PA8: Ersk . . . . . . .2H 57
Sandilands Cres. ML1: Moth . . . .4D 142
Sandilands St. G32: Glas . . . . . . . .6B 86
Sandmill St. G21: Glas . . . . . . . . . .2C 84
Sandpiper Dr. G75: E Kil . . . . . . . .6C 148
Sandpiper Pl. G75: E Kil . . . . . . . .6C 148
Sandpiper Way ML4: Bell . . . . . . .5A 110
Sandra Rd. G64: B'rig . . . . . . . . . .5E 49
Sandra Way PA2: Pais . . . . . . . . . .6H 97
Sandringham Av.
G77: Newt M . . . . . . . . . . . . . .3G 133
Sandringham Ct.
G77: Newt M . . . . . . . . . . . . . .4G 133
Sandringham Dr. PA5: Eld . . . . . . .4H 95
Sandwood G52: Glas . . . . . . . . . . .6A 80
Sandwood Cres. G52: Glas . . . . . . .6A 80
Sandwood Path G52: Glas . . . . . . .6A 80
Sandwood Rd. G52: Glas . . . . . . .1A 100
Sandyfaulds Sq. G5: Glas . . . . . . .1G 103
Sandyfaulds St. G5: Glas . . . . . . .1H 103
Sandyford Av. ML1: N'hse . . . . . .5D 112
Sandyford Pl. G3: Glas . . . . . . . . . .3C 82
(off Claremont St.)
ML1: N'hse . . . . . . . . . . . . . . .6D 112
Sandyford Pl. La. G3: Glas . . . . . . .3C 82
Sandyford Rd. G3: Glas . . . . . . . . .3A 82
ML1: N'hse . . . . . . . . . . . . . . .6D 112
PA3: Pais . . . . . . . . . . . . . . . . . .3C 78
SANDYHILLS . . . . . . . . . . . . . . .1D 106
Sandyhills Cres. G32: Glas . . . . . .2B 106
Sandyhills Dr. G32: Glas . . . . . . .2B 106
Sandyhills Gro. G32: Glas . . . . . .3B 106
Sandyhills Pl. G32: Glas . . . . . . . .2B 106
Sandyhills Rd. G32: Glas . . . . . . .2B 106
Sandyknowes Rd. G67: Cumb . . . .5A 36
Sandy La. G11: Glas . . . . . . . . . . . .1G 81
Sandy Rd. G11: Glas . . . . . . . . . . .1G 81
ML8: Carl . . . . . . . . . . . . . . . . .3F 165
PA4: Renf . . . . . . . . . . . . . . . . . .2E 79
Sannox Dr. ML1: Moth . . . . . . . . .2D 142
Sannox Gdns. G31: Glas . . . . . . . . .3D 84
Sanquhar Dr. G53: Glas . . . . . . . .5A 100
Sanquhar Gdns. G53: Glas . . . . . .5A 100
G72: Blan . . . . . . . . . . . . . . . .5H 123
Sanquhar Pl. G53: Glas . . . . . . . .5A 100
Sanquhar Rd. G53: Glas . . . . . . . .5A 100
Sanson La. ML8: Carl . . . . . . . . . .5H 165
Sapphire Rd. ML4: Bell . . . . . . . .4C 126
Saracen Head La.
G1: Glas . . . . . . . . . . . . . . . . . . .5A 84
Saracen St. G22: Glas . . . . . . . . . .6G 63
Sarazen Ct. ML1: Cle . . . . . . . . . .1E 145
Sardinia La. G12: Glas . . . . . . . . . .6B 62
Saskatoon Pl. G75: E Kil . . . . . . .2D 148
Saucel Hill Ter. PA2: Pais . . . . . . .2A 98
Saucel St. PA1: Pais . . . . . . . . . . .1A 98
Sauchiehall Cen. G2: Glas . . . . . . . .3C 4
Sauchiehall La. G2: Glas . . .3E 83 (3A 4)
(not continuous)
Sauchiehall St. G3: Glas . . .2B 82 (2A 4)
Sauchiesmoor Rd. ML8: Carl . . . .5G 165
Saughs Av. G33: Glas . . . . . . . . . .3H 65
Saughs Dr. G33: Glas . . . . . . . . . .3H 65
Saughs Ga. G33: Glas . . . . . . . . . .3H 65
Saughs Pl. G33: Glas . . . . . . . . . .3H 65
Saughs Rd. G33: Glas . . . . . . . . . .3H 65
G33: Mille . . . . . . . . . . . . . . . . .3A 66
Saughton St. G32: Glas . . . . . . . . .4G 85
Saunders Ct. G78: Barr . . . . . . . .4D 114
Savoy Cen. G2: Glas . . . . . .3F 83 (3C 4)
Savoy St. G40: Glas . . . . . . . . . . .1B 104
Sawmillfield St. G4: Glas . . . . . . . .1F 83
Sawmill Rd. G11: Glas . . . . . . . . . .1F 81
Saxon Rd. G13: Glas . . . . . . . . . . .2D 60
Scadlock Rd. PA3: Pais . . . . . . . . .5F 77
Scalpay G74: E Kil . . . . . . . . . . . .2C 150
Scalpay Pas. G22: Glas . . . . . . . . .2H 63
Scalpay Pl. G22: Glas . . . . . . . . . .2H 63
Scalpay St. G22: Glas . . . . . . . . . .2G 63
Scapa St. G23: Glas . . . . . . . . . . .1C 62
Scapesland Ter. G82: Dumb . . . . .3G 17
Scaraway Dr. G22: Glas . . . . . . . . .1H 63
Scaraway Pl. G22: Glas . . . . . . . . .1H 63
Scaraway St. G22: Glas . . . . . . . . .1G 63
Scaraway Ter. G22: Glas . . . . . . . .1H 63
Scarba Dr. G43: Glas . . . . . . . . .2H 117
Scarba Quad. ML2: Wis . . . . . . . .2E 157
Scarffe Av. PA3: Lin . . . . . . . . . . .6F 75
Scarhill Av. ML6: Air . . . . . . . . . . .6H 91
Scarhill La. ML6: Air . . . . . . . . . . .6A 92
Scarhill St. ML1: Cle . . . . . . . . . .5H 129
ML5: Coat . . . . . . . . . . . . . . . .2B 110
Scarrel Dr. G45: Glas . . . . . . . . .3C 120
Scarrel Gdns. G45: Glas . . . . . . . .3C 120
Scarrel Rd. G45: Glas . . . . . . . . .3C 120
Scarrel Ter. G45: Glas . . . . . . . . .3C 120
Scavaig Cres. G15: Glas . . . . . . . .3G 43
Schaw Ct. G61: Bear . . . . . . . . . . .1E 45
Schaw Dr. G61: Bear . . . . . . . . . . .1D 44
G81: Faif . . . . . . . . . . . . . . . . . .6G 23
Schaw Rd. PA3: Pais . . . . . . . . . . .5C 78
Scholar's Ga. G75: E Kil . . . . . . . .5F 149
School Av. G72: Camb . . . . . . . . .2B 122
Schoolhouse La. G72: Blan . . . . .3A 140
School La. G66: Len . . . . . . . . . . . .3F 7
G66: Milt C . . . . . . . . . . . . . . . . . .5C 8
G82: Dumb . . . . . . . . . . . . . . . .3D 16
ML8: Carl . . . . . . . . . . . . . . . .4E 165
School Quad. ML6: Air . . . . . . . . .1H 91
School Rd. G33: Step . . . . . . . . . .3E 67
G64: Torr . . . . . . . . . . . . . . . . . .4E 29
G77: Newt M . . . . . . . . . . . . . .5D 132
ML2: Newm . . . . . . . . . . . . . . .5F 147
(Morningside)
ML2: Newm . . . . . . . . . . . . . . .5E 147
(Newmains)
PA1: Pais . . . . . . . . . . . . . . . . . .6G 79
School St. ML3: Ham . . . . . . . . . .2H 153
ML5: Coat . . . . . . . . . . . . . . . .1C 110
ML6: Chap . . . . . . . . . . . . . . . .3D 112
School Wynd PA1: Pais . . . . . . . . .6A 78
Scioncroft Av. G73: Ruth . . . . . . .6E 105
Scone Pl. G74: E Kil . . . . . . . . . .6F 137
G77: Newt M . . . . . . . . . . . . . .5H 133
Scone St. G21: Glas . . . . . . . . . . .6G 63
Scone Wlk. G69: Bail . . . . . . . . . .2G 107
Sconser PA8: Ersk . . . . . . . . . . . .2G 57
Sconser St. G23: Glas . . . . . . . . . .6C 46
Scorton Gdns. G69: Bail . . . . . . . .1F 107
Scotcart Indoor Kart Racing . . . . .1C 122
Scotia Cres. ML9: Lark . . . . . . . . .4E 161
Scotia Gdns. ML3: Ham . . . . . . . .4G 153
Scotia St. ML1: Moth . . . . . . . . .2E 143
Scotland St. G5: Glas . . . . . . . . . .6D 82
Scotland Street School Mus. . . . .6D 82
Scotland St. W. G41: Glas . . . . . . .6B 82
Scotsblair Av. G66: Kirk . . . . . . . .1C 50
Scotsburn Rd. G21: Glas . . . . . . . .5E 65
SCOTSTOUN . . . . . . . . . . . . . . . .5B 60
Scotstoun Athletic Track . . . . . . .5C 60
SCOTSTOUNHILL . . . . . . . . . . . .3B 60
Scotstounhill Station (Rail) . . . . .4B 60
Scotstoun Leisure Cen. . . . . . . . .5D 60
Scotstoun St. G14: Glas . . . . . . . .6C 60
Scott Av. G60: Bowl . . . . . . . . . . .5B 20
G66: Milt C . . . . . . . . . . . . . . . . .5C 8
PA5: John . . . . . . . . . . . . . . . . .5E 95
Scott Cres. G67: Cumb . . . . . . . . .6F 35
Scott Dr. G61: Bear . . . . . . . . . . . .1C 44
G67: Cumb . . . . . . . . . . . . . . . .6F 35
Scott Gro. ML3: Ham . . . . . . . . . .1H 153
Scott Hill G74: E Kil . . . . . . . . . .6A 138
Scott Ho. G67: Cumb . . . . . . . . . . .2A 36
Scottish Enterprise Technology Pk.
G75: E Kil . . . . . . . . . . . . . . . .4A 150
Scottish Exhibition & Conference Cen.
. . . . . . . . . . . . . . . . . . . . . .4B 82
Scottish Maritime Mus.
Dumbarton . . . . . . . . . . . . . . .4F 17
Renfrew . . . . . . . . . . . . . . . . . .6A 60
Scottish National Football Mus.
. . . . . . . . . . . . . . . . . . . . .6F 103
Scott Pl. ML4: Bell . . . . . . . . . . .6D 110
PA5: John . . . . . . . . . . . . . . . . .5E 95
Scott Rd. G52: Hill . . . . . . . . . . . .3H 79
Scott's Pl. ML6: Air . . . . . . . . . . . .3B 92
Scott's Rd. PA2: Pais . . . . . . . . . .2D 98
Scott St. G3: Glas . . . . . . . . .3E 83 (3B 4)
G69: Bail . . . . . . . . . . . . . . . . .1H 107
G81: Clyd . . . . . . . . . . . . . . . . .3A 42
ML1: Moth . . . . . . . . . . . . . . .2G 143
ML3: Ham . . . . . . . . . . . . . . . .2H 153
ML9: Lark . . . . . . . . . . . . . . . .3F 161
SEAFAR . . . . . . . . . . . . . . . . . . .3G 35
Seafar Rd. G67: Cumb . . . . . . . . .5G 35
SEAFAR RDBT. . . . . . . . . . . . . . .5G 35
Seafield Av. G61: Bear . . . . . . . . . .6F 25
Seafield Cres. G68: Cumb . . . . . . .4A 34
Seafield Dr. G73: Ruth . . . . . . . . .4F 121
Seaforth Cres. G78: Barr . . . . . . .2D 114
Seaforth La. G69: Mood . . . . . . . . .5E 53
Seaforth Pl. ML4: Bell . . . . . . . . .4B 126
Seaforth Rd. G52: Hill . . . . . . . . . .4A 80
G81: Clyd . . . . . . . . . . . . . . . . .6D 42
Seaforth Rd. Nth. G52: Hill . . . . . .4A 80
Seaforth Rd. Sth. G52: Hill . . . . . .4A 80
Seagrove St. G32: Glas . . . . . . . . .5F 85
Seamill Gdns. G74: E Kil . . . . . . .1F 149
Seamill Path G53: Glas . . . . . . . .2H 115
Seamill St. G53: Glas . . . . . . . . .2H 115
Seamore St. G20: Glas . . . . . . . . .1D 82
Seath Av. ML6: Air . . . . . . . . . . . .4G 91
Seath Rd. G73: Ruth . . . . . . . . . .4C 104
Seath St. G42: Glas . . . . . . . . . .3G 103
Seaton Ter. ML3: Ham . . . . . . . . .5E 141
Seaward Pl. G41: Glas . . . . . . . . . .6D 82
Seaward St. G41: Glas . . . . . . . . . .6C 82
(not continuous)
SEAWARD ST. INTERCHANGE . . . .6C 82
Second Av. G33: Mille . . . . . . . . . .4B 66
G44: Glas . . . . . . . . . . . . . . . .1F 119
G61: Bear . . . . . . . . . . . . . . . . .4F 45
G66: Auch . . . . . . . . . . . . . . . . .6C 50
G71: Tann . . . . . . . . . . . . . . . .4C 108
G81: Clyd . . . . . . . . . . . . . . . . .4B 42
G82: Dumb . . . . . . . . . . . . . . . .3C 18
PA4: Renf . . . . . . . . . . . . . . . . .2E 79
Second Av. La. G44: Glas . . . . . . .6F 103
Second Gdns. G41: Glas . . . . . . . .1G 101
Second Rd. G72: Blan . . . . . . . . . .4C 140
Second St. G71: Tann . . . . . . . . . .5D 108
SEEDHILL . . . . . . . . . . . . . . . . . .1C 98
Seedhill PA1: Pais . . . . . . . . . . . .1B 98
Seedhill Rd. PA1: Pais . . . . . . . . . .1B 98
Seggielea La. G13: Glas . . . . . . . .3D 60
(off Helensburgh Dr.)
Seggielea Rd. G13: Glas . . . . . . . .3D 60
Seil Dr. G44: Glas . . . . . . . . . . . .3F 119
Selborne Pl. G13: Glas . . . . . . . . . .4E 61
Selborne Pl. La. G13: Glas . . . . . . .4E 61
Selborne Rd. G13: Glas . . . . . . . . .4E 61
Selby Gdns. G32: Glas . . . . . . . . . .6D 86
Selby Pl. ML5: Coat . . . . . . . . . . . .1H 89
Selby St. ML5: Coat . . . . . . . . . . . .1H 89
Selkirk Av. G52: Glas . . . . . . . . . .1C 100
PA2: Pais . . . . . . . . . . . . . . . . .4E 97
Selkirk Dr. G73: Ruth . . . . . . . . . .6E 105
Selkirk Pl. G74: E Kil . . . . . . . . . .6D 138
ML3: Ham . . . . . . . . . . . . . . . .1A 154
Selkirk St. G72: Blan . . . . . . . . . .2B 140
ML2: Wis . . . . . . . . . . . . . . . . .4A 146
ML3: Ham . . . . . . . . . . . . . . . .1A 154
Selkirk Way ML4: Bell . . . . . . . . .6D 110
ML5: Coat . . . . . . . . . . . . . . . .2G 111
Sella Rd. G64: B'rig . . . . . . . . . . . .5F 49
Selvieland Rd. G52: Glas . . . . . . . .6H 79
Semphill Gdns. G74: E Kil . . . . . .1B 150
Sempie St. ML3: Ham . . . . . . . . . .5D 140
Sempill Av. PA8: Ersk . . . . . . . . . . .5D 40
Semple Av. PA7: B'ton . . . . . . . . . .4H 39
Semple Pl. PA3: Lin . . . . . . . . . . . .4H 75
Senga Cres. ML4: Bell . . . . . . . . .6C 110
Seres Rd. G76: Clar . . . . . . . . . . .1B 134
Sergeantlaw Rd. PA2: Pais . . . . . . .6E 97
Service St. G66: Len . . . . . . . . . . . .2E 7
Seton Ter. G31: Glas . . . . . . . . . . .4B 84
Settle Gdns. G69: Bail . . . . . . . . .1F 107
Seven Sisters G66: Lenz . . . . . . . .2E 51
Seventh Av. G71: Tann . . . . . . . . .5D 108
Seventh Rd. G72: Blan . . . . . . . . .4C 140
Severn Rd. G75: E Kil . . . . . . . . .4B 148
Seymour Grn. G75: E Kil . . . . . . .3D 148
Seyton Av. G46: Giff . . . . . . . . . .6A 118
Seyton Ct. G46: Giff . . . . . . . . . .6A 118
Seyton La. G74: E Kil . . . . . . . . .6G 137
Shaftesbury Av. G81: Clyd . . . . . . .5B 42
Shaftesbury Ct. G74: E Kil . . . . . .4C 138
Shaftesbury Cres. ML1: N'hill . . .4D 128
Shafton Pl. G13: Glas . . . . . . . . . .1E 61
Shafton Rd. G13: Glas . . . . . . . . . .1E 61
Shaftesbury St. G3: Glas . . . .3D 82 (4A 4)
(not continuous)
Shakespeare Av. G81: Clyd . . . . . .3B 42
Shakespeare St. G20: Glas . . . . . . .4C 62
Shamrock St. G4: Glas . . . . .2E 83 (1B 4)
G66: Kirk . . . . . . . . . . . . . . . . .5D 30
Shandon Cres. ML4: Bell . . . . . . .6C 110
Shandon Ter. ML3: Ham . . . . . . . .6D 140
Shand Pl. ML8: Carl . . . . . . . . . . .2F 165
Shand St. ML2: Wis . . . . . . . . . . .6H 145
Shandwick Sq. G34: Glas . . . . . . . .3G 87
Shandwick St. G34: Glas . . . . . . . .3G 87
Shanks Av. G78: Barr . . . . . . . . . .5E 115
Shanks Cres. PA5: John . . . . . . . . .3E 95
Shanks Pk. Ind. Est.
G78: Barr . . . . . . . . . . . . . . . .3E 115
Shanks St. G20: Glas . . . . . . . . . . .4C 62
ML6: Air . . . . . . . . . . . . . . . . . .2A 92
Shanks Way G78: Barr . . . . . . . . .2E 115
Shannon St. G20: Glas . . . . . . . . . .4D 62
Shapinsay St. G22: Glas . . . . . . . . .1H 63
Sharmanka Kinetic Gallery & Theatre
. . . . . . . . . . . . . . . . . . . . . .5G 83
(off Trongate)
Sharp Av. ML5: Coat . . . . . . . . . .1G 109
Sharp St. ML1: Moth . . . . . . . . . .2D 142
Shaw Av. PA7: B'ton . . . . . . . . . . .4A 40
Shawbridge Arc. G43: Glas . . . . . .5A 102
Shawbridge Ind. Est.
G43: Glas . . . . . . . . . . . . . . . .6A 102
Shawbridge St. G43: Glas . . . . . .6H 101
Shawburn Cres. ML3: Ham . . . . . .5F 141
Shawburn St. ML3: Ham . . . . . . . .5F 141
Shaw Ct. G77: Newt M . . . . . . . . .5F 133
PA8: Ersk . . . . . . . . . . . . . . . . .4D 40
Shaw Cres. ML2: Wis . . . . . . . . . .2D 156
SHAWFIELD . . . . . . . . . . . . . . . .3B 104
Shawfield Cres. ML8: Law . . . . . . .6D 158

Shawfield Dr. G5: Glas . . . . . . . .3A 104
Shawfield Ind. Est. G73: Ruth . .3B 104
Shawfield Rd. G73: Ruth . . . . .3B 104
Shawfield Stadium . . . . . . . . .3B 104
Shawgill Ct. ML8: Law . . . . . . .1H 163
SHAWHEAD . . . . . . . . . . . . . . .2B 110
Shawhead Av. ML5: Coat . . . . . .1D 110
Shawhead Cotts. ML5: Coat . . .3D 110
Shawhead Ind. Est. ML5: Coat . .2E 111
Shawhill Cres. G77: Newt M . . .6E 133
Shawhill Rd. G41: Glas . . . . . . .5A 102
G43: Glas . . . . . . . . . . . . .5A 102
Shawholm Cres. G43: Glas . . . .6H 101
(not continuous)
SHAWLANDS . . . . . . . . . . . . . .5C 102
Shawlands Arc. G41: Glas . . . . .5B 102
Shawlands Station (Rail) . . . .5B 102
Shawmoss Rd. G41: Glas . . . . . .4A 102
Shawpark St. G20: Glas . . . . . . .3C 62
Shaw Pl. PA3: Lin . . . . . . . . . . .6H 75
Shawrigg Rd. ML9: Lark . . . . . .3G 161
Shaw Rd. G62: Miln . . . . . . . . . .5G 25
G77: Newt M . . . . . . . . . . .5E 133
SHAWSBURN . . . . . . . . . . . . . .3A 162
Shaws Rd. ML9: Lark . . . . . . . .6F 161
Shaw St. G51: Glas . . . . . . . . . . .3G 81
ML9: Lark . . . . . . . . . . . . .5F 161
Shawwood Cres.
G77: Newt M . . . . . . . . . . .6E 133
Shearer Dr. ML3: Ham . . . . . . .4G 153
Shears La. PA4: Renf . . . . . . . . .6F 59
Sheddens Pl. G32: Glas . . . . . . .6G 85
Sheepburn Rd. G71: Udd . . . . .6C 108
Sheila St. G33: Glas . . . . . . . . . .5G 65
Sheiling Hill ML3: Ham . . . . . . .5A 142
Sheldaig Rd. G22: Glas . . . . . . .1F 63
Sheldrake Pl. PA5: John . . . . . .6D 94
Shelley Ct. G12: Glas . . . . . . . . .4G 61
Shelley Dr. G71: Both . . . . . . . .4F 125
G81: Clyd . . . . . . . . . . . . . .3C 42
Shelley Rd. G12: Glas . . . . . . . . .4F 61
Shells Rd. G66: Kirk . . . . . . . . . .4E 31
Sherbrooke Av. G41: Glas . . . . .2A 102
Sherbrooke Dr. G41: Glas . . . . .1A 102
Sherbrooke Gdns. G41: Glas . . .2A 102
Sherbrooke Pl. G75: E Kil . . . . .2E 149
Sherdale Av. ML6: Chap . . . . . .3D 112
Sheriff Pk. Av. G73: Ruth . . . . .6C 104
Sherry Av. ML1: Holy . . . . . . . .2H 127
Sherry Dr. ML3: Ham . . . . . . . .2E 153
Sherry Hgts. G72: Camb . . . . . .1A 122
Sherwood Av. G71: Udd . . . . . .2E 125
PA1: Pais . . . . . . . . . . . . . .5C 78
Sherwood Dr. G46: T'bnk . . . . .4G 117
Sherwood Pl. G15: Glas . . . . . .4B 44
Shetland Dr. G44: Glas . . . . . . .3F 119
SHETTLESTON . . . . . . . . . . . . .6B 86
Shettleston Rd. G31: Glas . . . . .5E 85
Shettleston Station (Rail) . . . . .6B 86
Shiel Av. G74: E Kil . . . . . . . . . .6H 137
Shielbridge Gdns. G23: Glas . . .6C 46
Shiel Ct. G78: Barr . . . . . . . . . .2D 114
Shieldburn Rd. G51: Glas . . . . .4C 80
SHIELDHALL . . . . . . . . . . . . . .3C 80
Shieldhall Gdns. G51: Glas . . . .4C 80
Shieldhall Rd. G51: Glas . . . . . .3B 80
Shieldhill G75: E Kil . . . . . . . . .4H 149
Shieldhill Rd. ML8: Carl . . . . . .5E 165
Shieldmuir Station (Rail) . . . . .5C 144
Shieldmuir St. ML2: Wis . . . . . .5C 144
Shiel Dr. ML9: Lark . . . . . . . . . .6H 155
Shields Ct. ML1: Moth . . . . . . . .6B 144
Shields Dr. ML1: Moth . . . . . . . .6B 144
Shields Rd. G41: Glas . . . . . . . .3C 102
G75: E Kil . . . . . . . . . . . . .6E 149
ML1: Moth . . . . . . . . . . . . .5A 144
Shields Rd. Station (Und.) . . . .6D 82
Shields Twr. ML1: Moth . . . . . . .6B 144
Shiel Pl. G74: E Kil . . . . . . . . . .6H 137
ML5: Coat . . . . . . . . . . . . . .6F 91
Shiel Rd. G64: B'rig . . . . . . . . . .6D 48
Shiel Ter. ML2: Newm . . . . . . . .3D 146
Shilford Av. G13: Glas . . . . . . . .2A 60
Shillay St. G22: Glas . . . . . . . . .1A 64
Shillingworth Pl. PA11: Bri W . . .5F 73
Shilton Dr. G53: Glas . . . . . . . . .2C 116
Shilton La. PA7: B'ton . . . . . . . .3C 40
Shinwell Av. G81: Clyd . . . . . . . .6F 43
Shipbank La. G1: Glas . . . . . . .5G 83
(off Clyde St.)
Shira Ter. G74: E Kil . . . . . . . . .2B 150
Shirley Quad. ML1: Moth . . . . . .6F 143
SHIRREL . . . . . . . . . . . . . . . . . .6C 110
Shirrel Av. ML4: Bell . . . . . . . . .6C 110
Shirrel Rd. ML1: Holy . . . . . . . .3A 128
Shirva Lea G65: Twe . . . . . . . . .1D 32
Shiskine Pl. G20: Glas . . . . . . . .1A 62
Shiskine St. G20: Glas . . . . . . . .1A 62

Sholto Cres. ML4: Bell . . . . . . . .6H 109
Shore St. G40: Glas . . . . . . . . . .3B 104
Shortridge St. G20: Glas . . . . . .4C 62
SHORTROODS . . . . . . . . . . . . . .4A 78
Shortroods Av. PA3: Pais . . . . . .4H 77
Shortroods Cres. PA3: Pais . . . .4H 77
Shortroods Rd. PA3: Pais . . . . . .4H 77
Shotts St. G33: Glas . . . . . . . . . .3D 86
Showcase Cinema
Kirkwood . . . . . . . . . . . . . . .1F 109
Paisley . . . . . . . . . . . . . . . .6C 76
Shuna Gdns. G20: Glas . . . . . . .4C 62
Shuna Pl. G20: Glas . . . . . . . . . .4C 62
G77: Newt M . . . . . . . . . . .3B 132
Shuna St. G20: Glas . . . . . . . . . .3C 62
Shuttle St. G1: Glas . . . .4H 83 (6G 5)
G65: Kils . . . . . . . . . . . . . . .3H 11
PA1: Pais . . . . . . . . . . . . . . .1A 98
PA10: Kilb . . . . . . . . . . . . . .1A 94
Sidland Rd. G21: Glas . . . . . . . .4E 65
Sidlaw Av. G78: Barr . . . . . . . . .6E 115
ML3: Ham . . . . . . . . . . . . .1D 152
Sidlaw Ct. ML5: Coat . . . . . . . . .2E 111
Sidlaw Dr. ML2: Wis . . . . . . . . . .6F 145
Sidlaw Rd. G61: Bear . . . . . . . . .1B 44
Sidlaw Way ML6: Chap . . . . . . .4F 113
ML9: Lark . . . . . . . . . . . . .6H 155
Sielga Pl. G34: Glas . . . . . . . . . .3G 87
Siemens Pl. G21: Glas . . . . . . . .1D 84
Siemens St. G21: Glas . . . . . . . .1D 84
Sievewright St. G73: Ruth . . . . .4E 105
SIGHTHILL . . . . . . . . . . . . . . . .1A 84
Sighthill Loan ML9: Lark . . . . . .1F 161
(off Muirshot Rd.)
SIKESIDE . . . . . . . . . . . . . . . . . .6F 91
Sikeside Pl. ML5: Coat . . . . . . . .6F 91
Sikeside St. ML5: Coat . . . . . . . .6F 91
Silkin Av. G81: Clyd . . . . . . . . . .6F 43
Silk St. PA1: Pais . . . . . . . . . . . .6B 78
Silvan Pl. G76: Busby . . . . . . . . .4E 135
SILVERBANK . . . . . . . . . . . . . . .1G 121
Silverburn Cres. ML1: N'hill . . . .4D 128
Silverburn St. G33: Glas . . . . . . .3G 85
Silverdale G74: E Kil . . . . . . . . .6E 137
Silverdale St. G40: Glas . . . . . . .1E 105
Silverfir Ct. G5: Glas . . . . . . . . .1H 103
Silver Firs ML1: N'hill . . . . . . . .4C 128
Silverfir St. G5: Glas . . . . . . . . .2H 103
Silver Glade G52: Glas . . . . . . . .1B 100
Silvergrove St. G40: Glas . . . . . .1A 104
SILVERTON . . . . . . . . . . . . . . . .4H 17
Silverton Av. G82: Dumb . . . . . .4H 17
SILVERTONHILL . . . . . . . . . . . . .1B 154
Silvertonhill Av. ML3: Ham . . . .3A 154
Silvertonhill La. G82: Dumb . . .4H 17
Silvertonhill Pl. ML3: Ham . . . . .4H 153
SILVERWELLS . . . . . . . . . . . . . .6E 125
Silverwells G71: Both . . . . . . . . .6E 125
Silverwells Ct. G71: Both . . . . . .6E 125
Silverwells Cres. G71: Both . . . . .6E 125
Silverwood Ct. G71: Both . . . . . .6F 125
Simons Cres. PA4: Renf . . . . . . .4F 59
Simpson Ct. G71: Udd . . . . . . . .1D 124
G81: Clyd . . . . . . . . . . . . . .5C 42
Simpson Dr. G75: E Kil . . . . . . .4F 149
Simpson Gdns. G78: Barr . . . . .5D 114
Simpson Hgts. G4: Glas . . . . . .4A 84
(off John Knox St.)
Simpson Pl. G75: E Kil . . . . . . . .4F 149
Simpson Way ML4: Bell . . . . . . .6E 111
Simshill Rd. G44: Glas . . . . . . . .4F 119
Sinclair Av. G61: Bear . . . . . . . .1E 45
Sinclair Dr. G42: Glas . . . . . . . .6D 102
ML5: Coat . . . . . . . . . . . . . .4H 89
Sinclair Gdns. G64: B'rig . . . . . .1D 64
Sinclair Gro. ML4: Bell . . . . . . .5B 126
Sinclair Pk. G75: E Kil . . . . . . . .3H 149
Sinclair Pl. G75: E Kil . . . . . . . .3H 149
Sinclair St. G62: Miln . . . . . . . . .3G 25
G81: Clyd . . . . . . . . . . . . . .1F 59
Singer Rd. G75: E Kil . . . . . . . .5H 149
G81: Clyd . . . . . . . . . . . . . .4B 42
Singer Station (Rail) . . . . . . . . .5D 42
Singer St. G81: Clyd . . . . . . . . . .4D 42
Sir Matt Busby Sports Complex
. . . . . . . . . . . . . . . . . . . . . . .2B 126
Sir Michael Pl. PA1: Pais . . . . . .1H 97
Sixth Av. PA4: Renf . . . . . . . . . .2E 79
Sixth St. G71: Tann . . . . . . . . . .4C 108
Skaethorn Rd. G20: Glas . . . . . .2H 61
Skara Wlk. ML2: Newm . . . . . . .2D 146
(off Kildonan Ct.)
Skaterigg Dr. G13: Glas . . . . . . .4F 61
Skaterigg Gdns. G13: Glas . . . . .4F 61
Skaterigg La. G13: Glas . . . . . . .4F 61
(off Chamberlain Rd.)
Skelbo Path G34: Glas . . . . . . . .2B 88
Skelbo Pl. G34: Glas . . . . . . . . . .2B 88
Skellyton Cres. ML9: Lark . . . . .3F 161

Skene Rd. G51: Glas . . . . . . . . . .6H 81
Skerne Gro. G75: E Kil . . . . . . . .5B 148
Skerray Quad. G22: Glas . . . . . .1G 63
Skerray St. G22: Glas . . . . . . . . .1G 63
Skerryvore Pl. G33: Glas . . . . . .3B 86
Skerryvore Rd. G33: Glas . . . . .3B 86
Skibo La. G46: T'bnk . . . . . . . . . .4E 117
Skimmers Hill G66: Milt C . . . . .1B 30
Skipness Av. ML8: Carl . . . . . . .5G 165
Skipness Dr. G51: Glas . . . . . . .4D 80
Skirsa Ct. G23: Glas . . . . . . . . . .1E 63
Skirsa Pl. G23: Glas . . . . . . . . . .2D 62
Skirsa Sq. G23: Glas . . . . . . . . . .2E 63
Skirsa St. G23: Glas . . . . . . . . . .1D 62
Skirving St. G41: Glas . . . . . . . . .5C 102
Skovlunde Way G75: E Kil . . . . .5G 149
Skye Av. PA4: Renf . . . . . . . . . . .2E 79
Skye Ct. G67: Cumb . . . . . . . . . .5F 35
Skye Cres. G60: Old K . . . . . . . .2G 41
PA2: Pais . . . . . . . . . . . . . .6H 97
Skye Dr. G60: Old K . . . . . . . . . .2G 41
G67: Cumb . . . . . . . . . . . . .5F 35
Skye Gdns. G61: Bear . . . . . . . .1B 44
Skye Pl. G67: Cumb . . . . . . . . . .5F 35
Skye Quad. ML2: Wis . . . . . . . . .4C 146
Skye Rd. G67: Cumb . . . . . . . . .5F 35
G73: Ruth . . . . . . . . . . . . . .4F 121
Skye Wynd ML3: Ham . . . . . . . .2D 152
Slakiewood Av. G69: G'csh . . . . .2C 68
Slatefield G66: Len . . . . . . . . . . .3F 7
Slatefield Ct. G31: Glas . . . . . . .5C 84
(off Slatefield St.)
Slatefield St. G31: Glas . . . . . . .5C 84
Sleaford Av. ML1: Moth . . . . . . .5F 143
Slenavon Av. G73: Ruth . . . . . . .4F 121
Slessor Dr. G75: E Kil . . . . . . . .4G 149
Slioch Sq. ML1: N'hill . . . . . . . .3C 128
Sloy St. G22: Glas . . . . . . . . . . .5H 63
ML2: Wis . . . . . . . . . . . . . .2G 157
Small Cres. G72: Blan . . . . . . . .2B 140
Smeaton Av. G64: Torr . . . . . . . .5D 28
Smeaton Dr. G64: B'rig . . . . . . . .3C 48
Smeaton St. G20: Glas . . . . . . . .3D 62
Smith Av. ML2: Wis . . . . . . . . . .4G 157
Smith Cl. G64: B'rig . . . . . . . . . .1F 65
Smith Cres. G81: Hard . . . . . . . .2D 42
Smith Gdns. G64: B'rig . . . . . . . .1F 65
Smith Gro. G64: B'rig . . . . . . . . .1F 65
Smithhills St. PA1: Pais . . . . . . . .6A 78
Smith Pk. Pl. G76: Busby . . . . . .4D 134
Smith Quad. ML5: Coat . . . . . . .4E 91
Smith's La. PA3: Pais . . . . . . . . .5A 78
SMITHSTONE . . . . . . . . . . . . . .2B 34
Smithstone Cres. G65: Croy . . . .6A 12
Smithstone Rd. G68: Cumb . . . .3B 34
Smith St. G14: Glas . . . . . . . . . .1E 81
(not continuous)
Smithview ML2: Over . . . . . . . . .4A 158
Smith Way G64: B'rig . . . . . . . . .1F 65
Smithycroft ML3: Ham . . . . . . . .1C 154
Smithycroft Rd. G33: Glas . . . . .3F 85
Smithyends G67: Cumb . . . . . . .6B 14
Smollett Rd. G82: Dumb . . . . . . .4H 17
Snaefell Av. G73: Ruth . . . . . . . .3E 121
Snaefell Cres. G73: Ruth . . . . . .2E 121
Snead Vw. ML1: Cle . . . . . . . . . .6E 129
Sneddon Av. ML2: Wis . . . . . . . .2A 158
Sneddon St. ML3: Ham . . . . . . . .3D 140
Sneddon Ter. ML3: Ham . . . . . . .3D 140
Snowdon Pl. G5: Glas . . . . . . . .1H 103
Snowdon St. G5: Glas . . . . . . . .1H 103
Snuff Mill Rd. G44: Glas . . . . . .2E 119
Society St. G31: Glas . . . . . . . . . .6D 84
Solar Ct. ML9: Lark . . . . . . . . . .5F 161
Sollas Pl. G13: Glas . . . . . . . . . .1G 59
Solsgirth Gdns. G66: Kirk . . . . .4H 31
Solway Ct. ML3: Ham . . . . . . . . .3F 153
Solway Pl. G69: Chry . . . . . . . . .6B 52
Solway Rd. G64: B'rig . . . . . . . . .5F 49
Solway St. G40: Glas . . . . . . . . .3B 104
Somerford Rd. G61: Bear . . . . . .6F 45
Somerled Av. PA3: Pais . . . . . . .2B 78
Somerset Av. ML3: Ham . . . . . . .5F 141
Somerset Pl. G3: Glas . . . . . . . .2D 82
Somerset Pl. M. G3: Glas . . . . .2D 82
(off Somerset Pl.)
Somervell St. G72: Camb . . . . . .1H 121
Somerville Dr. G42: Glas . . . . . .5F 103
G75: E Kil . . . . . . . . . . . . . .4G 149
Somerville La. G75: E Kil . . . . . .4H 149
Somerville Ter. G75: E Kil . . . . .4G 149
Sorby St. G31: Glas . . . . . . . . . .6F 85
Sorley St. G11: Glas . . . . . . . . . .1F 81
Sorn St. G40: Glas . . . . . . . . . . .2D 104
Souterhouse Path ML5: Coat . . .6B 90
Souterhouse Rd. ML5: Coat . . . .6B 90
Southampton Dr. G12: Glas . . . .3H 61

Southampton La. G12: Glas . . . . .3H [cut]
(off Burlington A[cut])
Sth. Annandale St. G42: Glas . . .3F 1[cut]
South Av. G72: Blan . . . . . . . . . .4B 1[cut]
G81: Clyd . . . . . . . . . . . . . .5C 4[cut]
ML8: Carl . . . . . . . . . . . . . .4E 16[cut]
PA2: Pais . . . . . . . . . . . . . .5B 9[cut]
PA4: Renf . . . . . . . . . . . . . .6F 5[cut]
Southbank Bus. Pk. G66: Kirk . .6C 3[cut]
Southbank Dr. G66: Kirk . . . . . .6C 3[cut]
Southbank Rd. G66: Kirk . . . . . .6B 3[cut]
Southbank St. G31: Glas . . . . . .6F 8[cut]
Sth. Bank St. G81: Clyd . . . . . . . .2E 5[cut]
SOUTHBAR . . . . . . . . . . . . . . . .1E 5[cut]
Southbar Av. G13: Glas . . . . . . .2A 6[cut]
Southbar Rd. PA4: Inch . . . . . . . .3E 5[cut]
SOUTH BARRWOOD . . . . . . . . .4A 1[cut]
Sth. Barrwood Rd. G65: Kils . . . .4A 1[cut]
Sth. Biggar Rd. ML6: Air . . . . . . .4B 9[cut]
South Brae G66: Len . . . . . . . . . .5E [cut]
Southbrae Av. PA11: Bri W . . . . .4D 7[cut]
Southbrae Dr. G13: Glas . . . . . . .4C 6[cut]
Southbrae La. G13: Glas . . . . . . .4E 6[cut]
(off Selborne R[cut])
Sth. Bridge St. ML6: Air . . . . . . . .3A 9[cut]
Sth. Burn Rd. ML6: Air . . . . . . . .4F 9[cut]
Sth. Caldeen Rd. ML5: Coat . . . .6D 9[cut]
Sth. Calder ML1: Moth . . . . . . . .1H 14[cut]
Sth. Campbell St. PA2: Pais . . . .2A 9[cut]
Sth. Carbrain Rd. G67: Cumb . . .5H 3[cut]
SOUTH CARDONALD . . . . . . . . .1C 10[cut]
Sth. Chester St. G32: Glas . . . . .6A 8[cut]
Sth. Circular Rd. ML5: Coat . . . .4C 9[cut]
Sth. Claremont La. G62: Miln . . .4G 2[cut]
Sth. Commonhead Av. ML6: Air . .2H 9[cut]
Southcroft Rd. G73: Ruth . . . . . .4A 10[cut]
Southcroft St. G51: Glas . . . . . . .4H 8[cut]
Sth. Crosshill Rd. G64: B'rig . . . .6C 4[cut]
Sth. Dean Pk. Av. G71: Both . . . .5E 12[cut]
Southdeen Av. G15: Glas . . . . . .4A 4[cut]
Southdeen Rd. G15: Glas . . . . . .4A 4[cut]
Sth. Douglas St. G81: Clyd . . . . .1E 5[cut]
South Dr. PA3: Lin . . . . . . . . . . .5H 7[cut]
Sth. Dumbreck Rd. G65: Kils . . .3F 1[cut]
Sth. Elgin Pl. G81: Clyd . . . . . . . .2E 5[cut]
Sth. Elgin St. G81: Clyd . . . . . . . .2E 5[cut]
Southend Pl. ML4: Bell . . . . . . . .3B 12[cut]
Southend Rd. G81: Hard . . . . . . .2D 4[cut]
Southern Av. G73: Ruth . . . . . . .2D 12[cut]
Southerness Dr. G68: Cumb . . . .6A 1[cut]
Sth. Erskine Pk. G61: Bear . . . . .2D 4[cut]
Southesk Av. G64: B'rig . . . . . . . .4B 4[cut]
Southesk Gdns. G64: B'rig . . . . .4B 4[cut]
Sth. Exchange Ct. G1: Glas . . . . .6E [cut]
Southfield Av. PA2: Pais . . . . . . .5A 9[cut]
Southfield Cres. G53: Glas . . . . .5C 10[cut]
ML5: Coat . . . . . . . . . . . . . .6E 9[cut]
Southfield Rd. G68: Cumb . . . . .4E 3[cut]
Sth. Frederick St.
G1: Glas . . . . . . . . . . . .4G 83 (5F 5[cut]
Southgate G62: Miln . . . . . . . . . .4G 2[cut]
G74: E Kil . . . . . . . . . . . . . .2G 14[cut]
(off Olympia St[cut])
Sth. Glassford St. G62: Miln . . . .4H 2[cut]
Sth. Hallhill Rd. G32: Glas . . . . .6B 8[cut]
Southhill Av. G73: Ruth . . . . . . . .1E 12[cut]
Southinch Av. G14: Glas . . . . . . .3G 5[cut]
Southlea Av. G46: T'bnk . . . . . . .4G 11[cut]
South Loan G69: Chry . . . . . . . . .1B 6[cut]
Southloch Gdns. G21: Glas . . . . .6B 6[cut]
Southloch St. G21: Glas . . . . . . .6B 6[cut]
Sth. Mains Rd. G62: Miln . . . . . .4F 2[cut]
Sth. Medrox St. ML5: Glenb . . . .2G 6[cut]
Sth. Moraine La. G15: Glas . . . . .5C 4[cut]
South Mound PA6: Hous . . . . . . .1A 7[cut]
Sth. Muirhead Rd. G67: Cumb . . .3A 3[cut]
Southmuir Pl. G20: Glas . . . . . . .4B 6[cut]
Sth. Nimmo St. ML6: Air . . . . . . .4B 9[cut]
SOUTH NITSHILL . . . . . . . . . . . .3A 11[cut]
South Pk. ML3: Ham . . . . . . . . . .1H 15[cut]
Southpark Av. G12: Glas . . . . . . .1B 8[cut]
Sth. Park Av. G78: Barr . . . . . . . .4D 11[cut]
Sth. Park Dr. PA2: Pais . . . . . . . .3A 9[cut]
Sth. Park Gro. ML3: Ham . . . . . .6H 14[cut]
Sth. Park La. G12: Glas . . . . . . . .1C 8[cut]
Sth. Park Ter. G12: Glas . . . . . . .1C 8[cut]
South Pl. ML4: Bell . . . . . . . . . . .3B 12[cut]
South Portland St. G5: Glas . . . .5F 8[cut]
Sth. Portland La. G5: Glas . . . . .6F 8[cut]
(not continuous[cut])
South Rd. G76: Busby . . . . . . . . .4E 13[cut]
Sth. Robertson Pl. ML6: Air . . . .4G 9[cut]
Sth. Scott St. G69: Bail . . . . . . .1H 10[cut]
Southside Cres. G5: Glas . . . . . .1G 10[cut]
Sth. Spiers Wharf
G4: Glas . . . . . . . . . . . .1F 83 (1D 4[cut]
Sth. St. G14: Glas . . . . . . . . . . .5A 6[cut]
PA4: Inch . . . . . . . . . . . . . .5F 5[cut]
PA6: Hous . . . . . . . . . . . . . .1A 7[cut]
Sth. Vesalius St. G32: Glas . . . . .6A 8[cut]

South Vw.—Stock St.


outh Vw. G72: Blan 6A 124
G81: Clyd 4B 42
ML4: Bell 3A 126
outhview Av. G76: Busby 4D 134
outhview Ct. G64: B'rig 2B 64
outhview Cres. PA11: Bri W 2F 73
outhview Dr. G61: Bear 2C 44
outhview Gro. G61: Bear 2C 44
outhview Pl. G69: G'csh 3C 68
outhview Ter. G64: B'rig 2B 64
h. William St. PA5: John 3F 95
outhwold Rd. PA1: Pais 6G 79
outhwood Dr. G44: Glas 2G 119
h. Woodside Rd. G20: Glas 6D 62
G4: Glas 1C 82
outra Pl. G33: Glas 3B 86
overeigns Ga. G71: Both 5C 124
palehall Dr. ML1: N'hill 4F 129
PATESTON 6C 94
pateston Rd. PA5: John 6C 94
pean Av. G74: E Kil 2B 150
pean St. G44: Glas 6E 103
pectrum Ho. G81: Clyd 5D 42
peirsfield Ct. PA1: Pais 2H 97
peirsfield Gdns. PA2: Pais 2A 98
peirshall Cl. G14: Glas 4H 59
peirshall Ter. G14: Glas 3G 59
peirs Rd. G61: Bear 4G 45
PA5: John 2H 95
pencer Dr. PA2: Pais 5B 96
pencerfield Gdns.
ML3: Ham 6B 142
pencer St. G13: Glas 2F 61
G81: Clyd 4C 42
pence St. G20: Glas 1A 62
pey Av. PA2: Pais 5C 96
pey Ct. ML2: Newm 3D 146
ML6: Air 6C 92
pey Dr. ML5: Coat 1A 110
PA4: Renf 1G 79
pey Gdns. ML3: Ham 3F 153
pey Gro. G75: E Kil 4A 148
pey Pl. PA5: John 5C 94
pey Rd. G61: Bear 5C 44
pey St. G33: Glas 3H 85
pey Ter. G75: E Kil 4B 148
pey Wlk. *G67: Cumb 4H 35*
*(in Cumbernauld Shop. Cen.)*
ML1: Holy 1C 128
pey Wynd ML9: Lark 5E 161
piersbridge Av. G46: T'bnk 5E 117
(Nitshill Rd.)
G46: T'bnk 4F 117
(Spiersbridge Rd.)
piersbridge Bus. Pk.
G46: T'bnk 4E 117
piersbridge La. G46: T'bnk 4E 117
piersbridge Rd. G46: T'bnk 5F 117
piersbridge Ter. G46: T'bnk 4E 117
piers Gro. G46: T'bnk 4F 117
piers Pl. PA3: Lin 4A 76
piers Rd. G61: Bear 4H 45
PA6: Hous 1B 74
piers Wharf G4: Glas 1F 83 (1D 4)
pindlehowe Rd. G71: Tann 1E 125
G71: Udd 2D 124
pinners Gdns. PA2: Pais 2F 97
pinners La. G81: Hard 6D 22
PITTAL 2B 120
pittal Rd. G73: Ruth 3B 120
pittal Ter. G72: Flem 5H 123
poolers Rd. PA1: Pais 2F 97
poutmouth G1: Glas 5H 83
pringbank Rd. PA3: Pais 4H 77
pringbank St. G20: Glas 5D 62
pringbank Ter. PA3: Pais 4H 77
PRINGBOIG 5C 86
pringboig Av. G32: Glas 5C 86
pringboig Rd. G32: Glas 4C 86
PRINGBURN 5B 64
pringburn Leisure Cen. 5B 64
pringburn Mus. *5B 64*
*(off Ayr St.)*
pringburn Pl. G74: E Kil 6C 136
pringburn Rd. G21: Glas 2A 84
pringburn Shop. Cen.
G21: Glas 5B 64
pringburn Station (Rail) 5B 64
pringburn Way G21: Glas 5A 64
pringcroft Av. G69: Bail 5H 87
pringcroft Cres. G69: Bail 5H 87
pringcroft Dr. G69: Bail 5G 87
pringcroft Gdns. G69: Bail 5A 88
pringcroft Gro. G69: Bail 5H 87
pringcroft Wynd G69: Bail 5H 87
pringfield Av. G64: B'rig 1C 64
G71: Udd 2D 124
PA1: Pais 1D 98
pringfield Ct. G1: Glas 4G 83 (6E 5)
G64: B'rig 6D 48
Springfield Cres. G64: B'rig 1C 64
G71: Udd 2D 124
G72: Blan 2A 140
ML8: Carl 5F 165
Springfield Dr. G78: Barr 6G 115
Springfield Gro. G78: Barr 6F 115
Springfield Pk. PA5: John 3G 95
Springfield Pk. Rd. G73: Ruth 1E 121
Springfield Quay G5: Glas 5D 82
Springfield Rd. G31: Glas 1E 105
G40: Glas 2C 104
G64: B'rig 6C 48
G67: Cumb 1A 36
G78: Barr, Neil 2F 131
ML6: Air 3E 93
Springfield Sq. G64: B'rig 1C 64
Springfield Woods PA5: John 3G 95
SPRINGHALL 3F 121
Springhall Ct. *G73: Ruth 4F 121*
*(off Slenavon Av.)*
SPRINGHILL 1G 131
Springhill Av. ML5: Coat 1G 109
ML6: Air 3B 92
Springhill Dr. Sth. G69: Bail 5G 87
Springhill Farm Gro. G69: Bail 5G 87
Springhill Farm Pl. G69: Bail 5G 87
Springhill Farm Rd. G69: Bail 5G 87
Springhill Farm Way G69: Bail 5G 87
Springhill Gdns. G41: Glas 4C 102
Springhill Parkway G69: Bail 5G 87
Springhill Pl. ML5: Coat 1G 109
Springhill Rd. G69: Bail 6F 87
G76: Busby 2D 134
G78: Barr 5D 114
G78: Neil 4G 131
Springholm Dr. ML6: Air 1H 91
Springkell Av. G41: Glas 2H 101
Springkell Dr. G41: Glas 3H 101
Springkell Gdns. G41: Glas 3B 102
Springkell Ga. G41: Glas 3B 102
Springside Gdns. G15: Glas 3A 44
Springside Pl. G15: Glas 3A 44
Springvale Dr. PA2: Pais 3D 96
Springvale Ter. G21: Glas 5A 64
SPRINGWELL 4D 122
Springwell Cres. G72: Blan 2D 140
SPRINGWELLS 3D 140
Springwells Av. ML6: Air 3C 92
Springwells Cres. ML6: Air 3C 92
Spruce Av. G72: Blan 1A 140
ML3: Ham 1A 154
PA5: John 4G 95
Spruce Ct. ML3: Ham 2A 154
ML5: Coat 1B 110
Spruce Dr. G66: Lenz 2A 50
G72: Flem 3F 123
Spruce Rd. G67: Cumb 1D 36
G71: View 4G 109
Spruce St. G22: Glas 4H 63
Spruce Way G72: Flem 3F 123
ML1: Holy 3B 128
Spynie Pl. G64: B'rig 5F 49
Spynie Way *ML2: Newm 3D 146*
*(off Iona Rd.)*
Squire St. G14: Glas 1D 80
Sraehouse Wynd ML8: Carl 4H 165
Stabcross Bus. Pk. *G3: Glas 3C 82*
*(off St Vincent Cres.)*
Stable Gro. PA1: Pais 2F 97
Stable Pl. G62: Miln 2F 25
Stable Rd. G62: Miln 2F 25
Staffa G74: E Kil 3C 150
Staffa Av. PA4: Renf 2E 79
Staffa Dr. G66: Kirk 5H 31
ML6: Air 4F 93
PA2: Pais 6A 98
Staffa Rd. G72: Camb 4H 121
Staffa St. G31: Glas 3D 84
Staffin Dr. G23: Glas 6B 46
Staffin Path *G23: Glas 6C 46*
*(off Staffin St.)*
Staffin St. G23: Glas 6C 46
Stafford St. G4: Glas 2G 83 (2G 5)
ML4: Bell 3B 126
Stag Ct. G71: View 1G 125
Stag St. G51: Glas 4H 81
Staig Wynd ML1: Moth 5A 144
Staineybraes Pl. ML6: Air 1H 91
Stalker St. ML2: Wis 5C 144
Stamford Pl. G31: Glas 6D 84
Stamford Rd. G31: Glas 6D 84
Stamford St. G31: Glas 6D 84
G40: Glas 6D 84
STAMPERLAND 6D 118
Stamperland Av. G76: Clar 2D 134
Stamperland Cres. G76: Clar 1C 134
Stamperland Dr. G76: Clar 2D 134
Stamperland Gdns. G76: Clar 6D 118
Stamperland Hill G76: Clar 1C 134
Stanalane St. G46: T'bnk 3F 117
Standburn Rd. G21: Glas 2F 65
Stand Comedy Club, The 1C 82
Standford Hall *G72: Camb 1A 122*
*(off Main St.)*
Staneacre Pk. ML3: Ham 6B 142
Stanecraigs Pl. ML2: Newm 3D 146
Stanefield Dr. ML1: N'hill 3E 129
Stanely Av. PA2: Pais 5F 97
Stanely Cres. PA2: Pais 5F 97
Stanely Dr. PA2: Pais 4G 97
Stanely Rd. PA2: Pais 4G 97
Stanford St. G81: Clyd 6E 43
Stanhope Dr. G73: Ruth 2F 121
Stanhope Pl. ML2: Wis 4G 157
Stanistone Rd. ML8: Carl 3G 165
Stanka Av. PA2: Pais 2G 97
STANLEY 4G 97
Stanley Blvd. G72: Blan 5B 140
Stanley Dr. G64: B'rig 5D 48
ML4: Bell 1C 126
PA5: Brkfld 6C 74
Stanley Gro. PA2: Pais 5F 97
Stanley La. PA5: Brkfld 6C 74
Stanley Pk. ML6: Air 3B 92
Stanley Pl. G72: Blan 6B 124
Stanley Rd. PA2: Pais 3H 97
Stanley St. G41: Glas 6C 82
ML3: Ham 5D 140
Stanley St. La. G41: Glas 6C 82
Stanmore Rd. G42: Glas 5F 103
Stanrigg St. ML6: Plain 1G 93
Stark Av. G81: Dun 1A 42
Starling Way ML4: Bell 5A 110
Startpoint St. G33: Glas 3A 86
Station Brae G78: Neil 1C 130
Station Bldgs. G67: Cumb 5A 36
Station Cres. PA4: Renf 5G 59
Station Pk. G69: Bail 1A 108
Station Pl. ML8: Law 5E 159
Station Rd. G20: Glas 1A 62
G33: Mille 4A 66
G33: Step 4D 66
G46: Giff 4A 118
G60: Old K 1F 41
G61: Bear 3C 44
G62: Bard 6E 27
G62: Miln 3G 25
G65: Kils 2H 11
G66: Len 3F 7
G66: Lenz 3C 50
G69: Bail 1A 108
G69: Muirh 2A 68
G71: Both 5E 125
G71: Udd 1C 124
G72: Blan 1C 140
G76: Busby 4E 135
G78: Neil 2D 130
G82: Dumb 3E 17
ML1: Cle 6H 129
ML1: New S 4B 128
ML2: Wis 1G 157
ML6: Air 3E 93
ML6: Plain 1H 93
ML8: Carl 4E 165
ML8: Law 6D 158
ML9: Lark 1F 161
PA1: Pais 2E 97
PA10: Kilb 3A 94
PA11: Bri W 4G 73
PA4: Renf 5F 59
PA7: B'ton 5H 39
Station Row ML8: Law 5E 159
Station Way G71: Udd 1D 124
Station Wynd PA10: Kilb 3B 94
Staybrae Dr. G53: Glas 4H 99
Staybrae Gro. G53: Glas 4H 99
Steading, The ML2: Wis 4H 145
Steel St. G1: Glas 5H 83
ML2: Wis 1H 157
Steeple Sq. PA10: Kilb 2A 94
Steeple St. PA10: Kilb 2A 94
Stemac La. ML6: Plain 1G 93
Stenhouse Av. G69: Muirh 2A 68
Stenton Cres. ML2: Wis 2D 156
Stenton Pl. ML2: Wis 2D 156
Stenton St. G32: Glas 4G 85
Stepends Rd. ML6: Air 5H 93
Stepford Path G33: Glas 4G 87
Stepford Pl. G33: Glas 4F 87
Stepford Rd. G33: Glas 4F 87
Stepford Sports Pk. 5G 87
Stephen Cres. G69: Bail 6F 87
Stephenson Pl. G75: E Kil 3F 149
Stephenson Sq. G75: E Kil 3F 149
Stephenson St. G52: Hill 3G 79
Stephenson Ter. G75: E Kil 3F 149
STEPPS 4C 66
Steppshill Ter. G33: Step 4C 66
Stepps Rd. G33: Glas 2C 86
G66: Auch 5E 51
STEPPS RD. INTERCHANGE 2C 86
Stepps Station (Rail) 4E 67
Stevens La. ML1: New S 4A 128
Stevenson Pl. ML4: Bell 6D 110
Stevenson St. G40: Glas 5A 84
(not continuous)
G81: Clyd 3B 42
ML8: Carl 3E 165
PA2: Pais 2A 98
Stevenston Ct. ML1: New S 3A 128
Stevenston St. ML1: New S 3A 128
Stewart Av. G72: Blan 2A 140
G77: Newt M 3E 133
PA4: Renf 2D 78
Stewart Ct. G73: Ruth 6E 105
G78: Barr 3E 115
*ML5: Coat 5E 91*
*(off Clifton Pl.)*
Stewart Cres. G78: Barr 3F 115
ML2: Newm 3E 147
Stewart Dr. G69: Barg 5F 89
G76: Clar 1B 134
G81: Hard 1D 42
STEWARTFIELD 5E 137
Stewartfield Dr. G74: E Kil 5F 137
Stewartfield Rd. G74: E Kil 6E 137
Stewartfield Way G74: E Kil 6A 136
Stewart Gdns ML5: Coat 4E 91
Stewart Gill Pl. ML9: Ashg 4B 162
Stewarton Dr. G72: Camb 2G 121
Stewarton Ho. *ML2: Wis 1H 157*
*(off Stewarton St.)*
Stewarton Rd. G46: T'bnk 6D 116
G77: Newt M 4A 132
Stewarton St. ML2: Wis 1H 157
Stewarton Ter. ML2: Wis 1H 157
Stewart Pl. G78: Barr 3F 115
ML8: Carl 3F 165
Stewart Quad. ML1: Holy 1B 128
Stewart Rd. PA2: Pais 5B 98
Stewarts La. ML2: Wis 6A 146
Stewart St. G4: Glas 2F 83 (1D 4)
G62: Miln 4G 25
G78: Barr 3F 115
G81: Clyd 4A 42
ML3: Ham 4E 141
(not continuous)
ML4: Moss 2E 127
ML5: Coat 3C 90
ML8: Carl 2E 165
Stewartville St. G11: Glas 1H 81
Stirling Av. G61: Bear 5E 45
Stirling Dr. G61: Bear 1D 44
G64: B'rig 4A 48
G73: Ruth 2D 120
G74: E Kil 6A 138
ML3: Ham 5C 140
PA3: Lin 6F 75
PA5: John 3D 94
Stirlingfauld Pl. G5: Glas 6F 83
Stirling Gdns. G64: B'rig 4A 48
Stirling Ho. G81: Clyd 5D 42
Stirling Pl. G66: Len 3G 7
Stirling Rd. G4: Glas 3H 83 (4H 5)
G65: Kils 2A 12
G66: Kirk 4D 30
G82: Dumb, Milt 1G 17
ML6: Air, Rigg 1B 92
ML6: Chap 1D 112
ML8: Carl 1E 165
Stirling Rd. Ind. Est.
ML6: Air 1B 92
Stirling St. G67: Cumb 1B 36
ML1: Moth 5B 144
ML5: Coat 1H 109
ML6: Air 4H 91
Stirling Way G69: Bail 1G 107
PA4: Renf 2F 79
Stirrat St. G20: Glas 3A 62
PA3: Pais 4F 77
Stobcross Rd. G3: Glas 3A 82
Stobcross St. G3: Glas 4C 82 (5A 4)
ML5: Coat 5C 90
Stobcross Wynd G3: Glas 4B 82
Stobhill Cotts. G21: Glas 2C 64
Stobhill Rd. G21: Glas 2B 64
Stobo G74: E Kil 5C 138
Stobo Ct. G74: E Kil 5C 138
Stobo St. ML2: Wis 4A 146
Stobs Dr. G78: Barr 2D 114
Stobs Pl. G34: Glas 2A 88
Stock Av. PA2: Pais 2A 98
Stock Exchange G2: Glas 5E 5
Stockholm Cres. PA2: Pais 2A 98
Stockiemuir Av. G61: Bear 6D 24
Stockiemuir Ct. G61: Bear 6E 25
Stockiemuir Rd. G61: Bear 1D 44
G62: Miln 3C 24
Stocks Rd. ML1: Cle 1D 146
Stock St. PA2: Pais 3A 98

Stockwell Pl.—Symington Sq.

**Stockwell Pl.** G1: Glas .5G **83**
**Stockwell St.** G1: Glas .5G **83** (6F **5**)
**Stoddard Sq.** PA5: Eld .2B **96**
**Stonebyres Ct.** ML3: Ham .6E **141**
**Stonecraig Rd.** ML2: Wis .1H **157**
**Stonedyke Cres.** ML8: Carl .2G **165**
**Stonedyke Gro.** G15: Glas .5B **44**
**Stonedyke Rd.** ML8: Carl .2G **165**
STONEFIELD .1C **140**
**Stonefield Av.** G12: Glas .3A **62**
PA2: Pais .4B **98**
**Stonefield Cres.** G72: Blan .3A **140**
G76: Clar .1A **134**
PA2: Pais .4B **98**
**Stonefield Dr.** PA2: Pais .4B **98**
**Stonefield Gdns.** ML8: Carl .2F **165**
PA2: Pais .4B **98**
**Stonefield Grn.** PA2: Pais .4A **98**
**Stonefield Gro.** PA2: Pais .4A **98**
**Stonefield Pk.** PA2: Pais .5A **98**
**Stonefield Pk. Gdns.**
G72: Blan .1C **140**
**Stonefield Pl.** G72: Blan .3H **139**
**Stonefield Rd.** G72: Blan .2A **140**
**Stonefield St.** ML6: Air .2A **92**
**Stonehall Av.** ML3: Ham .1F **153**
**Stonehaven Cres.** ML6: Air .6G **91**
**Stonelaw Dr.** G73: Ruth .6D **104**
**Stonelaw Rd.** G73: Ruth .6D **104**
**Stonelaw Towers** G73: Ruth .1E **121**
**Stoneside Dr.** G43: Glas .1G **117**
**Stoneside Sq.** G43: Glas .1G **117**
**Stoney Brae** PA2: Pais .5A **98**
(not continuous)
**Stoneyetts Rd.** G69: Mood .4D **52**
**Stoneymeadow Rd.** G72: Blan .3E **139**
G74: E Kil .5B **138**
**Stony Brae** PA1: Pais .6A **78**
PA3: Pais .6A **78**
**Stonyflatt Av.** G82: Dumb .2H **17**
**Stonyflatt Rd.** G82: Dumb .2H **17**
**Stonyhurst St.** G22: Glas .5F **63**
(not continuous)
**Stonylee Rd.** G67: Cumb .4A **36**
**Storie St.** PA1: Pais .1A **98**
(not continuous)
**Stormyland Way** G78: Barr .5E **115**
**Stornoway Cres.** ML2: Wis .4C **146**
**Stornoway St.** G22: Glas .1G **63**
**Stow Brae** PA1: Pais .1A **98**
**Stow St.** PA1: Pais .1A **98**
**Strachan St.** ML4: Bell .3C **126**
**Strachur St.** G22: Glas .2E **63**
**Strain Cres.** ML6: Air .5B **92**
**Straiton Dr.** ML3: Ham .1B **152**
**Straiton Pl.** G72: Blan .1B **140**
**Straiton St.** G32: Glas .4G **85**
**Stranraer Dr.** G15: Glas .5C **44**
**Stratford** G74: E Kil .4D **138**
**Stratford St.** G20: Glas .4B **62**
**Strathallan Gdns.** *G66: Kirk .5D* ***30***
*(off Willowbank Gdns.)*
**Strathallon Pl.** *G73: Ruth .4F* ***121***
*(off St Stephen's Av.)*
**Strathaven Rd.** G75: E Kil .3A **150**
ML3: Ham .6G **153**
**Strathavon Cres.** ML6: Air .1A **92**
**Strathblane Cres.** ML6: Air .6H **71**
**Strathblane Dr.** G75: E Kil .3A **148**
**Strathblane Gdns.** G13: Glas .1E **61**
**Strathblane Rd.** G62: Miln .3H **25**
G66: Cam G .1A **6**
**Strathbran St.** G31: Glas .1F **105**
STRATHBUNGO .3D **102**
**Strathcairn Cres.** ML6: Air .6H **71**
**Strath Carron** ML8: Law .6E **159**
**Strathcarron Cres.** PA2: Pais .5D **98**
**Strathcarron Dr.** PA2: Pais .4D **98**
**Strathcarron Pl.** G20: Glas .3B **62**
PA2: Pais .5D **98**
**Strathcarron Rd.** PA2: Pais .5D **98**
**Strathcarron Way** PA2: Pais .4D **98**
Strathclyde Arts Cen. .6A **4**
**Strathclyde Bus. Cen.**
G72: Flem .4E **123**
**Strathclyde Bus. Pk.** ML4: Bell .5A **110**
Strathclyde Country Pk. .1A **142**
**Strathclyde Dr.** G73: Ruth .6C **104**
Strathclyde Homes Stadium .5G **17**
**Strathclyde Path** G71: Udd .1C **124**
**Strathclyde Rd.** G82: Dumb .2G **17**
ML1: Moth .3D **142**
**Strathclyde St.** G40: Glas .3C **104**
**Strathclyde Vw.** G71: Both .6F **125**
**Strathcona Dr.** G13: Glas .2F **61**
**Strathcona Gdns.** G13: Glas .2G **61**
**Strathcona La.** G75: E Kil .4G **149**
**Strathcona Pl.** G73: Ruth .3F **121**
G75: E Kil .4G **149**
**Strathcona St.** G13: Glas .3F **61**
**Strathconon Gdns.** *G75: E Kil .2A* ***148***
*(off Strathnairn Dr.)*
**Strath Dearn** ML8: Law .6E **159**
**Strathdearn Gro.** G75: E Kil .3A **148**
**Strathdee Av.** G81: Hard .2D **42**
**Strathdee Rd.** G44: Neth .5C **118**
**Strathdon Av.** G44: Neth .5C **118**
PA2: Pais .3G **97**
**Strathdon Dr.** G44: Neth .5D **118**
**Strathdon Pl.** *G75: E Kil .3A* ***148***
*(off Strathnairn Dr.)*
**Strathearn Gro.** G66: Kirk .4H **31**
**Strathearn Rd.** G76: Clar .3C **134**
**Strath Elgin** ML8: Law .6D **158**
**Strathendrick Dr.** G44: Glas .3C **118**
**Strathfillan Rd.** G74: E Kil .1F **149**
**Strath Halladale** ML8: Law .6E **159**
**Strathhalladale Ct.** *G75: E Kil .3A* ***148***
*(off Strathmore Gro.)*
**Strathkelvin Av.** G64: B'rig .2B **64**
**Strathkelvin La.** G75: E Kil .3A **148**
**Strathkelvin Retail Pk.**
G64: B'rig .3E **49**
**Strathlachan Av.** ML8: Carl .4G **165**
**Strathleven Pl.** G82: Dumb .4F **17**
**Strathmore Av.** G72: Blan .6A **124**
PA1: Pais .1F **99**
**Strathmore Cres.** ML6: Air .1A **92**
**Strathmore Gdns.** G73: Ruth .3F **121**
**Strathmore Gro.** G75: E Kil .3A **148**
**Strathmore Ho.** *G74: E Kil .2G* ***149***
*(off Princess Sq.)*
**Strathmore Pl.** ML5: Coat .6F **91**
**Strathmore Rd.** G22: Glas .2F **63**
ML3: Ham .6A **142**
**Strathmore Wlk.** ML5: Coat .6F **91**
**Strathmungo Cres.** ML6: Air .1H **91**
**Strath Nairn** ML8: Law .6E **159**
**Strathnairn Av.** G75: E Kil .3A **148**
**Strathnairn Ct.** G75: E Kil .3A **148**
**Strathnairn Dr.** G75: E Kil .3A **148**
**Strathnairn Way** G75: E Kil .3A **148**
**Strath Naver** ML8: Law .6E **159**
**Strathnaver Gdns.** G75: E Kil .3A **148**
**Strathord Pl.** G69: Mood .3E **53**
**Strathord St.** G32: Glas .2A **106**
**Strath Peffer** ML8: Law .6D **158**
**Strathpeffer Cres.** ML6: Air .1A **92**
**Strathpeffer Dr.** *G75: E Kil .3A* ***148***
*(off Strathnairn Dr.)*
**Strathspey Av.** G75: E Kil .3A **148**
**Strathspey Cres.** ML6: Air .6H **71**
**Strathtay Av.** G44: Neth .5C **118**
G75: E Kil .3A **148**
**Strathtummel Cres.** ML6: Air .6H **71**
**Strathview Gro.** G44: Neth .5C **118**
**Strathview Pk.** G44: Neth .5C **118**
**Strathview Rd.** ML4: Bell .4A **126**
**Strathy Pl.** G20: Glas .3B **62**
**Strathyre Gdns.** G61: Bear .2H **45**
G69: Mood .4E **53**
G75: E Kil .3A **148**
ML6: Glenm .4H **71**
**Strathyre Rd.** G72: Blan .3D **140**
**Strathyre St.** G41: Glas .5C **102**
**Stratton Dr.** G46: Giff .5H **117**
**Strauss Av.** G81: Clyd .6G **43**
**Stravaig Path** PA2: Pais .6E **97**
**Stravaig Wlk.** PA2: Pais .6E **97**
**Stravanan Ct.** G45: Glas .5A **120**
**Stravanan Gdns.** G45: Glas .5H **119**
**Stravanan Pl.** G45: Glas .5H **119**
**Stravanan Rd.** G45: Glas .6H **119**
**Stravanan St.** G45: Glas .5H **119**
**Stravanan Ter.** G45: Glas .5H **119**
**Stravenhouse Rd.** ML8: Law .1G **163**
**Strawberry Fld. Rd.** PA6: C'lee .2B **74**
**Strawhill Ct.** G76: Busby .2D **134**
**Strawhill Rd.** G76: Clar .2C **134**
**Strayhgryffe Cres.** PA11: Bri W .2E **73**
**Streamfield Gdns.** G33: Glas .2G **65**
**Streamfield Ga.** G33: Glas .2F **65**
**Streamfield Lea** *G33: Glas .1G* ***65***
*(off Brookfield Dr.)*
**Streamfield Pl.** G33: Glas .2G **65**
**Strenabey Av.** G73: Ruth .3F **121**
**Striven Ct.** ML5: Coat .2D **110**
**Striven Cres.** ML2: Wis .2G **157**
**Striven Gdns.** G20: Glas .6D **62**
**Striven Ter.** ML3: Ham .2E **153**
**Stroma St.** G21: Glas .1D **84**
**Stromness St.** G5: Glas .1E **103**
**Strone Gdns.** G65: Kils .3F **11**
**Stronend St.** G22: Glas .4F **63**
**Strone Path** ML5: Glenb .3G **69**
**Strone Pl.** ML6: Air .6C **92**
**Strone Rd.** G33: Glas .4B **86**
**Stronsay Pl.** G64: B'rig .5F **49**
**Stronsay St.** G21: Glas .1D **84**
**Stronvar Dr.** G14: Glas .5B **60**
**Stronvar La.** G14: Glas .5B **60**
**Stroud Rd.** G75: E Kil .6E **149**
**Strowan Cres.** G32: Glas .1B **106**
**Strowan's Rd.** G82: Dumb .2C **18**
**Strowan St.** G32: Glas .1B **106**
**Strowan's Well Rd.**
G82: Dumb .2C **18**
**Struan Av.** G46: Giff .4A **118**
**Struan Gdns.** G44: Glas .2E **119**
**Struan Rd.** G44: Glas .2E **119**
**Struie St.** G34: Glas .3G **87**
**Struma Dr.** G76: Clar .1A **134**
**Struther & Swinhill Rd.**
ML9: Lark .6G **161**
STRUTHERHILL .5F **161**
**Strutherhill** ML9: Lark .4F **161**
**Strutherhill Ind. Est.**
ML9: Lark .5G **161**
**Struthers Cres.** G74: E Kil .5B **138**
**Struther St.** ML9: Lark .5F **161**
**Stuart Av.** G60: Old K .2F **41**
G73: Ruth .2D **120**
**Stuart Dr.** G64: B'rig .1A **64**
ML9: Lark .4G **161**
**Stuart Ho.** G67: Cumb .2B **36**
**Stuarton Pk.** G74: E Kil .1G **149**
**Stuart Quad.** ML2: Wis .2E **157**
**Stuart Rd.** G76: Crmck .1H **135**
G82: Dumb .1C **18**
PA7: B'ton .3H **39**
**Stuart St.** G60: Old K .2F **41**
G74: E Kil .1H **149**
**Stuartville** ML5: Coat .4D **90**
**Succoth St.** G13: Glas .2F **61**
**Sudbury Cres.** G75: E Kil .2D **148**
**Suffolk St.** G40: Glas .5H **83**
**Sugworth Av.** G69: Bail .6H **87**
**Suisnish** PA8: Ersk .2G **57**
**Sumburgh St.** G33: Glas .4H **85**
**Summerfield Cotts.** G14: Glas .1E **81**
**Summerfield Rd.** G67: Cumb .1C **54**
**Summerfield St.** G40: Glas .2D **104**
**Summerhill & Garngibbock Rd.**
G67: Cumb .5E **55**
**Summerhill Av.** ML9: Lark .3E **161**
**Summerhill Dr.** G15: Glas .3B **44**
**Summerhill Gdns.** G15: Glas .3B **44**
**Summerhill Pl.** G15: Glas .3B **44**
**Summerhill Rd.** G15: Glas .3A **44**
G76: Busby .2D **134**
**Summerhill Way** ML4: Bell .3B **126**
**Summerlea Rd.** G46: T'bnk .3F **117**
SUMMERLEE .3B **90**
**Summerlee Cotts.** ML5: Coat .4B **90**
Summerlee Heritage Trust .3B **90**
**Summerlee Rd.** ML2: Wis .5C **144**
ML9: Lark .6H **155**
**Summerlee St.** G33: Glas .3C **86**
ML5: Coat .4B **90**
SUMMERSTON .6B **46**
Summerston Station (Rail) .1B **62**
**Summer St.** G40: Glas .6B **84**
**Summertown Path** G51: Glas .4H **81**
**Summertown Rd.** G51: Glas .4H **81**
**Summyside Oval** PA2: Pais .4A **98**
**Sunart Av.** PA4: Renf .5D **58**
**Sunart Ct.** ML3: Ham .2E **153**
**Sunart Gdns.** G64: B'rig .6E **49**
**Sunart Rd.** G52: Glas .6E **81**
G64: B'rig .6E **49**
**Sunart St.** ML2: Wis .2G **157**
**Sunbury Av.** G76: Clar .2A **134**
**Sundale Av.** G76: Clar .3B **134**
**Sunderland Av.** G82: Dumb .3C **16**
**Sunflower Gdns.** ML1: Moth .1F **143**
**Sunningdale Av.** G77: Newt M .4F **133**
**Sunningdale Dr.** PA11: Bri W .5E **73**
**Sunningdale Rd.** G23: Glas .1B **62**
**Sunningdale Wynd** G71: Both .4C **124**
**Sunnybank Dr.** G76: Clar .3B **134**
**Sunnybank Gro.** G76: Clar .3B **134**
**Sunnybank St.** G40: Glas .2D **104**
**Sunnyhill** G65: Twe .2D **32**
**Sunnylaw Dr.** PA2: Pais .3F **97**
**Sunnylaw St.** G22: Glas .5F **63**
SUNNYSIDE .3C **90**
**Sunnyside Av.** G71: Udd .2D **124**
ML1: Holy .2B **128**
**Sunnyside Cres.** ML1: Holy .2A **128**
**Sunnyside Dr.** G15: Glas .6A **44**
G69: Barg .6D **88**
G76: Clar .1B **134**
**Sunnyside Pl.** G15: Glas .6A **44**
G78: Barr .5D **114**
ML1: Holy .2A **128**
**Sunnyside Rd.** ML1: Cle .1H **145**
ML3: Ham, Quar .3A **160**
ML5: Coat .4C **90**
ML9: Lark .2B **160**
PA2: Pais .4H **97**
**Sunnyside St.** ML9: Lark .1D **1**
**Sunnyside Ter.** ML1: Holy .2A **1**
**Surrey La.** G5: Glas .1F **10**
**Surrey St.** G5: Glas .1F **10**
**Sussex St.** G41: Glas .6C **8**
**Sutcliffe Ct.** G13: Glas .2E **6**
**Sutcliffe Rd.** G13: Glas .2E **6**
**Sutherland Av.** G41: Glas .2H **10**
G61: Bear .6E **2**
**Sutherland Ct.** G41: Glas .1C **10**
**Sutherland Cres.** ML3: Ham .5E **14**
**Sutherland Dr.** G46: Giff .6B **1**
G82: Dumb .2C **1**
ML6: Air .6G **9**
**Sutherland La.** G12: Glas .1B **8**
**Sutherland Pl.** ML4: Bell .5B **1**
**Sutherland Rd.** G81: Clyd .5D **4**
**Sutherland St.** G72: Blan .4A **14**
PA1: Pais .6H **7**
**Sutherland Way** G74: E Kil .6C **13**
**Sutherness Dr.** G33: Glas .4A **8**
**Swaledale** G74: E Kil .6E **13**
**Swallow Dr.** PA5: John .6C **9**
**Swallow Gdns.** G13: Glas .2H **5**
**Swallow Rd.** G81: Faif .6F **2**
ML2: Wis .5H **14**
**Swan Pl.** PA5: John .6C **9**
**Swanston St.** G40: Glas .3C **10**
**Swan St.** G4: Glas .2G **83** (1F 5
G81: Clyd .4B **4**
**Swan Way** ML8: Law .1H **16**
**Sween Av.** G44: Glas .3E **11**
**Sween Dr.** ML3: Ham .2E **15**
**Sween Path** *ML4: Bell .4E* ***12***
*(off Millbank Av*
**Sweethill Ter.** ML5: Coat .2F **11**
**Sweethill Wlk.** ML4: Bell .6E **11**
**Sweethope Gdns.** G71: Both .5F **12**
**Sweethope Pl.** G71: Both .4E **12**
**Swift Bank** ML3: Ham .2C **15**
**Swift Cl.** ML2: Wis .6H **14**
**Swift Cres.** G13: Glas .1H **5**
**Swift Pl.** G75: E Kil .5A **14**
PA5: John .6D **9**
**Swindon St.** G81: Clyd .4A **4**
SWINHILL .6G **16**
**Swinstie Rd.** ML1: Cle .1A **14**
SWINTON .5G **8**
**Swinton Av.** G69: Bail .6A **8**
**Swinton Cres.** G69: Bail .6A **8**
ML5: Coat .1F **10**
**Swinton Dr.** G52: Glas .6B **8**
**Swinton Gdns.** G69: Bail .6B **8**
**Swinton Path** G69: Bail .6B **8**
**Swinton Pl.** G52: Glas .6B **8**
*ML5: Coat .1F* ***10***
*(off Swinton Cres.*
**Swinton Rd.** G69: Bail .6A **8**
**Swinton Vw.** G69: Bail .6B **8**
**Swisscot Av.** ML3: Ham .3F **15**
**Swisscot Wlk.** ML3: Ham .3F **15**
**Switchback Rd.** G61: Bear .5F **4**
**Swordale Path** *G34: Glas .3G* ***8***
*(off Kildermorie Rd*
**Swordale Pl.** G34: Glas .3G **8**
**Sword St.** G31: Glas .5B **8**
ML6: Air .4H **9**
**Sycamore Av.** G66: Lenz .2D **5**
G71: View .6G **10**
PA5: John .4G **9**
**Sycamore Ct.** G75: E Kil .5F **14**
*ML5: Coat .1B* ***11***
*(off Ailsa Rd.*
**Sycamore Cres.** G75: E Kil .5E **14**
ML6: Air .5D **9**
**Sycamore Dr.** G81: Clyd .3C **4**
ML3: Ham .1B **15**
ML6: Air .5D **9**
**Sycamore Gro.** G72: Blan .1A **14**
**Sycamore Pl.** G75: E Kil .5F **14**
ML1: N'hill .4C **12**
**Sycamore Way** G66: Milt C .6C **8**
G72: Flem .3F **12**
G76: Crmck .2H **13**
**Sydenham Ct.** *G12: Glas .5H* ***6***
*(off Westbourne Gdns. La.*
**Sydenham La.** G12: Glas .6A **6**
**Sydenham Rd.** G12: Glas .6A **6**
**Sydes Brae** G72: Blan .5H **13**
**Sydney Dr.** G75: E Kil .4E **14**
**Sydney Pl.** G75: E Kil .3E **14**
**Sydney St.** G31: Glas .5A **8**
G81: Clyd .3H **4**
**Sykehead Av.** ML4: Bell .2D **12**
**Sykeside Rd.** ML6: Air .1G **11**
**Sykes Ter.** G78: Neil .2F **13**
**Sylvania Way** G81: Clyd .5D **4**
**Sylvania Way Sth.** G81: Clyd .6D **4**
**Symington Dr.** G81: Clyd .5C **4**
**Symington Sq.** G75: E Kil .3H **14**

Syriam Pl.—Tiree Grange

riam Pl. G21: Glas 5B 64
riam St. G21: Glas 4B 64

## T

oard Pl. G13: Glas 1C 60
oard Rd. G13: Glas 1C 60
bernacle La. G72: Camb 2A 122
bernacle St. G72: Camb 2A 122
ggart Rd. G65: Croy 2B 34
g Rd. G66: Kirk 6H 31
t Av. G78: Barr 3F 115
kmadoon Rd. G65: Kils 2A 12
lbot G74: E Kil 5C 138
lbot Ct. G13: Glas 4B 60
lbot Dr. G13: Glas 4B 60
lbot Pl. G13: Glas 4B 60
lbot Ter. G13: Glas 4B 60
G71: Tann 5C 108
lisman Av. G82: Dumb 3C 16
isman Cres. ML1: Moth 5F 127
isman Rd. G13: Glas 3C 60
PA2: Pais 6C 96
llant Rd. G15: Glas 4B 44
llant Ter. G15: Glas 4C 44
lla Rd. G52: Glas 5A 80
l Ship at Glasgow Harbour, The 3A 82
marack Cres. G71: View 4G 109
mar Dr. G75: E Kil 5B 148
mbowie Av. G62: Miln 3F 25
mbowie Cres. G62: Miln 3F 25
mbowie St. G13: Glas 1E 61
mshill St. G20: Glas 3D 62
nar Av. PA4: Renf 2G 79
nar Way PA4: Renf 1G 79
NDLEHILL 3B 94
ndlehill Rd. PA10: Kilb 4A 94
nera Av. G44: Glas 2G 119
nfield Pl. G32: Glas 4C 86
nfield St. G32: Glas 4C 86
nkerland Rd. G44: Glas 1E 119
nnadice Av. G52: Glas 2C 100
nnadice Path *G52: Glas 1C 100*
*(off Tannadice Av.)*
nna Dr. G52: Glas 2F 101
nnahill Cen. PA3: Pais 5E 77
nnahill Cres. PA5: John 4E 95
(not continuous)
nnahill Dr. G74: E Kil 6C 138
nnahill Rd. G43: Glas 1D 118
PA3: Pais 5F 77
nnahill's Cottage 1G 97
nnahill Ter. PA3: Pais 5F 77
nnoch Dr. G62: Miln 2G 25
G67: Cumb 6H 35
nnoch Pl. G67: Cumb 6H 35
NNOCHSIDE 4F 109
nnochside Dr. G71: Tann 4E 109
nnochside Pk. G71: Tann 4F 109
nnock St. G22: Glas 5F 63
ntallon Ct. ML8: Carl 2E 165
ntallon Dr. ML5: Coat 2G 89
PA2: Pais 4E 97
ntallon Pk. G74: E Kil 1F 149
ntallon Rd. G41: Glas 5C 102
G69: Bail 2G 107
G71: Both 4F 125
nzieknowe Av. G72: Camb 4B 122
nzieknowe Dr. G72: Camb 4B 122
nzieknowe Pl. G72: Camb 4A 122
nzieknowe Rd. G72: Camb 4A 122
ransay St. G51: Glas 3G 81
rbert Av. G72: Blan 5A 124
ML2: Wis 2G 157
rbert Ct. ML3: Ham 2E 153
rbert Pl. ML8: Carl 4G 165
rbert Way ML5: Coat 1A 110
rbolton G74: E Kil 6D 138
rbolton Cres. ML6: Chap 5D 112
rbolton Dr. G81: Clyd 4E 43
rbolton Path ML9: Lark 2D 160
rbolton Rd. G43: Glas 1B 118
G67: Cumb 3B 36
rbolton Sq. G81: Clyd 4F 43
rbrax Way ML3: Ham 6E 141
rfside Av. G52: Glas 1C 100
rfside Gdns. G52: Glas 1D 100
rfside Oval G52: Glas 1D 100
rget Rd. ML6: Air 5B 92
rland St. G51: Glas 5F 81
rn Gro. G33: Glas 1G 65
rras Dr. PA4: Renf 2G 79
rras Pl. G72: Camb 2D 122
sman Dr. G75: E Kil 4D 148
smania Quad. ML2: Wis 6C 146
ssie Pl. G74: E Kil 1A 150
ssie St. G41: Glas 5B 102
ttershall Rd. G33: Glas 1C 86
Tavistock Dr. G43: Glas 2B 118
Tay Av. PA4: Renf 6G 59
Tay Ct. G75: E Kil 4A 148
Tay Cres. G33: Glas 2G 85
G64: B'rig 6D 48
Tay Gdns. ML3: Ham 3F 153
Tay Gro. G75: E Kil 4A 148
Tayinloan Dr. ML8: Carl 5H 165
Tay La. ML2: Newm 4E 147
Tay Loan *ML1: Holy 2A 128*
*(off Windsor Rd.)*
Taylor Av. ML1: Carf 5D 128
PA10: Kilb 2A 94
Taylor Pl. G4: Glas 3H 83 (3H 5)
Taylor St. G4: Glas 3H 83 (4H 5)
(not continuous)
G81: Clyd 1E 59
Taymouth St. G32: Glas 2B 106
Taynish Dr. G44: Glas 3F 119
Tay Pl. G75: E Kil 4A 148
G82: Dumb 1H 17
ML9: Lark 5E 161
PA5: John 5C 94
Tay Rd. G61: Bear 5D 44
G64: B'rig 6D 48
Tayside ML6: Air 2H 91
Tay St. ML5: Coat 2G 89
Tay Ter. G75: E Kil 3A 148
Tay Wlk. *G67: Cumb 4H 35*
*(in Cumbernauld Shop. Cen.)*
Teak Pl. G71: View 4H 109
Teal Ct. ML4: Bell 5A 110
Teal Cres. G75: E Kil 6B 148
Teal Dr. G13: Glas 2A 60
Tealing Av. G52: Glas 1C 100
Tealing Cres. G52: Glas 1C 100
Teasel Av. G53: Glas 4B 116
Teawell Rd. G77: Newt M 4D 132
Technology Av. G72: Blan 5A 140
Teesdale G74: E Kil 6E 137
Teign Gro. G75: E Kil 5B 148
Teith Av. PA4: Renf 1H 79
Teith Dr. G61: Bear 4D 44
Teith Pl. G72: Camb 2D 122
Teith St. G33: Glas 2G 85
Telephone La. *G12: Glas 1A 82*
*(off Highburgh Rd.)*
Telford Av. ML9: Lark 5G 161
Telford Ct. G81: Clyd 5C 42
Telford Pl. G67: Cumb 5A 36
Telford Rd. G67: Cumb 5A 36
G75: E Kil 3F 149
Telford St. ML4: Bell 1C 126
Telford Ter. *G75: E Kil 3H 149*
*(off Telford Rd.)*
Teme Pl. G75: E Kil 4B 148
Templar Av. G13: Glas 6D 44
TEMPLE 2F 61
Temple Gdns. G13: Glas 2F 61
Templeland G53: Glas 3C 100
Templeland Rd. G53: Glas 3C 100
Temple Locks Ct. G13: Glas 2F 61
Temple Locks Pl. G13: Glas 2F 61
Temple Rd. G13: Glas 2G 61
Templeton Bus. Cen.
G40: Glas 6A 84
Templeton St. G40: Glas 6A 84
Tenement Ho. G3: Glas 2E 83 (2A 4)
Tennant Av. G74: E Kil 1C 148
Tennant Complex, The
G74: E Kil 1C 148
Tennant St. PA4: Renf 5F 59
Tennent St. ML5: Coat 6D 90
Tennyson Dr. G31: Glas 1G 105
Tenters Way PA2: Pais 2F 97
Tern Pl. PA5: John 6D 94
Terregles Av. G41: Glas 3H 101
Terregles Cres. G41: Glas 3A 102
Terregles Dr. G41: Glas 3A 102
Teviot Av. G64: B'rig 4C 48
PA2: Pais 5C 96
Teviot Cres. G61: Bear 5D 44
Teviotdale *G74: E Kil 1F 149*
*(off Strathfillan Rd.)*
G77: Newt M 4H 133
Teviot Dr. PA7: B'ton 5A 40
Teviot Path G72: Blan 2A 140
Teviot Pl. G72: Camb 2E 123
Teviot Sq. *G67: Cumb 4H 35*
*(in Cumbernauld Shop. Cen.)*
Teviot St. G3: Glas 3A 82
ML5: Coat 1H 89
Teviot Ter. PA5: John 5C 94
Teviot Wlk. *G67: Cumb 4H 35*
*(in Cumbernauld Shop. Cen.)*
Teviot Way *G67: Cumb 4H 35*
*(in Cumbernauld Shop. Cen.)*
Tewkesbury Rd. G74: E Kil 4D 138
Thane Rd. G13: Glas 3C 60
Thanes Ga. G71: Both 2C 124
Thankerton Av. ML1: Holy 2H 127
Thankerton Rd. ML9: Lark 4F 161
Tharsis St. G21: Glas 2B 84
Theatre Royal 3F 83 (3D 4)
Third Av. G33: Mille 4B 66
G44: Glas 6F 103
G66: Auch 5D 50
G82: Dumb 3C 18
PA4: Renf 1E 79
Third Av. La. G44: Glas 6F 103
Third Gdns. G41: Glas 1G 101
Thirdpart Cres. G13: Glas 2G 59
Third Rd. G72: Blan 4C 140
Third St. G71: Tann 5D 108
Thirlmere G75: E Kil 6B 148
Thistle Bank G66: Lenz 3D 50
Thistlebank PA11: Bri W 2E 73
Thistlebank Gdns.
ML5: Coat 2A 110
Thistle Cres. ML9: Lark 3F 161
Thistledown Gro.
ML5: Coat 5E 91
Thistle Gdns. ML1: Holy 2A 128
Thistleneuk G60: Old K 6E 21
Thistle Pl. G74: E Kil 6G 137
Thistle Quad. ML6: Air 2B 92
Thistle Rd. ML1: New S 4A 128
Thistle St. G5: Glas 6G 83
G66: Kirk 5D 30
ML1: Cle 6H 129
ML6: Air 2B 92
PA2: Pais 3G 97
Thistle Ter. G5: Glas 1G 103
Thomas Muir Av. G64: B'rig 1C 64
Thomas Muir Mus. 6C 48
Thomas St. PA1: Pais 1F 97
Thompson Av. G66: Kirk 5E 31
Thompson Brae PA1: Pais 2A 98
Thompson Pl. G81: Hard 1E 43
Thompson St. PA4: Renf 1E 79
Thomson Av. ML2: Wis 2D 156
PA5: John 2E 95
Thomson Dr. G61: Bear 1F 45
ML1: Moth 4F 143
ML4: Bell 2H 125
ML6: Air 5H 91
Thomson Gro. G72: Camb 6A 106
Thomson St. G31: Glas 5C 84
ML8: Carl 3F 165
PA5: John 3E 95
Thorn Av. G74: T'hall 6G 135
Thornbank St. G3: Glas 3A 82
Thornbridge Av. G12: Glas 4A 62
G69: Bail 6H 87
Thornbridge Gdns. G69: Bail 6G 87
Thornbridge Rd. G69: Bail 6G 87
Thorncliffe Gdns. G41: Glas 3C 102
Thorncroft Dr. G44: Glas 3H 119
Thorndale Gdns. FK4: Alla 1H 15
Thorndean Av. ML4: Bell 3D 126
Thorndean Cres. ML4: Bell 3D 126
Thorndene PA5: Eld 2H 95
Thorndene Av. ML1: Carf 5C 128
Thornden La. G14: Glas 5A 60
Thorn Dr. G61: Bear 1D 44
G73: Ruth 3E 121
Thorndyke G74: E Kil 4C 138
Thorne Brae PA5: John 2G 95
Thornhill PA5: John 3H 95
Thornhill Av. G72: Blan 1B 140
PA5: Eld 3H 95
Thornhill Dr. PA5: Eld 3H 95
Thornhill Gdns. G77: Newt M 6D 132
PA5: John 2G 95
Thornhill La. G71: Both 4F 125
Thornhill Path G31: Glas 6F 85
Thornhill Rd. ML3: Ham 5C 140
Thornhill Way ML5: Coat 2F 111
Thorniecroft Dr. G67: Cumb 1E 55
Thorniecroft Pl. G67: Cumb 1E 55
Thornielee G74: E Kil 1B 150
Thorniewood Gdns. G71: Tann 6E 109
Thorniewood Rd. G71: Tann 5D 108
Thornkip Pl. ML5: Coat 6F 91
Thornlea Dr. G46: Giff 3B 118
Thornlea St. ML8: Carl 5G 165
Thornley Av. G13: Glas 3B 60
THORNLIEBANK 4F 117
Thornliebank Ind. Est.
G46: T'bnk 4E 117
Thornliebank Rd. G43: Glas 1H 117
Thornliebank Station (Rail) 3G 117
Thornlie Gill ML2: Wis 1H 157
THORNLY PARK 5B 98
Thornly Pk. Av. PA2: Pais 5B 98
Thornly Pk. Dr. PA2: Pais 5B 98
Thornly Pk. Gdns. PA2: Pais 4B 98
Thornly Pk. Rd. PA2: Pais 4A 98
Thorn Rd. G61: Bear 2C 44
ML4: Bell 2D 126
Thornside Rd. PA5: John 2G 95
THORNTONHALL 6G 135
Thorntonhall Station (Rail)
6F 135
Thornton La. G20: Glas 2C 62
Thornton Pl. ML3: Ham 5H 153
Thornton Rd. G74: T'hall 6G 135
Thornton St. G20: Glas 2B 62
ML5: Coat 1H 89
Thorntree Av. ML3: Ham 4D 140
Thorntree Way G71: Both 4F 125
Thornwood Av. G11: Glas 1G 81
G66: Lenz 2A 50
Thornwood Cres. G11: Glas 6F 61
Thornwood Dr. G11: Glas 1F 81
(not continuous)
PA11: Bri W 4D 72
PA2: Pais 3F 97
Thornwood Gdns. G11: Glas 1F 81
Thornwood Pl. G11: Glas 6F 61
(not continuous)
Thornwood Quad. G11: Glas 6F 61
Thornwood Rd. G11: Glas 1F 81
Thornwood Ter. G11: Glas 1F 81
Thornyburn Dr. G69: Bail 1B 108
Thornyburn Pl. G69: Bail 1A 108
Thorny Pk. Ct. PA2: Pais 5A 98
Thorp Ct. PA5: John 3G 95
THRASHBUSH 1A 92
Thrashbush Av. ML2: Wis 5B 146
Thrashbush Cres. ML2: Wis 5B 146
Thrashbush Rd. ML2: Wis 5B 146
Threave Ct. ML8: Carl 2E 165
Threave Pl. G77: Newt M 4B 132
Three Queens Sq. G81: Clyd 6D 42
Three Rivers Wlk. G75: E Kil 3D 148
Threestonehill Av. G32: Glas 5B 86
Threshold Pk. G74: E Kil 1A 150
Threshold Rd. G74: E Kil 1A 150
Thriplee Rd. PA11: Bri W 3E 73
Thrnyland Way PA8: Ersk 2F 57
Thrums G74: E Kil 4D 138
Thrums Av. G64: B'rig 6E 49
Thrums Gdns. G64: B'rig 6E 49
Thrushbush La. ML6: Air 1B 92
Thrushbush Quad. ML6: Air 1A 92
Thrushbush Rd. ML6: Air 1A 92
Thrushcraig Cres. PA2: Pais 3B 98
Thrush Pl. PA5: John 6D 94
Thurso St. G11: Glas 2A 82
Thurston Rd. G52: Glas 6A 80
Thyme Sq. ML1: Moth 1G 143
Tianavaig PA8: Ersk 2G 57
Tibbermore Rd. G11: Glas 6G 61
Tiber Av. ML1: Moth 6E 127
Tighnasheen Way G72: Blan 1B 140
Tillanburn Rd. ML1: N'hill 4F 129
Tillet Oval PA3: Pais 4H 77
Tillie St. G20: Glas 6D 62
Till St. ML2: Wis 3H 145
Tillycairn Av. G33: Glas 1D 86
Tillycairn Dr. G33: Glas 1D 86
Tillycairn Pl. G33: Glas 1E 87
Tillycairn Rd. G33: Glas 1E 87
Tillycairn St. G33: Glas 1E 87
Tilt Rd. ML2: Newm 3D 146
Tilt St. G33: Glas 1G 85
Time Capsule, The 5B 90
Timmons Gro. ML4: Moss 2F 127
Timmons Ter. ML6: Chap 4D 112
Tinker's La. ML1: Moth 3E 143
Tintagel Gdns. G69: Mood 4D 52
TINTOCK 3A 32
Tintock Dr. G66: Kirk 4F 31
Tintock Pl. G68: Dull 5F 13
Tintock Rd. G66: Kirk 3H 31
Tinto Ct. ML5: Coat 2E 111
Tinto Cres. ML2: Wis 1A 158
Tinto Dr. G78: Barr 6D 114
Tinto Rd. G43: Glas 2A 118
G61: Bear 1B 44
G64: B'rig 6F 49
ML6: Air 5B 92
Tinto Sq. PA4: Renf 2D 78
Tinto St. ML2: Wis 1A 158
Tinto Vw. ML3: Ham 3A 154
Tinto Vw. Rd. ML9: Shaw 6H 161
Tinto Way G75: E Kil 6D 148
ML1: Cle 5H 129
Tinwald Path G52: Glas 6A 80
Tiree G74: E Kil 4C 150
Tiree Av. PA2: Pais 6H 97
PA4: Renf 3E 79
Tiree Ct. G67: Cumb 5F 35
Tiree Cres. ML2: Newm 2D 146
Tiree Dr. G67: Cumb 5F 35
Tiree Gdns. G60: Old K 1G 41
G61: Bear 1B 44
ML6: Glenm 4H 71
Tiree Grange ML3: Ham 2D 152

Veitches Ct.—Weavers Ct.


itches Ct. G81: Dun .......... 1C 42
itch Pl. G66: Len .......... 3F 7
nnacher Rd. PA4: Renf .......... 5C 58
nnard Gdns. G41: Glas .......... 3C 102
rmont Av. G73: Ruth .......... 6C 104
rmont St. G41: Glas .......... 6B 82
rnon Bank G74: E Kil .......... 6G 137
rnon Dr. PA3: Lin .......... 5G 75
rona Av. G14: Glas .......... 5C 60
rona Gdns. G14: Glas .......... 5C 60
rona La. G14: Glas .......... 5C 60
salius St. G32: Glas .......... 6A 86
aduct Rd. G76: Busby .......... 2D 134
carfield St. G51: Glas .......... 4H 81
CARLAND .......... 2A 122
carland Pl. G72: Camb .......... 3A 122
carland Rd. G72: Camb .......... 2A 122
cars Wlk. G72: Camb .......... 2B 122
ckers St. ML1: Moth .......... 1D 142
ctoria Av. G78: Barr .......... 3D 114
ML8: Carl .......... 4E 165
ctoria Baths .......... 5F 59
ctoria Bri. G5: Glas .......... 5G 83
ctoria Cir. G12: Glas .......... 6A 62
ctoria Ct. ML9: Lark .......... 1E 161
ctoria Cres. G65: Kils .......... 3F 11
G76: Busby .......... 2D 134
G78: Barr .......... 3D 114
ML2: Wis .......... 5D 144
ML6: Air .......... 5G 91
ctoria Cres. La. G12: Glas .......... 6A 62
ctoria Cres. Pl. G12: Glas .......... 6A 62
ctoria Cres. Rd. G12: Glas .......... 6A 62
ctoria Cross G42: Glas .......... 3E 103
ctoria Dr. G78: Barr .......... 3D 114
ctoria Dr. E. PA4: Renf .......... 1E 79
ctoria Dr. W. PA4: Renf .......... 6D 58
ctoria Gdns. G78: Barr .......... 3D 114
ML6: Air .......... 4H 91
PA2: Pais .......... 3G 97
ctoria Glade G68: Dull .......... 5F 13
ctoria Gro. G78: Barr .......... 3D 114
ctoria Pk. G65: Kils .......... 3F 11
ctoria Pk. Cnr. G14: Glas .......... 6D 60
ctoria Pk. Dr. Nth.
G14: Glas .......... 5D 60
ctoria Pk. Dr. Sth.
G14: Glas .......... 6D 60
(not continuous)
ctoria Pk. Gdns. Nth.
G11: Glas .......... 6F 61
ctoria Pk. Gdns. Sth.
G11: Glas .......... 6F 61
ctoria Pk. La. Nth. G14: Glas .......... 6D 60
ctoria Pk. La. Sth. *G14: Glas* .......... *6D 60*
*(off Westland Dr.)*
ctoria Pk. St. G14: Glas .......... 6D 60
ctoria Pl. G62: Miln .......... 4H 25
G65: Kils .......... 3G 11
*G73: Ruth* .......... *5C 104*
*(off King St.)*
G78: Barr .......... 3E 115
G81: Hard .......... 1D 42
ML4: Bell .......... 3B 126
ML6: Air .......... 5G 91
ictoria Quad. ML1: Holy .......... 2H 127
ctoria Rd. G33: Step .......... 4C 66
G42: Glas .......... 4E 103
G66: Lenz .......... 3C 50
G68: Dull .......... 5F 13
G73: Ruth .......... 1D 120
G78: Barr .......... 3D 114
PA2: Pais .......... 3G 97
PA5: Brkfld .......... 6D 74
ictoria St. G66: Kirk .......... 5C 30
G72: Blan .......... 3B 140
G73: Ruth .......... 5C 104
G82: Dumb .......... 5G 17
ML2: Newm .......... 5E 147
ML3: Ham .......... 3F 141
ML9: Lark .......... 2E 161
ictoria Ter. G68: Dull .......... 5F 13
ictor St. ML6: Plain .......... 1G 93
ictory Dr. PA10: Kilb .......... 1A 94
ICTORY GARDENS .......... 1E 79
ictory Way G69: Bail .......... 1H 107
iewbank G46: T'bnk .......... 4G 117
iewbank Av. ML6: C'bnk .......... 3B 112
iewbank St. ML5: Glenb .......... 4B 70
IEWFIELD .......... 4B 126
iewfield G69: Mood .......... 3C 52
ML6: Air .......... 5G 91
iewfield Av. G64: B'rig .......... 1A 64
G66: Lenz .......... 2C 50
G66: Milt C .......... 6B 8
G69: Bail .......... 6F 87
G72: Blan .......... 6C 124
iewfield Dr. G64: B'rig .......... 1A 64
G69: Bail .......... 6F 87
iewfield La. G12: Glas .......... 1C 82
Viewfield Rd. FK4: Bank .......... 1D 14
G64: B'rig .......... 1A 64
ML4: Bell .......... 4B 126
ML5: Coat .......... 1F 109
Viewglen Ct. G45: Glas .......... 6H 119
Viewmount Dr. G20: Glas .......... 2B 62
VIEWPARK .......... 6G 109
Viewpark G62: Miln .......... 4H 25
Viewpark Av. G31: Glas .......... 3D 84
Viewpark Ct. G73: Ruth .......... 1E 121
Viewpark Dr. G73: Ruth .......... 1D 120
Viewpark Gardens .......... 1F 125
Viewpark Gdns. PA4: Renf .......... 1D 78
Viewpark Pl. ML1: Moth .......... 3E 143
Viewpark Rd. ML1: Moth .......... 3E 143
Viewpark Shop. Cen.
G71: View .......... 1H 125
Viewpoint Pl. G21: Glas .......... 3B 64
Viewpoint Rd. G21: Glas .......... 3B 64
Vigilant Ho. PA3: Pais .......... 4A 78
Viking Cres. PA6: C'lee .......... 3D 74
Viking Rd. ML6: Air .......... 6B 92
Viking Ter. G75: E Kil .......... 5G 149
Viking Way G46: T'bnk .......... 2F 117
PA4: Renf .......... 2E 79
Villafield Av. G64: B'rig .......... 4C 48
Villafield Dr. G64: B'rig .......... 4C 48
Villafield Loan G64: B'rig .......... 4C 48
Village Gdns. G72: Blan .......... 6C 124
Village Rd. G72: Flem .......... 2E 123
Vincent Ct. *ML4: Bell* .......... *3C 126*
*(off Gardenside)*
Vine St. G11: Glas .......... 1H 81
Vinicombe La. *G12: Glas* .......... *6B 62*
*(off Vinicombe St.)*
Vinicombe St. G12: Glas .......... 6B 62
Vintner St. G4: Glas .......... 1G 83
Viola Pl. G64: Torr .......... 5E 29
Violet Gdns. ML8: Carl .......... 5E 165
Violet Pl. ML1: Holy .......... 1B 128
Violet St. PA1: Pais .......... 1C 98
Virginia Ct. G1: Glas .......... 4G 83 (6E 5)
Virginia Gdns. G62: Miln .......... 5A 26
Virginia Pl. G1: Glas .......... 4G 83 (6F 5)
Virginia St. G1: Glas .......... 4G 83 (6F 5)
Viscount Av. PA4: Renf .......... 2E 79
Viscount Ga. G71: Both .......... 2C 124
Vivian Av. G62: Miln .......... 4F 25
Voil Dr. G44: Glas .......... 3E 119
Vorlich Ct. G78: Barr .......... 6E 115
Vorlich Gdns. G61: Bear .......... 6C 24
Vorlich Wynd ML1: N'hill .......... 3C 128
Vulcan St. G21: Glas .......... 5A 64
(not continuous)
ML1: Moth .......... 1G 143

## W

Waddell Av. ML6: Glenm .......... 5F 71
Waddell Ct. G5: Glas .......... 6H 83
Waddell St. G5: Glas .......... 1H 103
ML6: Air .......... 2A 92
Waid Av. G77: Newt M .......... 3C 132
Waldemar Rd. G13: Glas .......... 2C 60
Waldo St. G13: Glas .......... 2F 61
Walkerburn Dr. ML2: Wis .......... 3A 146
Walkerburn Rd. G52: Glas .......... 1B 100
Walker Ct. G11: Glas .......... 2H 81
Walker Dr. PA5: Eld .......... 3H 95
Walker Path G71: Tann .......... 5E 109
Walker St. G11: Glas .......... 2H 81
PA1: Pais .......... 1H 97
Walkinshaw Rd. PA4: Inch .......... 6F 57
Walkinshaw St. G40: Glas .......... 1C 104
PA5: John .......... 2F 95
(Collier St.)
PA5: John .......... 2F 95
(High St.)
Walkinshaw Way PA3: Pais .......... 4A 78
Wallace Av. PA5: Eld .......... 2A 96
PA7: B'ton .......... 4H 39
Wallace Dr. G33: B'rig .......... 1F 65
ML9: Lark .......... 3G 161
Wallacegait PA4: Renf .......... 6D 58
Wallace Gdns. G64: Torr .......... 4D 28
Wallace Ga. G33: B'rig .......... 1F 65
Wallace Ho. G67: Cumb .......... 3G 35
Wallace Pl. G33: B'rig .......... 1F 65
G72: Blan .......... 6C 124
ML3: Ham .......... 1C 154
Wallace Rd. ML1: New S .......... 5B 128
PA4: Renf .......... 2C 78
Wallace St. G5: Glas .......... 5E 83
G33: B'rig .......... 1F 65
G73: Ruth .......... 6C 104
G81: Clyd .......... 1D 58
G82: Dumb .......... 5G 17
ML1: Moth .......... 2F 143
ML5: Coat .......... 6C 90
Wallace St. ML6: Plain .......... 1G 93
PA3: Pais .......... 5A 78
Wallacewell Cres. G21: Glas .......... 4D 64
Wallacewell Pl. G21: Glas .......... 4D 64
Wallacewell Quad.
G21: Glas .......... 3E 65
Wallacewell Rd. G21: Glas .......... 4C 64
Wallace Wynd ML8: Law .......... 5E 159
Wallbrae Rd. G67: Cumb .......... 5A 36
Waller Gdns. G41: Glas .......... 4B 102
Wallneuk PA3: Pais .......... 6B 78
Wallneuk Rd. PA3: Pais .......... 6B 78
Walls St. G1: Glas .......... 4H 83 (6G 5)
Walmer Cres. G51: Glas .......... 5A 82
Walnut Ct. G66: Milt C .......... 6B 8
Walnut Cres. G22: Glas .......... 4H 63
PA5: John .......... 4H 95
Walnut Dr. G66: Lenz .......... 1B 50
Walnut Ga. G72: Flem .......... 3F 123
Walnut Pl. G22: Glas .......... 4G 63
G71: View .......... 4G 109
Walnut Rd. G22: Glas .......... 4G 63
Walpole Pl. PA5: John .......... 6D 94
Walter St. G31: Glas .......... 4D 84
ML2: Wis .......... 6B 146
Walton Av. G77: Newt M .......... 3C 132
Walton Ct. G46: Giff .......... 5A 118
Walton St. G41: Glas .......... 5C 102
G78: Barr .......... 4E 115
Wamba Av. G13: Glas .......... 1E 61
Wamba Pl. G13: Glas .......... 1E 61
Wamphray Pl. G75: E Kil .......... 4A 148
Wandilla Av. G81: Clyd .......... 5F 43
Wanlock St. G51: Glas .......... 3G 81
Wardend Rd. G64: Torr .......... 4D 28
Warden Rd. G13: Glas .......... 2D 60
Wardhill Rd. G21: Glas .......... 4D 64
Wardhouse Rd. PA2: Pais .......... 6G 97
Wardie Path G33: Glas .......... 4F 87
Wardie Pl. G33: Glas .......... 4F 87
Wardie Rd. G33: Glas .......... 4F 87
Wardlaw Av. G73: Ruth .......... 6D 104
Wardlaw Cres. G75: E Kil .......... 4H 149
Wardlaw Dr. G73: Ruth .......... 5D 104
Wardlaw Rd. G61: Bear .......... 6F 45
WARDPARK .......... 4C 14
Wardpark Ct. G67: Cumb .......... 5D 14
Wardpark E. Ind. Est.
G68: Cumb .......... 3E 15
Wardpark Nth. Ind. Est.
G68: Cumb .......... 4C 14
Wardpark Pl. G67: Cumb .......... 5D 14
Wardpark Rd. G67: Cumb .......... 5C 14
WARDPARK RDBT. .......... 4D 14
Wardpark Sth. Ind. Est.
G67: Cumb .......... 5D 14
Wardrop Pl. G74: E Kil .......... 6H 137
Wardrop St. G51: Glas .......... 3G 81
PA1: Pais .......... 1A 98
Wards Cres. ML5: Coat .......... 6A 90
Ware Rd. G34: Glas .......... 4F 87
Warilda Av. G81: Clyd .......... 5E 43
Warlock Dr. PA11: Bri W .......... 2F 73
Warlock Rd. PA11: Bri W .......... 2F 73
Warnock Cres. ML4: Bell .......... 3D 126
Warnock Rd. G77: Newt M .......... 3C 132
Warnock St. G31: Glas .......... 3A 84
Warren Rd. ML3: Ham .......... 3H 153
Warren St. G42: Glas .......... 4F 103
Warren Wlk. G66: Len .......... 4G 7
Warrington Ct. G33: Glas .......... 3H 85
Warriston Cres. G33: Glas .......... 3F 85
Warriston Pl. G32: Glas .......... 4B 86
Warriston St. G33: Glas .......... 3F 85
Warriston Way *G73: Ruth* .......... *3F 121*
*(off Kilbride Rd.)*
Warroch St. G3: Glas .......... 4D 82
Warwick G74: E Kil .......... 5C 138
Warwick Gro. ML3: Ham .......... 4C 140
Warwick Vs. *G81: Clyd* .......... *2G 59*
*(off Edward St.)*
Washington Rd. G66: Kirk .......... 5B 30
PA3: Pais .......... 3B 78
Washington St. G3: Glas .......... 4E 83 (6A 4)
Watchmeal Cres. G81: Faif .......... 6E 23
Waterbank Rd. G76: Crmck .......... 3H 135
WATERFOOT .......... 6B 134
Waterfoot Av. G53: Glas .......... 5C 100
Waterfoot Bank G74: T'hall .......... 6C 134
Waterfoot Rd. G74: T'hall .......... 6C 134
Waterfoot Rd. G77: Newt M .......... 6F 133
Waterfoot Row G76: Water .......... 6B 134
Waterfoot Ter. *G53: Glas* .......... *5C 100*
*(off Waterfoot Av.)*
Waterford Rd. G46: Giff .......... 4H 117
Waterhaughs Gdns. G33: Glas .......... 2F 65
Waterhaughs Gro. G33: Glas .......... 2F 65
Waterhaughs Pl. G33: Glas .......... 2F 65
Waterlands Gdns. ML8: Carl .......... 2G 165
Waterlands Pl. ML8: Law .......... 1A 164
Waterlands Rd. ML8: Law .......... 5F 159
WATERLOO .......... 2B 158
Waterloo Cl. G66: Kirk .......... 4D 30
Waterloo Gdns. *G66: Kirk* .......... *4D 30*
*(off John St.)*
Waterloo La. G2: Glas .......... 4F 83 (5C 4)
Waterloo St. G2: Glas .......... 4E 83 (5B 4)
G66: Kirk .......... 4D 30
Watermill Av. G66: Lenz .......... 3D 50
Water Rd. G78: Barr .......... 4E 115
Water Row G51: Glas .......... 3G 81
Watershaugh Dr. ML1: Cle .......... 5H 129
WATERSIDE
Barrhead .......... 2G 115
Kirkintilloch .......... 6H 31
Waterside Av. G77: Newt M .......... 5C 132
Waterside Cotts. G66: Kirk .......... 6H 31
Waterside Ct. G76: Crmck .......... 2H 135
Waterside Dr. G77: Newt M .......... 5C 132
Waterside Gdns. G72: Flem .......... 4E 123
G76: Crmck .......... 2H 135
ML3: Ham .......... 2A 154
Waterside La. PA10: John .......... 3C 94
Waterside Rd. G66: Kirk .......... 6E 31
(not continuous)
G76: Crmck .......... 4H 135
Waterside St. G5: Glas .......... 1H 103
Waterside Ter. *PA10: Kilb* .......... *3C 94*
*(off Kilbarchan Rd.)*
Waterside Way PA10: Kilb .......... 3C 94
Water Sports Cen. .......... 3C 142
Watling Pl. G75: E Kil .......... 2C 148
Watling St. G71: Tann .......... 4C 108
ML1: Moth .......... 6D 126
Watson Av. G73: Ruth .......... 6B 104
PA3: Lin .......... 5H 75
Watson Cres. G65: Kils .......... 3A 12
Watson Pl. G72: Blan .......... 2H 139
Watson St. G1: Glas .......... 5H 83 (6H 5)
G71: Udd .......... 2D 124
G72: Blan .......... 2H 139
ML1: Moth .......... 4G 143
ML9: Lark .......... 2D 160
Watsonville Pk. ML1: Moth .......... 3G 143
Watt Cres. ML4: Bell .......... 6D 110
Watt La. PA11: Bri W .......... 4G 73
Watt Low Av. G73: Ruth .......... 1B 120
Watt Pl. G62: Miln .......... 2F 25
G72: Blan .......... 5A 140
Watt Rd. G52: Hill .......... 4H 79
PA11: Bri W .......... 4F 73
Watt St. G5: Glas .......... 5D 82
ML6: Air .......... 2C 92
Waukglen Av. G53: Glas .......... 5B 116
Waukglen Cres. G53: Glas .......... 4C 116
Waukglen Dr. G53: Glas .......... 4B 116
Waukglen Gdns. G53: Glas .......... 5B 116
Waukglen Path G53: Glas .......... 4B 116
Waukglen Pl. G53: Glas .......... 4B 116
Waukglen Rd. G53: Glas .......... 4B 116
Waulking Mill Rd.
G81: Faif, Hard .......... 6E 23
Waulkmill Av. G78: Barr .......... 3F 115
Waulkmill St. G46: T'bnk .......... 3E 117
Waulkmill Way G78: Barr .......... 3F 115
Waverley G74: E Kil .......... 5D 138
G81: Clyd .......... 5E 43
Waverley Ct. G71: Both .......... 5E 125
PA2: Pais .......... 5D 96
Waverley Cres. G66: Kirk .......... 5E 31
G67: Cumb .......... 6F 35
ML3: Ham .......... 5D 140
Waverley Dr. G73: Ruth .......... 6E 105
ML2: Wis .......... 5H 145
ML6: Air .......... 2B 92
Waverley Gdns. G41: Glas .......... 4C 102
PA5: Eld .......... 3B 96
WAVERLEY PARK .......... 4B 102
Waverley Pk. G66: Kirk .......... 5D 30
Waverley Rd. PA2: Pais .......... 6D 96
Waverley St. G41: Glas .......... 4C 102
ML3: Ham .......... 5D 140
ML5: Coat .......... 2D 90
ML9: Lark .......... 5E 161
Waverley Ter. G72: Blan .......... 4A 140
G82: Dumb .......... 3B 16
Waverley Way PA2: Pais .......... 6D 96
Weardale La. G33: Glas .......... 3C 86
Weardale St. G33: Glas .......... 3C 86
Weaver Av. G77: Newt M .......... 2C 132
Weaver Cres. ML6: Air .......... 6A 92
Weaver La. PA10: Kilb .......... 1A 94
Weaver Pl. G75: E Kil .......... 4A 148
Weavers Av. PA2: Pais .......... 2F 97
Weaver's Cottage .......... *2A 94*
*(off Weavers Ct.)*
Weaver's Cottage Mus., The .......... 3A 92
Weavers Ct. *G74: E Kil* .......... *1H 149*
*(off Parkhall St.)*
PA10: Kilb .......... 2A 94

Weaver's Ga.—Whitacres Path

Weaver's Ga. PA1: Pais . . . . . . . . .2E 97
Weavers Rd. PA2: Pais . . . . . . . . . .2F 97
Weaver St. G4: Glas . . . . . .4H 83 (5H 5)
Weaver Ter. PA2: Pais . . . . . . . . . .2C 98
Webster Groves ML2: Wis . . . . . .4B 146
Webster St. G40: Glas . . . . . . . . .2C 104
G81: Clyd . . . . . . . . . . . . . . . .1G 59
Wedderlea Dr. G52: Glas . . . . . . . .6A 80
Wedsley Ct. G41: Glas . . . . . . . . .1C 102
Weensmoor Rd. G53: Glas . . . . . .3H 115
Weeple Dr. PA3: Lin . . . . . . . . . . .5G 75
Weighhouse Cl. PA1: Pais . . . . . . .1A 98
Weigh Ho. Rd. ML8: Carl . . . . . . .2E 165
Weir Av. G78: Barr . . . . . . . . . . . .5E 115
Weir Pl. ML8: Law . . . . . . . . . . . .1H 163
Weir's La. ML8: Carl . . . . . . . . . . .3F 165
Weir St. ML5: Coat . . . . . . . . . . . .4C 90
PA3: Pais . . . . . . . . . . . . . . . .6B 78
Weirwood Av. G69: Bail . . . . . . . .1F 107
Weirwood Gdns. G69: Bail . . . . . .1F 107
Welbeck Rd. G53: Glas . . . . . . . . .2B 116
Weldon Pl. G65: Croy . . . . . . . . . .2B 34
Welfare Av. G72: Camb . . . . . . . .3D 122
Welland Pl. G75: E Kil . . . . . . . . .4A 148
Wellbank Pl. G71: Udd . . . . . . . . .2D 124
Wellbeck Ho. G74: E Kil . . . . . . . .1H 149
(off Stuart St.)
Wellbrae Hill ML9: Lark . . . . . . . .3E 161
Wellbrae Rd. ML3: Ham . . . . . . . .2F 153
Wellbrae Ter. G69: Mood . . . . . . . .5D 52
Wellcroft Pl. G5: Glas . . . . . . . . . .1F 103
(not continuous)
Wellcroft Rd. ML3: Ham . . . . . . . .6C 140
Wellcroft Ter. ML3: Ham . . . . . . .6C 140
Wellesley Cres. G68: Cumb . . . . . .4A 34
G75: E Kil . . . . . . . . . . . . . . .4B 148
Wellesley Dr. G68: Cumb . . . . . . . .4H 33
G75: E Kil . . . . . . . . . . . . . . .3B 148
Wellesley Pl. G68: Cumb . . . . . . . .4H 33
Wellfield Av. G46: Giff . . . . . . . . .4H 117
Wellfield St. G21: Glas . . . . . . . . . .5B 64
Wellgate Ct. ML9: Lark . . . . . . . . .1E 161
Wellgate St. ML9: Lark . . . . . . . . .1E 161
Well Grn. G43: Glas . . . . . . . . . . .5A 102
Well Grn. Ct. G43: Glas . . . . . . . .5A 102
(off Well Grn.)
Wellhall Ct. ML3: Ham . . . . . . . . .5F 141
Wellhall Rd. ML3: Ham . . . . . . . . .1C 152
Wellhouse Cres. G33: Glas . . . . . . .4E 87
Wellhouse Gdns. G33: Glas . . . . . .4F 87
Wellhouse Gro. G33: Glas . . . . . . .4F 87
Wellhouse Path G34: Glas . . . . . . .4F 87
Wellhouse Rd. G33: Glas . . . . . . . .3F 87
Wellington G75: E Kil . . . . . . . . . .4D 148
Wellington La. G2: Glas . . .4E 83 (5B 4)
(not continuous)
Wellington Path G69: Bail . . . . . .1H 107
Wellington Pl. G81: Clyd . . . . . . . .4H 41
ML2: Wis . . . . . . . . . . . . . . .3B 158
ML5: Coat . . . . . . . . . . . . . . . .6G 89
Wellington Rd. G64: B'rig . . . . . . .3D 48
Wellington St. G2: Glas . . . .4F 83 (6C 4)
ML2: Wis . . . . . . . . . . . . . . . .4C 144
ML6: Air . . . . . . . . . . . . . . . . .2A 92
PA3: Pais . . . . . . . . . . . . . . . .5H 77
Wellington Way PA4: Renf . . . . . . .2E 79
Wellknowe Av. G74: T'hall . . . . . .6G 135
Wellknowe Pl. G74: T'hall . . . . . . .6F 135
Wellknowe Rd. G74: T'hall . . . . . .6G 135
Well La. G66: Len . . . . . . . . . . . . . . .3F 7
Wellmeadow Cl. G77: Newt M . . .4D 132
Wellmeadow Grn.
G77: Newt M . . . . . . . . . . . .3D 132
Wellmeadow Rd. G43: Glas . . . . .1H 117
Wellmeadow St. PA1: Pais . . . . . . .1H 97
Wellmeadow Way
G77: Newt M . . . . . . . . . . . .4D 132
Wellpark La. G78: Neil . . . . . . . . .3D 130
Wellpark Rd. FK4: Bank . . . . . . . . .1D 14
ML1: Moth . . . . . . . . . . . . . . .3E 143
Wellpark St. G31: Glas . . . . . . . . . .4A 84
Wellpark Ter. G78: Neil . . . . . . . . .3D 130
Well Rd. PA10: Kilb . . . . . . . . . . . .2A 94
Wellshot Cotts. G65: Kils . . . . . . . .4H 11
Wellshot Dr. G72: Camb . . . . . . . .2H 121
Wellshot Rd. G32: Glas . . . . . . . . .2H 105
WELLSIDE . . . . . . . . . . . . . . . . .3D 122
Wellside Av. ML6: Air . . . . . . . . . . .2A 92
Wellside Dr. G72: Camb . . . . . . . .3C 122
Wellside La. ML6: Air . . . . . . . . . . .2B 92
Wellside Quad. ML6: Air . . . . . . . . .1A 92
Wellsquarry Rd. G76: Crmck . . . .5E 137
Wells St. G81: Clyd . . . . . . . . . . . .4B 42
Well St. PA1: Pais . . . . . . . . . . . . .6G 77
PA3: Pais . . . . . . . . . . . . . . . .6G 77
Wellview Dr. ML1: Moth . . . . . . . .3F 143
Wellwynd ML6: Air . . . . . . . . . . . . .3H 91
Wellwynd Gdns. ML6: Air . . . . . . .3H 91
Welsh Dr. G72: Blan . . . . . . . . . . .3B 140
ML3: Ham . . . . . . . . . . . . . . .4G 153
Welsh Row ML6: C'bnk . . . . . . . .2C 112
Wemyss Av. G77: Newt M . . . . . .2C 132
Wemyss Dr. G68: Cumb . . . . . . . . .4A 34
Wemyss Gdns. G69: Bail . . . . . . .2G 107
Wendur Way PA3: Pais . . . . . . . . . .3A 78
Wenlock Rd. PA2: Pais . . . . . . . . . .3B 98
Wensleydale G74: E Kil . . . . . . . .6E 137
Wentworth Dr. G23: Glas . . . . . . . .6C 46
Wesley St. ML6: Air . . . . . . . . . . . .4H 91
Westacres Rd. G77: Newt M . . . .5A 132
WEST ARTHURLIE . . . . . . . . . . .6C 114
West Av. G33: Step . . . . . . . . . . . .4D 66
G71: View . . . . . . . . . . . . . . .1F 125
G72: Blan . . . . . . . . . . . . . . .4C 140
ML1: New S . . . . . . . . . . . . . .5A 128
ML6: Plain . . . . . . . . . . . . . . .1G 93
ML8: Carl . . . . . . . . . . . . . . .4D 164
PA1: Pais . . . . . . . . . . . . . . . .1B 96
PA4: Renf . . . . . . . . . . . . . . . .6F 59
WEST BALGROCHAN . . . . . . . . . .3D 28
W. Balgrochan Rd. G64: Torr . . . . .4D 28
Westbank Ct. G12: Glas . . . . . . . . .1C 82
(off Westbank Quad.)
Westbank La. G12: Glas . . . . . . . . .1C 82
(off Gibson St.)
Westbank Quad. G12: Glas . . . . . . .1C 82
Westbourne Cres. G61: Bear . . . . .2C 44
Westbourne Dr. G61: Bear . . . . . . .2C 44
Westbourne Gdns. La.
G12: Glas . . . . . . . . . . . . . . . . .5A 62
Westbourne Gdns. Nth.
G12: Glas . . . . . . . . . . . . . . . . .5A 62
Westbourne Gdns. Sth.
G12: Glas . . . . . . . . . . . . . . . . .5A 62
Westbourne Gdns. W.
G12: Glas . . . . . . . . . . . . . . . . .5H 61
Westbourne Rd. G12: Glas . . . . . . .5H 61
Westbourne Ter. La. Nth.
G12: Glas . . . . . . . . . . . . . . . . .5H 61
Westbourne Ter. La. Sth.
G12: Glas . . . . . . . . . . . . . . . . .5H 61
West Brae PA1: Pais . . . . . . . . . . . .1H 97
Westbrae Dr. G14: Glas . . . . . . . . .5E 61
Westbrae Rd. G77: Newt M . . . . .3F 133
West Bridgend G82: Dumb . . . . . . .3E 17
W. Buchanan Pl. PA1: Pais . . . . . .1H 97
WESTBURN . . . . . . . . . . . . . . .1E 123
Westburn Av. G72: Camb . . . . . . .1D 122
PA3: Pais . . . . . . . . . . . . . . . .6E 77
Westburn Cres. G73: Ruth . . . . . .6B 104
G81: Hard . . . . . . . . . . . . . . . .6D 22
Westburn Dr. G72: Camb . . . . . . .6B 106
Westburn Farm Rd.
G72: Camb . . . . . . . . . . . . . .1B 122
Westburn Rd.
G72: Camb, Newt . . . . . . . . .2B 122
W. Burnside St. G65: Kils . . . . . . .3H 11
W. Campbell St. G2: Glas . .4E 83 (6B 4)
PA1: Pais . . . . . . . . . . . . . . . .1F 97
W. Canal St. ML5: Coat . . . . . . . . .5B 90
Westcastle Ct. G45: Glas . . . . . . .4H 119
Westcastle Cres. G45: Glas . . . . .4H 119
Westcastle Gdns. G45: Glas . . . . .4H 119
Westcastle Gro. G45: Glas . . . . . .4H 119
W. Chapelton Av. G61: Bear . . . . . .3F 45
W. Chapelton Cres. G61: Bear . . . .3F 45
W. Chapelton Dr. G61: Bear . . . . . .3F 45
W. Chapelton La. G61: Bear . . . . . .3F 45
Westcliff G82: Dumb . . . . . . . . . . .3B 16
W. Clyde St. ML9: Lark . . . . . . . . .3F 161
Westclyffe St. G41: Glas . . . . . . . .4C 102
W. Coats Rd. G72: Camb . . . . . . .3H 121
West Ct. G81: Clyd . . . . . . . . . . . .3A 42
PA1: Pais . . . . . . . . . . . . . . . .1E 97
WEST CRAIGEND . . . . . . . . . . . .6E 41
WEST CRINDLEDYKE . . . . . . . . .3D 146
West Cross ML2: Wis . . . . . . . . . .6G 145
West Dr. ML6: Air . . . . . . . . . . . . .5E 93
WEST DRUMOYNE . . . . . . . . . . .4D 80
Westend G61: Bear . . . . . . . . . . . .5G 45
Westend Ct. ML8: Law . . . . . . . . .1H 163
W. End Dr. ML4: Bell . . . . . . . . . .3A 126
Westend Pk. St. G3: Glas . . . . . . . .2D 82
W. End Pl. ML4: Bell . . . . . . . . . .3B 126
WESTER AUCHINLOCH . . . . . . . .6D 50
Westerburn St. G32: Glas . . . . . . . .5H 85
Wester Carriagehill PA2: Pais . . . .3H 97
Wester Cleddens Rd.
G64: B'rig . . . . . . . . . . . . . . . .5C 48
Wester Cochno Holdings
G81: Hard . . . . . . . . . . . . . . . .5D 22
Wester Comn. Dr. G22: Glas . . . . .5E 63
Wester Comn. Rd. G22: Glas . . . . .5E 63
Westercraigs G31: Glas . . . . . . . . .4B 84
Westercraigs Ct. G31: Glas . . . . . .4B 84
Westerdale G74: E Kil . . . . . . . . .6E 137
Westerfield Rd. G76: Crmck . . . . .5H 135
Westergate Shop. Cen. G2: Glas . . .6C 4
Wester Gill ML6: Air . . . . . . . . . . . .5E 93
Westergreens Av. G66: Kirk . . . . . .1B 50
Westerhill Rd. G64: B'rig . . . . . . . .3D 48
WESTER HOLYTOWN . . . . . . . . . .2G 127
Westerhouse Ct. ML8: Carl . . . . . .3D 164
Westerhouse Path G34: Glas . . . . .3G 87
(off Arnisdale Rd.)
Westerhouse Rd. G34: Glas . . . . . .3F 87
WESTERHOUSE ROAD INTERCHANGE
. . . . . . . . . . . . . . . . . . . . . . .3F 87
Westerkirk Dr. G23: Glas . . . . . . . .6C 46
Westerlands G12: Glas . . . . . . . . . .3G 61
Westerlands Dr. G77: Newt M . . .5B 132
Westerlands Gdns.
G77: Newt M . . . . . . . . . . . . .5B 132
Westerlands Gro.
G77: Newt M . . . . . . . . . . . . .5B 132
Westerlands Pl. G77: Newt M . . .4B 132
Westermains Av. G66: Kirk . . . . . .6B 30
Wester Mavisbank Av. ML6: Air . . .3G 91
Wester Moffat Av. ML6: Air . . . . . .3E 93
Wester Moffat Cres. ML6: Air . . . . .4E 93
Wester Myvot Rd. G67: Cumb . . . .3C 54
Western Av. G73: Ruth . . . . . . . . .5B 104
Western Baths Club . . . . . . . . . . .6B 62
Western Isles Rd. G60: Old K . . . .1G 41
Western Rd. G72: Camb . . . . . . . .3G 121
Wester Rd. G32: Glas . . . . . . . . . .1D 106
Westerton G66: Len . . . . . . . . . . . . .3H 7
Westerton Av. G61: Bear . . . . . . . . .1F 61
G76: Busby . . . . . . . . . . . . . . .4E 135
ML9: Lark . . . . . . . . . . . . . . .4E 161
Westerton Ct. G76: Busby . . . . . .4E 135
Westerton La. G76: Busby . . . . . .4E 135
Westerton Rd. G68: Dull . . . . . . . . .5F 13
Westerton Station (Rail) . . . . . . .6E 45
WESTERWOOD . . . . . . . . . . . . . .6A 14
W. Fairholm St. ML9: Lark . . . . . .6H 155
WEST FERRY INTERCHANGE . . . .1A 38
WESTFIELD
Cumbernauld . . . . . . . . . . . .6B 34
Kilsyth . . . . . . . . . . . . . . . . .2F 11
Westfield G82: Dumb . . . . . . . . . . .3C 16
Westfield Av. G73: Ruth . . . . . . . .6B 104
Westfield Cres. G61: Bear . . . . . . .5E 45
Westfield Dr. G52: Glas . . . . . . . . .6A 80
G61: Bear . . . . . . . . . . . . . . . .5E 45
G68: Cumb . . . . . . . . . . . . . . .6A 34
Westfield Ind. Area G68: Cumb . . .1H 53
Westfield Ind. Est. G68: Cumb . . . .2A 54
Westfield Pl. G68: Cumb . . . . . . . .1H 53
Westfield Rd. G46: T'bnk . . . . . . .5G 117
G65: Kils . . . . . . . . . . . . . . . . .2F 11
G68: Cumb . . . . . . . . . . . . . . .1H 53
ML1: N'hse . . . . . . . . . . . . . .6C 112
Westfields G64: B'rig . . . . . . . . . .4A 48
Westgarth Pl. G74: E Kil . . . . . . .6C 136
West Ga. ML2: Wis . . . . . . . . . . .6B 146
Westgate Way ML4: Bell . . . . . . .3B 126
W. George La. G2: Glas . . . .3E 83 (4A 4)
W. George St. G2: Glas . . . .3E 83 (4A 4)
(not continuous)
ML5: Coat . . . . . . . . . . . . . . . .3C 90
W. Glebe Ter. ML3: Ham . . . . . . .1G 153
W. Graham St. G4: Glas . . .2E 83 (1B 4)
W. Greenhill Pl. G3: Glas . . . . . . . .3C 82
W. Hamilton St. ML1: Moth . . . . .3G 143
W. High St. G66: Kirk . . . . . . . . . .4C 30
Westhorn Dr. G32: Glas . . . . . . . .4A 106
Westhouse Av. G73: Ruth . . . . . .6A 104
Westhouse Gdns. G73: Ruth . . . . .6A 104
W. Kirk St. ML6: Air . . . . . . . . . . . .4H 91
Westknowe Gdns. G73: Ruth . . . .2D 120
Westland Dr. G14: Glas . . . . . . . . .6D 60
Westland Dr. La. G14: Glas . . . . . .6D 60
(off Westland Dr.)
Westlands Gdns. PA2: Pais . . . . . .3H 97
West La. PA1: Pais . . . . . . . . . . . .1F 97
Westlea Pl. ML6: Air . . . . . . . . . . .5B 92
W. Lodge Rd. PA4: Renf . . . . . . . .5D 58
WEST MAINS . . . . . . . . . . . . . . .1D 148
W. Mains Rd. G74: E Kil . . . . . . . .1D 148
WEST MARYSTON . . . . . . . . . . . .4B 88
Westminster Ter. G3: Glas . . . . . . .3C 82
(off Royal Cres.)
Westmoreland St. G42: Glas . . . .3E 103
Westmuir Pl. G73: Ruth . . . . . . . .5B 104
Westmuir St. G31: Glas . . . . . . . . .6F 85
W. Nile St. G1: Glas . . . . . .4F 83 (5D 4)
G2: Glas . . . . . . . . . . . .3F 83 (4D 4)
West of Scotland Go-Kart Circuit
. . . . . . . . . . . . . . . . . . . . . . .5A 156
West of Scotland Indoor Bowling Club
. . . . . . . . . . . . . . . . . . . . . . .3A 104
West of Scotland R.U.F.C. . . . . . .5H 25
Westpark Dr. PA3: Pais . . . . . . . . .6F 77
West Pl. ML2: Newm . . . . . . . . . .4E 147
Westport G75: E Kil . . . . . . . . . . .2C 148
WEST PORTON . . . . . . . . . . . . . .3G 39
W. Porton Pl. PA7: B'ton . . . . . . . .3F 39
Westport St. G65: Kils . . . . . . . . . .3H 11
W. Prince's La. G4: Glas . . . . . . . .1C 82
W. Prince's St. G4: Glas . . .1D 82 (1A
Westray Av. G77: Newt M . . . . . . .2C 1
Westray Cir. G22: Glas . . . . . . . . . .3G 6
Westray Ct. G67: Cumb . . . . . . . . .5G 3
Westray Pl. G22: Glas . . . . . . . . . .2H 6
G64: B'rig . . . . . . . . . . . . . . . . .5F 4
Westray Rd. G67: Cumb . . . . . . . . .5G 3
Westray Sq. G22: Glas . . . . . . . . . .2G 6
Westray St. G22: Glas . . . . . . . . . .2G 6
Westray Wynd ML2: Newm . . . . .3D 1
(off Iona Rd
W. Regent La. G2: Glas . . . .3F 83 (4C
W. Regent St. G2: Glas . . . .3E 83 (3B
(not continuou
West Rd. G64: Torr . . . . . . . . . . . .4D 2
PA10: Kilb . . . . . . . . . . . . . . . .1A 9
W. Scott Ter. ML3: Ham . . . . . . . .2H 15
Westside Gdns. G11: Glas . . . . . . .1H 8
W. Stewart St. ML3: Ham . . . . . .5G 14
West St. G5: Glas . . . . . . . . . . . . .1E 10
G81: Clyd . . . . . . . . . . . . . . . . .1G 5
PA1: Pais . . . . . . . . . . . . . . . . .1G 9
WEST ST. INTERCHANGE . . . . . . .6D 8
West Street Station (Und.) . . . . . .6E 8
W. Thomson St. G81: Clyd . . . . . . .4C 4
W. Thornlie St. ML2: Wis . . . . . . .1G 15
W. Westbrae Cres. ML3: Ham . . .2F 15
W. Whitby St. G31: Glas . . . . . . . .1E 10
WESTWOOD . . . . . . . . . . . . . . . .3D 14
Westwood Av. G46: Giff . . . . . . . .4H 11
Westwood Cres. ML3: Ham . . . . .1F 15
Westwood Gdns. PA3: Pais . . . . . . .6F 7
Westwood Hill G75: E Kil . . . . . . .3D 14
Westwood Quad. G81: Clyd . . . . . .6F 4
Westwood Rd. G43: Glas . . . . . . .1H 11
G75: E Kil . . . . . . . . . . . . . . . .2D 14
ML2: Newm . . . . . . . . . . . . . .2D 14
Westwood Sq. G75: E Kil . . . . . . .3D 14
Weymouth Dr. G12: Glas . . . . . . . .3G 6
Weymouth La. G12: Glas . . . . . . . .4H 6
(off Chelmsford Dr
Whamflet Av. G69: Bail . . . . . . . . . .4A 8
Whamond Twr. ML1: Moth . . . . . .4G 14
Wheatfield Rd. G61: Bear . . . . . . .4D 4
Wheatholm Cres. ML6: Air . . . . . . .2B 9
Wheatholm St. ML6: Air . . . . . . . . .2B 9
Wheatland Av. G72: Blan . . . . . . .1A 14
Wheatlandhead Ct. G72: Blan . . .1A 14
WHEATLANDS . . . . . . . . . . . . . .1A 14
Wheatlands Dr. PA10: Kilb . . . . . . .1A 9
Wheatlands Farm Rd.
PA10: Kilb . . . . . . . . . . . . . . . .1A 9
Wheatley Ct. G32: Glas . . . . . . . . .6A 8
Wheatley Cres. G65: Kils . . . . . . . .4H 1
Wheatley Dr. G32: Glas . . . . . . . . .6A 8
Wheatley Loan G64: B'rig . . . . . . . .1E 6
Wheatley Pl. G32: Glas . . . . . . . . .6A 8
WHIFFLET . . . . . . . . . . . . . . . . . .6D 9
Whifflet Ct. ML5: Coat . . . . . . . . . .6D 9
(off Whifflet St
Whifflet Station (Rail) . . . . . . . . .6D 9
Whifflet St. ML5: Coat . . . . . . . . .2C 11
Whin Av. G78: Barr . . . . . . . . . . . .3D 11
Whinfell Dr. G75: E Kil . . . . . . . . .5C 14
Whinfell Gdns. G75: E Kil . . . . . . .5C 14
Whinfield Av. G72: Camb . . . . . . .6G 10
Whinfield Rd. G53: Glas . . . . . . . .3A 11
WHINHALL . . . . . . . . . . . . . . . . .2G 9
Whinhall Av. ML6: Air . . . . . . . . . .2G 9
Whinhall Rd. ML6: Air . . . . . . . . . .2G 9
Whin Hill G74: E Kil . . . . . . . . . . .5B 13
Whinhill Pl. G53: Glas . . . . . . . . .2A 10
Whinhill Rd. G53: Glas . . . . . . . . .2A 10
PA2: Pais . . . . . . . . . . . . . . . . .3D 9
WHINKNOWE . . . . . . . . . . . . . . .5C 16
Whinknowe ML9: Ashg . . . . . . . . .5B 16
Whin Loan G65: Queen . . . . . . . . .2A 1
Whinney Gro. ML2: Wis . . . . . . . .5C 14
Whinnie Knowe ML9: Lark . . . . . .4D 16
Whinpark Av. ML4: Bell . . . . . . . .4B 12
Whin Pl. G74: E Kil . . . . . . . . . . .4B 13
Whins Rd. G41: Glas . . . . . . . . . .4A 10
Whin St. G81: Clyd . . . . . . . . . . . .3C 4
Whirlie Ct. PA6: C'lee . . . . . . . . . .2C 7
Whirlie Dr. PA6: C'lee . . . . . . . . . .3B 7
Whirlie Rd. PA6: C'lee . . . . . . . . . .2B 7
WHIRLIES RDBT., THE . . . . . . . . .5A 13
Whirlow Gdns. G69: Bail . . . . . . . .6G 8
Whirlow Rd. G69: Bail . . . . . . . . . .6G 8
Whistleberry Cres. ML3: Ham . . .2F 14
Whistleberry Dr. ML3: Ham . . . . .2E 14
Whistleberry Ind. Pk.
ML3: Ham . . . . . . . . . . . . . . . .2E 14
Whistleberry Pk. ML3: Ham . . . . .2E 14
Whistleberry Retail Pk.
G72: Blan . . . . . . . . . . . . . . . .2D 14
Whistleberry Rd. G72: Blan . . . . .2D 14
ML3: Ham . . . . . . . . . . . . . . . .2E 14
Whistlefield Ct. G61: Bear . . . . . . .4E 4
Whitacres Path G53: Glas . . . . . . .3A 11

# HOSPITALS and HOSPICES
## covered by this atlas
### with their map square reference

N.B. Where Hospitals and Hospices are not named on the map, the reference given is for the road in which they are situated.

CORD HOSPICE —3E **99**
awkhead Hospital Grounds
awkhead Rd.
AISLEY
enfrewshire
A2 7BL
el: 0141 5812000

ORN STREET DAY HOSPITAL —1B **104**
3 Acorn St.
LASGOW
40 4AN
el: 0141 5564789

RBLES ROAD CENTRE —4H **143**
9 Airbles Rd.
OTHERWELL
1L1 2TJ
el: 01698 261331

EXANDER HOSPITAL —3A **90**
lair Rd.
OATBRIDGE
anarkshire
IL5 2EW
el: 01236 422661

AWARTHILL HOSPITAL —3A **60**
29 Holehouse Dr.
LASGOW
13 3TG
el: 0141 211 9000

NNIESBURN HOSPITAL —5E **45**
witchback Rd.
earsden
LASGOW
61 1QL
el: 0141 2115600

ELAND HOSPITAL —1A **146**
ellside Rd.
leland
OTHERWELL
anarkshire
1L1 5NR
el: 01698 245000

ATHILL HOSPITAL —1C **110**
ospital St.
OATBRIDGE
anarkshire
IL5 4DN
el: 01698 245000

WGLEN HOSPITAL —6D **100**
0 Boystone Rd.
LASGOW
53 6XJ
el: 0141 2119200

RUMCHAPEL HOSPITAL —5B **44**
29 Drumchapel Rd.
GLASGOW
15 6PX
el: 0141 2116000

UMBARTON JOINT HOSPITAL —3C **16**
ardross Rd.
UMBARTON
82 5JA
el: 01389 762317

YKEBAR HOSPITAL —6D **98**
Grahamston Rd.
PAISLEY
Renfrewshire
A2 7DE
el: 0141 8845122

SKINE HOSPITAL (PRINCESS LOUISE SCOTTISH HOSPITAL) —2C **40**
Bishopton
BISHOPTON
Renfrewshire
A7 5PU
el: 0141 8121100

ARTNAVEL GENERAL HOSPITAL —5G **61**
053 Gt. Western Rd.
GLASGOW
12 0YN
el: 0141 2113000

ARTNAVEL ROYAL HOSPITAL —4F **61**
055 Gt. Western Rd.
GLASGOW
12 0XH
el: 0141 2113600

GLASGOW DENTAL HOSPITAL —3E **83** (3B **4**)
378 Sauchiehall St.
GLASGOW
G2 3JZ
Tel: 0141 2119600

GLASGOW HOMOEOPATHIC HOSPITAL —5G **61**
1053 Gt. Western Rd.
GLASGOW
G12 0YN
Tel: 0141 2111600

GLASGOW NUFFIELD HOSPITAL, THE —4H **61**
25 Beaconsfield Rd.
GLASGOW
G12 0PJ
Tel: 0141 3349441

GLASGOW ROYAL INFIRMARY —3A **84**
84 Castle St.
GLASGOW
G4 0SF
Tel: 0141 2114000

GOLDEN JUBILEE NATIONAL HOSPITAL —5A **42**
Beardmore St.
CLYDEBANK
G81 4HX
Tel: 0141 9515000

HAIRMYRES HOSPITAL —2B **148**
Eaglesham Rd.
East Kilbride
GLASGOW
G75 8RG
Tel: 01355 220292

HAWKHEAD HOSPITAL —3E **99**
Hawkhead Rd.
PAISLEY
Renfrewshire
PA2 7BL
Tel: 0141 8898151

JOHNSTONE HOSPITAL —1G **95**
Bridge of Weir Rd.
JOHNSTONE
PA5 8YX
Tel: 01505 331471

KIRKLANDS HOSPITAL —3F **125**
Fallside Rd., Bothwell
GLASGOW
G71 8BB
Tel: 01698 245000

LENNOX CASTLE HOSPITAL —2C **6**
Glen Rd., Lennoxtown
GLASGOW
G66 7LB
Tel: 01360 329200

LEVERNDALE HOSPITAL —3H **99**
Crookston Rd.
GLASGOW
G53 7TU
Tel: 0141 2116400

LIGHTBURN HOSPITAL —4B **86**
966 Carntyne Rd.
GLASGOW
G32 6ND
Tel: 0141 2111500

MANSIONHOUSE UNIT, THE —5D **102**
100 Mansionhouse Rd.
GLASGOW
G41 3DX
Tel: 0141 2016161

MARIE CURIE CENTRE, HUNTERS HILL —3B **64**
107 Belmont Rd., GLASGOW
G21 3AY
Tel: 0141 5582555

MERCHISTON HOSPITAL —6E **75**
Bridge of Weir Rd., Brookfield
JOHNSTONE
Renfrewshire
PA5 8TY
Tel: 01505 328261

MONKLANDS DISTRICT GENERAL HOSPITAL —4G **91**
Monkscourt Av.
AIRDRIE
Lanarkshire
ML6 0JS
Tel: 01236 748748

PARKHEAD HOSPITAL —6F **85**
81 Salamanca St.
GLASGOW
G31 5ES
Tel: 0141 211 8300

PRINCE & PRINCESS OF WALES HOSPICE —5F **83**
71 Carlton Pl.
GLASGOW
G5 9TD
Tel: 0141 4295599

PRIORY HOSPITAL, GLASGOW, THE —5D **102**
38 Mansionhouse Rd.
GLASGOW
G41 3DW
Tel: 0141 6366116

QUEEN MOTHER'S MATERNITY HOSPITAL —2A **82**
Dalnair St.
Yorkhill
GLASGOW
G3 8SH
Tel: 0141 2010550

RED DEER DAY HOSPITAL —3E **149**
Alberta Av.
East Kilbride
GLASGOW
G75 8NH
Tel: 01355 244254

ROADMEETINGS HOSPITAL —5H **165**
Goremire Rd.
CARLUKE
Lanarkshire
NL8 4PS
Tel: 01555 77221

ROSS HALL HOSPITAL —2A **100**
221 Crookston Rd.
GLASGOW
G52 3NQ
Tel: 0141 8103151

ROYAL ALEXANDRA HOSPITAL —3H **97**
Corsebar Rd.
PAISLEY
Renfrewshire
PA2 9PN
Tel: 0141 887 9111

ROYAL HOSPITAL FOR SICK CHILDREN —2A **82**
Dalnair St.
Yorkhill
GLASGOW
G3 8SJ
Tel: 0141 2010000

ST ANDREW'S HOSPICE —3A **92**
Henderson St.
AIRDRIE
Lanarkshire
ML6 6DJ
Tel: 01236 766951

ST MARGARET'S HOSPICE —2F **59**
East Barns St.
CLYDEBANK
Dunbartonshire
G81 1EG
Tel: 0141 9521141

ST VINCENT'S HOSPICE —6B **94**
Midton Rd.
Howwood
JOHNSTONE
Renfrewshire
PA9 1AF
Tel: 01505 705635

SHETTLESTON DAY HOSPITAL —1H **105**
152 Wellshot Rd.
GLASGOW
G32 7AX
Tel: 0141 3038800

SOUTHERN GENERAL HOSPITAL —3D **80**
Govan Rd.
GLASGOW
G51 4TF
Tel: 0141 2011100

STOBHILL GENERAL HOSPITAL —3C **64**
133 Balornock Rd.
GLASGOW
G21 3UW
Tel: 0141 2013000

STRATHCLYDE HOSPITAL —4F **143**
Airbles Rd.
MOTHERWELL
Lanarkshire
ML1 3BW
Tel: 01698 245000

UDSTON HOSPITAL —5D **140**
Farm Rd.
HAMILTON
Lanarkshire
ML3 9LA
Tel: 01698 245000

VICTORIA INFIRMARY —5E **103**
Langside Rd.
GLASGOW
G42 9TY
Tel: 0141 2016000

VICTORIA MEMORIAL COTTAGE HOSPITAL —3F **11**
19 Glasgow Rd.
Kilsyth
GLASGOW
G65 9AG
Tel: 01236 822172

WESTER MOFFAT HOSPITAL —3F **93**
Towers Rd.
AIRDRIE
Lanarkshire
ML6 8LW
Tel: 01236 763377

WESTERN INFIRMARY —1A **82**
Dumbarton Rd.
GLASGOW
G11 6NT
Tel: 0141 2112000

WISHAW GENERAL HOSPITAL —6E **145**
Netherton St.
WISHAW
Lanarkshire
ML2 0DP
Tel: 01698 361100